AF278346

THE BEATS

Kerouac. Ginsberg. Burroughs. These are the most famous names of the Beat Generation – but in fact they were only the front line of a much more wide-ranging literary and cultural movement. This critical history takes readers through key works by these authors, but also radiates out to discuss dozens more writers and their works, showing how they all contributed to one of the most far-reaching literary movements of the post–World War II era. Moving from the early 1940s to the late 1960s, this book explores key aesthetic and thematic innovations of the Beat writers, the pervasiveness of the Beatnik caricature, the role of the counterculture in the postwar era, the involvement of women in the Beat project, and the changing face of Beat political engagement during the Vietnam War era.

STEVEN BELLETTO is Professor of English at Lafayette College. He is author of *No Accident, Comrade: Chance and Design in Cold War American Narratives* (2012) and editor of *The Cambridge Companion to the Beats* (2017) and *American Literature in Transition, 1950–1960* (2018). He is also co-editor of *Neocolonial Fictions of the Global Cold War* (2019) and *American Literature and Culture in an Age of Cold War: A Critical Reassessment* (2012). He is currently an editor for the journal *Contemporary Literature*.

THE BEATS

A Literary History

STEVEN BELLETTO

Lafayette College

CAMBRIDGE
UNIVERSITY PRESS

CAMBRIDGE
UNIVERSITY PRESS

University Printing House, Cambridge CB2 8BS, United Kingdom

One Liberty Plaza, 20th Floor, New York, NY 10006, USA

477 Williamstown Road, Port Melbourne, VIC 3207, Australia

314–321, 3rd Floor, Plot 3, Splendor Forum, Jasola District Centre, New Delhi – 110025, India

79 Anson Road, #06–04/06, Singapore 079906

Cambridge University Press is part of the University of Cambridge.

It furthers the University's mission by disseminating knowledge in the pursuit of education, learning, and research at the highest international levels of excellence.

www.cambridge.org
Information on this title: www.cambridge.org/9781107176683
DOI: 10.1017/9781316817179

© Steven Belletto 2020

This publication is in copyright. Subject to statutory exception and to the provisions of relevant collective licensing agreements, no reproduction of any part may take place without the written permission of Cambridge University Press.

First published 2020

A catalogue record for this publication is available from the British Library.

Library of Congress Cataloging-in-Publication Data
Names: Belletto, Steven, author.
TITLE: The Beats : a literary history / Steven Belletto.
DESCRIPTION: Cambridge ; New York : Cambridge University Press, 2020. | Includes bibliographical references and index.
IDENTIFIERS: LCCN 2019038672 (print) | LCCN 2019038673 (ebook) | ISBN 9781107176683 (hardback) | ISBN 9781316629918 (paperback) | ISBN 9781316817179 (epub)
SUBJECTS: LCSH: Beats (Persons)–Philosophy. | American literature–20th century–History and criticism. | Counterculture–United States–History–20th century.
CLASSIFICATION: LCC PS228.B6 B485 2020 (print) | LCC PS228.B6 (ebook) | DDC 810.9/0054–dc23
LC record available at https://lccn.loc.gov/2019038672
LC ebook record available at https://lccn.loc.gov/2019038673

ISBN 978-1-107-17668-3 Hardback

Cambridge University Press has no responsibility for the persistence or accuracy of URLs for external or third-party internet websites referred to in this publication and does not guarantee that any content on such websites is, or will remain, accurate or appropriate.

Then there's a BG manufactured by brazen, shameless academic hustlers who write silly books about it, third hand, and give courses on it in somnambulistic college classrooms.

Chandler Brossard

Contents

vii

Figures

Preface

This book is a literary history of the Beat movement, which had its roots in New York City in the mid-1940s, its zenith in the late 1950s, and its legacy secured in the 1990s and after. The story I want to tell isn't predominantly focused on the biographical exploits that have become legendary in certain circles – the details of such exploits are easily found in popular histories, encyclopedias, and on the internet. Instead, this book explores something like a Beat republic of letters, an informal association of writers and artists that germinated aesthetic innovations and encouraged considerations of once-taboo subjects. This network, which existed always in tension with the underground and what dominant culture thought about the underground, was responsible for producing some of the most recognizable literary works in postwar America. My basic assumption is that the richest way to appreciate individual Beat texts is in relation to one another, so that their achievement may be seen as at once singular and of a piece with more widespread preoccupations; as the great Beat scholar Oliver Harris has put it in the context of William S. Burroughs's "early texts," one would be ill-advised to imagine that discrete texts are best "read outside the Beat context, taken out like a picture from an old frame."[1] What follows is a book-length examination of texts and contexts during which the concept of "Beat" emerges as a character in its own right, an elusive and ever-shifting idea that floats through these pages naming constellations of aesthetics, attitudes, formal techniques, and styles that mutated across time and space.

Readers of this book are probably already familiar with the more celebrated Beat writers: Jack Kerouac (1922–1969), Allen Ginsberg (1926–1997), and William S. Burroughs (1914–1997). Originally from Massachusetts, New Jersey, and Missouri, respectively, in the early 1940s, these three converged in and around Columbia University in New York City, forming a circle of friends that would be the roots of the so-called Beat Generation. They were first brought together by Columbia undergraduate Lucien Carr, and as I explain in the first chapter, his shocking murder of a mutual friend gave the aspiring writers their first collective subject matter. Another irresistible subject would arrive from Denver in 1946: Neal Cassady, a manic raconteur and womanizer whose boundless energy inspired the character of Dean Moriarty in Kerouac's *On the Road*, and who would be anointed the "secret hero" of Ginsberg's "Howl." John Clellon Holmes, a fourth early chronicler of the Beat ethos in both fiction and nonfiction, entered the frame in 1948. Rounding out the group was Gregory Corso, a younger poet Ginsberg met in 1950; a decade later Corso would be routinely grouped with Kerouac, Ginsberg, and Burroughs as the four most important Beat figures. As the original generation, we can look to these writers to understand the most consequential features of Beat literary achievement – at least according to the common story.

In fact, this group was only the front line of a much more diffuse avant-garde literary and cultural movement. Peruse this book's Table of Contents and you'll get a quick sense of how from small beginnings in the New York underground, the Beat sensibility shifted and adapted as widening circles chased their own artistic visions while associating with others doing the same. To more fully appreciate the depths of the Beat movement, then, it is necessary to look at familiar writers as well as those lesser known, and to read their work in the context of one another, as pieces of a gathering postwar sensibility some called the "new consciousness." While I do offer readings of stalwarts like *On the Road*, "Howl," and *Naked Lunch*, these readings aren't intended to be flashily ingenious, but rather to show how they contributed to the rise of the Beat novel or Beat poetry. In terms of word count, much attention is given to the Big Three writers – and, to a lesser extent, Holmes and Corso – and the book tries to reckon with the decades-long critical conversations that scholars have had about these writers. But the balance of the book concerns a broader diversity of writers and texts, some of whom have received comparatively little scholarly attention, with the hope of bringing wider and more complex Beat networks into better focus. Of course, even a good-faith effort to take a wide-angle approach cannot be totally comprehensive, for as became dauntingly clear when writing this book, there are always negotiations between telling sweeping stories and drilling down into the specifics of particular texts, of acknowledging and exploring the nuances of major writers while filling in details about those who might be more obscure but still of interest (no, said my editor, it's long enough). Thus for all my visions of inclusion, there are inevitable omissions or short shrifts that are products of my own biases, tastes, and scope of knowledge. But what follows is, I hope, a capacious, not-too-shameless journey through a significant literary movement as told by its writing, a movement that is in my view among the more far-reaching of the latter twentieth century.

Acknowledgments

To paraphrase Neil Young when he walked on stage to sing with The Band for their farewell concert: it's been one of the pleasures of my life to be able to spend time reading and writing about the Beats. Of course this book would not exist at all without the intrepid work of those scholars who had to convince others that the Beats were worthy of study, and who went against the academic grain to give them a fair hearing. I'm standing – tottering – on the shoulders of these giants. My experience editing *The Cambridge Companion to the Beats* led to this book, and was a humbling one as I learned so much from all its contributors, who must have centuries of expertise between them. For various conversations and kindnesses, I would like to thank in particular Nancy M. Grace, Oliver Harris, Tim Hunt, Bob Lee, Todd Tietchen, and Regina Weinreich. Double thanks to Erik Mortenson, who heroically read the entire manuscript and talked it through with me. I am also grateful to Steven Moore for sharing his apparently limitless knowledge, and to Hettie Jones for granting permission to reprint images from *Yugen*.

Ray Ryan is the Malcolm Cowley of contemporary literary studies, an industrious editor and fearless champion, and I can't thank him enough for his confidence in me. Mike LeMahieu, who I've always said knows everything that I do plus a bunch of philosophy and critical theory, went through this book with laser focus and came up with some inspired suggestions.

Diane Shaw, as director of Special Collections at Lafayette College, worked with me to build a small but mighty Beat collection, which has been invaluable for my scholarship and a real treat for my students, who deeply appreciate the opportunity to work with rare editions and obscure publications. Karen Haduck, Lafayette's Interlibrary Loan maven, was able to conjure items even if they are owned by a mere handful of libraries around the world. I owe many of the images reproduced to Paul Miller, and I thank him for his assistance. I would also like to thank Lafayette's

Academic Research Committee for awarding me a Richard King Mellon Research Fellowship, affording me the opportunity travel to archives at the Bancroft Library at UC-Berkeley, the Beinecke at Yale, and the Fales at NYU. The Friends of the Princeton University Library awarded me a University Library Research Grant, which allowed me to spend some very pleasant time in the rare books room at the Firestone. I also benefited from the research assistance of Mailinda Hoxha, my EXCEL Scholar at Lafayette.

It's not a given that you'll be gifted with generous and sympathetic colleagues in the workplace, but I've been lucky to have known a few. Carrie Rohman has been my brilliant friend for more than a decade, and has helped me think through the shape and scope of this book. Paul Cefalu is a model scholar and unblinking advocate, so it's not been too bad being across the hall from him. It's a privilege to call Lee Upton my friend and mentor: she is the kind of rare person one can only hope to emulate.

Cheers to all those friends who helped me do anything but write a book – the Whole Sick Crew under the stairs, Simba the Salmon King, the East Coast's leading authority on Robin Zander, et al. One time Travis came with me down to the Bowery to listen to some poetry, and who knew we would ever get to hear The Fugs play live? Maisie and Nina were close by as I wrote pretty much every word of this book, and it wouldn't be the same without them. This is also true of Katie, whose spirit infuses these pages; Katie: this book is for you.

PART I

Get Hip, My Soul: How It All Got Started (1944–1948)

CHAPTER I

The Wild Outré Gang of Columbia Campus
The Beginnings of a Movement

The most cinematic way to begin a book about the Beats is with a murder. It's easy enough to establish the scene by imagining upper Manhattan's Riverside Park in the close and humid early hours of August 14, 1944. There and then, on the grassy banks of the Hudson, Lucien Carr, a Columbia University sophomore, found himself in a drunken argument with his friend David Kammerer. The men had known each other for years, and after Carr had matriculated at Columbia, the older Kammerer trailed him to New York, where they both fell into a social circle of students and others interested in art, literature, and culture – and the more carnal pleasures of drugs, alcohol, and sex. Whatever transpired between them that night, we remember it now because Carr wound up stabbing Kammerer in the chest with his old Boy Scout knife, and then dragged the body into the river, where it sank only with the help of stones found nearby. At a loss for what to do next, Carr went straight to others in the social circle, first to William Burroughs, who gave him some cash and advised him to seek legal counsel, and then to Jack Kerouac, who accompanied Carr on a surreal tour of the city before the latter eventually turned himself in to authorities. In the papers, the sensational story punctuated unending dispatches from the Pacific and European fronts, updating readers when Burroughs and Kerouac were arrested as material witnesses. Another close friend, Allen Ginsberg, managed to avoid legal entanglements but was as devastated as they all were, striking a plaintive note in his journal: "The libertine circle is destroyed with the death of Kammerer."[1] Although the killing did have the direct effect of busting up the circle and dispersing the friends to far-flung locales, at least temporarily, from our vantage it is historically significant because it draws together, in a most lurid and spectacular way, the Big Three writers of what was not yet called the Beat Generation. In fifteen years, Ginsberg, Kerouac, and Burroughs would all be famous avatars of literary iconoclasm, and so this early incident seems a natural starting point for understanding the movement they engendered.

Were it not for the later fame of those involved, Kammerer's death would almost certainly have been lost to history as one among countless forgotten tragedies of the urban nightscape. From at least the mid-1970s, when critical work on the Beats began to appear with some regularity, the Carr–Kammerer confrontation provided a recognizable origin story, as in Aaron Latham's gossipy *New York Magazine* piece, "The Columbia Murder That Gave Birth to the Beats" (1976), which dubs Carr the "founding father of the movement," through to *The Typewriter Is Holy* (2010), Bill Morgan's "complete, uncensored history" of the Beats, which declares that the murder is where "the story of the Beat Generation really begins."[2] In such cases, the seamy contours of real life are what captivate, and the desire to learn more about the details might drive inquisitive minds to the literature – *Kill Your Darlings*, a 2013 feature film about these events, virtually ignores writing to dramatize instead, as its tagline announced, "A True Story of Obsession and Murder."[3] Although many a reader has cracked a Beat book to discover the "true story" of its author's turbulent life, so doing reinforces the widespread but erroneous notion that these writers merely wrote down what happened to them transparently and with little discrimination. This assumption is flawed, and leads to a fundamental misunderstanding of the Beats. Real-life events notwithstanding, they are of course relevant today – of interest to readers, enshrined at their own dedicated museum, subjects of admiring films and countless tribute songs, and paid serious attention in scholarly books, biographies, and at academic conferences – not for their exploits alone but for the force of their writing, which excelled at mythologizing and elevating such exploits. When thinking about the Beats, it is therefore essential to foreground questions of representation, to recognize that however much real life inspired and informed literary production, their achievement rests finally in the nature of this production, in the distinctive ways they explored and experimented with language.

I begin with a murder, then, not because writers later celebrated were embroiled in scandal, but because it was the first event that Ginsberg, Kerouac, and Burroughs collectively *wrote* about, which in turn made it a founding moment in and of Beat lore. A mere six weeks after Carr was sentenced for his crime, for example, eighteen-year-old Ginsberg began drafting a novel inspired by Kammerer's murder called "The Bloodsong." That manuscript didn't get very far because the beset administration at Columbia asked Ginsberg to drop the project, but he would return to the incident more indirectly in later work, notably "Howl" (published 1956), which includes among its subterranean catalogues "great suicidal dramas on the apartment cliff-banks of the Hudson under the wartime blue floodlight of the moon & their heads shall be crowned with laurel in oblivion."[4] The "oblivion" here refers both to Kammerer's literal death and to the way Ginsberg had moved from the quasi-ethnographic account in "The Bloodsong" to a lyrical though oblique reference in "Howl," where Carr and Kammerer remain unnamed but "crowned with laurel" against the romantic wash of moonlight. Like many lines in "Howl," the specifics of the "suicidal dramas" are purposively left unsaid, contributing to the event's subsequent status as something only insiders really knew about.

While "The Bloodsong" was abandoned, in the immediate aftermath of the murder, Kerouac and Burroughs decided to collaborate on their own novel about the incident, so it is fair to say that if the killing "destroyed" the circle, it also provided these three writers with generative material (corresponding from jail that September, Carr told Ginsberg that he also wanted to lay claim to the event in an autobiographical novel he was planning).[5] By the winter of 1944, Kerouac and Burroughs were making headway on their novel, ultimately called *And the Hippos Were Boiled in Their Tanks*, which featured alternately written chapters narrated by fictionalized versions of themselves. The book was drafted by spring of 1945, and Kerouac for one thought highly of it, boasting to his sister that Columbia Pictures wanted movie rights, but that, despite its dramatic content, *Hippos* wasn't really "movie material" so much as a "portrait of the 'lost' segment of our generation, hardboiled, honest, and sensationally real."[6] While both collaborators were interested in the commercial viability of the novel – perhaps explaining its "hardboiled" quality – it is telling that Kerouac frames the effort in terms of the "'lost' segment of our generation," as this phrase draws a line from an earlier literary era, the Lost Generation, to his own "generation," a word that would be famously attached to "Beat" in the coming years.[7]

Kerouac's sense that there was a wider generational story to be told via the Carr–Kammerer affair was persistent enough that soon after *Hippos* was written, he reimagined the material in a new project called "I Wish I Were You." Never published as a stand-alone book, "I Wish I Were You" focuses on social context rather than on the "sensationally real" murder – the plot is in fact all prelude to the killing, another telling change as it suggests it was the portrait of his "generation" which seemed most consequential to Kerouac on second thought.[8] In rereading Kerouac's body of work, one might indeed be struck by the way the killing indexes wider cultural discontent in a range of books, as when it appears, sanitized, in his first published novel, *The Town and the City* (1950) or when in his masterpiece *Visions of Cody* (1951–1952; published 1972), a fascinated Neal Cassady wants to know about the "novel ... about the death."[9] A bookend to *Hippos*, Kerouac's last substantive work, *Vanity of Duluoz* (1967), devotes a lengthy section to those months in 1944 not merely because of the murder but because his experiences with the legal system shaped his sensibility as a young writer.[10] (Burroughs would likewise characterize the death as somehow symptomatic of his "generation," as when he wrote in the mid-1950s, "Certainly I would be atypical of my generation if I didn't die with my boots on. Dave Kammerer stabbed by his boy with a scout knife."[11])

The murder was thus significant not simply because of the obvious personal impact it had on the group but also because it seemed to Ginsberg, Kerouac, and Burroughs enigmatically indicative of shifting cultural winds, making it all but irresistible as subject matter. Thinking in terms of representation helps us see that the murder as such was immediately spun into a legible story, first by Burroughs, then by the media and by Carr's lawyers – by the time Burroughs and Kerouac began to draft *Hippos*, such stories were practically impossible to sort out from the event itself. When *Hippos* was finally published in 2008, many readers assumed it was nothing more than a straightforward account of what had really happened, but in fact it turns on the very distances between real life and representation, an abiding interest of much Beat writing, as I show throughout this book.[12] Put differently, *Hippos* unsettles the official story circulated in the media and maintained by Carr's legal defense. This unsettling depends on an interplay of real life and fictional stories, meaning that one cannot read *Hippos* hermetically, by bracketing biographical and cultural contexts, a truism that applies to essentially all Beat literature. But even if one accepts this truism as such, it does not in turn follow that *Hippos* is naïve history, real life with the names changed, but it is rather an exploration of the problems that come with representing anything via language. For these reasons, *Hippos* is a useful entry point into Beat literature – while far from the finest example of this literature, the collaborative novel is a rich illustration of how the Beats have been handcuffed to both media accounts of their "generation" and to the perceptions of their most strident critics, and so I'll linger over some of its details before describing the wider literary and cultural landscape from which Beat writing emerged.

1.1 Unsettling the Official Story

From a literary historian's point of view, *Hippos* sutures New York in 1944 – a place and time in which the Beat Generation was embryonic and as-yet unnamed – to the post-"Howl," post–*On the Road* (1957), post–*Naked Lunch* (1959) literary landscape in which Ginsberg, Kerouac, Burroughs, and others were characterized as Beat, which meant that they became somewhat infamous but widely misunderstood. This is because though completed in 1945, the manuscript remained unpublished until 2008, three years after Carr's death. There are numerous reasons for this half-century interlude, not the least of which was Carr's desire to disassociate himself from the Beats and their fascination with the murder – "Isn't it enough that the past is there," he said to Ginsberg in 1962, "without your returning again and again and again to nuzzle, smell, wallow, guzzle and paint yourself blue with it? ... As far as it affects me, can't you word bandiers stick to your own ghosts and leave mine alone?"[13] Given the allure of such ghosts, it was perhaps inevitable that they would eventually be disturbed again, and Beat enthusiasts had long anticipated the manuscript's publication, as it had been alluded to in biographies and other criticism, and evoked by Kerouac in one of his last interviews as a kind of buried treasure still "hidden under the floorboards."[14] When finally published, *Hippos* was accompanied by a lengthy afterword by James Grauerholz, Burroughs's literary executor, who rightly pointed out: "For better or worse, *Hippos* comes to you now as a 'framed' work: *The Columbia murder that gave birth to the Beats! A lost Kerouac book! A lost Burroughs book!*"[15] This observation was borne out by the novel's reception, which tended to be lukewarm and focused on the intimate biographical details it supposedly provided.

To find a visible critical reaction we need look no further than Michiko Kakutani's *New York Times* review, which panned *Hippos* for being little more than poorly written gossip. Calling *Hippos* a "flimsy piece of work," Kakutani laments that none of its "one-dimensional slackers are remotely interesting as individuals," but concedes that it captures "the seedy, artsy world Kerouac and Burroughs inhabited in New York ... before they found their voices and became bohemian brand names."[16] Such a perspective certainly fulfills Grauerholz's prediction that readers would be drawn to the novel because of the "brand names" attached to it, and Kakutani imagines these readers happily combing chapters for biographical and historical tidbits.

But Kakutani's perspective assumes that *Hippos* is best understood as an historical relic, even though its very form evades claims to historical knowledge. Although *inspired* by the murder and featuring characters recognizably drawn from real life, *Hippos* exists in generic limbo somewhere between fiction, history, and autobiography, and is conspicuously coy about its central motivating plot point: *Why* did one friend kill another?

With respect to the real-life murder, the standard line for several decades was that Kammerer had a dangerous obsession with the much-younger Carr, who finally had no choice but to violently fend off unwelcome sexual advances. This is the story told, for instance, in John Tytell's *Naked Angels* (1976), a groundbreaking and widely cited study of the Big Three Beat writers:

> Using incorrigible deceptions, he [Kammerer] had relentlessly pursued Carr to New York, declaring his love and his desire to possess him exclusively. He would shadow Carr about the streets, haunt the bars that he frequented, ingratiate himself with his friends, and suddenly appear at parties. On August 13, 1944, after an evening of drinking at the West End, Kammarer [*sic*] accosted Carr in Riverside Park, insisting that they make love. Carr retaliated by stabbing his antagonist repeatedly in the chest with his scout knife.[17]

This general narrative is repeated in most subsequent accounts, which tend to emphasize both Kammerer's "obsession" and "reckless" behavior, and that Carr was far younger and, as Ginsberg's biographer puts it, "decisively heterosexual."[18] There is little doubt that Kammerer was romantically interested in Carr, but it is worth pointing out that while the scenario Tytell describes is plausible, it is not finally verifiable or really knowable. This is what Joyce Johnson notes in her study of Kerouac when she observes, "No one ever knew exactly what happened there, especially what went on in Lucien's mind – not definitively."[19] As it turns out, it was this very epistemological uncertainty that Kerouac and Burroughs faced as they composed *Hippos*, which does not grant readers access to the moment of killing – as the authors themselves did not have access – but treats it instead in terms of the stories that were told about it. Rather than looking to *Hippos* to find out what "really happened," then, we should read it for the ways it navigates those narratives that were immediately attached to the murder.

In *Hippos*, characters modeled on Carr and Kammerer are called Phillip Tourian and Ramsay Allen, respectively. Their story is told by two narrators, Mike Ryko, whose chapters are written by Kerouac, and Will Dennison, whose chapters are written by Burroughs. The story of the "libertine circle" is fictionalized, and details about the killing are changed so as to obscure the novel's inspiration. One effect of having two first-person narrators is that crucial information depends on perspective and interpretation, which emphasizes the elusive nature of "truth" in the novel. Such elusiveness is underscored formally as readers are never taken to the scene of the crime, but only hear about it third-hand, as Dennison recounts the story as he remembers Tourian telling it.

In one of Dennison's chapters, readers learn that directly after the murder, Tourian shows up to seek advice, and explains to Dennision what happened:

> "I found a hatchet and broke some windows with it.
> "Later we were up on the roof. Al [Allen] kept saying he wanted to ship out with me. I got mad and gave him a shove. He nearly went over. He looked at me and said, 'I want to do the things you do. I want to write poetry and go to sea and all that.'" Phillip stopped and looked at me. "I can see you don't believe me."
> "Go on," I [Dennison] said.
> "Well, so I said to him, 'Do you want to die?' and he said, 'Yes.' He made a couple of wisecracks and tried to put his arm around me. I still had the hatchet in my hand, so I hit him on the forehead. He fell down. He was dead."[20]

Leaving aside for the moment the changes in murder weapon and venue, we might note that nowhere in Dennison's account of Tourian's story is Allen threatening or aggressive, and so the motive for his actions remains inexplicable. Far from seeming like a crime of passion or desperation, the killing appears in this telling markedly dispassionate and therefore markedly disturbing: we learn only that Allen "was dead," not *why* he was killed.

In fact, it is Dennison who supplies the motive, and the accompanying details that will get Tourian a light sentence in the novel: "Do you know what happened to you, Phil?" Dennison says. "You were attacked. Al attacked you. He tried to rape you. You lost your head. Everything went black. You hit him. He stumbled back and fell off the roof. You were in a panic. Your only thought was to get away. Get a good lawyer, you'll be out in two years" (163). Historically speaking, this is the story that was repeated in newspapers, accepted by the criminal justice system, and confirmed by biographers and literary critics (and Carr actually did get out of prison in two years).

In *Hippos*, however, the idea that Tourian was defending himself against Allen's attempted "rape" is presented not as historical fact but as an invention by Dennison. His short, declarative sentences match those in Tourian's own account, and Dennison's opening question, "Do you know what happened to you, Phil?," is immediately followed by authoritative answers that he himself supplies, casting doubt on their status as "real," even in the world of the novel. Kerouac's ensuing chapter also raises such doubts when Ryko notes that "Phillip *gave me the story* he'd told Dennison earlier in the morning" (169; my emphasis). Ryko then reassures the distraught Tourian by repeating the story once more, like a mantra: "Al was queer. He chased you over continents. He screwed up your life. The police will understand that" (170).

In real life, the police did indeed understand this story, as Carr doubled down on it to make the killing explicable and even justifiable to a largely homophobic culture.[21] This was a culture in which homosexuality was a great taboo, seen by many as evidence not simply of immorality but of inhumanity. Consider, for instance, that in the very month of Kammerer's death, San Francisco poet – and, in later years, Beat associate – Robert Duncan published a brief but significant piece in *Politics* titled "The Homosexual in Society." This piece criticized both mainstream society for its homophobia and those living closeted gay lives, taking the latter to task for retreating into cliques rather than demanding human recognition and civil rights from dominant culture.[22] In the course of his essay, Duncan refers to another sensational murder case concerning a man named Wayne Lonergan, who had been arrested for bludgeoning his heiress wife with a candelabra. Increasingly desperate during his trial, Lonergan disclosed homosexual relationships as part of his (failed) defense – one *Daily News* headline read: "Lonergan Alibi: Twisted Sex."[23] Duncan's thoughts on the Lonergan case might as easily apply to Kammerer's murder, and help us see those stories attached to it by the lights of mid-century homophobia:

> The law has declared homosexuality secret, non-human, unnatural.... The law itself sees in it a crime, not in the sense that murder, thievery, seduction of children or rape is seen as a crime – but in an occult sense. In the recent Lonergan case it was clear that murder was a *human crime*, but homosexuality was *non-human*. It was not a crime against man but a crime against "the way of nature," as defined in the Christian religion, a crime against God.[24]

If Duncan's analysis is even broadly accurate, and I think it is, then the *New York Times* coverage of Kammerer's death adheres perfectly to this cultural logic. The *Times* first established Carr as "a quiet, well-behaved, intellectual type" and Kammerer simply as "a homosexual," then presented a version of the story much like the one Dennison suggests to Tourian in *Hippos*:

> Carr said that several times during their acquaintance Kammerer had made improper advances toward him but that he had always rebuffed the older man.... [The night of the murder] Kammerer once more made an offensive proposal.... Carr said that he rejected it indignantly and that a fight ensued ... [the] slight youth ... [was] no match for the burly former physical education instructor ... [and so] In desperation, Carr pulled out of his pocket his Boy Scout knife, a relic of his boyhood.[25]

This story was refined by Carr's legal defense, who insisted that Kammerer had "hounded" Carr and overwhelmed him with "improper advances."[26] In real life, then, homosexuality – according to the logic Duncan describes a "secret, non-human, unnatural" crime against humanity – was invoked so as to make manslaughter understandable if not acceptable, and this story was repeated so often that it seemed, in the end, unvarnished truth. In its coverage of Carr's sentencing that October, for instance, the *Daily Mirror* reported that the judge declared that a jury would likely have acquitted Carr, and that the Elmira Reformatory "may release him when he has entirely recovered from the evil influence to which he had been subjected."[27] In this narrative, Carr is fixed as the straight victim to Kammerer's homosexual predation, which, bearing out Duncan's theories, is construed as a crime far worse than murder.

But this is not the case in *Hippos*, where the truth refuses to be fixed so neatly. There are, for instance, numerous suggestions that Tourian's sexuality is more fluid than Dennison's cover story allows: Ryko observes that "a lot of people ... looked at him suspiciously as if they thought he might be a dope fiend or a fag" (14), and wonders why, despite "necking with her for months" (128), Tourian and a girlfriend never actually have sex (43). Burroughs's chapter echoes this fluidity, as when the pair frequent "queer place[s]" (101) or when Dennison tells a lovesick Allen that "Phillip isn't queer. He might sleep with you, which I doubt altogether, but anything permanent is impossible" (28). This conversation proposes a distinction between one's sexual behavior and being identified a "fag" or a "queer" (categories that Burroughs would explore more subtly in later work), with both Ryko and Dennison indicating that while Tourian "might sleep" with men, he isn't "queer."

The most striking challenge to the official narrative about the murder comes when *Hippos* offers the exact inverse of the cover story suggested by

Dennison: that it was Tourian, not Allen, who was the sexual aggressor. Early in the novel, Allen comes to Dennison to tell him about another incident between Tourian and Allen that took place on a rooftop (thus implying a parallel to the rooftop murder); as Allen recounts to Dennison:

> "Well, when we got up on the roof, Phillip rushed over to the edge like he was going to jump off, and I got worried and yelled at him, but he stopped suddenly and dropped a glass down. I went over and stood on the edge with him and said 'What's the matter?' and started to put my arm around him. Then Phil turned around and kissed me very passionately, on the mouth, and dragged me down with him on the roof."
>
> I [Dennison] said, "It looks like you're getting there, after four years. Well go on – what happened then?"
>
> "He kissed me several times, then suddenly he pushed me away and got up." (26)

The novel never demonstrates – or even hints – that Allen is lying here, retaining the possibility that he and Tourian had a romantic relationship about which Tourian was conflicted, in turn suggesting that shame, not self-defense, could have been the true motive for the murder. In other words, unlike the official narrative of the real-life event, its fictionalization in *Hippos* introduces competing stories that account for Allen's murder, but refuses to verify any of them, rendering it finally inexplicable.

1.2   The Beats, Evasion, and the Underground

The enigma at the heart of *Hippos* helps us see how the book and the circumstances of its composition draw together three threads that characterize Beat literature broadly imagined. First, we have a group of writers emphasizing the precarious relationship between language and "the real" in an attempt to define themselves against representations by the media, a mirror and mouthpiece of dominant culture. It is possible to trace this emphasis through much Beat writing, and as I explain throughout this book, in order to see Beat writers collectively, one has to account for popular representations of them as such, including by journalists and critics generally dismissive of them.

Second, there is the sense that these competing representations are not merely semantic squabbles, but rather that they have serious consequences in people's lives: obviously, Carr himself was affected by the way his relationship with Kammerer was represented in public, but similar representations had wider impacts on various kinds of "underground" cultures that existed at the time. As the Carr–Kammerer story may suggest, there were from those early days blurred lines between underground queer culture and what would become the Beat underground, a notion that may surprise readers who see the avatar of the Beat Generation in *On the Road*'s womanizing protagonist. Maria Damon has framed these blurred lines like this: "What the Beats did for the gay community was goad it into visibility – a visibility that would eventually become politicized – by exemplifying flamboyant resistance to an oppressive norm. What the gay culture did for the Beats was to offer them a model for fluid relationships, outlaw culture and a high regard for the relatively apolitical politics of 'lifestyle.'"[28] As elaborated throughout this book, Damon's final point about the politicizing of lifestyle is absolutely central to understanding the Beats and their contributions to US letters and culture. Their lives and literatures resisted hard distinctions among the personal and political, private and public, in ways that would shift the very meaning of what "politics" could mean or be – a shift that became in later decades very nearly mainstream.

Third, there is the sense that what made the Beats a group, whether a tight-knit "libertine circle" or seemingly diffuse generation or movement, was their evasions of dominant culture. But despite such evasions, it became difficult – probably impossible – to discuss the counterculture without discussing dominant culture, meaning that Beat counterculture became collectively visible when seen *against* dominant culture, even as this collectivity was never itself entirely cohesive or internally consistent.

In light of these three threads, we might see how *Hippos* is a prototypic-ally Beat, underground book. For now, I'll use the term "underground" broadly, and will wait until Part II to detail the historical specificities and shades of meaning necessary for understanding how the Beat sensibility emerged from the New York underground of the mid- to late 1940s. In the meantime, it suffices to think in terms reminiscent of those in Dick Hebdige's influential account of postwar "youth subcultures," which argues that in such subcultures, style – variously construed but always constitutive – "signals a Refusal" of "dominant ideologies."[29] For Hebdige, refusal is a hallmark of the various subcultures he discusses; in the case of the Beats specifically, I would suggest it was manifest in the particular evasions evinced in *Hippos* and in the more general evasions of social and cultural ideologies then dominant. After all, in the first public theorization of the Beats (1952), John Clellon Holmes claimed that even in "the wildest hipster, ... there is no desire to shatter the 'square' society in which he lives, only to elude it."[30] We might then say that the epistemological unsettling staged in *Hippos* illustrates one of Beat literature's fundamental premises: that one should approach dominant narratives or ideologies with skepticism, and privilege instead the messier truths of idiosyncratic, subjective experience. But as attention to the very concept of "subculture" reminds us, these individual experiences occurred in the context of a group or community: a "libertine circle" which became a literary coterie, which in time radiated out to a loosely associated movement of regional, then national, then international import. As I explain in the following pages, attending to figurations of community is therefore crucial for understanding the seeming paradox of the Beats as highly individualistic writers who nonetheless constituted a collective underground literary movement.

CHAPTER 2

Write for Them about Them Personally
The Beats and Avant-Garde Literary Communities at Mid-Century

In popular imagination, mid-century America tends to be characterized by the national unity of the war years and the conformity and consumerism of the long 1950s – but most literary and cultural historians would agree that in the realms of literature and the arts, the postwar years were in fact subject to pretty radical changes.[1] One way such change has been described is via the communities of writers and artists that emerged around the United States to mount collective assaults on what they perceived as the restrictive norms of ossified tradition. Alan Golding, for one, has encouraged readers to see "literary history not only as a history of individual careers, important books, and competing discourses but also as a history of writing *communities*."[2] As I explain below, thinking in terms of "writing communities" has been especially useful for mapping the terrain of postwar poetry deemed avant-garde, and in this respect critics have pointed not only to the Beats, but in particular to the poets associated with Black Mountain College, the San Francisco Renaissance, and the New York School, communities that all had important connections to the Beats.

When I use "community" in this context, I'm thinking of it in the sense articulated by Stephen Voyce, who takes the word "to mean the network of poets, cultural spaces, and institutional frameworks that enable a group's collaborative work."[3] Voyce's definition of community is a useful starting point, but embedded in this formulation is the premise that such networks applied only to *poetic* communities, a widespread critical assumption that has had the effect of obscuring the importance of community to other kinds of literary production. The Beats, of course, worked in a range of genres, from poetry and prose to plays, letters, and genre-smashing texts such as cut-ups; one reason I began with *Hippos* is to illustrate that the Beat literary community was hardly limited to poets. In fact, the chapters to follow will illustrate that Beat writing is purposively pugnacious and promiscuous when it comes to questions of genre, with many writers moving among different genres, redefining and repurposing those genres – or simply inventing their own.

Before exploring how the Beat movement emerged from a wider field of avant-garde literary communities, I want to register one other caveat, that it is reasonable to be skeptical of any literary community as a bounded, discrete phenomenon, especially when to say "community" is to name a collectivity of individualist iconoclasts.[4] As suggested by Voyce's use of the term, one way to think more capaciously about community is to do so in terms of "networks." In this regard, I'm following the lead of Jimmy Fazzino, whose recent study of the "worlding" of Beat literature uses networks to think about community far beyond ones like the libertine circle to recognize "expression[s] of felt solidarity and mutual understanding" outside national bounds.[5] For Fazzino, "subterranean" is a generative "image of creation and connectivity, where vast underground networks of influence and inspiration proliferate"; the term represents an "ever-expanding network ... of hidden synchronicity and syncretism" (42). As he explains, "Where the subterranean is concerned, the multiple always trumps the singular, and a particular movement – literary, social, or otherwise – can be meaningful and effective only insofar as it can recognize and link up with an outside-of-itself" (47). Fazzino's terms are useful for illuminating the underground as a space where creation and connectivity are watchwords, but where multiplicity means that varied sensibilities and forms of expression can proliferate simultaneously.[6]

Thinking about multiplicity in particular underscores the crucial point that when we talk about literary communities, we are not necessarily talking about a uniform aesthetic or unchanging sensibility even within those communities, but rather about social and ideological spaces that foster idiosyncratic expression, disagreement, and difference. Lytle Shaw characterizes poetic communities "as temporary, tactical social compositions based on contingent rather than organic bonds, dissipating and reforming themselves frequently ... collectivity does not mean consensus."[7] Viewing poetic communities in this way means that were one to search for stable definitions of, say, Black Mountain poetry or New York School poetry, one might only discover axiomatic characteristics subject to complication or refinement when confronted with the particulars of work produced across time by different writers.

Thus although *The Beats: A Literary History* is of course predicated on the assumption that there is such a thing as a Beat literary movement, I want to stress that this thing is mutable and protean, and so part of my purpose is to track its various changes across time, text, and author to explore shifting though identifiable Beat sensibilities. In so doing, I won't claim that the Beats were unique in their challenge to dominant culture or literary convention, as writers associated with the groups named above (and others) have claims on like challenges. That said, I do think it is useful to frame this study in terms of a diffuse Beat movement and its attendant sensibilities because doing so emphasizes the degree to which the Beats often had simultaneous audiences in mind: a small audience of intimates and a much broader, public audience – what we might call posterity – that could recognize these intimates as the successors to the Lost Generation.

2.1   The Dual Audiences for Beat Work

I didn't put it in these terms earlier, but one way to understand the registers of meaning in *Hippos* is to recognize that the book plays on tensions between its intimate audience – those familiar with the murder and its principals prior to reading its fictionalization – and a broad or public audience – those who come to the fictionalization from positions outside the circle. The irony is that for those in the circle, the novel has the effect of unsettling the official narrative they knew to be incomplete, while for those in the broader audience (who probably cannot distinguish between what really happened and the way it is represented), the novel appears to draw readers into a circle of intimates by promising access to private truths. This performance of intimacy is one way scholars have tried to distinguish Beat literature as such; writing about Kerouac, for example, Ann Douglas has described what she calls his "poetics of intimacy," his canny ability to pull "the reader inside the story as well."[8] Thinking about Beat writing in the context of postwar literary communities helps us see that while it was most intelligible at first to the inner circle, it was also often composed with an eye toward broader audiences who might identify these writers as a movement and believe them significant for their membership in same. Accordingly, throughout this book I explore how both familiar and lesser known Beat works navigate their intimate and broader audiences insofar as they describe underground spaces or heterodox attitudes only to invite – or *seem* to invite – outside readers into such spaces.

By 1950, communal intimacy not only was foundational to the libertine circle and groups such as Black Mountain, the San Francisco Renaissance, and the New York School, but had been proposed as a necessary condition for avant-garde literary and aesthetic production to occur at all. At the time, this claim was made most plainly by Paul Goodman, a poet, social critic, and polymath connected at various times to each of these communities as he had at different moments taught at Black Mountain College, run with the New York Intellectuals, and read with the Beats, even being counted among them in the formative anthology *The Beat Scene* (1960). He is probably best-known today for *Growing Up Absurd*, a series of social analyses of "problems of youth in the organized society" published the same year as *The Beat Scene* (and that singled out the Beats for special consideration).[9]

But I want take us back to an essay Goodman published almost a decade prior to *Growing Up Absurd* because it offers an influential articulation of how vital community could be to the development of an American avant-garde. The essay, "Advance-Guard Writing 1900–1950," surveys the literary scene spanning those years, and culminates with a discussion of what Goodman considers unique about his contemporary moment, the years after World War II – the very ones when the libertine circle would be transfigured into the Beat Generation. True to the martial metaphor of the avant-garde or advance-guard, Goodman sees the most significant avant-garde movements as assaults on established norms – Naturalism, for example, aims "to attack and reform by letting the facts speak for themselves," and the Modernist "revolution of the word" entails a "concentrated attack on the formal attitudes of literature, the vocabulary, syntax, genre, method of narration, judgment of what is real and what is fantasy."[10] Following this brief tour of the prior half-century, Goodman turns to his present moment and describes what he sees as the necessary conditions for a contemporary avant-garde. First, he notes, "serious writers … have more and more been describing marginal personalities – criminals, perverts, drunkards, underground people" (372). By way of illustration, he cites French writer and enfant terrible Jean Genet, great hero of the Beats, as one who "assert[s] the marginal and prove[s] its justification, thereby demolishing the norm" (373). Goodman then goes on to make what has become a well-known claim about the postwar avant-garde, that it is "the physical reestablishment of community":

> In literary terms this means: *to write for them about them personally*.... But such personal writing about the audience itself can occur only in a small community of acquaintances, where everybody knows and understands what is at stake.... The point is that the advance-guard action helps create such community, starting with the artist's primary friends. The community comes to exist by having *its* culture. (375–376)

This view not only underscores the importance of the intimate audience for groups of writers, but places it at the very center of avant-garde practice, so that the assurance of this audience is the very thing that encourages experimentation or innovation. Predicated as it is on the existence of common social spaces, webs of literary references, and entangled personal histories, Goodman's theory also emphasizes the necessarily *personal* nature of the avant-garde writer's subject matter, which helps to account for one of the broad shifts we find in postwar literature, toward what Mark McGurl calls "the increasingly widespread concern with the voice of the storyteller."[11]

In Goodman's model, the postwar avant-garde is inextricable from "a small community of acquaintances," a suggestive connection for those interested in understanding how and why what are called literary "movements" or "schools" are often coupled with claims about experimentation or innovation. In the case of the Beats in particular, the question of how (or whether) to account for them collectively has been especially acute since they became famous precisely because they were characterized as a "generation" by detractors in the academy and the media who used this very sense of collectivity as pretext to ridicule them. As explained in the coming chapters, the Beats began the rise to national prominence in 1956 and 1957 thanks to an obscenity trial connected to Ginsberg's *Howl and Other Poems* (1956) and then to the release of Kerouac's *On the Road*, which was marketed as the bible of the younger, disaffected generation. As these books spawned a lifestyle movement concomitant with a literary one, amused critics were quick to point out the ironies inherent in asserting individualism collectively. By 1960, poet and longtime *Saturday Review* editor John Ciardi would have great fun claiming that "the Beat Generation is marked by an orthodoxy as rigid as the blue laws. The Beats wear identical uniforms.... They practice an identical aversion to soap and water. They live in the same drab dives listening to the same blaring jazz with identical blanked-out expressions on their identical faces."[12] While Beat literature may have initially sprung from the impulse to write "*for them about them personally*," by the end of the 1950s, Ciardi and many other skeptics distorted this fact to cast this literature *only* in terms of its social symbolism, meaning that it tended to be read not for any potential literary or aesthetic merit but as one among many items in a list of rebellious or antiestablishment activities that included wearing sandals, listening to jazz, and neglecting personal hygiene. Michael Davidson zeroes in on this conflation when he notes that "subordination of actual literary practice to lifestyle is a standard pattern among literary historians" interested in the Beats.[13] Davidson was writing in the late 1980s, and although the intervening years have produced a flowering of scholarship that explores Beat literary practice in depth, there remains a pervasive tendency to view writing as one among so many props of a bohemian lifestyle. This is of course a misperception, but a misperception crucial to understanding Beat writing and its reception.

This book aims to offer an account of individual writers in relation to others, but does so by focusing primarily on language rather than on biographies or social bonds – a differing focus that has, at times, served as a stand-in for textual analysis in critical work on the Beats. In order to do so, this book operates inductively, so that over the course of the following discussions and analyses, certain themes, aesthetic practices, and attitudes toward language will emerge that, when taken together, point toward identifiable, distinctive Beat sensibilities. This strategy means that while I discuss in depth a range of work by Kerouac, Ginsberg, and Burroughs, I also take seriously work by many others, including their lesser known texts, because the very development of the libertine circle into a literary movement demands consideration of a wider array of figures. For the purposes of this book, then, I don't view those beyond the inner circle as "latecomer[s]" or "pryer-intoer[s] of our genuine literary movement" – as Kerouac once grumbled about John Clellon Holmes, considered by virtually all scholars a significant Beat writer – but as progenitors in their own right. My hope is that by offering a wider-angle view, readers may discover a multivalent, sometimes contradictory sense of Beat writing that seems identifiable as such without being quarantined from other energies in mid-century aesthetics and politics.[14] As suggested above, attending to this multiplicity requires that we do not seal Beat literature off from other schools or movements, and that we open ourselves to recognizing potential synergies among this writing and other literary, philosophical, or aesthetic developments in the postwar world. Such an openness might allow us to see the Beats not as a quirky social footnote in the story of postwar letters, but rather as a diffuse movement at the very center of the postwar avant-garde, for their writerly innovations and cultural postures had an incalculable influence on subsequent generations of writers.

2.2   Black Mountain College into *Black Mountain Review*

In the waning years of the 1940s and into the early 1950s, as Kerouac, Ginsberg, and Burroughs were finding the voices and techniques that would inform their most consequential works, they were also cultivating wider networks of friends and fellow travelers with whom they would enjoy reciprocal influence and inspiration. In this way, the story of the Beat emergence is really the story of multiple coteries that would at various moments come into contact with the Beats, who in turn learned from, incorporated, or challenged ideas or paradigms associated with these other coteries. This was the case, for example, with the writers associated with Black Mountain College. As Kaplan Harris has put it, the poets of the so-called Black Mountain School "have been packaged as a more or less coherent group" since their appearance together in Donald Allen's field-defining anthology *The New American Poetry* (1960).[15] Like the Beats, individual writers of the Black Mountain School shared broad sympathies but produced work less coherent than pat labeling allows, and yet – again like the Beats – they have nonetheless come to be discussed primarily in terms of their "membership" in this group. With a qualification about the poverty of labels in mind, it is nonetheless fair to say that Black Mountain played an important role in shaping – and distributing – the inchoate Beat sensibility.[16]

Black Mountain College was a small, experimental, arts school founded in North Carolina in 1933, and by the late 1940s could boast such luminous faculty as composer John Cage, choreographer Merce Cunningham, and painter Robert Rauschenberg. Poet Charles Olson began teaching there in 1948, and would be prove to be a singular influence on the small but surprisingly talented group of student-poets who came through the campus. As Martin Duberman has observed, the "wonder" is that "from a handful of students (from 1952 to 1956 the *total* winter enrollment at Black Mountain averaged about twenty) would emerge poets of the caliber of Joel Oppenheimer, John Wieners, Michael Rumaker, Ed Dorn, and Jonathan Williams."[17] There was also Robert Creeley, who after corresponding with Olson finally ventured to North Carolina in 1954 amid his work on a new magazine that would help advertise the insolvent college's unique merits.

As befits Black Mountain as a "packaged" literary school, there is a manifesto encapsulating the college's intervention in literary history, Olson's highly influential essay, "Projective Verse vs. the Non-Projective," published in 1950 (and later reprinted as a stand-alone pamphlet, *Projective Verse*, in 1959).[18] For a younger generation of writers, including the proto-Beats, Olson's concept of "Projective Verse" was like a shockwave through the literary establishment, challenging as it did what he calls the "closed form" then fashionable in venues like university quarterlies. In contrast to closed form, often embodied by T. S. Eliot and shorthand for mastery of older poetic forms, Olson favors "kinetic" poetry: "A poem is energy transferred from where the poet got it (he will have some several causations), by way of the poem itself to, all the way over to, the reader."[19] He further argues that poets who are "open" may achieve such transfer by viewing the poem as like an extension of their body, meaning, for instance, that line length reflects the length of one's breath. Olson insists continually on the "part that breath plays in verse," concluding that "verse will only do in which a poet manages to register both the acquisitions of his ear *and* the pressure of his breath" (241). From this premise, Olson suggests that form and even syntax must submit to the "LAW OF THE LINE," so that "the conventions which logic has forced on syntax must be broken open as quietly as must the too set feet of the old line" (244). Otherwise put, Olson was calling for a reenergizing of poetry that depended on a kind of immediacy associated with spontaneity and speed – "fast, there's the dogma," he insisted (240).

Those readers even passingly familiar with Beat aesthetics might note some affinities with Olson's declarations, and again and again one finds a wide range of Beat-associated writers insisting on his essay's importance, from Robert Duncan, who claimed to "carry it like people carried *Pilgrim's Progress*," to Michael McClure, who remarked, "When I found Charles' essay on 'Projective Verse,' I found one of the bases of my own poetics," to Joanne Kyger, who marveled at Olson's emphasis on the poet's body:

> Olson's PROJECTIVE VERSE hits me like a whallop. Poetry is true stuff the way he writes of it.
>
> The *Head* by way of the EAR to the SYLLABLE.
> the *Heart* by way of the BREATH to the LINE.[20]

For some later critics, Kerouac's "spontaneous prose" seems to have the most obvious synergy with Olson's projective verse – Ginsberg would in fact later remark, "I don't think Olson would claim that Kerouac was writing projective verse. I think that Olson would say that 'projective verse' is his terminology for this kind of writing."[21] I discuss Kerouac's development of spontaneous prose in some detail later in this book, but I quote Ginsberg here to point both to the sometimes-overlapping aesthetic project of Black Mountain and the Beats and to Ginsberg's willingness to obscure distinctions between "projective verse" and "spontaneous prose," a move that underscores a shared avant-garde project more invested in invigorating language than in reifying labels (although Ginsberg was *also* canny about marketing the Beat Generation as such, as I also explain throughout this book).

As influential as Olson was – for Ginsberg he was "the head peer of the East Coast bohemian hipster-authors post-Pound" – it is tempting, though surely reductive, to see the 1956 folding of Black Mountain College as the moment when the torch was passed from Olson and his circle to the Beats, who would become far more visible embodiments of the literary avant-garde by the end of the 1950s.[22] Those inclined toward such an argument could point to the fact that after Robert Creeley had come to Black Mountain, he did indeed start a little magazine, *Black Mountain Review* (*BMR*) which ran for only seven issues (1954–1957), but had an outsized impact on those hungry for a new poetics.[23] During its run, *BMR* tended to print work by those associated with the College, and was seen as a venue for acolytes of projective verse, even as its contents were in fact always more varied.

The final issue of *BMR* is particularly illustrative of the connections among Black Mountain and the Beats, for it was produced after the College closed and Creeley had moved briefly to San Francisco, where he met Ginsberg and others. In fact, that issue, *BMR* 7 (1957), counted both Olson and Ginsberg among its contributing editors. The huge issue clocked in at over 240 pages, and while it boasted a variety of work, including by those associated with the College, it also presented what Creeley later called "unequivocally a shift and opening of the previous center."[24] Creeley meant the shift to Beat writing, which frames *BMR* 7 even as it was not explicitly labeled as such. For example, after an exchange of letters between Edward Dahlberg and Herbert Read, the first three pieces were Ginsberg's "America," excerpts from Kerouac's "October in the Railroad Earth," and Edward Marshall's "Leave the Word Alone," all key examples of Beat aesthetics. The issue featured also a contribution from William Burroughs (writing as William Lee) titled "from Naked Lunch, Book III: In Search of Yage," as well as poetry by Michael McClure, Philip Whalen, and Gary Snyder. The last three pieces were Kerouac's aesthetic manifesto "Essentials of Spontaneous Prose," Michael Rumaker's review of *Howl and Other Poems*, and a preface that William Carlos Williams had written in 1952 for Ginsberg's book *Empty Mirror*, a collection of early poems that wasn't in fact published until 1961.

Probably thanks to Ginsberg's influence, these were hardly random choices, but rather showcased a range of Beat aesthetic practice. In "America," included in *Howl and Other Poems*, Ginsberg evocatively indicts contemporary political and social mores, and for its publication in *BMR*, he added a new second part that declared, among other things, that "Walt Whitman alone of all American poets was completely hip" and that "Nowadays only teaheads have any idea what Democracy means."[25] "October in the Railroad Earth" is one of the finest examples of Kerouac's spontaneous prose, proceeding as it does from what he calls in "Essentials" a "jewel center of interest," eschewing linear plot to pursue vertical chains of associations (in this way, the piece is a prose illustration of Olson's dictum in

"Projective Verse" that "ONE PERCEPTION MUST IMMEDIATELY AND DIRECTLY LEAD TO A FURTHER PERCEPTION").[26] While Edward Marshall is a less familiar name than Kerouac or Ginsberg, the latter called him "the best of the young poets" on the strength of his "long mad poem," "Leave the Word Alone," which like much Beat work wrestles with themes of institutionalization, particularly in asylums; the nature of self in an unsympathetic society; and what it means to write in the wake of various literary traditions (the speaker hears "a spoken word telling / me to read this and that – / Williams and Olson / I suppose that is the punishment").[27] Burroughs contributed a letter he wrote to Ginsberg from Peru in 1953, in which he recounts his experiences with the hallucinogenic root ayahuasca, or yagé, memorably calling it "space time travel."[28] In terms of Beat literary history, this letter also opens a window onto the chaotic and ever-shifting mass of text that would become *Naked Lunch*; although advertised as an excerpt from "Part III" of the as-yet unpublished novel, in fact this text wound up as part of another book, *The Yage Letters* (1963), with only a few lines making their way into the version of *Naked Lunch* finally published in 1959. The presence of McClure, Whalen, and Snyder in *BMR 7* is also noteworthy because they were among the best of the younger writers associated with the Beat wing of the San Francisco Renaissance. One could reasonably say, then, that with *BMR 7*, Beat writing was given a kind of avant-garde imprimatur that not only would legitimate it in those circles moving forward, but also muddied distinctions among these purportedly divergent schools.[29]

2.3   Anarchy and Poetry in San Francisco

Just as Black Mountain was a major arts community that had a multifaceted and mutually generative relationship with the emerging Beat writers, so too did the poetic and artistic phenomenon that came to be dubbed the San Francisco Renaissance. The Beat sensibility would eventually saturate the San Francisco literary scene so completely that the caricature of the "beatnik" was born there in the late 1950s, and many subsequent readers have accordingly assumed that the San Francisco Renaissance, the Beat Generation, and even the image of the bongo-playing beatnik are one and the same. This widespread misperception is why the first thing Michael Davidson does in his definitive book on the San Francisco Renaissance is dispel the myth that the Renaissance "began" on October 7, 1955, when Ginsberg read "Howl" publicly for the first time at the 6 Gallery (a reading that also featured McClure, Snyder, Whalen, and Philip Lamantia).

Davidson shows that despite the myth-building around this event, notably in Kerouac's *The Dharma Bums* (1958), in fact "the San Francisco Renaissance was by no means unified, nor did it necessarily revolve around the figures who read at the Six Gallery ... Sectarian rivalries among persons, manifestoes, and subgroups within the city fragmented the scene, and when journalists attempted to define some kind of common ground, they had to fall back on vague references to exotic religions and anti-establishment attitudes."[30] As suggested in the preceding pages, this insight could as well apply to the Beat movement, which Davidson notes is "only one strand in a much more diverse and eclectic movement" whose diversity means that it has claims on many of the figures he discusses, particularly Kenneth Rexroth, William Everson, Lawrence Ferlinghetti, Joanne Kyger, Diane di Prima, and Lenore Kandel (60). The major figures Davidson leaves out of his discussion are Bob Kaufman and ruth weiss, both of whom I discuss in more detail later in this book, along with a range of Beat-associated writers working in the Bay Area by the late 1950s, including Ron Loewinsohn, Sheri Martinelli, C. V. J. Anderson, William J. Margolis, and David Meltzer. Merely listing these names gives, I think, a taste of the variety of Beat-associated energies in the city, and as I discuss them in more depth throughout this book, it will illustrate the widening of the movement into ever-expanding circles and networks of connection and collaboration.

Although a Beat scene wouldn't develop in San Francisco until some ten years after Kammerer's murder, there was a robust literary counterculture there long before Ginsberg, Kerouac, and others ever ventured west. The city had been a bohemian enclave for decades, but the dawning of World War II clarified for many writers and artists antiestablishment attitudes that would eventually influence the Beats. Some of these writers, notably William Everson and Kenneth Patchen, were even interned in conscientious-objector camps during the war, where they strengthened communal bonds that would persist in later years, when many settled around the Bay Area. In those years, the area's literary scene came to be dominated by a "countercultural" ethos – insofar as that term can mean a literary and cultural sensibility informed by anarcho-pacifism, a stance Todd Tietchen has described as the belief that "militarized nation-states ... posed a significant threat to the future of the planet ... [that] mass culture and modern nationalism [should be viewed] as simultaneous events that had seriously eroded human potential ... [and a] neo-Romantic call for new subjectivities and modes of collective life that were unsutured from wartime public culture and the formation of dutiful national subjects."[31]

Such a position is exemplified by William Everson's *War Elegies* (1944), a poetry collection published by Untide, a small press he and others started while interned at a conscientious-objector camp in Oregon. *War Elegies* announces the poet's "vow not to wantonly ever take life," and the final poem is particularly suggestive of Everson's later connections to the Beats.[32] Written amid "The Internment, Waldport, Oregon; January, 1943," "War Elegy XI" provides the book with its final lines:

> We perceive our place in the terrible pattern,
> And temper with pity the fierce gall,
> Hearing the sadness,
> The loss and the utter desolation,
> Howl at the heart of the world.

The final image, so redolent of the Beat Generation's most famous poem, suggests in hindsight another meaning of a remark in the book's headnote, that "all these elegies are merely a prelude" (n.p.). The sensibility articulated in *War Elegies* was indeed prelude to a Beat one, distinctive yet in some ways made possible by the elder countercultural generation. After the war, Kenneth Rexroth, Everson's friend and collaborator, was widely held to be the center of San Francisco literary counterculture, so much so that when Ginsberg did finally arrive there in the mid-1950s, he presented Rexroth with a letter of introduction from William Carlos Williams, granting him access to a different community of writers that would stimulate his work in new ways.[33]

But in those immediate postwar years, when Kerouac was lighting out on the road, Ginsberg was in and out of Columbia, and Burroughs was trying his hand at gentleman farming in Texas, Rexroth and his circle were forging a literary ethos that would have a profound effect on the direction of Beat writing and politics. Such an effect is illustrated in *The Ark*, a little magazine that, like *Black Mountain Review*, encapsulates a critical and aesthetic posture the Beats would later appreciate and refine. An avowedly committed venue for work with an anarcho-pacifist cast, the first issue of *The Ark* appeared in spring 1947, and in addition to Rexroth and Everson, featured work by Kenneth Patchen, Robert Duncan, Paul Goodman, e. e. cummings, and William Carlos Williams, among others. Readers familiar with Beat literature might note also the inclusion of San Francisco native Philip Lamantia, a boy wonder who had already published his first book of poetry, *Erotic Poems* (1946) at age nineteen, and who would go on to recite his dead friend John Hoffman's poems at the 6 Gallery reading; or Thomas Parkinson, poet and scholar who would assume a professorship at UC

Berkeley and give some measure of academic credence to the Beats with the still-useful collection, *A Casebook on the Beat* (1961), the first sustained scholarly consideration of them.[34] Ties to *The Ark* and its sensibility are thus even clearer in hindsight, and given the Beats' unwarranted reputation for political apathy, the editorial statement that opens the first issue is particularly useful for contextualizing the literary field into which they would enter:

> In direct opposition to the debasement of human values made flauntingly evident by the war, there is rising among writers in America, as elsewhere, a social consciousness which recognizes the integrity of the personality as the most substantial and considerable of values.. . .
>
> Present day society, which is becoming more and more subject to the State with its many forms of corrupt power and oppression, has become the real enemy of individual liberty.. . .
>
> We believe that social transformation must be the aim of any revolutionary viewpoint, but we recognize the organic, spontaneous revolt of individuals as presupposing such a transformation.[35]

The editors frame the ensuing work as oppositional, so it can therefore be viewed as broadly "antiestablishment" – but they are also much more pointed and specific than this. They charge "the State" with being inherently corrupt and anathema to "individual liberty," envisioning, in contrast, "social transformation" effected by an "organic, spontaneous revolt of individuals." In the context of *The Ark* as a whole, then, the individual contributions are claimed to "do" something by contributing to potential social transformation, a notion directly descended from the radical left tradition.[36]

Such a tradition was never entirely absent from even the earliest Beat texts and positions: part of the plot of *Hippos* concerns Ryko and Tourian trying to validate their cards at the National Maritime Union Hall, where, for instance, members can browse a bookstand stocked with "varied pamphlets of the left-wing type, and the *Daily Worker*" (66). Ginsberg was known even back in high school as the bookish kid who "hated dull teachers and Republicans."[37] And while it is true that radical politics tended to remain submerged in the earliest Beat writing, after their forays in the San Francisco scene, for many – though not all – writers, such politics became increasingly visible and explicit. In "America," Ginsberg's contribution to *Black Mountain Review* 7 (written in Berkeley in early 1956), the speaker describes youthful outings to "Communist Cell meetings," which recall for him still deeper histories of radicalism, when the Party seemed to promise the sort of "social transformation" striven for by *The Ark*'s editors.[38]

This is all to suggest that noting the wider networks in and against which the Beats wrote allows us to recognize aspects of the literature sometimes obscured when viewed only in a bounded context often stained by popular misperceptions. As I explain throughout this book, for instance, while Beat writing is generally less overtly political than the work in *The Ark*, it is hardly apolitical, and one abiding argument advanced is that the Beats, informed by traditions like the one in *The Ark*'s editorial statement, were changing the very notion of what "politics" could look like. This is why, to take one example, in the mid-1950s, Michael McClure and James Harmon resurrected the sensibility of *The Ark*, a publication they considered "the first coherent expression of a new aesthetic and social freedom ... of the post war II generation" (n.p.). Their new magazine, *Ark II Moby I*, became an important articulation of a Beat ethos just before it broke into the national consciousness, and showcases work certainly interested in social transformation, but in less strident terms than those of their forebears.[39]

Beyond incubating magazines like *Ark II Moby I*, San Francisco became an important center of Beat activity thanks in no small part to sympathetic publishers headquartered there, most importantly Lawrence Ferlinghetti's City Lights Books. Originally from New York – he attended Columbia during the same years as the libertine circle, graduating in 1946 – Ferlinghetti came in the early 1950s via France to San Francisco. Deeply invested in the arts, he soon fell in with Rexroth and his circle, during which time he became, as Neeli Cherkovski puts it, "spiritual godson" of writers like Rexroth, Patchen, and Henry Miller.[40] In the coming years, Ferlinghetti would prove himself an important poet in his own right, but his prominence in the Beat movement reaches far beyond his own work as he published and championed a number of seminal Beat texts. In 1953, Ferlinghetti co-founded City Lights Bookstore, and when he bought out his partner in 1955, he established a publishing enterprise that Todd Tietchen has characterized as "a bridge between the ideas of wartime anarcho-pacifists and the animating causes of the New Left and New Social movements to come."[41] This enterprise, City Lights Books, was launched with the Pocket Poets series (inexpensive paperbacks designed to fit in a back pocket), the first four titles of which were Ferlinghetti's own *Pictures of the Gone World* (1955), Rexroth's translations of *Thirty Spanish Poems of Love and Exile* (1956), Patchen's *Poems of Humor and Protest* (1956), and, most enduringly, Ginsberg's *Howl and Other Poems* (1956). While never restricted to Beat texts, City Lights and the Pocket Poets series in particular became firmly associated with them after 1957, when Ferlinghetti and bookseller Shigeyoshi Murao were hit with obscenity charges for selling *Howl*. City Lights also published inexpensive broadsides such as Gregory Corso's "Bomb" and Bob Kaufman's "Abomunist Manifesto," which helped bring a sense of street immediacy to this work, as well as little magazines such as *Journal for the Protection of All Beings* (1961–1978) and *City Lights Journal* (first run: 1963–1966). The San Francisco area, then, became an ideal place for the flourishing of the Beat aesthetic in no small part because of the publishing outlets available there, not only City Lights but, as I explain later, even smaller but vital houses such as Dave Haselwood's Auerhahn Press, and communal centers of energy such as the Bread & Wine Mission, which in 1959 was the staging ground for *Beatitude*, the most important Beat-associated little magazine out of San Francisco in the late 1950s.

2.4 Personism and the New York School

Returning to the original locus of Beatdom, New York City, in the late 1940s, we find one more literary community that, like Black Mountain and the San Francisco Renaissance, illuminates particular facets of the Beat movement. This community, what later came to be known as the New York School, was a circle of young poets including John Ashbery, Kenneth Koch, Frank O'Hara, and James Schuyler. Critic David Lehman has characterized this circle in terms that would not be out of place in most accounts of the Beats: "The poets of the New York School were as heterodox, as belligerent toward the literary establishment and as loyal to each other, as their Parisian predecessors had been."[42] Although, like the Beats, those of the New York School weren't characterized as a group until later years, Lehman dates the "school's" putative launch to June 1948, when Ashbery mailed a poem, "The Painter," to Koch (7). I find it suggestive that this foundational moment occurred within a few weeks of John Clellon Holmes's introduction to Kerouac and Ginsberg, an event that represents an important widening of the Beat circle, since, as I mentioned earlier, virtually every critic considers Holmes a significant Beat writer (Ann and Samuel Charters have argued that Holmes's first novel, *Go* [1952], is "still the most honest . . . [and] darkest portrayal of the Beat scene").[43]

I won't spend as much time on the New York School as Black Mountain and the San Francisco Renaissance because their ties to the Beat movement weren't as deep and varied, partly because many New York School writers felt, as Lehman puts it, "the Beats were too provincial, unsophisticated, narcissistic, and self-mythologizing" (335). Despite such judgments, perhaps the most well-known New York School associate was also at times affiliated with the Beats: Frank O'Hara, a major twentieth-century American poet who revolutionized the use of the vernacular in poetry in ways broadly comparable to the Beats. Like Ginsberg, O'Hara was something of a bon vivant and social operator, and had a wide network of friends and aesthetic confidants in the New York scene – and his Beat connection again highlights the centrality of the personal in Beat writing.

Indeed, like Olson's "Projective Verse" and *The Ark*'s inaugural editorial statement – which, as we have seen, suggest certain affinities among their respective literary communities and the Beats – O'Hara's "Personism: A Manifesto" is a useful articulation of those dimensions of New York School poetics in conversation with the Beat project. Written at the end of the 1950s, "Personism: A Manifesto" was in fact born of O'Hara's interactions with Beat writers, and so while he is generally discussed in connection with the New York School, "Personism" might be seen as a kind of crossover statement that emphasizes the importance of intimate coteries to the development of avant-garde poetics. Writing with particular reference to LeRoi Jones, whose editorial energies in New York in the late 1950s did much to promote and disseminate Beat literature, O'Hara proposes a half-serious poetic declaration about what coterie audiences might mean in terms of poems themselves, as one of Personism's central tenets is to "address itself to one person (other than the poet himself), thus evoking overtones of love without destroying love's life-giving vulgarity, and sustaining the poet's feelings towards the poem."[44] If this seems to return us to Paul Goodman's claim that the contemporary avant-garde ought to write "*for them about them personally*," it's because O'Hara had read "Advance-Guard Writing" back when it first appeared, and was so impressed that he wrote to a friend: "I read Paul Goodman's current manifesto in *Kenyon Review* and if you haven't devoured its delicious little message, rush to your nearest newsstand!"[45] Hardly surprising, then, that numerous critics have heard echoes of Goodman in "Personism"; Andrew Epstein glosses several who note in "Advance-Guard Writing" the "origins of O'Hara's distinctive poetic stance: in particular, his penchant for writing poems to and about his friends, his preference for occasional poetry, and his notorious, controversial practice of nonchalantly citing his friends' proper names in his poems, leaving some to wonder how the reader is supposed to have any idea who 'Jane' or 'John' are."[46] Although Epstein calls these features evidence of O'Hara's "distinctive poetic stance," they also apply to a range of Beat work – both poetry and prose – and it is also significant that while "Personism" is about intimate address to one other person, O'Hara also frames the essay in terms of a broader collective.

While he invokes the term "movement" only half-seriously, playing on the critic's impulse to label and categorize, "Personism" does gesture beyond O'Hara and his friends to imply wider aesthetic energies so that it becomes about *both* addressing "one person" and intervening in literary history. Like so much Beat writing, then, O'Hara's poetics are predicated on intimate address with the awareness of a broader audience always present in the background.

We can clarify what O'Hara is doing with "Personism" by looking at "Personal Poem," the piece that explains the circumstances of the "lunch with LeRoi Jones on August 27, 1959" that inspired his aesthetic philosophy.[47] In that poem – which appeared alongside Goodman's work in *The Beat Scene* and then in O'Hara's celebrated City Lights book *Lunch Poems* (1964) – O'Hara uses the mundane setting of lunch to explore his relationship with LeRoi Jones.[48] This relationship is of course "personal," but it indexes also shared literary and aesthetic principles: "we go eat some fish and some ale it's / cool but crowded we don't like Lionel Trilling / we decide, we like Don Allen we don't like / Henry James so much we like Herman Melville."[49] Although the poem's occasion is a private meeting over lunch, the discussion eventually veers toward the antagonism between competing literary traditions represented by conservative Columbia English professor Lionel Trilling in one camp, and progressive Grove Press editor Don Allen in the other (at the time this lunch took place, Allen was putting the finishing touches on *The New American Poetry*, an anthology that would blow open the literary world by collecting groupings of Black Mountain, San Francisco, and Beat poets). Thus if "Personal Poem" addresses itself to "one person," it also keeps an eye on posterity, on those broader audiences who care more about shifts in poetic trends than the particular relationship between O'Hara and Jones, or between the speaker and the poem's addressee, Vincent Warren, O'Hara's love interest at the time.

In later years, "Personism" even became shorthand for the way some Beat writers thought about the broader literary import of the "poetics of intimacy." For example, in a 1972 assessment of Kerouac's achievement in *Visions of Cody* – a book all about wrestling with how to represent the personal – Ginsberg draws together several strands I've been discussing: "The style ... [of *Visions of Cody*] was simultaneous and later much explored, exploited artfully & gracefully & embellished as in N.Y. school, & Projective verse.... [It was a] breakthru & historic first incidence of that later-universal American style of 'Anything we *do* is art.' Read Frank O'Hara on *Personism*."[50] Writing with some historical distance, Ginsberg emphasizes the links among the avant-garde poetics of the Beats (represented by *Visions of Cody*), Black Mountain (represented by Projective Verse), and the New York School (represented by "Personism") to suggest that the shared project of forging new forms to better explore the personal and to recognize the embodied nature of writing itself was a "historic" literary development, so that speaking one person to another, as Kerouac literally does in *Visions of Cody* when he tape records conversations with Neal Cassady, can be understood as an intervention in literary history and thus of interest to readers beyond the circle.

This is all to say that thinking about the Beats in the context of postwar avant-garde communities allows us to see their affinities with these communities, affinities that can be obscured with the assumption that the Beats somehow materialized from thin air to explode the mores and minds of conservative America.[51] This was the standard line on the Beats for decades, and although a robust body of criticism has overturned this notion, it lingers in the idea that the Beats' primary importance lies in their social postures, a view that figures them first as rebels whose writing is only a tool of such rebellion. While I don't want to diminish the Beats' contribution to postwar social progress, in the pages to follow I want to focus primarily on the writing itself, on what these writers thought they were doing when they explored a "new consciousness" via styles, forms, and breakthroughs they believed would change the very notion of what "literature" could mean or be.

PART II

Underground to Literary Celebrity
(1948–1957)

CHAPTER 3

Hipsters in the Zoo
How the Beats Came Up from the Underground

As explained in Part I, in the mid-1940s, when most of the country was preoccupied with waging global war, Jack Kerouac, Allen Ginsberg, and William Burroughs were venturing into an imagined space called the "underground" and then inventing their own version of its sensibility to help them articulate new visions for American letters. Ironically, by the later part of the decade, cultural observers in New York City were already claiming that the underground was becoming mainstream and therefore passé, and singled out for special ridicule its most visible embodiment, the hipster. As one might gather from the "angelheaded hipsters" of "Howl" (*Howl: Original*, 3), "the sordid hipsters of America, a new beat generation" of *On the Road*, or even the mockery of the "square [who] wants to come on hip" in *Naked Lunch*, figurations of hipsters or the hip are crucial for understanding the emergence of Beat literature, which was inspired by hipsters but strove to be distinguished from them.[1]

In 1948, Anatole Broyard, a writer and critic widely held to be among the more promising literary voices in postwar New York, anatomized the avatar of the underground in a *Partisan Review* piece called "A Portrait of the Hipster." In that article, later a touchstone for those seeking to understand the hip sensibility of the late 1940s, Broyard at once identified the hipster and proclaimed his irrelevance.[2] He began by framing the hipster in literary terms, claiming that as "the illegitimate son of the Lost Generation, the hipster was really *nowhere*."[3] Broyard's italicized use of the slang word "nowhere" isn't incidental as he emphasizes the hipster's reliance on "jive language," arguing that his clipped vocabulary hamstrings thought and expression – years later, LeRoi Jones's "A Poem for Speculative Hipsters" would echo Broyard in imagining a similarly barren linguistic dreamscape containing "Only ideas, / and their opposites / Like, / he was *really* / nowhere."[4] For Broyard, the hipster's peculiar language is both his most distinctive feature and that which radically limits his potential for meaningful personal expression, let alone his capacity to create art: "the hipster banished all comparatives, qualifiers, and other syntactical uncertainties. Everything was dichotomously *solid, gone, out of this world,* or *nowhere, sad, beat,* a *drag*" (722). His own dichotomous hyperbole here notwithstanding, Broyard claims that such language had infected the hipster's very being so that the "external world was greatly simplified ... to schematic proportions which could be easily manipulated" (726).

Claiming this easy though ultimately empty posture meant that the hipster enjoyed brief currency in New York's Greenwich Village, where he was "received as an oracle" while at the same time being roundly ignored by dominant culture (726). For Broyard, because the Village provided the hipster a context receptive to his "schematic" observations, it ironically put him on the road to ruin, for he "got what he wanted; he stopped protesting, reacting ... The hipster – once an unregenerate individualist, an underground poet, a guerrilla – had become a pretentious poet laureate.... He was bought and placed in the zoo" (727). If hipsters must exude an air of disaffected individualism, Broyard identifies the paradox in the notion of a *hipster community* (the underground), that the very existence of such a community means that the hipster has compromised true individuality for a performative caricature of authenticity, something that, as mentioned in Part I, would also become central to criticism of the Beats by the end of the 1950s. Hardly surprising, then, that when the Beats began receiving national attention, Broyard was roundly dismissive of them, a position that Burroughs, for one, saw as rooted in jealousy and resentment: Broyard "hates the Beats," Burroughs said in 1985; "He started out as a Beat writer and didn't make it.... he hates the whole thing. It's very personal."[5]

Although the charge of individual groupthink may seem especially suited to the Beatnik caricature that metastasized across the States after 1957, as Broyard's article suggests, critics were dismissing hipsters in much the same way a decade earlier. In fact, there was some interest in New York literary circles in distinguishing the hipster as a species apart even from the artistic bohemian types that had long populated Greenwich Village. In 1948, the same year Broyard's article appeared, his friend and noted hip character Milton Klonsky (his collected essays would be called *A Discourse on Hip* [1990]) put such a distinction in sharper focus, arguing that hipsters were "a circle apart" from the rest of the Village: "Hipster societies – if they are such, since nobody in them think they belong – may be considered the draft-dodgers of commercial civilization, just as Villagers, in general, are the loyal opposition or 'conscientious objectors.'"[6] Like his pal Broyard, Klonsky can't help but hedge when identifying a *collective* phenomenon, even as he goes on to describe hipsters as a "circle" to be found in "coteries" or "societies." For Klonsky, the oppositional posture of the hipster radiated out to infect everything, including literary or artistic production, so that in his telling bona fide hipsters cared so little for commitments of any kind that it was impossible for them to be writers or artists. Such a view of hipsters would later be applied to the Beats, and even in the early 1950s, before the Beat Generation was public knowledge, these writers found themselves pushing back against not only dominant culture, but those widely held opinions of the New York intelligentsia that hipsters were pseudo-intellectuals deservedly mocked for their hypocritical identification as a group.

3.1 1948: Cool Hipsters Turn Hot

As is well known to students of Beat literature, 1948 was also the year when Kerouac first defined the "Beat Generation," a term that might seem, like "hipster societies," oxymoronic on its face. As John Clellon Holmes later recalled, during a conversation that fall, Kerouac remarked that they were both members of a "generation of furtives" invisible to "the 'public.'" Although Kerouac insisted on "inner knowledge," about "all the forms, all the conventions of the world," what seemed important was that this inner knowledge was shared, thus forming the basis of a collective sensibility, a "*beat* generation."[7] In the context of the long 1950s, it is easy to see why Kerouac might be thinking about sweepingly naming a generation, for there was a pervasive urge to label what W. H. Auden called the "Age of Anxiety" or Irving Howe the "Age of Conformity" or Gregory Corso the "Hung-Up Age" – it was like the Age of Ages.[8] This impulse to label seemed doubly true for literary critics, for as a young William Styron complained in 1954, "Critics are always linking writers to 'schools.' If they couldn't link people to schools, they'd die. When what they condescendingly call 'a genuinely fresh talent' arrives on the scene, the critics rarely try to point out what makes him fresh or genuine but concentrate instead on how he behaves in accordance with their preconceived notion of what school he belongs to."[9]

Literary critics are of course easy targets, but the phenomenon Styron complains about could also cut both ways, and the writers we now call Beat did in the late 1940s and early 1950s think of themselves in terms of a "literary movement," and so one problem became how to frame this movement so it was not overshadowed or otherwise defined by its intersections with hipsters and their environs. By April 1950, for example, Holmes was insisting to Kerouac that "it's time we thought about our material. Call them hipsters, the 'beat generation,' 'postwar kids,' or our own displaced persons whatever you will."[10] In his own effort to think more about "our material" and how it related to the hipster underground, Kerouac sometimes thought of them in the same breath, as in 1957 when the called the Beats "a generation of crazy, illuminated hipsters" (*Portable Kerouac*, 559) while at other times insisting on a distinction between them, as in 1959, when he noted: "When I first saw the hipsters creeping around Times Square in 1944, I didn't like them either. One of them, [Herbert] Huncke of Chicago, came up to me and said 'Man, I'm beat.'"[11] In this view, even Huncke, hipster extraordinaire and later a famed Beat muse, seemed to Kerouac an avatar of another kind of sensibility.

Probably the best way to make sense of this is to say that for Kerouac, the hipster is parent to the Beat but distinct from him. He theorized the difference between hipsters and Beats in terms of "cool and hot":

> Much of the misunderstanding about hipsters and the Beat Generation . . . derives from the fact that there are two distinct styles of hipsterism: the cool today is your bearded laconic sage . . . whose speech is low and unfriendly, whose girls say nothing and wear black: the "hot" today is the crazy talkative shining eyed (often innocent and openhearted) nut who runs from bar to bar, pad to pad looking for everybody, shouting, restless, lushy, trying to "make it" with the subterranean beatniks who ignore him. Most Beat Generation artists belong to the hot school. (*Portable Kerouac*, 569–570)

It's clear, then, that Kerouac conceptualized "cool" in terms of the hipsters as Broyard and Klonsky thought of them back in 1948, whereas the Beats were related but more energized, "crazy talkative shining eyed." But because the image of "the hipster" was already a relatively well-known cultural trope before the Beats published their first works, it tended to be confused in public perception (and critical reception) with what the Beats were trying to do, which is why by the end of the 1950s, Kerouac felt the need to insist on a schematic distinction between them.

CHAPTER 4

The Rise of the Beat Novel
Factualism to Spontaneity

Despite the presuppositions that attached themselves to Beat writing from the moment of their publication – and sometimes before – those reading the work coming out of the immediate postwar years could have identified the initial stirrings of a new sensibility that would attain full flower in the middle and latter part of the 1950s. Several novels were published in the early 1950s that described the lives of the inner circle, directly named the Beats or the Beat Generation, or took as their subject an underground populated by characters that seemed at first blush merely hip, but were in fact something else, the first literary depictions of a Beat sensibility.

Kerouac's first novel, *The Town and the City* (1950), is an expansive saga of the Martin family structured around the social and ideological differences between Galloway – a version of his hometown of Lowell, Massachusetts – and New York City, specifically Greenwich Village and Times Square, home to hipsters and stomping grounds of characters modeled on Ginsberg, Burroughs, Carr, Kammerer, and Huncke. Despite Kerouac's fictionalization of these characters and his use of the word "beat" in *The Town and the City*, John Clellon Holmes's first novel, *Go* (1952), is often credited with being the first "Beat novel," not only because it was the first to name the Beat Generation, but also because its main characters are modeled on Holmes himself, as well as Ginsberg, Kerouac, Cassady, Huncke, and another mutual friend, William Cannastra. Such claims are bolstered by the fact that *Go* was the first published novel to record what would become central moments of Beat lore, including Ginsberg's visions of William Blake, his arrest and subsequent stint in a psychiatric institution, Cassady's bursting onto the New York scene from Denver, and Cannastra's shocking death in a subway accident. Burroughs's first solo novels, *Junky* (1953) and *Queer* (written as an offshoot of *Junky* but not published until 1985), fictionalize his experiences in the drug underworld, self-consciously playing with figurations of the hipster and featuring specific locales found in Kerouac's and Holmes's books, as well as some of the same characters, notably those modeled on Huncke. Following these books, Burroughs developed his singular style with the stories in *Interzone*, a collection that would eventually morph into *Naked Lunch*, the key novel of his career and one of the most influential of the later twentieth century. *Naked Lunch* and Kerouac's *On the Road* are of course the breakthrough Beat novels of the 1950s. First drafted in 1951 but not published until 1957, *On the Road* would thereafter enshrine the Beat Generation as a cultural phenomenon and successor to the Lost Generation. And as central as *On the Road* is to Beat literature, many critics consider his subsequent revision, *Visions of Cody*, written 1951–1952, to be a purer articulation of his aesthetic vision. Published in pieces in 1960 and in its entirety only after Kerouac's death, *Visions of Cody* is far more radical than *On the Road* in terms of formal experimentation, and is important for its display of spontaneous prose, one of Kerouac's signature aesthetic innovations. It is instructive to read these early novels by Kerouac, Holmes, and Burroughs together as much for their mosaic depiction of the underground as for the formal and aesthetic disruptions they collectively initiate.

The following pages thus describe an arc from *The Town and the City* to *Naked Lunch* and *Visions of Cody* not to suggest a clear line of development, but rather a constellation of overlapping characters, philosophical and political ideas, and aesthetic experimentations that suggest how it is possible to consider such discrete and distinctive writing as examples of a literary movement. Because this work emerged from the hip underworld only to resist identification with it, I touch more briefly on two other contemporaneous hipster novels tangential to the inner circle, George Mandel's *Flee the Angry Strangers* and Chandler Brossard's *Who Walk in Darkness* (both 1952). Appearing as they did the same year as *Go*, both of these novels are set in the New York City underground and have at various moments been labeled "the first Beat novel" – despite the fact that when read today they don't seem especially Beat. As I'll explain, I think this has less to do with subject matter and more to do with style and with the authors' sense of their place relative to literary history, two factors that are crucial in thinking about a novel in terms of that elusive idea of "Beat."

4.1   *The Town and the City*: Children of the Sad American Paradise

To appreciate Kerouac's overall achievement, we have to take his first novel seriously on its own terms as much as for the ways it differs from his later, more well-known work. As Tim Hunt has noted, the "usual narrative of Kerouac's development" sees *The Town and the City* as "the promising but conventional apprenticeship and *On the Road* the breakthrough to originality and the paradigm for the work that followed."[1] He goes on to argue that such an account is "misleading" because while *The Town and the City* may seem conventional relative to Kerouac's later works, it was not so conventional relative to other novels being published by "ambitious young fiction writer[s]" in 1950 (34, 35). It is true, for example, that, as many readers have observed, *The Town and the City* takes inspiration from the lyrical realist mode of Thomas Wolfe and his door-stopper novels like *Look Homeward, Angel* (1929); but as Hunt points out, to write in such a mode was itself to buck the established literary wisdom of the late 1940s, which held that Ernest Hemingway's spare unsentimentality was the gold standard to be imitated, not Wolfe's lush romanticism. As such, even if we consider it an apprentice work, *The Town and the City* certainly bears Kerouac's special stamp, and is significant in the context of Beat literary history not only because it was the first in print to fictionalize versions of Kerouac, Ginsberg, Burroughs, and Carr, but also for the way it presents twentieth-century intellectual history. Throughout the novel, Kerouac explicitly delineates the differences between strands of "contemporary thought" associated with Modernism, and a more soul-infused, romantically inclined engagement with the contemporary situation, a sensibility that formed the philosophical and emotional core of what would soon be known as the Beat Generation.

Ranging from the early 1930s to just after World War II, *The Town and the City* follows the fortunes of the Martins, a large family from the working-class town of Galloway, Massachusetts. Most of the plot concerns the growth of three Martin brothers, Joe, Francis, and Peter, and so while *Look Homeward, Angel* is indeed a key influence, fans of Fyodor Dostoyevsky might also find traces of *The Brothers Karamazov* (1880). As Ginsberg later put it, Kerouac was inspired to divide "himself up somewhat similarly into Dostoyevsky characters. Joe would be the equivalent of Dmitri, a solid, all-American ... [Francis would correlate to] Ivan the intellectual, the mentalist, somewhat like Burroughs ... [a] city intellectual.... The third [brother, Peter] is the sensitive Kerouac. Neither the decadent nor the all-American Joe, but the Christian saint or Buddhist bodhisattva [correlating to Alyosha in *The Brothers Karamazov*]."[2] While Ginsberg is inclined to associate Francis's cold intellectualism with Burroughs, the novel also locates this intellectualism in a broadly Modernist literary and philosophical genealogy. For our purposes, I'll focus on the distinction the novel draws between Francis and Peter because it illustrates Kerouac's critique of a Modernist sensibility associated with Francis in favor of the restless, neoromantic sensibility – let's call it "proto-beat" – associated with Peter. In the context of Kerouac's work specifically and Beat literary history more generally, *The Town and the City* is thus tremendously suggestive as it reflects Kerouac's thinking about literature and aesthetics in the late 1940s, when he saw his and his friends' work as inaugurating the next great literary leap forward.

Significantly, it is Francis, not Peter, who seems to have the first claims to being a proto-Beat in *The Town and the City*. Still mired in what he considers a cultural backwater, Francis haunts Galloway's public library looking for intellectual nourishment, and there he runs into a man passing through town on a business trip. Wilfred Engels – Carlo Marx would not appear until *On the Road* – is a cosmopolitan Leftist who introduces Francis to a whole body of thought beyond the provincial mores of Galloway. If Francis had long felt isolated and out of sync with society, Engels shows him that he is hardly alone in such feelings, and exposes the budding intellectual to a republic of letters predicated on a shared disaffection from the mainstream. Through Engels, Francis will learn "the articulate fluent language of 'contemporary thought' … [and] 'modern consciousness.'"[3] As Francis swims deeper in the waters of modernity, his "misty indistinct feelings" are given shape by psychoanalytic and Marxist theories, existentialism, and the masters of Modernist literature, and his worldview is clarified thanks to a new critical vocabulary: "'compulsive neurosis,' 'oedipus complex,' 'anxiety,' 'economic exploitation,'" and the like (116). Growing up in Galloway means that such terms are deeply foreign to Francis, and although he considers the ideas they represent as an "invisible revolt in America" challenging "society and its conventions and traditions" (116), the novel underscores that such a revolt is only invisible to small-town America. In other words, if Francis's eyes are opened to a wider philosophical or cultural "revolt," it is not one happening in what Broyard or Klonsky called the underground, but rather is becoming increasingly de rigueur for anyone – solvent middle-class or not – desperate to claim distinction from the masses.

The same year *The Town and the City* was published, for example, novelist Robert Lowry identified a species he labeled "Underground Man Model 1950": he "wears a tie, buys shoeshines, gets his hair trimmed every ten days, washes his armpits," and so on, and yet he "is sure that his opinions are contra the world's."[4] For Lowry, this clean-cut Underground Man defines himself against prevailing taste and opinion, whether mainstream or countercultural, and thus busies himself "disdaining both the Greenwich Village neurotics and the uptown successes but shuttling between the two at least three or four times a week" (18). Of course the basic irony in Lowry's observation is that one could fancy himself "an underground man and hold a majority opinion" (19), and so as Klonsky would delight in needling "hipster societies," Lowry lambasts the Underground Man Model 1950 "for a solidly obscure underground opinion, a really radical, rascally attitude that will knock the Sears, Roebuck socks of the fuddy-duddy old man back in Oswego" (19–20).[5]

As Francis leaves Galloway for Harvard and then New York City, he becomes more immersed in the sort of "modern consciousness" increasingly adopted by part-time bohemians and pseudo-intellectuals in the nation's urban centers. Far from being invisible, Engels's heroes read like a Who's Who of Modernism, a universe of "strange names and stars that constellated it: Freud, Krafft-Ebing, Kafka, Jung, Rilke, Kierkegaard, Eliot, Gide, Auden, Huxley, Joyce ... Picasso, Braque, Cocteau, Heidegger, Tchelitchev, Henry Miller, Isherwood" (116). As the novel unfolds, it becomes increasingly clear that Kerouac is associating Francis with a particular strand of "contemporary thought" that had from the turn of the century to World War II radically changed how the world was understood. Though these figures are "strange" to Francis, they are of course central to Western modernity, so much so that by the immediate postwar years they had become "mainstreamed" – this is why Lowry could complain that by 1950, even a "home-town" housewife "wanted to know more about George Orwell, William Faulkner and Ezra Pound – seems she'd been reading about them in the Luce publications [*Time* and *Life*]" (17).

After Francis has assimilated what had been revolutionary thought for a previous generation, his intellectual development reaches an ironic apotheosis when he encounters the *New Yorker*. Despite that magazine's highbrow pretentions, those working on the more avant-garde edges of "modern consciousness" tended to view it as of a piece with mainstream publications of little substance or retrograde taste: in 1949 Marshall McLuhan grouped it with *Time* and *Life* as "our psychological bureaucracy, inhabited by well-paid artist-apes" and in 1952 Seymour Krim with *Harper's Bazaar* and *Mademoiselle* as "sleek bourgeois magazines – bourgeois in lack of daring, lack of purpose."[6] It is from this general perspective that Kerouac has Francis fawn over the magazine:

> The sentences themselves were so fresh and glossy and new, "the latest," the very smartest somehow, the last thing in the whole huge scene that was New York and even Washington and Boston and Chicago, all connected together somehow by networks of rails and dining-cars on which people read the *New Yorker* and sipped martinis, a world connected by rumor, excitement, news, style, opinion, fashion, smart talk. (462)

By this late point in the novel, Francis has been seduced by the trappings of bourgeois life, so the once revolutionary concepts represented by Freud and Joyce become flattened in the "glossy" pages of the *New Yorker*, figured like martinis as a prop of well-off pseudo-intellectuals interested not in "revolt" but in rumor and anodyne opinion. In place of the paradigm-shattering lights of Modernism that first drew Francis from Galloway is a "scene" held together by the well-written gossip of the *New Yorker*, and Francis's attachment to it signals that his dissatisfaction "with society and its conventions and traditions" has itself become a kind of convention (in a 1948 outline of the novel, Kerouac underscores the idea that Francis "indulges in literary diatribes against American culture in the little chi-chi publications of the city").[7] A final word on this change comes from younger brother Mickey, who on a visit to the city defines Francis by his material successes: "What a nice apartment Francis lives in . . . right in the middle of New York, and what a nice blonde he's got. . . . Imagine having a girl like that right in the middle of New York, and a good job, and go out at night to big restaurants. . . . Yow! What a lucky guy!" (468). Francis, the one-time critic of convention and tradition, has become their very avatar.

While Francis's intellectual odyssey culminates in a good job and nice Midtown apartment, Peter's leads him to decidedly Beat horizons, notably the bohemian Lower East Side and beyond. In contrast to his brother's bloodless forays into "modern thought," Peter is introduced to literature and philosophy by his childhood friend Alexander Panos, whose interest in books leads him not to analytic abstraction but to "things for the sake of themselves." He speaks of "'ideals,' 'beauty,' and 'truth,'" so it is fitting that "One of the first things young Alex did was to read him [Peter] Keats' 'Ode to a Grecian Urn' [*sic*] . . . and their friendship opened up into a springtime of wonder and knowledge" (131). Peter's New York will accordingly look quite different from Francis's, as portended by his first visit there, where he and Alexander "drank beer in longshoremen's bars, stood vigil on Brooklyn Bridge in the dead of night, visited museums and theaters, sailed on the ferry to Staten Island, and quoted poetry at dawn in scraggly streets" (141). If this loose mix of tourism and "great cries to the rising sun" (142) seems Beat-like, it is perhaps because it is exactly the sort of behavior Ginsberg would celebrate in "Howl," whose subjects "talked continuously seventy hours from park to pad to bar to Bellevue to museum to the Brooklyn Bridge" (*Howl: Original*, 3).

The divergence between the brothers is further clarified toward the end of the novel, in what Kerouac later called its "hipster chapters."[8] This is the part that seems most familiar to fans of Beat writing as it is when Peter takes up with characters modeled on the libertine circle. Peter is drawn into the world of Leon Levinsky and Junkey, characters modeled on Ginsberg and Huncke, respectively. Levinsky first appears decked in a "Paisley scarf, and dark-rimmed glasses with the air of an intellectual," and at his side is the "dope addict, whose only known name was Junkey" (364). In a move that would be repeated in many other Beat novels, Kerouac figures these characters not merely as eccentric individuals but as embodiments or representations of a more widespread underground scene. Levinsky, for example, "'knew everybody' and 'knew everything,' was always bearing tidings and messages from 'the others,' full of catastrophe. He brimmed and flooded over day and night with a thousand different thoughts and conversations." These others – "everyone Peter knew, [and] a few thousand others Peter did not know" – make up "the 'scene'" (365), the underground counterpoint to the "whole huge scene" of bourgeois *New Yorker* readers (462). Levinsky's scene is the geographical and social context for the Beat Generation, "All the cats and characters ... looking for something, waiting for something, forever moving around" (362), and by the end of the decade the word "scene" itself would be launched into wider usage as signaling the hip world, as in the 1960 anthology *The Beat Scene*.

True to form, Levinsky takes Peter on a tour of what he hypes as "a great symbol among all of us" (371), an "amusement center" called the Nickel-O, probably modeled on the Pokerino Palace, one of Huncke's Times Square haunts and a favorite spot of Ginsberg's at the time:[9]

> when you go in there among all the children of the sad American paradise, you can only stare at them, in a Benzedrine depression ... It goes on all night, everyone milling around uncertainly among the ruins of bourgeois civilization, seeking each other, ... but so stultified by their upbringings somehow, or by the disease of the age, that they can only stumble about and stare indignantly at one another. (369)

Unlike Francis, who begins in similar alienation only to flourish in "bourgeois civilization," Levinsky's people are both defined and rejected by "the sad American paradise." For Levinsky, it is their "upbringings" and the "disease of the age" that have left them bereft of human connection and seemingly alienated from even themselves. This suggests, as we will see throughout this book, that even in early depictions of Beatness or proto-Beatness, there is a dynamic connection to dominant culture rather than a total rejection of it.

In this existential context Peter encounters Junkey, who tells him, "I'm beat and I need some sleep if I'm also going to score with the doctors for everybody around here" (402). This is the sense of "beat" that Kerouac later attributed to Huncke circa 1944, when he recalled it as part of "a new language."[10] In the novel as in real life, this word takes on a greater portability when the narrator uses it to describe New York's underground scene, the context for using the word "beat" in its fuller sense, to describe Francis and Peter's sister, Liz, who winds up a "hip-chick" in the city (449). As he describes how Liz was drawn into the hipster lifestyle, Kerouac tosses out the sort of hip words Broyard had identified in his article: she spends her nights "wandering 'beat' around the city ... When you were loaded with loot and having your kicks, that was living; but when you were hung up without gold and left beyond the reach of kicks, that was a drag" (451). Here the word "beat" is placed in quotation marks to signal that it is being used as an adjective to describe a world characterized also by slang such as "kicks," "hung up," and "drag." By the later 1950s, such jargon would be repeated to the point of parody, but for Kerouac at this time it was still "a new language" useful for demarcating and distinguishing a subculture he was interested in exploring.

Although the end of *The Town and the City* includes a version of Kammerer's murder (Kerouac turns the death into a suicide), it actually closes on a positive note that offers a link to his later work. If those in Levinsky's circle are the clearest Beat or proto-Beat characters in the book, there is another, far more subtle presence that is perhaps more significant in retrospect for the ways it prefigures *On the Road* and *Visions of Cody*: Neal Cassady. In the fall of 1946, a mutual friend from Denver, Hal Chase, had introduced Cassady to Kerouac, Ginsberg, Huncke, and others in their circle.[11] His frenetic energy, sexual prowess, and ability to write letters in the manic way he spoke would have an incalculable effect on the direction of Beat literature.

Cassady makes an oblique though significant appearance in *The Town and the City* as the inspiration for Peter's existential journey. Reflecting on the novel in a long letter to Cassady in 1951, Kerouac claimed that "the whole story of Peter Martin, as such, is contained in this one dream" in which Peter fantasizes about lighting out on the road (*Selected Letters, 1940–1956*, 305). The scene is near the middle of the book, when Peter dreams of "his father's car, the old Plymouth, and his father himself sitting in it and smoking a cigar and looking at a roadmap ... in the great light of a plain, with mountains beyond" (395). Singling out this scene for Cassady, Kerouac proceeds to analyze it for him:

> the only reason why – the ONLY reason – I threw in ... the part about plains and mountains, in other words, Colorado and Denver itself, because

you came from there. I'm saying to you, when I wrote that last line of the paragraph in my "Town & City" labors, I was specifically referring (tho not mentioning) with respect to you, so that you too stood around the tractor plow with Joe and Charley. This is how you are therefore strangely connected with the scene of these events in my life twenty four years ago, in haunted old sad Lowell of time. (306)

The dream is the germ of Peter's desire to see the wider world, and he in fact realizes it in the final short section of the novel, when he sets off to hitchhike "on the road" (498). Cassady is thus the unspoken link between Kerouac's first two published novels. While very different in style, tone, and aim, when read together and especially in the context of the hipster underground sketched earlier, we might actually note some commonalities between these two texts that remind us that one hallmark of Beat literature is the sort of subterranean connections Kerouac points out to his friend and muse.

4.2 *Flee the Angry Strangers* and *Who Walk in Darkness*: Underground Calling

The New York City underground scene described in the last section of *The Town and the City* was of interest to novelists in the early 1950s, especially since the underground could serve as a catch-all word linked to several hot-button social issues of those years, including drug use, juvenile delinquency, and sexual promiscuity. As in Kerouac's Greenwich Village and Times Square, such people were often lumped together with jazz musicians and bohemian writers and artists as part of a vaguely associated hip underworld, a perennial object of fascination for the solid-citizen reading public.[12]

Two novels worth mentioning in this context are George Mandel's *Flee the Angry Strangers* and Chandler Brossard's *Who Walk in Darkness*, both of which appeared in the middle of 1952, and both of which explore undergrounds similar to the one in *The Town and the City*. These books represent differing approaches to the scene: like an ethnographer immersed in his culture of study, Mandel moved to the Lower East Side with the express purpose of gathering material for a book, which accordingly has an objective, documentary feel (a mode Burroughs would adopt but undermine in *Junky*). Brossard, by contrast, was an old Village resident with ties to the Beat scene. Interested at the time in existentialism and the French *nouveau roman* that aimed to overturn conventional expectations about genre, Brossard used the underground as a setting for philosophical explorations of individuals and how they relate or not to their environment.

After serving in World War II, George Mandel returned to his native New York City, where he was drawn to the underground as object of study.[13] Although not originally associated with the inner circle, when the Beats became a media sensation after 1957, Mandel was not only classed as such by anthologists, but he traded on the sudden notoriety with *Beatville, U.S.A.* (1961), a book of cartoon sketches gently lampooning the supposed Beatnik lifestyle. As the cover announced, it was "a hilarious, opinionated and uncensored view of the Beat Generation by a noted author who saw it coming – and ducked!"[14] If Mandel was "noted" by 1961, it was on the strength of *Flee the Angry Strangers* and his sophomore effort, *The Breakwater* (1960). He would go on to have a long career, but his best-known novel remains his first, largely due to its perceived connection with the Beats: in 2003, the 50th anniversary edition declared it "the first Beat novel."[15]

But when *Flee* appeared in 1952, hipsters figured as Beat were only to be found lurking in the latter pages of *The Town and the City*, and were still unnamed as a "generation" in Holmes's *Go*, so there was no deliberate link to the inner circle in the novel itself. Mandel was, however, interested in a social phenomenon headquartered in the Village, and he spent five years there, conducting what he called "research" that "occurred incidentally while I was sitting it out with painters, dreamers, and dope fiends."[16] *Flee* thus reads as though Mandel is an ethnographer observing the strange habitat of "drug addicts and their world" – the subtitle emblazoned on the dust jacket – and outlets like the *New York Times* and *Time* were at once shocked and fascinated by his "clinical" and "documentary" mode. Read in the context of early Beat novel, we might say *Flee* is the straight version of the junk underground that Burroughs turns inside out in *Junky*, published a year later.

Reminiscent of the characters Levinsky describes haunting the Nickel-O, those who populate *Flee the Angry Strangers* are "dope fiends and philosophers, prostitutes and poets, artists and hoods, darlings, dreamers, derelicts and every American variety of displaced person, all together in a debris of Babel."[17] And as in *The Town and the City*, Mandel emphasizes the sense of these people both as a subculture *and* as Americans, so that the stories of his particular characters read as indices of a more diffuse underground phenomenon. Mandel takes pains to depict a panoply of characters who comprise his underground, from Stoney, a "shaggy" painter who mugs for slumming tourists from uptown, to Dincher, a musician whose speech is clogged with "like" and assorted slang ("Like-he's good for a sixer-like"), to Lukey the Swede, whose half-thought politics amount to complaining that "everybody dominated me . . . We got to eliminate the dominance in life. When the big kicks the small he's gonna get kicked when the small gets larger" (17, 32, 60). Each of these characters represents a facet of the hip scene, and in their comic flatness sometimes anticipate Beatnik caricatures popular by the end of the 1950s (and that Mandel would himself indulge in *Beatville, U.S.A.*). Stoney doesn't so much paint as perform the role of painter, while Lukey the Swede, tired of being "dominated," thinks up a credo he calls "escapology," a social and political refusal that is a light version of what Kenneth Rexroth liked to call "disaffiliation." Clearly the novel is poking fun at certain members of the scene, but the tone takes a much darker turn with the story of Diane Lattimer, an eighteen-year-old who sweeps into the Village after having busted out of a youth home.

Much of the novel concerns Diane and her descent into hell as she gets increasingly entangled with this cast of underground characters. We soon learn that Diane was a rebellious teenager – so much so that she has an illegitimate son and a penchant for marijuana. Her mother (such an embodiment of dominant culture that she works as the manager of the copy-editing department at an advertising agency [186]) tries to get Diane back on track, but to no avail. The plot follows Diane as she moves from marijuana and casual sex to heroin and prostitution, and the cutesy depictions of hipsters and bohemians in the first part give way to the physical and existential horror visited upon her as she sinks deeper into the underground. With its unrelenting, unflinching descriptions of death, addiction, and crime, *Flee* makes the most of its clinical, documentary mode that stands as a warning against the corrupting influences of illegal drugs. As one of the novel's more level-headed characters remarks, "this narcotics kick is all over town – all over the country for all I know. Diane was caught up in it. School kids are using it" (374). Thus while the novel is set in some of the same social spaces from which the Beat movement emerged, and includes visible markers of hipsterdom like jazz, marijuana use, and what reviewers called a "weird vocabulary," the "special jargon of drug addiction," *Flee* does not finally read as particularly Beat as it contains none of the joy or inventive language that marks later work, and is basically a warning against the call of that kind of life.[18]

Whereas *Flee the Angry Strangers* is notable for its "clinical," ethnographic treatment of the underground as threat to regular folk, the other hipster novel of these months, Chandler Brossard's *Who Walk in Darkness*, explores the scene more subtly, in terms of performance. For Brossard, the hip underground is not merely a world apart from respectable culture, but a contingent social space where figurations of identity are mutable and therefore unstable. Set as it is in the Village in the late 1940s, *Who Walk in Darkness*, like *Flee*, has been dubbed the first Beat novel. Unlike Mandel, though, Brossard was consistently vocal about distancing himself from the Beat Generation, claiming instead affinities with a "less publicized group" that immediately preceded them. This group includes the real-life models for writers and intellectuals he describes in *Who Walk*, people who knew the inner circle and even shared some of their aesthetic goals; as Brossard later remarked: "These people were the first 'beats,' if you like, and their scene was the Village in the middle and late forties, and I was there among them and part of them before, during, and after the writing of my first novel."[19]

Despite Brossard's insistence that he was not a "member" of the Beats, readers of *The Town and the City* will encounter suggestive echoes in *Who Walk in Darkness* ("Tentative," 7). His hesitancy to be pigeonholed as a Beat writer – especially in the Beatnik Era and after – is understandable, but his own experiences in New York during the period belie his claims to hard distinctions between his work and that of the Beats. In fact, Brossard lived in the same building as David Kammerer, and according to Barry Miles, the two were "close friends" who saw each other "constantly" the summer Kammerer was killed.[20] Brossard even turns up in *Hippos*, the original Beat collaboration, as Chris Rivers, "a chronic deadbeat and sanitary problem" (182).[21] Such personal and aesthetic connections are why Brossard was collected in the very first Beat anthology, and why he was included in Ann Charters's landmark critical collection *The Beats* (1983), in which Samuel Charters concluded that *Who Walk* "will continue to be discussed as a document of the early Beat movement, if not as an example of Beat writing, then for the glimpse it gives of emerging Beat consciousness."[22] I am less interested in claiming Brossard as a "member" of this or that group than I am in noting the ways in which *Who Walk* uses the Village underground as both setting and metaphor for the way social milieu puts pressure on people's outward expressions of self, even as we all like to cling to our own senses of autonomy. The hipster is in fact the ideal figure to explore such an idea, since, as Broyard and Klonsky argue, his very raison d'être is to blanch at society, a paradox that motivates Brossard's analyses of the mandates of the underground at that time and place.

Despite Brossard's later complaints about being associated with the Beats, in *Who Walk* he consciously sets out to map a new social phenomenon, for as the jacket copy on the first edition announced: "Here for the first time the new generation of American bohemians are presented in fiction."[23] Such claims of generational bohemianism could of course apply to the Beats as much as Brossard's characters, but the novel itself is more subtle in its handling of hipsterism. The narrator, Blake Williams, knows a lot of hipsters but tries to maintain a certain arch aloofness from them, describing himself as "partly underground" (114).[24] The novel opens with Williams's conflicted description of Henry Porter, at once a hip ladies' man and social wit who can boast "some literary status" (5), and a shameless social climber who steps on those who might interfere with his ambitions. In Porter's general orbit are the hipster extraordinaire Max Glazer, the "Hamlet of the Underground" (56); and Harry Lees, a New Englander who doesn't seem naturally cool, but desperately wants to be liked, and so knows enough to claim an interest in the right sort of hip preoccupations. As Williams deadpans early on, he and his circle dislike certain bars because they attract the wrong clientele: "We did not like the people who went to them. We did not think they were very hip" (5). Brossard thought of the book variously as an "antinovel" and "existential novel" and as such the plot is purposively aimless, concerning mainly drinking and philosophical discussions punctuated by visits to New Jersey to watch a young boxer train.[25] The most dramatic moments are when Porter's girlfriend, Grace, comes to Williams for assistance with an abortion (unbeknownst to Porter), and they wind up falling for each other. Although not much happens in *Who Walk*, Brossard remarked that it is "about what people do to one another when their sustaining sociological context collapses," and we might think of the particular context as the hip underground, and the way it collapses Brossard's critique of this context's effect on people ("Tentative," 22).

Given his interest in French existentialism and the "antinovel" as form, Brossard always stressed these dimensions of the novel even as readers thought they spotted a straightforward roman à clef and so read it on those terms. As critic Delmore Schwartz put it at the time, "Brossard draws directly from life and often the prototypes are so unmistakable that the reader must feel that only one thing is lacking: the telephone numbers of the human beings whom the novelist has in mind."[26] The real people from whom Brossard drew inspiration include none other than Anatole Broyard, on whom Harry Porter was modeled, as well as Milton Klonsky (Max Glazer), and a then-unknown writer named William Gaddis (Harry Lees).

At the time, Gaddis, who is today widely considered a heavyweight of postwar writing, had yet to publish his first book, what would become the massive encyclopedic novel, *The Recognitions* (1955). Although Gaddis is usually thought of as exemplifying a postmodern aesthetic rather than a

Beat one, his writing developed in the same New York underground that gave birth to the Beats – he once shared a Village apartment with Brossard – and *The Recognitions*, for all its knotty philosophical density, features also the same bars, parties, and conversations that animate books like *The Town and the City* and *Go*, a tapestry one character calls the "rags and relics below Fourteenth Street."[27] Such intersections were obvious to the *Time* reviewer, for one, who panned Gaddis's bleak tone, claiming, "To the small army of 'beat generation' characters in *The Recognitions*, dawn never comes."[28] In *The Recognitions*, Gaddis, like Kerouac or Holmes, takes pains to suggest his characters are indices of a more widespread underground phenomenon, and so depicts Village bars as overrun by hipsters, "poets here who painted; painters who criticized music; composers who reviewed novels, unpublished novelists who wrote poetry," a group characterized as "an ill-dressed, underfed, overdrunken group of squatters with minds so highly developed that they were excused from good manners, tastes so refined in one direction that they were excused for having none in any other, emotions so cultivated that the only aberration was normality, all afloat here on sodden pools of depravity calculated only to manifest the pricelessness of what they were throwing away" (305). Thus if it makes sense to discuss Kerouac, Burroughs, and Holmes as a community of writers responding to and emerging from the same geographic and intellectual spaces, then it likewise makes sense to recognize that books like *Who Walk in Darkness* and *The Recognitions*, while as stylistically and formally distinct as *The Town and the City* and *Naked Lunch*, are nonetheless connected to the hip underground, and would benefit from further study in that context.

Although in 1952, Gaddis was too obscure to raise any eyebrows among the New York literati, Anatole Broyard was well known, and the fact that Harry Porter was obviously inspired by Broyard caused a minor scandal prior to *Who Walk*'s publication. Like Porter, Broyard was known as something of a social climber, a smooth talker who, also like Porter, had the Gatsbyesque habit of calling people "sport."[29] Brossard belabors Porter's attempts to "to dress like a Harvard man" (3) because he "wanted to be taken for a Harvard type" (4). But scandal brewed not merely because Brossard had used real-life people recognizable to some, but because of a particular dimension of the novel encapsulated in its very first line: "People said Henry Porter was a 'passed' negro" (1). Given that Porter was otherwise so recognizably modeled on Broyard, Schwartz and others thought the novel could damage Broyard's reputation, and encouraged James Laughlin at New Directions to delay its publication until

Brossard revised out mentions of Porter's possible blackness.[30] As published in 1952, *Who Walk* opened with the line "People said Henry Porter was an illegitimate," which inevitably led to some odd moments later in the book, since illegitimacy didn't carry quite the same social force as racial passing: toward the end of the novel, for instance, Harry demands of Porter, "Are you really an illegitimate? ... Everybody I know cares."[31]

Contemporary controversies aside, the expurgated race plot is central to what Brossard is doing with the underground, for if the importance of racial difference can be destabilized by passing, hipsterism can likewise be seen as dependent on performance. Brossard's version of the "underground man" is sketched at the Sporting Club – a Village bar modeled on the famed San Remo – where a tourist from Midtown gets a glimpse of hipster society. Harry Lees introduces the group to Russell Goodwin, "an account executive [who] makes four hundred a week" (99) and hence a stand-in for square America – Max correctly guesses that Goodwin reads "the *New Yorker* regularly and think[s] it is really terrific" (106). Goodwin's visit to the Sporting Club is an opportunity for Brossard to define his terms: "What do you mean by the underground man?" asks Goodwin (102). Lees and Porter spar over an answer:

> "The man who will do anything [said Lees]. He's a spiritual desperado."
>
> "He means Max Glazer," Porter said, "He's a very smart guy. Really very hip."
>
> "I didn't say he wasn't. He is a desperado, though. Do you know what his ideal is? His ideal is to look like a street-corner hoodlum and be the finest lyric poet in America at the same time." (102)

Lees's characterization echoes one in a nonfiction piece Brossard had published in 1950, which offers a portrait of a "young Jewish poet who wants to seem like an underworld character, ... his every public move calculated to encourage this personality myth."[32] As in Lees's description of Glazer, in this essay Brossard zeroes in on a performative falsity associated with hipsterism: although hipness seems to mean exuding a natural cool without concern for what others think, in *Who Walk* it in fact means a constant awareness of everyone else's opinion, thus compromising the hipster's claim to easy authenticity. If, for Lees, Max is "the real Modern Man," he is so because the modernity of Francis's idols in *The Town and the City* has been replaced by the impulse to live underground, which in Max's case means that "He acts the way he feels like acting" (56); the repetition of "acts" and "acting" is not incidental as the novel glosses hipsterism as a posture, another kind of social game. This is why Max's "racket" (213) is to teach "a rich woman how to write poetry" (90), thereby selling out both idealistic notions of poetry and himself, in much the same way that Porter dons an Ivy League costume as if to will himself into a different social stratum. After the scene with Goodwin the slumming tourist, both Williams and Lees are left more confused; as Lees says: "It is like a joke become serious.... I don't know when to take this underground business as a laugh or when to take it as the real thing" (114). *Who Walk in Darkness* is finally evasive about the existence of any underground at all, for it could be a figment built on shifting sands, one that has an evocative power but that is not born from anything genuine or authentic. For a writer interested in the existentialist bent of what would become known as the *nouveau roman*, "the hipster" is the ideal figure since his identity seems to be premised on claims to unmediated authenticity but is in fact legible mainly via performance.

4.3   *Go*: A New Season about to Break

If Brossard managed to write a hipster novel while routinely disavowing his ties to the Beat Generation, John Clellon Holmes went out of his way to advertise his connections with this generation, naming in it in his debut novel, *Go*, and a companion essay he published in the *New York Times*. Born in Massachusetts on March 12, 1926 (four years to the day after Kerouac), Holmes missed out on the formation of the original libertine circle as he had been drafted into the Navy. After serving a stint in the Hospital Corps, he moved to New York with his wife, Marian, and tried to plug in to the literary scene loosely associated with Columbia University. By June 1948, he had achieved modest success as a poet, having published work in mainstays such as *Poetry* and *Partisan Review*. And yet despite being able to pass for an academic poet, Holmes was drawn to the underground scene via his interest in jazz, which he would eventually develop into his second novel, *The Horn* (1958), about saxophonist Edgar Pool and others living on the edges of respectable society.

The Horn had a precursor in "Tea for Two," a story Holmes published in the summer of 1948, the title a seeming nod to the popular song of the same name, but for those in the know really alluding to the marijuana or "tea" smoked by the story's two characters. Filled with the sort of slang that would come to mark Beat work – and later fascinate critics – "Tea for Two" dramatizes an encounter between a jazz musician, Beeker, and an unnamed woman who wanders into his club. The woman interests Beeker because she exudes a strange energy, earnestly telling him: "Life is just some of your friends and some tea to you; but with me there has to be something else, that makes it mean something, that gives it dimension.... I want to paint, and live if possible ... so I take a trip to a place I've never been to and live another life in which I don't believe."[33] Substitute "write" for "paint" and these lines could have been spoken by Sal Paradise in *On the Road*, suggesting that Holmes had been exploring a like sensibility before he ever encountered the members of the inner circle.

In fact, "Tea for Two" was like a countercultural credential for Holmes as it appeared not in a stuffy university quarterly, but in *Neurotica*, a bootstrapped magazine out of St. Louis whose editor, Jay Landesman, imagined it as an outlet for the "man who has been forced to live underground, and yet lights an utter darkness with his music, poetry, painting and writing."[34] Landesman would later characterize the magazine explicitly in the generational terms set forth by Ginsberg in the opening lines of "Howl": "I was determined to bring the best and most original minds of our generation to *Neurotica*. I eventually brought together an unholy alliance of existentialists, surrealists, radical sociologists, psychoanalysts, playwrights and musicians to create the first underground critique of American life."[35] (*Neurotica* even met with Brossard's approval, as he called it "the most original and inspired magazine of the time."[36]) *Neurotica* ran from 1948 to 1952 and was an important venue for the hip sensibility of the moment, featuring the likes of Brossard, Broyard, and Carl Solomon (Solomon appeared under the names Carl Goy and Carl Gentile). *Neurotica* also has the distinction of being the first non-student publication to print Ginsberg's poetry, a brief collaboration with (uncredited) Kerouac, "Song: Fie My Fum," the first line of which would be repurposed for the title of a later collaborative Beat film, *Pull My Daisy* (1959), discussed in Part III. In 1981, Landesman would reprint the nine issues of the magazine in book form, giving it the subtitle of "The Authentic Voice of the Beat Generation." Although that book included an introduction by Holmes, the subtitle is marketing hyperbole: while Landesman certainly was an early champion of Beat-associated writers, they were a minority part of an eclectic group that included everyone from composer Leonard Bernstein to pop philosopher Marshall McLuhan; as Beat scholar R. J. Ellis has put it, "it is more accurate to think of *Neurotica* not so much as a Beat magazine, as an influence upon the Beats."[37]

That said, publishing in *Neurotica* only boosted Holmes's image in the eyes of other hungry writers. Recalling his first encounter with Ginsberg over the July Fourth weekend, 1948, Holmes felt glad-handed for his "useable connections" since, as he wrote, Ginsberg was never one to "pass up on an opportunity to cultivate anyone who might be helpful."[38]

His introduction to Ginsberg was only one of four that weekend that would change the direction of Holmes's literary life. Jay Landesman had blown into New York from St. Louis, enlisting Holmes's help recruiting new talent for *Neurotica*. Landesman in turn introduced Holmes to Gershon Legman, who became *Neurotica*'s co-editor for later issues. Over the same frenetic weekend, Holmes also met not only Ginsberg, but this "Karawak" person he had been hearing about from fellow writer Alan Harrington, who claimed the prolific Kerouac could "quote whole speeches [from *The Brothers Karamazov*] with great accuracy," and so Holmes had some idea of who he was when the two finally met.[39] Both Kerouac and Ginsberg made an immediate impression on Holmes, and over the next few years, he spent a great deal of time with the pair, especially Kerouac, and was introduced to the circle that included Cassady, Huncke, Solomon, William Cannastra, Joan Haverty, and Alan Ansen, among others. While Holmes shared Kerouac and Ginsberg's literary ambitions as well as their constitutional disaffection, he never quite understood the more outré behavior of people like Cassady, Cannastra, and Huncke, and was sometimes seen as a judgmental observer rather than full-fledged participant in the underground scene. True to his observational tendencies, during the late 1940s and early 1950s, Holmes kept detailed journals describing this circle, notes that would form the basis of *Go*, his self-described "*roman a clef* in the strictest sense of that term, for very little in it is fictionalized."[40]

Structured as it is around his newfound circle and their exploits, *Go* obviously has affinities with *On the Road*, which was written around the same time, but not published for another five years (Holmes completed his first draft of *Go* in February 1951; the scroll version of *On the Road* was written that April).[41] Both novels feature characters modeled on the same people, and even describe some of the same incidents. In a short appraisal, Gilbert Millstein – who would later write the over-the-top review of *On the Road* that helped propel Kerouac to literary celebrity – singled out *Go*'s most vivid characters: "a burly individual called Pasternak, who writes a presumably good novel, or at least one that gets sold; Stofsky, a homosexual and literary whirling dervish; Hart, a frantic character from out of town."[42] These descriptions are of course immediately familiar as characters modeled on Kerouac, Ginsberg, and Cassady, respectively, all of whom would become far more celebrated than Holmes by the end of the 1950s. In addition to these characters, significant portions of the novel concern the often caustic behavior of Bill Agatson, a character modeled on Cannastra, whose death at the end of *Go* marks a sober fallout from his frenetic lifestyle (in 1950, Cannastra had stuck his head out of a moving subway car and been killed). Holmes later recalled that he wanted "to show the destructiveness in this kind of experience, not just [as] . . . reflected in Agatson but also the destructiveness that is implicit to me in Hart Kennedy and some of the Beat stuff too."[43] *Go* can thus be seen as a counterweight to *On the Road*'s generally celebratory tone (although as I explain below, Kerouac does build in a crucial critique of both Sal Paradise and Dean Moriarty).

Holmes develops his more "objective" view by centering the novel's emotional core on the relationship between Paul and Kathryn Hobbes, modeled on Holmes and his wife, whose marriage is severely strained by their forays into the polyamorous underground, which inspires Paul to coolly rationalize extramarital sex: "'Sex isn't quantitative.... If I *wanted* another woman, I'd certainly have her. It wouldn't have anything to do with love. Don't you see what I mean?'" (61). This seems like an airtight intellectual stance – until it crumbles when Kathryn actually has sex with Pasternak and Paul suffers a mental block when attempting to seduce another woman. By anchoring the novel in a relatively normal married couple living in an established domestic space, Holmes shows the ways in which the thin philosophy of the Beats – the nihilism of Agatson, the aggressive sexuality of Kennedy, or the unfocused spirituality of Stofsky – has consequences about which the novel is finally ambivalent. Although Hobbes is fascinated by these characters, he is also put off by them, and after the parties and arrests and affairs and deaths, the novel ends with him and Kathryn more adrift than in the beginning.

Although he characterizes it differently from the way Kerouac or Ginsberg would in their more well-known works, Holmes was the first to deliberately label the circle *as* a circle, naming it the "Beat Generation" in *Go* and announcing a more widespread phenomenon in a *New York Times Magazine* piece boldly titled "This Is the Beat Generation" (November 1952). In fact, the working title for *Go* was "The Beat Generation," but Kerouac, claiming ownership of the phrase, suggested "The Beat Ones" instead.[44] Holmes thus occupies an unusual position in Beat literary history as he was not involved in the original libertine circle, but nonetheless ran with the impulse to name its members as indicative of a broader "generation." Conventional wisdom is that this situation inevitably led to some tension between Holmes and Kerouac.[45] The maturing writers had grown closer and mutually supportive of each other's work in 1948–1949, but Holmes was envious when *The Town and the City* was accepted for publication (on the very same day his first novel, "The Transgressors," was rejected), and later, when *Go* was accepted, Kerouac felt that Holmes was exploiting a scene he had come to belatedly. After reading the draft of *Go*, Kerouac praised it to Holmes, but then turned around to complain to Ginsberg that Holmes was "really riding our wagon without knowing where actually it's headed (but you know and I know)."[46] Kerouac had a point since Holmes certainly did capitalize on the concept of a "Beat Generation" before anyone else – although he was careful to attribute the origin of the term to Kerouac in "This Is the Beat Generation": "It was John Kerouac, the author of a fine, neglected novel *The Town and the City*, who finally came up with it. It was several years ago, when the face was harder to recognize, but he has a sharp, sympathetic eye, and one day he said, 'You know, this is really a *beat* generation.'"[47]

In later years, after the interest spawned by *Howl and Other Poems* and *On the Road*, Holmes continued to locate the origin of the term "Beat Generation" in a conversation he had with Kerouac in 1948, during which Kerouac remarked, "It's a sort of furtiveness. . . . Like we were a generation of furtives. You know, with an inner knowledge there's no use flaunting on that level, the level of the 'public,' a kind of beatness – I mean . . . we all *really* know where we are – and a weariness with all the forms, all the conventions of the world. . . . So I guess you might say we're a *beat* generation."[48] This conversation is fictionalized in *Go* as the narrator remarks, "Once Pasternak said to [Hobbes] with peculiar clarity: 'You know, everyone I know is kind of furtive, kind of beat. They all go along the street like they are guilty of something, but didn't believe in guilt. I can spot them immediately! And it's happening all over the country, to everyone; a sort of revolution of the soul, I guess *you*'d call it!'" (36). The particulars here are telling since Pasternak retains Kerouac's sense of a generation being "furtive," thus emphasizing the importance of Beat insiderness, but he ends by saying that *Hobbes* would label the phenomenon "a revolution of the soul." In other words, Holmes's Kerouac emphasizes the noun "*beat*," whereas his Pasternak emphasizes the actor ("*you*'d"). The change is significant because while the idea of "everyone I know" being "kind of beat" remains attributed to Pasternak, the impulse to "call it" something, to classify the group as an analyzable object, is ironically foisted onto Hobbes, the novel's awkward participant-observer. *Go* thus has it both ways by crediting its Kerouac figure with the term "beat," but leaving it to Hobbes and the novel as a whole to describe and define it.

The nature of Hobbes's descriptions is unusual relative to other Beat literature insofar as it comes via an even-tempered, ethnographic style markedly different from, say, Sal Paradise's pop-eyed rhapsodies about

Dean and America in *On the Road*. As Ann Charters has observed, Holmes named his fictional self after philosopher Thomas Hobbes because it signaled Paul Hobbes's "rationality and emotional detachment from the antics of the other characters."[49] Throughout *Go*, Holmes emphasizes this detachment, as Hobbes tends to observe situations with "clinical fascination" (78) or "no particular feelings" (103), qualities that set him apart from the inner circle, who operate "on feelings, sudden reactions" (35). In the novel, the term "Beat Generation" first appears in a letter to Liza Adler, Hobbes's extramarital love interest, and he uses it not to claim membership in the Beat underground but to dwell on his exclusion from it, noting that his "effort to transcribe his feelings of discovery [had] somehow failed." In place of true articulation, he offers a faltering exclamation: "this beat generation, this underground life!" (126). Hobbes's failure to really connect with the scene is partly explained by his having missed out, as did Holmes in real life, on the group's formative era, "the frantic, wartime years at Columbia," which further explains why "he did not have their thirsty avidity for raw experience, their paradigmatic quest for the unusual, the 'real,' the crazy" (35).

A reserved, ethnographic mode is not limited to Hobbes's perspective, however, and *Go's* most significant formal feature, at least when held against *On the Road* or "Howl" or even *Naked Lunch*, all of which begin with the word "I," is that it is written in the third person. The third-person omniscient narrator shares with Hobbes a kind of academic detachment that has led many observers to read the book as what Seymour Krim calls a "sourcebook," a "true 'document' saved from the fire."[50] But however much *Go* may read like a "sourcebook," it is not finally a documentary, and Holmes's objective narrative style actually tells us a lot about the way the nascent Beat Generation had to be packaged for public consumption circa 1952. Whereas Kerouac gives us this generation through the admiring eyes of Sal Paradise, whose descriptions of Dean Moriarty and his world are so dreamy that it is easy to miss the novel's fundamental distance from him, Holmes adopts an outsider's position that remains peripheral throughout the story, so very little in *Go* explains Hart Kennedy's appeal for Pasternak and Stofsky, and the antics of the Beat Generation come off like desperate existential fallout from the modern world rather than something to be celebrated.

We see this first in those passages that set the stage for the book's action:

> [Hobbes] came to know their world, at first only indirectly. It was a world of dingy backstairs "pads," Times Square cafeterias, bebop joints,

> night-long wanderings, meetings on street-corners, hitchhiking, a myriad of "hip" bars all over the city, and the streets themselves. It was inhabited by people "hungup" with drugs and other habits, searching out a new degree of craziness; and connected to the invisible threads of need, petty crimes of long ago, or a strange recognition of affinity. They kept going all the time, living by night, rushing around to "make contact," suddenly disappearing into jail or on the road only to turn up again and search one another out. They had a view of life that was underground, mysterious, and they seemed unaware of anything outside the realities of deals, a pad to stay in, "digging the frantic jazz," and keeping everything going. (36)

Notice that the passage is focalized through Hobbes's sensibility, underscoring his remove from "their world," and offering a description that alights on the identifiable features of this world, rather than focusing on his own participation. It's all here: the hipster slang jarringly set off in quotation marks, the habitats and haunts, and the characteristic behavior – notably drug use, "digging the frantic jazz," and an anxious need to keep moving (at publication only a handful of people could have gotten the reference to Kerouac's as-yet unpublished novel in the nod to those disappeared "on the road"). What binds these people, what makes their world a world, is that their experiences are "underground, mysterious" from a mainstream point of view. *Go*'s introductory definition of the Beat Generation is a square's perception, figured here as the slightly unsettling realization that these people exist "all over the city" bound by a "strange recognition of affinity" that outsiders don't share. The result is that readers are not so much brought into this "underground urgency" (120), but are rather invited to behold it from afar, a perceptual remove that the novel never really succeeds in crossing.

Although this narrative strategy makes it harder for Holmes to create the sense of intimacy between reader and character (or author) for which Beat texts are known, it does have certain advantages when it comes to representing the more ethically dubious behavior in the book. The role of women is particularly notable in this regard, for just as their contact with the underground stretches Paul and Kathryn's marriage to the breaking point – John and Marian Holmes would be divorced before *Go* was published – men like Hart Kennedy conduct themselves with a casual physical and emotional violence toward the women in their orbit. In describing the interactions between the men and women in the novel, Holmes's objective narrator cuts through the characters' perceptions and self-delusions to find, as Cynthia Hamilton puts it, the "uncritical affirmation of all experience unacceptable."[51] The virtues of the formal choice to have Hobbes remain detached are clear if one compares the treatment of the same incident in *Go* and *On the Road.*

In the middle of *Go*, Kennedy rockets into town with Dinah, a character modeled on LuAnne Henderson, whom Neal Cassady married when she was fifteen – only to then divorce her amid his involvement with Carolyn Robinson (later Carolyn Cassady), among others. *Go* stages an argument between Kennedy and Dinah over his affairs with other women. Although she had been maintaining a façade of nonchalance regarding his constant womanizing (a pose Diane di Prima would later diagnose as the "eternal, tiresome rule of cool," discussed in Part III), Dinah finally loses her cool and snaps, "What *are* you! What *are* you!" This challenge infuriates Kennedy and he lashes to strike her "viciously with his fist" (176). The narrator lingers over this viciousness in order to ironize Kennedy's immediate perversion of the act: "A cut had opened on her forehead and blood was, indeed, pulsing out of it, mingling on her cheeks with the tears. She was sobbing softly, moaning to herself. [Kennedy says:] 'Baby, look what we did! . . . Are you all right, baby? It'll stop in a minute. Look, look, honey! I broke my thumb on you!'" (177). Kennedy's expressions of concern for Dinah pale against his framing of the violence as what "we did," a sneaky rhetorical move that allows him to shift the focus to his own injury and putative suffering. It is easy to see through Kennedy at this moment, for as he kisses Dinah in apology, his "lips are stained with her blood," even as she inevitably falls victim to his emotional manipulations ("'What a foolish baby you have!'" she says; "What was I doing!" [177]).

This incident is framed very differently in *On the Road*, in which Dean describes to Sal how he hit Marylou (also modeled on Henderson) during an argument:

> "I hit Marylou on the brow on February twenty-sixth at six o'clock in the evening – in fact six-ten, because I remember I had to make my hotshot freight in an hour and twenty minutes – the last time we met and the last time we decided everything, and now listen to this: my thumb only deflected off her brow and she didn't even have a bruise and in fact laughed, but my thumb broke above the wrist and a horrible doctor made a setting of the bones that was difficult and took three separate castings, twenty-three combined hours of sitting on hard benches waiting . . . in April when they took off the cast the pin infected my bone and I developed osteomyelitis which has become chronic, and after an operation which failed and a month in a cast the result was the amputation of a wee bare piece off the tip-ass end." (185)

Like other parts of *On the Road*, this account incorporates verbatim language from a letter Cassady had written to Kerouac: "I hit LuAnne on the forehead on Feb. 2nd and broke my left thumb just above the wrist. The setting of the bones was difficult and took three separate castings, 23 combined hours of sitting on hard benches waiting etc.... In April when they took the cast off the pin infected my bone and I developed osteomyelitis which has become chronic."[52] Neither Holmes nor Kerouac actually witnessed the incident, and since Cassady's letter doesn't bother describing LuAnne's injuries, the differing fictionalizations in *Go* and *On the Road* are particularly revealing. Missing from Holmes's "clinical" account is Cassady's distinctive voice, which in his letter and in *On the Road* unwinds a somehow charming, sad-sack story laden with impressive detail. Holmes, on the other hand, strips Kennedy of such rhetorical flourishes in his version of scene, and Kennedy comes across as cruel, selfish, and transparently manipulative. Dean Moriarty shares these qualities, but they exist in tension with his magnetism and rhetorical prowess, especially as Kerouac invents a detail not found in Cassady's letter, that his "thumb only deflected off her brow and she didn't even have a bruise and in fact laughed." Although Dean isn't exactly exonerated in the novel's eyes – a couple of pages later Sal realizes that "all these women were spending months of loneliness and womanliness together, chatting about the madness of the men" (187) – it is much easier to empathize or identify with Dean than it is with Kennedy.[53]

Thus while both novels present the Cassady character in critical lights, Holmes's third-person narrative is more obviously negative, and readers are left with little sense of why Cassady seemed so charismatic to so many people. *On the Road*'s Dean Moriarty, by contrast, seduces Sal *and* the reader, so we share Sal's sense of betrayal when Dean eventually abandons him, wracked with dysentery in Mexico City, a sense of intimate identification that as I've said is a hallmark of Beat literature. In thinking about the rise of the Beat novel, then, we see that the third-person, objective style adopted in *The Town and the City* and *Go* affords a more clear-eyed representation that can be read as overly analytic and clinical, whereas testing the possibilities of the first person was a step toward Beat literature's most important breakthroughs, not only *On the Road*, but the early novels of William Burroughs, which seem at first blush as clinical as Hobbes's observations, but conceal in fact more complex insights about the relationship between representation and reality.

4.4 *Junky*: The Hip Sensibility Mutates

If *Go* presents the Beat Generation focalized through Paul Hobbes, an outsider who never quite commits himself to "raw experience" (35),

William Burroughs's first novel, *Junky* (1953), reads like a guide to the underworld by a sensibility *defined* by raw experience, a person who has gone to deep and dangerous places and lived to tell the tale. Ostensibly a book about addiction to "junk" – by which Burroughs means "opium or derivatives of opium; morphine, heroin, pantopon, Dilaudid, codeine" – *Junky* is written in a deceptively straight narrative style in keeping with an aesthetic principle he called "factualism." As he explained to Ginsberg in 1948, when working in a factualist mode, "All arguments, all nonsensical considerations as to what people 'should do,' are irrelevant. Ultimately there is only facts on all levels, and the more one argues, verbalizes, moralizes the less he will see and feel of fact."[54] Such interest in "facts on all levels" helps explain *Junky*'s generally flat, sometimes pseudo-academic style that Burroughs insisted was nothing "but an accurate account of what I experienced during the time I was on the junk" (*Letters, 1945–1959*, 83).

But the further one gets into the novel, the clearer it becomes that Burroughs is exploiting a tension between two of its keywords, "facts" and "experience." Narrator William Lee continually claims authority based on his "own experience," from the opening sentence ("My first experience with junk was during the War, about 1944 or 1945" [1]) to the last page ("I know from my own experience that telepathy is a fact" [127]). At first, it may seem somewhat counterintuitive for Burroughs to write a book concerned with "facts" in the first person rather than the "clinical" third person of *Go* or *Flee the Angry Strangers*. But it is precisely Burroughs's manipulation of the authorial "I" that makes the book Beat: he has fun with factualism by creating a narrative in which readers think they are on stable ground and gaining access to the authentic underground experience, but are in fact subjected to subtle screens and manipulations.[55] In *Interzone*, Burroughs would write about his interest in a "novel that consists of the facts as I see and feel them" (*Interzone*, 73), a figuration that so radically qualifies facts – "as I see and feel them" – that they are associated with his idiosyncratic authorial subjectivity rather than with any pretense to some ideal of disembodied objectivity. Even in the lines quoted above, Lee's straightforward, declarative statements are weakened by his inability to recall even the year he first experienced junk or by the presumption that his "own experience" mandates that we regard telepathy as "fact." This dynamic and ever-shifting play between narrative stability and instability extends from Burroughs's depiction of specific drug use to the underground more broadly, and what he calls the "hip sensibility."[56] Square readers may pick up the book wanting "facts," but such facts have meaning only in terms of Burroughs's experience, and it is never exactly clear how this experience should be interpreted.

Having abandoned the United States for Mexico, Burroughs completed a draft of what he called his "book about junk" in late 1950, and passed along a version to Lucien Carr to shop around in New York City. In September 1951, one of the most significant events in Burroughs's life occurred: during a drunken game of William Tell, he attempted to shoot a shot glass off his wife Joan's head, but missed and killed her. Much later, Burroughs would claim that he was "forced to the appalling conclusion that I would never have become a writer but for Joan's death," and that her killing clarified for him a "constant need to escape from possession, from Control."[57] He wound up leaving Mexico in the aftermath of the killing, and during this tumultuous time he continued to revise his junk manuscript, convinced that it would see publication due to "current interest in the subject" (*Letters, 1945–1959*, 113). Despite the contemporary curiosity about the drug underworld, the book may have never been published without Ginsberg's networking talents. Just as he acted as Kerouac's informal agent, Ginsberg was also keen to talk up Burroughs's work around town, and showed the junk manuscript to Carl Solomon, who in turn brought it to his uncle, A. A. Wyn, publisher of Ace Books.[58] Wyn had already rejected Holmes's *Go*, but took a chance on *Junky* because he thought it might sell.

Wyn was indeed thinking in terms of commerce, not aesthetic achievement, when he published *Junky*, packaging it as part of an Ace Double Book, binding it together with a reprint of Maurice Helbrant's 1941 memoir, *Narcotic Agent*. Such packaging of course suggests that it was the subject of drug addiction, not necessarily Burroughs's treatment of this subject, that was the book's main appeal so far as its publisher was concerned. Although Burroughs had been in contact with New Directions, a more avant-garde, "literary" publisher, Ace's interest proved tempting enough that he convinced himself the book would fare better at a "strictly commercial" press, simply because he would likely make more money.[59] He was determined to get the book into "saleable form" and made numerous changes at Ace's request, including the now-famous prologue that purports to offer a forthright biographical sketch (perhaps it is thus fitting that the definition of "beat" in *Junky*'s glossary is "To take someone's money" [129]).[60] Because of the book's purported fidelity to "the facts," Burroughs published it pseudonymously, concerned that it would scandalize his family. In a bit of trivia that speaks to the way the fictionalized "Burroughs image" was circulating even prior to the publication of his own writing, he first considered using the pseudonym Will Dennison, the name used for a version of the Burroughs character in *Hippos* and both *The Town and the City* and *Go*, before deciding it might be "a little transparent" to readers of those books.[61] Finally, despite Burroughs's hesitation that "Bill Lee is a little too close" to his real name, in April 1953, Ace published the book under the name William Lee, adding the subtitle *Confessions of an Unredeemed Drug Addict* without his permission.[62]

For Ginsberg, *Junky's* imminent publication was a chance to publicize the Beat Generation, for he thought that with *The Town and the City* and *Go* it could be viewed as the vanguard of a literary movement so labeled. Attempting to build on Holmes's *New York Times* article the year before – which, incidentally, Burroughs found "O.K. in an obvious way" – Ginsberg sensed a marketing opportunity in *Junky*, and so in February 1953 wrote a press release intended for *Times* critic David Dempsey, author of the chatty column "In and Out of Books."[63] The idea was to drum up interest in Burroughs and his book by linking them to the Beat Generation, a technique Ginsberg would perfect in the coming years, when his promotional acumen was essential to the cohesion of the movement. *The Town and the City* and *Go* notwithstanding, in 1953 the Beats were not really on the public's radar, but Ginsberg was determined to change this by announcing the existence of a rising movement that cultured people needed to know about. *Junky*, with its cast of sordid, underworld characters, was the embodiment of Ginsberg's vision of the Beat Generation circa 1953. Here is how he contextualized the book:

> JOHN KEROUAC AND Clellon Holmes, both experts on the Beat Generation, Holmes through his recent *Times Magazine* section controversy, say that they "dig" the pseudonymous William Lee as one of the key figures of the Beat Generation.

> Lee first appeared lurking in the shadows of both of their books, respectively *The Town and the City* and *Go*, portrayed as an underground character. Lee's professional debut in the open on his own as an author is announced by Ace Double Books with the publication of *Junkey* [*sic*]: *The Confessions of an Unredeemed Junk Addict*, which comes up from underground April 15.

> Author-Junky Lee has not stayed around to gather whatever plaudits are due and was last heard from on an expedition into the Amazon basin in search of a rare narcotic.[64]

Ginsberg's teaser doesn't merely acknowledge the sensational aspects of the Beat Generation, it figures them as its defining characteristics, so what makes *Junky* of interest is its tantalizing connection to "controversy," the "shadows," and the "underground."

This is likewise the case in Carl Solomon's "publisher's note," which was included in the first edition; Solomon frames the book as a "pitilessly factual and hard-boiled" account of an "anonymous underworld" populated by "moochers, fags, four-flushers, stool pigeons, thieves . . . all are a 'beat, nowhere bunch of guys,' seemingly without past and no future. There has never been a criminal confession better calculated to discourage imitation by thrill-hungry teen-agers" (150). Solomon's note is presumably present to assure readers – or official watchdogs – that Ace does not condone the use of illicit drugs and is therefore presenting the novel as a way to "discourage imitation." But, like Ginsberg, Solomon also understands narrator William Lee and his fellow junkies as part of a larger "underworld," a subculture he too labels "beat" by singling out a phrase from the book, when Lee refers to his fellow patients in a sanitarium as "a beat, nowhere bunch of people" (83).

True to the book's refusal to submit authentic hipness, however, Lee doesn't use the adjective "beat" to describe hipster junkies who "knew the score," but in fact their inverse, a "pretty square and sorry lot . . . The type psychiatrists like" (83). Thus despite Ginsberg's eagerness to claim *Junky* for the Beat Generation and Solomon's linking of the two through selective quotation, the novel itself takes pains to distinguish "hipster-bebop junkies" from what Lee considers authentic junkies, as when he describes the "junk territory" at 103rd and Broadway in New York City, insisting that "The hipster-bebop junkies never showed at 103rd Street. The 103rd Street boys were all oldtimers" (24–25).[65] Even though Ginsberg and Solomon want extend the gritty "authenticity" of the junk underworld to the Beat Generation, the book itself resists the label "Beat" by describing an even deeper, "oldtimer" sensibility closed off from the sort of "hipster-bebop junkies" who would populate "Howl."[66]

In keeping with his statement that *Junky* is best read as an "accurate account" of his experiences, in his much later introduction to *Queer*, Burroughs again asserted that his "motivation" for writing his first book was "comparatively simple: to put down in the most accurate and simple terms my experiences as an addict."[67] Writing some thirty-five years after *Junky* was composed – and after he had become celebrated for far stranger texts like *Naked Lunch* – Burroughs uses the word "simple" twice in a single sentence about *Junky*'s genesis, thereby doubling down on his insistence that readers see it as near ethnography. As he recounts various interactions with those in the underground, Lee often pauses over technical information on the effects of a given drug, or to describe the finer points of etiquette when it comes to buying drugs, stealing money to buy drugs, or convincing doctors to write helpful prescriptions. Not much happens in the way of character development or rising action: aside from brief sketches of memorable characters, readers pretty much just drift with Lee through vignettes about pick-pocketing or "taking the cure" at a rehab facility. There's a nod to development or change in final page, when Lee announces he will embark on a search for yagé, a hallucinogenic that "may be the final fix" (128).

Summarized this way, *Junky* may not seem particularly literary or even interesting, and yet for those who have read the book carefully, such a summary seems impoverished, for although the subject of junk addiction may tantalize at first, it is that subtly odd first-person narrative that compels on rereading. In pointing this out, I'm following the lead of Burroughs's most attentive critics, who have been skeptical of reading *Junky* as merely an "accurate and simple" description of certain moments in Burroughs's life.[68] Oliver Harris has been especially introspective about this possibility, writing, "It's tempting to conclude that Burroughs' chillingly cool and seductive book is complex and ironic, to say that its apparent simplicity is a sophisticated ruse to fool you, but this is too simple and won't do either. In fact, Burroughs' first novel is both absolutely distinct from everything he would write after it, and yet impossible to read without encountering at every turn phantom traces of the writing to follow. It's like reading two books simultaneously, one atypically straight, the other characteristically twisted."[69] Claiming that one must attend to the "phantom traces" of Burroughs's later writing helps Harris attune himself both to the novel's matter-of-fact reportage *and* its undeniable ironic turns, a simultaneity that leads him to conclude that "*Junky* is in embryonic form an exploratory novel, an *experimental* text, like all those Burroughs would write after it, and the final lines of the introduction he cut could stand as the maxim for his entire oeuvre. 'I am using the known facts as a starting point in an attempt to reach facts that are not known'" (xxv). In Part I, I explained how *Hippos* exploits tensions between coterie and broader audiences by describing David Kammerer's murder in ways that evade the official account of the event; *Junky* is likewise a book ostensibly written to make the facts known to curious readers, and yet it continually defers knowledge by shifting the contexts for these facts.

Consider, for example, the opening paragraph, which begins with that straightforward declarative statement quoted above:

> My first experience with junk was during the War, about 1944 or 1945. I had made the acquaintance of a man named Norton who was working in a shipyard at the time. Norton, whose real name was Morelli or something like that, had been discharged from the peacetime Army for forging a pay check, and was classified 4-F for reasons of bad character. He looked like

George Raft, but was taller. Norton was trying to improve his English and achieve a smooth, affable manner. Affability, however, did not come natural to him. In repose, his expression was sullen and mean, and you knew he always had that mean look when you turned your back. (1)

As I have said, while this appears to be a simple, "accurate account" of an "experience with junk," the very first sentence throws such accuracy into doubt as the narrator is unsure of the exact year of this experience. This uncertainty characterizes the rest of the paragraph: we learn that Lee's first junk connection was Norton – but that his "real name was Morelli or something like that." For a narrator supposedly concerned with the "facts," Lee is surprisingly cavalier about both the year of his first experience and the name of his first connection. Or it may not be so surprising if we read this opening paragraph in terms of the novel's larger resistance to offering access to the unmediated underground, so Lee goes on to associate Norton with imitations of the real thing: he is a forger classified as 4-F (i.e., mentally unfit to serve) who resembles George Raft, a movie actor known for playing underworld hoods in gangster flicks, and he presents himself as something he's not, imitating "affability" even though it is hardly "natural to him." If this wasn't enough, the description itself is an imitation of one Burroughs had done in *Hippos*, in which Will Dennison's gangster underworld connection is Danny Borman, "a defense worker who looks like George Raft."[70]

After all this, the last sentence does not return to Lee's "first experience with junk" or even to Lee himself, but to Norton's "mean look" surfacing from beneath his strained veneer of affability. *Junky's* opening paragraph is thus written in the apparently simple, declarative style that has made it seem, like *Go*, a "sourcebook" to the junk underground, and yet this simplicity unravels as the facts themselves are unstable. Lurking just under the guise of straightforwardness – or behind the reader's back – are funhouse distortions of the facts, a world of forgery, images confused with reality, and "bad character," what Harris calls "a matter of refusals, absences, negations" (*Secret*, 69). Following this paragraph, Lee continues for several more pages describing his entry into the underground, specifically a seedy bar frequented by "42nd Street hustlers" like Herman, a character modeled on Herbert Huncke, and then declares, "A few nights after meeting Roy and Herman, I used one of the syrettes, which was my first experience with junk" (6). This line again calls into question the supposed factual statement in the novel's opening line in that readers are invited to wonder whether "experience" – the foundational trope of the whole book – means the experience of being around junk, of selling junk, of using junk, or of something else (perhaps addiction to junk?).

This play between the seeming solidity of fact-based "experience" and the unstable contexts for interpreting this experience characterizes *Junky* as a whole. The book's famous prologue opens with the line "I was born in 1914 in a solid, three-story, brick house in a large Midwest city" (xxxv), initially characterizing Lee as hailing from an aggressively normal upbringing unshakable both physically and figuratively, thus setting the stage for the kind of *drug addiction could happen to anyone!* narrative found in a novel like *Flee the Angry Strangers*. But as soon as Burroughs proposes this setup, he challenges it, describing his childhood "lawn … backyard with a garden, … shiny Lincoln and drives in the park" not as evidence of a privileged childhood, but as false markers, precursors to Norton's propensities toward forgery, calling them "All the props of a safe, comfortable way of life" (xxxv). In fact, the prologue's second paragraph introduces his "earliest memories … colored by a fear of nightmares" and the third the idea that he was "subject to hallucinations as a child." The strangeness of the prologue thus establishes one strategy of the novel as a whole, which is, as Harris has argued, "not to authorize the straight-dealing narrative that follows … but to expose claims to truth as contingent and rhetorical, by revealing the author's own manipulations and the manipulations of authorship" (*Secret*, 75).

Interested readers can locate such manipulation and instability throughout *Junky*, and I would note the ways it extends beyond Lee's characterizations of his personal "experience" to the wider "underground" such experience ostensibly typifies. As much as the novel can be read in terms of Ginsberg's eagerness to claim it as an underground document specifically exemplifying something called the Beat Generation, Lee not only plays with his own relationship with normality, he also blurs distinctions between dominant and underground cultures. As many readers have noted, one of the starkest examples of such blurring is Bill Gains, a character who "came from a 'good family'" and was "a vague respectable presence" (35). Despite his solid background – "his father had been a bank president somewhere in Maryland" – Gains is actually among the more sinister characters in the novel, as he "was one of the few junkies who really took a special pleasure in seeing non-users get a habit" (35). Although Gains may seem like merely another cautionary tale for those who think their respectable upbringing will shield them from narcotics addiction, he also serves a more existential function insofar as he questions what, if anything, distinguishes a junky from a non-junky – or, by extension, the hip world from the square.

Burroughs twists such distinctions throughout the book, as when Lee, scouting the subway for marks to pickpocket, uses the *New York Times* as a prop to "look like a businessman" (31), or when an older doctor chooses to write illegal prescriptions because "he had reached the point where he could change the appearance of things to suit his needs and when he looked out there [in his waiting room] he saw a distinguished and diversified clientele, probably well-dressed in 1910 style, instead of a bunch of ratty-looking junkies come to hit him for a morphine script" (8) – in *Naked Lunch*, Bill Gains himself turns up "huddled in someone else's overcoat looking like a 1910 banker with paresis" (5). Such willingness to "change the appearance of things" extends to *Junky* as a whole, which offers discretely accurate "facts," but then changes the context for these facts so it is difficult to interpret them. By the novel's final pages, categories become so muddled that a young hipster-junky can lament that even federal narcotics agents have become indistinguishable from true junkies: "I mean these guys are hips themselves. Guys just like you and me with one small difference – they work for Uncle [Sam]" (121). Lee considers this phenomenon of "addict-agents" (121) a dark sign that the United States is collapsing into a "state of complete chaos where you never know who is who or where you stand" (120), and so decides to leave for Mexico.[71] Not only is it ironic that federal agents and not junkies occasion a "state of complete chaos," but the merging of the two questions the whole notion of an underground, so while *Junky* opens a window onto Burroughs's "experience" with junk, it also challenges the seemingly logical conclusion that such experience indexes a wider phenomenon.

Junky's reluctance to pin down meaning is perhaps most visible in the book's "Glossary," in theory the most straightforward and objective part of a book that appears to insist on objectivity. The point of the glossary is to explain the "jive talk" (129) used in the book, apparently so that readers can be brought inside the junk underworld and better understand it. And yet a key concept, "Hep or Hip," is described like this: "Someone who knows the score. Someone who understands 'jive talk.' Someone who is 'with it.' The expression is not subject to definition because, if you don't 'dig' what it means, no one can ever tell you" (130). Comparable to later Beat work like Bob Kaufman's "The Abomunist Manifesto" (discussed in Part III), this is a parody of a definition that refuses to define, so what ought to be the most objective or factual feature of the book is again unstable and open to revision. Indeed, the glossary ends with the observation that "the meanings of these words are subject to rapid changes, and . . . a word that has one hip meaning one year may have another the next. The hip sensibility mutates. . . . Not only do the words change meanings but meanings vary locally at the same time. A final glossary, therefore, cannot be made of words whose intentions are fugitive" (133). Given the premise that the "hip sensibility mutates," it makes a certain sense that what seems most hip in *Junky* is a coy reluctance to really offer anything to those who don't already "dig."

4.5 *Queer*: The Routine Artist Outdoes Himself

By April 1952, when he was still tinkering with *Junky*, Burroughs was "working day and night on *Queer*," material he variously thought of as "part II of *Junk*" or even the final part of "one novel."[72] Despite such early optimism, *Queer* would not in fact be published until 1985, during the intervening decades enjoying status as an actual underground – that is, unpublished – novel increasingly infamous for those who had heard about it or even read it in manuscript. Picking up on the promise of *Junky*'s intriguing final line, "Yage may be the final fix" (128), *Queer* begins with the same protagonist, William Lee, in Mexico City, suffering from junk withdrawal and planning a trip to Ecuador in the hope of finding yagé, the powerful hallucinogenic long used by indigenous peoples in religious rites. "When we get to where the Yage is," Lee says in his best impression of a cartoon hipster-junky, "we'll dig a hip cat and ask him, 'Where can we score for Yage?'"[73] As he's knocking about the expatriate bars in Mexico City, Lee becomes infatuated with a younger man named Eugene Allerton, modeled on Adelbert Lewis Marker, whom Burroughs had met in the summer of 1951 when he was thirty-seven and Marker twenty-one.[74] *Queer*, like *Junky*, is short on character development or rising action, focusing instead on Lee's attempts to convince the reluctant Allerton to accompany him to Ecuador through a mix of bribes and improvised spoken "routines": comic, often grotesque stories.

In terms of Burroughs's career trajectory, most critics from Alan Ansen on have noted *Queer*'s use of what Ansen identified as "a new form, the routine," an important aesthetic innovation insofar as it helped Burroughs free himself from the constraints of plot.[75] Although *Queer* is nominally structured around Lee's dual pursuit of Allerton and yagé, the real stars are these routines; Burroughs continued to experiment with routines in the material collected in *The Yage Letters* (written 1953 and after; published 1963) and *Interzone* (written 1953–1958; published 1989), portions of which would make their way into *Naked Lunch*, which famously shed all interest in linear plot.[76] Because the routines are so intimately linked to Lee's distinctive voice, it may seem somewhat surprising that Burroughs shifts from *Junky*'s first-person narrative to the third person. But this change allows him to illustrate the performative dimension of the routines by emphasizing Allerton's role as Lee's "audience," which aligns him with Burroughs's audience of readers. As *Queer*'s third-person narrator writes:

> Allerton disliked commitments and had never been in love or had a close friend. He was forced to ask himself: "What does he want from me?" It did not occur to him that Lee was queer, as he associated queerness with at least some degree of overt effeminacy. Allerton was intelligent and surprisingly perceptive for a person so self-centered, but his experience was limited. He decided finally that Lee valued him as an audience. (24–25)

As in *Junky*, in which the presumed reader's "experience was limited," Allerton serves as a relative innocent who might be seduced by Lee's routines. If, as Burroughs remarked to Ginsberg, routines were originally conceived as a "*means* to make contact with Allerton and to interest him" (*Letters, 1945–1959*, 126), then in the context of a novel they are by extension a means to seduce readers. As Burroughs would put it in *Interzone*: "The routine artist is always trying to outdo himself, to go a little further, to commit some incredible but appropriate excess. A routine, like a bullfight, needs an audience. In fact the audience is an integral part of the routine. But unlike a bullfight, the routine can endanger the audience" (127). The idea of a routine's hazardousness is literalized in *Queer*, as "Allerton felt at times oppressed by Lee, as though Lee's presence shut off everything else" (24).[77] As Burroughs explored the routine as form, he became more interested in the notion that "Routines are uncontrollable, unpredictable, charged with potential danger for Lee himself, and anyone close to him is liable to be caught in the line of fire" (*Interzone*, 127). This sort of uncontrolled unpredictability becomes part of the point, so what compels in a Burroughs routine is how he will get from A to B, usually via questionable logical leaps or imagistic associations. In *Queer*, this experience is literally dangerous for Allerton as it puts him in physical proximity to Lee in remote locations where Lee fantasizes about subjecting Allerton to "thought control" (80) and vows that "Someday I am going to have things just like I want.... And if any moralizing son of a bitch gives me any static, they will fish him out of the river" (87). More abstractly, routines might be dangerous for the reader because they give primacy to "The Word," unrestrained so that by the time we get to *Naked Lunch*, it "will leap on you with leopard man iron claws" (*Naked Lunch*, 192).

   Queer's use of the third person allows Burroughs to better illustrate the routine's potential danger by offering glimpses into Allerton's consciousness, something that would not be possible were the book written in the first person. Via Allerton's negative reactions, the novel can cast Lee as overbearing and even predatory when he offers the younger man gifts and money as part of a "contract" for sexual favors. In this way, *Queer* replicates the dynamic found between Phillip Tourian and Ramsay Allen in *Hippos*: an older man doggedly pursues a younger one who claims not to be "queer," but who tolerates sexual advances because of material gain. In one sober moment in *Queer*, Lee "forced himself to look at the facts. Allerton was not queer enough to make a reciprocal relation possible" (52), a situation that echoes Dennison's advice to the love-struck Allen in *Hippos*: "Facts, man, it's time to face facts.... Phillip isn't queer. He might sleep with you, which I doubt altogether, but anything permanent is impossible" (29, 28). Whether Burroughs saw affinities with his own seemingly futile pursuit of Marker and his friend Kammerer's ultimately fatal pursuit of Carr, it is worth asking why he chooses to frame the relationship in these terms in a novel boldly titled *Queer* – nothing in the book is affirmative, and far from offering portraits of same-sex love or even of "reciprocal" sexual desire, it focuses instead on Lee's constantly thwarted attempts to win over a largely indifferent Allerton. Thus when Burroughs puts Allerton in the role of Lee's "audience," he serves as a kind of proxy for the likely audience of a book called *Queer*: just as *Junky* turns on playing to but ultimately frustrating social expectations about junkies and their underground, so *Queer* does with respect to the homosexual "underground." If Lee is a figure both in and out of the junk world, he occupies a like position with respect to homosexuality, often decrying labels such as "fag" while engaging in physical and emotional behavior condemned by the dominant, heterosexual culture.[78]

To understand what Burroughs is doing with *Queer*, we have to keep in mind that at this moment in the United States, homosexuality was seen in pathological terms, much the same way drug addiction was, and just as a novel like *Flee the Angry Strangers* reflects broad cultural anxieties about the corrupting influences of narcotics, so too was homosexuality figured as a threat to cultural stability, not only to heterosexuality but to the nuclear family and indeed to the integrity of the nation itself.[79] Burroughs was of course acutely aware of and personally affected by this context, and much of his writing pushes back against these figurations, often quite aggressively. For example, in a letter describing his "new novel" *Queer* to Ginsberg, he disapprovingly cites Donald Webster Cory's influential book *The Homosexual in America* (1951): "Enough to turn a man's gut," writes Burroughs, "This citizen says a queer learns humility, learns to turn the other cheek, and returns love for hate. Let him learn that sort of thing if he wants to. I never swallowed the other cheek routine."[80] In *Queer*, we have a depiction of the "homosexual in Mexico" presented in a seemingly straightforward manner but filtered through a posture that at times mimics conventional wisdom about homosexuality so stridently that it finally punctures its logic.

Burroughs's adoption of mainstream homophobic attitudes first occurs in *Junky*, when Lee visits a "queer bar" and remarks, "A room full of fags gives me the horrors. They jerk around like puppets on invisible strings, galvanized into hideous activity that is the negation of everything living and spontaneous" (*Junky*, 60). This is a startling statement about the corruptive potential of homosexuality – the passage goes on to claim that the very lives of homosexuals are taken over by a nebulous "something" (their flamboyant sexuality?) so they have become ventriloquists' dummies lacking will of their own. And yet immediately following this declaration, Lee admits that he "backslide[s] now and then" and proceeds to arrange a liaison with a younger man he meets at the bar. Thus it is not the sexual act itself that gives Lee "the horrors," but a certain kind of performative queerness, a "yapping" that takes over all other aspects of one's personality in an affirmation of homosexuality. In fact, the word "fag" was at the time for Burroughs a marker of the unmanly humility or meekness he so despised in Cory's characterizations – when Carl Solomon floated the idea of titling the *Queer* manuscript "Fag," an appalled Burroughs wrote to Ginsberg: "That's just what I been trying to put down uh I mean *over*, is the distinction between us strong, manly, noble types and the leaping, jumping, window dressing cocksucker."[81] Aligning himself with conventional notions of masculinity – here the strong, silent type – Burroughs casts himself in the role of straight American male who has sex with men.

In *Queer*, Lee initiates his courtship of Allerton with a routine that seems to argue that homosexuality represents an existential threat to Lee's sense of masculinity: "I shall never forget the unspeakable horror . . . when the baneful word seared my reeling brain: *homosexual*. I was a homosexual. . . . Nobler, I thought, to die a man than live on, a sex monster. It was a wise old Queen – Bobo, we called her – who taught me that I had a duty to live and to bear my burden proudly for all to see" (35). As in his letter to Ginsberg, Burroughs counterpoints the "unspeakable horror" of homosexuality to the nobility of certain ideas of manliness. This is the sort of logic that might make sense to the homophobic cultural narrative rife at the time, and yet as this passage continues, it becomes clear that it is merely the opening of a routine for Allerton's amusement, that it is actually Lee satirizing those who treat homosexuality as a pathology. As Lee continues, we see that Bobo's counsel is of a piece with the clichéd brand of advice that reduces life to the hokey flatness of greeting card optimism ("to conquer prejudice and ignorance and hate with knowledge and sincerity and love" [35–36]). Indeed, following this statement, Bobo meets a comically grotesque end in a car accident, "completely gutted, leaving an empty shell sitting there on the giraffe-skin upholstery" (36). Despite the seeming wisdom of the platitudinous advice, then, Bobo ends up no better than those "empty shells" in the gay bar. At this point, like Allerton, we are meant to understand the sentiments as a routine, and so are encouraged to recontextualize the seemingly straight declarations about homosexuality that kicked it off.[82]

Another layer of irony in *Queer* is that as Lee adopts the voice of the homophobic culture only to undercut it, he also uses it to announce his queerness to Allerton. Throughout the novel, Lee insists that he is the farthest thing from those "simpering female impersonators" who gave him the horrors, and attempts to prove it by adopting the brashest and ugliest traits of hypermasculine US culture, from a facility with imperial racism to the lust for complete control mentioned above.[83] One reason for Lee's interest in yagé is that it symbolizes the potential for ultimate control, as its supposedly telepathic qualities might allow him to infiltrate Allerton's mind as well as his body: "Think of it: thought control. Take anyone apart and rebuild to your taste.... I could think of a few changes I might make in you, doll.... You'd be so much *nicer* after a few alterations" (80). Read in the context of Lee's comments about homosexuality in both *Junky* and *Queer*, we can view this as an extension of his performance of normative American traits best understood not as earnest reproduction but as ironic critique. This is perhaps the queerest thing about *Queer*, that in its formal strangeness it is not so much a defense of homosexuality as a distorted mirror on a society in which control is viewed as a good in and of itself – and as we'll see below, Burroughs explores a similar dynamic in *Naked Lunch*.

The composition of *Queer* is tangled up with the letters that would form the book *The Yage Letters* as well as some of the material later collected in *Interzone* (a working title for *Naked Lunch*). Like *Queer*, *Interzone* was not published until the 1980s, but as James Grauerholz argues, it is a useful text for readers interested in "how the precise, laconic and deadpan writer of *Junky* and *Queer* transformed himself into the uncompromising prophet and seer of *Naked Lunch* ... readers may now be able to see that transformation take place in the course of one volume."[84] As constituted in the 1980s, *Interzone* consists of three sections: "Stories," "Lee's

Journals," and "Word." The first section contains what is generally acknowledged as Burroughs's first writing, a short piece called "Twilight's Last Gleaming" composed with his friend Kells Elvins in 1938. Set aboard a sinking ship – inspired by the real-life sinking of the *Morro Castle* in 1935 – this story is notable as it features Dr. Benway of *Naked Lunch* fame performing a drunken appendectomy. Other stories of interest include "The Finger," a fictional version of the 1939 incident when Burroughs cut off his finger to impress a romantic interest at the time, Jack Anderson (in the story, Lee's love interest is a woman [17]); and "In the Café Central" and "International Zone," early descriptions of the scene in Tangier. "Lee's Journals" includes routines and vignettes in Mexico City, Tangier, and elsewhere. For Grauerholz, the final section, "Word," is particularly illuminating as it reads like a compressed version of *Naked Lunch*, and includes characters, routines, and images that finally did appear there, including the frequently cited assertion that "This book spill off the page in all directions" (135; *Naked Lunch*, 191). Grauerholz claims that "Word" "shows the complete transformation of the straightforward style of the two early novels into a manic, surreal, willfully disgusting and violently purgative regurgitation of seemingly random images" (xxi–xxii). While, as I've explained, I don't see *Junky* or *Queer* as exactly "straightforward," Grauerholz is right to note the importance of "Word" in Burroughs's body of work, especially as it prefigures *Naked Lunch*'s formal strangeness.

4.6   *Naked Lunch*: The Word Will Leap on You

It is not surprising that Grauerholz should draw attention to the ways *Interzone* anticipates *Naked Lunch*'s interest in "seemingly random images," for this is the most well known and most remarked-on aspect of the latter book, even for those who have never read it. When Grauerholz singles out certain parts of *Interzone*, he in turn emphasizes certain parts of *Naked Lunch* that can be traced to commentary about the nature of writing featured in "Lee's Journals": "What am I trying to do in writing? This novel is about transitions, larval forms, emergent telepathic faculty, attempts to control and stifle new forms" (69); "the fragmentary, unconnected quality of my work is inherent in the method, and will resolve itself as far as is necessary" (89); "how can I ever write a 'novel'? I can't and won't. The 'novel' is a dead form, rigid and arbitrary. I can't use it" (*Interzone*, 126). This sense of Burroughs's ongoing project as characterized by its "fragmentary, unconnected quality" appears also in the ways he described the mutating manuscript to friends, as when he told Kerouac that "the novel form is completely inadequate to express what I have to say" or Ginsberg that "The MS. in present form does not hold together as a novel for the simple reason that it is not a novel."[85] Such statements have encouraged generations of critics to locate *Naked Lunch*'s importance in its subversion and resistance, to characterize it as an aggressive repudiation of generic and aesthetic norms, as well as established formal "literary" techniques.[86]

To this end, perhaps the most quoted line in *Naked Lunch* criticism comes from the "Atrophied Preface" toward the end of the book: "You can cut into *Naked Lunch* at any intersection point ..." (187, ellipses in original). This line has been of particular interest to those who argue that *Naked Lunch* is important to literary history because it doesn't prioritize character or plot, or even basic notions of linearity – as Burroughs writes a few pages later, "I do not presume to impose 'story' 'plot' 'continuity'" (184). To this way of thinking, if a reader really could "cut into *Naked Lunch* at any intersection point," then it must not be a novel at all but a new kind of writing, an exemplar of literary "development" that has been linked not only to the Beats but to postmodernism and poststructuralism. Writing in 1987, during the heyday of deconstructive practices in American literary criticism, Robin Lydenberg argued that Burroughs's work has affinities with "contemporary radical theorists such as Jacques Derrida, Roland Barthes, Julia Kristeva, and others. These critics challenge, as does Burroughs, our conventional notions about the status of the author in the text, about the referentiality of language, and about the dualism of Western thought."[87] One needn't wade into the intricacies of these theorists' work to understand the broad comparisons Lydenberg is making regarding their "challenge" to accepted wisdom about language: that its meaning arises from an author, that it must refer to or signify something, that if an utterance denotes X it cannot also denote Y, and so on. Burroughs's work seemed especially suited to such a critical environment as he claimed to restrain his own influence as author and argued for the multiplicity and irreducibility of "The Word" – also, broadly speaking, one of the fundamental projects of Derridean deconstruction. As Lydenberg wrote of *Naked Lunch*: "Burroughs' radical text ... is a non-hierarchical network, its parts are interchangeable and reversible" (43).[88]

While it is of course essential to recognize the "radical" aspects of *Naked Lunch*, other critics have cautioned against taking this recognition too far to read the book as a literally random assemblage. Once again, Oliver Harris is a useful guide as he points out that the "mythology" of *Naked Lunch* "is its natural accomplice, its viral double, there from the very beginning, bait for rubes and cognoscenti alike."[89] This mythology comes partly from the manuscript's underground status throughout the 1950s (boldly announced in the dedication to *Howl and Other Poems*, when Ginsberg acclaimed the unpublished "*Naked Lunch*, an endless novel which will drive everybody mad"), and partly from Burroughs's own assertions that the text was somehow self-generating: "I have no precise memory of writing the notes which have now been published under the title *Naked Lunch*. The title was suggested by Jack Kerouac. I did not understand what the title meant until my recent recovery [from opioid addiction]."[90] Such a statement evacuates the writer's authority so completely that the text seems to have a life of its own: if Burroughs's name is on the book, he claims no "precise memory" of writing it, so much so that he insists not to have understood something so fundamental as the title itself. Harris argues that this sort of myth-making – he calls Ginsberg's dedication an "agent's act of marketing" ("Beginnings," 15) – has remained so powerful that it shapes fundamentally how readers approach *Naked Lunch* even today. Focusing on the title, for instance, Harris explores a well-known piece of Beat lore, that Kerouac's suggestion came from mishearing Ginsberg read aloud the phrase "naked lust," which Burroughs had supposedly used in *Hippos*. For Harris, the purportedly "slapdash origins of its title implies a reading of Burroughs' whole book in the same terms, as simply thrown together by chance and error – a crudely reductive reading that has nonetheless stuck" ("Beginnings," 18). Harris then goes on to offer a corrective both to this story about the title's origins and to the idea that *Naked Lunch* is best approached as though it was "simply thrown together by chance and error."

Building on such correctives, it is tempting to say that the most perverse – and thus most Burroughsian – way to read the novel is straight through from the first page to the last. After all, despite its protracted and confusing composition history, if you want to read *Naked Lunch* today, you can pick up a copy of the "restored text," which, like any book of its length, has a page 3 and a page 104 and a page 196.[91] Even if these pages don't necessarily constitute a beginning, middle, and end in terms of conventional plot arcs or character development, one way to read against the grain is to *not* cut into the book at random, but to proceed through the text as presented. This approach has some affordances when considering *Naked Lunch* in the context of Beat literary history because it helps us see it as a catalogue and encyclopedia of underground experience. Readers of *Junky* and *Queer* will recall those books' similar interest in "experience," and *Naked Lunch* certainly follows suit. Consider, for instance, that the "cut into *Naked Lunch* at any intersection point" line is followed by a passage asserting that the text "is a blueprint, a How-To Book . . . How-To extend levels of experience by opening the door at the end of a long hall" (187). The metaphor of an instructional manual explaining "levels of experience" might help us recognize that *Naked Lunch*'s goal is not only to describe and annotate an exhibition of "underground" experience – a goal it shares with other Beat texts like Holmes's *Go* or Ginsberg's "Howl" – but to ask readers to reorient the very way they understand "experience" relative to their own lives, a reorientation that depends on the sort of "radical" form and language praised by critics.

When read as part of the rise of the Beat novel, it's easier to see that *Naked Lunch* opens with familiar underground experiences, only to take away this familiarity in short order. Indeed, if you had just finished *Junky* and picked up *Naked Lunch*, the first few pages wouldn't seem all that strange: a junky is evading an undercover "narcotics dick" by vaulting a turnstile in the Washington Square subway station (one that serves Greenwich Village), a scene that was in fact imported from *Junky*. In the opening page of *Naked Lunch*, Will Lee, writing in first person, dismisses the "square [who] wants to come on hip," who "Talks about 'pod,' and smokes it now and then, and keeps some around to offer the fast Hollywood types" (3). Readers wised-up to the underground scene via books like *The Town and the City* or *Go* can share Lee's derision of the square trying to be cool, and can also appreciate Lee's refusal to even name himself as "hip," instead blurting out stereotypical criminal slang for the benefit of an onlooker in the subway: "'So long flatfoot!' I yell, giving the fruit his B production" (3).

From there, the opening chapter revisits techniques found in *Junky* such as connecting junk to deeper kinds of meaning (it is "surrounded by magic and taboos, curses and amulets" [6]), as well as offering factual asides that have the objective tone of a pharmacopoeia ("Note: Catnip smells like marijuana when it burns. Frequently passed on the incautious or uninstructed" [5]). But this version of the underground lasts for only twenty pages or so, and at a certain point, perhaps after finishing the whole book, readers realize that the ostensible familiarity of the introductory pages was a put-on, reminiscent of those passages in *Queer* that seem at first sincere depictions of queer life only to be revealed as routines that don't actually tell us anything sociologically substantive. The opening of *Naked Lunch* likewise gives voyeuristic readers what the junk underground is *assumed* to be like, an ironic reworking and dismissal of what Burroughs was doing in *Junky*. Those who "cut into" *Naked Lunch* with its opening line move from the literal underground beneath Greenwich Village in the first section to sketches of underground characters like "the vigilante," a junky "prosecuted in Federal Court under a lynch bill" whose "human lines" are transformed into a twisted nightmare: "sex organs sprout anywhere . . . rectums open, defecate and close . . . the entire organism changes color and consistency in split-second adjustments" (9, ellipses in original). After a few scant pages, then, readers are denied the hardboiled factualism that dominated *Junky* and are taken instead into a bizarre realm where the rules of reality don't seem to obtain. Did this literally happen to the vigilante? Is it a metaphor for the results of his incarceration? Is it both? Neither? Do questions of "reality" perhaps not apply? *Naked Lunch* raises such questions but doesn't answer them, a large part of how and why it unsettles.

Following "the vigilante" section, there is one called "the rube," in which Lee moves across the United States and finally into Mexico in a kind of parody of *On the Road* that showcases the worst and darkest aspects of the United States, from the "vast subdivision" of "lifeproof houses" in the Midwest (11) to the racist sheriffs of Texas (14). A long way from the romantic odes to America in which Kerouac sometimes indulges, the America in *Naked Lunch* is neither youthful nor full of promise: "America is not a young land: it is old and dirty and evil before the settlers, before the Indians. The evil is there waiting" (11). This perspective sets the tone for the novel's political and social critiques, which as I'll explain are bound up in its "radical" style and loose form.

The book doesn't in fact remain in the States for long, and its most well-known sections are set in Interzone, a fictitious political and psychic space inspired by Tangier, Morocco. In the mid-1950s, when Burroughs lived in Tangier, it was an International Zone with quarters administered by a host of European countries and the United States, making it a confluence of diverse nationalities, religions, and ethnicities. In *Naked Lunch*, Interzone is a staging ground for distorted reflections of how culture and civilization spawn bureaucracies, which necessitate politicians and their parties, invariably leading to individuals being subject to varying degrees of control. Burroughs has various characters purport to be "agents" for these parties, as well as for an entity called Islam Inc., for which Lee himself works, although he claims not to know why (121); as he admits, "The exact objectives of Islam Inc. are obscure. Needless to say everyone involved has a different angle, and they all intend to cross each other up somewhere along the line" (134). The political landscape of *Naked Lunch*, such as it is, amounts to a dizzying romp in which these many parties are thrust into the foreground to "cross each other up" – and yet it is never totally clear who is "really" aligned with which party, or for that matter how these parties are finally differentiated. In Interzone, the point is the experience, the game of playing politics, which seems to always have the final effect of curtailing individual freedoms.

It isn't necessary for our purposes to parse what may be minute differences among these parties to see that they are all connected to fantasies of control. One speaker imagines, for instance, a near-distant future in which "Shortly after birth a surgeon could install connections in the brain. A miniature radio receiver could be plugged in and the subject controlled from State-controlled transmitters" (136). For the political parties of Interzone, the watchword is control, a fact that has led numerous critics to see a repudiation of control as *Naked Lunch*'s central project. As Timothy Murphy has argued, for example, Burroughs's "early novels ... address the accelerating dialectic of capitalist control of American society, a form of control that functions by transforming the individual into the 'addict agent' who is the mirror image of the controller."[92]

Such a critique is introduced following the "familiar" opening sketches, when readers encounter Dr. Benway, a character who, as mentioned above, goes all the way back to 1938 and Burroughs's first crack at writing. In *Naked Lunch*, Dr. Benway has become an "advisor" to a place called Freeland, where his "first act was to abolish concentration camps, mass arrest and, except under certain limited and special circumstances, the use of torture" (19). Except for the torture part, this *sounds* pretty good, but we soon discover that Benway is "a manipulator and coordinator of symbol systems, an expert on all phases of interrogation, brainwashing and control" (19), and as such practices forms of control that don't necessarily *look* like control: "The subject must not realize that the mistreatment is a deliberate attack of an anti-human enemy on his personal identity" (19). Benway puts it more baldly later: "A *functioning* police state needs no police" (31). For all its surreal weirdness – as, for instance, when Benway performs operations with a baboon assistant (27) – the obvious way to read Freeland is as a perverse reflection of the postwar United States, in which, to take one example, people are seduced by lust for material goods, which ironically makes them less individualized as they come to depend more and more on these goods (witness the "American Housewife" who complains that her box of detergent isn't automated enough to render her obsolete: "Why don't it have an electric eye the box flip open when it see me and hand itself to the Automat Handy Man" [104]).

Getting toward the middle of the "restored text," readers are faced with an onslaught of outré scenes occurring in spaces such "hassan's rumpus room," "a.j.'s annual party," and "the market." These sections contain the book's most notorious descriptions of unbridled libidinal activities, from graphic sex in all combinations, hangings, and decapitations involving "The blood and substance of many races, Negro, Polynesian, Mountain Mongrel, Desert Nomad, Polyglot Near East, Indian, races as yet unconceived and unborn" (92; see also 62–70, 74–87, 89–101). There's a lot to say about these scenes, but for our purposes, I want to emphasize that the outrageous behavior depicted is teasingly connected both to figurations of "hipsters" and to theories about language and spontaneity. With respect to the first point: among the people in Hassan's rumpus room are those whose "Clothes and hairdo suggest existentialist bars of all the world cities" (75), implying a version of hipsterism familiar from a book like *Who Walk in Darkness*. Moreover, once in "the market," we learn that "Hipsters with smooth copper-colored faces lounge in doorways twisting shrunk heads on gold chains, their faces blank with an insect's unseeing calm" (89). The detail of the "shrunk heads on gold chains" marks these hipsters as a long way from the ones in *The Town and the City* or even Burroughs's own *Junky*, but their named presence tells us we are in a distorted, surreal version of those books' underground scenes. Indeed, a lengthy section of "the market" is devoted to a "vicious, fruity old Saint applying pancake from an alabaster bowl" (94), who touts "the New Religion" during "The Prophet's Hour," a parody of Evangelical Christian radio sermons. Fuzzily defined, this New Religion seems to amount to the Saint breezily dismissing the world's great religious leaders (Christ is a "cheap ham" [94], Buddha a "notorious metabolic junky" [95], and Mohammed "dreamed up by the Mecca Chamber of Commerce" [96]) by using cartoon Beat slang: "Now some citizens really wig when they make with the New Religion.... So we gotta play it cool, you dig, cool" (96). Given such coy connections to the Beat sensibility, one way to read the infamous scenes of sex and violence in *Naked Lunch* is as the hip pose taken to its most extreme, ridiculous ends: if the counterculture is about repudiating mainstream norms, then those in the rumpus room or the market don't merely evade normative culture, they forsake it ad absurdum.

And as it turns out, the parodic use of slang in "The Prophet's Hour" is hardly incidental as it reminds us that *Naked Lunch* is always foregrounding The Word and how it shapes – or infects – what we call the real. Toward the end of his monologue, the "fruity old Saint" implies that the New Religion is bound up in a new perspective on language: "So I got an exclusive why don't I make with the live word? The word cannot be expressed direct ... It can perhaps be indicated by mosaic of juxtaposition like articles abandoned in a hotel drawer, defined by negatives and absence" (97, ellipses in original). The phrase "mosaic of juxtaposition" is an apt enough way to describe the form of *Naked Lunch* that one critic borrowed it for the title of a study about Burroughs's "narrative revolution."[93] The collage-like aspect of the book is moreover what Gregory Corso hit on as being particularly innovative: "When I read it [*Naked Lunch*] ... I saw that we were all wrong to be upset or driving on his connecting the events; the events ARE connected, like something glued that doesn't need string to hold it together, the string is not necessary."[94] Corso's insight is that *Naked Lunch* conceptualizes "expression" in a way that proceeds according that "mosaic of juxtaposition" logic (some of Burroughs's other contemporaries were not as astute as Corso on this point: writing about excerpts from *Naked Lunch* he had just seen in a little magazine, Norman Mailer declared them "more arresting ... than anything I've read by an American in years," but thought the forthcoming book would be good only "if the novel proves to be a novel and not a collage of extraordinary fragments").[95]

What is potentially disturbing about Burroughs's "mosaic of juxtaposition" is that the book refuses to offer the basic ground from which to judge or interpret the actions it describes. In the rumpus room, to take one example, young boys are described as being raped and then hung (65), scenes that certainly do not conform to social, cultural, and ethical norms, but it's hard to argue that they are positive or just. And yet the book presents such scenes without moral judgment. Is Burroughs endorsing such actions? Condemning them? Is it satire? After all, he claimed in 1960 that the book is "a tract against Capital Punishment in the manner of Jonathan Swift's *Modest Proposal* ... intended to reveal capital punishment as the obscene, barbaric and disgusting anachronism that it is ... If civilized countries want to return to Druid Hanging Rites in the Sacred Grove or to drink blood with the Aztecs and feed their Gods with blood of human sacrifice, let them see what they actually eat and drink" (*Naked Lunch*, 205).

This is a basically sensible, logically consistent position, which is why we should be suspicious of it as the key to *Naked Lunch*. Reading the book as Swiftian satire renders it knowable and safe: disgusting at times, sure, but for the right reasons. But Burroughs repeatedly states that the reader is unsafe, that The Word itself is dangerous: "The Word will leap on you [the reader] with leopard man iron claws, it will cut off fingers and toes like an opportunist land crab" (192). This sense of The Word is in fact purposively connected to those shocking sex scenes, as its "pieces can be had in any order being tied up back and forth in and out fore and aft like an innaresting sex arrangement. This book spill off the page in all directions, kaleidoscope of vistas, medley of tunes and street noises, farts and riot yips" (191). In this view, the profuse potentialities of The Word are directly compared to the "innaresting sex arrangement[s]" found throughout the book, linking the physical to the abstract to better illustrate why the latter can be disturbing and dangerous.

With respect to Beat literary history, it is significant that Burroughs often frames the disruptive potentialities of The Word in terms of spontaneity. The notion of spontaneity is more often connected with Kerouac and his development of spontaneous prose, but Burroughs was drawn to the potential of spontaneity and how it might counter forms of control represented by Dr. Benway or the parties of Interzone. This is literalized in a scene in which Dr. Benway is performing one of his questionable operations and the following happens:

> A young man leaps down into the operating theater and, whipping out a scalpel, advances on the patient.
> DR. BENWAY: "An *espontáneo*! Stop him before he guts my patient!"
> (*Espontáneo* is a bull-fighting term for a member of the audience who leaps down into the ring, pulls out a concealed cape and attempts a few passes with the bull before he is dragged out of the ring.)
> The orderlies scuffle with the *espontáneo*, who is finally ejected from the hall. The anesthetist takes advantage of the confusion to pry a large gold filling from the patient's mouth. (52)

In *Naked Lunch* as in the Spanish bullfighting arena, the *espontáneo* is the personification of spontaneity, a force that disrupts the impulses for control represented by Benway. But if the *espontáneo* embodies a rebuke of order, this rebuke is itself dangerous, as a real-life *espontáneo* would put himself in harm's way in the hopes of achieving glory (Burroughs's *espontáneo* wields a scalpel with no clear motive but disruption). Via the logic underpinning the book's "mosaic of juxtaposition" aesthetic, the *espontáneo* is connected figuratively to "The Word" through the image of the leopard man quoted above, who will "leap" on the reader just as the *espontáneo* "leaps" into the frame, and points to why *Naked Lunch* remains so unsettling: it certainly presents a rebuke or evasion of control, but does so differently from other examples of Beat literature, which tend to figure dominant culture negatively and the underground positively. But in *Naked Lunch*, by contrast, The Word-as-disruptive force is dangerous *because* it subjects readers to the disturbing "kaleidoscope of vistas," without orientating them as to what they "mean." The book leaves readers with a kind of spontaneity that rebukes or evades not just the political systems in

Interzone, but *any* political or social order associated with the state (indeed, the "road to follow" in *Naked Lunch* is the "cooperative," which "*can* live without the state ... The building up of independent units to meet needs of the people who participate in the functioning of the unit. A bureau operates on opposite principle of *inventing needs* to justify its existence" [112]).

One of the most famous set-pieces in the book occurs when Dr. Benway describes a man who taught his asshole how to talk, a section that ends with a withering view of democracy: "Democracy is cancerous, and bureaus are its cancer. A bureau takes root anywhere in the state, turns malignant like the Narcotic Bureau, and grows and grows.... Bureaucracy is wrong as a cancer, a turning away from the human evolutionary direction of infinite potentials and differentiation and independent spontaneous action to the complete parasitism of a virus" (112). Again the book counterpoints a political system with "independent spontaneous action" – and the system in question is not fascism or Soviet-style totalitarianism, but democracy, emphasizing the fact that while democracy is figured in the West as an idealized political model, its contemporary form depends on bureaucracies, which are finally antithetical to "independent spontaneous action." One way to think about *Naked Lunch*, by contrast, is that it presents spontaneous action without bureaucratic oversight. As Will Lee remarks toward the end of the book: "Push your mind too hard and it will fuck up like an overloaded switchboard, or turn on you with sabotage ... Americans have a special horror of giving up control, of letting things happen in their own way without interference" (179). *Naked Lunch* is designed to push the mind too hard, to short-circuit it into producing spontaneous thought.

4.7   *On the Road*: Sordid Hipsters of America

Although from 1950 on, there were those quieter developments in the Beat novel with Chandler Brossard's antinovel or Burroughs's "straight" underground books, by 1959 *Naked Lunch* had forged a path that might have rendered the very term "novel" obsolete. After *The Town and the City*, Kerouac went down a like path with his breakthrough work, *On the Road*, and especially with its reimagining, *Visions of Cody*, both of which exist in a generically fuzzy space that draws on the resources of fiction, memoir, and history.

Arguably the most celebrated Beat text to this day, *On the Road* was an immediate best-seller, and once *New York Times* reviewer Gilbert Millstein declared its publication a "historic occasion" and "testament" of the Beat Generation, it was saddled with cultural baggage that Kerouac himself didn't anticipate or necessarily want – as Ann Charters has put it, "it would seem he had spent the first part of his career trying to write the book and get it published, and the rest of his life trying to live it down."[96] What Kerouac was trying to live down was partly the effects of how Viking chose to market *On the Road*: rightly noting curiosity about the bohemian writers in the Ginsberg–Kerouac orbit after the furor over *Howl and Other Poems* in San Francisco, the jacket copy announced that "After World War I a certain group of restless searching Americans came to be called 'The Lost Generation'.... For a good many of the same reasons after World War II another group, roaming America in a wild, desperate search for identity and purpose, became known as 'The Beat Generation.' Jack Kerouac is the voice of this group, and this is his novel."[97] The evocative proclamation is certainly the most pithy example of the dynamic that came to characterize how the "Beat Generation" accrued meaning in American culture in the late 1950s: as an outsider, underground sensibility nonetheless packaged, disseminated, and given shape by mainstream publishing outlets such as Viking Press and the *New York Times*.

While Kerouac did indeed have larger social phenomena in mind as he drew exuberant portraits inspired by his friends, he was dismayed when the writing itself was eclipsed by this phenomenon – or misunderstandings of this phenomenon – an eventuality suggested by Millstein's claim that *On the Road* was "the most important utterance yet made by the generation Kerouac himself named years ago as 'beat,' and whose principal avatar he is."[98] Such a pronouncement insisted on Kerouac's importance, but did so in terms of his cultural position rather than his literary achievement. Many enthusiastic readers in 1957 and after followed Millstein's lead, coming to *On the Road* for its buoyant style, its descriptions of an America strange to the middle class and thus seemingly more authentic or "pure," and its recognizable portrayals of figures already associated with the new, hip generation: not only Neal Cassady, on whom the character of Dean Moriarty is based, but also Allen Ginsberg, William Burroughs, Herbert Huncke, John Clellon Holmes, and others. One of the great successes of the novel is that Kerouac is able to invite readers into a world populated by these characters: I alluded in Part I to Kerouac's "poetics of intimacy," an approach that gives the impression that he merely transcribed what happened to him and his buddies, a notion reinforced by the much-circulated story that he had written the book with blazing speed, completing it in only three weeks.[99]

As compelling a story as this is, it obscures the real circumstances of the novel's composition, in turn making it more difficult to see Kerouac's importance as a literary artist as well as the cultural "avatar" Millstein claims. *On the Road*'s significance as a social event notwithstanding, most Kerouac scholars now insist that we view the novel in the context of his larger body of work.[100] This has been difficult to do partly because the legend surrounding *On the Road*'s composition is so well known, if not exactly correct. Although it is true, for example, that Kerouac wrote a version of the book in just twenty days, from April 2 to 22, 1951, on long strips of paper threaded through his typewriter, some persistent myths have clouded how generations of readers have approached the novel. In a meticulous essay in which he tries to separate reality from legend, Matt Theado identifies what he calls the "most significant of the long-lasting myths" about *On the Road*'s composition, which I think are worth repeating in the context of this book:

> that Kerouac wrote the novel while he was high on Benzedrine; that he wrote the scroll on teletype paper; that the typescript's prose was unpunctuated; that Kerouac was unwilling to revise; that the reaction of his editor, Robert Giroux, upon seeing the scroll format caused Kerouac to withdraw the novel, refusing to change a word; and that the prose style of the scroll was significantly different from Viking's 1957 publication.[101]

Theado shows that none of these myths is strictly accurate, correcting the more picayune misperceptions by noting that Kerouac insisted that he was drinking only coffee during his marathon writing session, telling Ginsberg that "Road was not written on benny, on coffee" (qtd. in Theado, "Revisions," 15), and that despite Kerouac's 1959 remark on *The Steve Allen Show* that he wrote on "teletype paper," the scroll was composed on eight strips of "translucent paper . . . somewhat rattly or crackly" (14) and ranged from around 11′ 8″ long to 16′ 10½″ long, taped together after he had typed each individual section (18). From there, Theado moves into correctives that help us rethink Kerouac's aesthetic project, as when he reminds us that although the scroll typescript was written as one long paragraph, it was conventionally punctuated (21), or when he explains that Kerouac's encounter at Giroux's office, in which he supposedly unfurled the scroll with a flourish, declaring that he would never change a single word, is greatly exaggerated (19).

Indeed, the most persistent – and pernicious – myth about *On the Road* is that Kerouac never revised it, a notion firmly rooted in pop culture ideas about the Beats, but debunked many times over by scholars. Before discussing the published text, then, it is useful to clarify some aspects of its composition history. In addition to the scroll, there are numerous extant drafts, typescripts, and associated notebooks connected to *On the Road*'s composition, material that was not readily available for public study until 2006, after the Berg Collection at the New York Public Library purchased the bulk of Kerouac's archive. Access to this archive has been a windfall for Kerouac devotees, and the most useful guide to it is Isaac Gewirtz's *Beatific Soul: Jack Kerouac on the Road* (2007), published to coincide with NYPL's exhibit of the same name that ran from November 9, 2007, to March 16, 2008. Gewirtz takes readers through the most important "proto-versions" of *On the Road* collected in the Berg, the first of which is catalogued, per Kerouac's labeling, as "Ray Smith Novel of Fall 1948," and contains scenes later retained in *On the Road*, using a name for his protagonist (Ray Smith) he wound up reserving for *The Dharma Bums*. As Gewirtz makes clear, "*Ray Smith* is only the first of at least a half dozen proto-versions of *On the Road*, each of which is represented in the Archive by anywhere from a few to several dozen drafts, as well as scores of fragments and hundreds of pages of working notes."[102] Thus even those who cannot make the trip to the Berg now know that Kerouac relied on the detailed notes he kept regarding his road trips from 1947 to 1949, and used them to generate a range of texts prior to the scroll, which may therefore be understood as a clarification of material he had been working with for years.[103] After the scroll version, Kerouac wrote at least two more full typescripts of *On the Road*, refining its voice and narrative structure. The first, called the "'second' typescript" by Gewirtz (112) and T2 by Theado, was written according to Theado immediately after the scroll version, from April 22 to May 22, 1951 (32–33); following this, the "'third' typescript" (Gewirtz, *Beatific Soul*, 118) or T3 (Theado, "Revisions," 33) "was the one that Kerouac submitted to Viking as his final draft; it was then emended further – according to Kerouac, without consulting him – by his Viking editors, [Malcolm] Cowley and Keith Jennison . . . It is the product of at least two different drafts, the first of which was created in 1953–1954" (Gewirtz *Beatific Soul*, 118).

As I hope is evident from this briefest of tours through the Kerouac archive, the composition history of *On the Road* is complex and tricky to sort out definitively, and though the broad strokes remain similar enough from the scroll to the published version that Theado can insist that their "prose style" is not "significantly different" (11), it is likewise the case that there certainly are changes that other readers might interpret as significant. For our present purpose, I won't wade too deeply into the minutiae of proto-versions or drafts, except when quoting from them is useful in illustrating my claims about what the novel is doing, or how it fits into both Kerouac's body of work and the rise of the Beat novel more broadly conceived.

So, while the scroll was exhilarating to Kerouac because its energy seemed closer to the spirit of his experiences, it isn't necessarily the most "authentic" version of *On the Road*. Moreover, when placed in terms of his larger body of work, most scholars agree that despite the novel's compelling style, perfected across a range of versions, it does not yet reflect what many see as Kerouac's most significant aesthetic innovation, spontaneous prose.[104] As Tim Hunt reminds us, when we're discussing Kerouac's development of spontaneous prose, we're not simply talking about speedy composition as in the scroll version, but rather about a "new game entirely."[105] For Hunt, *On the Road* changed the rules of the literary game with its free-flowing style and treatment of taboo subject matter, but it was the subsequent development of spontaneous prose, exemplified in *Visions of Cody* and later work, that would change the game itself. I'll explain the method of spontaneous prose after my discussion of *On the Road*, but for now it may be useful to bear in mind Kerouac's quick schematic distinction between *On the Road* and *Visions of Cody*: "Instead of just a horizontal account of travels on the road, I wanted a vertical, metaphysical study of Cody's [Cassady's] character and its relationship to the general 'America'" (n.p.). In this view, "horizontal" writing (*On the Road*), however wild or digressive in sensibility, is still motivated primarily by the architectures of plot, what he would later frame negatively as "craft." By contrast, "vertical" writing (*Visions of Cody*) is not concerned with plot or character development in the traditional sense, and is thus free to pursue not merely digressions, but imagistic associations, wordplay, and the momentum or "swing" of the sentence without a planned idea of where the sentence will end. As he elaborated in "Essentials of Spontaneous Prose," to write vertically is to "begin not from preconceived idea of what to say about image but from jewel center of interest in subject of image at *moment* of writing, and write outwards swimming in sea of language to peripheral release and exhaustion."[106] This reliance on a "jewel center of interest," followed outward according to the writer's own subjective response to the "image" at that particular moment in time, characterizes a signal development in Kerouac's aesthetics post–*On the Road*.[107]

As a horizontal novel, the plot of *On the Road* is straightforward: in the late 1940s, a young, comparatively "mainstream" writer, Sal Paradise, meets Dean Moriarty, a hip petty thief, womanizer, and inveterate talker who inspires him to take four road trips across the United States and finally into Mexico. Along the way, Sal encounters a cast of characters who challenge his ideas about what is right or normal, and his romanticized portraits of hobos, migrant workers, drug addicts, petty criminals, sexually open couples, and the like form an underground community more or less invisible to dominant culture, a community that would on the novel's publication be lumped together as the Beat Generation. This is partly because as Kerouac was thinking about how best to frame his road material, he was also thinking about how his characters' adventures might be illuminated or not by the concepts of "beat" and Beat Generation. In the second typescript, for example, Kerouac opens the novel like this: "I first met Dean not long after [my father died and I thought everything was dead. My knowledge of the beat generation and the road began. Before] that I'd always dreamed of going west, seeing the country, planning and never taking off."[108] According to Gewirtz, the second typescript is notable partly because "it bears witness to a panicked Kerouac unmercifully mutilating his novel . . . in the hope of removing anything that Viking might find objectionable" (120). If it's true that on some level Kerouac had publishability in mind during this round of revisions, it is telling that in addition to excising material, he added this explicit reference to the "beat generation" in the opening lines, suggesting as it does that Kerouac thought such a label might ensure sales. Although the addition didn't make it into the published novel, its insertion here further suggests that Kerouac was thinking about the book in both individual and generational terms, and that when he invests Dean with an increasingly larger-than-life aura, he does so to make him an emblem of the "mystic signification" he associated with the "beat" people he had encountered in his travels (121).

In reading the original scroll version against the published one, we find Kerouac emphasizing that Sal casts Dean not only in mystic but also in mythic terms. In the scroll, for example, Dean (still named Neal) is introduced like this: "My first impression of Neal was of a young Gene Autry—trim, thin-hipped, blue eyes, with a real Oklahoma accent."[109] Compare this with the published version: "My first impression of Dean was of a young Gene Autry – trim, thin-hipped, blue-eyed, with a real Oklahoma accent – a sideburned hero of the snowy West" (5).[110] The addition of the final clause elevates Dean to the realm of the archetypal, and reminds us that On the Road is not merely Kerouac's factualist recounting of his experiences, but a fiction based on these experiences, told through the admiring, naïve perspective of Sal Paradise. It is Dean, not Sal, who the novel figures as avatar of "the sordid hipsters of America, a new beat generation that I [Sal] was slowly joining" (54). Throughout the novel, in fact, Sal is continually searching for the authentic Beat experience, but is never quite able to find it, as it seems most vivid in the past or in some phantom place a step ahead of him, symbolized by the elusiveness of Elmer Hassel, a hipster junky inspired by Herbert Huncke.

Dean, though, embodies a magnetic energy irresistible to Sal, and is always telling him stories about good old days with the inner circle of Hassel, Bull Lee (inspired by Burroughs), and Carlo Marx (inspired by Ginsberg). Reminiscing about his "Houston days in 1947," for example, Dean characterizes these figures archetypally, so while he was busy trying to bed a "real gone dumb girl" whose "beautiful body was matched only by her idiot mind," "Bull was drunk trying to get this young Mexican kid drunk. Carlo was writing poetry on heroin. Hassel didn't show up till midnight" (158). These pithy descriptions were based, as Kerouac put it in his journals, on Neal "reminiscing of former beat adventures with Hunkey [*sic*]" (*Windblown*, 331), and serve in the novel to underscore the "mystic signification" Kerouac associated with Beatness by compressing these figures into mythic caricature: Dean is chasing girls, Bull is chasing boys, Carlo is composing poetry in altered states, and Hassel has lately disappeared. Sal of course romanticizes this past, always deferred or filtered through Dean's memory, and it only whets his desire to have a "pure" experience himself.

Given that Sal – like Kerouac – is a writer who aspires to make his mark on literary history, as *On the Road* unfolds, we find that he casts such mythologization in terms of a "generation" contrasted to the Lost Generation. In fact, Sal not-so-subtly holds the earlier Lost Generation against the contemporary Beat Generation via his friend Roland Major, who writes "Hemingwayan short stories" (41) and brags about his European adventures that reenact *The Sun Also Rises* (1926), as when he paraphrases Jake Barnes and company's practice of cooling their wine in the river: "Straight out of Hemingway, it was," Sal observes (53). It is only a page later that Sal explicitly contrasts Roland's friends to Dean and Sal, providing a fuller context for *On the Road*'s first mention of the Beat Generation: "I wished Dean and Carlo were there – then I realized they'd be out of place and unhappy. They were like the man with the dungeon stone and the gloom [from Beethoven's opera *Fidelio*], the sordid hipsters of America, a new beat generation that I was slowly joining" (54). From Sal's writerly point of view, then, the Beat Generation is "new" specifically because it moves beyond the mores of Hemingway's Lost Generation.

For Kerouac, a crucial difference between his work and earlier work exemplified by, say, Hemingway, is his handling of Sal's voice, which is essential to understanding what he's doing in *On the Road*. As the novel's most attentive readers have noticed, to assume simply that Sal equals Kerouac is to miss the ironic distance between the implied author and the narrator.[111] In some moments this distance is obvious, as in the first few pages when Sal gushes about his plans to take an epic road trip, only to fail miserably; this is Sal as what Nancy M. Grace calls the "comic fool . . . someone with whom the reader can initially identify yet feel a bit superior."[112] In other moments the distance is clarified by studying versions of *On the Road*, as in the example above, when Kerouac underscores Sal's hero-worship of Dean by revising descriptions of their first encounter. Generally speaking, though, readers need only the published text to note the distinctions between Sal and the implied author that suggest the book's ethical perspective on the events it describes. While such distinctions may be easy to miss since the novel's style encourages forward momentum, stopping to read carefully, pausing to savor certain passages as Sal himself pauses to savor certain vistas, helps us to see that although *On the Road* is horizontal, it is far from a straightforward, diaristic account of what really happened to Kerouac.

My goal in the following pages isn't to offer a wholesale reinterpretation of *On the Road*, but to focus attention on an aspect that I think opens up Kerouac's general methods. I find it suggestive, for instance, that one of the most discussed sections in the novel concerns Sal meeting Terry, a Chicana agricultural worker in California's Central Valley. In 1955, Kerouac published a version of this section as "The Mexican Girl" in *The Paris Review*, and it was apparently so evocative to him that, as then-wife Joan Haverty later recalled, while he was retyping this part of the scroll, he suddenly woke her up to demand sex, aroused not by Joan but by "what was in the typewriter . . . his description of Terry, the Mexican girl he knew in California, and the pity he felt for her."[113] Sal's interlude with Terry has also had an especially robust afterlife, as many critics have zeroed-in on their relationship as the book's most problematic, and it even inspired Tim Z. Hernandez's *Mañana Means Heaven* (2013), a book blending fact and fiction that imagines the real-life relationship between Kerouac and Bea Franco, on whom Terry was modeled.

In *On the Road*, Sal falls for Terry and spends a couple of weeks living in her world, picking cotton for subsistence wages and moving into a migrant worker's tent where he plays husband to Terry and father to her young son – "There were a bed, a stove, and a cracked mirror hanging from a pole; it was delightful. I had to stoop to get in, and when I did there was my baby and my baby boy" (94). This isn't marriage, but its parody; as Sal remarks at the outset, "For the next fifteen days we were together for better or for worse" (85). That the time frame specified in the first part of this sentence undercuts the promise of the second half is clear when, after some days idealizing his impoverished life with Terry, Sal feels "the pull of my own life calling me back," and so shoots his aunt "a penny postcard across the land and asked for another fifty" (98). Critics have often pointed to the Terry section to underscore a problem with Kerouac's vision, that he glamorizes poverty without having to really suffer its consequences, that he and the other Beats were slumming when they interacted with those whom Sal dubs the "great fellahin peoples of the world" (98).[114] This problem is compounded, the argument goes, by the fact that Kerouac is writing from a white, comparatively privileged position, and the impoverished people he romanticizes most, whether Terry or the "old Negro couple in the field" (96), are people of color not in a position to effortlessly conjure a month's wages with a postcard. Sal's interactions with and descriptions of Terry are certainly problematic, but I think that the novel is aware of this problem while Sal remains oblivious, at least initially, and so it is not quite correct to collapse the novel's point of view with Sal's, as some critics have done.[115] To collapse the implied author and narrator is to ignore the distinction between what the novel knows and what Sal knows, a key result of Kerouac's shift from third person in *The Town and the City* to first-person narration, and essential to understanding how the novel ironizes Sal precisely by questioning his behavior with Terry.

Such a distance between narrator and implied author is clarified by attending to the particulars of the Terry section. When Sal first enters the Central Valley, where he is about to encounter Terry for the first time, he waxes poetic: "Soon it got dusk, a grapy dusk, a purple dusk over tangerine groves and long melon fields; the sun the color of pressed grapes, slashed with burgundy red, the fields the color of love and Spanish mysteries" (80). In the introductory clause, Sal describes dusk with no adjective, and then offers two quick variations on this description, both connected to grapes, and we soon learn that this description, written, after all, retrospectively, is framed by Sal's knowledge that Terry is a grape-picker, and that for him the Central Valley will always be associated with Terry and therefore grapes. Thus although the sentence may seem merely repetitive, in fact it develops a motif: the valley is associated with grapes, then the color of grapes, then the sun itself is the color of "pressed grapes" and "burgundy red," reminding us that the grapes are a product that will be turned into wine, thereby nodding to the economics underlying Terry's and her family's labor. (Sal later points to "variation" as a key formal characteristic of a "jazz-session" [200], praising a musician who liked "the surprise of a new simple variation of a chorus" [201].)

This sentence in fact has a dual function in *On the Road*: for Sal, it is a way to wistfully describe a romantic landscape; for Kerouac, it is a way to begin viewing the Central Valley in economic terms, providing a broader context for his narrator's experiences there, although Sal himself remains largely oblivious. Reading *On the Road* alongside *Junky* makes it tempting to see a more strident economic critique in the former if Kerouac's Central Valley echoes Burroughs's mention in the latter book of the Rio Grande Valley, which as he wrote in 1948, depends "entirely on Mexican laborers who enter the Country illegally with our aid and connivance. The 'civil liberties' of these workers are often violated repeatedly. They are often kept on the job at gun point.... Workers who try to leave the field are shot."[116] Whether or not Kerouac was consciously evoking Burroughs, *On the Road* does repeatedly allude to the economics underlying Terry's labor conditions, even as Sal romanticizes them. The sentence quoted above, for example, is connected to others in this section via a cluster of imagistic associations that together yield meaning outside the romance plot in which Sal seems stuck. For example, we learn that Terry's relatives "were grape-pickers and lived in a shack in the vineyards" (82), and that "The thought of living in a tent and picking grapes in the cool California mornings hit me right" (89), lines that inform a later reprise of "grapy dusk," when "purple dusk descended over the grape country" (92). The dreamy sense of "grape country" is again underscored, and in fact extended to Terry herself, whose skin Sal describes as "brown as grapes" (84). After this freighted simile, Sal spends the next fifteen pages describing his time with Terry, and following a failure to find grape-picking work himself, his meditations on the cotton picking he does seem especially tone-deaf as he calls the enterprise "beautiful," and lingers over "an old Negro couple" who "picked cotton with the same God-blessed patience their grandfathers had practiced in ante-bellum Alabama" (96). If that weren't startling enough, at the end of his work day, resting in the tent, Sal characterizes himself as contentedly "sighing like an old Negro cotton-picker" (97).

Many readers have rightly raised an eyebrow at sentences such as these, but my sense is that Kerouac *wants* readers to be taken aback, that this is evidence of the distance between the implied author and the narrator.[117] This is apparent partly in the revisions from the scroll version to the published one: Kerouac changed the scroll's "prewar Alabama" (*Original*

Scroll, 197) to "ante-bellum Alabama" to eliminate any ambiguity about which war is being referred to, as "ante-bellum" is traditionally used to refer to pre–Civil War times. This small change suggests that Kerouac was trying to call attention to Sal's romanticization of enslaved cotton pickers, thereby making his lack of historical awareness even more pointed.

This general lack of awareness informs Sal's interpretation of Terry and her situation, for although he does register her poverty, he does so in romanticized and therefore naïve terms. Describing that "shack in the vineyards" (82), for example, he writes: "I couldn't imagine how the whole family managed to live in there. Flies flew over the sink. There were no screens, just like in the song, 'The window she is broken and the rain she is coming in.' Terry was at home now and puttering around pots" (99). Sal succeeds in simultaneously noting extreme poverty and yet failing to witness it or to engage with it in an ethical or humane way. This is partly because he reads the scene through a lyric in a popular song, "Mañana (Is Soon Enough for Me)" (1947), performed by (white) singer Peggy Lee in a caricatured Mexican accent. The song proceeds in broken English to describe a living situation very much like Terry's, but puts the blame on the speaker's comically lazy family, destitute because they put work off until "mañana," or tomorrow (as does Terry's brother Rickey, whose mantra is "*Mañana,* man, we make it; have another beer" [92]). Sal's quotation from a song in which a white performer mimics a Mexican speaker thus mirrors Sal's own mimicry of Terry's life – at one point he remarks that some "Okies . . . thought I was a Mexican, of course; and in a way I am" (97) – and from the novel's point of view, both "Mañana (Is Soon Enough for Me)" and Sal's claim to be "in a way" Mexican are problematic as they represent a privileged slumming rather than an authentic engagement or "pure" experience.

Near the end of the Terry section, Kerouac emphasizes this point by returning again to the grape motif, having Sal observe that "In California you chew the juice out of grapes and spit the skin away, a real luxury . . . I hid in the grapevines, digging it all. I felt like a million dollars; I was adventuring in the crazy American night" (100). The financial simile is apt as the novel associates Sal with privilege or "luxury" even in those moments when he thinks he is hanging out with the "beatest characters in the country" (85): he is able to "feel like a million dollars" because he can summon money from his aunt whenever he wants. He has the luxury to spit out the grape skins just as he spits out Terry, whose skin, recall, he sees as "brown as grapes" (84).[118]

As the novel's forward momentum continues, Kerouac puts a finer point on Sal's lack of awareness about those Beat characters he glorifies.

During one of their subsequent road trips, for example, Sal and Dean happen to pass again by Terry's hometown, where Sal notes he "had lived and loved and worked in the spectral past" (169). Sal's nostalgia seems to register a pang of guilt, but it is only a page later when Marylou, one of Dean's women, says to Sal: "You see what a bastard he is? ... Dean will leave you out in the cold any time it's in his interest" (170). This is a moment when as a reader, you want Sal to draw a connection between Marylou's criticism of Dean and Sal's own treatment of Terry, but Sal himself doesn't do so.

It isn't until the end of the novel, when the road takes him into Mexico, that Sal finally sees through his fantasies concerning the "great fellahin peoples of the world" (98). Kerouac primes Sal for this breakthrough on one of the final stops before the border, at a hospital in San Antonio, when he observes a room full of "poor Mexican women, some of them pregnant, some of them sick or bringing their little sick kiddies. It was sad. I thought of poor Terry and wondered what she was doing now" (272). This fleeting concern for Terry seems to disappear once they get over the border to "the magic land at the end of the road" (276). Unmoored from the oppressiveness of Cold War America, as they venture deeper into Mexico, Sal, Dean, and another travel buddy get drunk and high and are brought to brothels teeming with young brown women; Dean is awestruck: "We've finally got to heaven" (278). But it is in one of these brothels that Sal sees a person he takes to be the most pitiable in the room, a young, obviously desperate prostitute. Rather than underscoring that this girl embodies "the Fellahin Indians of the world, the essential strain of the basic primitive" (280), or romanticizing her poverty as he does with Terry or the various hobos he has encountered, Sal suddenly sees her situation more clearly: "Of all the girls in there she needed the money most; maybe her mother had come to get money from her for her little infant sisters and brothers. Mexicans are poor. It never, never occurred to me just to approach her and give her some money" (290). Sal's self-recrimination stems from his recognition that he has been exploiting people in Mexico, and that he has been able to do so precisely because of his position of wealth relative to the fellaheen poor in "real beat huts" (277). This is why Kerouac echoes Sal's earlier boast that he ironically "felt like a million dollars" (100) with Terry: in Mexico he can "thr[o]w money" at women unabashedly, since "I didn't know the value of Mexican money; for all I knew I had a million pesos" (288). Sal's realization that a truly sympathetic person might just give over some money without expecting anything in return leads to his epiphany in the brothel, when "somewhere I heard a baby wail in a sudden lull, remembering I was in Mexico after all and not in a pornographic hasheesh daydream in heaven" (291). Finally Sal is able to distinguish "Mexico" from "heaven" – that is, to apprehend the reality of rural poverty as such, rather than romanticizing it as a means to his own self-actualization (the irony that this recognition nonetheless still leads to Sal's self-actualization is perhaps lost on the novel).[119] Kerouac underscores this point in the final scene in Mexico City, when Dean abandons a dangerously ill Sal because, as he says, "Gotta get back to my life" (302), an echo of Sal's earlier abandonment of Terry, when he felt "the pull of my own life calling me back" (98). And if Sal had earlier lingered over Terry's scarred, "poor belly" (84), alone and feverish in Mexico, he is now associated with her, clutching the "cramps in my belly" (302), finally realizing "what a rat" Dean is (303).

I have spent time on the details of the Terry section and its chains of echoes and associations throughout *On the Road* to stress that reading Sal as Kerouac with a different name means glimpsing only a piece of the novel's achievement. Although many readers have been drawn to the novel for its romantic exuberance and characterization of an alternative, underground America, the very energy of the writing itself is what compels many on second look. It wouldn't be surprising, for example, if as a teenager one came to *On the Road* for its energy and sense of adventure, but returned to it later for its style, not only Kerouac's facility with images like the grape motif discussed above, but his ability to wind out long, lyrical sentences that carry the reader along as though down a highway. This interest in style itself, in the notion that language could become the real star of a book, takes center stage as Kerouac developed a new writing technique he called spontaneous prose.

4.8 Developing Spontaneous Prose

Kerouac's next major work, *Visions of Cody*, moved away from plot to experiment instead with what a "vertical" novel might look like. As it turned out, this verticality could be achieved only if he moved even farther afield from the style of *The Town and the City*, dropping any pretense to the conventional beginning, middle, and end still evident in *On the Road*. Instead, Kerouac ran with the spontaneous aesthetic inspired by a piece of Neal Cassady's own writing, an eighteen-page dispatch from his frenetic world that was later dubbed the "Joan Anderson letter." Over the course of this bravura letter, written in December 1950, Cassady detailed his romances with two women, Joan Anderson and "Cherry Mary," writing with what he called a "sense of careless freedom"; according to Charters, Kerouac was "literally overwhelmed" not merely by Cassady's free-form, conversational style, but by the idea that such a style could sustain an "extended narrative."[120] Here, for example, is Cassady describing his narrow escape through a bathroom window after a parent of the child Mary was babysitting returned home unexpectedly: "I could hardly reach outside to work on the screen – since the window opened outward – but I pushed and making a hellova noise, split the screen enough to open the window. Now the impossible compressing of my frame for the squeeze. I thought if I could get my head through I could make it; I just was able to, by bending the tough metal bar the slightest cunthair (in those days I cleaned and jerked 220 lbs.) and of course, I almost tore off my pride-and-joy as I wiggled into the cold November air."[121] These few sentences illustrate the letter's rakish voice and point of view, which is carried along by an engagingly offhand energy and self-deprecating humor.

In his reply to Cassady, Kerouac called the letter "among the best things ever written in America" – he was so enthusiastic because he thought Cassady was finally writing with "the muscular rush of [his] own narrative style and excitement," what Kerouac called "kickwriting" (*Selected Letters, 1940–1956*, 242).[122] Because of this over-the-top response, the lore around the "Joan Anderson letter" is that it shocked Kerouac out of the mode he had used in *The Town and the City* by demonstrating the power of spontaneous prose, resulting in a narrative breakthrough with *On the Road*. Anyone who has read *The Town and the City*, the "Joan Anderson letter," and *On the Road* can see that *On the Road* has more of the first-person energy and buoyancy of Cassady's letter, which surely did encourage Kerouac's experimentations with voice. But the real work with spontaneous prose came after *On the Road* was drafted, when Kerouac began experimenting with "sketching" in October 1951 – about seven months after he had written the scroll version. As Tim Hunt explains, "In sketching, the writer does not compose a representation of the scene; instead, the writer performs his attention to the scene through the details as he records them in writing. The sketch that results is literally a recording of the process of the writer engaging the scene" (*Textuality*, 106). Otherwise put, sketching abandons fiction's seemingly fundamental need for plot by foregrounding the writer's idiosyncratic perspective, which itself becomes the real subject of the sketch.

It was from the idea of sketching that Kerouac would develop more elaborate theories and techniques of spontaneous prose, whose principles he explained in "Essentials of Spontaneous Prose" (published in 1957 in

Black Mountain Review 7 but written in 1953 at the behest of Ginsberg and Burroughs). He listed nine "essentials," the explanations of which tended toward the metaphorical and elliptical: Set-Up, Procedure, Method, Scoping, Lag in Procedure, Timing, Center of Interest, Structure of Work, Mental State. As with sketching, a basic goal of spontaneous prose is to showcase the writer's subjectivity, and "Essentials" is filled with assertions about writing such that it should be an "undisturbed flow from the mind of personal secret idea-words" or that the writer ought not "pause to think of proper word but the infantile pileup of scatological buildup words till satisfaction is gained."[123] In order to achieve such "undisturbed flow," Kerouac recommends specific formal techniques: "No periods separating sentence-structures already arbitrarily riddled by false colons and timid usually needless commas" (484) or "Never afterthink to 'improve' or defray impressions, as, the best writing is always the most painful personal wrung-out tossed from cradle warm protective mind ... always honest, ('ludicrous'), spontaneous, 'confessional' interesting, because not 'crafted.' Craft *is* craft" (485).[124]

In "Essentials," Kerouac offered a method for sketching with the idea of the "jewel center of interest": "Begin not from preconceived idea of what to say about image but from jewel center of interest in subject of image at *moment* of writing, and write outwards swimming in sea of language" (585). What Kerouac is proposing here is a different way to think about fiction: rather than work from a larger narrative plan – plot – the "jewel center of interest" names an object, image, or idea set before the writer's mind ("set-up"), and the writer then trusts him- or herself to radiate out from this jewel center via imagistic or linguistic associations, even if that means letting the unconscious take over, as in automatic writing; he advised: "Follow roughly outlines in out-fanning movement over subject, as river rock, so mindflow over jewel-center" (485).

One of the finest illustrations of this technique is "The Railroad Earth" (sometimes titled "October in the Railroad Earth") (1952), which begins with a "jewel-center of interest" and radiates out – the piece has no plot except, as Hunt puts it, "the process of the writer engaging the scene" (*Textuality*, 106). Here are the opening lines: "There was a little alley in San Francisco back of the Southern Pacific station at Third and Townsend in redbrick of drowsy lazy afternoons with everybody at work in offices in the air you feel the impending rush of their commuter frenzy."[125] Kerouac read this piece on *The Steve Allen Show* in 1959, and hearing it aloud emphasizes its linguistic play, interest in sound, and imagistic chains and associations that are not building to an end point so much as revealing the "fanning movement" of Kerouac's perceptions: "It was the fantastic drowse and drum hum of lum mum afternoon nathin' to do, ole Frisco with end of land sadness" (*Lonesome*, 38). In addition to "The Railroad Earth" and *Visions of Cody*, Kerouac experimented with spontaneous prose most effectively in *The Subterraneans* and *Old Angel Midnight*, both of which are discussed in more detail in Part III.

4.9   *Visions of Cody*: A Vertical, Metaphysical Study

Visions of Cody was Kerouac's first sustained exploration of what spontaneous prose could do, and although he held out great hope that it would propel what he called the "American Literary Renaissance" forward, the book was so strange that even Ginsberg didn't quite get it when he first read the manuscript in 1952.[126] He wrote to Kerouac: "I don't see how it will ever be published, it's so personal, . . . so full of our local mythological references, I don't know if it would make sense to any publisher. . . . I can't see anyone, New Directions, Europe, putting it out as it is."[127] Ginsberg was right that Kerouac would have trouble placing the whole manuscript "as it is," but James Laughlin's New Directions did eventually publish a condensed version in 1960 (limited to 750 copies), and portions appeared in a range of publications during Kerouac's lifetime.[128] But it wasn't until 1972, three years after Kerouac's death, that the full manuscript was finally published, complete with an afterword by Ginsberg, who by then had come around to appreciate the book, offering annotations explaining the "rightness" of its prose.[129]

Like *Naked Lunch*, *Visions of Cody* doesn't seem to cohere in conventional senses – but it does, also like *Naked Lunch*, conform to its own logic of spontaneity. In the 1952 letter quoted above, Ginsberg went on to fault *Visions* for "blowing on sounds and refusing to make sense," a reference to Kerouac's comparisons of spontaneous prose to the techniques of jazz musicians – "*blowing* (as per jazz musician) on subject of image," as he would put it in "Essentials of Spontaneous Prose" (484). Although Ginsberg didn't appreciate it at first, "blowing" was a way for Kerouac to stretch his mind, to give himself permission to experiment, to revel in language and play with literary history. *Visions of Cody* "makes sense" in terms of the experience of Kerouac's mind as it interacts with Cassady and images of Cassady – these interactions are the "visions" of the title. "This is all like bop," Kerouac writes, "we're getting to it indirectly" (296), and a later riff on Miles Davis is better understood as an indirect statement on his method in *Visions of Cody*:

Miles Davis, like the sun; or the sun, like Miles Davis, blows on with his raw little horn ... to flesh some of its fine raw sound, some wild abstract new ideas developed around a growing theme that started off like a tree and became a structure of iron on which tremendous phrases can be strung and hung and long pauses goofed, kicked along, whaled, touched with hidden and active meanings. (323–324)

This passage about Davis applies as well to *Visions*, revealing that it operates from its own idiosyncratic logic – "abstract new ideas" – which are often pursued and developed in ways that seem opaque if one is merely reading for, say, "Neal's history," as Ginsberg put it in his initial critique of the book.[130]

Instead, Kerouac had much larger aims in mind, and in the context of the rise of the Beat novel, *Visions of Cody* is a particularly rich text because, taken as a whole, it amounts to a 400-page experimental writing lab in which he tries out various strategies of representation. The published book is divided into three main parts narrated by Jack Duluoz, with unnumbered sections or chapters within those parts. Part One (3–43) consists of sketches that are inspired by Cody or somehow evocative of him; the opening line is "This is an old diner like the ones Cody and his father ate in" (3) and proceeds from that jewel center of interest.[131] Part Two (47–116) takes readers to Duluoz's imagistic impressions of Cody's childhood.[132] Part Three opens with a section titled "Frisco: The Tape" (119–247), transcriptions of real-life tape recordings Kerouac had made of his marijuana-infused conversations with Cassady. This lengthy section is followed by "Imitation of the Tape" (249–274), in which Duluoz takes on various voices and reimagines the transcriptions not as what was actually spoken but as what *might have* been thought or felt. There is a final titled section, "Joan Rawshanks in the Fog" (275–290), a set piece describing a real-life incident when Kerouac stumbled on Joan Crawford filming a movie in Russian Hill, San Francisco. This set piece is followed by various "visions" (290–337), the most memorable of which concerns Cody and the Three Stooges (304–306). After all this, the final section of the book (338–398) is a retelling of some events depicted in *On the Road*: the line "I first met Cody in 1947 but I didn't travel on the road with him till 1948" (338) signals that Kerouac is reworking earlier versions of the road book, the first of which opens: "I first met Neal not long after my father died" (*On the Road: Original*, 109). These sections are connected insofar as they showcase what Kerouac called in the preface to *Visions* "the world of raging action and folly and also of gentle sweetness seen through the keyhole of his eye" – with an emphasis not on plot or even on Cody as such, but rather on the way Cody activates Kerouac's subjectivity and writerly perceptions, the "keyhole of his eye."

For those readers looking forward to nothing but spontaneous prose, the most bewildering part of *Visions of Cody* is likely the lengthy "Frisco: The Tape" section at its center, a section that is, for the most part, dispassionate transcriptions of tape recordings. Given the way Kerouac was inspired by Cassady's voice in the "Joan Anderson letter," the tape transcriptions do make a certain sense as they are a way to capture this voice in its raw immediacy. The tape transcriptions thus do present "spontaneity" insofar as they capture extemporaneous speaking, but the writing itself is not of course an example of spontaneous prose; as Hunt puts it: "Kerouac's use of the tape recorder can be seen as an attempt to finesse, and preferably avoid, composing. But sketching records the inner action of the self's attention to the outer; the tape records the self oriented outward to engage an other in dialogue" (*Textuality*, 203 n. 6). In fact, I would suggest that in the context of *Visions of Cody* as a whole, the "Frisco: The Tape" section represents a meditation on the nature of spontaneity and how it can be manifest in writing.

For starters, it is not really the case that the tape recorder is unobtrusively capturing what is naturally occurring. Instead, Jack has prompted Cody by asking him to tell old stories about "Bull" (Burroughs) and "Huck" (Huncke), and so the section opens with Cody *performing* for the recorder and once again reifying the mythology of the Beat inner circle (237–241). Ten pages into the transcription, Cody himself recognizes the performative aspect of his story-telling, remarking that "we're still aware of ourselves, even when we're high" (129). This self-awareness actually becomes an impediment to spontaneous monologues or conversation, and on the second night of recording, Cody says: "I know you got the recorder on ... if I acted as if I didn't know it was on, why then, there'd been an ambiguity of ... of, ah, ulterial motives" (132–133, second set of ellipses in original). As it turns out, Cody's self-consciousness becomes incommensurate with the supposed objectivity of the tape recording, particularly when Kerouac converts these recordings into writing. Moments after Cody notes his awareness of the recorder, for example, the men begin to read the transcript Kerouac had typed up of the previous night's conversation, and Cody pauses over Kerouac's insertion of the phrase "demurely downward look" to describe Cody's expression as he spoke. This insertion leads to a lengthy debate about whether Cody had "really" (133) looked this way, the final result of which is that "the real" seems to be something that writing can never definitively capture.[133]

Thus although a tape recording *seems* to be the best way to capture spontaneity – just push play and act natural! – in fact its presence induces Cody to self-conscious performance, and even the most seemingly innocuous insertion drives a wedge between the signifier and signified. This is all to say that Kerouac included the "Frisco: The Tape" as an earnest experiment that does not finally succeed, and it sets the stage for what spontaneous prose can achieve that ostensible objectivity cannot.

After the tape transcriptions, Part Three opens with a section called "Imitation of the Tape" that thematizes the self-conscious nature of representation by referencing numerous types of expression, from school "Composition" themes (249) to newspapers and lists (250) to B-movies (251) and comic strips (261). Rather than pretending toward objectivity as in "Frisco: The Tape," Duluoz's imitation announces that he will redouble his effort to flex his own radical subjectivity and explore "visions" of Cody that are inextricable from this subjectivity. As he writes: "So now I sit and stew in a sophistication which has taken hold of me just exactly like a disease and makes me lie around like a bum all day long and stay up all night goofing with myself" (259). This idea of "goofing" is one way that Kerouac glosses a change from the sketching techniques found in Part One: goofing marks an even freer technique than sketching insofar as its practitioner isn't necessarily bound to the jewel center of interest but instead works promiscuously as he follows sounds, associations, and flights of thought and image. Kerouac put it simply in the Beat film *Pull My Daisy*: "goofing means I'm playing around with words."[134] In *Visions of Cody*, goofing becomes an end in and of itself: "YOU'VE GOT TO MAKE UP YOUR GODDAMN MIND IF YOU WANT TO GOOF OR DON'T WANT TO GOOF OR WANT TO STAY ON ONE LEVEL KICK OR GOOF" (255). Duluoz decides to deviate from the "ONE LEVEL" and instead "GOOF," which means breaking even from his own bounded subject position to take on different voices and styles of writing, from his friends and family to Kerouac's own past writing (e.g., "Galloway rolls on" [262] reimagines the opening of *The Town and the City*: "The town is Galloway" [3]), and he goofs in voices ranging from Gary Cooper (269) to "Owlhorn Mountain Ski Instructor" (270). This crashing cacophony of voices represents that which has come to Kerouac's attention, and he draws it into *Visions of Cody* as context for his own eccentric "visions" of Cody. As Gerald Nicosia notes, in the "Imitation" section, "Kerouac is parodying Joyce, . . . just as Joyce parodied all his fellow English writers in the 'Oxen of the Sun' section of *Ulysses*" (376), and he further locates parodies of Shakespeare, Dickens, Yeats, Twain,

Gertrude Stein, Hemingway, Steinbeck, Jesus Christ, Arthur Conan Doyle, W. C. Fields, Milton Berle, and Billie Holiday (*Memory Babe*, 373). One doesn't necessarily need to know the details of these allusions to see what Kerouac is doing with them: he's demonstrating all the reading he has done, signaling the stylistic and thematic influences that have informed his own putatively original voice.[135]

The idea that in *Visions of Cody* Kerouac includes that which has come to his attention is evident also in the lengthy set piece mentioned above, "Joan Rawshanks in the Fog." This section is apparently unconnected to Cody, but indirectly demonstrates how Kerouac's writerly consciousness can apprehend an event from real life and then develop its "hidden and active meanings" (324) in ways superior even to movie cameras. This section describes an actual moment when Kerouac had happened on Joan Crawford filming *Sudden Fear* (1952), specifically a scene in which she is fumbling with her keys while trying to open a door. Kerouac uses the incident to meditate on real life events and how we capture them, what he calls the "actual TAKE" (281). Joan Rawshanks does the same action over and over with the hope of achieving the perfect take, but this isn't possible *because* the camera is rolling (a situation that mirrors the note of performative falsity in the "Frisco: The Tape" section): "the thing, the Take, the actual juice suction of the camera catching a vastly planned action, the moment when we all know that the camera is germinating, a thing is being born whether we planned it right or not" (281). As in the "Frisco: The Tape" section, Kerouac is reflecting on the way the recording medium impinges on notions of spontaneity, so that the "thing" being germinated must necessarily be tainted and informed by the medium: it may be fascinating and worthy of attention, but it isn't real.

A way out of this apparent trap is to forget trying to capture the object external to the writerly consciousness – whether Crawford's performance or Cody's – and to instead explore a different kind of truth, the "visions" of the book's title. This is why the final turn of the book is away from the failed objectivity of "Frisco: The Tape" to the rabbit hole of Duluoz's "visions": "I've had several visions of Cody," he writes in a section after "Joan Rawshanks in the Fog," "most of the great ones in the middle of a tea-high and the greatest on jazz tea-high, matched only by the vision I had of him in Mexico" (295). These subsequent "visions" make up the last part of the book and are pointedly not attempts to represent Cassady's spontaneous talking, but rather the writer's "mindflow" – hence the insistence here that the best visions were born of marijuana use, which helps the writer "remove literary, grammatical and syntactical inhibition," an injunction in "Belief & Technique for Modern Prose" that Kerouac couples with the advice to "Like Proust be an old teahead of time" (483).

A well-known example of the book's latter "visions" is a riff on Cody and the Three Stooges, who in contrast to Joan Rawshanks are not trying to represent "the real," but rather are inventing their own slapstick, goofing logic that delights without having to be laden with "meaning":

> Supposing the Three Stooges were real? (and so I saw them spring into being at the side of Cody in the street right there front of the Station, Curly, Moe and Larry, that's his bloody name, *Larry*; Moe the leader, mopish, mowbry, mope-mouthed, mealy, mad, hanking, making the others quake; whacking Curly on the iron pate, backhanding Larry (who wonders); picking up a sledgehammer, honk, and ramming it down nozzle first on the flatpan of Curly's skull, boing, and all big dumb convict Curly does is muckle and yukkle and squeal, pressing his lips, shaking his old butt like jelly, knotting his Jell-o fists, eyeing Moe. (304)

Here Kerouac lets "stooge logic" carry his writing, and so revels in the sounds of made-up words that are onomatopoeic echoes of the Stooges whaling on each other – the point of the passage is not of course to get to the end, to find out what happens, but to be present in the moment, experiencing the kinetics of living with the Stooges. Thus although from a historical or biographical point of view, Cody's imagined romp with the Three Stooges is less "real" than Kerouac's dutiful transcriptions in "Frisco: The Tape," Kerouac's whole point is that such a view is wrong-headed when it comes to the relationship between representation and the thing being represented; according to his theories of spontaneous prose, the vision of Cody and the Three Stooges is actually truer than the tape transcription because it showcases the spirit of Cody's performative presentism that avoids the false note of Cassady performing for the tape.

Indeed, although goofing can be a non-serious end in itself, Kerouac, ever-anxious about the stakes of the "genuine literary movement" he helped launch, was also keen to signal how his seemingly dumb visions were in fact a shot across the bow of the literary establishment. He ends the Cody and the Stooges vision by pugnaciously repudiating the "outside world," whose literary critics he knows would dismiss such visions out of hand: "all the goofs he felt in him were justified in the outside world and he had nothing to reproach himself for, bonk, boing, crash, skittely boom, pow, slam, bang, boom, wham, blam, crack, frap, kerplunk, clatter, clap, blap, fap, slapmap, splat, crunch, crowsh, bong, splat, splat,

BONG!" (306). After this moment, in which narrative representation has been stripped away so readers are left in the realm of imaginative wordplay, and for a defiant length of time, Kerouac puts a finer point on just to whom in the "outside world" he might feel compelled to justify his work:

> "Obviously, an image which is immediately and unintentionally ridiculous is merely a fancy," – T. S. Eliot, *Selected Essays, 1917–1932*, Harcourt, Brace and Company, 383 Madison Avenue, New York 17, New York, Fifth Printing, June 1942, when little Cody Pomeray was sixteen.... There were no images springing up in the brain of Cody Pomeray that were repugnant to him at their outset. (306)

This quotation seems at first a straight-faced reference to Eliot, one of the reigning adjudicators of literary taste at mid-century, but as it keeps going, Kerouac pushes academic conventions ad absurdum so it ends in a parody of scholarly meticulousness.[136] But the parody has a point: in the quoted line Eliot is condemning the very thing that Kerouac has just spent pages doing in the Cody and Stooges section, and the fact that Eliot's *Selected Essays* is in its fifth printing suggests the reach of such a pronouncement. For Eliot, it is obvious that "ridiculous" images are mere fancy – the quoted line is excerpted from a passage explaining "the difference between imagination and fancy" – and yet Kerouac has just presented readers with a "vision" that is a ridiculous flight of imagination *and* integral to the work of the novel for that very reason. Eliot thus functions in *Visions of Cody* as the voice of literary tradition who sees "the literary" as circumscribed by seriousness of purpose and methodical planning; Cody, by contrast, represents an alternative perspective, an embodiment of the new consciousness who does not suffer images "repugnant to him at their outset" precisely because he values spontaneity and presentism. By underscoring the temporal correlation between the fifth printing of Eliot's *Selected Essays* and Cody's growing maturity, Kerouac suggests that Cody's perspective will supplant Eliot's, that if Eliot was a primary theorist of an earlier literary generation, Cody embodies what comes after, and *Visions of Cody*, inspired as it was by Cassady's own letters, which rebuked no image as prima facie "repugnant," is a key text in the rise of the Beat novel, and in a sea change in American letters.

CHAPTER 5

The Rise of Beat Poetry
Raw Experience Meets Raw Language

During the years the Beat novel rose, the American poetry scene was crackling with voices who bucked the perceived "tradition" venerated in academic or university poetry and embodied by none other than T. S. Eliot, object of Kerouac's parodic scorn in *Visions of Cody*. Part I canvassed three poetic schools or movements with important ties to the Beats – Black Mountain, San Francisco Renaissance, and the New York School, all of which were finding new routes from what they took to be the formally "closed" academic poetry that tended to be showcased in established university quarterlies and rewarded with prestigious prizes. By 1960, these routes would in fact be *defined* by what they were not: Donald Allen's *The New American Poetry* was the first anthology to present poets associated with Black Mountain, the San Francisco Renaissance, the New York School, and the Beats alongside one another, and as varied as this poetry was, Allen argued that they shared "one common characteristic: a total rejection of all those qualities typical of academic verse."[1] Allen does not elaborate what he means by "academic verse," and by 1960 the word "academic" became an epithet in the poetry circles Allen counts as "the new American poetry" – although vaguely defined, the word served as a kind of monolith against which avant-garde writing supposedly occurred.[2] As I'll explain in depth in Part III, in the latter 1950s, "academic verse" became with New Criticism a favorite target of Beat writers and editors, and they liked to position themselves against these concepts in order to suggest the freshness and vitality of their own work. Allen's anthology thus didn't invent his organizing categories so much as it gave recognition and shape to shifts that had been happening in American poetry throughout the 1950s. But it is true that the book provided a handy way to think about the contemporary literary scene as a dichotomy, with differing energies flourishing outside the academy while those perceived as "establishment" remained somehow invested in perfecting familiar forms or worn-out ideas. While the reality was of course messier and more complicated, this dichotomy was a neat shorthand that writers and cultural observers used and continue to use to describe developments in postwar American poetry.[3]

The same year that *The New American Poetry* appeared, for example, poet Robert Lowell proposed a now-famous distinction between two "competing" poetries on the American scene, "a cooked and a raw" – we might see the latter as a corollary to the "thirsty avidity for raw experience" Holmes identified in the Beat underground (*Go*, 35). As Lowell explains: "The cooked, marvelously expert, often seems laboriously concocted to be tasted and digested by a graduate seminar. The raw, huge blood-dripping gobbets of unseasoned experience are dished up for midnight listeners. There is a poetry that can only be studied, and a poetry that can only be declaimed, a poetry of pedantry, and a poetry of scandal."[4] Lowell's distinction has been seen by many critics to encapsulate the story of 1950s poetry, that an academic faction, conceived, it seemed, to be "digested by a graduate seminar," remained intent on producing "cooked" poetry, dense and well-made but failing to move the aesthetic needle in terms of form or content. "Raw" poetry, on the other hand, was generally written by those dismissed by the academy, was more visceral and often more readily accessible, interested in "unseasoned experience" that required new forms and modes of expression. It is the raw poetry that has since been associated with the postwar avant-garde and sifted into various analyzable "schools" codified in *The New American Poetry*.

5.1   Allen Ginsberg: Poetry in the Raw

Coming of age amid an extraordinarily creative time for American poetry, Allen Ginsberg was absolutely convinced that he and his friends could mount what his biographer calls an assault on "the bland, conservative sensibilities of American literature."[5] Acting on this belief, he not only served as informal agent for Kerouac and Burroughs, attempting, as we have seen, to stitch their work together as exemplars of a new vision called the Beat Generation, he also dedicated himself to disseminating his own work. In 1952, for example, he had William Carlos Williams give Marianne Moore a manuscript called "Empty Mirror" with the idea that her influence could help him get a book deal (it turned out she found the poems "too literal").[6] Moore's negative reaction to the manuscript proved typical in that no publisher would take it, and despite his early ambition to rock the literary world, Ginsberg would have to wait until *Howl and Other Poems* in 1956 – which did of course rock the literary world.

His trouble placing whole books aside, in the early 1950s, Ginsberg was beginning to publish poetry in outlets not connected to Columbia University. As mentioned in Part III, his first poem, "Fie My Fum," co-written with Kerouac but not attributed as such, appeared in *Neurotica* in spring 1950; over the next few years, he published a handful of poems in *New Directions in Prose and Poetry* (1953) – notably "The Bricklayer's Lunch Hour" – and in small reviews such as *Variegation* and *Occident*. This was modest success, especially compared to his friends with book contracts, but his work from this period is worth reading for both biographical and aesthetic reasons. Those interested in seminal moments in the lives of Ginsberg and his circle might be drawn to "Vision 1948" (about his famous vision of William Blake) or "In Memoriam: William Cannastra, 1922–1950" (his response to Bill Cannastra's death, also fictionalized in *Go* and Alan Harrington's *The Secret Swinger*).

In terms of aesthetic achievement, I would single out "Paterson" (1949), a nod to Williams's epic masterpiece, *Paterson* (1946–1958), that nonetheless evinces a shift in subject matter that makes it feel very Ginsbergian.[7] The speaker announces himself as a nonconformist, decrying "rooms papered with visions of money" and "employment bureaus, magazine hallways, statistical cubicles, factory stairways." In provocative contrast to what he calls "commonplace obsession," the speaker unfurls long lines redolent of the "unseasoned experience" Robert Lowell identified as "raw" poetry: "I would rather go mad, gone down the dark road to Mexico, heroin dripping in my veins, / eyes and ears full of marijuana, / eating the god Peyote on the floor of a mudhut on the border" (*Collected Poems*, 48). With respect to Ginsberg's changing sensibility, "Paterson" is of note as it celebrates the sort of underground scene that would comprise the first part of "Howl," thematizing drugs, sex, and lighting out on the road as ways to "annihilat[e] reality." Fellow poet Louis Simpson calls "Paterson" a "touchstone of [Ginsberg's] style," and observes that "The rhythms . . . are a chant; the long rushing lines overwhelm the listener and make him share the poet's emotion," a technique that Ginsberg would exploit to great effect in "Howl."[8]

In later years, Ginsberg himself often drew attention to two poems written in 1953 that he thought were particularly significant to his aesthetic development: "Sakyamuni Coming Out from the Mountain" and "The Green Automobile."[9] The first poem is notable in terms of both content and form, as it is an early sympathetic engagement with Buddhism and uses Williams's triadic line – in which each line is broken into three indented, descending parts – as a way to explore the long line as a measure of the breath, an interest that also speaks to Charles Olson's influence, and one Ginsberg would pursue and refine throughout his career, as for instance in *Mind Breaths* (1978).[10] Ginsberg in fact later linked the technique in "Sakyamuni" with what he would do in "Howl," a poem in which, as he said, "the verse line breaks down under weight of associations and extended breath ... the original intention was to build on the triadic ladder form established by W. C. Williams, imitated by the author in 'Sakyamuni'" (*Howl: Original*, 11). Titled after a twelfth-century ink scroll by Liang Kai, "Sakyamuni Descending the Mountain after Asceticism," Ginsberg's poem imagines Sakyamuni (Buddha) exhausted after his quest for enlightenment:

> how painful to be born again
> > wearing a fine beard,
> > > reentering the world
>
> a bitter wreck of a sage:
> > earth before him his only path.
> > > We can see his soul,
>
> he knows nothing
> > like a god:
> > > shaken
>
> meek wretch –
> > humility is beatness
> > > before the absolute World.
> > > > (*Collected Poems*, 98–99)

The long lines are broken into Williams's triads as a way to approximate the measure of speech, and Ginsberg later recalled he would read the poem aloud "with that slight pause between phrases" (*Best Minds*, 378). This technique lends a modern interpretation to a centuries-old depiction of an ancient story, a move that unites Ginsberg's own contemporary speech patterns with the story of Sakyamuni. And this association is not incidental, as the characterization "exhausted, at the bottom of the world, looking up or out, sleepless, wide-eyed, perceptive, rejected by society, on your own" was also how Ginsberg has elsewhere described Beatness.[11] Indeed, the poem repeats the phrase "humility is beatness" three times, suggesting that Sakyamuni, "meek wretch" and "a bitter wreck of a sage," is being figured as spiritual forefather of the Beat Generation. Like Sakyamuni, who "drags his bare feet / out of a cave" (98), those exhausted seekers are found in "Howl," "dragging themselves through the negro streets at dawn" (*Howl: Original*, 3).

A version of the long line extended to quatrains is found in "The Green Automobile," Ginsberg's answer to the unpublished *On the Road* that imagines a cross-country road trip with Neal Cassady in the titular car "which I have invented / imagined and visioned / on the roads of the world" (*Collected Poems*, 92). Although both Ginsberg and Kerouac had by that time experienced intense relationships with Cassady, this poem is written entirely in the wistful subjunctive mood that is more about what the speaker wishes were real than reality itself. The poem characterizes Cassady in terms similar to the opening pages of *On the Road*, in which Dean Moriarty is cast as a "sideburned hero of the snowy West" (5); in Ginsberg's formulation, Cassady is most "heroic" when living in the poet's imagination: "He'd come running out / to my car full of heroic beer / and jump screaming at the wheel / for he is the greater driver" (*Collected Poems*, 91). The allusion to T. S. Eliot's *The Waste Land*, famously dedicated to Ezra Pound, "Il Miglior Fabbro," generally translated as "the greater craftsman," puts Cassady into the role of aesthetic collaborator not on a textual collage of Western civilization's greatest hits, but on the road trip to Denver and the Rockies, part of Cassady's mythic origins. Just as in *Visions of Cody*, where Kerouac supplants Eliot's aesthetic pronouncements with Cody's energy, here too the philologist-poet finds himself replaced by the visceral driver. In light of other works by Kerouac and Holmes that likewise fictionalized Cassady, this poem can be read as winking at the mythologizing tendencies that we have already seen in early Beat novels, and that would of course characterize Beat writing writ large in the coming years.[12]

5.2   Peter Orlovsky: Pure American

One event that would profoundly affect Ginsberg's life occurred in December 1954 during a visit to painter Robert LaVigne's studio in San Francisco. There Ginsberg saw a striking portrait titled "Nude with Onions," and when he asked about the model, LaVigne explained that the young man lived with him, and called over Peter Orlovsky. Just twenty-one at the time, Orlovsky was originally from New York, had already been honorably discharged from the army (as psychologically unfit), and had chosen to remain in San Francisco where he had been stationed, partly because of his relationship with LaVigne. The older painter had taken Orlovsky under his wing, helping him transition from military life and introducing him to San Francisco's artistic scene and queer underground. Ginsberg was immediately drawn to Orlovsky, and after a breakup with LaVigne, Orlovsky and Ginsberg got together and would remain partners for more than forty years, until Ginsberg's death in 1997.[13]

Because of his long and highly visible relationship with Ginsberg –
in the early 1960s, Richard Avedon's photograph of the nude couple
embracing became a much-circulated image of gay liberation – Orlovsky
is usually mentioned in Beat criticism as a companion or muse rather than
as a writer in his own right. This is a reasonable position, since while
Orlovsky did write poetry and keep journals, he did not see himself
primarily as a writer, and published only one book of poetry, *Clean Asshole
Poems & Smiling Vegetable Songs* (1978), which collected work from
1957 up until 1978 (his first published poem was in *Yugen* 3 in 1958).[14]
In 2014, some four years after Orlovsky's death, Bill Morgan edited a new
volume of his journals and letters ranging from 1954 to 1994, material that
provides Orlovsky's perspective on Beat events of that forty-year span.
Given his importance to Ginsberg's life, Orlovsky is a key figure in Beat
history, but beyond this romantic connection, he did also develop his own
idiosyncratic poetic style that, while arguably slighter than the work of
some of his well-known associates, does nonetheless possess a singular
charm that seems quintessentially Beat.

In the late 1950s, after the Beat Generation had entered into national
consciousness, Orlovsky frequently turned up in newspaper articles and
critical appraisals, but it tended to be unclear as to whether he was a Beat
associate, romantic companion, or fellow poet – or all three. In Alfred
Aronowitz's twelve-part *New York Post* series on the "Beat Generation"
(1959), Orlovsky is described as Ginsberg's roommate, "a tall, friendly,
and good-looking young man."[15] Such a description seems to place
Orlovsky's importance only relative to Ginsberg, his status as "roommate"
coyly implying their romantic involvement; and yet that same page prominently features a photograph of Orlovsky reading before a rapt crowd, the
caption announcing: "ROOMMATE ORLOVSKY ... Poetry reading at
Brooklyn College" (ibid., ellipses in original). As in many other accounts,
here Orlovsky's looks and personality are foregrounded while his writing
seems secondary: he's pictured reading a poem, and yet the *Post*'s readers
could have no way of knowing what that poem might be about. Orlovsky's
participation therefore seems more like a prop of the supposed Beat
lifestyle rather than a true instance of literary production. This is likewise
the case in *Life* magazine's famously critical 1959 article about the Beats,
which asserted that "Ginsberg's leading disciple is Gregory Corso, who
shares a dingy slum apartment off Manhattan's Bowery with him and a
tousled, sheeplike young man named Peter Orlovsky (Orlovsky, who
occasionally writes a poem of his own, is noted mostly for being Ginsberg's
constant companion)."[16]

While those writing about the Beats from the outside tended to repeat the sense that Orlovsky's role was principally as roommate or "constant companion," those inside the Beat circle were wont to insist on his importance as a poet. In 1957, for example, Kerouac pronounced Orlovsky "a great American Surrealistic Poet of the First Magnitude," and in 1960, Ray Bremser declared, "Best poets alive are me, Ginsberg, [LeRoi] Jones, Kerouac, Orlovsky & Corso."[17] In 1959, a symposium was premised on the notion that the "leading Beat poets" were Ginsberg, Corso, and Orlovsky.[18] At the time, such aesthetic judgments were made largely on the strength of the poems Orlovsky read or circulated in manuscript (all of which were given Ginsberg's enthusiastic imprimatur): by the late 1950s, he had published only a few things in Beat-associated little magazines such as *Yugen* and *Beatitude*, and yet his reputation was such that Donald Allen included one of his poems in *The New American Poetry*, thus contributing to Orlovsky's standing as a significant practitioner of the new poetry – even as he had written little and published even less.

The poem included in *The New American Poetry* is "Second Poem," written in 1957 and first published in *Yugen* 4 (1959). Like much of Orlovsky's poetry, it exudes naïve charm and surprising juxtapositions ("Morning again, nothing has to be done, / maybe buy a piano or make fudge") and memorable images ("life splits faster than sissors").[19] But the first thing most readers probably notice in Orlovsky's work is his eccentric spelling and grammar: in "Second Poem," for instance, one finds not only "sissors" for "scissors," but "nock" for "knock," "aney" for "any," "knowtice" for "notice," and so on (11). Such spellings are rife in *Clean Asshole Poems*, from the first poem, actually titled "Frist Poem," through to work from the late 1970s such as "Write It Down – Allen Said" (118–120). For those on board with the Beat mission to repudiate "closed form" and the well-made poem, such moments are evidence that Orlovsky was "pledged to spontaneity," as Ann Charters has put it ("Foreword," xiv). Bill Morgan in fact suggests that Orlovsky wrote in this way specifically under Ginsberg's tutelage, as he encouraged Orlovsky "to just 'write it down' without worrying about conventional grammar and spelling, all for the sake of spontaneity" ("Introduction," xxix).[20] The unpremeditated nature of Orlovsky's language invites readers to feel as though they have access to the poet's unfiltered thoughts and emotions at specific moments in time, and as such his poetry was held up by many Beats as enacting a distinctly American, straightforward, and unadorned spontaneity. In *Desolation Angels*, for instance, Kerouac devotes many pages to Simon

Darlovsky, his character inspired by Orlovsky, and includes a scene in which the younger poets visit William Carlos Williams, who "loves Simon's poems and later writes in a review that Simon is actually the most interesting new poet in America," and supports this judgment with very close approximations of lines from "Frist Poem" and "Second Poem" (290). As Corso later recalled, Williams praised Orlovsky's "natural voice," remarking of "Frist Poem" that there was "Nothing English about it – pure American."[21]

Orlovsky's poems have a distinct knack for drawing on "natural" language – even down to those notorious misspellings – in order to invite readers into his emotional life. In this regard, fans of Beat writing might be particularly interested in those poems that thematize subjects that his fellow writers also explored, such as drug use ("Great Balls of Heroin Feeling," "A Cool Typewriter Is in the Icebox," "High on H"); the strange, dehumanizing nature of mental institutions ("Mental Hospital Julius," "Morris," "Creedmore State Hospital"); or the many varieties of sexual experience ("Woe – Its Waring Time Again in the Armey," "Trying My Best to Walk around Paris," "Frist Woman Lay"). I would also draw particular attention to those poems that explore Orlovsky's relationship with Ginsberg – not only their romantic relationship, but their differing approaches to writing and their relative stature in the literary world. In "Peter's Jealous of Allen," for example, Orlovsky recounts a "trauma-like dream" in which he is trapped with a clique who "all regarded Allen as / the most important person in the room" (25). The poem illustrates Orlovsky's anxiety about always being what the articles quoted above called a "constant companion" or "roommate" to Ginsberg. The poem explains the emotional toll of this situation: "I was scared, frightened & ancious to prove my worth" (25), and finally proposes spectacular self-harm as the only way to gain attention: "I wanted to bleed to death slowly in front of them – / for here I would be the main figure of attention / & not Allen – or the other poets" (26). The imagined death is a metaphor for how one could feel marginalized by existing in Ginsberg's orbit – even the person supposedly closest to him, a notion that in fact speaks to Orlovsky's general position in the Beat movement: that he was seen but not necessarily appreciated. He was a constant presence in accounts of the Beats and participated in readings and later in political protests, and yet his work is less read than many of his counterparts. But he is central to the rise of Beat poetry, a quirky figure who injected a refreshing vitality into the scene, and who will accordingly turn up at various points throughout this book.

5.3 Gregory Corso: The Reluctant Hipster

Orlovsky knew better than anyone that a close association with Ginsberg could be a double-edged sword, as his fame could at times overwhelm personal relationships. For Gregory Corso, Ginsberg's friendship was a boon insofar as it helped the younger poet's entry into the literary underground of the early 1950s. The two had met in late 1950 at a bar called the Pony Stable in the Village. Recently out of jail – and thus appropriately abject for Ginsberg's tastes – Corso had been writing poetry at a table when the two hit it off as like-minded literary confreres. Born on Bleecker Street in 1930, Corso's troubled life among orphanages, reform schools, and finally the Clinton Correctional Facility intrigued Ginsberg – as did Corso's early poetic efforts – and Ginsberg introduced the younger poet to the inner circle. Corso soon became like a kid brother to the slightly older Ginsberg and Kerouac, and he cultivated a rambling, street tough persona that appealed to both men. Indeed, by the end of the 1950s, Corso would be routinely grouped with Kerouac, Ginsberg, and Burroughs as the four most important Beat writers. As "L'Enfant Terrible of the Beat Generation," his pugnacious poetry smashed convention as he sought to remake the real on his own terms.[22]

In the early 1950s, Corso had a renewed sense of possibility after being released from prison, and he took the opportunity to throw himself headlong into the literary life, where he enjoyed some initial success. In fact, prior to the publication of *Howl and Other Poems*, it looked as though Corso might be the first Beat poet to break into literary stardom: in the summer of 1955, Kerouac was surprised to hear veteran editor extraordinaire Malcolm Cowley mention Corso as an up-and-coming poet who seemed to be working in the same broad mode as Kerouac. Ginsberg was shocked when Kerouac told him this ("I don't understand Corso's celebrity," he complained), and Kerouac had to explain that "Corso's celebrity obtains from enclosed POEM book [*The Vestal Lady on Brattle*].... Also, he wrote a play which he was going to entitle Beat Generation, changed to *This Hung-Up Age* when he saw my *New World* shot – one act play, it was produced at Harvard, big hit."[23] Corso would go on to establish a national reputation with his collection *Gasoline* (1958), but Kerouac was correct that he was making a name for himself on the underground scene with that first poetry collection, *The Vestal Lady on Brattle* (1955), and a one-act play, *In This Hung-Up Age*, written in 1954 and performed in Cambridge, Massachusetts, in 1955.[24]

In 1953, Corso had gone to Cambridge at the invitation of V. R. "Bunny" Lang, poet, playwright and bon vivant who saw in Corso a breath of fresh air – and an opportunity to rattle the generally conservative literary scene in and around Harvard (ironically, Corso's first appearance in print was in *The Harvard Advocate* in 1954).[25] As Nora Sayre recalled, "planting Corso in Cambridge was probably a deliberate act of sedition. No one at Harvard – not even the New Yorkers – had met anyone like him, and she [Lang] took him to starchy gatherings and urged him to be insolent."[26] Corso's seditious streak by turns fascinated and repulsed the genteel literary scene, and he fell in with the Poet's Theater, what Sayre calls "a loose affiliation of poets living in Cambridge" (195) that, for her, had "an exciting aura of a counterculture, which was very hard to locate in the Fifties" (199). It was via his introduction to this "loose affiliation" of writers that Corso eventually managed to solicit donations to publish his first poetry collection, *The Vestal Lady on Brattle*, in a limited run of 500 copies, as well as to produce his short "farce," *In This Hung-Up Age*. As John Tytell points out, Corso's feat of publishing *Vestal* through a kind of subscription model was particularly impressive, "rare in any national literary history and had not occurred in ours since Edgar Allen [*sic*] Poe a century earlier persuaded over 100 fellow cadets at West Point to pay for the publication of his first book of poems."[27]

Its unusual background notwithstanding, *The Vestal Lady on Brattle* doesn't showcase quite the distinctive vigor of Corso's subsequent work such as *Gasoline* and *The Happy Birthday of Death* (1960), but it does evince a broadly countercultural sensibility insofar as its speakers tend to feel out of sync with the mores of polite society – one baffled reviewer wrote that "the collection, I'm sure, will be huzzahed by the type [of] people who say they understand progressive jazz and abstract painting."[28] Part of this reviewer's confusion comes from the provocatively surreal – or "unreal" – moments in *Vestal*, where Corso breaks down sense in order to encourage readers to see new ways of approaching experience.

Indeed, *Vestal* announces Corso's presence on the literary scene by exploring, in part, figurations of the underground. There are poems, for instance, which contrast the reserved nature of Cambridge to the poet's countercultural posture, as in "Cambridge, First Impressions," in which the speaker notes that "It is not easy to walk / these Cambridge streets" because of their "Better carpets" – the implication being that he is more accustomed to the hard-surfaced life on the streets."[29] Likewise in "In the Tunnel-Bone of Cambridge," the speaker specifically figures himself as an underground character, noting the "hipster-tone of my vision agent," and lamenting that he feels out of place in Cambridge, "a subterranean / lashed to a pinnacle" (72), with Harvard representing the supposed pinnacle of intellectual achievement (Ginsberg thought that with that poem in particular Corso was "displaying his rough trade, gangster, or jailboy background to the Cambridge aesthetes").[30]

Aside from deploying keywords like "hipster" and "subterranean," Corso put his own spin on Beat preoccupations such as the uncaring nature of society ("Greenwich Village Suicide") or the recognition of bop's importance ("Requiem for 'Bird' Parker, Musician"). Gregory Stephenson has argued that the "central motif" of *Vestal* is "a predatory devouring or destruction of innocence and beauty," a motif that Corso would explore throughout his career as he forged his own version of a Beat aesthetic.[31] "Greenwich Village Suicide," which for Stephenson "presents the destruction of another innocent by the forces of sterility and death . . . manifested in ordinary people, in society-at-large" (*Exiled*, 16), ends with a hard-nosed look at "society-at-large"; after a young girl leaps to her death, the world grinds on without a second thought: "They take her away with a Daily News on her face / And a storekeeper throws hot water on the sidewalk" (*Vestal*, 67). The newspaper shielding the girl's face from others on the street signals also the media tools of the dominant culture, especially as just before she jumps, the woman thinks of "New Yorker cartoons."

Beyond *Vestal*, the best example of Corso's mid-decade explorations of hipness is a short play, *In This Hung-Up Age* – a piece whose very existence again underscores the willingness of Beat writers to work across genres.[32] Recall that in Holmes's *Go*, the underground was "inhabited by people 'hungup' with drugs" (36); Corso takes the slang term "hung up" as a starting point, and uses it to mock both the dominant culture and hipsterdom. With this play, Corso presented himself as a hip interlocutor of sorts: when it was reprinted in *Encounter* in 1962, he appended a short note insisting that it "pre-dates anything ever written about the Hipster and hip-talk, the Square, and the advent of San Francisco's 'poesy re-birth'" ("Note," 90). Writing in 1962 from a position of relative notoriety, Corso wanted to retroactively claim *In This Hung-Up Age* as *the* originary statement on hipness – "I was truly a hipster," he claims – but we know from the previous chapter that this is hyperbole, as novels from *The Town and the City*, *Go*, and *Who Walk in Darkness* featured hipster characters of the sort dissected in essays by Broyard, Klonsky, and Holmes. Nonetheless, it seems to me suggestive of the long reach of the Beatnik caricature – discussed in depth in Part III – that from his perch in 1962, Corso should claim that way back in 1954, prior to national awareness of the Beat

Generation, it was he who inaugurated the hipster phenomenon, a move that at once asserts his own hip authority while simultaneously disavowing hipsterdom, as he "saw the advent [of hipsterdom] and deemed it farce" (90).

In This Hung-Up Age is about what happens when a bus carrying an allegorical cross-section of society breaks down en route from New York City to San Francisco. The characters are all purposively flat and function as comic embodiments of dominant culture (Tourist, Mrs. Kindhead, College Girl), hip and literary cultures (Hipster, Poetman), the mythic American past (Apache), and unobtainable abstraction (Beauty).[33] To give you an idea of the broadness of these characters: Tourist's default position is to rail against "commies" (84); the earnest College Girl advises Poetman to "learn a trade" (85); and Apache speaks in the broken English of a cartoon Indian, interjecting things like "Poetman got heap talent" (88) and "We all go to happy-hunting-ground" (89).

But perhaps more relevant to understanding the pose Corso cultivated at this time is how he skewers those associated with the counterculture. Poetman, for instance, doesn't seem devoted to poetry so much as to monetizing verse, drunkenly asserting: "if you want to know why this age is hung-up, is because people are too damn cheap to buy a poetry magazine" (86). Like J. D. Salinger's Holden Caulfield, Poetman isn't shy about pointing out middle-class phoniness – but, also like Holden, he isn't much better. "A lot of people," he says, "hang up Picasso prints and all that just to show how modern and intellectual they are, but just once, just once would I like to see them buy a poetry magazine. They're phoneys, cheats, penny pinchers! That's why this age is hung-up, it's because of them!" (87). Far from being the antidote to bourgeois values represented by Tourist, College Girl, and the good-natured but vapid Mrs. Kindhead (who likes to assure everyone that "I'm for progress, any kind" [84]), Poetman is figured as ironically bourgeois in his own obsessions with sales and public recognition (given that he was in the process of soliciting contributions for *Vestal*, it would make sense if there's a little of Corso in Poetman's preoccupations).

Corso's Hipster is a decidedly nonliterary member of the hip scene, and exists mainly to crack wise in caricatured argot. Described in the notes as "A New York City lower East Side delinquent, tough and endowed with slang and jazz talk" (83), Hipster's first line, "What a drag" (83), encapsulates his general outlook; at one point, he says, "Like face it, man, a great Poetman's gotta be hoid. Widout a audience the cat's like a chicken widout a head – beat – nowhere, dead, man, dead" (84). Echoing *Junky's*

Lee, who dubs his fellow sanitarium patients "a beat, nowhere bunch of people" (83), Corso's Hipster trades on the term "beat" mainly to signal his disaffiliation and linguistic estrangement from the rest of the group (his speech is played for laughs throughout). The dramatic climax of the play occurs when the broken-down bus and its stranded passengers are trampled by a "berserk buffalo" (89), suggesting that the whole hung-up age, both Beat and square, deserves to be swept under the leveling force of some Adamic American past. In the context of the rise of the Beat aesthetic, *In This Hung-Up Age* is worthy of mention as a humorous exploration of the entanglements of the dominant and underground cultures that predate Beat celebrity, and yet evinces Corso's reluctance to be totally identified with any group at all.

5.4 San Francisco and the Rise of Beat Poetry

It was of course not incidental that the characters in Corso's play were traveling from New York to San Francisco, since the Bay Area was, as explained in Part I, home to a confluence of artistic and poetic energies that would eventually help propel the Beats into national consciousness. This energy is partly indicated by the concentration of avant-garde little magazines centered there, from earlier periodicals such as *Circle* (1944–1948), *The Ark* (1947), and *Contour* (1947–1949), to their mid-1950s descendants such as *The Miscellaneous Man* (1954–1959), *Semina* (1955–1964), *The Needle* (1956), and *Ark II Moby I* (1956–1957).[34] These magazines all showcased varieties of what would, at the end of the decade, be called the "new poetry." Concomitant with the sort of "raw" poetry found in their pages, these magazines also traded on versions of the countercultural posture the Beats would later fold into their literary brand.

In *The Miscellaneous Man*, for example, poet and editor William J. Margolis – who in 1959 would go on to become one of the editors of *Beatitude* – explained his magazine's title as a label for those who loathe labels: "The miscellaneous man is the individual man . . . who, as a dynamic entity, never quite fits under any label and is constantly bulging out of categories."[35] Margolis echoes this perspective in a poetic contribution, "Manacle . . . Or Man?," which anticipates the Moloch section of "Howl," with its images of "caged" mankind being consumed by machines: "a mass man / a centralized product / of a centralized machine / society."[36]

Ark II Moby I, edited by Michael McClure and James Harmon, took its inspiration directly from the anarcho-pacifist sensibilities of *The Ark*, and is more explicitly linked to the Beat movement. Like the later and more well-known "San Francisco Scene" issue of *Evergreen Review* (1957), *Ark II Moby I* is an important volume of the new poetry that includes work by Ferlinghetti, Snyder, Ginsberg, Whalen, and Rexroth. In terms of the rise of Beat poetry, one of the most significant contributions is an excerpt from Kerouac's *Mexico City Blues* (written 1955; published 1959), a key volume of Beat poetry that draws on some of the same techniques as *Visions of Cody*.[37] The book consists of 242 linked "choruses" in which Kerouac spontaneously ranges over such topics as his own life story, his inheritances from literary history, the nature of addiction, and, importantly, his deepening explorations of Buddhism – the excerpt included in *Ark II Moby* I opens: "Buddhists are the only people who don't lie / In the Sacred Diamond Sutra / Mention is made that God will die – " (19). Formally, *Mexico City Blues* is of interest as each page presents snapshots in time that are nonetheless linked to the greater texture of the book as a whole; as Kerouac explained:

> In my system, the form of blues choruses is limited by the small page of a breastpocket notebook in which they are written, like the form of a set number of bars in a jazz blues chorus, so sometimes the word-meaning can carry from one chorus into another, or not, just like the phrase-meaning can carry harmonically from one chorus to the other . . . so that . . . the form is determined by time, and by the musician's spontaneous phrasing.[38]

In its explorations of "spontaneous phrasing," *Mexico City Blues* emphasizes orality, sometimes reproducing the speech of notorious Mexico City junky Bill Garver, as it demonstrates the various possibilities of voice as in *Visions of Cody*. The book likewise incorporates the ideas of Corso, Burroughs, Ginsberg, Solomon, and others, and counterpoints Kerouac's poetic techniques to academic poets: "They got nothing on me / at the university / Them clever poets . . . / With charcoal suits."[39] *Mexico City Blues* is a wholesale repudiation of clever university poets and an important expression of the spontaneous method, which Kerouac would push even further in one of his strangest works, *Old Angel Midnight*, which I will discuss in more detail later.

Although based in New York, *Evergreen Review* contributed to San Francisco's visibility as an epicenter of the new poetry thanks to its second issue, emblazoned on the cover with "San Francisco Scene" over a green-hued cityscape. *Evergreen Review* was founded by Barney Rosset – who would go on to publish a long list of Beat and Beat-related work through Grove Press – but the first two issues were edited by Rosset and Donald Allen, the energetic champion of the new poetry who was then living in San Francisco. Allen had sent Rosset a copy of *Howl and Other Poems*, and the "San Francisco Scene" issue cohered around a reprinting of "Howl" together with a range of work by Rexroth, Everson (as Brother Antoninus), Ferlinghetti, McClure, Snyder, Whalen, and Kerouac. The issue was, as Loren Glass puts it, a "big hit in the Bay Area," and Rosset capitalized on its popularity by organizing "Evergreen Book Week" in the spring of 1958, which featured talks and readings by writers from the area that helped clarify the city's status as the "nation's cultural capital," as one of Rosset's press releases claimed.[40]

Beyond a robust culture of little magazines and their associated writers, more sustained ventures such as the Pocket Poets series, edited by Lawrence Ferlinghetti at City Lights Books, did much to distribute Beat writing, and to help make San Francisco an epicenter of Beatdom in the mid-1950s and after. Ferlinghetti's own *Pictures of the Gone World* (1955) was the inaugural volume in the Pocket Poets series, and helped to establish him as a major poetic voice associated with the Beats, a precursor to hot-selling work such as *A Coney Island of the Mind* (1958). The poems in *Pictures* range purposively across the page, stretching out their lines and making use of negative space as the poet stretches out his thoughts, as in this example:

> "Truth is not the secret of a few"
> $\qquad\qquad$ yet
> you would maybe think so
> $\qquad\qquad$ the way some
> $\qquad$ librarians
> and cultural ambassadors and
> $\qquad\qquad$ especially museum directors
> $\qquad\qquad\qquad$ act.[41]

A playful rebuke of those who would fancy themselves gatekeepers of culture and arbiters of taste, this poem's cerebral humor is characteristic of much of Ferlinghetti's poetry. *Pictures* also suggests the way in which Ferlinghetti would thematize bohemian San Francisco, a theme he would often return to in later work, when he himself became one of the more visible fixtures on this scene:

> Dada would have liked a day like this
> $\qquad\qquad$ with its various very realistic
> $\qquad$ unrealities
> $\qquad\qquad$ each about to become
> too real for its locality
> $\qquad\qquad$ which is never quite remote enough
> to be Bohemia. $\qquad\qquad$ (n.p.)

These "unrealities" – presumably so to the "cultural ambassadors" and "museum directors" of the previous poem – are apt ways to characterize the version of bohemia percolating at the time in Ferlinghetti's adopted city, an environment ripe for testing the limits of the real and its ability to be represented, and as such likewise ripe for the ascension of the Beat sensibility. And ascend it did.

5.5   Charming Event: The 6 Gallery Reading

An episode often seen as a culmination of the literary and artistic energy in San Francisco in the mid-1950s was the 6 Gallery reading on October 7, 1955, an evening that was quickly mythologized as a touchstone moment in Beat lore. The reading featured Ginsberg, Philip Whalen, Philip Lamantia, Michael McClure, and Gary Snyder; Rexroth served as emcee, with Kerouac and Cassady whipping up enthusiasm in the audience. The star of the evening was Ginsberg, who publicly read from "Howl" for the first time – Ferlinghetti was so impressed by what he heard that he sent Ginsberg a telegram echoing what Ralph Waldo Emerson wrote to Walt Whitman on reading *Leaves of Grass* (1855) almost exactly one hundred years earlier: "I GREET YOU AT THE BEGINNING OF A GREAT CAREER. WHEN DO I GET MANUSCRIPT OF 'HOWL'?"[42]

Looking back with just two years' hindsight, in November 1957, the Dutch review *Litterair Paspoort* published a stock-taking of the contemporary literary avant-garde called "The Literary Revolution in America" that singled out the 6 Gallery reading as paradigm-shifting. This essay, attributed solely to Gregory Corso but largely ghostwritten by Ginsberg, was an early act of myth-making by one of the 6 Gallery participants.[43] First, Corso/Ginsberg emphasize that the reading was intended "to defy the system of academic poetry, official reviews, New York publishing machinery, national sobriety and generally accepted standards to good taste."[44] Taking up the avant-garde as anti-academic stance discussed earlier in this chapter and with respect to particular instances in the Beat novel, Corso/Ginsberg portray the reading as an act of defiance that flouts all manner of "accepted standards," and in such defiance creates a deliberate countercultural community. This is why they go on to emphasize that there was no admission fee, that it took place in the "Negro section" of the city, and that it was advertised in the bohemian enclave of North Beach. In other words, the evening is characterized not as a mere reading but as an instance of community-building that would radiate out to be seen as a foundational moment in and for the Beat Generation. A year later,

Kerouac published what became a much more well-known depiction of the reading in *The Dharma Bums* (1958), calling it "a great night, a historic night."[45] In fact, Kerouac's lightly fictionalized version is largely responsible for the later impression that the San Francisco Renaissance somehow emerged whole-cloth from this moment he dubbed "the night of the birth of the San Francisco Poetry Renaissance" (13).

Kerouac's bold pronouncements notwithstanding, Corso/Ginsberg invest the event with a slightly different kind of hyperbole that links the younger poets to Rexroth, the "well known Frisco Anarchist resident poet," which accords the reading countercultural legitimacy, even as other locally known poets such as Robert Duncan, Jack Spicer, and Robin Blaser were not invited.[46] And although "The Literary Revolution in America" counterpoints the 6 Gallery poets to the academic establishment, it doesn't follow that these writers were depicted as emerging sui generis as *The Dharma Bums* implies. Instead, Corso/Ginsberg identify the poets in terms of their broad affiliations or poetic influences, so Lamantia is "a surrealist blood poet, former member of San Francisco Anarchist group" (195); McClure is characterized as a "representative of the Black Mountain School" (195); Whalen is "a Zen Buddhist Bodhisattva" (195); and Snyder is "a bearded youth of 26 ... who had lived with American Indians and taken the religious drug peyote with them, and who is now occupied in the study of Chinese and Japanese ... in Japan" (196). In this telling, then, the 6 Gallery poets stand as representatives of certain aesthetic, philosophical, and intellectual traditions, but traditions that exist outside circles deemed acceptable to academic literary culture in the mid-1950s. I discuss Lamantia, McClure, Whalen, and Snyder in more detail in Part III, including some of the work they read that night at 6 Gallery; for now, I just want to point out that their participation in the reading underscores their presence on the Beat scene in earlier years, prior to its participants' later notoriety.

5.6 "Howl" and Its Aftermath

The magnum opus of the 6 Gallery reading was, of course, Ginsberg's "Howl," a tour de force now considered both a masterpiece of Beat literature and one of the most important poems of the twentieth century. As was rather immodestly asserted in the *Litterair Paspoort* essay, "The most brilliant shock of the evening was the declamation of the now-famous rhapsody, *Howl*, by Allen Ginsberg – a poet subsequently notorious for this one poem, which achieved instantaneous national recognition – attack, praise, banning by customs authorities" (195). I think it is fair to say that those in the 1950s who were affected by the poem, either positively or negatively, were so because of its frank language and depictions of an underground rife with ideas and activities anathema to polite society.[47] This is what LeRoi Jones (writing as Amiri Baraka) put his finger on when he recalled, "I had been moved by *Howl* because it talked about a world I could identify with and relate to. His language and rhythms were real to me. Unlike the cold edges and exclusiveness of the New Yorker poem ... Ginsberg talked of a different world."[48] The poem's reputation for evoking an entirely "different world" rests largely on its first part, where Ginsberg runs with his experiments with longer lines in a poem like "Paterson" to offer the lengthy catalogue naming the "best minds" of his generation. But there are three other parts as well, and although many of the poem's most evocative images and memorable lines are in part I, these moments can only really be understood in the context of the poem as a whole.

While it should go without saying that in trying to understand a work of literature, a good reader should strive to account for as much of that work as possible, the more salacious lines in "Howl" blinded many contemporary critics to its overall structure. After *Howl and Other Poems* was published, for example, Ginsberg's old friend and Columbia classmate John Hollander blasted "the utter lack of decorum of any kind in his dreadful little volume."[49] In an extensive, irritated response, Ginsberg took Hollander to task for missing "the fucking obvious construction of the poem."[50] For all the poem's shocking moments, Ginsberg was always clear that attention to form was a way to see the "lack of decorum" as a part of a larger statement rather than as an end in and of itself.

5.7   The Obvious Construction of "Howl"

In order to see what Ginsberg is doing in the poem, then, it is necessary to familiarize ourselves with its "obvious construction," and once again the poet himself is a useful guide, particularly in the detailed letter he wrote explaining how he structured "Howl." The letter was written to poet Richard Eberhart, who had come to San Francisco in spring 1956 to cover the poetry scene there for the *New York Times*.[51] Eberhart had heard "Howl" read aloud in Berkeley, and had even spoken to Ginsberg about it; but after Ginsberg thought about their conversation, he wrote Eberhart what became, according to Bill Morgan, his "most famous letter" explicating the poem's construction, hoping to sway Eberhart's opinion of the poem as he worked on the *Times* piece.[52] The letter begins by questioning a remark Eberhart had apparently made to Ginsberg in Berkeley, that the poem is "a negative howl of protest." Instead, Ginsberg insisted: "the poem itself is an act of sympathy, not rejection ... I am saying that what seems 'mad' in America is our expression of natural ecstasy.... I have taken a leap of detachment from the artificial preoccupations and preconceptions of what is acceptable and normal and given my yea to the specific type of madness listed in the Who section [part I]."[53] Even before the poem's publication, then, Ginsberg found himself defending it against those who thought it merely rejecting society, an accusation that would become deafening by the end of the decade, when the Beatnik eclipsed the Beat. In *Interzone* – which Ginsberg had been editing in the months leading up to writing "Howl" – Burroughs compares society to a penal colony in which "any spontaneous expression of feeling brings the harshest punishment" (44). Echoing this sort of thinking to Eberhart, Ginsberg sets the stage for his meticulous explanation of how the poem asks readers to reimagine "acceptable and normal" society by figuring it as a monstrous pathology.

Part I opens with what is probably the most famous line in all of Beat literature: "I saw the best minds of my generation destroyed by madness, starving hysterical naked, dragging themselves through the negro streets at dawn looking for an angry fix" (3). This continues on for another seventy-eight very long lines, so that the whole of part I consists of a single sentence that catalogues these "best minds," those "Who were expelled from the academies for crazy" (3), "who disappeared into the volcanoes of Mexico" (4), "who let themselves be fucked in the ass by saintly motorcyclists, and screamed with joy" (4), "who demanded sanity trials accusing the radio of hypnotism" (5), "who threw potato salad at CCNY lecturers on Dadaism" (5), and on and on. Taking those earlier experiments with the long line to the extreme, Ginsberg draws readers into a world by turns exhausted and energized, introducing figures sensitive to and passionate about life, but also desperate and fearful, misunderstood and pathologized by the dominant culture and its institutions. Together these lines constitute a portrait of Ginsberg's "generation," an ambitious undertaking that audaciously transforms the experiences of his group of friends into a literary-historical generational experience.

After part I takes readers on a tour of Ginsberg's "generation," what Eliot Katz calls "an implicit countercultural community," part II presents a personification of the dominant society that has caused the destruction catalogued in part I.[54] This personification is Moloch, a Canaanite fire god "whose worship," Ginsberg later explained, "was marked by parents' burning their children as propitiatory sacrifice" (*Howl: Original*, 139). In part II, Moloch functions as a multilayered metaphor for the culture that has marginalized the people in part I, demanding either their assimilation or institutionalization as criminal or crazy. As Ginsberg noted to Eberhart, "Moloch is the vision of the mechanical feelingless inhuman world we live in and accept – and the key line finally is 'Moloch whom I abandon'" (132). Part II opens by asking: "What sphinx of cement and aluminum bashed open their skulls and ate up their brains and imagination?" and answers with successive figurations of Moloch: "Moloch whose mind is pure machinery! Moloch whose blood is running money! Moloch whose fingers are ten armies! Moloch whose breast is a cannibal dynamo!" (6). Moloch is the horrific embodiment of "acceptable and normal" society exposed as such *because* it comes after part I. In other words, the catalogue of Beat characters in part I encourages readers to imaginatively inhabit and sympathize with the underground before they get to part II, thus encouraging them to see "acceptable and normal" as accordingly strange: "Moloch! Moloch! Robot apartments! invisible suburbs! skeleton treasuries! blind capitals! demonic industries! spectral nations! invincible madhouses! granite cocks! monstrous bombs!" (7). The very markers of modern civilization, apartments or suburbs or treasuries or industries, are cast in stark exclamations, making them not evidence of humanity but that which threatens it.

The figure of "Moloch" was floating around in the late 1940s underground culture described earlier, as suggested by Anatole Broyard's 1950 essay, "Village Café," which purports to depict the wild goings-on at a Greenwich Village café frequented by bohemian types: "Someone – he's not here – shouted something about the machinery of production, rattled the workers' ghostly chains, but the others know that the machinery of production is for beer and bombs, and they'll take beer. Art? – The art of self-defense! God – Moloch, the jukebox!"[55] Such correspondences suggest that Ginsberg wasn't necessarily inventing his social criticism from nothing, and apparently after taking peyote in San Francisco in 1954, he saw the façade of the Francis Drake Hotel transform into Moloch, which he subsequently used in "Howl."

Likewise, Kenneth Rexroth's poem "Thou Shalt Not Kill" (1953) offers a litany of those both figuratively and literally crushed by similar "machinery" embodied by Moloch:

> All over the world
> The same disembodied hand
> Strikes us down.
>
> . . .
> Three generations of infants
> Stuffed down the maw of Moloch.[56]

Figure 5.1   In Fritz Lang's *Metropolis* (1927), the dynamo at the heart of a factory transforms into Moloch, who demands the literal sacrifice of the workers. Image courtesy of Murnau Stiftung

In part II of "Howl," Ginsberg takes the trope of Moloch as leveler of difference or resistance and makes it even more vivid, borrowing also the image of Moloch as an embodiment of technologized civilization consuming individuals from Fritz Lang's classic film *Metropolis* (1927). This film is set in a dystopia in which the labor of the masses is exploited for the gain of the wealthy few. In one hallucinatory scene, a dynamo at the heart of an immense factory transforms into Moloch, who then consumes the factory workers in his fiery maw – this is the "cannibal dynamo" of "Howl" and evocatively encapsulates the poem's rebuke of dominant culture (see Figure 5.1).

Part III turns explicitly to the poem's dedicatee, Carl Solomon, whom Ginsberg had met at the New York State Psychiatric Institute in 1949.[57] The poem's speaker repeats "I am with you in Rockland" – another psychiatric institution in New York whose name was more punchily suggestive than the one in which they'd actually met. The phrase becomes like a mantra, what Ginsberg thought of as a "bachlike fugue built up" that might salve the horrors depicted in first two parts (*Howl: Original*, 150). Part III moves from Solomon being alienated by Moloch as crazy to being brought into Ginsberg's creative fold. The opening lines are:

> Carl Solomon! I'm with you in Rockland
>   where you're madder than I am
> I'm with you in Rockland
>   where you must feel very strange
>
> (7)

If Solomon is "madder than I am" and "very strange" according to the norms of acceptable society, by the end of part III and the poem proper, Ginsberg asserts his powers of imagination as more formidable than Moloch, so Solomon's supposed strangeness is embraced by like-minded community: "I'm with you in Rockland / in my dreams you walk dripping from a sea-journey on the highway across America in tears to the door of my cottage in the Western night" (8). These final lines represent an imaginative jailbreak from Rockland, whisking Solomon all the way across the continent to the speaker's "cottage," a reference to the real place where Ginsberg was living in Berkeley as he was working on parts II and III. Jonah Raskin calls that cottage "a commune of sorts – the perfect place to envision a more perfect world and more perfect human beings" and notes that Philip Whalen and Jack Kerouac lived there at times.[58] In "Howl," then, the reference to this specific cottage signals that Ginsberg is welcoming Solomon into an artistic community that could counter the norms upheld by the Moloch-tinged "acceptable and normal" society – as Ginsberg told Eberhart, part III is "a litany of active acceptance of the suffering of soul of C. Solomon, saying in effect I am *still* your amigo tho you are in trouble and think yourself in a void" (132).

This sense of community is underscored in the poem's final part, "Footnote to Howl," which playfully echoes the "footnotes" that T. S. Eliot had appended to *The Waste Land* when it was published in book form. In those footnotes, Eliot toys with scholarly convention by seeming to undermine his own references with not-so-informative glosses such as, "I do not know the origins of the ballad from which these lines are taken" or "The following lines were stimulated by the account of one of the Antarctic expeditions (I forget which; but I think one of Shackleton's)."[59] Doing Eliot one better, Ginsberg's footnotes dispense with all pretense to academic objectivity by declaring, "Everything is holy! everybody's holy! everywhere is holy!" (8). In the course of announcing "everybody's" holiness, he names specific people linking Solomon to Ginsberg's circle, the real-life embodiments of the Beat Generation: "Holy Peter holy Allen holy Solomon holy Lucien holy Kerouac holy Huncke holy Burroughs holy Cassady" (8). Although this is the poem's most obvious mention of real people, in fact "Howl" stitches together incidents from the lives of a wider range of people Ginsberg thought of as embodiments of the Beat Generation, so the poem can also be read as a kind of secret history of hipness.

5.8 "Howl" as Secret History of the Beat Generation

Decades after "Howl" was published, Ginsberg remarked that it was "written for the people who read *Time* magazine as well as for the bohemian left" (*Best Minds*, 394) and that "There was some conscious intention to make a cultural breakthrough, to talk in public as we talked in private. How we behave in private is actually the ultimate politics. So the original literary inspiration was to behave in public as we do in private."[60] These comments are immensely suggestive of how Ginsberg figured a relatively small circle of friends as a whole "generation" – writing the way he "talked in private" means not only using colloquial language and the like, but also building the poem around references to persons and events known only those in a "private" circle. Thus readers of *Time* magazine and those on the "bohemian left" would experience "Howl" in different ways, and this difference would ironically turn on the ways that the poem mythologizes these specifics to make them stand in for greater cultural shifts; as Marjorie Perloff has put it, "persons and places in 'Howl' are so much larger than life that they come to occupy a mythic, rather than everyday, domain."[61] In thinking of "Howl" as *the* paradigmatic "Beat poem," I want to emphasize how it flickers between broader generational claims and close attention to a far smaller, insider community.[62]

To illustrate Ginsberg's dual-pronged approach, it is instructive to consider successive drafts, and look at one passage in particular that refers to "N.C., secret hero of these poems, cocksman and Adonis of Denver" (4). While now it is common knowledge that these initials refer to Neal Cassady, when the poem was published, such a reference was coy and mysterious, even as the first edition was dedicated to Kerouac, Burroughs, Carr, and Cassady, "author of *The First Third*, an autobiography (1949) which enlightened Buddha" (*Howl and Other Poems*, n.p.). In the early drafts, the mention of Cassady is explicit, and delivered in an onrush of other names:

> who read ~~Marx Spengler Antonin Artaud Gne Gneet Genet Gurj ieff~~
> Genet Gurjieff Spengler Dostoievsky ~~Antonin Artaud~~ Rimbaud
> ~~Wolfe~~ Louis Ferdinand Celine Proust Wolfe Whitman Buddha
> Ginsberg Kerouac Burroughs & Neal Cassady, I name them all,
> except Lu~~cien~~ Carr who ~~took to journalism so they must~~
> ~~have read him too~~ ...
> who sweetened the cunt of t a million girls trembling in the sunset.[63]
> (23)

The impulse to "name them all" suggests Ginsberg's desire to define "the best minds of my generation" in explicit terms – not only all the people to whom he would eventually dedicate *Howl and Other Poems*, but his circle's favorite and most consequential thinkers, poets, novelists, and religious figures. In subsequent drafts, Ginsberg excised what he called "this ponderous lineage" (*Howl: Original*, 136) and retained only the following image, found in the third draft: "who sweetened the snatch of a million girls trembling in the sunset, flashing buttocks under barns" (29). By this draft, the litany of names, Ginsberg's real-life circle of friends and their constellation of aesthetic, philosophical, and religious darlings, are replaced by the line about copulation, suggesting that this action was somehow connected in Ginsberg's mind to all these names, just as Kerouac counterpointed Eliot's aesthetic authority to Cassady's manic energy at the end of *Visions of Cody*. The fourth draft offers the first glimpse of "N.C.," who, when reading the drafts in succession, seems to be all those names telescoped into two initials: "N.C., secret hero of these poems, cocksman and Adonis of Denver, our long old love, heart of ten thousand bodies on either coast, joy to the memory of his innumerable lays of girls in empty lots and diners, backyards" (38). If Cassady is being made to bear all that literary and philosophical weight, it makes sense that he would accordingly be figured as the "secret hero of these poems." According to the draft sequence as presented in the *Original Draft Facsimile*, Cassady disappeared from the fifth draft – which generically describes those "who went out whoring through midwest in myriad stolen night cars, joy to the memory of his innumerable lays of girls in empty lots & diners" (49) – but he makes it back in for the final draft (see *Howl: Original*, 4). I read this apparent ambivalence as an instance of Ginsberg trying to figure out whether the poem would be most successful with specific people named or with a more generalized sense of myth-making. That he finally settled on mentioning Cassady without directly naming him is, I think, indicative of the larger strategy at work, in which Ginsberg takes specific events and people and describes them in a mythological light – the result is that if you are a reader of *Time* magazine, you might think the poem an encyclopedic account of the younger, disaffected "generation," while if you were "in" on the bohemian left, you might recognize this as a smaller group, and might even know some of the people and events alluded to.

In fact, one of the most consistently compelling aspects of the poem is the way it depicts those whom Ginsberg calls "persons obliquely modeled in the poem"; when he attempted to give the keys to the poem for the annotated edition, he tended to focus often on those lines modeled on real people (123). The effect of such focus is twofold: it draws attention to the importance of real people but also reminds us that it's not really possible to understand the poem without reading promiscuously, that it depends for its very efficacy on context outside itself. In this way, it is a rebuke of New Critical norms that dictated, as Cleanth Brooks put it, that "poetry must be wrested from the context ... must be given a place of permanence among the stars"; in "Howl," by contrast, the poetry and its contexts cannot be wrested apart.[64]

In part I, for example, we find the line: "who bared their brains to Heaven under the El and saw Mohammedan angels staggering on tenement roofs illuminated" (3). This is evocative, and suggestive on its own of a particularized, religious vision occurring in tenements. But in the original facsimile version, Ginsberg points readers to Philip Lamantia, and quotes him as saying that he had been "reading the Koran on a couch, one night, I was suddenly physically laid out by a powerful force beyond my volition ... consciousness was contracted to a single point at the top of my head ... I floated toward an endless-looking universe of misty, lighted color forms" (*Howl: Original*, 124). Unlike the "N.C., secret hero of these poems" line, it would have been basically impossible to know, in 1956, that this line refers "obliquely" to Lamantia – unless of course you happen to be Lamantia, or a friend of Lamantia's, or had heard this reference anecdotally. Fifty years later, with his own scholarly edition, Ginsberg rendered such personal relationships far less important, so that any reader can know intimate details by consulting the notes. Crucially, this doesn't mean that the poem no longer works in terms of the inside and the outside, but that the nature of these categories has radically shifted, creating a far wider fiction of Beat insiderness.

The original version of "Howl" published in 1956 was coy about its references and encouraged readers to speculate or gossip about the poem, trading stories or theories about who Ginsberg is "really" talking about in a given line, thus encouraging readers to feel as though drawn into an imaginative Beat community. With the original facsimile edition, Ginsberg was able to frame his work through decades of renown, offering authoritative comments on previously obscure lines. By performing the role of academic expert on his own work, Ginsberg draws more and more people into the "inside" fold, ironically deploying the scholarly apparatus for Beat ends.[65]

5.9 The Trial

Beyond the layers within the poem itself, "Howl" is of course also important to literary history because, after its publication in book form, it was subject to a well-publicized obscenity trial. This trial has been exhaustively depicted in scholarly books, collations of primary documents, and even in the film *Howl* (2010), which dramatizes courtroom scenes using language from court transcripts.[66] Because of the plenitude of available work on the trial, I won't take readers point by point through this history, but instead want to emphasize that the trial was like a hinge into the Beatnik Era, the subject of Part III and the period when the Beat Movement exploded.

Here is a quick sketch of the major events: the official publication date of *Howl and Other Poems* was November 1, 1956. The first runs were printed in France, on March 25, 1957, and the San Francisco Collector of Customs was able to seize copies of the second run being imported, claiming it was obscene. On June 3, Shigeyoshi Murao, a bookseller at City Lights Books, was arrested for selling copies of *Howl and Other Poems* to undercover agents; a warrant for Ferlinghetti's arrest was also issued, and he turned himself in on June 6. From August to October 1957, a trial was held in connection with *Howl and Other Poems*; the charges against Murao were dismissed early on, and after expert witnesses such as Mark Schorer, Kenneth Rexroth, and Walter Van Tilberg Clark, among others, testified to the book's literary merits, Judge Clayton Horn eventually ruled that Ferlinghetti was not guilty of publishing and selling obscene writing.[67] In terms of literary history broadly imagined, the trial was significant as another blow against censorship: once Ferlinghetti was found not guilty, *Howl and Other Poems* joined an illustrious list of previous work that had been subject to like obscenity trials but eventually cleared, including James Joyce's *Ulysses* (1922), D. H. Lawrence's *Lady Chatterley's Lover* (1928), and Henry Miller's *Tropic of Cancer* (1934).

In terms of Beat literary history in particular, the trial was significant because it stirred public interest in Ginsberg and the "generation" he described in the poem. As John G. Fuller, regular columnist for the *Saturday Review of Literature*, observed in October 1957: "the trial has boomeranged completely at this point, and the poem is receiving many times the attention it would have received" and noted that the man on trial, with Ginsberg, could be "considered part of the nebulous group which has become known as ... the San Francisco Renaissance [...] ... the New Generation of Revolt ... the Beat Generation ... or various other combinations of phrases."[68] As Fuller's column suggests, not only did the trial confirm the truism that banning or censoring something only draws more attention to that thing, it also helped clarify the poem and its "best minds" as part of something larger, a "nebulous group" that would soon shrug off these other possible labels to be known simply as the Beat Generation. Kerouac had of course specifically named the "Beat Generation" in *On the Road*, which had been published that September, something Fuller himself underscores later in that same column, when he briefly notes his interview with Kerouac, "a peripatetic member of the San Francisco group": "'I guess I was the one who named us the 'Beat Generation,' he said. 'This includes anyone from fifteen to fifty-five who digs everything, man.... The Beat Generation loves every thing, man. We go around digging everything'" (6). Fuller's use of the "Howl" trial to pivot into discussing the wider Beat Generation portends a movement about to break: in the coming months and years, the words "Beat," "Beat Generation," and "Beatnik" ricocheted throughout American culture, naming a phenomenon that would grow and grow in the latter 1950s and beyond, attracting as many champions as detractors, and inspiring a more diffuse literary and cultural movement that would mutate far beyond what those friends who met at Columbia in the early 1940s could have imagined.

PART III

The Beatnik Era and the Profusion of Beat Literature (1958–1962)

CHAPTER 6

The Establishment Strikes Back
Beat Becomes Beatnik

It's not really possible to understand what happened to the Beats after 1957 without accounting for the widespread backlash against them, a kind of cultural counterattack founded on the popularized image of the "Beatnik," a term coined by San Francisco *Chronicle* columnist Herb Caen in the spring of 1958.[1] Although Caen first used the word as an aside, saddling the bohemians taking over North Beach with the suffix "nik" to suggest a whiff of communism and probably poor hygiene, the epithet stuck and worked its way across the nation, morphing into the image of the bearded, beret-wearing doper who could hardly manage to tap out rhythm on a pair of bongos, let alone create anything resembling literary art. The irony, of course, is that as this image circulated, it only meant more attention and fame for Kerouac, Ginsberg, and company, affording even the most casual media consumer an easy point of reference regarding the strange "generation" described in *On the Road* and "Howl." But such attention came with a price: while slick magazine exposés of the Beatniks beamed the names Kerouac or Ginsberg or Corso to the farthest reaches of the United States, they were generally described as avatars of a cartoon sketch – Caen's Beatnik run amok – which meant that these and other associated writers found themselves perennially disentangling what they were actually doing in their writing from what the public assumed they must be doing based on the Beatnik caricature.

The blame – or credit, depending on your politics – for the rise of the Beatnik thus goes to the mass media itself, which seemed at once fascinated and repulsed by the Beats, and refined a narrative that confused the specifics of the literature with the most sensational aspects of the imagined Beatnik lifestyle. Widely read publications such as *Time, Newsweek, Look,* and *Life* all ran negative features or recurring short items about the Beats built on scant treatment of the writing in favor of amused critical commentary about the antics of the "beard-and-sandal set."[2] *Time* in particular reserved its snarkiest phrases for Beat figures, as Kerouac was dubbed "latrine laureate of Hobohemia," Ginsberg the "recognized leader of the pack of oddballs who celebrate booze, dope, sex and despair," and Corso a "shaggy, dark little man who boasts that he has never combed his hair."[3] Almost two years to the week after Millstein's glowing review of *On the Road*, *Time* seemed particularly dismayed over what Kerouac had wrought, assuring its readers that though the Beats were undeniably weird, they probably wouldn't disrupt the smooth functioning of a normal suburb: "The bearded, sandaled beat likes to be with his own kind, to riffle through his quarterlies, write craggy poetry, paint crusty pictures, and pursue his never-ending quest for the ultimate in sex and protest. When deterred from such pleasures by the goggle-eyed from Squaresville, the beatnik packs his pot (marijuana), shorts and bongo drums, grabs his black-hosed, pony-tailed beatchicks and cuts out."[4] Portraits such as these were typical of the way *Time* buried the Beat under the caricature of the Beatnik: they were seen first as adolescent buffoons and second as creative "artists" in name only whose work was consistently lazy and predictably poor. Thus despite the tangled relationship between the dominant and countercultures described throughout this book and explored in much Beat writing, after 1957, middlebrow outlets such as *Time* invested themselves in proving Beatniks a species apart from modern man, a strange, unshowered lot comprehensible only to their "own kind."

As implied in such comical descriptions of the Beats, one recurring criticism leveled by publications like *Time* was that despite all their outward signs of social dissent, the Beat rebellion was anemic and hardly new or original, a criticism used to likewise justify dismissal of work such as "Howl" and *On the Road*. An illustrated 1958 *Look* story, "The Bored, the Bearded and the Beat," for example, wasted little time on writing, instead arguing that "There's nothing really new about the Beat philosophy. It consists merely of the average American's value scale – turned inside out. The goals of the Beats are *not* watching TV, *not* wearing gray flannel, *not* owning a home in the suburbs and especially – *not* working."[5] *Not* supported by quoting any writing or well-known Beat figures, this assertion is backed by photographs of bearded and black-clad couples sitting on the floor and looking sullen or through slice-of-life shots with captions like, "Linda is lifted to momentary ecstasy by the savage drumbeat that fills the rooms" (67). The article criticizes "the Beat," but quotes no Beat writers, and is content instead to conclude that "it is really neither a generation nor a movement. Of deeper significance is the overblown national furor and fascination it has caused" (68). *Look* therefore had it both ways: it dismissed "Beat philosophy" as unoriginal and facile while denying there is such a thing as a movement at all, wagging its finger at regular Americans who sensationalize substance-less Bohemians – exactly, of course, what the article itself was doing.

The reflexive move of media blaming media for the popularity of the vapid Beatniks is likewise evident in what has become the most notorious popular take-down of the Beats, the November 1959 *Life* story, "The Only Rebellion Around." Staff writer Paul O'Neil's sprawling, illustrated feature on the Beats recognizes that they can hardly be extricated from media perceptions about them: "[the Beats are] seldom out of the news for long, and there are few Americans today to whom the word Beat or the derisive term, Beatnik, does not conjure up some sort of image – usually a hot-eyed fellow in beard and sandals, or a 'chick' with scraggly hair, long black stockings, heavy eye make-up."[6] Although O'Neil mentions a wider range of writers than the *Look* piece, not only Kerouac ("Beatdom's Grand Old Man"), but Ginsberg (photographed making "a scary face" at Corso), Philip Lamantia, Michael McClure, Lawrence Ferlinghetti, and William Burroughs ("ex-dope addict"), he quotes only a few fragments, and the article reinforces rather than complicates the caricatured "image" of Beatdom about which he complains.

O'Neil's article is visually dominated by a large-format photograph titled "The Well-Equipped Pad" (see Figure 6.1). This photograph is captioned with the explanation that it represents "A Beat's entire 'pad' or household, as re-created in a studio shot using paid models, contains all the essentials of uncomfortable living and consists of the following":

> 1. Beat chick dressed in black ... 3. naked light bulb, 4. hot plate for warming espresso coffee pot and bean cans, 5. marijuana for smoking, 6. posters from old poetry readings and jazz concerts, 7. paperback library of Beat classics, 8. crates which serve as tables and closets ... 10. typewriter with half-finished poem ... 11. bearded Beat wearing sandals, chinos and turtlenecked sweater and studying a record by the late saxophonist Charlie Parker ... 18. Beat poetry leaflet (*Abomunist Manifesto*) ... 22. Beat baby, who has gone to sleep on floor after playing with beer cans. (114–115)

There could hardly be a better example than this photograph of the postmodern theory of simulacrum, which names a moment "when the distinction between representation and reality – between signs and what they refer to in the real world – breaks down."[7] The carefully staged photograph is a representation of a caricature presented as documentary evidence of the way Beats live. Although it certainly has light-hearted aspects, there is nothing in the article to contradict the sense that these "paid models" posing in a studio accurately represent what real people are

Figure 6.1   "The Well-Equipped Pad," photograph by Bert Stern, *Life*
(November 30, 1959).
Image courtesy of Lafayette College

doing in real places like Greenwich Village or North Beach. In fact, O'Neil is sure to underscore his belief that the known figures of Beatdom reflect what is depicted in the opening photograph. Borrowing the exact (though unattributed) phrase *Time* used earlier that year, for example, O'Neil informs readers that Corso "boasts that he has never combed his hair" (123) and that when poet Edith Sitwell interviewed Ginsberg in England, she immediately said to him: "My, you *do* smell bad, don't you?" – a story that was dismissed as untrue, "vulgar," and "insane" by Sitwell herself in a subsequent issue of *Life*.[8]

After taking readers on a tour of the infelicities of the purported Beat lifestyle, O'Neil turns his attention to writing, claiming that "The bulk of Beat writers are undisciplined and slovenly amateurs who … rejected the form, style and attitudes of previous generations and have seized upon obscenity as an expression of 'total personality'" (124). In other words, what is striking about Beat authors is that they are no better than the "undisciplined and slovenly" types found in the photograph, a statement that implies that their work can likewise be described using the same adjectives. Despite this salvo, O'Neil seems for a paragraph willing to admit some virtues of Beat writing: Ginsberg's "excitement," Bob Kaufman's "humor," Kerouac's "real feeling for life," and Burroughs's "vengeful sense of drama" (126). But rather than elaborating these attributes for readers who may have not read the literature, O'Neil offers brief summaries of *On the Road*, "Howl," *Naked Lunch*, and a couple of poems by Corso and McClure, and concludes that what's most interesting about them is that they are real-life embodiments of the fictional characters in the studio photograph. The portraits of the Beats offered in *Life* – alongside those in the *Time* and *Look* features discussed above – have little to do with Beat authors aside from using them as examples of bad behavior, so it is hardly surprising that the impression of the Beats by the general public was not one of literary creativity or worthwhile engagement of any kind, but of willfully lazy, borderline psychotic nonconformity and nonproductivity.

Little wonder, then, that by 1960, novelist Herbert Gold could argue that "the anonymous scribes at *Time* and *Life* have labored to create nothing from a something which was merely *almost* nothing. They have invented the Beatnik.… The beatnik is the hipster squeezed into shape by the popular media, seen as through a gloss darkly by radio, television, films, and magazines."[9] It seems intentional that Gold refrains from listing novels or poetry as outlets responsible for "glossing" the Beats for mainstream America, for as we have seen, the depictions in places like *Time* and *Life* had hardly deigned to mention writing at all. "The beatnik," writes Gold, "is the hipster parodied and packaged as a commercial product. It is a commodity" (136, 137).

Gold's observation is everywhere evident in American popular culture during the Beatnik Era. The most recognizable Beatnik caricature was probably the character of Maynard G. Krebs in the television program *The Many Loves of Doby Gillis*, which debuted in September 1959. Krebs (Bob Denver) was the foil to the strait-laced, all-American Doby (Dwayne Hickman): exhibiting all the features of the Beatnik found in the pages of *Time* and *Life*, Maynard was shabbily attired, an aficionado of jazz, and prone to mumbling hipster slang. That Maynard became the most popular character on the show speaks to the general hold the Beatnik image had on American culture during this moment, and in fact there were a great many other examples from Hollywood that exploited the Beatnik caricature and his supposed environment. Films such as *The Beat Generation* (1959) (and the companion novelization by producer Albert Zugsmith [1959]), *The Bloody Brood* (1959), *The Rebel Set* (1959), and *The Beatniks* (1960) not only trafficked in the shaggy stereotypes embodied by Maynard G. Krebs, but took them a step further by associating Beatniks with violence as their plots concerned a serial rapist, armed robbery, and murders, respectively. In all of these representations, Beat-related artwork is treated as a joke, in some cases as dangerous as the crimes themselves: in *A Bucket of Blood* (1959) – directed by Roger Corman of *The Little Shop of Horrors* (1960) fame – a wannabe Beatnik artist exhibits a dead cat as sculpture; when his fellow bohemians lavish praise on the piece, he winds up killing human beings and exhibiting them in order to gain validation from a self-identified artistic community that can't in fact seem to distinguish good art from murder.

If such work has little – or nothing – to do with Beat literary production, other examples of popular culture from the Beatnik Era traded on the assumption that free love and athletic sex added up to the sum total of Beat experience. There was, for example, a whole cottage industry producing adult-themed paperback novels such as John Schuyler's *Beatnik Party* (1959), James Rowe's *Artist Colony* (1962), and Don Elliott's *Beatnik Wanton* (1964), all of which argued that Beat chicks were loose-moraled and overly sexualized – every square male's dream.[10]

A step above such novels were those written by people connected to the scene who traded on Beat notoriety to boost sales. This is the case, for example, in Bonnie Golightly's novel *Beat Girl* (1959). Golightly was owner of the Park Bookshop in Greenwich Village, a haunt for bohemian types, and so knew a wide range of writers, including poet Harold Norse, whom she briefly dated after her divorce (Truman Capote would eventually borrow her last name for the heroine of *Breakfast at Tiffany's* [1958]).[11] By the Beatnik Era, Golightly could draw on her knowledge of the scene for *Beat Girl*, a potboiler about a nice normal girl who falls in with the "true-blue children of the Beat Generation" via her involvement with a "West Coast displaced poet cum philosopher cum jazz aficionado – primitive jazz, of course – going to Columbia on thin air."[12] Golightly's "children of the Beat Generation" are sketchily drawn, but it hardly mattered since the type was so well known by 1959 that shorthand would suffice to conjure a whole subculture photographed in *Look* and *Life*.

As in the Hollywood versions of the Beat Scene, in novels like *Beat Girl*, art is dismissed as but a pretext for bad behavior. The cover of *Artist Colony* shrilly declared: "Their 'ART' was an excuse to indulge themselves in orgies!"[13] This cover and many others are reproduced in the illustrated book *Beatsville* (2003), which takes readers on a tour of the surprising examples of kitsch and popular culture from the Beatnik Era and after, including not only the films and books mentioned above, but countless record albums (*The Cool Scene: Twelve New Ways to Fly* [1959], Ray Baudic and Nappy Lamare's *Two-Beat Generation*, and Saroff and the Cool Ones' *Like Beat Man* [1959]) that took a more light-hearted approach to the Beatnik craze. In this era, Beatnik kitsch mushroomed, so faddish consumers could buy a "Beatnik Kit," featuring a beret, beard, heavy-rimmed glasses, and a cigarette holder, or could collect a set of ceramic Beatnik figurines, each with unique placards with phrases like "Dad, whatever it is, I'm against it" (see *Beatsville*, 23, 50). In this tongue-in-cheek vein, humor magazines such as *Mad* published books skewering the Beats, including *Like, MAD* ("Are you a member of 'The Beat Generation?' If You Are, This Book Is Definitely Not for You!!").[14] Readers of illustrated humor books such as William F. Brown's *Beat Beat Beat* (1959) and George Mandel's *Beatville, U.S.A.* (1961) would likewise be treated to absurdist characterizations of the supposed lifestyle that relied on and reinforced popular misconceptions, creating an echo chamber where "the Beatnik" was endlessly reproduced.[15] In Greenwich Village, tourists could even seek out Café Bizarre, a Beatnik-themed space designed to deliver on expectations born of images found everywhere from television to the pages of popular magazines.

6.1 How the New Criticism Savaged Beat Writing

During the Beatnik Era, this widespread dismissal, by turns derisive of grubby pads and horrified at the potential for Beat violence, was not confined to paperback racks or television and movie screens. In fact, critics writing for highbrow reviews and thus supposedly more interested in literary craft tended to collapse what poet John Ciardi called the "set of antics" of the Beat lifestyle with the merits – or lack thereof – of the writing ("Epitaph," 11). When critics did wade into discussions of language, they tended to dismiss it in much the same terms that the cartoon Beatniks were dismissed: the writing was lazy, undisciplined, and too reliant on "hip" slang. Highbrow and middlebrow critics alike seemed fascinated by the Beat appropriation of black jazz slang, and pointed to its use in Beat poetry and prose as evidence of impoverished expression. The effect of this focus on slang or hipster jargon was that critics blinkered themselves to alternative kinds of meaning and structure in Beat works that may have been perceptible had they been approached from more generous points of view. Certain keywords – "slang," "spontaneity," "obscenity" – became proxies for meaningful engagement with Beat writing. Thus, in *The New Republic*, William Raymond Smith announced he was going to undertake textual analysis to get to the bottom of the Beat phenomenon, but rather than interpret real samples of writing, he offers instead a portrait of an imagined hipster who is "characterized, like all hipsters, by an inarticulateness of expression in language. They continually rephrase what they say: 'You're nowhere, man, like I mean, you don't know, I mean, you don't know why.'"[16] If Smith's made-up hipster can't even say what he means without a thousand false starts, there is little hope for written expression, for a premise of Smith's essay is that the unshowered, sandaled Beat and his poem are essentially indistinguishable. For Smith, as for a great many other critics writing in this period, Beat writing was "loose and undiscriminating" because the Beats themselves were loose and undiscriminating, a fatal fault according to the norms of the reigning New Criticism.[17]

The hold that New Criticism had on literary analysis at the time goes a long way in explaining the hostile reception the Beats encountered in the academy and in those highbrow venues informed by the academy's critical norms. "New Criticism" names a school of formal literary theory that by the 1950s ruled in American universities, and its precepts for what counted as worthwhile literature lurked behind nearly every dismissal of Beat writing during the Beatnik Era. Having been elaborated in John Crowe Ransom's *The New Criticism* (1941) and elsewhere, this method of literary analysis sought to unlock the complexities of literary form, and is responsible for the popularity, even today, of "close reading" in literature classrooms. New Critics taught that a good reader ought to shun biographical or historical contexts in favor of close reading for literary devices such as irony, ambiguity, paradox, images, and symbols.

Especially important for understanding how New Critical norms led to a dismissal of Beat writing is New Criticism's emphasis on formal unity. In their highly influential textbook, *Understanding Fiction* (1943), for example, Cleanth Brooks and Robert Penn Warren argue that "successful" fiction depends on "something in the nature of the story as story – on whether the motivation is acceptable, on how characters are related to the plot, on the degree of plausibility in incidents."[18] In the second edition of *Understanding Fiction*, the idea of "unity" was emphasized further:

"When we say '*a* novel,' '*a* story,' or '*a* plot,' we instinctively imply the idea of unity. We imply that the parts, the various individual events, hang together.... If we can detect no reasonable connection between them, if there is no 'logic' whatever, we lose interest."[19] With the New Critical emphasis on unity and logic and "reasonable connection" in mind, it is easier to understand why critics who deemed Beat texts "loose and undiscriminating" were damning them as worthless or not "real" writing.

In 1958, for example, critic John Roberts argued that because the Beats themselves are undisciplined, their writing lacks structure and unity:

> to write (really write, not just jot down unassimilated impressions) you must feel, then organize and impose a viewpoint. If, occasionally, the hipster lapses from coolness to commit to paper some nightmare induced by weed, bennies or wine . . . he must avoid any rational analysis or unifying theme; to do otherwise would be square, then which oblivion would be preferable.[20]

Roberts's use of terms like "unifying theme" allows him to claim that it is the Beat's very tendency to write impressionistically that dooms his work to structural failure according to the logic of New Criticism. As explained in Part II, there are many kinds of meaning available in work that does not conform to New Critical norms, but if one relies primarily on these norms, as Roberts and other critics did, then such meaning is rendered effectively invisible. It is telling indeed that Roberts should continue on to quote a short passage from Kerouac's *The Subterraneans* (1958) in which narrator Leo Percepied is arguing with a character whom Roberts calls a "serious square young writer." The writer says to Percepied: "'Well, I believe that the most important thing is selectivity,'" a statement at which Percepied "blew up and said 'Ah don't give me all that high school stuff I've heard it and heard it long before you were born almost for krissakes and really now, say something interesting and new about writing.'"[21] Roberts cites this passage in order to show that Kerouac's novel is an "unselective jumble of words" and therefore worthless, whereas Kerouac includes the exchange specifically as a dig against New Critical standards of "literariness." Equating the younger writer's interest in "selectivity" with "all the high school stuff" is a way for Percepied to point to *Understanding Fiction*, by the late 1950s a standard pedagogical text that assured students that the only route to a literary, unified work of fiction was through "selectivity." As Brooks and Warren write:

> We have several times referred to *selection*. But this principle applies not only to exposition and description; it applies with equal force to plot

structure. The individual items in the chain of events which presumably the character of a story would participate in real life, during the span of time of the story, are not of equal significance; ... [the writer] selects the events which have meaning, and meaning in terms of the basic impulse of the story, not simply in isolation or in relation to some idea not involved in the story. (576)

With such New Critical statements in mind, it is easier to see that when Kerouac stages a brief debate between Percepied and the young writer in *The Subterraneans*, he does so in part to dismiss the standards by which his own work would be attacked in highbrow and middlebrow publications. For Kerouac, to rely on New Critical terms like "selectivity" is to be stuck recycling tired ideas about what fiction must do or be. In this view, contemporary critics like Roberts are likewise stuck claiming Kerouac's work is an "unselective jumble of words" precisely because Kerouac's writing doesn't begin from the premise that some events are more significant than others. We saw in Part II that as he worked on spontaneous prose, Kerouac was purposively pushing back against what was considered good or worthwhile literature, and attention to the New Critical context allows us to see one of his most well-known aesthetic statements in a different light: "Not 'selectivity' of expression but following free deviation (association) of mind into limitless blow-on-subject seas of thought" – here Kerouac pointedly opposes his theories of writing against those popularized by Brooks and Warren (which is also why, in a 1950 letter to Neal Cassady, Kerouac praised Cassady's writing by contrasting it to Warren's).[22]

Kerouac's methods were not merely opposed to New Critical norms for the sake of being rebellious, but were rather ways to access what he took to be more truthful, radically subjective experiences that he saw as obscured by the "craft" advocated by critics like Brooks and Warren. He elaborated this view in a 1959 column for *Escapade* magazine:

My position in the current American literary scene is simply that I got sick and tired of the conventional English sentence which seemed to me so ironbound in its rules, so inadmissible with reference to the actual format of my mind as I had learned to probe it in the modern spirit of Freud and Jung, that I couldn't express myself through that form any more. How many sentences do you see in current novels that say, "The snow was on the ground, and it was difficult for the car to climb the hill"? By the childish device of taking what was originally two short sentences, and sticking in a comma with an "and," these great contemporary prose "craftsmen" think they have labored out a sentence. As far as I can see it is two short sets of imagery belonging to a much longer sentence the total imagery of which would finally say something we never heard before if the writer dared to utter it out.[23]

This is an explanation of the synergy between form and content in Kerouac's own, apparently unselective writing, contrasted specifically against the style he recognizes as approved by contemporary critics: short, declarative sentences obviously inherited from Hemingway. Turning the tables on those who cast the Beats as adolescent and undisciplined, Kerouac calls his example sentence "childish" because its putative "craft" is derivative and closes the language off from the writer's mind for the sake of seeming voguishly "contemporary." In Kerouac's view, this sort of writing is less literary than his own as it merely applies a formula, thereby removing the "actual format of [the writer's] mind" from the writing itself. After this statement, he goes on to connect his rejection of the "conventional English sentence" to that of like-minded writers he sees as producing the most consequential "current" work – Burroughs, whose *Naked Lunch* "may prove repulsive to many . . . but in time will mellow in their minds"; Corso, "a fabulous young American poet of the very first magnitude"; and Ginsberg, whose unpublished, "wild little notebooks," he declares "perfect" (146–147).[24] So not only does Kerouac forcefully reject the Hemingwayan mode, he underscores the sense of a literary movement built on like rejections by connecting his own work to three of the most famous Beat figures – and he also points to a "rich *school* of writing" that one could locate in decidedly nonacademic little magazines like *Evergreen Review* or *Yugen* (147).

Despite such even-tempered explication on Kerouac's part, the general critical attitude during the Beatnik Era was blind to such potential in his writing, and in fact used this writing and the wider Beat dismissal of New Criticism as evidence for the movement's lack of merit. As professor John Sisk argued in 1959, the "unhappy conviction that it is impossible to 'make,' in the traditional artist's sense, without corrupting . . . [explains] the Beat writers' violent and surrealist dislike of the New Critics and the university poets."[25] Yet it was not that the Beats were loath to "make," but that they were loath to make in the particular ways prescribed by the New Criticism, which for a critic like Sisk is indistinguishable from the "traditional artist's sense," as though it is impossible to imagine meaningful art that is not "traditional" or exemplary of New Critical measures of literariness.

The reach of New Criticism is also helpful in contextualizing the reasoning found in what is today the best-remembered hatchet job on the Beats: Norman Podhoretz's "The Know-Nothing Bohemians" (1958). This piece appeared in *Partisan Review*, a venerable literary and cultural magazine that had by the late 1950s moved slightly right of center and became even more invested in curating high culture. Podhoretz's essay is a thorough critique that has since been widely anthologized as the representative example of establishment criticism of the Beats.[26] When Podhoretz complains, "Nothing that happens [in *On the Road*] has any dramatic reason for happening," he echoes the kind of logic quoted above, when Brooks and Warren insist that a good writer selectively narrates events that are significant and discards those that are not.[27] Moreover, Podhoretz concludes that Kerouac's spontaneous prose radically hamstrings his ability to express complex thoughts or emotions: "The only method he has of describing an object is to summon up the same half-dozen adjectives over and over again: 'greatest,' 'tremendous,' 'crazy,' 'mad,' 'wild,' and perhaps one or two others. When it's more than just mad or crazy or wild, it becomes 'really mad' or 'really crazy' or 'really wild'" (153). Ginsberg was thus probably within his rights to criticize Podhoretz's "diatribes on spontaneous bop prosody" for "confusing it with the use of hip talk not realizing it refers to rhythmical construction of phrases and sentences."[28]

Indeed, even though Podhoretz actually does quote at length from *On the Road* and *The Subterraneans* (unlike a great many other critics who scarcely bothered to engage the writing they attacked), he does so to prove that Kerouac lacks a depth of feeling, and that because he supposedly crams his novels with "everything" that happened in real life, regardless of whether those things have a "dramatic reason" for being so included, his books can only hope to destroy "the distinction between life and literature," in that very destruction failing to achieve formal unity (155). This confusion of "life and literature" is what Podhoretz finds most problematic about Beat writing because he thinks it has led or will inevitably lead to a more fundamental lack of moral structure in the younger generation. Once he decides, for example, that *On the Road* and *The Subterraneans* lack conventional formal architectures or a flair for what he calls the "right words," Podhoretz concludes: "What you get in these two books is a man proclaiming that he is *alive* and offering every trivial experience he has ever had in evidence.... But if it meant something, ... why can't you explain what it meant, and why do you have to insist so? I think it is legitimate to say, then, that the Beat Generation's worship of primitivism and spontaneity is more than a cover for hostility to intelligence; it arises from a pathetic poverty of feeling as well" (155–156). When Podhoretz refers here to "intelligence," he implies a particular kind of knowledge and knowledge production associated with enlightenment values, rationality, and academic inquiry – not to mention New Critical measures of literary worth – and what ultimately bothers him is not the Beat writer's undisciplined use of language, but how this lack of discipline is manifest in the declining moral attitudes of contemporary youth.

In fact, Podhoretz is ultimately concerned that Kerouac's failure to conform to New Critical standards of literariness does not merely make him a bad writer, but that it indicates a personal moral failing, as well as a greater moral failing of the generation for whom Kerouac was thought to speak. Podhoretz writes, for example, that "the spirit of hipsterism and the Beat Generation strikes me as the same spirit which animates the young savages in leather jackets who have been running amok in the last few years with their switchblades and zip guns" (156–157). He then goes on to accuse the Beats of promoting violence, claiming that "even the relatively mild ethos of Kerouac's books can spill over easily into brutality" (157). Such a position, that the Beat writers' interest in atypical literary forms and taboo themes meant that they somehow relished or otherwise advocated violence, became widespread during the Beatnik Era. Yet it was hardly the case. If there is violence in *On the Road, The Subterraneans*, or "Howl" (the three texts on which Podhoretz focuses), it is violence done to the Beats by others; even in *Naked Lunch*, which Podhoretz mentions but hadn't yet read, the excessive violence is a reflection of a sick society, not something to be emulated – as Kenneth Rexroth put it in 1957, "'The Poetry of the New Violence'? It isn't at all violent. It is *your* violence it is talking about."[29]

Podhoretz's idea that the Beats are of "the same spirit" as those "young savages in leather jackets" comes not so much from the writing itself – which contains scenes of car stealing and shoplifting, yes, but not of the gang-like criminal violence Podhoretz names – but from one of the most notorious analyses of "the hipster" in the 1950s: Norman Mailer's "The White Negro" (1957). Mailer's provocative essay claimed that the hipster "had absorbed the existential synapses of the Negro" because African Americans had historically been forced into the role of cultural outsider in the United States.[30] Drawing on the vocabulary found in Robert Lindner's widely cited *Rebel without a Cause – The Hypnoanalysis of a Criminal Psychopath* (1944), Mailer used terms like "violence" and "criminality" and "psychopath" to describe those "existential synapses" on which the hipster supposedly modeled his existence: "Hated from the outside and therefore hating himself, the Negro was forced into the position of exploring all those moral wildernesses of civilized life which the Square automatically condemns as delinquent or evil or immature or

morbid or self-destructive or corrupt" (348). Whereas Mailer saw generative potential in such energies, Podhoretz only affirms his agreement with
the string of adjectives a square might use to condemn hipsters. Thus when
Podhoretz ends his essay by wondering what Mailer himself would think
of "those wretched kids," the "savages in leather jackets," he tips his hand
to the fact that he is drawing his final conclusions not from the texts
themselves, but from conflating the Beats with those savages that he
thinks, without a trace of irony, are "running amok" with knives and
guns. If Podhoretz, a professional literary and cultural critic, could so easily
confuse the import of Beat writing with the actions of street gangs, it
suggests the power of the wider misperception, for although he uses the
term "Beat Generation," it wasn't entirely clear what counted as that
"generation" beyond the orbit of Kerouac and Ginsberg. Indeed, in a
follow-up to "The Know-Nothing Bohemians" published a few months
later in *Esquire*, Podhoretz throws up his hands to characterize the Beats
as veritable horsemen of the apocalypse: "Isn't the Beat Generation a
conspiracy to overthrow civilization ... to replace it [with] the world of
the adolescent street gang?"[31]

During the Beatnik Era, many commentators took such violence seriously and insisted that it could best explain what exactly counted as Beat.
Catholic World thought "the Beat carry on their search in a convulsion
of brassy sound and deaf-dumb violence" and *Commonweal* that they
were "full of violence"; *The Nation* dubbed Ginsberg "poet of the New
Violence," and the *Sewanee Review* declared that "everyone in Ginsberg's
book [*Howl and Other Poems*] is hopped-up on benzedrine, reefers, or
whiskey, and is doing something as violently and loudly as he can, in
'protest' or 'fulfillment.'"[32] Such depictions were why, a mere five months
after *On the Road*'s publication, Kerouac, as the media-crowned King of
the Beats, already felt the need to defend himself against claims of violence:
"The Beat Generation is no hoodlumism. As the man who suddenly
thought of that word 'beat' to describe our generation, I would like to
have my little say about it before everyone else in the writing field begins to
call it 'roughneck,' 'violent,' 'heedless,' 'rootless'.... My favorite Beat
buddies were all *kind*, good kids, eager, sincere."[33] Such defenses hardly
mattered, though, as most media outlets, led by *Time* and *Life* and given
intellectual heft by both Norman Mailer's blithely confident proclam-
ations about the hipster and by more nuanced arguments in the *Partisan
Review* and other academic quarterlies, had by 1959 collectively made up
their mind to dismiss the Beats as adolescent navel-gazers at best, deranged
violent offenders at worst.

6.2 Early Critical Sympathy

But swimming against this powerful current of anti-Beatnik dismissal was a handful of broadly positive and sympathetic accounts of the Beats that presaged the more serious scholarly engagements of later decades. Some of these accounts indulged in the caricatures found in the publications mentioned above, but did so with enthusiasm rather than studied revulsion. In February 1959, for example, *Playboy* magazine, ever on the lookout for the hip bachelor aesthetic, published essays by Herbert Gold and Noel Clad attempting to make sense of the Beat Generation. The stories proved interesting enough to readers that in June *Playboy* printed Kerouac's corrective to popular conceptions of the Beat Generation ("Beatific"), and in July had yet another feature on Beat writing, "The Sound of Beat," featuring work by three "leading Beatnik poets": Kerouac ("To Harpo Marx"), Ginsberg ("To Lindsay"), and Corso ("Made by Hand").[34] A few pages after these poems, *Playboy* presented their first-ever "Beat Playmate," Yvette Vickers, who was claimed to have been found "sipping espresso" in a Los Angeles "beat coffee house." According to her biographical sketch, Vickers was "interested in serious acting, ballet, the poetry of Dylan Thomas, classical music ... and is more than a bit of a rebel, frowning prettily on conformity."[35] In her centerfold spread, Vickers was pictured lying on a sofa with the requisite Beat paraphernalia strewn about: sandals, poetry manuscript, booze, cigarettes, jazz records, and an album about Zen. *Playboy* was clearly capitalizing on the pop culture version of the Beatnik, and did so with an "open-mindedness" predicated on figuring women as adornments or accessories, something that, as we will see, is an unfortunate characteristic of many contemporary accounts of the Beats, even broadly positive ones.

Going further than the sympathetic but superficial treatments in men's magazines, other documents from the Beatnik Era further explored the specifically literary innovations of Beat-associated writing. The most visible journalistic account of the movement, at least in New York City, was Alfred Aronowitz's twelve-part series, "The Beat Generation," which appeared across as many issues in the *New York Post* in March 1959. Like the negative depictions discussed above, Aronowitz begins with some of the more sensational moments from Beat lore, as when Ginsberg took off all his clothes during a poetry reading, or when Burroughs accidentally shot his wife Joan Vollmer (in his sketches of these events, neither Ginsberg nor Burroughs are named). Aronowitz also offers readers wink-wink portraits of youthful hangers-on like the nineteen-year-old girl wearing a turtleneck sweater and dark stockings who says, "Of course I'm a member of the Beat Generation," but who has never heard of Ginsberg and is only dimly aware that Kerouac is a writer.[36] But rather than letting these stories stand for the meaning of the Beat Generation as *Time* or *Life* would, Aronowitz allows its central figures to speak for themselves, thereby rendering a more complex and sympathetic portrait than the ones available in the Beatnik-obsessed slicks.

In the first installment, Aronowitz recounts the story of Holmes and Kerouac's 1948 conversation in which the term "Beat Generation" was coined, but then quickly questions the notion that there is such a thing as a coherent generation at all. Dutifully following up on the standard comparison between the Beats and the Lost Generation, Aronowitz even interviewed Hemingway himself, who thought that "The difference between the alleged, so-called Lost Generation and this one . . . is that this one promotes itself by publicity and makes a movement. . . . I think these guys have a lot of talent and I wish them all the luck they can have" (40). Ever astute, Hemingway put his finger on publicity as a signal characteristic of Beat phenomenon; as we have seen, the "Beat Generation" came to be important culturally not when Kerouac made an offhand remark about a circle of friends who traded manuscripts, but when these friends began to receive media attention, first Holmes's *Go* and *New York Times* article, then "Howl" and its ensuing controversy, then *On the Road* and Millstein's rave review, and finally the protracted backlash that conflated a semi-imaginary Beatnik lifestyle with the literary achievement of these writers. And just as Hemingway was cagey about the "alleged, so-called Lost Generation," so too were many Beat-associated writers cagey about declaring their participation in or association with that group since it had been so effectively packaged, then roundly dismissed by the mass media.

Rather than recycling the Luce publications' line on the unwashed, psychopathic Beatnik, Aronowitz focused attention on profiling Kerouac, Cassady, Ginsberg, Ray Bremser, Corso, Snyder, Pierre Delattre, and Eric Nord, the "Big Daddy of the Beatniks."[37] Over the course of these twelve installments, Aronowitz made a good-faith effort to take the Beat writers on their own terms, to let them speak for themselves and correct what most of them perceived as an inaccurate public record. For example, Aronowitz quotes Ginsberg's response to accounts like the ones described earlier: "we're not interested in the sociology of it . . . The Beat Generation is a literary movement, and if the public associates it with violence or juvenile delinquency, it's the fault of the critics. It is they who have put the worst kind of violence to our poetry, in such a way that they have betrayed the muse. The violence in my poetry and Kerouac's poetry is no greater than that in Rabelais or Shakespeare" (40). In later installments, Aronowitz returns to the subject of violence in more depth in his profiles of Bremser and Corso, showing that while they had indeed committed crimes and served jail time in their younger years, poetry was actually keeping them from continuing down a criminal path. He emphasizes how after spending time in jail, Bremser took correspondence courses in journalism, became head librarian, and wrote reams of poetry and prose. Corso is depicted as a troubled foster kid who discovered literature in jail, and who finds in poetry a means of sense-making and escape from the cycle of poverty-driven crime. Through Ginsberg, Aronowitz shows, both poets were connected to the wider underground poetry scene, thus suggesting its redemptive potential. As for violence, Corso put his own spin on the term: "Violence? Creativity is a manifestation of violence. Creativity in art is not a destructive type of violence, but it's violent nevertheless. True creativity is violent because it's unorganized and chaotic."[38] For Corso, poetry – good poetry – is only "violent" insofar as it is disruptive: it amounts to an aesthetic violence that might "make it new" in the Modernist tradition – hardly the physical violence perpetrated by hoodlums lurking in the shadows.

The first in-depth profile in the series is of Kerouac. Aronowitz visited the Long Island home Kerouac was then sharing with his mother, who walks in and out of the interview, endearingly referring to her son as "a good boy" and informing Aronowitz that she had made it only to page thirty-four of *On the Road*.[39] Amid this maternal affection, Kerouac drinks constantly and dismisses the "Beat Generation" as "not important, it's a fad" (4). Instead, he wants to talk about the virtues of spontaneous prose, whose origins he credits to Neal Cassady's "Joan Anderson letter," discussed in Part II, what Kerouac dubs "a great literary masterpiece," and about his "serious writing," which involves real people and events because "the way to write is to get excited in telling a real story" (64). Far from a madman of the road or a violent delinquent, Kerouac is portrayed as an eccentric homebody who drinks too much and sincerely believes in the transformative potential of literature.

In his conversations with Aronowitz, Ginsberg echoes both Kerouac's trepidation in viewing the "Beat Generation" as a cohesive movement and his insistence on focusing on the functions or innovations of their writing rather than on their "antics." Aronowitz goes on to characterize the "Beat Generation" not as a bounded movement with identifiable members and nonmembers but as a network of like-minded writers who were more often than not connected to Ginsberg in some way. Ginsberg is indeed depicted as a linchpin of the Beat underground, a mover and shaker of inexhaustible energy whose desk overflowed with correspondence suturing the far-flung outposts of the scene: "The letters both ways are usually filled with copies of poems so that in San Francisco, Denver, Chicago, New Orleans, Mexico City, Paris, Majorca, Tangier, and other extensions of the road, the underground knows what is being written in New York and vice versa" (32). Rather than a movement that comically prescribes certain attitudes and even costumes as *Life* and *Time* suggested, Aronowitz presented the Beats as experimental writers critical of middle-class values and "the academic poets" – while simultaneously interested in literary recognition – and, in the case of Kerouac, ironically living with one foot in the suburban, middle-class life.[40]

The Aronowitz piece marks a noteworthy critical profile on the Beats, but given its appearance in the *New York Post*, its impact was more localized and ephemeral, and so it didn't have the more widespread reach of the first book-length description of the Beat Generation, Lawrence Lipton's *The Holy Barbarians* (1959), a kind of amateur ethnography. Lipton had published novels and poetry collections in earlier decades, but his own writing hadn't been particularly underground. However, by the latter 1950s, he was living and working around the bohemian scene in Venice Beach, California. Appearing as it did at the height of the Beatnik Era, *The Holy Barbarians* was advertised as the first book "to give a true, inside view of the controversial 'beats.'"[41] Although Lipton tends to take the Beats more seriously than *Time*, *Life*, or the *Partisan Review*, *The Holy Barbarians* nonetheless focuses nearly all of its 300-plus pages on the Beat lifestyle with almost no attention paid to writing – in a profile piece for *The Village Voice*, Suzanne Kiplinger paraphrased Lipton as saying "the big commercial market is for books like his *about* the Beat, rather than the creative writing itself."[42] As such, there are chapters devoted to casual sex ("The Loveways of the Beat Generation"), drug use ("'God's Medicine': The Euphoric Fix"), the refusal to work ("Down with the Rat Race: The New Poverty"), and the widespread interest in jazz. "To sneer at success," proclaimed an advertisement for the book, "monogamy, cleanliness and order – that's beat."[43] Hardly surprising, then, that Kerouac found the book "awful, all about his [Lipton's] own barefooted bearded non-working art friends who don't write but just talk and show off and the things about us who started it all are pejorative."[44]

Kerouac reacted negatively to *The Holy Barbarians* because Lipton didn't focus on those connected to the original inner circle, but on a different community, the one he knew in Venice Beach. It is at once a virtue and a problem that Lipton chooses not give pride of place to the inner circle or locate the energies of the movement primarily in New York or San Francisco – it is a virtue because it represents a wider view of the social phenomenon, a problem because it tends to ignore literary achievement in favor of sociological tidbits. Reading the book retrospectively, one gets the sense that Lipton wanted to cash in on media interest in the Beat orbit around Kerouac and Ginsberg, but as an outsider himself to this orbit, the sixty-year-old Lipton played up Venice as a third geographical and conceptual space where the Beat lifestyle flourished.[45] The general effect of this framing is that Lipton himself becomes the center of a Beat revolution happening in Venice, a rhetorical move that was successful to the extent that for a brief period after the book's publication, he was seen by some as the spokesperson for the Beat Generation. Even though he was never a widely read creative writer, Lipton can be found in photographs from the Beatnik Era performing poetry to jazz accompaniment in bohemian coffee houses, and in 1960 he even appeared in the campy horror film *The Hypnotic Eye* as "King of the Beatniks."

Yet if *The Holy Barbarians* recirculates some clichéd ideas about the Beats in order to recast Lipton himself as their leader or elder statesmen, one notable aspect of the book is that it takes Beat "disaffiliation" seriously as political critique. As one of his subjects puts it with respect to "political solutions": "What are they but election tactics, lies, deceptions, trickery, mass manipulation? All parties use the same tricks, so what choice is there between them?"[46] As I have explained, such a fundamental refusal to participate in elections and other venues of mainstream politics was seen by many observers as adolescent and intellectually lazy, and yet Lipton is willing to entertain the notion that it could have positive political content. In other words, Lipton recognizes that to "disaffiliate" was to be political – yet it was a politics invisible to those commentators with a more circum-scribed view of political engagement. Lipton claims, for example, that "there is almost universal agreement among them [the Beats] that militarism and war is the biggest shuck of all."[47] The condemnation of "militarism and war" in this sentence refers mainly to the Korean War, the Arms Race, and general postwar triumphalism mandated by the Cold War, a mandate that would have its most far-reaching expression in the protracted Vietnam War (and as we will see in Part IV, by the mid-1960s, to question the intrinsic virtue of "the system" itself became the very core of the countercultural movement, as high-level decisions pertaining to the Vietnam War seemed damning evidence of the system's endemic failures). To disaffiliate, in this view, is not to claim exemption from politics, but to question the very terms of the (political) discussion: "Disaffiliation is a voluntary self-alienation from the family cult, from Moneytheism and all its works and ways. The disaffiliate has no blueprint for the future. He joins no political parties. He is free to make his own inner-directed decisions. If he fails to vote altogether, that, too, is a form of political action ... it is a no-confidence vote."[48] Lipton brings together language from David Riesman's highly influential work of sociology, *The Lonely Crowd* (1950), which proposed a distinction between "other directed" personalities and "inner directed" personalities, and the basic ideas of Kenneth Rexroth. Lipton quotes Rexroth as saying "[The Beat] isn't disaffiliated from society, he is disaffiliated from the social order, from the state and capitalist system."[49] For Rexroth, the state is invested in promoting the "social lie," and part of the work of this lie is to collapse the social and the state; by disaffiliating, the Beats refused to accord the state naming power over the social itself. Lipton actually fails to follow up on this possibility in *The Holy Barbarians*, but the book marks a moment when Beat disaffiliation was connected to a refusal of the "social lie" – which helps us begin to see political dimensions of the Beat sensibility before it became more clearly involved with legislative politics in the 1960s.

An attempt to take the Beats more seriously than the dismissive work surveyed above is found in two other important artifacts from the spring of 1959: English professor Warren Tallman's essay, "Kerouac's Sound," published in the Canadian journal *Tamarack Review*, and *Wagner Literary Magazine*'s symposium on "The Beat Poets." Tallman's was the first scholarly treatment of Kerouac and the Beats that saw real literary merit in their work, and is notable for theorizing exactly what spontaneous prose could accomplish. Tallman's essay begins familiarly enough, with the notion that the Beats are working from the assumption that they are living "in something like the ruins of our civilization, ... [and that] to swing is to enter into full alliance with the moment and to do this is to triumph over the squares who otherwise rule the world."[50] But rather than remain in the realm of the sociological, Tallman turns to an analysis of the ways in which Kerouac's innovative methods helped him develop a prose style that could effectively respond to a civilization in crisis. Whereas Podhoretz complained that in Kerouac's writing, "Nothing happens [that] has any dramatic reason for happening," Tallman sees narrative flights of fancy as integral to how his work has meaning and is inherited from such recognizably legitimate writers as James Joyce, Franz Kafka, Virginia Woolf, and William Faulkner, who had all noted the "deviousness and imprecision in our language because an evident fragmentation has overtaken meanings in our time" (550). The problem with earlier writers like Joyce and Eliot is that for "most persons" such work is "so circuitously difficult" that there has been a "distinct breakdown of any vital connection with our best literature" (550). So what is a contemporary writer aware of language's slippery imprecision to do? The "solution," writes Tallman, "is to be Beat. To be Beat is to let your life come tumbling down into a humpty-dumpty heap ... the humpty-dumpty meanings which language attempts to sustain" (550). Thus far from faulting the Beats for being paralyzed nihilists, Tallman sees their writing as broadly generative, as inheriting the avant-garde spirit of Modernism but marshaling it into work more accessible to a greater readership.

For Tallman, *The Subterraneans* is Kerouac's "most important novel" because in it he has most successfully exploited the method that has allowed him "to tap his imagination in spontaneous ways" so that "the narrative line has tended to weaken, merge with, and be dominated by the sum of variations" (556, 549–550). In order to show how this works, Tallman analyzes the second paragraph of *The Subterraneans*, which begins by introducing Julien Alexander, "the angel of the subterraneans" (1), but then shoots off into several lines of variation and repetition concerning the connection between Leo and Mardou, whose romance forms the emotional core of the novel. For a New Critic looking for the principles of unity, the shifts in the paragraph might indicate a lack of literary merit, but for Tallman, attuned as he was to the improvisational nature of jazz and the contemporary awareness of language's slipperiness, such shifts are, on the contrary, the great strength of the novel. As he writes, "The narrative line follows the brief love-affair between Percepied and Mardou while the improvised details move, as the title would suggest, down into the clutter of their lives among the guilts and shames which come up from the subterranean depths to steal their love from them. The truth is in the improvisations" (556). Tallman's analysis is important to Beat literary history because it was the first in print to recognize what Kerouac was trying to do with spontaneous prose, and as such is ancestor to those subsequent generations of scholars who have analyzed the complex architectures of Kerouac's work in minute detail.[51]

Although Tallman's essay certainly ran counter to the majority of literary critics writing during the Beatnik Era, he was not entirely alone in his more sympathetic treatment. *Wagner Literary Magazine* was a student-run publication at Wagner College, a small liberal arts institution on Staten Island. Despite its limited reach, *Wagner Literary Magazine* is of interest for our purposes because in 1959 the editors had managed to convince a range of luminaries to respond to "some typical writings of the leading Beat poets (Ginsberg, Corso, and Peter Orlovsky)," and printed these responses together with work by the three poets as well as reflective essays by Wagner students.[52] There was brief commentary from the likes of *Partisan Review* editor Philip Rahv ("the stuff seems pretty vacuous to me" [20]), theologian Paul Tillich ("I think it is valuable insofar as it enriches the possibilities for more organic forms of expression" [20]), literary critics Marius Bewley ("as a movement, 'beat' poetry belongs to the history of publicity, not of literature" [20]) and Lionel Trilling ("I have no admiration for 'beat' literature" [23]), poet Robert Lowell ("I've read nothing by the beats *remotely* comparable in genius and intelligence to say, Salinger, Mary McCarthy and Flannery O'Connor in prose, to Jarrell, Shapiro and Elizabeth Bishop in poetry" [24]), and Norman Mailer, who directed the students to his own essays, especially "The White Negro." In addition to these thoughts, there are also comments by Marianne Moore, William Carlos Williams, e. e. cummings, and others that are generally positive – as well as a rambling "reply" by Corso, Ginsberg, and Orlovsky.[53] Although the respondents are hardly uniformly enamored of Beat writing, their commentary is much more measured and nuanced than what one encountered in *Life* or *Time*. When read together, then, the commentary in the *Wagner Literary Magazine* symposium represents an early example of critical response that was, like Aronowitz's *Post* series, more willing to take the Beats seriously as writers, even if the final assessment of this writing was conflicted (the symposium even earned the "Wagner College literary circle" a cameo in *The Hipsters* [1961], Ted Joans's bizarre, collage-like appraisal of the Beat Scene).[54]

CHAPTER 7

Little Magazines and Subterranean Networks

From about 1958 to 1962, third-party accounts of the Beats, whether positive or negative, tended to focus on those in the immediate orbit of Kerouac and Ginsberg, even while the literary movement associated with them was widening to encompass a greater diversity of texts and figures. Thus when we retrospectively discuss the literary movement that flourished during these years, it is imperative to recognize not merely writers who were personally close to Kerouac and Ginsberg or self-identified as Beat, but also those participating in and contributing to a phenomenon that encompassed aesthetic and ideological affinities as well as social ones. In fact, while the media-constructed version of the Beatnik was powerful enough that I'm calling these years the "Beatnik Era," there is an important counternarrative about how a Beat sensibility cohered not only around nationally visible books such as *On the Road* or *Howl and Other Poems*, but also in the pages of little magazines and in the publications of small independent presses. As much as the Beatnik caricature dominated popular imagination in the late 1950s, these years were also the dawn of the mimeographic revolution, when it became feasible to publish broadsides, chapbooks, and literary magazines on shoestring budgets, arranging layouts on kitchen tables with the help of friends. Rather than being habitually faced with rejection from mainstream venues, by the latter part of the decade, Beats and Beat associates founded their own literary magazines and small presses, the proliferation of which helped place their work before ever greater audiences. Little magazines were often the first venues in which many Beat writers were published, and looking at them from issue to issue, journal to journal, we discover the tissue of the late 1950s literary underground: not only the visions of individual works, but also a sustained cross talk among editors, readers, and writers that exemplifies the emergence of a new sensibility.

7.1   LeRoi and Hettie Jones, *Yugen,* and the New Consciousness

The most important and consistently high-quality Beat-associated little magazine from this period was founded by LeRoi and Hettie Jones on the Lower East Side in the spring of 1958. They called the magazine *Yugen: A New Consciousness in Arts and Letters,* and it ran for eight issues until 1962. The name means "elegance, beauty, grace, transcendence of these things, and also nothing at all," and the "new consciousness" of the subtitle was intended to repudiate what the Joneses considered the stale aesthetic of venues like the *Partisan Review,* where Hettie was working as a subscription manager, much to the amusement of her bohemian circle. *Yugen* 1 was in fact published at the same time as Podhoretz's "The Know-Nothing Bohemians," and over its life, the magazine would go on to champion everything that Podhoretz had lambasted. In her later memoir, Hettie explicitly opposed *Yugen*'s sensibility to that of the New Critics, whom she figures as a kind of aesthetic judicial system: "I imagined the nine letters of N.e.w. C.r.i.t.i.c. as the nine Supreme Court justices, presiding over all that was robed and respectable.... Where was the guide to my situation, cultural or political – where was my life in these pages [of the *Partisan Review*]?"[1] Her husband LeRoi, for his part, recalled that he had been motivated to start a different kind of literary magazine because he "was getting beat over the head with New Criticism."[2]

The Joneses didn't set out to create an exclusively Beat magazine, but rather to reflect and promote a new sensibility that bridled against not only middle-class American values, but also the aesthetic norms of the New Criticism. Of course, there were many possible routes to such a critique of normative cultural and aesthetic values, but as Hettie describes in her memoir, that moment in the Village was dominated by "the 'Beats' – ambiguous enough to include anyone" (45). After the publication of *Howl and Other Poems,* LeRoi had written to Ginsberg in Paris to see if Ginsberg was "for real" and to announce a plan to launch a literary magazine. Ginsberg replied favorably and suggested writers for the project, including those who were not in New York at the time, such as Philip Whalen, Gary Snyder, and Corso. The Joneses were also active at readings and other events in New York and so were well positioned to represent the broad strokes of a "new consciousness" in the pages of *Yugen.*[3] By 1959, Ginsberg thought that *Yugen* was "the best avant-garde poetry magazine in the country," and in 1960, Burroughs praised it as a "no-paying far-out" magazine.[4] In the first year of *Yugen*'s run, Corso would remark to Paul Blackburn that "when I write a poem ... I send it to friends, Don Allen of

Grove, or Wieners of *Measure* or *Yugen* but never to non-friends or connections," and to Diane di Prima that the magazine "indicates an awakening rose."[5] Corso felt among friends at *Yugen* because over its eight issues, it tended to publish again and again writers who shared his basic anti-establishment sensibility, and who, not incidentally, would later populate anthologies of Beat writing: Ginsberg, Snyder, Michael McClure, Kerouac, Corso, Whalen, Ray Bremser, and di Prima, among others (di Prima in fact frequently assisted in the production of the magazine).

By 1960, midway through *Yugen*'s life, the magazine's Beat sensibility was so pronounced that an interviewer asked LeRoi Jones why it seemed to be a "clique" magazine that "publishes a fairly restricted group of so-called 'Beat,' 'San Francisco,' and 'New York' writers." Jones responded that he and Hettie were not interested in labels so much as individual writers who were productively exploiting new themes and techniques:

> If it turns out to be a coterie – well, it turns out to be that way.... The writers I publish are really not all "Beat" or "San Francisco" or "New York." There are various people who could also fit into other groups – for instance, the people who went to Black Mountain College – and others not affiliated with any real group. But they have some kind of affinity with the other so-called groups – their writing fits into a certain kind of broad category.[6]

Jones's response is typical of many Beat-associated writers who were generally reluctant to affiliate themselves definitively with the Beat or any other literary movement. Jones likewise resists group labels, but does finally conclude that taken together, the writing in *Yugen* does share particular characteristics, that it "fits into a certain kind of broad category." Hettie echoes this assessment retrospectively, insisting on the dialogue among "so-called" Beats and other writers:

> From a quick first look at *Yugen 4* you'd say Beat, as the three Beat gurus – Kerouac, Corso, and Ginsberg – were represented. Except the "new consciousness in arts and letters" was more inclusive. Like Basil King, Joel Oppenheimer, and Fielding Dawson, the poets Robert Creeley, John Wieners, and Charles Olson were out of Black Mountain College, where Olson was the last rector. Frank O'Hara, like the painters he knew, was a poet of the "New York School." Gilbert Sorrentino lived in Brooklyn, Gary Snyder in Japan, Ray Bremser in a Trenton, New Jersey, prison (*How I Became*, 74)

So although literary and cultural critics have retroactively applied the label "Beat" to *Yugen*, seemingly affixing its meaning in place, it is useful to reiterate that it was never the case that the Beats were like the Masons, with initiations and tiered memberships: beyond the "inner circle," it was always a loose affiliation, an unofficial network easier seen in hindsight. If by the mid-1970s critic Jim Burns could note that "*Yugen* was an archetypal publication of the beat years" and in 2000 Barry Miles could claim, "Suddenly LeRoi was at the center of Beat Generation small-press publishing and . . . *Yugen* . . . became one of the most influential of all Beat periodicals," in the late 1950s, the Joneses were focused on capturing what Hettie later called "the new consciousness that everyone downtown agreed was just what the world needed" – "everyone downtown" of course being the bohemian set mixed with the Beat characters, but also the New York School poets, and those associated with the lately defunct Black Mountain College.[7] In the context of a literary history of the Beats, it is useful to think about the eight issues of *Yugen* as an aesthetic project comprised of its constituent poems and prose pieces that did not so much *reflect* a Beat sensibility but that rather helped *shape* exactly what such a sensibility might be. Indeed, one thing we find when looking at *Yugen* from above is that there was much more cross talk and fluidity among these seemingly disparate groups or movements than the retroactive cordoning of them into discrete schools would suggest.

Despite the fact that *Yugen* did not limit itself to self-identified Beats, it is true the Joneses did publish a relatively small "clique" of writers, and one of the magazine's distinguishing characteristics is that some of the work published refers to the other writers in this clique in the same kind of intimate and oblique ways we saw in earlier work by Holmes, Burroughs, Ginsberg, and Kerouac. The second poem printed in *Yugen*, for example, Philip Whalen's "Takeout, 4: ii: 58" (meaning it is a poem about February 4, 1958), includes the parenthetical line: "(Olson, in conversation, 'That wall, it has / to be there!')."[8] Likewise in *Yugen* 3, Whalen's poem "Soufflé" describes an incident in Berkeley in 1957: "I drank myself into a crying jag face down / On Ginsberg's woolly green rug / Roaring, 'Gone, everything gone,' . . . The Messers. Ginsberg & Kerouac, also juiced / Wrapped me in blankets while I froze & squalled."[9] In these two examples, we have a so-called San Francisco poet referring to his close association with a so-called Black Mountain poet (Olson), as well as his intimate relationships with the Beat inner circle (Ginsberg and Kerouac). Writing of the appearance of Whalen's "Soufflé," critic R. J. Ellis notes that in *Yugen* "a certain Beat-oriented introspectiveness did emerge, itself a sign of the Beats' embrace of confessional exposure. The autobiographical centre of . . . 'Soufflé' . . . substantially depends upon the reader's ability to recognize its protagonists as Ginsberg and Kerouac."[10] Given Ginsberg's and Kerouac's notoriety by 1958, and the fact that they are named in the poem, "Soufflé" depends not so much on a reader's ability to recognize these figures, but rather on advertising Whalen's links to the Beats, so the confessional, autobiographical poem about drinking too much takes on another layer of literary texture because it has unfolded in the presence of these countercultural stars.

This is similarly the case in Gary Snyder's poem "On Vulture Peak," which includes the line: "J.K. & me sitting naked and sandy / At McClure Beach steaming mussels."[11] In this poem, the intimacy the speaker shares with J.K. "sitting naked and sandy" is extended to the reader who recognizes these initials as Jack Kerouac's, so as is the case with the oblique references to Neal Cassady in "Howl" ("N.C., secret hero of these poems"), Snyder demonstrates his connections to the Beat inner circle, likewise inviting readers who recognize "J.K." to also feel as though they themselves are peering into this circle. More oblique is a poem like Diane di Prima's "The Lovers," which alludes to her affair with married LeRoi Jones; after discussing the unnamed man's desire to raise the "stakes" of "poetry," the speaker asks: "why lie to me I'm not your wife."[12] Di Prima would later imply that work like "The Lovers" represented an extended conversation between herself and *Yugen*'s co-editor: "LeRoi and I began a dialogue – often painful – in our poems that went on for many years.... And parts of that dialogue found their way into the issues of *Yugen* that we pasted up together."[13] Although only an intimate of Jones or di Prima could recognize the figures in this poem, it exhibits its interest in confessionalism through communal connection found throughout *Yugen*'s pages.

As these examples from Whalen, Snyder, and di Prima may suggest, throughout *Yugen*'s run, one can locate poetry that refers to a relatively small clique of other writers, some virtually unknown to readers beyond intimate circles in New York City or San Francisco, others so famous by the late 1950s that the mere initials "J.K." would send a tingle of recognition through the spine of even quasi-hip lovers of the new literature. But as *Yugen* expanded from twenty-five pages in its first issue to more than sixty in its last, the writers who turn up multiple times (Ginsberg, Corso, Kerouac, O'Hara, McClure, Sorrentino) became more identifiable as a group, if not simply as "Beat writers," then as counterexamples to what LeRoi Jones called in *Yugen*'s pages the "simplemindedness &/or immaturity of the official literary hierarchy."[14] By these later issues, *Yugen*'s "new consciousness" was more explicitly framed as a reaction to and attack on what the editors perceived as a university-centered "literary hierarchy" that dismissed writing hostile to academic, broadly New Critical norms.

Rebukes of New Critical norms are found throughout the pages of *Yugen*, as for example in Michael McClure's important poem "Rant

Block," which oscillates between seemingly earnest, block-lettered declarations on the nature of form and language, and the poet's comic, idiosyncratic struggles to relate to others. Pugnaciously critical of conventional wisdom on proper poetic form, McClure writes:

THERE IS NO FORM BUT SHAPE! NO LOGIC BUT SEQUENCE!
· · ·
FORM IS AN EVASION! POETRY
A PATTERN TO BE FILLED BY FAGGOTS
· · ·
all of this is ugliness and talk not freedom
OH SHIT HELL FUCK THAT WE ARE BLOCKED
in striving by what we hate
surrounding us. And do not break it in our strike
at it. The part of us
so trained to live in filth and never stir.
THAT I WAIT FOR YOU TO RAISE YOUR HAND FIRST
(to me)
This is sickness. This is what
I hate within
Myself. This
Is the war I battle in. This neverending instant.
· · ·
Never let them stand stemmed by form again. Let
my face be radiant and give off light!
Never allow sign of love where hatred dwells!
If there are bastions, let my love be walls![15]

A poem about the limitation of poetic "form," "Rant Block" enacts, often humorously, the poet bumping up against such norms of literariness as he attempts to express himself honestly. McClure accuses "form" and "pattern" – those mainstays of academic poetry – as impinging on questions of "freedom."

Looking back on his career in the early 1980s, McClure called "Rant Block" his "breakthrough" poem because it explores the concept of "shape" as a counterpoint to form, and in the poem he realized that attention to shape allowed him to write a poem that could function like an organic expression of his own body: "I saw the Bulk, and the Bulk is the Body of what we are and what we strive for ... I felt that our lives were lines of synaptic stars – literally – and it seemed *that* simple – and it is – and *that* brutal. It is life, not beauty, that we are after, for if there is beauty (and we do live in beauty) it is our perceptions raining lightning upon our fleshly pads that is glorious" (ellipses and emphasis in original).[16] For McClure, as for many contributors to *Yugen*, the enemy is staid form; as he pleads, "Never let them stand stemmed by form again." He explores not only the power of our perceptions but also how the strictures of language limit one's ability to communicate with others. Hence the final declaration quoted above amounts to an assault on human experience articulated through form and pattern – that is, through conventional poetry – and he offers instead love, part of what he later called the "living bio-alchemical organism" of the shape of the poet's life made manifest through language, as a bulwark against meaninglessness (*Scratching*, 89).

Pointed confrontations between academic poetry and the new consciousness reverberate throughout the pages of *Yugen*, manifest not only in the prose and poetry of the kind discussed in the preceding pages, but also in the advertisements and other ephemera that French literary theorist Gerard Genette called "paratext." Recognizing such dimensions of *Yugen* itself is helpful in understanding the work in its pages in its cultural and literary moment, and attending to these dimensions reinforces the sensibility or "vibe" of the magazine as a whole. In *Yugen* 5, for example, one finds a biting visual art piece that echoes the opposition between the two literary circles that intensified as the magazine developed, as shown in Figure 7.1.

This image is a playful attack on the poetic tradition approved by New Critic Cleanth Brooks. The image repurposes an old advertisement for Brooke's "Monkey Brand" soap, and recontextualizes the motto "ALWAYS READ DIRECTIONS" and the drawing of a monkey gazing at his own reflection in a hand mirror. The implications are hard to miss, especially when we recall the pervasiveness of Brooks and Warren's *Understanding Poetry* in providing "directions" for good poetry.[17] Beneath this picture, the editors promise to award Hafaz Fellowships – half-assed fellowships – to the University Poet crowd, including W. D. Snodgrass (winner of the 1960 Pulitzer Prize for his first poetry collection, *Heart's Needle* [1959]), Alfred Alvarez (then poetry editor at *The Observer*), Norman Podhoretz (who had of course recently published "The Know-Nothing Bohemians"), and Truman Capote, who had just sneered on the television program *Open End* that "None of these people [the "Beat Generation"] have anything interesting to say and none of them can write."[18] If the *Yugen* clique was not exclusively made up of Beat writers, then one way to define such a clique would be as whatever was not connected to Brooks, Warren, the University Poets, or to those respectable little reviews that tended to publish them such as the *Partisan Review*, *Hudson Review*, or *Sewanee Review*, magazines *Yugen*'s editors had elsewhere collapsed into a conglomerate journal called "Parhudnee Review," depicted as worshipping the monolith of tradition.

HAFAZ FELLOWSHIPS
(for outstanding achievement in 19th-century English verse)
to Wm. Meridith, John Hollander, Pack-Simpson & co., Stan Kunitz, May
Swenson, W. D. Snodgrass, David Galler & all the professors who've ever waxed
(& for outstanding work in psycholeptic criticism)
Alfred Alvarez, Norman Podhoretz
(and for staying as sweet as he is)
Truman Capote

Figure 7.1   Fun with New Criticism: a duded-up monkey represents those "hafaz"
(half-assed) poets who merely perform old conventions from nineteenth-century poetry.
From *Yugen* 5 (1959): 13.
Image courtesy of Princeton University Library

This assault takes a different form in another aspect of *Yugen* that one would notice if one paged through entire issues: its advertisements for books or other magazines. The prominent and recurring ads for periodicals like *Evergreen Review* and *Big Table* demonstrated to *Yugen*'s readers what they should track down if they wanted to deepen their readings of hip or underground literature. Much of the paratextual material in *Yugen* in fact functions as training manuals for those interested in becoming hip readers: having gone from the poetry and prose of a relatively small clique of writers in *Yugen*'s pages, readers could then look to the advice from the editors on where to go next.

To cite just one example of such advice, consider the "Addenda" to *Yugen* 6, as shown in Figure 7.2. This dense chunk of information, so detailed that it even provides mailing addresses for purchasing harder-to-find titles, is set over another, smaller cartoon of Brooke's Monkey Brand Soap, so the motto "A NEW DAY COMING" again pointedly refers to the day when the Brooks-style New Critical norms may no longer reign. Although at bottom a bibliography, this addendum still adopts a chatty tone that seems to give readers access to insider information, not only

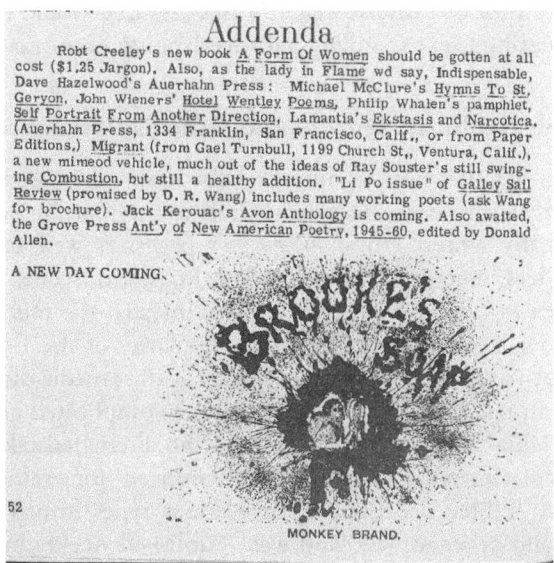

Figure 7.2 "Addenda" to *Yugen* 6: Subterranean networking in action. Note the reference to "Brooke's Soap," which pits this network against New Critical norms. Kerouac's planned *Avon Anthology* of Beat writing never materialized. From *Yugen* 6 (1960): 52.
Image courtesy of Princeton University Library

through private jokes ("as the lady in *Flame* wd say" refers to Lilith Lorraine, pseudonym for Mary M. Wright, who published the avant-garde little magazine *Flame* from 1954 to 1963), but also through reference to works that hadn't yet appeared in print. Just as Robert Creeley's latest work ought to be "gotten at all cost," the editors are eager to promote the Auerhahn Press – which, like the Joneses' own Totem Press, was invested in publishing the Beat-associated writers frequently found in *Yugen* (I discuss Auerhahn in more detail later). The editors likewise point readers to Allen's *The New American Poetry* and the volume Kerouac had planned but never completed, *The Avon Anthology of Beat Literature*. The "Addenda" amounts to a digest of the latest books that the hip or aspiring hip ought to own; sustaining the label "Beat" becomes less important than recognizing particular styles or sensibilities.

In the realm of little magazines, then, *Yugen* deserves special recognition as an influential Beat publication of the Beatnik Era. Although earlier publications such as *Neurotica* or *Ark II Moby I* had significant Beat energies, *Yugen* was the first informed by and invested in promoting a Beat sensibility – with all the qualifications about cross talk among other so-called literary "groups" described in the foregoing pages – and it set the stage for other Beat or Beat-associated magazines that would be absolutely crucial in fostering ever-expanding and overlapping networks of writers.

7.2   Bob Kaufman, *Beatitude*, and the San Francisco Scene

While *Yugen* was the most significant boot-strapped magazine based in New York City at this time, *Beatitude* was its counterpart in San Francisco, publishing many writers found in *Yugen*'s pages, as well as a clique of others who had emerged from the San Francisco scene. Named for Kerouac's idea in *On the Road* that "BEAT [means] the root, the soul of Beatific" (195), *Beatitude* traded on the popularity of the Beat phenomenon circa 1959 and self-consciously set itself against media distortions and Beatnik caricatures. Editorship of *Beatitude* is a complicated question, as it was the brainchild of a number of people who alternated taking the lead editing particular issues. The first issue announced, for example, that the magazine was "Edited cooperatively by various types from Grant Street, Mill Valley, and other scenes," and was "Published weekly by John Kelly from offices at 14 Bannam Alley San Francisco 11, California."[19] Poet John Kelly is indeed listed as editor of the first few issues, but there was from the inception strong editorial guidance from others, notably poets Bob Kaufman and William J. Margolis.[20] Note, for example, the photograph

Figure 7.3   This photograph appeared in *Beatitude* 29 (1979) with the caption: "First printing of Beatitude magazine at the Bread and Wine Mission, Greenwich and Grant Ave. S.F. April 1959. L to R Bill Margolis, Eileen & Bob Kaufman."
Image courtesy of Princeton University Library

in Figure 7.3 shows the first printing of *Beatitude* presided over by Margolis and Bob and Eileen Kaufman.

Printed in runs of about 1,000, *Beatitude* was published weekly from issues 1 to 5 (May 9 to June 6, 1959), and then appeared about once a month for the next year (issues 6–15 [June 17, 1960]). Two more issues were produced, 16 (September–October 1960) and 17 (October–November 1960), which were the last ones printed until 1966; after this time it was revived sporadically by different editors.[21] By issue 8 (August 15, 1959), *Beatitude* was headquartered at the Bread & Wine Mission, a hangout for Beat scenesters, what Pierre Delattre called "a place for the North Beach 'beatnik' community to gather in search of the moral and spiritual dimension of their art," where crowds would come to get fed, "sit on [the] floor, listen to music and poetry, drum, but mostly just to talk."[22] With issue 8, *Beatitude* also carried an affiliation with City Lights Books, which printed issue 17, the last of the initial 1959–1960 run.

Over the course of its first run from 1959 to 1960, *Beatitude* published many significant Beat writers, including Bob Kaufman, Corso, Ferlinghetti, Ginsberg, Lenore Kandel, Kerouac, Sheri Martinelli, McClure, Orlovsky, Whalen, and ruth weiss. In addition to these writers, the magazine frequently printed the work of the "young reinforcements," a clique of Beat associates based in San Francisco, but not as widely known outside the underground literary culture there and seldom discussed today; of these people, I would single out C. V. J. Anderson, William J. Margolis, and Pierre Delattre as deserving of further critical attention.[23] In addition to the work itself, *Beatitude* is notable for the strong sense of community it exuded – by this I mean it read as a kind of literary newsletter dispatched from the bohemian streets of San Francisco. As John Kelly put it in the "Publisher's Letter" prefacing the second issue, "The overwhelming response to our magazine and the flood of poems coming into our office has made us realize that there are very likely more poets per square foot here in North Beach than anywhere else in the world. It looks as if San Francisco had become de facto the poetry center of the human race."[24]

Given that North Beach had by 1959 long been an object of touristic fascination, it is perhaps unsurprising that as the "official" organ of the "poetry center of the human race," *Beatitude* should want to define itself on its own terms, against the media caricatures of the Beatnik already rampant. It did this by consistently publishing both work by Ginsberg and other well-known names of the Beat movement, as well as work that thematizes the scene or the movement directly, either deflating stereotypes or exploring Beat networks from sympathetic perspectives. Thus when the title page announced that it was to be "A weekly miscellany of poetry and other jazz designed to extol beauty and promote the beatific or poetic life," it did so to promote its own version of this beatific life in contrast to what was presented in venues like *Life* magazine.[25]

The first issue announced its bona fides by opening with Ginsberg's "Hymn from Kaddish" and two poems by Kaufman, but a striking amount of work in that issue concerned the scene itself, "the beatific or poetic life" described in the magazine's mission statement. For example, Margolis's "Poem to My Self – But I'll Clue You In, Too," plays with figurations of that "life" as the caricatured Beatnik scene; it begins: "Like, what's happening, man? / Is the fuzz hassling the scene?" From there, the poem goes on to indulge in further clichéd lines such as, "Is there a fine & fresh / chick who knows the scene," and ends with the stanza:

> Like, why is this scene
> in Cassandra's
>   the Gallery
>   the Place
> all these temples
> of the fragile seekers –
> why is this scene so hopeless?[26]

As is the case in work by more recognizable poets such as Ted Joans or Diane di Prima, Margolis draws on cartoon Beat slang ("Like, what's happening, man?") not to offer insider access to this world but to mock those who think such language could possibly mark insider access. Margolis's poem suggests that *Beatitude* is addressing itself to an audience who already knows and mocks such suppositions, who can see that the poem appears to use slang as a "straight" reflection of a Beat sensibility, when it fact it is an ironic performance of square assumptions about the Beatnik. When Margolis name checks all the cool places, he does so to acknowledge their cachet but then disavow it, so they are figured not as hotspots to experience the authentic "scene," but false "temples" for gawkers of the hip.[27]

This posture is present all over *Beatitude* 1 in work such as Mark Green's "A Night in the Coffee Gallery," a poem about a place filled with "Friends repeating the same words each drunken time," which concludes, "Make the scene / but, the scene is bugging." In "A Reason," Carol Mann likewise follows a local character "making the Mission scene"; and Pierre Delattre, a locally famous North Beach personality, offers a portrait of a "Woman in a Bohemian Bar" staring "at fragments, / Torn posters, scratched out / Sexual hints, disconnected numbers." Such work exists in a precarious tension with popular distortions of their authors' lives and writing: as much as these poems mock or disavow Beatnik caricatures, there is abiding insistence that such an underground scene does exist, but that it is a moving target difficult or impossible to characterize in its fullness.

Beyond the first issue, readers of *Beatitude* encountered recurring meditations on the "Beat Generation," work that usually argued that it was passé, misguided, or simply didn't exist at all. True to *Beatitude*'s communal spirit, such work was often sourced from local, unknown poets or even from anonymous notes that had been left around town, and frets over the act of labeling or categorizing a movement as such. In a poem "to sociologists & publicists of the beat generation," for example, a person signed only as "joy" argues that writing about "the beat" necessarily misses the point: "these things are lived / not sociologized," and the greatest folly is to "try to explain the beat / or utmost: hip / in academic words."[28] In "Beat Congo," two poets signed "francine & alice / gruesome twosome" cheekily announce: "I lost religion, I made the big decision / I joined with the rebels in a mood of inhibition."[29] *Beatitude* 15 featured an "open letter to the beats from a spy deep in enemy territory," which, as the editors noted, "was found tacked to the wall at City Lights" (20). The poem takes the Beats to task for assuming a zero-sum choice in life: "you can / be a factory slave office zombie suburbanite / OR a hip free brother ragpicker," and goes on to assert that there is a middle way, that one could have a job and then rail against society from a position of comfort.[30] The piece evidently struck a chord with the editors, who responded with a call for dialogue: "We hope the author will eventually step forth and accept responsibility for his words. We also hope someone else will choose to argue with the author. The pages of BEATITUDE are open for such an argument" (20). As these and other examples suggest, *Beatitude* was not only a venue for Beat writing, but a forum for working through the very notions of Beatness, something that was often done more explicitly than in *Yugen*, largely because North Beach had by then become ground zero for the Beatnik lifestyle in popular imagination. Consider, for example, the playful cover of *Yugen* 7 (Figure 7.4), which spells out "Beetitood" the way a caricatured hipster might say it, and whose "Bored of Directours" is comprised of twisted allusions to Ginsberg ("A. Ginsboig"), Kerouac ("J. Korewax"), and Orlovsky ("P. Onoroffkey"), among others. Note that the motto in the upper right above the drawing of the hepcat reads: "zmoke Beetituud it tastes like an Abomunist shoed."

While such engagements with the meaning of the Beat Generation and its distinctions from the Beatniks offer intriguing snapshots of a moment, *Beatitude* is notable in terms of literary history for the richer work it showcased. Of this work, some of the most enduring was produced by Bob Kaufman, one of the three most significant African American Beat writers (with Ted Joans and LeRoi Jones), a fixture on the North Beach bohemian scene, and a founding editor of *Beatitude*. As critic Maria Damon put it in her introduction to a 2002 issue of *Callaloo* devoted to Kaufman, he was "one of the founding architects and living examples of the sensibility of the Beat Generation, a counter-cultural phenomenon of the Cold War which attempted to embody dissent from the tyranny of consensus in its artistic and everyday practice."[31] Damon notes also that Kaufman has been overshadowed by his contemporaries, a fact that does indeed have to do with race, as she suggests, as well as with Kaufman's lack of interest in self-promotion, and in his position as a "street poet" working in the oral tradition. Writing for that issue of *Callaloo*, Aldon Lynn Nielsen has observed that "African-American writing was erased from the public history of the Beats even as the Beats themselves loudly and persistently proclaimed the centrality of black culture to their lives and works."[32] Following the work of Damon, Nielsen, and others, I want to turn to some of Kaufman's writing to underscore his importance as a progenitor of the San Franciscan Beat sensibility.

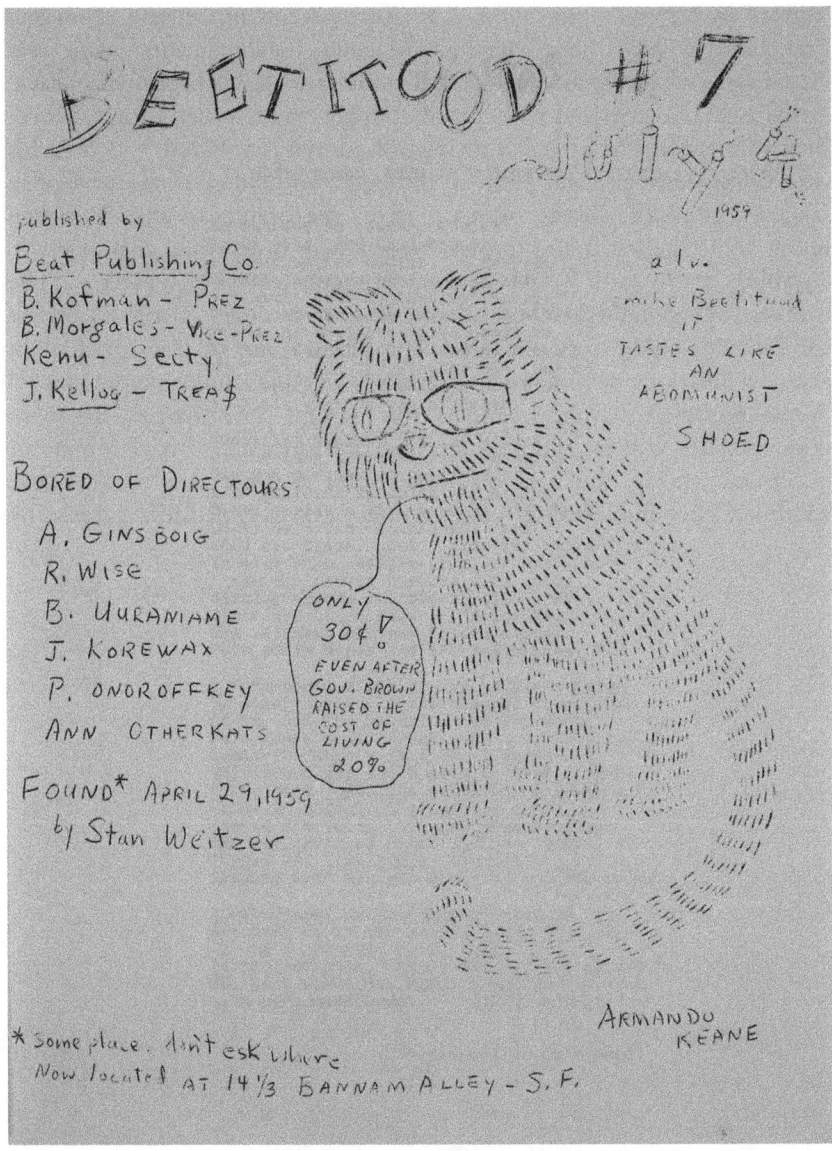

Figure 7.4   Cover for *Beatitude* 7 (July 4, 1959), spelled out in the way a caricatured hipster might say it: "Beetitood."
Image courtesy of Princeton University Library

Born in New Orleans in 1925, Kaufman eventually wound up in San Francisco (by way of the Merchant Marines, bohemian New York, and elsewhere), where he had achieved by the late 1950s near-mythological status as an oral poet and master extemporizer, the so-called King of North Beach (for a Sheri Martinelli drawing of Kaufman, see Figure 7.5).[33] As his wife Eileen later recalled, "Bob would begin to hold court in the Coffee Gallery [in North Beach] about 7:30 in the evenings, and for several hours while the locals and tourists bought him beer, wine, champagne – anything, he, in turn, would speak spontaneously on any subject.... The tourists were delighted to buy . . . anything we wanted – just to be part of the Life emanating from our table. The Life was, for the most part, Bob, and his hilarious monologues, sparkling wit and funky comments."[34] While Kaufman became legendary for his oral performances, his work does translate well on the page, and we are fortunate to have a body of published writing, much of it appearing for the first time in *Beatitude*. Kaufman later published in other venues such as broadsides printed by

Figure 7.5   Sheri Martinelli's drawing of Bob Kaufman, from *Anagogic & Paideumic Review*. The caption reads, "Sanctus Sandalium Bomkoff / Sandal footed Saint Bomkoff," a reference to the caricature of the Beatnik supposedly embodied by Kaufman. In fact, he existed in ironic tension with such a caricature.
Image courtesy of Beinecke Rare Book and Manuscript Library, Yale University

City Lights Books – "Abomunist Manifesto" (1959), "Second April" (1959), and "Does the Secret Mind Whisper?" (1960) – as well as in the three poetry collections released during his lifetime, *Solitudes Crowded with Loneliness* (1965), *Golden Sardine* (1967), and *The Ancient Rain, Poems 1956–1978* (1981).[35] On the strength of this work, Kaufman is now recognized as a significant Beat writer, and in the decades after his heyday in North Beach, his reputation has only grown among his peers; as Ted Joans put it in a tribute poem in 1979: "Once if I remember Kerouacian / Epoch well, we all drank from / Kaufman's hip hot Bop word well."[36]

In terms of the Beat context, Kaufman's most important work is "Abomunist Manifesto," first published in pieces in *Beatitude*, then as a City Lights broadside, then in *Solitudes Crowded with Loneliness*. "Abomunist Manifesto" is a central text of the Beat movement, and was prominent enough even in Squaresville that *Life* had named it an essential feature of the Beatnik's pad in that notorious November 1959 story discussed earlier. True to its title, "Abomunist Manifesto" announces itself as a creed of something called Abomunism, a surreal, Dadaesque anti-political, anti-social, political and social position. There are disparate parts and addenda to the work, including "Notes" and "Lexicon" entries, and although contemporary readers must now come to them as part of a finished whole, for those first encountering it in 1959, a key characteristic of what we now call the "Abomunist Manifesto" was that it appeared in fragments across many issues of *Beatitude*. The first issues of *Beatitude* were in fact all framed by parts of "Abomunist Manifesto," and they typically appeared on the last page or endpaper as the final word of a given issue. Unlike other work in the issue – including other poems by Kaufman – these fragments didn't necessarily present themselves as poetry, but rather as supporting documents pertaining to a philosophy or way of life, and were of a piece with the communal ethos of the magazine.

For example, *Beatitude* 1 ends with declarative excerpts from "Abomunist Manifesto" such as "ABOMUNISTS REJECT EVERYTHING EXCEPT SNOWMEN" (n.p.), a teasing, surrealist anti-stance that stretched into the second issue and beyond. The last piece in *Beatitude* 2 is "Notes Dis- and Re- Garding Abomunism" by Bomkauf (one of Kaufman's pen names), which informs readers that they can be Abomunist "By telling psychometric poets two heads are better than none," "By calling taxis dirty names, while ordering fifths of milk," "By using real names at false hotels," and other Dadaesque acts.[37] Such statements don't so much set out to "define" what Abomunism is but to pretend it is a widely practiced or at least widely known phenomenon, and takes readers into lexical playfields where words seemed loosed from their denotative moorings, a prerequisite for Abomunism. The fragmentary approach continues in *Beatitude* 3, which closes with "Further Notes Dis- and Re- Garding Abomunism" and a sampling of "Abomunus Craxioms":

> Egyptian mummies are lousy dancers.
>> Alcoholics cannot make it on root beer.
> Jazz never made it back down the river.
>> Licking postage stamps depletes the body fluids.
> Fat automobiles laugh more than others, and frink.

Is this poetry? Are they hip axioms? Are they nonsense statements, as they seem at first blush? Looking over them again, we may realize that it is in fact technically true that "mummies are lousy dancers" or that alcoholics crave alcohol, and so may then wonder about the implications of these statements, perhaps something about the drawbacks of being wound too tightly or, in the case of the third line, about appropriations of African American art forms. While it may not be finally clear what such lines "mean," their presence in *Beatitude* – and in the wider Beat movement – suggest they are pieces of an attitude, a pose of refusal that extends even to logic or semantic regularity (which is also why Abomunism required new language such as "frink," discussed below).

Given that "Abomunist Manifesto" appeared weekly in *Beatitude*, then as inexpensive broadsides, it makes sense to read it as a text that circulated communally. John Kelly teasingly suggested that a "movement" even cohered around Abomunism, which he saw as something beyond the text itself; as he put it in the "Publisher's Letter" prefacing *Beatitude* 3, "The ABOMUNIST MOVEMENT, as far as I can dig it, is a PLOT on the part of poets to change society. Doctors scientists engineers and other groups have started movements to run things their way. Why shouldn't poets?"[38] In this view, Kaufman's work becomes the "official" manifesto of those literary types who want to "change society," and as such is an absurdist descendent of earlier manifestos from San Francisco such as the anarcho-pacifist statement that opened the little magazine *The Ark* in 1947. Akin in spirit to Frank O'Hara's more contemporaneous piece, "Personism: a Manifesto," the "Abomunist Manifesto" is best understood as a tongue-in-cheek declaration of the aims and values of countercultural communities – whether Abomunist or Beat – and like any good satire, it conceals serious aims.

Obviously suggesting a coy connection with communism, the creeping menace of Cold War American culture, the "Abomunist Manifesto" does not provide a rational theory as *The Communist Manifesto* does, but instead asserts a series of pointedly irrational declarations that imply an ethos:

ABOMUNISTS JOIN NOTHING BUT THEIR HANDS OR LEGS, OR
OTHER SAME.
ABOMUNISTS SPIT ANTI-POETRY FOR POETIC REASONS AND
FRINK.
ABOMUNISTS DO NOT LOOK AT PICTURES PAINTED BY
PRESIDENTS AND UNEMPLOYED PRIME MINISTERS.
IN TIMES OF NATIONAL PERIL, ABOMUNISTS, AS REALITY
AMERICANS, STAND READY TO DRINK THEMSELVES TO DEATH
FOR THEIR COUNTRY.
ABOMUNISTS DO NOT FEEL PAIN, NO MATTER HOW MUCH IT
HURTS.
ABOMUNISTS DO NOT USE THE WORD SQUARE EXCEPT WHEN
TALKING TO SQUARES.
ABOMUNISTS READ NEWSPAPERS ONLY TO ASCERTAIN THEIR
ABOMINUBILITY.
ABOMUNISTS NEVER CARRY MORE THAN FIFTY DOLLARS IN
DEBTS ON THEM.
. . .
ABOMUNIST POETS, CONFIDENT THAT THE NEW LITERARY
FORM "FOOT-PRINTISM" HAS FREED THE ARTIST OF
OUTMODED RESTRICTIONS, SUCH AS: THE ABILITY TO READ
AND WRITE, OR THE DESIRE TO COMMUNICATE, MUST BE
PREPARED TO READ THEIR WORK AT DENTAL COLLEGES,
EMBALMING SCHOOLS, HOMES FOR UNWED MOTHERS,
HOMES FOR WED MOTHERS, INSANE ASYLUMS, USO CANTEENS,
KINDERGARTENS, AND COUNTY JAILS. ABOMUNISTS NEVER
COMPROMISE THEIR REJECTIONARY PHILOSOPHY.[39]

Like some other work in *Beatitude* already discussed, this is deft play between what Kaufman thinks of those on the scene and the perceptions and stereotypes accorded those people from outside, by tourists or reporters. If there is a through-line in these statements, it is refusal, Kaufman's version of Rexroth's idea of "disaffiliation." The first line states that Abomunists "JOIN NOTHING" and so cannot paradoxically be a group at all (the first tenet of the "Abomunist Election Manifesto" is "Abomunists vote against everyone by not voting for anyone" [Kaufman, *Solitudes*, 81]). Then, as though poking fun at the New Critical reader trained in hunting for subtle paradoxes in poetry, the work goes on to list obvious paradoxes that do not make sense rationally, but rather suggest aspects of Abomunism that echo characteristics of the Beat sensibility already elaborated in this book: a willingness to engage in absurdity, to "SPIT ANTI-POETRY FOR

POETIC PURPOSES," and a refusal of the terms of national identification, whether it be admiring the oils of amateur painter Dwight Eisenhower or fighting for one's country "IN TIMES OF NATIONAL PERIL." The poem mocks the orthodoxies of mainstream American life without offering any counter orthodoxies, and its brilliance is in this withholding: Kaufman never offers earnest responses to repressive norms, but a relentlessly comic rejection of everything "EXCEPT SNOWMEN."

Like others associated with the Beat movement, Kaufman viewed poetry as a site of this rejection; as O'Hara's Personism names a cheeky-yet-truthful description of his poetic methodology, Kaufman's "FOOT-PRINTISM" claims itself a poetic breakthrough that has "FREED THE ARTIST OF OUTMODED RESTRICTIONS." But rather than explain what exactly foot-printism entails, Kaufman strikes at the most fundamental level of what writing is supposed to do (communicate), and claims instead that Abomunist poets do not even possess the ability to read or write – a ridiculous statement until we remember it is exactly the charge leveled at Beat writers by a range of mainstream publications. Rather than defend against such attacks head-on as, say, LeRoi Jones would do in the pages of *Yugen*, Kaufman absorbs this criticism into his work, claiming it as his own and presenting it back in a confidently declarative style that is serious and joking at the same time.

Other pieces of "Abomunist Manifesto" continue in the half-serious vein, and include "Excerpts from the LEXICON ABOMUNON," which mimics the informative authority of the dictionary without being particularly informative or authoritative. Consider, for example: "*Abommunity*: n. Grant Avenue & other frinky places . . . / *Abomunicate*: v. To dig (Slang: to frink.) / . . . *Frink*: v. To (censored). n. (censored) and (censored). / *Frinky*: adj. Like (censored)."[40] Playing on touristic fascination with Beat argot characteristic of the Beatnik Era, Kaufman offers a lexicon of circular definitions that have been redacted by the imaginary hand of authority. "Frink," for example, is a word that means everything and nothing. In this way, the "Lexicon Abomunon" parodies real books like *Poor Richard's Guide to Non-Tourist San Francisco* (1958), which included a section on "'Beat Generation' Bohemia" with advice like "*do* dress casually. If you go tripping down there [North Beach] in your mink or tux, someone is liable to spit on you," and dutifully lists phone numbers and addresses of the best places to glimpse "thin chested young men with beards making intense conversation to long haired girls in pulled up black stockings over red wine."[41] Not as palpably useful as the guidebook to "non-tourist" San Francisco, the "Lexicon Abomunon" captures a mood or ethos, not so much providing information on theories or principles by which Abomunists live, but rather sketching an attitude of rebellion. In an irony that applies broadly to much Beat writing, this attitude is at once anti-establishment and the very center of Americanness, so the pieces of "Abomunist Manifesto" scattered across issues of *Beatitude* and published in *Solitudes Crowded with Loneliness* include the "Abomunist Election Manifesto" and "Abomunist Documents" such as a letter from John Hancock to John Adams about the Boston Tea Party: "it will be cooler if we make the Scene dressed as Indians, the British Fuzz, will not know who the Tea-Heads are" (86). As Huck Finn is both fugitive from American civilization and a paradigmatic American character, adherents to Abomunism are actually extensions of the deeply American tradition of dissent.

In addition to "Abomunist Manifesto," other poetry Kaufman published in *Beatitude* concerns engagements with the scene that poke fun at both the media understandings of the Beats and the often too-self-conscious posturing of the writers, musicians, and intellectuals so identified. These poems include "San Francisco Beat," "A Remembered Beat" (dedicated to John Hoffman), and "Bagel Shop Jazz."[42] Of these, "Bagel Shop Jazz" is the most well known today, and the first thing to note about the poem is that it refers to the Co-Existence Bagel Shop, probably the most famous Beat gathering place in San Francisco at this time, a place Sheri Martinelli once parodied as "PissFul Co-egiztant Beagle & Loks."[43]

Kaufman often held forth and extemporized poetry at Co-Existence, and "Bagel Shop Jazz" is a portrait of the social scene there, from "Mulberry-eyed girls in black stockings" to "Turtle-neck angel guys" to "Coffee-faced Ivy Leaguers ... / Whose personal Harvard was a Fillmore district step" (*Solitudes*, 14–15). While at first blush a shared commitment to bohemianism seems to obliterate the gender or racial differences of these people, the poem suggests rather that superficial talk of "Bird and Diz and Miles" may in fact stall connection or understanding, so the "Coffee-faced" customers harbor

> the secret terrible hurts,
> Wrapped in cool hipster smiles,
> Telling themselves, under the talk,
> This shot must be the end,
> Hoping the beat is really the truth.[44]

By ending the poem with the "secret, terrible hurts" of the African American hipsters at the Bagel Shop, the poem describes, as Maria Damon puts it, "a tense negotiation between nonequals, who, drawn together by mutual yearning for a new society, have had to put up a united front against the 'guilty police' – the normative world" (60).[45] Thus although the counterculture may appear a "united front" from an establishment point of view, "Bagel Shop Jazz" is interested in the unequal striations within this community; in this way the poem is comparable to work by Ted Joans and LeRoi Jones, whose respective first books, *Jazz Poems* and *Preface to a Twenty Volume Suicide Note*, also explore the additional layers of alienation or estrangement that come with being a black Beat.

Kaufman's explorations of race are sometimes more oblique than Joans's or Jones's, as in "West Coast Sounds – 1956," a poem that seems on first read to be just another lament about the authentic bohemian culture of San Francisco being diluted by outsiders:

> San Fran, hipster land,
> Jazz sounds, wig sounds,
> Earthquake sounds, others,
> Allen on Chestnut Street,
> Giving poetry to squares,
> Corso on knees, pleading,
> God eyes.
> Rexroth, Ferlinghetti,
> Swinging, in cellars,
> Kerouac at Locke's
> Writing Neil [Neal Cassady]
> On high typewriter,
> Neil, booting a choo-choo,
> On zigzag tracks.
> Now, many cats
> Falling in,
> New York cats,
> Too many cats,
> Monterey scene cooler,
> San Franers, falling down.
> Canneries closing.
> Sardines splitting
> For Mexico.
> Me too.
>
> (*Solitudes*, 11)

The first way one might read this poem is as yet another example of an author writing himself into a mythological inner circle by name-dropping all the famous people he knows, a circle that is then assailed by latecomers or tourists. But another way to read it is to notice that none of the figures named was originally from San Francisco, and all are white. In this reading, the well-known figures such as Kerouac, Ginsberg, Corso, Cassady, and Ferlinghetti do not constitute an authentic hip coterie, but rather are interlopers themselves, white men who had come to San Francisco and worshipped black "Jazz sounds" which, thanks to their patronage and subsequent fame, have become synonymous with the "West Coast Sounds" of the poem's title. Recalling the line from "Abomunist Manifesto" that "Jazz never made it back down the river," we might read "West Coast Sounds – 1956" as a poem that at once celebrates Beat energy, underscored by the poem's formal sense of movement, but also acknowledges an element of white appropriation of a black art form, so that jazz's origins "down the river" (i.e., New Orleans) are obscured by its more celebrated white champions. This reading figures Kerouac and others as further examples of the "many cats / Falling in," making them complicit in turning the city into a bohemian Disneyland, a "hipster land." The poem's speaker is unmarked, but if we assume a rough reflection of a black Beat poet, we have the sense that the hipster land isn't made authentic by the presence of these white hipsters, but rather more carnivalesque, so the only recourse is to flee to "cooler" climes, the fellaheen space of Mexico.

Despite the sense in "West Coast Sounds" that San Francisco had been inundated with outsiders, it was there that Kaufman became one of the most original poetic voices of the Beat movement, and there that *Beatitude* was launched, underlining other networks of Beat-associated writers besides the original libertine circle. And although Kaufman is now the most well-known writer associated with *Beatitude*, several others recur throughout its pages and constitute another group associated with the Beat movement; such writers have received little to no scholarly attention, but they were instrumental in promoting their own versions of Beatness in the Bay Area in the late 1950s.

The first writer to know about is William J. Margolis, pictured in Figure 7.3 working on the first issue of *Beatitude* with Bob and Eileen Kaufman. Although seldom discussed today, Margolis had been a presence on the Bay Area poetry scene since at least 1954, when he edited *Miscellaneous Man*, a little magazine out of Berkeley invested in alternative, avant-garde sensibilities. His poetry collection, *The Anteroom of Hell* (1957), predates Kaufman's first broadsides and features work that feels Beat in its neoromanticism, as in "I am a Child" or in its distrust of language, as in the Buddhist-inspired "A Word Is But a Finger Pointing."[46] *The Anteroom of Hell* also evinces connections to San Francisco's anarcho-pacifist traditions, as in "Upon a Friend's Being Found Criminally Sane," which is dedicated to Vern Davidson, "an imprisoned conscientious objector to war" (12–13; quotation on 12).

Like Margolis, C. V. J. (Chester) Anderson was another force on the San Francisco scene who published lots of work in *Beatitude* and edited some issues in the summer of 1960. When he returned to New York, Anderson even edited *Beatitude*'s sister magazine, *Beatitude/east* (1960–1961), an endeavor that tried to suture the sensibilities on both coasts. As one issue explained: "There are now, by subtle agreements, at least two kinds of Beatitude, east and west.... Hardly Christ could manage so many. But then, he preceded offset lithography by many years, and thus lacked some of our conveniences."[47] Anderson's first book, *Colloquy* (1960), was published in an edition of 300 by the Bread & Wine Press, and featured artwork by Sheri Martinelli. The book's "Biographical Note" specifies that "Anderson has spent much of his life wandering across America as a musician, composer, and poet," and that the work collected is culled from presentations at "Bay Area readings during the last two years."[48] In other words, Anderson was styling himself a classic poet-wanderer, and emphasizing his connection to the San Francisco scene. With respect to his association with Beatdom, I'll draw attention to four poems in particular – "Summa contra Beatniks," "For Bob Kaufman, on the Death from Leukemia of His Infant Nephew," "La Martinelli Talks of Ezra," and "The Soul's Identity" – all of which originally appeared in *Beatitude*. "Summa contra Beatniks," the title a play on Thomas Aquinas's *Summa contra Gentiles*, is about those itinerant souls who "walked / on poems, every step a haiku and every path / a lyric of incredible delight" (9). "La Martinelli Talks of Ezra," collected in Anderson's second book, *A Liturgy for Dragons* (1961), is a dramatic monologue in Sheri Martinelli's voice imagining that she and Ezra Pound would run off together once he was released from St. Elizabeths.[49]

In 1959, *Beatitude* published Anderson's "The Soul's Identity," which he considered "a public poem, an address, a statement to all the world of what I have found among the Beat and of what for good the Beat mean."[50] Anderson goes on to suggest that the Beats are descendants of the British Romantic poets insofar as they embody the "inevitable Child": "In this the Beat are holy: not that they have discovered the Goal, but that they have found the Road. All of their foolishness and unreasoned extremism (drugs, negativism, orientalism) have been signs only, caricatures, if you will, of the essential and inevitable Child."[51] "The Soul's Identity" itself is mainly a hymn to "We, children of the hidden light of years" and their "vital flame song," a contrast to the "negativism" he also sees in the Beats, what he calls in "Summa contra Beatniks," those who drink "the bitter coffee of despair" (*Colloquy*, 9).[52] Like Kaufman, then, Anderson's poetic work often reflects on the cultural circulation of "Beats" and "Beatniks," and couches its own authenticity in terms of its ironic self-awareness.

In addition to editing issues of *Beatitude* and *Beatitude/east*, in 1959 Anderson also co-founded (with Alan Dienstag) *Underhound*, a "monthly magazine of Commentary and Humor." Of interest for our purposes is the 1960 issue devoted to the Beat scene in San Francisco, in particular its skewering of the police force, who seemed to the editors and other Beats intent on harassment and intimidation via what was dubbed the "Beatnik Patrol." In "How Much Does a Cop Cost?" Anderson wonders how much he would need to lay out for a cop who would protect rather than harass him, noting that he heard Officer 67 using the nastiest racial epithet against "two Bagel Shop customers."[53] In a "Scherzo" "dedicated to our studious law enforcement officers," he declares:

> I'd like to be a Beatnik, but
> I
> don't
> know
> how.
> Two full years of Beatnik life
> have left me just as square as I began.
>
> (21)

Other work in this issue of *Underhound* likewise resonates with *Beatitude*, particularly insofar as it puzzled over the meaning of Beatness in the face of this apparently constant police pressure. See in particular "Notes on Neo-Beatnikism," which opens: "Quoth the Kaufman: 'The age of the irresponsible Beatnik is over,'" and then proceeds to puzzle over the implications of what it might mean to be a responsible – that is, politically engaged – Beatnik, a question that would become increasingly urgent during the Vietnam era.

One other figure worth brief mention in the context of the *Beatitude* circle is Padriec (Paddy) O'Sullivan, a figure whose Beatnik shtick was so successful that in 1959, Vesuvio's in North Beach offered a kitschy "Beatnik Kit" that included O'Sullivan's "epic poem" called "Howya Gonna Keep 'em Down on the Peninsula after They've Seen North Beach?"[54] O'Sullivan also published a book of poetry, *Weep Not My Children*, which is similarly teasing about the poet's connection to something called the Beat Generation. O'Sullivan's work isn't as dynamic as Kaufman's, but *Weep Not*'s preface, written by San Francisco *Chronicle* art critic Thomas J. Albright, takes pains to orient this work in and against the unfolding cultural phenomenon known as the Beat Generation. While O'Sullivan was clearly associated with the *Beatitude* writers, like Kaufman he plays on the touristic aspect of the Beatnik experience, so that his book is framed as an "answer to the Beat Generation."[55] As Albright writes: "Sired by Madison avenue, reared by a respectable tourist named Kerouac and nurtured by a society of pigeon-holers, the term 'Beat Generation' has become a handy catch-all which, at last report, includes everyone from Dylan Thomas to Elvis Presley.... 'Weep Not My Children' is a voice from the 'Beat Generation' telling the image-makers that the 'Beat Generation' does not exist" (n.p.). Writing against the Beatnik narrative, Albright grounds O'Sullivan in the traditions of Alexander Pope, Robert Browning, and Lord Byron: "Some members of the 'Beat Generation' will [put] O'Sullivan's work down as maudlin sentiment or interesting period pieces. Others [sic] members of the 'Beat' also – may find something here that speaks to them. There is no conformity in the pigeon-hole because there is really no one within it" (n.p.). While the ensuing poetry does not quite deliver on the weight of this tradition, O'Sullivan is clearly trying to stake out his own sense of bohemia – one poem is dedicated to Maxwell Bodenheim, the so-called King of the Greenwich Village bohemians in the earlier part of the twentieth century – and yet it is an individual expression that cannot ignore the force of the media-constructed "Beat Generation." By including a preface that explicitly disassociates himself from the Beats, O'Sullivan – like Kaufman and other *Beatitude* writers – of course gains traction from this very association, a paradoxical relationship that as we have seen informs the work of many Beat-associated poets throughout and following the Beatnik Era.[56]

7.3   Two Other Beat Little Magazines and Their Associated Writers: *The Floating Bear* and *Big Table*

Two other little magazines warrant mention as especially significant outlets for Beat-associated writing during the Beatnik Era. *The Floating Bear* (1961–1969) was an $8.5'' \times 11''$ mimeographed "newsletter" founded by LeRoi Jones and Diane di Prima and available by mailing list only, which consisted predominantly of other poets. As di Prima later recalled, the "techniques of poetry were changing very fast, and our sense of the urgency of getting the technological advances of, say, Olson, into the hands of, say, Creeley, within two weeks, back and forth, because the thing just kept growing at a mad rate out of that."[57] In contrast to *The Floating Bear*, which had a kind of street, insider immediacy to it, *Big Table* (1959–1960) was a perfect-bound, relatively well-funded and widely distributed magazine founded by Irving Rosenthal and Paul Carroll as a rebuke to the *Chicago Review*, which Rosenthal had edited until it had been suppressed by the University of Chicago for intending to publish work by Kerouac and Burroughs. Although they framed it in different ways, these periodicals shared a general interest in promoting the "new consciousness" of American letters, and their pages were populated by the same clique of writers and editors familiar to readers of *Yugen* (and, to some extent, *Beatitude* – di Prima noted that at the time they "didn't know too much about the West Coast writers except for a few well-publicized ones" ["Introduction," viii]).

The Floating Bear

The Floating Bear is significant both as an example of subterranean networking via little magazines and as a representation of how Beat sensibilities shifted over the course of the 1960s. Distributed free of charge (except for the last couple of years, when the mailing list had swelled to more than 1,300) to poets and others invested in the new poetry, the *Bear* was a site of community formation, what di Prima called the "linking of all of us through the magazine" (*Recollections*, 254). Initially, di Prima and Jones's goal was "speed: getting this new, exciting work into the hands of other writers as quickly as possible," and the *Bear* accordingly has a fresh and urgent feel, as though it represents the latest avant-garde work hot off the presses ("Introduction," x). Although they had some disagreements about what exactly to print, Jones and di Prima tended, at least in the earlier issues, to publish writers who were broadly affiliated with the Beat movement: the first piece in issue 1 was a Michael McClure poem, and Charles Olson was also featured; issue 2 featured Frank O'Hara, Robert Creeley, and Jones. Some issues were exclusively or predominantly devoted to the work of single writers, a move that announced these writers' importance to the *Bear*'s readership. Issue 3 (March 1961), for example, was a long poem by Ed Dorn, "The Landscape Below"; issue 10 (June 1961) was thirteen poems by John Wieners; issue 16 (December 1961) contained six poems by Ron Loewinsohn; issue 27 (November 1963), titled "The Art of Literature" and dedicated to Lew Welch, contained seventeen poems by Philip Whalen; issue 33 (February 1967) five poems by Janine Pommey (Janine Pommy Vega); and issue 35 (April 1968) eight poems by Philip Lamantia.

In addition to these and other familiar names such as Ginsberg, Orlovsky, Solomon, Huncke, Burroughs, Snyder, di Prima, and Jones, over its nine-year run, the *Bear* also displayed more eclectic tastes, which could be said to expand what we consider Beat-associated networks. Issue 13 (September 1961), for example, printed seven poems by A. B. Spellman, author of *The Beautiful Days* (1965), the first book published by the Poets Press, which di Prima had founded in 1965 (Poets Press also published Herbert Huncke's *Huncke's Journal* [1965] and Kirby Doyle's *Sapphobones* [1966], among others). The original intention had in fact been for di Prima to start a poetry magazine with Spellman, but he couldn't stomach rejecting anyone's manuscripts and so bowed out of editorial work, and the manuscripts they received for that venture became the seeds of *The Floating Bear* ("Introduction," vii). *The Beautiful Days* came with an introduction by Frank O'Hara and featured poems that seem to be working in a broadly Beat vein: "the simplest pleasure is getting high / in the afternoon with 2 fertile women."[58] Spellman's beautiful days are filled with love and sex, John Coltrane, and meditations on his scene, where "john w. [Wieners] drank as much as i do" (n.p.).

Jones and di Prima worked collaboratively on editing the *Bear* for its first two years of existence, and, in yet another example in a growing line of obscenity charges connected to Beat-associated literature, they were both arrested in October 1961 for mailing an issue containing excerpts from Jones's novel *The System of Dante's Hell* (1965) and Burroughs's "Routine: Roosevelt after Inauguration," which imagines Franklin D. Roosevelt's political appointees perpetrating "unspeakable indignities in the lavatories of the Pentagon" (88). Unlike the case connected to *Howl and Other Poems*, Jones and di Prima never went to trial, but the mere fact of their arrest lent the *Bear* a new sheen of countercultural respectability.

As did *Yugen*, the *Bear* sometimes featured work that expressly thematized the literary networks being forged, as for instance by printing letters from Jones to di Prima (issue 5) or Gilbert Sorrentino to Jones (issue 11) or Ginsberg and Orlovsky to Charles Olson (issue 21). Carl Solomon's "The Bughouse" concerns a familiar cast of characters, set as it is in "Allen Ginsberg's Apartment on the Lower East Side": "Peter Orlovsky: Now, Carl, that you're out of the hospital maybe you can do a little writin' / Carl Solomon: Well, I'm well fed. / Alexander Trocchi: I think you'd like this collage it's very interesting" (52). Such a passage is likely compelling mainly to readers already familiar with the players, and who probably know that "Howl" is a poem whose power depends in part on Solomon's being in the hospital. Trocchi is a less recognizable name to fans of "Howl," but his presence in Solomon's piece effects yet again a widening of the Beat circle to include this Scottish writer, a notorious raconteur and

longtime heroin addict whose contributions to the avant-garde underground include editing the short-lived but influential little magazine
Merlin (1952–1955). In the 1950s and 1960s, Trocchi was a visible
presence on the international Beat scene, and his apartment in New York
became an infamous "shooting gallery" and way station for people like
Ginsberg and Huncke – in *Sheeper* (1967), Irving Rosenthal would write
about the "play of truth and moral beauty" in that apartment, the free flow
of heroin and literary debate that unfolded in what he dubbed "Trocchi's
Pad."[59] Trocchi's most important literary achievement is the novel *Cain's
Book* (1960), which follows his alter ego Joe Necchi through his daily
existence as a junky in New York City.[60] Beyond the theme of junk
addiction, *Cain's Book* shares an interest in "spontaneous prose" – even if
it isn't written in such prose – and shirking "conventional classifica-
tions."[61] Given Trocchi's drawing together of the junk underground with
meditations on narrative innovation, it is fitting that by 1961, Solomon
would speak of him in the same breath as Orlovsky and Ginsberg, another
writer for the *Bear*'s hip readers to pursue.

Although the *Bear* ran until 1969, Jones left the project in 1963, after
which di Prima became the driving force behind the newsletter – while she
did occasionally engage guest editors for certain issues over the years, the
sensibilities of the issues in the mid-1960s and after reflect her editorial
tastes.[62] One of the notable shifts in the *Bear* from 1961 to 1969 is the
increase in overtly political work in the later issues, a shift that mirrors
broader changes in the Beat sensibility during the Vietnam era. Over the
course of the 1960s, di Prima became invested in antiwar and other
political activism, which informed both her own work and editorial decisions. In 1968, she published the first part of her poetic call to political
action, *Revolutionary Letters*, the same year she edited the collection *War
Poems*, which emphasized the political edge of the Beat movement with
antiwar work by Ginsberg, di Prima, Corso, Snyder, Jones, McClure,
Whalen, and others.[63] In the latter issues of the *Bear*, one likewise finds
politically inflected poetry such as Lamantia's "Politics Poem" or di
Prima's own "Song for My Spooks," which laments the "dark time on a
dark planet" (443). There are also less "literary" texts connected to calls for
direct political action such as a notice from the "Newark Black Survival
Committee" (issue 34; October 1967); race riots had broken out in
Newark that summer, and a plea later in that issue solicited funds for
the "legal defense of black people arrested in this summer's disturbances"
(477). The *Bear*'s final issue (37; March–July 1969) serves to dispel any
lingering notions that the late 1960s Beat sensibility was apolitical or

utterly disaffiliated, as it includes three political manifestoes by core Beat writers: LeRoi Jones's "What the Arts Need Now," Michael McClure's "Tear Gas," and Gary Snyder's "Buddhism & the Coming Revolution," the last of which sums up the ethos of the final issue by insisting that "No one today can afford to be innocent, or indulge himself in ignorance of the nature of contemporary governments, politics, and social orders" (539). Ultimately, then, *The Floating Bear* is one of the more significant Beat-associated little magazines of the 1960s and a testament to di Prima's editorial energies that sutured different aspects of the movement and delivered them to her network with admirable speed.[64]

Big Table

While *The Floating Bear* was circulated among those already connected to the new poetry, *Big Table* made a larger impact on public consciousness partly because it was subject of yet another obscenity controversy for printing episodes from *Naked Lunch*. *Big Table* rose from the ashes of the university-sanctioned *Chicago Review*, and enhancing its bohemian cachet, it in fact owed its very existence to institutional censorship. Until 1958, the *Chicago Review* was unique among university quarterlies for being entirely student-run, without a faculty advisor or editor. In the late 1950s, the students had expressed their interest in and support of pursuits such as Zen Buddhism, and the autumn 1958 issue featured San Francisco poets Brother Antoninus (William Everson) and Whalen, as well as Joel Oppenheimer, Paul Carroll, Ginsberg, and an excerpt from *Naked Lunch*. Trouble began when Chicago *Daily News* columnist Jack Mabley ran a piece attacking the issue as "Filthy Writing on the Midway." Mabley not only called the issue's contents "one of the foulest collections of printed filth I've seen publicly in circulation," but also labeled the writing "beat," calling it "obscure to the unbeat generation, [but] the beat generation has quite a representation on the Midway."[65] Because of this negative publicity, University of Chicago officials compelled the *Review*'s editor-in-chief, Irving Rosenthal, to submit the upcoming issue's table of contents for review. Rosenthal had planned to publish just three writers in the winter issue: Kerouac (excerpts from *Old Angel Midnight*), Burroughs (more excerpts from *Naked Lunch*), and Edward Dahlberg ("The Garment of Ra" and "Further Sorrows of Priapus"). After the administration reviewed the proposed issue, a dean told Rosenthal that "no Burroughs, Kerouac, or Dahlberg could be printed – regardless of the nature of the material. Those authors had been judged 'undesirable' for inclusion in *Chicago Review*"

(Podell, "Censorship," 81). The university also suggested a plan in which an institutional panel would vet proposed issues of the *Review*, and if this panel deemed the writing unsuitable it would not be published. When Rosenthal refused this arrangement, he and most of the editorial staff resigned. Rosenthal then founded *Big Table* – a name taken from a list of suggestions solicited from Kerouac – and printed its first issue with a pugnacious announcement on the front cover: "The Complete Contents of the Suppressed Winter 1959 *Chicago Review*."[66] The issue opened with an editorial by Rosenthal explaining the circumstances just described (along with an epigraph of sorts from Corso, which begins: "Dear Irving, what? Suppression?" [3]), then indeed prints the complete contents of the "suppressed" *Chicago Review* issue, adding a three-poem "supplement" by Corso for good measure.

Big Table's public visibility is why many Beat-associated writers were drawn to it as shorthand for avant-garde publishing assailed by close-minded authority. Tuli Kupferberg, for example, wrote his poem "The Man with the Scissors" (1962) "after reading about the Big Table case."[67] The poem imagines the mind of a censor:

> Is this the thing The President made and gave
> To have dominion over 1st Class Mail and packages;
>
> . . .
>
> What gulfs between him and the swinging cats!
> Slave of the wheel of constipation, what to him
> Are Ginsberg and the swing of Burroughs?
>
> . . .
>
> O postmasters, priests, and librarians in all lands,
> How will his Wife reckon with the Man?

The titular "Man with the Scissors" thus names the individual bureaucrat or functionary who implements the reflexive censorship on behalf of institutional mandates from the likes of the postal service, the university, or the federal government. *Big Table* also turns up in Douglas Woolf's short story, "Work in Flight Grounded," which appeared in LeRoi Jones's anthology *The Moderns*; there *Big Table* is counterpointed to *Look*, *Life*, and *Time*. In Lawrence Ferlinghetti's novel *Her* (1960), excerpts of which were originally published in *Big Table*, the narrator notes: "this all illusion again for I have slipped off again, pardon me, slipped off the true new Big Table of perception"; and in Ginsberg's poem "Television Was a Baby Crawling toward That Deathchamber" (1961), he writes: "Jet toward Chicago, Big Table empty this morning, / nothing but an old frog-looking editor worried about his Aesthetics."[68]

Trading on its conspicuousness, *Big Table* was greater than the sum of the actual writing it contained: like *Yugen* and *The Floating Bear*, it inserted itself into the bifurcation of the American poetic tradition, not merely by publishing controversial work but by explicitly framing this work in the us-versus-them terms of the "new poets" versus the stodgy university tradition. *Big Table* 4 (1960), for example, included a section titled "The New Poets," containing work by twenty-two poets, sixteen of which appeared in *The New American Poetry* that same year (of the remaining six poets, some – notably di Prima – *should* have been in Allen's anthology). Thanks in part to unusually successful fund-raising campaigns, physically *Big Table* looked more like the nationally distributed *Evergreen Review* than mimeographed *Floating Bear* or *Beatitude*, and it contained also professional-grade advertisements for what was by then identifiably "Beat literature," including prominent ads for the latest numbers in the Pocket Poets series as well as Kerouac's *The Dharma Bums*. These advertisements, like the addenda in *Yugen*, created a sense of a literary community beyond *Big Table*'s pages. And with its slick advertisements not found in the other little magazines discussed above, it is clear the magazine benefited from the popularity of the romanticized idea of the Beat Generation.

Unlike the other little magazines discussed, then, *Big Table* did not so much participate in creating and defining the Beat sensibility than it did in presenting this sensibility fully formed and consumable. Whereas the slightly earlier periodicals published many in Beat circles without trying to create a Beat-specific publication, *Big Table* owes its very existence to the notoriety of Kerouac and Burroughs *as* Beat writers, and its issues reflect the increasingly pervasive trend of the Beat image being packaged as such and commoditized – by others and by some writers themselves.

Despite the more obvious features of the work in *Big Table* 1 (the gritty depictions of sex in Burroughs's and Dahlberg's work; Kerouac's use of the word "fuck"), its publication was an important moment in the history of Beat literary publications not because of its defiant vulgarity but because it challenged what language or the literary could do or be. Burroughs's comic, grotesque "routines" tossed out not only polite subject matter, but basic notions of plot and characterization, and *Old Angel Midnight* is arguably Kerouac's most radical use of the spontaneous method. While *Big Table* is familiar to students of Beat lore for its championing of the controversial, potentially obscene subject matter, the deeper story is in the representational experiments it showcased. From our contemporary vantage, we have the luxury of not feeling scandalized by the appearance of a dirty word or graphic sex act, and so are better positioned to appreciate

Big Table's contribution in terms of avant-garde literary dimensions of Beat experimentation.

As I hope is clear from this discussion of *Yugen*, *The Floating Bear*, *Beatitude*, and *Big Table*, you can't get a good handle on the widening of the Beat movement in the late 1950s without paying serious attention to the work of little magazines. These publications were not only hotbeds of ideas, they had a unique ability to communicate breaking developments more quickly than publishing houses, and were the sites of ongoing, constantly fluctuating canon formation. Such magazines are essential aspects of postwar literary history because they offer alternative senses of the movement at once fuller and more varied than the ones found in anthologies conceived specifically to showcase something called "Beat literature." Capitalizing on the hunger for all things Beat, anthologies such as Gene Feldman and Max Gartenberg's *The Beat Generation and the Angry Young Men* (1958), Stanley Fisher's *Beat Coast East: An Anthology of Rebellion* (1960), Seymour Krim's *The Beats* (1960), Elias Wilentz's *The Beat Scene* (1960), and Gene Baro's *"Beat" Poets* (1961) likewise represented ongoing "canon formation," but were top-down in structure and had the benefit of at least some measure of hindsight. Little magazines, by contrast, were assembled on the fly, could perhaps be more promiscuous in their choices, and so have a more energetic feel than even the best of these anthologies. For instance, *The Beat Scene*, among the better early anthologies, seems when read against *Yugen* like a museum exhibit of representative characters and their writing, containing as it does Fred McDarrah's captivating photographs.[69] In little magazines, on the other hand, one finds diverse choruses of voices and sensibilities coming alive and crashing into one another, voices that, for all their idiosyncrasies and aesthetic differences, nonetheless do finally clarify into patchwork pieces of an identifiable though mutating Beat sensibility. The work found in these pages tends to be concerned with the "new consciousness," however differently particular writers might define such a concept; it tends to foreground the self, but recognizes that the meaning of selfhood might be best illuminated in relation to others, a conceptual warrant for the group myth-making in which so many writers engaged. Finally, work in Beat little magazines tends to revel in formal and linguistic play, adapting or refusing convention in ways that are both joking and serious, and that are slyly political without seeming to be. And what still compels about such work is that despite their broad commonalities, the best writers have their own distinctive visions and feel, as do the journals themselves.[70]

CHAPTER 8

The Opening of the Field

As my earlier discussion of little magazines paused over particular poems first published in *Yugen, Beatitude, The Floating Bear*, and others in order to sketch a messy though identifiable Beat sensibility and aesthetic, the following pages describe the widening of the Beat movement by looking at books published during the Beatnik Era, many of them the first full-length works by those whose writing had initially appeared in little magazines. On the one hand, these books are so varied and idiosyncratic that it hardly seems logical to read them together as part of a coherent movement; but, on the other, it is instructive to consider them as products not merely of a broadly imagined "historical moment," but of the much more concentrated Beat scene. The writers in this chapter and the next were mainly centered in New York City and the San Francisco Bay Area; they knew one another, moved in the same social spaces, traded manuscripts, published one another's work, and undertook critical and aesthetic conversations in their poetry, prose, and letters. In grouping these writers together, I want to underscore that while their work can be seen as part of the Beat movement as propelled by more famous counterparts such as Kerouac, Ginsberg, and Burroughs, it is crucial to keep in mind that these writers never allowed their own work to be *defined* by these other, more well-known figures. Like the original inner circle, writers who constitute a widening of the movement were at times conflicted about being labeled "Beat," and yet they all drew sustenance and creative energy from being so associated. Thus conceptualizing the movement as a more widespread phenomenon does not necessarily lead us to a bunch of derivative poseurs jumping on the Beat bandwagon – although this certainly did happen – but to the recognition of distinctive sensibilities that were invested in doing their own idiosyncratic work that can in hindsight be seen as what Corso once called "variations on a generation."[1] Attending to the writers and books in the coming pages helps us see them as co-progenitors of Beatness who, like the inner circle, discovered the Beatnik caricature always lurking behind them, and so created work informed but never defined by such caricature.

8.1 Gregory Corso: The Surreal-Real

As we have already seen, Gregory Corso was producing work of interest before the Beat Generation was launched into national consciousness, and by the late 1950s, his renown as a Beat writer was second only to Kerouac's and Ginsberg's. His work had also come into its own with his second and third books, *Gasoline* (1958) and *The Happy Birthday of Death* (1960). Published by City Lights, *Gasoline* sold fairly well and marks Corso's growing mastery of his abilities, but does not quite achieve the ironic power of his most famous poems such as "Bomb" or "Marriage," both of which were collected in *The Happy Birthday of Death*.

Almost protesting too much in its worldliness, *Gasoline* is oriented geographically, announcing the poet's global wanderings to many Beat-associated hotspots, from San Francisco ("Ode to Coit Tower") and Greenwich Village ("For Miles") to Europe ("Vision of Rotterdam" and "Paris") and Mexico ("Mexican Impressions" and "Puma in Chapultepec Zoo"). The poems range over meditations on art history, the poet's missing his cats, and jejune declarations such as the one in the well-known poem, "I am 25": "I HATE OLD POETMEN!"[2] In his introduction to *Gasoline*, Ginsberg famously – or notoriously, for Beat detractors – wrote that Corso "gets pure abstract poetry, the inside sound of language alone. But what is he *saying*? Who cares?! It's said!"[3] Despite Ginsberg's theatrical claims here (reproduced in many a negative article about the Beats), Corso was indeed interested in "saying" things beyond pure abstraction. Even in "Don't Shoot the Warthog," the poem Ginsberg singles out as "pure poetry," Corso draws on language and imagery evocative of "Howl" (a "fury of mothers and fathers / sank their teeth" into angelic children of "my generation" [41]). Corso, like Ginsberg, makes claims to speak for an entire "generation," a word repeated three times in the short poem, but rather than present an us-versus-them binary as in "Howl," "Don't Shoot" describes how members of Corso's generation appear likewise complicit in the death of a nameless child. Even the speaker kicks the child and curses his name, so that Ginsberg's figure of Moloch, the Establishment, becomes transfigured into a scream against humanity itself in which Corso condemns his own complicity and that of his "generation."

Corso showcased his singular sensibility to even greater effect in his next collection, *The Happy Birthday of Death* (1960). He shopped the book to

James Laughlin at New Directions after pulling it from City Lights over a disagreement regarding some of its content, particularly "Power," which Ferlinghetti thought fetishized power in ways reminiscent of fascism. Ferlinghetti's hesitation notwithstanding, in my view *Happy Birthday* is one of Corso's strongest books. Composed largely during the Beatnik Era, this volume contains work refracted by the media image of the scrubby Beat poet, as for example in "Poets Hitchhiking on the Highway," a paradigmatic example of Beat poetry. Ginsberg later recalled that the "actual situation was me and Gregory hitchhiking down around Big Sur in 1956, going to visit Henry Miller and not being able to get a ride."[4] In the poem, Corso depicts the two (unnamed) poets on the road and having a war of words in which the most nonsensical phrase wins:

> This time he laughed
>   and said: "Suppose the
>   strawberry were
>   pushed into a mountain."
> After that I knew the
>   war was on –
> So we fought:
>   . . .
> He said: "Mad street with no name."
> I said: "Bald killer! Bald killer! Bald killer!"
> He said, getting real mad,
>   "Firestoves! Gas! Couch!"[5]

While it is easy to dismiss such a poem as somehow non-aesthetic because irrational, it is precisely in this unshackling of meaning from rationality that the poem generates its charm. For Ginsberg, the "ultimate poetic moment" comes when the poets have exhausted the "opposite combinations" or "inside-out ideas" and reached a place where ordinary words seem reinvested with strange power: "We'd arrived at a point where contradiction was so obvious that reality itself was sufficient to be self-contradicting.... in our brains, just reality itself, a simple real word like 'couch' was, in this context, total solidification of poetry."[6]

This interest in reimagining the terms of "reality itself" characterizes *Happy Birthday* as a whole, so much so that Gregory Stephenson views a central tenant of Corso's poetics as "essentially a rejection of the tyranny of the real. It is an assertion of freedom from limitation and from causality, a mode of refashioning, reinterpreting, recreating the phenomenological universe, of imposing inner desire on the external world, and by these means a way of contradicting, counteracting, and countermanding the real."[7] In this view, one might understand "Poets Hitchhiking on the Highway" as an illustration of Corso's poetics, a poem *about* bravura performances that is also itself a bravura performance, and as such resonates not only with Corso's work but also with his public persona as romantic bad boy poet. As Corso wrote in "Power," "I contradict the real with the unreal" (*Happy Birthday*, 75), and he later extended such contradiction or disruption into the literary realm when he claimed to abandon "old iambics by the use of mixtures containing spontaneity 'bop prosody' surreal-real images jumps beats cool measures long rapidic vowels, long long lines, and, the main content, soul."[8] By having his hitchhiking poets trade "surreal-real images," then, Corso alludes to what he sees as a larger reproach of poetic traditions dominated by those tired "old iambics."

As Stephenson elaborates his claim that Corso's work amounts to a "rejection of the tyranny of the real," he does so in oppositional terms that could apply to the Beat project broadly conceived. Corso's particular contribution to this project is to imagine "the real" in terms of social norms that have been collapsed or confused with objective reality. Whether such norms pertain to social ideas such as marrying by a certain age, linguistic ideas such as syntactic regularity – what Gavin Selerie calls "non-biological grammatical structure" – or poetic decorum that undervalues the features of Beat poetry listed above, pugnacious Corso thrives on pushing back against the expected.[9] This is the case in some of the most successful poetry collected in *The Happy Birthday of Death*, work that addresses big topics such as "Marriage," "Food," "Death," "Power," "Army," "Police," and, of course, his most famous poem, "Bomb" – these are all poems he saw as central to the volume in its early planning stages, when its working title was *Starmeat*.[10]

"Marriage" is probably the book's clearest rebuke of social norms as the speaker imagines a series of comic scenes encapsulating what it might be like to court and then marry a nice, respectable girl. Opening with two staccato questions, existential on their own but funny when paired ("Should I get married? Should I be good?"), the poem immediately veers into odd territory by substituting romantic notions of courtship and marriage with faintly macabre ones: "Don't take her to movies but to cemeteries / tell about werewolf bathtubs and forked clarinets" (29). After tossing off a couple of "surreal-real images" that would have been impressive to the companions hitchhiking on the highway, the speaker imagines marriage not from the conventional point of view of romantic love or even in terms of a relationship between the speaker and his beloved, but in terms of uncomfortable social norms such as meeting the parents "back straightened, hair finally combed, strangled by a tie." This is marriage not as culmination of a love story, but as social ritual:

> After tea and homemade cookies they ask What do you do for a living?
>
> > Should I tell them? Would they like me then?
> > Say All right get married, we're losing a daughter
> > but we're gaining a son –
> > And should I ask then Where's the bathroom? (29)

From here the speaker goes on to imagine an anxiety-filled wedding ("And I trembling what to say say Pie Glue!" [29]), a cheesy honeymoon at Niagara Falls, and eventually a homestead in suburban Connecticut. Picking up on the counterintuitive thought to take a date to a cemetery instead of the movies, this part of the poem speculates not merely about the strangeness of weddings and honeymoons but also about how the speaker's fundamentally anti-establishment sensibility might work in a normative institution such as marriage. To explore this question, Corso turns again to "surreal-real images," trying them out in the context of what a "good" marriage is supposed to look like:

> But I should get married I should be good
> How nice it'd be to come home to her
> and sit by the fireplace and she in the kitchen
> aproned young and lovely wanting my baby
> and so happy about me she burns the roast beef
> and comes crying to me and I get up from my big papa chair
> saying Christmas teeth! Radiant brains! Apple deaf!
> God what a husband I'd make! Yes, I should get married!
>
> > > (30)

By "good" Corso means normative, and he plays this definition to devastating effect in this stanza, which characterizes marriage in terms of domesticity ("fireplace," "kitchen," "aproned," "baby"), meaning also that husband and wife merely perform stock gender roles, so she pines for a baby, cooks dutifully, and runs crying to "big papa" when she is so distracted by her doe-eyed love for him that she burns dinner. In this context, the zany poet shouting nonsense phrases does not seem all that weird or problematic, and the stanza ends with the speaker plotting Dadaesque hijinks in the suburbs like "hanging a picture of Rimbaud on the lawnmower." The poem continues in this vein until it reaches what is finally its point, that marriage as a social institution actually hamstrings love rather than affirms it: "O but what about love? I forgot love / not that

I am incapable of love / it's just that I see love as odd as wearing shoes" (32). In this wonderful final turn, we learn that far from disparaging love by questioning marriage, Corso is making a case for defamiliarizing love, for making it strange precisely to restore its potency; he finally concludes that "were a woman possible as I am possible" – that is, were he to meet a woman interested in defamiliarizing love as he defamiliarizes language through phrases such as "Apple deaf" – then he would be all for marriage as an institution in which he might live happily ever after.

Corso's most famous poem, and his masterpiece from this period, is "Bomb," a lengthy meditation on the atomic bomb and the vices of civilization more generally. Originally published as a broadside by City Lights in 1958, "Bomb" is arranged in the shape of a mushroom cloud, and was included in *Happy Birthday* as a foldout to retain this striking format. Corso composed the poem in Paris while staying at the Beat Hotel, and when he finished it he wrote to Ferlinghetti, declaring it a "Really great poem – best I've ever done," then confiding that he "had difficulty with the ending – didn't know whether to end on hopeful note or funny note or bitter note. I decided upon the last, alas."[11] Corso's ambivalence about the ending resonates with the poem as a whole, as one of its most notorious aspects is its tone, which vacillates among disgust, awe, love, and fear. Given that fear was certainly the prevailing attitude regarding nuclear weapons during the Cold War, one might expect an oppositional Beat poet to simply denounce the bomb's destructive power, to indict a society that created a technology capable of destroying the world, something on the order of Ginsberg's blunt statement in the poem "America": "Go fuck yourself with your atom bomb" (*Howl*, 39).

Instead, Corso's pugnaciousness extends even to a repudiation of the "expected" oppositional stance to the atomic bomb, so while the poem opens with lines indicating the weapon's sweeping historical import ("Budger of history Brake of time"), when the speaker is first introduced, he declares, "I cannot hate you," and as the poem unfolds makes startling assertions such as, "I sing thee Bomb" and "O Bomb I love you / I want to kiss your clank eat your boom." It was lines like these that surprised some readers and enraged certain audiences, but seeing the poem's ambivalence as emblematic of larger societal struggles with understanding the cultural and psychic consequences of the atomic bomb helps us see that declaring love for it is not quite the same thing as endorsing apocalyptic destruction.

In fact, part of the reason the tone veers so radically from line to line is because it reflects the impossibility of really coming to terms with the atomic bomb, the invention of which was, as historian Paul Boyer has shown, "a psychic event of almost unprecedented proportions."[12] In order to theorize this psychic event, some observers have referred to the idea of the "nuclear sublime": as Frances Ferguson put it in 1984, "the notion of the sublime is continuous with the notion of nuclear holocaust: to think the sublime would be to think the unthinkable and to exist in one's own nonexistence."[13] Were one to read Corso's "Bomb" in these terms – Tim Armstrong has noted in passing that the poem is a "representative example of the nuclear sublime" – then its unsettling tonal shifts can be seen as manifestations of larger cultural conundrums regarding nuclear bombs.[14] Corso once agreed with an interviewer's assessment that the poem is an attempt to "enter into the consciousness of the weapon, seeking to under-stand it, rather than retreating in absolute fear."[15] If the poem is approached as an exploration of the bomb's "consciousness," then we might understand the speaker's claims to love it not as a blanket admir-ation of destruction, but as an ironic alignment with what the bomb represents for American cultural consciousness. In other words, if the bomb is figured as civilization's next great destructive technology – it's compared with "Catapult Da Vinci   tomahawk Cochise   flintlock Kidd dagger Rathbone" – then it actually makes sense to be simultan-eously awed and terrified, to both love and revile it: the bomb's function is to unleash unimaginable destruction, and yet it embodies also the pinnacle of scientific achievement by way of the military-industrial complex. The poem's schizophrenic tone thus reflects the bomb's paradoxical cultural position.

The ending does not so much resolve this paradox as allow it to be overcome with death, and the poem itself erupts in a series of onomato-poeic explosions:

> BOOM   BOOM   BOOM   BOOM   BOOM
> BOOM ye skies and BOOM ye suns
> BOOM BOOM ye moons   ye stars BOOM
> nights ye BOOM   ye days ye BOOM.

These booms, part terrifying, part orgiastic, again underscore the poem's schizophrenic tone, and help us see it as precursor to later work that treated the bomb with equally dark humor, most notably Stanley Kubrick's film *Dr. Strangelove, or: How I Stopped Worrying and Learned to Love the Bomb* (1964), which ends in a montage of mushroom clouds scored with Vera Lynn singing "We'll Meet Again." Unlike Kubrick's mock love letter in his satire's final scenes, in "Bomb," the parting lines turn to the "bitter" note that Corso registered in his letter to Ferlinghetti:

> Know that the earth will madonna the Bomb
> that in the hearts of men to come more bombs will be born
> magisterial bombs wrapped in ermine   all beautiful
> and they'll sit plunk on earth's grumpy empires
> fierce with moustaches of gold.

As these lines suggest, if the speaker declares, "O Bomb I love you," it is only to conform (ironically) to the judgment of dominant culture and indeed capital-H History itself, which will continue to produce bombs and to elevate them to the realms of gods and kings, marked here by "madonna" and "ermine."[16] In this view, the speaker is drawn to the bomb as a historical inevitability, as both object and abstraction whose potential power to destroy humankind renders all else meaningless.

But there is another aspect of "Bomb" that I think is overlooked if we read it *only* as a poem about the nuclear sublime, about our collective inability to imagine or represent the "horrible Bombdeath" that *might* come to the world. As mentioned above, Corso wrote the poem while living in Paris, one of the great cities of Western civilization, as France was fighting to maintain control of one of its oldest colonies, known then as French Algeria. The Algerian War (1954–1962) would eventually lead to Algeria's independence, and Paris became particularly violent during Corso's time there, when an Algerian nationalist movement called the National Liberation Front (FLN), waged guerilla warfare in the streets of the city. Such bloody conflict led to much national soul-searching about France's colonial legacy, a context that adds another layer of meaning to the evocation of "earth's grumpy empires" in the penultimate line of "Bomb." Indeed, in his correspondence from September 1958, when he had just completed a draft of the poem, Corso refers often to the violence he was witnessing, sometimes in the same breath as "Bomb."

For example, he wrote to Peter Orlovsky:

> Paris in an uproar. Arabs FLN have taken to war in city, they have in past week killed ten cops and four soldiers (mostly on dark streets and in Metros). Yesterday they blew up a cafe around here and killed nine. Paris very uneasy. *No* Arab allowed on streets after nine o'clock, tourists are trembling, fleeing, situation bad.[17]

To Donald Allen:

> I mailed my *Bomb* poem to Allen [Ginsberg] to give to you for anthology [*The New American Poetry*] in exchange for *Power*. Paris teeming with war. Arabs killing police and soldiers and blowing up cafes.[18]

To Gary Snyder:

> Paris really like Germans were here, machine guns everywhere. Arabs to be in at nine – curfew. Police found shot every morning.... Hope you see my *Bomb* poem at City Lights.[19]

As these excerpts illustrate, while Corso was composing his half-ironic ode to the atomic bomb, couching it in metaphysical terms such as "Budger of history Brake of time," small bombs were going off all around him, killing actual people. Other poems collected in *The Happy Birthday of Death* explore such violence explicitly, as in "The Sacré-Coeur Café," in which French intellectual firebrands discuss the radical politics of the French Revolution while turning blind eyes to the "The bombed Algerians [who] observe each others' burning teeth" (66). Far from sublime abstraction, the bombs in this poem are connected directly to the "bad" political situation. That poem ends by noting: "And the Algerians / they don't go to the Sacré-Coeur Café" (66), emphasizing the distance between Paris's famed café culture as locus of ideas and discussion, and an antagonistic and disenfranchised Arab underclass.[20] Another poem, "Written in Nostalgia for Paris," is even more pointed about the inescapable effects of the Algerian War:

> How lovely that childgirl was!
> The street was wild with raiders
>   but France protected their youth.
> I ran to buy her a flower but a rioter
>   needed blood for the FLN;
>   St. Michel sold the flowers
>   but it was cut off by
>   the Garde républicaine.
>
>   (68)

Here romantic love, traditional subject of poetry, is interrupted by "raiders" and "rioter[s]" connected to the FLN. Apparently less sympathetic toward the Algerians than the "Sacré-Coeur Café," this poem figures France as under siege from FLN militants, the net result being that the City of Love had become the City of Blood. Geographically, the poem is set at the Place Saint-Michel, a square in the Latin Quarter notable for its large statue of Saint Michael brandishing his flaming sword. Just as the unfolding Algerian War might call to mind the concluding reference in "Bomb" to "earth's grumpy empires," so too might this depiction of FLN violence under the shadow of Saint Michael recall another evocative question in that poem: "hath not St. Michael a burning sword"? While it is certainly possible to read this statement more generically, as another comparison of the atomic bomb to destructive technologies of the past, "Written in Nostalgia for Paris" also marks Saint Michael and his flaming sword as a location of colonial violence. With this in mind, the examples of the atomic bomb's power to mix up or confuse the world might seem to echo colonial encounter:

> Penguins plunged against the Sphinx
> The top of the Empire State
> arrowed in a broccoli field in Sicily
> Eiffel shaped like a C in Magnolia Gardens
> St. Sophia peeling over Sudan.

Although such lines may read at first as merely "surreal-real images" found in much of Corso's poetry, they also depict a post-bomb world in which great civilizations, from Egyptian to French to Ottoman to American, are thrown into disarray. And given the historical conditions of the poem's composition, I do not think that the reference to "Empire" is incidental here, nor is the image of the Eiffel Tower being twisted beyond recognition in New Jersey. In another poem in *Happy Birthday*, "Looking at the Map of the World," Corso imaginatively ranges across the map to conclude: "America is the most promising of empires / – stamp collectors will have to re-germinate / their American albums" (70). With this poem, we find Corso interested not merely in France's status as a "grumpy empire" but with the status of the United States as well, and if "Bomb" resonates with violence being done by real-life bombs in Paris cafés, it casts the United States as a new seat of empire authorized by the atomic bomb. Given *Happy Birthday*'s constellation of associations among France's crumbling empire and the ascending empire of the United States, we might read "Bomb" as a sober reflection on the dangers of empire, even as its speaker embodies an imagined public sphere expected to joyfully embrace the weapon and its geopolitical consequences.

8.2 Diane di Prima: Vanguard in the Village

As suggested by her involvement with *Yugen* and *The Floating Bear*, Diane di Prima was at the center of the Village scene throughout much of the 1950s, and would add a powerful female voice to the Beat Generation with her first book, *This Kind of Bird Flies Backward* (1958), and in the large body of work she has produced over her long career.[21] Despite her productivity, di Prima has received relatively scant attention from literary critics; the first critical monograph on her work, David Stephen Calonne's *Diane di Prima: Visionary Poetics and the Hidden Religions*, didn't appear until 2019. For many readers, the reason for such neglect is simply that Beat criticism has tended to follow the lead of writers like Ginsberg, whose remark in a journal that "The social organization which is most true of itself to the artist is the boy gang" has been frequently and disapprovingly cited by critics.[22] Brenda Knight, Nancy M. Grace, Ronna C. Johnson, Mary Paniccia Carden, and others have tried to overturn such a notion, and it is important to understand how a figure like di Prima wrote herself into the movement even as her fellow writers – and subsequent critics – seemed to habitually pass over her importance. As with the male inner circle, who legitimated and mythologized themselves by constantly cross-referencing one another's writing, di Prima was canny about linking her work to well-known figures. Such a desire to advertise her connections is why di Prima contacted Ferlinghetti to write an introduction to *This Kind of Bird*, and even though it only amounts to six sentences, beginning, "I don't know her, never saw her, never heard her," merely carrying his name on the book's cover did the work of letting those hip readers know di Prima's work is cool enough to merit attention.[23]

One hallmark of *This Kind of Bird* is in fact di Prima's undermining what readers think they know about "coolness" and the underground scene. She includes work from as far back as 1953 (the titles of the poems in this section are all specific dates), which has the simultaneous effect of establishing di Prima as an authentic – that is, pre–*On the Road* and "Howl" – Beat writer, and allowing her to criticize certain aspects of the bohemian lifestyle.[24] Indeed, in her later *Memoirs of a Beatnik* (1969), di Prima would pointedly sketch her participation in the Village scene as pre-dating "Howl":

> As far as we knew, there was only a small handful of us – perhaps forty or fifty in the city – who knew what we knew: who raced about in Levis and work shirts, made art, smoked dope, dug the new jazz, and spoke a bastardization of the black argot. We surmised that there might be another fifty living in San Francisco, and perhaps a hundred more scattered throughout the country: Chicago, New Orleans, etc., but our isolation was total and impenetrable.... Our chief concern was to keep our integrity (much time and energy went into defining the concept of the "sellout") and to keep our cool.[25]

Here di Prima predicates her own circle's "integrity" on its isolation and impenetrability, characterizing them as a group of like-minded people whose informal creed was merely not selling out. It is immediately following this description that she introduces the famous names associated with the Beat Generation: "Then one evening," she writes, someone gave her a copy of *Howl and Other Poems*, a book that both "turned [her] on" and "put a certain heaviness" in her, as it seemed to portend the end of the small, isolated clique of which she had been a part. "I sensed," she writes, "that Allen was only, could only be, the vanguard of a much larger thing" (175–176). With this passage, di Prima reverses the claims of those who would see her as riding on the coattails of the more famous male writers. Instead, it is she and her friends who are the true hipsters, whereas Ginsberg represented a "new era" in which the "unself-conscious Bohemianism we had maintained at the pad" would inevitably be changed once thrust into the public eye.

We ought to keep this context in mind when reading *This Kind of Bird*, many of the poems in which are centered on relationships and love, and in them one finds what became a signature of di Prima's sensibility over the next several decades, an ability to skewer self-identified bohemian, progressive men who nonetheless behave in conventionally boorish ways when it comes to women or relationships. This is the case, for example, in "August 1955," which ends with the stanza: "Like man don't flip, I'm hip you cooled / this scene. But you can hock the jazz / guitar, in limbo they play ballads" (10). Here di Prima reproduces Beat slang, what she later called "street language," but she does so self-reflexively: it is a performance of such slang interested in what this language covers up.[26] In "August 1955," the speaker resorts to hipster argot to assure the man who has "cooled the scene" that everything is fine, that as a "hip chick," she would never hold him to square standards like commitment. But even as the speaker makes this declaration, the poem is ambivalent about its virtue as readers are left with the sense of callousness with which the man splits, thereby implying that far from rendering men and women sexual equals, bohemian fantasies of free love can actually wind up enforcing conventional gender norms as men flee from genuine connection.

Similar theories are explored throughout *This Kind of Bird*; in a pair of "Poems for Bret," for example, di Prima inverts what later feminist theorists called the "male gaze" by proclaiming, "I've got my eye on you" (34), an assertion of the power of female subjectivity that runs through much writing by Beat-associated women writers. The poem ends by framing such power according to the norms of the underground scene:

it's nice
to run a pad
where both of us
are cool enough
to know we're both
uncool.

(34)

As in many other poems in the book, here di Prima demonstrates her
fluency with Beat slang, but does so in order to dismantle and indeed
dispatch such coolness as an affected veneer that only occludes true
connection. Thus this poem – and the collection as a whole – relishes in
being "uncool" if it spells true connection. As she writes in the untitled
opening poem:

I don't forget things
fast enough, I sing
last summer's ballads
winter long

like that's uncool.

(2)

This poem suggests that the bohemian ideal of "cool" can be as normative
as the square injunction to monogamy. If to linger over human connection
too long is to be "uncool," then the speaker embraces such uncoolness,
however antithetical it may be to what good Beat chicks were supposed to
do according to what di Prima called in *Memoirs* "our eternal, tiresome rule
of Cool" (133). Ronna C. Johnson has explained the Beat rule of cool as "a
set of rules for comportment that mandates terse expression and withheld
emotion . . . it is a social code . . . that makes women de facto collaborators
with their own oppression, because the essence of cool is the appearance of
passivity, indifference, and lack of emotion."[27] A critique of this "social
code" is present throughout *This Kind of Bird*, in which di Prima stakes a
claim on her own idiosyncratic visions of love and relationships loosed
from both mainstream *and* bohemian values. This is perhaps most evident
in the way di Prima conceptualizes her "Love Poems," not as starry-eyed
odes to abdominal fluttering or the transformative joys of sex, but rather as
hard-nosed inversions of such clichés: "you are not quite / the air I breathe
/ thank god. / so go" (27). Such inversions are informed throughout the
book by a wry assessment of the power dynamics that accompany romantic
relationships, even in a bohemian milieu: "In case you put me down I put
you down / already, doll / I know the games you play" (24). *This Kind of*

Bird Flies Backward is thus a noteworthy moment in Beat publishing because it represents a female critique of Beat gender norms that comes earlier than the work in the 1960s, 1970s, and beyond with which most students of Beat literature tend to be familiar.

Dinners & Nightmares (1961) extends di Prima's insider's tour of the scene from a female perspective. A combination of sketches, play-like "conversations," and poetry, parts of which were recycled from her first book, *Dinners & Nightmares* lays claim to hipster authenticity while mocking some of its more dubious characteristics. Like *This Kind of Bird*, *Dinners & Nightmares* uses hip slang: it is dedicated to those with whom di Prima shared "pads," and features dialogue such as, "Like man I said you're being uncool" (78). It also nods to examples of "canonical" Beat works, such as the mention of shoplifting food that that echoes Holmes's descriptions in *Go*, and the visit from an unnamed poet just released from Rockland State mental institution, an allusion to one of the more haunting refrains from Ginsberg's "Howl," that the speaker is "with you in Rockland" (80–82).

Such moments aside, *Dinners & Nightmares* does not resort to name checking or rehashing well-trod events from Beat mythology. There are no thinly veiled depictions of the by-then famous male Beat writers, nor are there poems to or about others clearly labeled as Important Poets. Instead, the book draws readers into the daily life of Lower East Side bohemianism in the mid-1950s, before the advent of the Beatnik Era, a move that simultaneously underscores di Prima's authority as an "authentic" Beat voice and suggests a new shape to what exactly such bohemianism entails. As the flyleaf in the original volume claimed, "Here is a young and brilliant writer whose honesty will shock the romantic illusions of even the 'beat' generation. Di Prima strips away stylistic pretensions to evolve a prose that mirrors the language and attitudes of her youthful characters."[28] The watchwords here – "youthful" and "unsentimental" – unite two strands of the movement that generally tend to be separate, so that if Kerouac is interested in youth, he isn't exactly "unsentimental," and if Burroughs is unflinchingly unsentimental, he seems bored by the enthusiasm of the young. Thus what might have shocked the "romantic illusions" of even the Beat Generation is di Prima's cutting depictions of the bohemian domestic space, depictions that come with uncomfortable observations about the complex gender inequalities still underwriting a supposedly progressive avant-garde.

The first section, "Dinners," focuses on meals that di Prima recalls being especially significant to her life; comparable to Corso's food poems of the same period or Frank O'Hara's poetic elevation of the mundane in *Lunch Poems*, this section is grounded in specific dates and street addresses, sometimes even reproducing shopping lists for particular meals.[29] These sketches tend to emphasize the domestic labor necessary even in bohemian settings, and this very context in fact blinds men in particular to such labor. This is the case in an early sketch beginning with the shopping list and menu for "Thanksgiving, 1955," that is then followed by a guest list: "Dan who would rather have bean soup. Bill who would rather eat at Downey's. Michael who wishes there were oysters instead of clams and that we had made garlic bread" (14–15). The idea is that even among this collection of unconventional people – they "whimsically" marry, are actors and dancers – the time and care it takes to prepare such a "feast" is still invisible to men absorbed in their own self-involved tastes and desires. These local examples are indicative of the larger tenor of *Dinners & Nightmares*, which does not didactically rail against gender inequality, but rather presents di Prima's experiences in all their irony and inconsistency, thereby providing an often-humorous critique of "alternative lifestyles" from a female perspective.

As with *This Kind of Bird*, at bottom *Dinners & Nightmares* is interested in puncturing the "rule of cool"; for di Prima, this rule is often made visible by the domestic labor that men assume women will do without question. This is the case, for example, in "The Quarrel," which charts the speaker's simmering rage with her lover, Mark:

> I am sick I said to the woodpile of doing dishes.... Just because I happen to be a chick I thought.... I got up and went into the kitchen to do the dishes. And shit I thought I probably won't bother again. But I'll get bugged and not bother to tell you and after a while everything will be awful and I'll never say anything because it's so fucking uncool to talk about it. (74)

While, on the one hand, such an interior monologue might seem universal for its depiction of how lovers can shut down and harbor silent contempt for each other, di Prima continually emphasizes the bohemian context, characterized not just by lack of funds but also by near-constant creative production and a seemingly supportive community. Thus the speaker resents doing the dishes because she has "work to do too ... in fact I probably have just as much fucking work to do as you" (73). The "work" here is not domestic chores, but writing and other creative activities, which are depicted throughout *Dinners & Nightmares* as being habitually deferred in favor of the work necessary to keep the "pad" functioning. When "The Quarrel" ends with the oblivious Mark yelling into the kitchen "Hey hon ... It says here Picasso produces fourteen hours a day" (74), readers understand di Prima's desire to "produce" is compromised because she "happen[s] to be a chick."

If "The Quarrel" represents the breakdown of the connection of just two people, it doesn't seem to bode well for the possibilities of a wider creative community, and yet di Prima offers models of what such a community might look like. Despite the cluelessness of the male dinner guests depicted above, one such model comes through food, as in the description of "garbage soup which was everything cheap thrown in a pot. cooked in a four gallon kettle, enough for everybody, payment was always you brought up some wood for the fireplace. food was warm all night, you just took a bowl and sat down" (25). If food helps people to connect – whether a wider circle as depicted here or just two lovers – then it can actually serve as a creative outlet congruent with artistic production, as in the sketch in which the speaker makes a clam dinner for her lover, and while waiting for his arrival writes "a play by chance, which is a good way to pass time ... i called it six poets in search of a corkscrew" (37). Although such moments are not exactly ideal, they do suggest the extent to which a female Beat writer could participate in the experimental creative ferment while simultaneously managing expected domestic duties such as cooking; in this regard, *Dinners & Nightmares* demonstrates the undue burden on women, who had to worry about both their art and the maintenance of the home – something that, from the book's point of view, men can ignore so that they might indulge their wanderlust and artistic ambitions.[30]

8.3   LeRoi Jones: Black Bohemian

Although I have thus far discussed LeRoi Jones mainly in the context of his editorial work, he is also one of the most significant writers to emerge from the Beat movement, having by the mid-1960s produced everything from poetry (*Preface to a Twenty Volume Suicide Note* [1961] and *The Dead Lecturer* [1964]) to a novel (*The System of Dante's Hell* [1965]), plays (notably, *Dutchman* [1964]), essays on art and politics (*Home: Social Essays* [1966]) and an influential work of musicology (*Blues People* [1963]). As this list suggests, Jones was extremely prolific in the late 1950s and early 1960s, years that the editor of the *LeRoi Jones/Amiri Baraka Reader* (1991) breaks down into "The Beat Period" (1957–1962) and "The Transitional Period" (1963–1965). The second label is meant to indicate a profound shift in Jones's life and aesthetics: in 1963–1965 he was growing increasingly wary of the bohemian avant-garde scene he viewed as dominated by white people, and after the assassination of Malcolm X in 1965, he denounced his white friends (and Hettie Jones, his Jewish wife), changed his name to Amiri Baraka, and moved to Harlem where he became active in Black Nationalist and Black Arts movements. This biographical fact has led many critics to view the "Beat Period" as a stepping-stone on the way to becoming Amiri Baraka, so that, as A. Robert Lee has observed, "The Beat phase ... increasingly takes on the look of interlude, temporary creative mooring" for those who want to view Jones as Baraka, a writer whose work is most profitably understood in the context of later movements like Black Arts.[31] While there are good reasons for viewing Jones's work in other contexts, I'll emphasize the Beat one in this book, looking at work from 1957 to 1965 to explore not only how he, like di Prima and many others, was stimulated by the bohemian scene but how the limitations and contradictions of this scene motivated him to develop his work in new directions.[32]

Jones's early work is invested in announcing his connections to the underground, and attending to the particularities of this environment helps us see how it launched him away from the Beat counterculture and into the other social and aesthetic contexts mentioned above. Born in 1934 in New Jersey, Jones graduated from Howard University, and then saw some of the world in the Air Force, but it was his move to the Lower East Side that opened his eyes to the possibilities of the written word. As Jones later put it, as a young man, "the word 'bohemian' I thought of as intriguing, positive, something to be found out about and emulated ... I was drawn to all of them and all of it. Who knew that all of this sat in a particular way in the world of meaning? Who knew the significance of all of it measured against a real world?"[33] While in subsequent years Jones would famously criticize this world, mainly for reproducing retrograde assumptions about race, in the late 1950s, Village bohemianism still represented to him open-mindedness and progressive possibility.

Jones's first book of poetry, *Preface to a Twenty Volume Suicide Note*, consisting of work written between 1957 and 1961, can be read as an exploration of the bohemian "world of meaning" and the ways it could be "measured against a real world." In *Preface*, Jones does everything from wrestle with the virtues and limitations of bohemianism, to offer unconventional love poems, odes to popular culture, and ironic jabs at the perils of "turn[ing] out bad/ A J.D./ A Beatnik/ A [/] Typical wise-ass N.Y. kid" (unbracketed slashes in original).[34] *Preface* is a telling snapshot of Jones's Beat poetics, and written as it was when he was in the thick of the scene, editing *Yugen* and defending Kerouac's writing in the pages of *Evergreen*

Review, it's hardly surprising that he makes frequent references to this scene and its mores – just a few years later, the *Herald Tribune* would dub him "King of the East Village."[35]

Preface is dedicated to his wife Hettie Jones, a dedication echoed by subsequent poems "For Hettie" and "For Hettie in Her Fifth Month," so subscribers to *Yugen* could form a mental picture of a buzzing bohemian household where "terrible poems come in the mail" (15). And beyond references to his own immediate family, Jones repeatedly underscores his personal connections to the new poetry, and includes poems for Ginsberg (21–22), Gary Snyder (24), John Wieners (25), and Michael McClure (25). One of Jones's most anthologized poems, "In Memory of Radio," is so partly because its opening lines boldly proclaim affinity with Kerouac: "Who has ever stopped to think of the divinity of Lamont Cranston? / (Only Jack Kerouac, that I know of: & me. / The rest of you probably had on WCBS and Kate Smith, / Or something equally unattractive.)" (12). In this wistful paean to the golden age of radio, Jones declares his veneration of the spectral crime fighter The Shadow – Lamont Cranston's alter ego – over popular patriotic singer Kate Smith, an appreciation he shares with Kerouac, suggesting an insider sensibility starkly opposed to "the rest of you," consumers of tepid mass media.[36] The balance of the poem is a chatty tour through popular culture that probes the "divinity" of unexpected places that only a select few can apprehend, let alone appreciate. In this way, Jones defines bohemianism via a new consciousness that creates its own "world of meaning" distinct from that of dominant culture.

And yet, despite the nostalgic promise in a poem like "In Memory of Radio," a recurring concern of *Preface* is figurations of "bohemianism" itself and the ways it remains in danger of being absorbed into the mainstream. In fact, like di Prima, Jones is attuned to the fact that bohemianism may already have been so absorbed – after all, listening to "The Shadow" is possible only via engagement with mass media, and as K. C. Harrison has argued, understood in this light, the radio is less an object of nostalgia and more a tool of socialization, as it "has caused [Jones] to internalize white radio voices."[37] In this view, the seemingly simple fraternity of appreciating The Shadow with his fellow underground writers is compromised by the unifying racial and social politics at work in such widespread dissemination, and so a strategy one finds in *Preface* is to adopt and redeploy certain characteristics of the medium, so that, as Harrison argues, Jones finds in radio's "static, channel-switching, and confusion of voices a new model for his process of self-inquiry" (ibid.). Such "channel-switching" and "confusion of voices" is found throughout *Preface*, and helps us see the proliferation of voices in the collection as models of varied ways of being – bohemian, Beat, square, black, white – that constitute Jones's articulation of self as framed by the underground scene from which he wrote.

Considered in the context of the other work discussed in this book, the voices and personae in *Preface* can be read as an interrogation of "real" bohemianism – explored with the caveat that such bohemianism exists mainly in the imagination. If Hettie is characterized as authentically hip – "she's been a bohemian / all her life ... black stockings / refusing to take orders" (13, ellipses in original), others in *Preface* are poseurs, hangers-on, or squares who look to the status quo for guidance on how to live. In "Vice," for example, Jones explores the difficulty of self-expression given that such expression must be received and understood by others in order to have meaning. The opening lines assert: "Sometimes I feel I have to express myself / and then, whatever it is I have to express / falls out of my mouth like flakes of ash" (27). The speaker's expressive potential "falls" short because, unlike the scenario in "Radio," those who might appreciate what he has to say are becoming increasingly replaced by those who participate in institutionalized bohemianism, a paradox that leads to that most depressing of phenomena: "Organized fun" (27). Here the Beat bandwagon is in full effect: "Pot Smokers Institute is going on an outing tomorrow; my / corny sister, in her fake bohemian pants, is borrowing something" (27). The notion of "borrowing" or appropriation haunts much of *Preface* so that as Jones tries to carve out an authentic expression of self, he does so in constant awareness of his bohemian milieu, which is in turn increasingly alert to its position vis-à-vis dominant culture.

"One Night Stand," a poem dedicated to Ginsberg, reads as though Jones is channeling di Prima in his half-ironic concern for who gets to set the terms of "cool." The dedication isn't incidental as Jones had credited "Howl" for introducing him if not to the idea of cool, then to the notion that poetry could be of the moment, alive and relatable (*Autobiography*, 150). "One Night Stand" investigates the results of being brought into the Ginsbergian fold, and opens with a cadre of bohemians storming New York City like holy barbarian raiders: "We entered the city at noon! / ... We roared through the old gates" (21). From this opening declaration, readers may expect Jones to elaborate the "total assault on the culture" model of Beat aesthetic critique; but instead the poem is about those outsiders with "incredulousness" being monitored by denizens of the city, "old men watching us slyly / as we come in" (22). The final lines internalize this surveillance and use it to question pat figurations of bohemians versus dominant culture, or us versus them: "We *are* foreign seeming persons. Hats flopped so the sun / can't scald our beards; odd shoes, bags of books & chicken. / We have come a long way, & are uncertain which of the masks / is cool" (22). Evoking the familiar characterization of the Beats as the "beard-and-sandal set," Jones imagines how he and his friends appear to the old men, who zero in on their beards and "odd shoes." But rather than dismiss such an attitude as provincial or old-fashioned, Jones imagines it as part of the bohemian triumph, that they "have come a long way" *because* they are objects of suspicion by the old men. The last lines then recontextualize the interactions of social spheres once again, acknowledging that the idea of "cool" is relational insofar as it depends on the "old men" being not cool. But rather than finally affirming a kind of cool insiderness, Jones – like di Prima in *This Kind of Bird Flies Backward* – questions the stability and probably very existence of "cool." By associating cool with masks, Jones figures it in terms of performance, as a pose that is perhaps not so far in spirit from those wide-eyed members of the Pot Smokers Institute looking for fun – but not too much fun.

The "corny sister" in "Vice" makes another appearance in what is probably the most significant poem in *Preface*, "Hymn for Lanie Poo" (referring to the childhood nickname of Jones's sister, Sandra). This is one of the few poems in *Preface* that deal explicitly with race, and as such has been taken by many commentators as an important precursor to Jones's later work on this subject, especially as it understands the meaning of race quite differently from that of his post-1965 work. Crucially, Jones frames this exploration in terms of the distinction between underground and dominant cultures, and Lanie Poo's problem is that she is cut off from the black community because she patterns her taste and behavior after white, establishment culture. She is therefore comparable to the "corny sister" in "Vice" with her "fake bohemian pants," an imposter, counted among those whom Rimbaud, in the poem's epigraph, calls "*faux Négres*" (6). As Jones once remarked of the poem, "It's about what E. Franklin Frazier called the *Black Bourgeoisie*. It tries to equate modern life, modern Negro life in America, with the life . . . in some unknown African tribe."[38] The connection between "Lanie Poo" and Frazier's *Black Bourgeoisie* (1957) makes sense as that somewhat notorious book had met with criticism by black intellectuals for charging middle-class African Americans with modeling themselves on the most crass, materialistic aspects of the white middle class. Given this connection, Jones's poem is better understood not as a condemnation of a specific person but as an exploration of modes of blackness available at mid-century.

Of a piece with Frazier's black bourgeoisie, Lanie Poo actively pursues the material trappings of the white middle class, a pursuit, the poem suggests, that serves to erode her own racial identity and her connections to the black community.[39] In the first lines, for example, Lanie Poo has internalized caricatured notions of exotic Africanness, so that "wild-assed trees" are legible to her only after being turned into "charming wicker baskets" (6), the implication being that anything "wild" must be domesticated into trivial oblivion. While the transformation of the wild or exotic into banal home décor seems relatively innocuous, in the final section of the poem, Jones draws out how commitment to the material underpinnings of the middle class changes also Lanie Poo's existential sense of self. As she reveres the "generation of fictitious / Ofays" (11), Lanie Poo likewise internalizes white attitudes toward blackness; as the speaker observes:

> my sister drives a green jaguar
> my sister has her hair done twice a month
> my sister is a school teacher
> my sister took ballet lessons
> . . .
> my sister doesn't like to teach in Newark
>   because there are too many colored
>   in her classes.
>
>   (11)

Just as the "wild-assed trees" have been domesticated into "wicker baskets," exotic animals such as jaguars now only hold meaning as car makes, and as Lanie Poo mimics the white bourgeoisie by dutifully taming her hair, learning the supposedly civilized way to dance, and teaching school, she estranges herself from other black people to such an extent that interacting with them in the classroom is uncomfortable. The Lanie Poo sections of the poem, then, amount to a relatively straightforward accusation of black people imitating white people that would have been familiar to readers of *Black Bourgeoisie.*

But "Hymn for Lanie Poo" does not simply reproduce Frazier's thesis, for it looks also at modes of blackness vis-à-vis other social spheres, notably bohemia. In section 6, "die schwartze Bohemien," Jones counterpoints Lanie Poo's interest in the middle class with the experience of black bohemians circulating on the Village scene. The section is thus reminiscent of both those poems in *This Kind of Bird Flies Backward* that record a cacophony of bohemian voices and a poem like Bob Kaufman's "Bagel Shop Jazz," which describes the mingling of races and genders united by common social or aesthetic interests, but which remains finally skeptical about what such genteel talk covers up:

> They laught,
> and religion was something
> he fount in coffee shops, by God.
> It's not that I got enything
> against cotton, nosiree, by God
> It's just that ...
> Man lookatthatblonde
> whewee!
> I think they are not treating us like
> Mr. Lincun said they should
>
> or Mr. Gandhi
> For that matter. By God.
> ZEN
> is a bitch! Like "Bird" was,
> Cafe Olay
> for me, Miss.
> But white cats can't swing ...
> Or the way this guy kept patronizing me –
> like he was Bach or somebody
> Oh, I knew
> John Kasper when he hung around with shades ...
> She's a painter, Man.
> It's just that it's such a drag to go
> Way uptown for Bar B Cue,
> By God ...
> How much?
>
> (10–11, ellipses in original)

On its face, this vignette seems preferable to Lanie Poo's strivings since it describes an interracial social space informed by hip trends (Charlie Parker, Zen) and progressive attitudes about race. But on second look, this scene reveals its own limitations and contradictions: while it is no doubt better for a black speaker to enjoy the possibility of romance with a white woman – in contrast to Lanie Poo's disdain for "colored" students – his checking out the blonde is, like "ZEN," an interjection that serves as an inane distraction, another version of the Jaguar or ballet lessons. In this section, race apparently takes on less importance than mutual appreciation of the trending music or non-Western religion – and yet the final lines imply that such bonhomie comes at the expense of participating in a shared racial identity, so just as Lanie Poo is loath to teach in Newark because there are too many black students, so too is the black bohemian loath to travel up to Harlem for decent barbecue because it's "such a drag." The hipster argot conceals what Lanie Poo is simply more explicit about: that allegiance to the material trappings of a white sphere – in this case bohemia rather than dominant culture – means that black people are on some level alienated from themselves (this is underscored by the reference to John Kasper, a disciple of Ezra Pound who became most infamous for his fierce anti-Semitism and vocal opposition to integration). "Hymn for Lanie Poo" thus rejects bohemianism as an "antidote" to black imitation of the white middle class, imagining instead another variation of such imitation, all the more fraught as hipsterism was itself rooted in white imitation of blackness. This is perhaps why Jones wrote to Ron Loewinsohn in 1959: "I am so goddamned thoroughly tired of this beatnik shit I'm screaming."[40]

8.4   Jack Micheline: Poetics of the Street

In his autobiography, Jones contextualizes the work collected in *Preface to a Twenty Volume Suicide Note* in terms of "the poetry-reading circuit" then in full swing, and singles out one poet in particular, Jack Micheline, whom he calls "the great populist" (150). Jones's recollection of Micheline as avatar of the Village coffeehouse scene is apt as he became an almost folkloric figure who cultivated a reputation as a "street poet." Rumor even held that, as Don Katzman recalled, "at one time in his life he [Micheline] lived at the top of the Washington Square Arch . . . that he possessed the key to the door at the side of the Arch and would lend it out to poets down-and-out on their luck and looking for a place to stay."[41] However embellished such stories surely were, their persistence speaks to Micheline's countercultural stature, so it is not surprising that his first book, *River of Red Wine* (1958), was given, like *This Kind of Bird Flies Backward*, a Beat imprimatur when a famous author agreed to write an introduction. In Micheline's case, Kerouac himself contributed a short introduction to *River of Red Wine* invoking the expressly nonacademic poetic lineage on evidence in the little magazines discussed above: "Doctor William Carlos Williams I think would like him, if he heard him read aloud."[42] Kerouac goes on to praise Micheline's work for not being "premeditated and crafted and revised" and compares him to other "swinging" writers on the scene including Ginsberg, Burroughs, Corso, McClure, Duncan, Creeley, Whalen, and Snyder (7). *River of Red Wine* was thus packaged as a Beat book for its first printing (and the 1986 reprint redoubles this effort, proclaiming Micheline a "major, if not understood, voice of the BEAT GENERATION," and includes a blurb from Gerald Nicosia placing the book among "the best work of the Beat Generation"), and much of the mileage Micheline got in subsequent years was from his identification as a Beat writer. Indeed, Fred McDarrah's 1960 essay, "Anatomy of a Beatnik," identifies Micheline as a quintessential poet "associated with the Beat Movement," and quotes him as saying: "I might have been politically active but it's all corrupt. I want to see better things happen that would help this country.... I've been told that the vitality of my work is identified with the Beat Generation. I'm anti-materialistic, the way I love, the way I feel, the way I think."[43] As with the self-identified Beats interviewed in other venues like Lipton's *The Holy Barbarians*, Micheline pointedly exempts himself from engaging in politics narrowly conceived, but nonetheless claims his work as making a social intervention (he was also careful to distinguish the "Beat Generation" from a Beatnik, whom he defines as "somebody running away from himself" [7]).

As for the poems themselves, with di Prima's and Jones's work, they exist in tension with perceptions of the bohemian underground, even in the use of the word "beat" or "beating," which recurs numerous times across a range of poems. The first poem in *River of Red Wine*, for example, "Lets Sing a Song," ends "and they took me away / away / away / from the roar / and the beat / and the beat / the beat," and it is as though Micheline is daring readers not to associate the repetition of the word with the so-called Beat Generation, especially given Kerouac's introduction.[44] Beyond the use of the (perhaps-incidental?) word "beat," *River of Red Wine* shares some formal and thematic characteristics of the new poetry, including an interest in jazz. This is most obvious in the two poems about Charlie Parker, "Give Bird Love" and "Last Night I Found Bird," which link Micheline to the jazz-inspired sensibilities of Ray Bremser and Ted Joans, discussed below, as well as to sweeping moral indictments familiar to readers of "Howl" or *The Miscellaneous Man*: "Machine man blinded / and binded to the / comforts/ of their laziness" (20). This sort of attack on bourgeois normality ("stuffed on T.V. / commercial madness" [ibid.]) characterizes the collection as a whole, which was written in the seemingly non-premeditated style of which Kerouac approves.

The lengthiest poem in the collection, "The Last of the Bohemians," is notable not so much because it yields original insights into contemporary problems (Micheline observes: "The politicians have / fed you with promises / and left you with doubts" [42]), but because it picks up on and makes its own the basic critique of normative culture by extending it to the supposedly hip denizens of the Village. Taking somewhat banal observations and extending them to the reputedly countercultural sensibility of the Village – a technique that, to take one other example, Corso uses in *Gasoline* and elsewhere – Micheline refuses the distinct binary between dominant and counterculture on which the Beatnik caricature insisted. To declare "the last of the Bohemians is dead" laments the loss of the bohemian era of the 1920s but leaves it ultimately ambiguous as to whether it is "America" to blame for killing the spirit of bohemianism, or the Village's "Sicilian streets" themselves, which, the poem suggests, may have willingly bought in to the sickness of mid-century America.

Micheline's objection to American civilization informs his next two books, *I Kiss Angels* (1962) (poetry) and *In the Bronx and Other Stories* (1965) (short prose). The latter book explores an America Micheline characterizes as a "seduced land where money is God and goods have spoiled the people, crushed their spirits, proclaimed false Gods, raped the minds of its workers, taken the life from its very own land."[45] To illustrate this premise, Micheline mixes first-person vignettes resembling incidents from his own life with third-person portraits of people crushed by what he dubs "this glory called civilization." These are people ignored or ostracized by the imagined "mainstream" culture excoriated in *River of Red Wine*, people who are basically good, who want to make it in America, but who face obstacle after obstacle; such people as Mexican Americans ("Bolo"), Puerto Ricans ("Puerto Rican Lolo"), Greek immigrants ("Cosmos"), and Jews ("Hot Chicken Soup," "Mr. Greenbaum," "Bernie Abramowitz," "Lessick's Kid"), as well as panhandlers ("Crazy Louie"), jazz musicians ("Go Home and Blow"), and, significantly, poets and writers, of both the authentic and phony varieties.

Amid his wrenching portraits of the poor underclass trying to make a go of it in America, Micheline has great fun mocking those pretentious artsy types who imagine they are going to sit bestride the literary world without having any real experiences (contemporary readers may detect a whiff of pretention in Micheline's own prefatory "Statement of a Poet," which solemnly concludes: "I will illuminate the darkness" [viii]). "Irwin" is about a college boy who "wanted to be a writer and . . . dreamed of Hemingway at night" (26), but who succeeds only in internalizing the norms of capitalism, finally becoming expert in the stock market and resolving to "Be always on the move – always hunting. Be a winner" (27). A similar fate befalls the protagonist of "Kid Figaro," so nicknamed because he ensconces himself at bohemian hot-spot Café Figaro on Bleecker Street. He is "an excellent student of American literature" who, like Irwin, dreams of being a "great writer" (65). But Kid Figaro doesn't have an original idea in his head, and after an encounter with a mysterious man from Colorado, he realizes that "no one could write unless he had the courage to find out who he was," that "he could never be a writer unless he became a man first" (67). From these pieces one gets a strong sense of how *not* to be a real writer, and as they are counterpointed with first-person accounts that reflect Micheline's own experiences as a hard-drinking, brawling street poet, we have the converse illustrations of how to do it right.

In this regard, the two most important stories in *In the Bronx* are "This Glory Called Civilization" and "Whiskey, Madness and Bellevue," both of which depict the poet-protagonist butting heads with the institutions that form the bulwark of a sardonically glorious American "civilization." These stories also draw connections among the poet and the wider Beat movement: "This Glory Called Civilization" has him arrested for urinating outside the Co-Existence Bagel Shop in San Francisco, the Beat gathering place filled, in Micheline's rendering, with "sick, lost defeated kids of a nation" (35). In the poet's comic post-arrest odyssey, part Kafka, part Orwell, he is roughed up by detectives who call him "another fucking queer" (36) and brought before a judge who seems existentially offended by his behavior, sending him to the county hospital for a mental examination. The poet finally games the system by faking contrition, only to later boast of his accomplishment to friends. Likewise in "Whiskey, Madness and Bellevue," the narrator asserts that "To be a poet is to be mad," and in reaction to those "boring" literary parties populated by "bastards that play the game" (53), he proceeds to drunkenly attack some police, and is arrested and taken to Bellevue. Echoing Ginsberg, who wrote in "Howl" of those desperate souls "who demanded sanity trials" (*Howl: Original,* 5), the narrator is able to secure release only after "telling the doctors I was just a drunk poet, demanding my sanity" (56). In both these stories, as in the book as a whole, Micheline underscores the connection between poetry and madness – but "madness" is an establishment term reserved for those who rebuke the systems and institutions that comprise American civilization.

8.5 The Gaslight Poets

True to his renown as a so-called street poet, Micheline read not in lecture halls or at the stodgy "literary parties" described in *In the Bronx* (53), but in places like the Gaslight Café, an important venue for poetry and folk music that opened in Greenwich Village in 1958. Although it would later become more widely known for its folk music acts, notably by a young Bob Dylan – whose album *Live at the Gaslight 1962* marks his early presence there – during the Beatnik Era the Gaslight was familiar enough to hip writers and their readers that Tuli Kupferberg's poem "Greenwich Village of My Dreams" casts it as the setting for a fictional rapprochement between the academic and bohemian factions: "Lionel Trilling kissing Allen Ginsberg / after a great Reading in the Gaslight."[46]

On the media side, the association between and Beats and the Gaslight was emphasized by mainstream newsmen like Charles Kuralt, who in June 1959 led an expedition into the Village to explore the Gaslight's strange fauna, steadfastly reporting back to middle America:

> The poets in the Greenwich Village coffeehouses have won their battle against the lawgivers, the cops, and the squares. The coffeehouses, like the Gaslight here on MacDougal street, are still operating without what might be called their poetic license, and the poets, the Beat and conventional alike, are still filling the night with smoky, blank verse.[47]

After setting the scene, Kuralt turns the microphone over to one of MacDougal Street's well-known characters, William Morris, who reads a short poem, "Lyric for Children," culminating with the advice: "do not run from armies that have not the sincerity of a child's kiss."

Although Morris was a poet, painter, and willing public figure who in the late 1950s touted himself around the Village as a consummate Beatnik artist, he has since all but disappeared from the pages of literary history. This is partly because, in keeping with his street ethos, Morris never published a formal book, although he was included in the seminal collection *The Beat Scene*, which printed his "poem for a girl I booted," as well as a photograph of him sitting barefoot on a stage, cigarette and poetry in hand.[48] In 1959, Morris did circulate a short chapbook titled *4*, which contained four selections from a work in progress, four paintings, and four long poems. Like others, Morris telegraphed his street cred by associating himself with the nonacademic lineage in American poetry, and so *4*'s back cover reproduces a photograph of him reading to an attentive William Carlos Williams, and he dedicates the penultimate poem, "cantiba high," to "gregory corso / as beautiful as any paris."[49] Morris also stakes his claim as the Gaslight's poet-in-residence with the piece "What Really Happened at the Gasbag," a tongue-in-cheek recounting of how a poetry reading there devolved into an orgy, playfully confirming the suspicions of mainstream observers like Charles Kuralt.

And yet despite these associations, Morris was also well aware that the "Beat Generation" was shorthand for a handful of figures reified both by the media and by these figures themselves, so that he could be at once ubiquitous on the Village scene but also outside what he himself calls the "inner circle." In fact, a recurring theme throughout *4* is that when discussed as a group or social phenomenon, the Beat Generation is less about a shared aesthetic or political vision and more about who is favored by Kerouac and Ginsberg. One piece tells the story of a boy who "had risen in some two years to be *the* member of the inner circle of the Beat Generation," which Morris figures as dominated by the fame of John Lowell (Kerouac, the pseudonym referring to his birthplace) and Alvin Presley (Ginsberg, the pseudonym referring to his rock-star status after the *Howl* obscenity trial). Lowell is described as the "High Prophet" of the Beat Generation, a "mad lush, wild & hoodlum writer protesting against his homosexual tendencies by his intense love of the world," while Presley is his "long-trusted & very homosexual right hand … ruthless leader and crack poet; he marched on the road to Buddha." Although these descriptions depend on Morris's intimacy with Kerouac and Ginsberg's writing and personal lives – recall that Kerouac's aggressive heterosexuality was a matter of public record even as his private encounters suggested more complex sexual fluidity, that he had explicitly disassociated the Beats from "hoodlums" in his nonfiction, and that even in late 1959, despite Ginsberg and Orlovsky's relationship, *Life* magazine still confidently asserted that "Few Beats are homosexual" – Morris would also argue that his imagined young poet would always remain on the outside, however much he tries to ingratiate himself to Lowell and Presley.[50] Indeed, in Morris's view, "The boy was never in the confidence of the triumverate [*sic*].... The 'in-group' was pretty bigoted about which people entered inwards." Frustrated by the in-group's closing of ranks, the boy at once defames its members for being "false idols" and yet still remains paradoxically attracted to such celebrity, for "he wished to be one as well." This short piece thus describes an important, though often unremembered, dimension of the Beat movement: those figures who were briefly stars on a local scene, who seemed in fact to be the very embodiment of a Beatnik ethos, and yet because they were not close enough to those we now consider major figures, or because they themselves did not publish substantive bodies of work, have been obscured by time. These are figures, like San Francisco's Paddy O'Sullivan, whom we might justifiably call Beatnik writers rather than Beat writers, as they were more successful at promoting their personas than producing writing.[51]

Given that figures like Morris did not publish formal books, it is important to pause over what work we do have as it offers glimpses into aspects of the Beat movement that are hard to see at half a century's remove. In the case of the Gaslight, for example, it was not only media like CBS that associated it with the Beat phenomenon, but also its owner, John Mitchell, who self-published an anthology, *Poetry of the Beat Generation: As Read in the Gaslight*. Mitchell was a familiar character on the underground – he had even roomed for a time with Maxwell Bodenheim, an old bohemian poet much admired by the Beats – and his collection tried to establish the Gaslight as a locus of Beat activity in the Village.[52] The anthology includes the likes of Micheline writing about the "I don't give a damn generation," "poets in the wind," and the "Greenwich Village movie hero."[53] Also included is Morris ("Return to New York") and other important writers such as Ted Joans ("The Sermon") and Allen Ginsberg ("A Dream X August 28, 1958").

Poetry of the Beat Generation also included some less-familiar names that nonetheless comprise significant aspects of the Lower East Side poetry scene at the time, in particular Dan Propper, Barbara Moraff, Stephen Tropp, and Hugh Romney (who would be better known to the 1960s counterculture as Wavy Gravy). Other contributors are less significant to Beat literary history, but attention to them helps us see both how prominent figures like Ginsberg and Kerouac were characterized and how the figuration of "Beat" itself was stretched and explored, by turns taken seriously or satirized. For example, in "The Little Prophet," Clinton Nichols – who had also turned up in Stanley Fisher's anthology *Beat Coast East* (1960) – wrote an ode to an unnamed "rebel soul crying for answers" who is clearly Ginsberg; we learn, for instance, that "In jersey's sky one soul burned beauty" while "Rockland looks on" and "In the night angels howl."[54] In Claus Stamm's contribution, the triolet, an old-fashioned poetic form of eight lines in which the first, fourth, and seventh lines are the same, as are the second and last lines, is updated for the Beat Generation: "Triolets are very beat. / First you get, like, a refrain. / Dig? Then you, like, repeat: / 'Triolets are very beat.'"[55] This poem resurrects an obscure poetic form by recognizing the popular perception of Beat poetry as sing-songy and simple, and exploiting this perception to make an ironic commentary on the nature of this poetry. By writing a paradigmatically Beat (or Beatnik) poem in fusty traditional form, Stamm at once embodies and satirizes a Beat ethos, half-seriously bringing in cartoon slang (like, dig, grooves) and fitting it into the restrictive form of a triolet with results that sound pretty good in the end.

Of the other poets in *Poetry of the Beat Generation*, I would single out Moraff, Propper, and Tropp as figures who merit further study. Moraff was an important female voice during the Beatnik Era, who in addition to being a Gaslight poet was known at only eighteen for having read with the likes of Ginsberg, Corso, and Kerouac at the nearby Seven Arts Café, and as such was included in the foundational anthology *The Beat Scene* and published in venues like *Evergreen Review* and *Yugen* (I discuss Moraff at more length in Part IV).[56] In 1959, Seymour Krim tossed off a list of "raw" Beat poets, counting the more obscure Propper in the same breath as Ginsberg, Bremser, Joans, and Micheline, a move that again suggests the constantly shifting bounds of perceived Beat insiderness.[57] But Propper's first short book, *The Fable of the Final Hour and Other Poems* (1960), does seem identifiably Beat as its title poem counts down the last sixty minutes in the final hour of the world, hence the reason why Krim would place the poem between Holmes and Kerouac in his own anthology, *The Beats* (1960). Evidently inspired by "Howl," "The Fable of the Final Hour" strikes a similarly apocalyptic tone while borrowing Ginsberg's catalogue structure to run through all the strange things that happen as the world slips into oblivion, many of them involving favorite Beat touchstones:

> In the fourth minute of the final hour thousands of frenzied poets engaged in drunken roof-dancing atop Sutton Place....
>
> In the 25th minute of the final hour fire swept through a marijuana grove deep in the woods of Madison, Wisconsin, completely entrancing the entire Volunteer Fire Department....
>
> In the 32nd minute of the final hour 36 unreleased masters by Charlie Parker were unearthed in a Philadelphia cellar. They were, fortunately, trampled upon by the police before they could spread Disorder and Uncertainty....
>
> In the 48th minute of the final hour all of the road signs were altered to read "GO!"[58]

Few would find this poem as powerful as "Howl," and yet it is more accomplished than much of the work in *Poetry of the Beat Generation*, and demonstrates the sly humor and ability to skewer social mores in a single absurd vignette that would characterize Propper's later work. Although Propper seemed to make his mark on the Beat scene later, with books like *For Kerouac in Heaven* (1980), *Fable* reminds us that his was another of many voices on the scene with like-minded aesthetics and social critiques that taken together would amount to an identifiable Beat ethos.

This is likewise the case with Boston poet Stephen Tropp, who with wife Gloria appears frequently in Fred McDarrah's photographs of the scene, but who remains largely neglected, despite his inclusion in such collections as *Beat Coast East* (1960) or, later, Jack Micheline's *Six American Poets* (1964). His first book, *Mozart in Hell* (1959), was published by his friend Tuli Kupferberg's Poets Union Press (PUP), an "affiliate" of his Birth Press (discussed below). Mozart is presumably in hell because of the prominence of jazz and the jazz aesthetic in the new poetry – Chuck Berry's like-themed song "Roll Over Beethoven" charted in 1956 – and Tropp's book contains many overt references to jazz musicians such as "Poem Written to 'Bluing' by Miles Davis (Prestige 7012)" and "Elegy for a Broken Bird" – a poem for Charlie Parker, a subject taken up not only by Jack Micheline but by a range of writers from Corso to Frank O'Hara – as critic Maria Damon put it, "poems for Charlie Parker were practically de rigueur in hipster culture."[59] Picking up on the surreal strain of the Beat aesthetic, *Mozart* also contains work such as "My Wife Is My Shirt," which was the first poem printed in Stanley Fisher's anthology *Beat Coast East* (1960).

To my mind, the most successful poem in *Mozart in Hell* is "Uncle Tom's Cabin," a pointed rewriting of the character of Uncle Tom. Rather than being uncritically loyal to white people, Tropp's Uncle Tom tries out a "violent experimental method" when dealing with white people. At one point, his ghost appears to white teenagers who want to be hip; channeling Mailer's arguments in "The White Negro" and lampooning them as Ted Joans would, Tropp writes: "A jovial red spectre unfolds over Bohemia. On his [Uncle Tom's] . . . tail are clustered hordes of 15 & 16 year old girls squealing in ecstasy. The spectre giggles over & over in a bass voice: 'All ah wants to do is teach dem lil ole white gals some jazz sos dey know how to tap their dainty footsies in time.'"[60] Tropp's Uncle Tom signifies: speaking in over-the-top dialect, he claims merely to want to educate the "lil ole white gals" in the ways of dancing – that is, to give them some kind of access to authentic blackness that would in turn fashion them into real, hip bohemians. But of course Tropp knows such a figuration is an exaggerated image of blackness that nonetheless makes sense to white teenagers desperate for a rebellious experience that can remain nonthreatening.

8.6 Ray Bremser: Jailbird, "Best Poet of His Generation"

Taken together, the relatively "minor" poets associated with the Gaslight encourage us to see the Beat movement more capaciously, and to pause over how this movement was constituted by contemporaneous editors and anthologists. There was, however, another poet collected in *Poetry of the Beat Generation* who is a significant Beat voice: Gaslight regular Ray Bremser. For much of the mid-1950s, Bremser had been incarcerated at the New Jersey State Reformatory at Bordentown for an armed robbery he had committed in 1953 at the age of nineteen. While in prison, Bremser turned to reading and writing as a way to make sense of his situation; he explained to Alfred Aronowitz in 1959, "It was the desire to retain one's own sanity which prompted me to submerge myself in writing."[61] When Bremser read about the "Howl" trial happening out in San Francisco, he recognized a kindred spirit in Ginsberg, and in 1957 mailed what Ginsberg described as a "mad long Rimbaud letter."[62] Ginsberg in turn put Bremser in touch with LeRoi Jones, who published his first poetry in *Yugen*, introducing him to hip readership in New York City. In part because he seemed a living embodiment of an anti-establishment ethos, an imprisoned rebuke of the legal system, by the time Bremser was released from prison in 1958, he was a minor celebrity to the Village underground, and Jones threw him what amounted to a debutante party. Living on the Lower East Side for a time after his stint in prison, in 1959 he met Brenda Frazer – later Bonnie Bremser – while on a reading junket in Washington, DC, and the couple married three weeks later. By the end of the decade they had fled to Mexico in the hope of evading charges of parole violation, a period chronicled by Bonnie in *Troia: Mexican Memoirs* (1969), discussed below.

Although Bremser had written most of the material for his first two books, *Poems of Madness* (1965) and *Angel* (1967), during the Beatnik Era, owing in part to his frequent bouts with the law, they were not published in book form until the mid-1960s. But in the lead-up to these books, Bremser was included in many Beat anthologies, not only the Gaslight volume, but also *Beat Coast East*, *The Beat Scene*, and *The Beats*, and was perhaps conferred the most legitimacy by being featured in Allen's *The New American Poetry* in 1960. During this period, Bremser had emerged as a visceral and uncompromising underground poet whose raw and evocative work transcended the shaggy shtick of his Gaslight confrere William Morris. In 1962, Bonnie organized an "Open House for Ray Bremser" at the Living Theatre in New York to help pay legal expenses after yet another arrest; participants included di Prima, Huncke, Jones, Lamantia, Ed Marshall, Irving Rosenthal, John Wieners, and Ed Sanders, among others – that same year Sanders called Bremser "the outstanding American poet" (note the definite article).[63] Fellow poet and longtime friend Charles Plymell echoed this contemporary assessment on the occasion of Bremser's death in 1998, saying that he was "one of the original, if not one of the most authentic Beats, a hipster from the same vein as Herbert Huncke ... from the jazz subterranean world down the block to where Kerouac was blowin' ... His poetry had the same jazz, surrealist, existential, hip tones as did his 'street-beat' contemporaries, Jack Micheline and Bob Kaufman."[64]

Bremser's first published poem appeared in *Yugen* 3 (1958) under the title "Part III (Poems of the City Madness)." It is a conflicted ode to Caril Fugate, infamous in the 1950s for being the teenaged lover of Charles Starkweather, a Nebraskan man who went on a murdering spree with Fugate as his accomplice. Calling Fugate "the youngest ever martyr," Bremser imagines how she could have been charmed and cajoled into participating in the murders by Starkweather, and ends the poem with a sensual offer: "let me run my cool tongue / in your mouth on your tears through your difficult / washmachine beauty."[65] In its flirtation with one of the most scandalous offenders of the 1950s, this poem introduced Bremser to the underground as a writer who not only understood the criminal impulse intimately, but did so in terms of anti-establishment critique, an ability that went a long way in explaining his appeal in the context of the Beat movement.

Poems of Madness extends this critique by opening with a childhood memory of seeing a police officer "humping some young / indiscernable [*sic*] girl in the park," after which moment the speaker grew to hate "what passes as law."[66] From there, Bremser moves into a revised version of the Fugate poem that had appeared in *Yugen*, in which the speaker draws a more direct line between the famous criminal and himself: "i've never been ready for trial. / But Carole [*sic*] Fugate has! / Sweet youngest ever martyr" (2). Later in *Poems of Madness*, Bremser amplifies this provocation by bringing in Starkweather:

> Praises America!
> Praise to my country!
>
> Let me bequeath it all
> to another blazer – Charles Starkweather!
> He should know how to handle the infinite
> putrid condoms somebody's mother manufactures.
>
> (9–10)

It was this sort of gritty, hard-nosed realism that both won Bremser acclaim by the counterculture and provided fodder for those critics who saw the Beats as poets of the "new violence." But declarations like the above notwithstanding, Bremser is not endorsing violence so much as the generative potential of deviance, and he in fact immediately mitigates his paean to Starkweather by realizing that praising him amounts to "cutting corners" (10). What he really means to do is ennoble the sort of "best minds" Ginsberg catalogues in "Howl," for as he makes his "visionary journey out of jail," he realizes that

I prefer to run around with homosexual cats,
in drag, then suck on sallow
tinfoil tits of brittle broads born in
                              nebraska!
. . .
                              Give me your black
and miserable hides and I will untar them.
And I dig jazz, and hipsters.
                                                (10)

As Bremser revises the most well-known passage from Emma Lazarus's famed poem "The New Colossus" ("Give me your tired, your poor, / Your huddled masses"), he ironically extends the poem's promise of nondiscrimination by opening "my country" up to those who have deviated most shockingly from its norms.[67] Such a move is in keeping with a broader Beat ethos of love and acceptance, an idea Bremser himself recognized, as when he writes in *Angel*, "holy everything Allen says," finally asking, "what else can you do? I mean what else *is* there to be done? love everything. or at least, like the hip, try to . . . dig as much of everyone you can & count yourself lucky in the outcomes no matter what."[68] In *Poems of Madness*, the primary impediment to such love is the penal system, depicted as a perpetrator of violence on the order of the mental institution in work by Ginsberg or Solomon ("fuzzy is the dissonance / of their wrath!" [4]). This system breaks its prisoners according to its own peculiar logic, so the first part of the book ends with the speaker's desperate plea: "I will sign the confession of monstrous [*sic*] crime . . . I WILL SIGN!" (4). In this context, Bremser cultivates what he calls "a wild unpatriotic rebel attitude" (8), and it is not the best of America that leaves him feeling unpatriotic, but those darker impulses that underwrite his mistreatment in prison, the morbid cultural fascination with Starkweather and Fugate's celebrity – if not with their crimes – as well as a mainstream sensibility that reads violence in one's non-conformist hairstyle, as in the speaker's "cascades of violent pure-bred hair!" (8).

Poems of Madness can be divided into two broad parts: first, a series of long "Poems of Madness," which are of the gritty, somber type already discussed; and second, "blues for bonnie," which is marked by a shift in style and tone to a more jazzy, free-form, and lighthearted riff on love and the underground scene in general. As in work like Kerouac's *Old Angel Midnight*, in the "blues for bonnie" section, Bremser is often interested in exploring the sound of the language rather than its semantic meaning: "whallop, a / lalapalooza floozie / on via flamina piazza / masticating a ruddy pizza" (15). In addition to such playful riffing – which is probably indebted to Kerouac's experimentations – this section of *Poems of Madness*, written as it was after Bremser had met Ginsberg and his circle, makes an explicit effort to contextualize his work in the Beat movement.

In the "blues for bonnie" section in particular, Bremser took care to place himself into a select circle of writers, thereby according his poetry heft as progenitor of this sensibility. In order to do so, he first offers what might seem a standard or obvious definition of "funk," associating the term with a black jazz musician who seems preternaturally – and pointedly nonrationally – connected with his instrument: "anyway, funk is when / thelonius monk peeps / above the bamboo shades / to see the piana setting there" (17). When I say this definition is standard or obvious, I mean that it is so from the Beat or underground perspective: a musician like Thelonius Monk was interpreted as being originator and exemplar of the new consciousness, but the idea of "funk" is racially marked as well, a mode of expression that cannot be articulated through conventional language and that inheres especially in black expression, an idea found in statements from white writers such as Kerouac (in, for example, *The Subterraneans*) or Norman Mailer (in "The White Negro"), and then upheld but skewered by black writers such as Ted Joans (who added the word "Funky" to various editions of his early book, *Jazz Poems*).

In Bremser's conception, "funk" names another dimension of the hip experience, and following this description of Monk's cool attitude, which has him "perfectly zonked and / loafing on the stool" (17–18), Bremser, like the members of Monk's trio, launches into improvisational variations on the idea of "funk":

> KEROUAC: on funk.
> > "you jus don know."
> > "what don i know?"
> > "how good them bacon
> > and them eggs is . . ."
> > [. . .]
> ROI JONES: on funk
> > . . . but them colored guys
> > with the big dicks . . .
> > or,
> > those wicker-baskets would make
> > wild-ass trees.
> or
> PETER ORLOVSKY:
> > pissed your pants again, huh,
> > morris?

GREGORY CORSO:
> radiator soup.
> kangaroonian weep.

PHILIP WHALEN:
> (2 lines, canceled . . .)

MICHAL [*sic*] MC CLURE:
> whap whap
> whap whap whap whap whap
> whap
> whap . . . do you believe me
> now?

(18–19, unbracketed ellipses in original)

Beyond a mere list of Beat associated writers, this section of the poem is also a slyly humorous take on the essence of these writers' aesthetic sensibilities (as Ginsberg observed of Bremser, "he's funny; on Funk, funky").[69] Displaying his fluency with his friends' writing, Bremser quotes nearly verbatim from Kerouac's *Mexico City Blues*: "GOOFING AT THE TABLE / 'You just dont know.' / 'What dont I know?' / 'How good this ham n eggs / is,'" and verbatim from Whalen's "Self-Portrait, from Another Direction," which includes his Zen ambivalence about committing anything at all to paper with the repeated phrase "(*2 lines canceled*)."[70] Jones's half-ironic allusion to stereotypical aspects of black male sexuality turns up in some of his work from this period, notably his play *Dutchman* (1964), and Bremser inverts Lanie Poo's idle thoughts in "Hymn for Lanie Poo" that the "wild-assed" trees would make nice "wicker baskets," thoughts that for Jones index identification with bourgeois whiteness, if not the opposite of funk then something close to it. The Orlovsky allusion points to "Morris," one of his better-known poems of the late 1950s, but not collected until *Clean Asshole Poems & Smiling Vegetable Songs* (1978). "Morris," drawn from Orlovsky's time as an orderly, opens with the line "Go on Morris piss up your room."[71] Zeroing in on his famed nonsensical juxtapositions, Bremser's Corso simultaneously mocks and underscores the media's version of him, a position Corso himself was adept at occupying – he had used the phrase "radiator soup" in a list of "Saleable Titles" he included before the title page of *The Happy Birthday of Death*. Bremser's McClure emphasizes experimentation with pure language that reached its weirdest, most committed incarnation in his development of "beast language" – guttural, animalistic sounds he used to explore his interconnections with nonhumans, as in *Ghost Tantra*'s "WUB / WUB / WUB / WUB."[72] The satire here works precisely because Bremser is clearly intimate with these writers and their work, and can affectionately strike to the heart of their personas and aesthetic projects. And considered in the context of *Poems of Madness*, this section also represents Bremser's shift from an individual poetic consciousness, literally and metaphorically confined to penal institutions, to a sense of participating in an artistic movement: in the course of performing variations on the idea of "funk," he is likewise offering an on-the-fly characterization of the Beat movement, and thereby giving himself authority to speak in and for such a movement.[73]

8.7   Bonnie Bremser: Distorted Communities

Like her husband Ray, Bonnie Bremser's writing certainly bears the marks of the Beat movement, but it is not so quick to explicitly claim itself as an insider's view of this movement. Her most important work, *Troia: Mexican Memoirs* (1969), is an extraordinary account of a period during which she and Ray fled to Mexico to escape legal charges, and she supported him and their infant daughter by working as a prostitute. In addition to its startling, often disturbing content, the most striking thing about *Troia* is its form: like Ray's poetry, which is willing to promiscuously dance from image to image and chase sounds to unexpected places, Bonnie's work jumps imagistically around in time and space to yield, as critic Mary Paniccia Carden has put it, "a fragmented and disjointed text, riddled with gaps, understatements, and contradictions; at points . . . impossible to follow with any real degree of certainty," a form that reflects the chaotic nature of her life at the time.[74] As Bremser asserts in the opening lines of the book: "I know that continuity is necessary, and I do my best up to a point, but I believe in distortion."[75] Such distortion is a version of the Beat evasion seen throughout this book insofar as it means Bremser recounts her experiences without necessarily making sense of them either morally or narratively.

On the more localized level of sentence and scene, *Troia* can be understood as an emulation of Kerouac's spontaneous prose: "If I sound like Kerouac," Bremser later recalled, "it's because I tried to.... He had the knack of the long sentence, which is carried by emotional weight fueled by transcendent flashes of realization."[76] In *Troia*, Bremser describes her experiences via long sentences that bear the "emotional weight" of exploiting her body for the survival of her family. Some passages loudly echo Kerouac's, as in the line "I know that I am as much Mexican as I am New Yorker or even spade, Negro, Veracruzan" (39), which recalls Sal Paradise's remark in *On the Road* that "in a way I am [a Mexican]" (97).[77] Other references, such as to the "Mexcity time-snake" (68), suggest Bremser's familiarity with Kerouac's *Doctor Sax* and its "Great World Snake." (I also hear Burroughs in her paranoia about the "cop atmosphere" [81] and "the fuzz closing in" [124], echoes of "the heat closing in" from the opening line of *Naked Lunch* [3].) Thus while Bonnie does not directly name other writers as Ray does, her Beat aesthetic is manifest in both this range of reference and the book's spontaneous feel – as Ann Charters remarks, Bremser didn't model her writing on others in a systematic way, but rather "followed her instinct in using Kerouac's writing method" (v).[78]

From a more wide-angled perspective, *Troia*'s spontaneous feel is explicable insofar as it wasn't originally intended to be a book – its contents began life in March 1963 as a series of two-page letters written to Ray while he was in jail.[79] It was only at the end of the 1960s, and at Ray's behest, that Bonnie agreed to publish the material as a book, which was arranged by editor and critic Michael Perkins, who "picked and chose among the pieces," as she later put it ("Artista," 120). The title word, "troia," has several meanings, including "adventuress" and "courtesan," but also "slut" and "whore," a duality that speaks to the book's narrative arc: the Bremsers flee to Mexico, Bonnie begins working as a prostitute, Ray is in and out of jail, Bonnie loses custody of her daughter, Bonnie and Ray split, and, in the final pages, the couple reconciles as Bonnie "decided to stay" (*Troia*, 213).[80] From this summary alone, it is easy enough to characterize *Troia* as more Beat than even its stylistic model *On the Road*, for like Kerouac, Bremser depicts alternatives to the dominant US culture – which both books figure as oppressive – but Bremser remains far more downtrodden and outright abject than Sal Paradise, who has the luxury, as discussed earlier, of abandoning the migrant worker camp when it suits him.[81] Bremser has no such luxury, and the book is filled with descriptions of sexual encounters during which her body is reduced to a commodity to be traded. But true to the book's constant "distortion," Bremser doesn't necessarily portray herself as a victim to male predation, for she admits: "having let go completely I am somewhat ashamed at enjoying what I am paid for, enjoying it immensely at times" (50). In such moments, the nature of Bremser's sex work is figured more complexly as she asserts a kind of proto-feminist agency, an assertion that seems very Beat in its reveling in a position considered pretty dismal by the standards of dominant culture.

For our purposes, I want to think about how *Troia* figures community in contrast to how Ray does in his poetry. I explained above how Ray plays with the notion of Beat insiderness through explicitly naming other writers on the scene, a fairly standard Beat practice. *Troia* – as constituted by Perkins – seems at first as if it will present similar fictions of community. Its opening pages hold the promise of a Beat ex-pat community as the

Bremsers arrive in Mexico City after a long bus trip "on our way to make the scene at P's" (12). The initial stands for Philip Lamantia, who is never otherwise named, but affords the Bremsers entry into what Bonnie calls the "the whole Mexican crew," "all the groovy poets who dig us" (14). This crew of "groovy poets" suggests the possibility that *Troia* will be set in a Beat community that might function as an antidote to the aggressively oppressive US culture, another version of the "heaven" Sal Paradise discovers at the end of the road in Mexico.[82] This possibility is present throughout those opening pages, when Bremser reflects on being "thoroughly a member of the club" (15) or that she's "flattered to be included in the group" (20). But she soon learns that rather than being Ray's literary club come alive, in Mexico she and Ray are more or less on their own: "in New York everyone understands that when you get down to the bottom, you go without cigarettes, you eat at the Salvation Army, friends help you . . . In Mexico, it was nothing but me and the general public between us and starvation and the jailhouse" (33).

Although there seems to be a stark contrast here between the United States and Mexico, in fact what *Troia* illustrates is that countercultural or bohemian communities in either country are compromised by the long reach of capitalism. Bremser asserts in the book's first paragraph that "everything is personal" (1), and *Troia* is certainly her personal story, but this story also functions as a critique of capitalism, and how it impinges on the way people can connect (or not) to one another. As she writes: "isn't capitalism the big steal in reality? And anything I could even do would never counterbalance it. I would live a life of crime freely if it fit me, but this is only poetic justice I tamper with" (54). As it turns out, Bremser's "life of crime" doesn't "counterbalance" capitalism by plugging her into an alternative community, but it does offer a mode of resistance that adopts the logic of capitalism and then distorts it for her own ends. This is what I take her to mean when she remarked in later years, "I thought I was doing a revolutionary thing.... I felt righteous about being a prostitute" (Grace and Johnson, *Breaking*, 129–130). Likewise in *Troia*, Bremser describes herself as "a total revolutionary" (125) who "kept up my revolutionary talk whenever able" (197) – and yet when she has a chance to interact with actual "revolutionaries . . . on their American way to Cuba," she becomes "ungracious, not timid, but contemptuous. They are on their way to Cuba and idealism and here we are left to grope with the snake of time and capitalism growing; I wince every time I see a Coca-Cola sign" (55). Despite the fact that she shares political sympathies with the revolutionaries, Bremser does not seem to stand in particular solidarity with them (nor with the scene of "groovy poets" mentioned above); instead, *Troia* presents her idiosyncratic version of revolutionary critique: engaging in illegal acts of prostitution, which, via the perverse logic of exchange, afford her intermittent money and even pleasure.

That such actions also constitute engagement with a community is underscored toward the end of the book, when Bremser compares her own sex work with Ray's circulation in the literary underground. After a "A New York newspaper reporter [Al Aronowitz] had chronicled Ray as a beat (beatific) poet" (175), Bonnie suggests that he had been set on a path to prostitute himself: "The climax came when Ray himself started digging people and saying that it had something to do with poetry. In other words he was doing the same thing as I was but on an intellectual, emotional plane that was, in his description, more interesting, more valid, than the straight hustle I had learned" (174). Playing on the sexual and narrative senses of the word "climax," Bonnie depicts Ray's rising celebrity as an underground poet as the moment when she began to question her own sex work: "That's one of the main ways my head got twisted, for then it all became a lie" (174). In this view, Ray's literary prostitution is actually less honest than Bonnie's "straight hustle" because it claims to be more high-minded, more "intellectual, emotional." But in a world "built and monster-ized by capitalism" (81), writing poetry, even Beat poetry, is just another kind of hustle, and one of *Troia*'s surprising feats is to show how her prostitution could be just as "interesting" and "valid" as Ray's writing – a position that amounts to a different kind of revolutionary stance.

8.8 Ted Joans: Hipper than Thou

In an autobiographical sketch published in the mid-1990s, African American poet, painter, and musician Ted Joans looked back on his half-century career in the arts to argue that he was an early "Black Beat," by which he meant that he was a key participant on the scene as the Beats were being transfigured into cultural phenomena.[83] A poem called "I Too, at the Beginning" sums up his position:

> I am the early Black Beat
> I read with some of the
> Best Beat minds
> When the Apple was Beat Generating
> I lived in Greenwich Village
> . . .
> I wanted to change and transform
> The minds of conventional Americans.
> ("Je Me Vois," 227)

Born in Illinois in 1928, Joans studied painting at Indiana University and eventually moved to Harlem in 1951, where he slid into the arts and music scenes, even rooming for a time with Charlie Parker (Joans was the one responsible for scrawling "Bird Lives!" across New York City after Parker's death). He was eventually drawn to what he called the "atmosphere of democracy in Greenwich Village," and it was there that he first met Corso and then others, and found himself "an evergrowing popular poet amongst the Greenwich Village intellect" ("Je Me Vois," 220, 236). As he began to write more poetry in the later 1950s, Joans perfected a particular kind of Beatnik shtick that exploited the way others saw his blackness as a marker of authentic hipness. There were but "Three darker brothers," he wrote, "Born Beat and hipper-than-thou [/] Kaufman/Jones/& Joans [/] Amonst [sic] the white beatniks" (227; unbracketed slashes in original). Although plenty of other writers adopted an ironic distance from media caricatures of the Beatnik, Joans took such irony to another artistic plane, and it suffuses much of his writing, whether about race, sex, jazz, surrealism, or, later, global travel.

A canny performer, Joans played up his supposedly authentic hipness to comic effect in both poetry and cultural happenings such as his "bi-annual" birthday party, a flier for which featured a cartoon of Joans in beret, sunglasses, and goatee holding a briefcase labeled "Beat Poetry." The flier announced that "girls of the Beat Generation" should "bring other chicklets – chicks – and even hip hens."[84] This sort of half-ironic perform-ance reached its most famous heights in November 1959 when photog-rapher Fred McDarrah placed an ad in the *Village Voice* reading: "ADD ZEST TO YOUR TUXEDO PARK PARTY … RENT A BEATNIK Completely equipped: Beard, eye shades, old Army jacket."[85] Although McDarrah intended mainly to generate interest in the forthcoming book, *The Beat Scene* (1960), which featured his photographs, instead he got an "overwhelming" response to the ad, soon placed others, and did actually set up a small enterprise "renting genuine Beatniks." Unsurprisingly, Joans was a perfect fit for such an undertaking, and *The Beat Scene* includes a photograph of him at a Rent-a-Beatnik party paid for by wealthy suburban-ites in Scarsdale. As A. Robert Lee has argued: "Beat playing Beat, Joans playing himself, offers a simulation, its own kind of performance loop."[86]

Due in large part to this "performance loop," Joans was so well known in the Village throughout the late 1950s that in subsequent years his persona has sometimes eclipsed discussions of his work, which detractors have assumed are merely accompaniments to the Beatnik shtick. By 1959, Joans was famous enough to the hip crowd that music critic Robert

Reisner (who also ran the famed jazz club The Open Door and would go on to write the first biography of Charlie Parker) claimed that "In Greenwich Village you can't walk a block with him but that you have to stop while he receives the big hello. If he was walking with Eisenhower, the beats in the Village would say 'Who's that guy with Ted?'"[87] In many ways, then, Joans's image was circulated far more than his actual poetry, as in the well-known color photograph of a beret-clad Joans reading poetry in Café Bizarre, reproduced in the cover artwork for the soft-core porn Beatnik exploitation novel, *Like Crazy, Man* (1960).[88] The original photograph appeared in an article on the "Roaming Beatniks" that Kerouac wrote for a special New York–themed issue of *Holiday* magazine, and even in that piece Joans's poetry is not discussed or named except for the caption to the photograph: "Here, before an interested but informal audience, Ted Joans offers one of his creations."[89] It is thus tempting to say that Joans was a victim of his own simultaneous impersonation and undermining of the Beatnik persona, and the fact that he is less read than many of his counterparts speaks to what one recent observer dubbed his "literary non-career."[90] This is a shame because much of Joans's poetry is razor-sharp social commentary about not only the Beat scene but also the political, cultural, and especially racial matters of his times. His "black surrealist" sensibility allowed him to approach culture's conventional wisdom from a fresh, often humorous perspective; his poetry has a breezy, oral quality that nonetheless conceals trenchant insights about the demands made on black people by dominant culture *and* the counterculture.

Like many of his fellow writers, Joans invokes the inner circle ironically and to question what such writers are understood to represent. This technique is found in three books Joans published during this period, *Jazz Poems* (1959), *All of Ted Joans and No More: Beat Generation Jazz Poems* (1961), and *The Hipsters* (1961).[91] In one of his best poems, "The Sermon," Joans seems to offer practical advice for those who want to be hip:

> If you want to be hip my cute young hens, you
>   must own a copy of *Howl*
> you must read all the French Dada and Surrealist
>   literature, you must read Norman Mailer's
>   *White Negro*, you must own a copy of Jack
> Kerouac's *On The Road.*[92]

But it is not merely reading these most visible of texts that will make the young women "hip," for they are also urged to adopt the attitudes found in such work, even as Joans himself never seems to take them completely seriously. Joans therefore counsels would-be Beat chicks to "get rid of that umbilical cord that your drag- / assed prejudiced parents have around your neck . . . / If you want to be popular with real hipsters / don't talk so much and please don't ever argue" (n.p.). This is exactly the sort of advice that any writer for *Time* or *Life* or the *Partisan Review* would have seized on to prove the vacuity and immorality of the Beat lifestyle. And yet the specifics of the advice are hard to take seriously. When Joans urges his audience of "sweet angelic chicklets" to embrace all the cartoon aspects of the Beatnik counterculture, he is not so much endorsing a lifestyle as he is mocking those who imagine these features as the substance and totality of the bohemian scene. In this way, "The Sermon" is reminiscent of a work like Bob Kaufman's "The Abomunist Manifesto," a half-serious statement about what bohemianism entails: just as Joans absurdly suggests that girls "sleep with everybody but don't make it / with anybody but Santa Claus" (n.p.), so does Kaufman assure his readers that "ABOMUNISTS REJECT EVERYTHING EXCEPT SNOWMEN." To take either statement at face value is to misread their ironic play that skewers mainstream perceptions of the Beats by seeming to confirm them: while Joans's counsel to girls seems sexist and paternalistic, in the preface to *All of Ted Joans*, he writes, "Joans is after a moral revolution in the United States. And this he thinks shall come through the women of the United States, thus he continues to refuse to read in all-male universities" (n.p.). Which statement are we to take more seriously? Joans's Dada-inspired sensibility (as he wrote in *Jazz Poems*, "I am a . . . graduate of Dada University in Zurich") encourages us to see both statements as sincere and joking at the same time, a put-on couching serious claims about the way the Beats have been packaged and thereby dismissed.[93] In "Howl," the best minds of Ginsberg's generation "threw potato salad at CCNY lecturers on Dadism," a very Dadaesque protest the poem connects to its vision of social and political critique (*Howl: Original*, 5). Likewise in "The Sermon," the piling up of these supposedly Beatnik precepts points to Joans's critique of normative values, as aspiring hipsters also "must help free our people behind the Cotton / curtain as well as those unfortunates behind the Iron one / you must not live in Greenwich Village and pay / highass rent to greedy landlords" (n.p.). It is no more that Joans's imagined audience will participate in direct action in the Jim Crow South or materially assist potential defectors from the Soviet Union than they will make love to Santa Claus; but the mental attitude associated with being hip nevertheless helps one to "See the truth" behind the various instantiations of what Kenneth Rexroth called the "social lie."[94]

One notable aspect of Joans's work is its arrangement on the page, and that he sometimes mixed text with images to achieve a collage-like effect. In *Jazz Poems* and *The Hipsters* in particular, text must be read in conjunction with images, an aspect of his work that is lost when it is read in anthologies or even later collections such as *Teducation* (1999). In *Jazz Poems*, for example, "The Sermon" is as shown in Figure 8.1. The unexplained juxtaposition of image to text is at once absurd and telling: the quaint, old-fashioned drawing of a little girl reminds one that the imagined recipients of Joans's advice have not yet transformed into "hip little girls." The illustration from the medical textbook moreover suggests that the poem is dissecting the social mores that regulate human bodies.

Likewise in the poem "Uh Huh," an illustration of a dissected human hand accompanies text comprised of supposedly noncommunicative hipster slang: "uh huh / that's it / yes siree / Man this is it / the real thing" (n.p.). Readers don't know what "it" or "the real thing" refers to, and the poem continues in this chatty vein ("yep yep" and "no shit"), until the final lines: "Well I be damn / here now this is it Uh Huh uh huhuh huh uh huh uh huh / THE COLORED WAITING ROOM" (n.p.). The final line recontextualizes the fragmented slang before it as stunned reactions to the fact of segregation, implying legalized inequality is a far greater moral crime than the perceived degradation of the English language. This claim in turn suggests that the hipsters standing outside "mainstream" culture looking in actually occupy a moral high ground, and the illustration of a dissected hand stands as both a metaphor for the poet's work in dissecting culture and a reminder than the guts of all human beings are the same, regardless of race.

The social dissection continues in other poems such as "Extra Cool," in which the dropping of an H-bomb renders moot the racist gaze of neighbors who scoff at the black poet and his white partner (Joans's wife, Joyce, was white). There are also poems mentioning the NAACP and White Citizen Councils ("125 Ways to Sex"), and decolonizing Africa and Arkansas Governor Orval Faubus, who notoriously opposed the integration of the Little Rock School Distract ("Why Hurry?"). Thus while Joans's work may appear on first read an indiscriminate celebration of all things Beatnik, in fact in its elaborate play on popular expectations about the Beats it levels an ironic political critique of phenomena like institutionalized racism, which is, after all, a result of the same confident misapprehensions that assume all Beat-associated folk were accurately captured in the pages of *Life* magazine.

In 1961, Joans left New York City for other horizons, traveling to the Beat Hotel in Paris and other points in Europe, and then eventually to

THE Sermon

SO YOU WANT TO BE HIP LITTLE GIRLS?????????
SO YOU WANT TO LEARN TO SWING ?????????????
AND YOU WANT TO BE ABLE TO DIG AND TAKE IN
EVERYTHING YES DIG EVERYTHING AS POET ALLEN
GINSBERG SAID.....NOW DIG ME PRETTY BABIES...

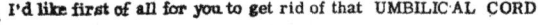

I'd like first of all for you to get rid of that UMBILICAL CORD
that your dragassed prejudice parents have around your neck
you dont need them to lay their ANTIQUEANGLOSAXONPURITANICAL
philosophy on you now...NO, pretty baby...for you are too slick to
have eyes for their late-ungreat-sick-scene, BUT love' em for
bringing you here....all you need is you.....real you, and people
that are hip
                    enough to dig whats happening.....So if your
neighborhood aint hip...SPLIT......Leave it for swinging , real
swinging surroundings.....So I want you chicks to be real hip
I want you babes to be turned on to the truth
I want you chicklets to get up off your lovely behinds and participate
in creative activity...I want you to find yourselves by doing
I want you to live it up...ACTION.....JAZZACTION
If you want to be hip, then Dig this SERMON

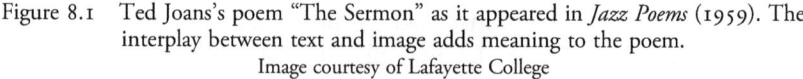

Figure 8.1   Ted Joans's poem "The Sermon" as it appeared in *Jazz Poems* (1959). The
interplay between text and image adds meaning to the poem.
Image courtesy of Lafayette College

Morocco and Mali, where he lived off and on for the next couple of
decades. Important later work includes *Black Pow Wow: Jazz Poems*
(1969), *Afrodisia* (1970), and *A Black Manifesto in Jazz Poetry and Prose*
(1971), the titles of which may suggest Joans's interest in exploring

a specifically black aesthetic, something on the order of what LeRoi Jones (writing as Amiri Baraka) called for in his influential poem "Black Art" (1965), which asserts, "We want a black poem. And a / Black World."[95] While Joans's later work isn't as pointed in its calls for violence (Baraka writes that "we want 'poems that kill.' / Assassin poems, Poems that shoot / guns"), he did become increasingly invested in the possibilities of a particularly black aesthetic, even as, unlike Baraka, he never renounced his connections to the Beats. Despite his evolving aesthetics and self-imposed exile, Joans is a key Beat writer, a figure whose accessible humor and surreal sensibility added an indispensable dimension to the movement.

8.9   Tuli Kupferberg: Beatnik Philosopher

Over the course of the 1950s, Joans became friendly with Tuli Kupferberg, a fellow writer and Village resident whom Joans liked to call his "Beat Brother of Hebraic Hipness."[96] Born in 1924, between Kerouac (1922) and Ginsberg (1926), Kupferberg was interested in writing from a young age, but his early work is more traditional in nature as he had not yet adopted the pugnacious and outré style that he perfected in the late 1950s and after. He later recalled that in the early 1950s, when he was still living in Brooklyn and writing "conventional romantic poetry," his literary world was blown apart by the Beats. "I developed a sneaking admiration for their force," he writes, "honesty & (misplaced) courage. I venally began to admire their audience, their popularity. I attended my first readings of poetry & jazz. The force & excitement of what was happening grabbed me."[97]

In the late 1950s, Kupferberg channeled this excitement into a whirl-wind of literary activity, starting a small publishing concern, Birth Press and the affiliated Poets Union Press (PUP), through which he published his own books and pamphlets such as *Snow Job: Poems, 1946–1959* (1959), *Selected Fruits & Nuts* (1959), and *The Rub-Ya-Out of Omore Diem* (1962), a parody of "The Rubaiyat of Omar Khayyam" that is, like Corso's "Bomb," a satiric ode to atomic weaponry: "WAKE! For the Bomb who scatter'd into flight / The Jets before him from the DEW of night."[98] An energetic editor, Kupferberg's press became known on the underground scene for quirky and avant-garde little magazines such as *Birth* (1958–1960); *Swing* (1960–1961), a magazine devoted to writings by children edited by Kupferberg and his wife Sylvia Topp; and the more well-known, politically minded *Yeah* (1961–1965). Kupferberg's unique blend of progressive politics and biting satirical humor is everywhere present in his own writing and editorial work, a sensibility that found its most influential expression in the rock band he founded with Ed Sanders in 1964 called The Fugs, whose most famous song, "Kill for Peace," was an anthem for those who opposed the war with theatrical acts of protest (it was written by Kupferberg). So while Kupferberg tends to be discussed in connection to a slightly later incarnation of Beatness, via The Fugs and antiwar work such as *1001 Ways to Beat the Draft* (1966) and *Fuck Nam: A Morality Play* (1967), his earlier work offers some of the era's most sustained engagements with the ideas of Beat and Beatnik.

During this time, Kupferberg became interested in theorizing the Beat phenomenon in light of the cultural misperceptions I have been discussing. The first issue of *Birth*, for example, concerns itself with figurations of the Beat Generation, a preoccupation to which Kupferberg would return in later work like *Beatniks, or The War against the Beats* (1961) and "The Function of Bohemia" (1962). Of particular interest is *Beating*, published in the summer of 1959, a treasure trove of analyses of the Beats as a social and literary movement. There are six sections: "The Subjects of Beat," "The Beat Attitude," "The Beat Ancestors," "Square Beat, Cult Beat, Commercial Beat," "Squaredom," and "Beat Poietics." The first section opens with a list of the subjects of Beat poetry:

1) sex
2) narcotics and alcohol
3) jazz
4) insanity
5) the Negro
6) homosexuality
7) hoboes & bums; travelling (new places)
8) anti-politics
9) anti-institutions (the army & war, the fuzz & prison, the mass media, the school, the job)
10) writing (& creative act) itself.[99]

Read with the caveat that plenty of other writers who had nothing to do with the Beats were interested in these topics, taken together, the list is actually a pretty good representation of a Beat sensibility circa 1959: while sex had been explored by, say, Grace Metalious in *Peyton Place* (1956), or "the Negro" by, say, Ralph Ellison in *Invisible Man* (1952), many Beats were indeed interested in those subjects as they related both to each other and to the whole constellation of concerns on

Kupferberg's list. Thus far from the titillating escapades in a middle-brow novel like *Peyton Place*, for Kupferberg, sex was always bound up in political and social questions, so that "sexual 'delinquency' . . . is one of the few healthy signs in American life today" (n.p.). While for Ellison blackness renders African Americans invisible to white America, for Kupferberg, blackness is connected to social and political revolution, as "The Beats link themselves & are linked to the new rising energies of Africa & Asia, to the primitive current life-loving peoples of Mexico & the Caribbean" (n.p.).

Even drug use is not for Kupferberg strictly recreational as it represents a sympathetic connection to those "on the outside."[100] Indeed, his characterizations of "Beat" hew to Kerouac's basic definition that connects the word to sympathy:

> Since the Beat is outside of society . . . he is sympathetic to, understanding with & seeks the friendship [of] . . . those others also on the outside:
>
> (poor) artists: (especially jazz musicians and "unsuccessful" painters)
> hoboes & hobohemians
> alcoholics and other addicts
> Negros
> homosexuals
> social (and political) minorities
> class minorities
> prisoners
> "insane people"
> children
> anyone trapped or crushed by, or fighting the ballbreaking, spirit enervating forces of society. (n.p.)

What Kupferberg is arguing, then, is that the "Beat Attitude" is at bottom one of inclusivity and acceptance, of recognizing the dangers and limitations of a mass culture that rejects difference to maintain the social and political status quo. This is quite a different view from that of disapproving commentators who associated the Beats primarily with laziness and violence – in fact, one could say Kupferberg argues that the Beats were shifting what could count as "political," if we understand sympathy toward and identification with those "outside of society" as a politically meaningful act.

Later in *Beating*, Kupferberg offers a subtle corrective to the notion that "unattached" means disengaged from society or politics: the "unattached Beat . . . is not merely anti-political . . . he is apolitical & doesn't pour his unexpressed emotions into a constipated eagle or a swinging swastika or

fall in love with a baby faced, clean shaven, fat jowled 'leader of nations'"
(n.p.). For Kupferberg, to be political is to identify or "fall in love" with
political parties or politicians, be they the Nazi Party or President Eisenhower; but as we have seen, because the Beats tended to refuse this sort of
identification, mainstream observers assumed they exempted themselves
from political considerations altogether. And yet when Kupferberg insists
that "The Beatnik is attempting a new society (a society of friends)" (n.p.),
he points to the inclusive model laid out above, an attempt that would
seem politically charged in all but the most doctrinaire senses of the word.
Indeed, one result of forging this kind of "society of friends" is that social
distinctions become irrelevant, not only between white/black, straight/gay,
middle class/poor, but even between adults and children. Thus *Birth* 2,
"Children's Writings" (summer 1959) is a compendium of poetry, stories,
diaries, and letters from children, sent to Kupferberg from around the
country, as well as some historical writing by children, an interest he
developed with *Swing*, which was entirely devoted to children's writing.
Part of the point of publishing children's writing is to divorce creative
writing from an academic context, and to rather present the material as
charming windows into children's minds – since they are, after all,
members of society.

In *Beating*, Kupferberg moves from social criticism to literary analysis in a section titled "Beat Poietics." There he takes "Howl" as
paradigmatic, confessing that his first reading of the poem mirrored
that of "America at large," so he was "repelled" and found it
"shocking," "disgusting," "exhibitionist," and "infantile." But since that
initial reaction, Kupferberg explains, he reexamined his attitudes and
realized "Howl" was necessary to the healthy functioning of contemporary America. He explains that because Ginsberg "takes himself
seriously and openly, he is willing to discuss & to air *him*self & his
writings . . . Because he is interested in creating a society of friends and
believes in poetry as an instrument of joy he wants the living contact of
the spoken word and the living audience" (n.p.). Again we find an
interest in "creating a society of friends," and it represents one way to
view what constituted the tissue of Beatdom in 1959: a willingness to
present oneself "seriously and openly" for the mutual benefit of a
community. Thus Kupferberg calls for "More Howls, more, more
horrible howls . . . More coming Kerouac lyricism . . . More Ted Joans
magnificent, magnanimous, strong humours . . . More Corso &
Orlovsky wordmake . . . More rushing and radiant Bremser. More
Abomunable Kaufman!" (n.p.).

In his own poetry, Kupferberg, like di Prima and Jones, connects to wider figurations of community by focusing on constructions and depictions of bohemianism. In *Snow Job*, for example, Kupferberg references the underground literary scene and how it does or does not fit into other literary trajectories. This is the case, for example, in "The Abominable Snow Job," which opens with a parody of the famous final line of *The Communist Manifesto* (1848) ("Workers of the World: Unite!"):

> Fuzz of all countries
> You bite!
> I'd like to turn you on!
> Whos gonna protect you guys fun yourselves?
> Certainly not the beat(niks)?
> Someday you all might arrest *each other*
> *Its not beyond the possibility of a doubt*
>
> Never underestimate the power of a poet
>
> . . .
>
> Authors note: I would of continued this
> poem more beatly but just
> as I'm writing this line
> the fuzz is entering the doo[101]

In these lines, Kupferberg plays with the distinctions between the mainstream and the Beats by inverting Marx and Engels's rallying cry to the world's exploited working classes. Here it is Kupferberg speaking with authority: it is not legal, political, or economic authority, but a kind of countercultural creative authority ("Never underestimate the power of a poet") that can confidently claim that the police, or "fuzz," bite. But however much this authority is asserted in the context of the poem itself, it is nonetheless ironically undercut in the poem's final line, when the "real world" intrudes in the form of a police raid, literally cutting the poet off mid-word.

Similar play is found in poems like "Washington Square," concerning "Tramps of feeling" and "The Bohemians [who] have gone into the sand-pit to drink sand" (n.p.); "For a Poet Scheduled to Die Young," which describes a "Landsman, cocksman, buddy of my balls" (n.p.); "The Ballad of the Rienzi Ladies," set at Café Rienzi, a bohemian hot-spot where earnest young men woo ladies with dubious lines like "I have changed you into a poem" (n.p.); and "Square," which reverses the popular notion that the Beats were violent by imputing such violence to the titular "Square":

> Tankstrut down the
> slippering street
> he'll bang you into
> a plateglass hell
>
> . . .
>
> Fags & beautiful poets
> watshit!he'll rune
> on you.
>
> (n.p.)

This is another version of Kupferberg's statement on "Squaredom" in *Beating*: "SQUARES are people who attack beats.... There is the casual kind who attacks by snide laughter.... Then there are his storm troopers fed from 2nd and 3rd immigrant generations ready to bust a head or break a fag any Saturday night in the Village" (n.p.). This conception explains how the poem "Square" inverts the media's idea of the Beats as violent, opposing squares to "beautiful poets" to underscore the cultural violence done to Beats by the dominant culture. Taken together, *Beating* and *Snow Job* comprise an important articulation of a Beat ethos during the Beatnik Era. These works illustrate Kupferberg's fluency not only with literary, cultural, and political history but also with the particular ways "Beat" was being circulated in contemporary US culture, and ought to be taken as commentaries on and correctives to such circulation. Indeed, the more obviously political contours of Kupferberg's work prefigure the direction of much Beat writing in the mid-1960s and after, when distinctions among aesthetics and politics, poetry and protest, began to break down.

CHAPTER 9

Revisions of the Real

As discussed in Parts I and II, San Francisco had a well-established avant-garde poetic community prior to the arrival of Ginsberg and Kerouac in the mid-1950s. Circles connected to Jack Spicer (who was always adamant about distancing himself from the Beats) or Kenneth Rexroth (who at times served as mentor to some writers like Ginsberg, while at other times pointedly criticized Kerouac or the whole Beat phenomenon) or Wallace Berman (who collaborated with and published many Beat-associated writers in his journal, *Semina*) existed concurrently with more recognizably Beat circles. But after the scandal of *Howl and Other Poems*, the notoriety of the Beat Generation inevitably colored literary production in San Francisco. Just as the Beat movement appreciably widened in New York City during the Beatnik Era, it radiated further out as San Francisco became the other main locus of Beat activity, not only through native West Coasters who wrote themselves into the movement, but through those from elsewhere who had migrated to the area. The following pages look at some noteworthy writers whose work illustrates how the Beat movement developed on the West Coast, becoming eventually an incarnation of Beatness that led to the 1960s counterculture unified, in part, by opposition to the Vietnam War.

9.1 Lawrence Ferlinghetti Says Things about Ontology

By 1960, Lawrence Ferlinghetti's City Lights Books was firmly established as the most visible publisher of Beat writing, thanks not only to the tremendous amount of publicity occasioned by the "Howl" trial, but also because Ferlinghetti was indefatigable in pushing his eclectic list, which included Ginsberg and Corso, as well as Marie Ponsot (*True Minds* [1956]), Denise Levertov (*Here and Now* [1957]), William Carlos Williams (*Kora in Hell* [1957]), and Nicanor Parra (*Anti-Poems* [1960]).[1] In the 1960s, he would publish the likes of Frank O'Hara, Philip Lamantia, Bob

Kaufman, Janine Pommy Vega, and Charles Upton, so his growing list is a good starting place for anyone interested in work that is, if not strictly "Beat," then certainly indicative of a "new consciousness" or broadly avant-garde sensibility as inflected by Ferlinghetti's particular tastes.

Ferlinghetti's own second book, *A Coney Island of the Mind* (1958), became one of the best-selling poetry books of the 1950s: by the book's nineteenth printing, there were 500,000 copies in circulation, an astounding achievement for any book of poetry.[2] Of course these sales can be partly explained by Ferlinghetti's fame as publisher of *Howl and Other Poems*, but the poetry stands on its own as some of the strongest that emerged from the Beat scene. *Coney Island* combines a finely tuned critical eye with a penchant for a humorous touch that seems deceptively breezy, and the result is deeply informed social and political commentary that is nonetheless broadly accessible.

Like many a work I've been discussing, *Coney Island* contains poems that turn on themselves to become about the nature of representation. This is the case in "Constantly risking absurdity," a poem so well known that one scholar used it as a title for a critical book on Ferlinghetti's work.[3] The poem's arrangement on the page mimics the delicate balancing act of good writing:

> Constantly risking absurdity
> and death
> whenever he performs
> above the heads
> of his audience
> the poet like an acrobat
> climbs on rime
> to a high wire of his own making
> and balancing on eyebeams
> above a sea of faces
> paces his way
> to the other side of day
> performing entrechats
> and sleight-of-foot tricks
> and other high theatrics
> and all without mistaking
> any thing
> for what it may not be.[4]

This is as charming a description of the writing process as one is likely to find: it captures the precarious position of the poet in society without taking itself too seriously. Ferlinghetti is interested in thematizing form, in drawing attention to the physical strictures of poetry. But the poem develops its controlling metaphor of poet as acrobat not only to underscore the difficulty of writing well but to reflect on the relationship between representation and reality: playing on John Keats's famous dictum from "Ode on a Grecian Urn" that "beauty is truth, truth beauty," Ferlinghetti imagines the poet walking the high wire of "taut truth" to get to where "Beauty stands and waits," the idea being that poetry is finally a way to make sense of the potential existential absurdity of "the empty air / of existence" (30). Just as an acrobat seems to affirm life by risking death, so too does a poet heighten life by daring to give it meaning and shape through form; as such, Michael Skau has said of this poem that it "finally stands as a testimony to Ferlinghetti himself."[5]

As suggested by the look of "Constantly risking absurdity" on the page, Ferlinghetti would with Charles Olson abandon "closed form" to take full advantage of the poetic field, an interest taken a step further in the second part of *A Coney Island of the Mind*, which was conceived, as he explains in a note, "specifically for jazz accompaniment and as such should be considered as spontaneously spoken 'oral messages' rather than as poems written for the printed page" (48). This section contains some of the poems Ferlinghetti read with Kenneth Rexroth at The Cellar in San Francisco, and ought therefore to be understood in the context of a wider interest in the aesthetic possibilities of fusing writing with formal innovations associated with jazz (one also finds this interest in work such as Kerouac's *The Subterraneans*, Holmes's *The Horn*, ruth weiss's *Steps* [1958], and Joans's *Jazz Poems*, all published within a year of *Coney Island*). But beyond merely the fact that these "oral messages" were meant to be heard aloud to jazz accompaniment, they also explore the speaker's subjectivity and relationship to his environment (see "Autobiography" in particular) as well as the nature of reality itself.

One of the best and most anthologized poems in *Coney Island* is an "oral message" titled "Dog," which takes a dog's-eye view of the streets of San Francisco, in so doing allowing the poet to reflect on "the real." Inspired by Ferlinghetti's real-life dog, Homer, the dog in the poem has "something to say / about ontology / something to say / about reality" (68).[6] The conceit of the dog trotting "freely in the street" to see reality as it is makes "Dog" broadly comparable to other Buddhist-inspired Beat works interested in apprehending *tathata* or the "world just as it is," loosed from linguistic or ideological coloration (some of these works are discussed in the coming pages).[7] But what's distinctive about Ferlinghetti is that he questions "the real" as a basis for explicit political critique: in "Dog" such critique remains relatively mild, but after *Coney Island*, his work would grow increasingly and unquestioningly political as he wrote about, say, Fidel Castro or Richard Nixon.[8] The San Francisco police department's reputation for aggressively dealing with those they perceived as Beatnik agitators hardly fazes the dog, who "doesn't hate cops / He merely has no use for them" (67). Likewise the dog has no use for conservative politicians as he trots the streets "touching and tasting and testing everything / investigating everything / without benefit of perjury" (68). The dog exists in "reality" and yet remains outside or beyond the legal and political parameters humans have instituted to circumscribe the real, and so his nonjudgmental wandering through the city amounts to a rebuke of those who collapse such parameters – ideology – with the "world just as it is," for the dog is a "a real realist / with a real tale to tell" (68).

"Dog" ends by alluding to the famous advertisement for Victor Records of a dog listening with a cocked ear to a gramophone so lifelike that he thinks it is actually "His Master's Voice" speaking to him. If the dog has "something to say / about ontology" it is because he does not mistake those false voices for reality, whether those authority figures glossed earlier in the poem or what humans as a species or culture take to be significant, for he finally looks "into the / the great gramaphone [sic] / of puzzling existence / with its wondrous hollow horn / which always seems / just about to spout forth / some Victorious answer / to everything" (68). But of course the "hollow" horn only "seems" about to spout answers to "puzzling existence," and Ferlinghetti's "real realist" dog – as opposed to the one in the staged photograph in the Victor Records ad – does not quite buy it, as he takes reality as it comes, without discrimination or judgment. In its basic critique of the way that ideologies are confused or conflated with reality, "Dog" and many poems in *A Coney Island of the Mind* share the sensibility of works like Kerouac's *The Dharma Bums* and Snyder's *Riprap*, discussed below. Kerouac indeed thought enough of the poem to write in *Old Angel Midnight* that "I will not rest no wont rest till Ferlinghetti's dog his day had does piss again on hydramatic stillness electrical ectroid" (51).

9.2   ruth weiss Keeps the Beat

ruth weiss is another important poet to emerge from this moment in San Francisco. Although she is well known to devotees of Beat literature as a poet and performance artist whose career, like Ferlinghetti's, spanned more than half a century, she is less familiar to the wider reading public, partly because she was not included in anthologies such as *The Portable Beat Reader*. Despite this unfortunate oversight, in recent years, weiss's work has garnered increasing critical attention that will likely develop further as time goes on, since, from one perspective, weiss personifies the Beat spirit more fully than others. As Preston Whaley has put it, she "wrote from the margin of the margin in the 1950s," and as such occupies that paradoxical position of a writer who has claims to being more Beat that her more famous male counterparts – and yet this very idea has meant that she has been less frequently read or taught.[9] Thus it is hard to disagree with Nancy M. Grace's assessment that "Few poets – male or female – can be said to embody Beat to the extent of the San Francisco jazz performance poet ruth weiss."[10]

Born in Germany in 1928 but emigrating in time to narrowly miss the full force of the Nazi regime, by 1950 weiss was self-possessed enough to hitchhike from her adopted home of Chicago to the Lower East Side of New York City. In 1952, she set out again, this time for her dream city of San Francisco, where she would live for a time in the Hotel Wentley, the shabby way station that lent John Wieners's first book of poetry its title. As weiss recalled, at the Hotel Wentley she wrote haiku with Kerouac until he was too drunk to continue, at which point Neal Cassady would show up to take them for rides in cars he had stolen.[11] By the mid-1950s, weiss had become interested in the aesthetic potential of connecting poetry with jazz, and despite the more visible example of Ferlinghetti and Rexroth reading at The Cellar, weiss would later claim that it was she who "started poetry and jazz" somewhere around "1955 or 6 or 7."[12] Whatever the particular origins of the very first pairing of jazz with writing, it is clear that weiss was working in the West Coast Beat scene from a comparatively early moment, and yet she has only recently been recognized as Beat progenitor by scholars and readers (and she herself has insisted on her connections to the Beats with her memoir *Can't Stop the Beat: The Life and Words of a Beat Poet* [2011]).

Such neglect was not limited to later chroniclers or anthologists, but extended to some of her contemporaries as well, for although weiss attended Rexroth's weekly salons and participated in readings at The Cellar, she recalled that when she approached Ferlinghetti about having City Lights publish *GALLERY OF WOMEN*, he turned her down, saying that he didn't publish women and that, besides, her poetry wasn't "political enough" (*Can't Stop*, 73).[13] Despite Ferlinghetti's refusal to support her work through City Lights, by 1959, weiss had self-published a chapbook, *Steps* (1958), and Adler Press in San Francisco brought out *GALLERY OF WOMEN*, *South Pacific* (both 1959), and *Blue in Green* (1960). These books, together with others such as di Prima's *This Kind of Bird Flies Backward*, and Lenore Kandel's *A Passing Dragon* and *An*

Exquisite Navel, constitute an important earlier moment of publishing by Beat-associated women, and they collectively challenge the notion that women's writing appeared on the Beat scene only later or retrospectively.

In this early work, there are two main ways that weiss explores her connections to the scene: by laying claim to bohemian San Francisco in *Steps*, and by initiating female-centered myth-making in *GALLERY OF WOMEN*, an imaginative construction that runs counter to the "boy gang" of Ginsberg and his circle. The first book, *Steps*, is a conflicted love letter to weiss's adopted city, and offers a female version of the sensibility made famous in *On the Road*:

> hitch-hiking across i found some [people]
> can't even begin to tell you how beautiful . . .
> they fed me
> and a deer-hunter shared his cantaloupes
> before depositing me on broadway and colombus [*sic*].
> he had stopped before the golden gate bridge
> to let me see the city on first-time entering.[14]

On the most basic level, the action of these lines challenges the standard notion that while men had the luxury of lighting out on the road, women simply didn't have that option for fear of personal safety. weiss, in contrast, depicts a beneficent nation in which the end of the road is the intersection of Broadway and Columbus in North Beach, mere steps from City Lights Books and what is now named Jack Kerouac Alley. San Francisco is indeed a geographic as well as psychic terminus for weiss – "one more step west is the sea" – and she understands its contemporary bohemian moment in terms of its history as an "outpost" on the edge of the continent. In this way, weiss shares with her male Beat counterparts like Kerouac and Ferlinghetti the sense of the city as an enclave of sympathetic people, but she worries about the fate of its soul:

> city, how close you are to
> water earth and tree
> and i love you for it.
> it is your saving;
> it will be your doom
> because you cannot quite accept yourself
> as you are.
> you have invited the webbed monster to connect you
> he has a cement and steel-greedy eye.
>
> (n.p.)

In this view, "city" becomes shorthand for its bohemian residents, and however enticing San Francisco is as an open and affirming place, it exists under threat from the "webbed monster," whose "cement and steel-greedy eye" echoes Ginsberg's Moloch, a "sphinx of cement and aluminum ... whose eyes are a thousand blind windows" (*Howl: Original*, 6). Via this connection to Ginsberg, weiss writes herself into the general Beat critique of establishment culture and values that might quash the spirit of the "wanderers" and "beautiful" people who populate the city. But given the collapse of population with place in her apostrophe to the "city," *Steps* also makes a case for self-love and self-actualization, so that the "you" in the lines "accept[ing] yourself / as you are" signals both San Francisco accepting its bohemian legacies, and its residents accepting themselves, thereby refusing the terms of the Moloch-like "webbed monster."

This idea of self-acceptance is on even greater display in weiss's next book, *GALLERY OF WOMEN* (1959), which as its title suggests is a collection of poems about and for women in her social and artistic circles, complemented by drawings by artist Sutter Marin that appear in the middle of the book.[15] As such, it makes sense to read the book as a counterpoint to the aggressive mutual mythologizing undertaken by the male Beats in the ways that I have described throughout this book. Although in *GALLERY OF WOMEN* weiss does not figure herself as Beat or a member Beat Generation, if one reads it looking back through the lens of her later work, one might be encouraged to interpret it as her explication of a poetic coterie at once contemporary to the Beats yet distinct from them. It wasn't really until later years that weiss began to play up her identification with the Beats, especially in her memoir, *Can't Stop the Beat*; but more than a decade earlier, she had also published another portrait gallery of women explicitly framed in terms of Beat, *For These Women of the Beat* (1997). This volume, written on the occasion of Brenda Knight's landmark anthology, *Women of the Beat Generation*, consists of short poems to the writers included therein, among others. As weiss writes in the foreword to *For These Women of the Beat*, "Many of my friends, some here some gone, belong in one more book. And then another."[16] In this spirit, we might read *GALLERY OF WOMEN* and *For These Women of the Beat* as bookends aimed at capturing a specifically female bohemian artistic and literary sensibility. weiss herself encourages this comparison as certain poems in the later book echo ones from way back in 1959. For example, in *GALLERY OF WOMEN*, her poem "Idell" (the pen name of poet Aya Tarlow) reads:

> "where have i been here before?
> look there are my footprints
> on the shore."
>
> the lily-face
> she closes in the shade
> she walks the shaded path
> the well-kept garden magics
> to jungle
> where strange flowers burst.
>   (n.p.)

Compare this with the poem "Aya Tarlow," written some fifty-two years later:

> the beat the beat the beat
> "where have i been here before
> look there are my footprints on the shore."
>   (*For These Women*, 30)

By reproducing the quoted line from "Idell," weiss draws a direct line from *GALLERY OF WOMEN* to *For These Women of the Beat*, encouraging readers to recognize the circles in which she wants her work to be contextualized. It is true that none of the names in *GALLERY OF WOMEN* is as readily familiar as those of the famous male Beats, and so the book represents an opportunity to shift how we understand the scene and who gets to be considered part of it. "Idell," for example, might take readers to the wonderful – and very Beat – work of a comparatively unknown poet, Aya Tarlow, whose books of this era, *Poems for Selected People* (1961) and *Marks of Asha* (1963), are useful companions to weiss's work.[17] weiss's poem for Tarlow is about a particular kind of feminine imagination that weiss identifies in Tarlow and many other women mentioned in both books. What makes the imagination feminine is not simply pronoun choice, but the use of tropes conventionally associated with femininity, which weiss deploys in order to twist such associations. In "Idell," for example, the "garden" is transformed from a space of maternal nurturing to a wild "jungle" – a transformation made possible via its subject's imagination, which "magics" a domesticated patch of land into something "strange" and ultimately much more curious. The idea is that a specifically female imagination or aesthetic has the power to transform the familiar into the strange, and much of the work in *GALLERY OF WOMEN* is concerned with this basic premise. In fact, keywords like "garden" or "flower" or "blossom" recur frequently throughout *GALLERY OF WOMEN*, and are generally connected to the subject's sense of self-actualization, as in "Sueko": "blossom / will you / be flower?" (n.p.). Such words and images also signal a kind of emotional specificity that is difficult for those outside the circle – perhaps men? – to understand, as in "Joan":

> (growth is pain
> and pain is passing)
> where the house
> was
> in a garden
> in the rain.
>
> (n.p.)

At other moments, garden imagery is used to suggest the ways that women are cut off or cut themselves off from others, as in "Dora," which ends with the lines: "the girl in the / secret garden chants her silence" (n.p.). For weiss, the imagination or female voice/agency is often invisible, hence the paradoxical sense of chanting silence. Given such an invisibility, the most obvious thing one can say about *GALLERY OF WOMEN* is that it aims to make a range of female subjectivity visible, and what makes it Beat is weiss's canny interest in creating a kind of counter-coterie to the men. weiss is thus a highly significant figure not only as a female Beat-associated writer on the scene comparatively early, but also because she changed the very terms of what this scene might encompass. When weiss is discussed, it tends to be in terms of later work such *DESERT JOURNAL* (written 1961–1968; published 1977) – which she considered her masterpiece – but it is also worth returning to her earlier work as it encourages us to continue reconsidering who or what comprised the tissue of Beatness in the late 1950s.[18]

9.3   Four Auerhahn Poets

As suggested by the energies surrounding City Lights, *Beatitude*, and the work of Ferlinghetti, Kaufman, and weiss, during the Beatnik Era, the West Coast poetry scene didn't merely flourish, it exploded with first books and other publications, as writers who had been working in San Francisco were finding wider readerships, partly through their perceived membership in the Beat Generation. Ferlinghetti's City Lights press – as well as his own book *A Coney Island of the Mind* – has rightly been credited for popularizing the San Francisco poetry scene during these years. But there were other outlets in San Francisco that were important venues for Beat-related publishing during this time, the most important of which was the Auerhahn Press. Founded by Dave Haselwood in 1958, Auerhahn would over the next several years publish significant books by writers crucial to the widening of the Beat movement.

Haselwood later recalled that in the summer of 1958, as "he drifted around San Francisco talking endlessly" to painters such as Robert LaVigne and poets such as Lamantia, McClure, and Wieners, he perceived a need for a press that struck a happy medium between large houses that were either "cowardly or controlled by the academies" and small presses that "simply didn't care what they printed long as it was by some vague definition poetry."[19] Auerhahn was intended to fill this void, and Haselwood quickly became a coveted publisher whose volumes were known to those on the scene as thoughtfully designed, beautifully produced aesthetic objects showcasing some of the finest voices of the "new poetry." During its short life (1958–1965), Auerhahn published several books connected to the Beat literary movement, the most consequential of which are John Wieners's *The Hotel Wentley Poems* (1958); Philip Lamantia's *Ekstasis* (1959), *Narcotica* (1959), and *Destroyed Works* (1962); Michael McClure's *Hymns to St. Geryon and Other Poems* (1959) and *Dark Brown* (1961); Philip Whalen's *Memoirs of an Interglacial Age* (1960); Lew Welch's *Wobbly Rock* (1960); William S. Burroughs and Brion Gysin's *The Exterminator* (1960); Edward Marshall's *Hellan, Hellan* (1960); and Diane di Prima's *The New Handbook of Heaven* (1963). Although these works vary as much in form and content as other writing under the Beat umbrella, they also share broad aesthetic affinities and are notable for their cross talk: as was the case with those based in New York, writers who were connected to San Francisco tended to know one another, read, and respond to one another's work, and there are various dialogic strands that can be traced through them.

John Wieners: The Poem Does Not Lie

The first title Auerhahn published was John Wieners's *The Hotel Wentley Poems*, the contents of which were written in June 1958 as Wieners stayed in Haselwood's room at the Hotel Wentley.[20] Born in the suburbs of Boston in 1934, Wieners had first been associated with the Black Mountain poets after he learned about Charles Olson in 1954, and went on to study at Black Mountain College from 1955 to 1956. Following his stint in North Carolina, Wieners returned briefly to Boston, where he launched *Measure*, a short-lived but noteworthy little magazine, and then moved to San Francisco, where he met Haselwood, Lamantia, and others, staying for a time at poet Joanne Kyger's apartment.[21]

Before discussing *The Hotel Wentley Poems*, it is useful to pause briefly over *Measure* as it helps us contextualize the work Wieners was doing at the time. *Measure* ran for three issues (no. 1, summer 1957; no. 2, winter 1958; no. 3, winter 1962), but despite this brief run, the magazine represents a conscious fusing of the Black Mountain, San Francisco, and Beat sensibilities; as Ginsberg noted as the first issue was in preparation, *Measure* was "trying to draw all threads together," its editor a "good poet himself, sort of an east coast Creeley-Olson axis but more humane digs Williams and Kerouac, and Gregory."[22] As Robert Dewhurst has explained, *Measure*'s "resonant title had two sources, which allusively established the magazine's genealogy and frontier: William Carlos Williams' essay 'On Measure – Statement for Cid Corman,' which had appeared in [Corman's magazine] *Origin* in 1954; and a line from Blake's 'The Proverbs of Hell' – 'Bring out number, weight and measure in a year of dearth" ("Measure," 9). With the final issue of *Black Mountain Review* having run in the autumn of 1957, *Measure* was a worthy successor, hewing to the dual senses of its title, giving voice to a range of writers dedicated to exploring what Williams called a contemporary "measure consonant with our time and not a mode so rotten it stinks" (quoted in Dewhurst, "Measure," 9).[23]

The first issue of *Measure*, published out of Boston, is populated mainly by the Black Mountain and San Francisco Renaissance crowds, and includes work by Olson, Edward Dorn, Robert Duncan, Robin Blaser, Jack Spicer, Michael Rumaker, and others. But by the second issue, published out of San Francisco, the Beat connection is clear, with work by Kerouac, Corso, and McClure in addition to many of the poets featured in issue 1. By the third issue – which appeared after a hiatus of four years, and thanks in part to fundraising readings by Ginsberg, McClure, and others – *Measure* had blended a range of supposedly distinct aesthetics, including not only contributors from previous issues, but those well known on the San Francisco scene like Philip Lamantia and Sheri Martinelli. It was in *Measure* that Kerouac declared, "I want to be considered a jazz poet blowing a long blues in an afternoon" in the headnote accompanying selections from *Mexico City Blues*, which had yet to be published in book form.[24] Across its three issues, Wieners's aesthetic tastes and poetic sensibility are on display – as are his sympathies with the Beat project.

But it was on the strength of 1958's *The Hotel Wentley Poems* that Wieners established his reputation as a singular practitioner of the new poetry, an affiliate of Black Mountain and the Beats, but hardly defined by either. As Al Filreis has said of the book: "Not quite Beat (although he was feeling beat – *out of it*, not *beatific* ...) and not quite Black Mountain, the poems ... do really well as more generally 'New American.'"[25] Filreis is alluding to the fact that Wieners had been included in Donald Allen's *The New American Poetry* anthology in 1960 (the selections were all from *Hotel Wentley*), and while his work, like that of any first-rate poet, is not reducible to broad-stroke labels, *Hotel Wentley* certainly does exude a Beat aura. Raymond Foye, Wieners's literary executor, went so far as to say that the book reads "like a résumé of Beat poetry and of late romanticism as a whole: urban despair, poverty, madness, homosexual love, narcotics and drug addiction, the fraternity of thieves and loveless transients."[26] The real-life Hotel Wentley served as both literal and symbolic shelter for those "loveless transients" Foye names, the bohemian haunt where ruth weiss and Jack Kerouac had written collaborative haiku, and which sat above the Foster's Cafeteria immortalized in some of Lamantia's poetry. Encapsulated by the image of this hotel, the book is a portrait of Wieners's time among those who could not quite find traction in mainstream society, those whose experiences would define what he later called "the beat streets of San Francisco."[27]

The poetry collected in *Hotel Wentley* is emotionally raw and unadorned, often matter-of-factly exploring marginal figures who were long objects of countercultural fascination, from junkies ("A poem for tea heads") to gay people ("A poem for cock suckers") to the mentally ill ("A poem for the insane"). In his journals of the period, Wieners declared, "All I am interested in is charting the progress of my own soul. And my poetics consist of marking down how each action unrolls" – as a gay man who struggled with drug addiction and mental illness at various points in his life, we might read work like the poems named above as simultaneously about the marginal populations to which they are addressed and about the poet's own experiences and emotional states.[28] In order to chart his soul's progress, Wieners tries to free his work from what he thought of as disingenuous artifice that might run the risk of distorting an "original emotion" or "real event" into "trashy romantic unreal self exploration" (Wieners, *Journal*, 21).

"A poem for painters," by far the longest in the book, opens with a plaintive question: "Our age bereft of nobility / How can our faces show it?" The speaker answers with emotionally direct sentences freed from old-fashioned notions about poetry's lofty pretensions, assuming instead, as Wieners once put it, that "a poem does not have to be a major thing."[29] As he writes in "A poem for painters":

My poems contain no
wilde beestes, no
lady of the lake, music
of the spheres, or organ chants.

Only the score of a man's
struggle to stay with
what is his own, what
lies within him to do.

Without which is nothing.
And I come to this
knowing the waste,

leaving the rest up to love
and its twisted faces,
my hands claw out at
only to draw back from the
blood already running there.[30]

It's not a stretch to read these lines as a statement of Wieners's poetics at the time. In the first stanza, he rejects fanciful beasts, mythical women, and the metaphysical "music of the spheres," thereby rejecting also their prominence in the English poetic tradition, alluding as he does to Chaucer ("wilde beestes"), Arthurian legend, and John Milton, who used the "music of the spheres" as a way to articulate the divine ordering of the cosmos.[31] Stripping his experience of any such mythological or religious valences, Wieners is left with just himself, his own intellect and emotions, at once humbled in contrast to the wider realms of the first stanza, but also insistent that exploring such idiosyncratic experience is central to poetry, "Without which is nothing." In the context of this unromanticized vision of the modern world, the final lines return to the poem's opening question to answer that "our faces" – the poet's own and those in his circle – are "twisted" even in love. Far from writing genteel poetry that transcends his embodied experience, the poet's hands become like claws that viscerally affirm his existence as an imperfect being "bereft of nobility" yet still capable of loving another imperfect being. It was this quality that helped get him in *The New American Poetry*, for as Charles Olson insisted to Donald Allen, Wieners had "love working for him."[32]

If Wieners aims to replace the harmonious "music of the spheres" with his own poetic "score," the poems in *Hotel Wentley* offer readers access to illicit scenes that comprise the raw twisted faces that populate his world. Thus in "A poem for tea heads," the speaker shares a Chinese meal with

"Jimmy the pusher" before the pair venture out to score drugs stashed in the wheel well of Jimmy's car. The poem is a wistful lament, so as quietly thrilling as is the drug run and the high it portends, the speaker acknowledges that "Soon I know the fuzz will inter- / rupt will arrest Jimmy and / I shall be placed on probation." Although the long arm of the law will inevitably take Jimmy away, it can never really prevail in a spiritual sense, an idea Wieners develops by counterpointing law with poetry, a technique that should be familiar from my earlier discussion of Bremser's and Kupferberg's work:

> The poem
> does not lie to us. We lie under its
> law, alive in the glamour of this hour
> able to enter into the sacred places
> of his dark people, who carry secrets
> glassed in their eyes and hide words
> under the roofs of their mouth.

In this conception, poetry ultimately displaces the legal system with its own mandates, its own "law." So long as it is true, poetry retains the power of the "sacred," and is invested with the possibility of communicating in ways invisible to "the fuzz" who would jail Jimmy the pusher. In its ironic valorization of poetry that itself creates a kind of community, "A poem for tea heads" shares with the best work in *Hotel Wentley* the urge to witness, to capture moments in time in those liminal spaces invisible to square America.

This is the case especially in "A poem for cock suckers," whose opening line, "Well we can go / in the queer bars," introduces a plural pronoun that could as easily refer to the speaker and a friend or lover as to the reader himself, who enters with the speaker into a world that is, to say the least, non-normative:

> On our right the fairies
> giggle in their lacquered
> voices & blow
> smoke in your eyes let them
> . . .
>   It is all here between
> the powdered legs & painted
> eyes of the fairy
> Friends who do not fail us
> Mary in our hour of
>   despair. Take not
> away from me the small fires
> I burn in the memory of love.

The poem is not merely a celebration of a queer space – though it certainly is this – it is an affirmation that the unspecified "we" belongs in, and in fact draws "strength" from, such a space. A place of belonging where "we can sing our songs / of love," the "queer bar" is the straight, "normal" world turned inside out, where acts like blowing smoke in one's eyes don't signal aggression so much a shared sense of community or flirtation. The idealized, bountiful imagery at the end of the second stanza – "The gifts do not desert us, / the fountains do not dry" – only seems to contrast to the more concrete description of the drag queen in the final stanza, for it is because of this strange beauty, rather than in spite of it, that the bar is a space where love and friendship can develop free from judgment and rancor. If this notion seems as idealized as the flowing mountain springs in the second stanza, it makes sense only in the bounded space of the bar, when "It is all here" and the outside world is suspended amid the smoke and "lacquered voices."

Wieners's interest in seeing queer spaces as poetic spaces is also evidenced in a poem he published in 1965, which lays bare the Beat context for this fusing. In "Memories of You," Wieners extends the non-normative space of "A poem for cock suckers" from the "queer bars" to an international queer scene connected by figures such as Ginsberg and Frank O'Hara: "Now back to New York and The Turkish Baths / which I find no fun, tho Frank O'Hara does, / and Allen Ginsberg sits in his white pajamas / and dreams of men as I do – and thinks of fame."[33] After this setup that names two of the most recognizable poets in America, Wieners says he will "travel back to San Francisco and blow them there, / 'get fucked in the ass by saintly motorcyclists.'" This poem revisits "A poem for cock suckers" insofar as the various cities on Wieners's international itinerary are linked via his sexual exploits, thereby exploding the closed, furtive spaces of "queer bars" into a global phenomenon. But it is, crucially, Ginsberg who articulates this action publicly, for by 1965 he has "fame," largely on the strength of "Howl," which defines the "best minds" of his generation as, in part, those "who let themselves be fucked in the ass by saintly motorcyclists" (*Howl: Original*, 4). In "Memories of You," Wieners associates himself with Ginsberg's "best minds" via his queerness; unlike "A poem for cock suckers," in which Wieners's sexuality is visible only in shared underground spaces, "Memories of You" suggests that such sexuality has been articulated and made more visible by Ginsberg, and Wieners writes himself into the Beat movement via an appropriation of Ginsberg's very language, so that the poem ends in the perverse wish that people "breed more children / so I can seduce them / and they can be seduced by / saintly motorcyclists in the dawn" (16).

Despite later pronouncements such as this, in *The Hotel Wentley Poems*, there are other elements of the real world that are not so amenable to fluid perspectives on sex or drugs or even definitions of the real. The final poem, for example, "A poem for the insane," is a kind of elegy for the people and personalities that comprise *Hotel Wentley's* underground, transient scene. There Wieners again refers explicitly to figures on the North Beach scene, particularly Eric "Big Daddy" Nord, a well-known club owner who personified the Beatnik ethos; the month Wieners wrote *The Hotel Wentley Poems*, San Francisco's mayor tried to make an example out of Nord by raiding his club and arresting him for operating without a license. "A poem for the insane" refers to the incident to symbolize the repression of the Beat ethos: the opening stanza returns to the speaker contemplating Edvard Munch's *Evening, Melancholy on the Beach* at the San Francisco Museum of Modern Art; after "big Eric [is] busted," the title of the lithograph seems to apply to North Beach:

> It is
> right, the Melancholy
> on the Beach. I do not
> > split
>
> I hold on to the demon
> tree, while shadows drift
> around me.

Thus despite all the promise San Francisco held for Wieners as a city dedicated to free living and the avant-garde arts – "I've got to go live there" he had written to Olson in August 1957 – the end of *The Hotel Wentley Poems* makes it clear that the general "Melancholy / on the Beach" seems a fitting physical manifestation of the poet's own coming resurgence of depression, and indeed by January 1960 he would be a patient at Medfield State (Psychiatric) Hospital back in Massachusetts, his dream of golden California turned into drifting shadows.[34]

Philip Lamantia: Surreal Mystic

After *The Hotel Wentley Poems*, Auerhahn turned attention to Philip Lamantia's second book of poetry, *Ekstasis*, and later his notorious exploration of drug use, *Narcotica*. By the late 1950s, Lamantia was by reputation a recognized part of the Beat scene – having participated in the

6 Gallery reading in 1955 and inspired passages in "Howl," *Junky*, and *The Subterraneans* – but he had not published any work in book form since his first collection, *Erotic Poems*, back in 1946. This was due in part to a renunciation of poetry that came with his return to Catholicism in 1954, his struggles with heroin addiction, and his generally peripatetic life throughout the 1950s, during which he lived in Mexico, San Francisco, New York, Morocco, and Paris. It was in Mexico where Lamantia had been experimenting with drug use with substances such as peyote and yahnah, a powerful tobacco used in rituals by the Cora Indians, and where he almost died from a scorpion sting.[35] In the throes of death, he cried out for the Virgin Mary, an event that, as the introduction to his *Collected Poems* puts it, "led to Lamantia's subsequent fervent embrace of the religion into which he was born; this had serious implications for his poetry, as he began to view his preconversion writings as blasphemous."[36] In 1955, some of those "preconversion writings," a manuscript called "Tau," had been in an "advanced stage of preparation" for publication by Bern Porter, publisher of his first book, but would not in fact see print until 2008, in a joint edition with John Hoffman's work.[37] Yet by the late 1950s, it is possible to trace some writing to which Lamantia had returned, including poems for Pope John XXIII: he sent this work to Paul Carroll at *Big Table*, who rejected them, explaining that "it didn't get under my skin."[38] Despite the misses with "Tau" and *Big Table*, by the end of the decade his work was once again turning up in little magazines such as *Beatitude*, and by 1959, Haselwood thought it his privilege to publish *Ekstasis*, as he felt a special kinship with Lamantia's poems, remarking that "they are written in the air and possess me entirely."[39]

Ekstasis contains material dated from 1948 to 1958, and is saturated with Christian images often merged with abstractly mystical ones. In "Scorpion Bite," a reference to his near-death experience, Lamantia declares: "light beams entangled, heaven and the god enter my breast / Christ IS the marvelous!" (the importance of the scorpion sting is suggested also by the small scorpion motif in the running title header on every page of a later book, *Destroyed Works* [1962]).[40] Looking back on this period toward the end of his life, Lamantia emphasized the connection between this particular view of the "marvelous" and the surreal cast of his earlier work such as *Erotic Poems*: "In *Ekstasis*, I wrote 'Christ IS the marvelous!' so yes, I felt a continuity between surrealism and mysticism. I believe that erotic love and spiritual love are essentially the same."[41] As suggested by its title, the Greek word for "ecstasy" but connoting especially the trancelike experience of being outside one's body, *Ekstasis* is interested in the ineffable nature of religious, mystic experience, what Lamantia defines as "the experience of having something previously unknown reveal itself to you, a direct communication with God. One in which you feel God's love in an ecstatic, physical way" ("Last Interview"). In the first part of the book in particular, the poems are shot through with the language of salvation, and are concerned with meditating on the nature of the divine. In "Mysterium Mysticus Ecclesia," for example, the speaker imagines the physical trappings of the Catholic Church, "The immensity coming back upon itself," and wonders about its connection to mystic experience. Likewise, "The Poor Paradoxes" explores the relationship between the individual and God in ways that resonate with the "continuity between surrealism and mysticism" (n.p.).

While the second half of *Ekstasis* does not abandon these interests, there is a notable change as it radiates out from the poet's own intensely personal religious experiences to explore connections with others, particularly his fellow writers, from Sheri Martinelli and Michael McClure to Ginsberg, Corso, Kerouac – and of course John Hoffman, whose poems he had read at 6 Gallery in 1955. If there is a way to link these two broad dimensions of *Ekstasis*, it is through the idea of experience as "holy" that became central to Kerouac and Ginsberg's version of the Beat Generation, and that would transform into a more recognizable political stance in Lamantia's and many others' work in the early 1960s and beyond.

The opening piece in *Ekstasis* is a concrete poem in the shape of a cross that begins "Death, sunrises / beatific the winter's / rise" (n.p.). Although this poem was written prior to the Beatnik Era, on its publication in 1959, its emphasis on Christ as "beatific" could no longer be read as incidental to the Beat scene, especially as *Time* magazine paired Lamantia with Kerouac as two "Beat mystics" in 1958. In that interview with journalist Mike Wallace, Kerouac said that Beat mystics "believe in love. They love children ... they love women, they love animals, they love everything ... We're an empty vision – in one mind."[42] Wallace then asked Lamantia to gloss a line of poetry he had written:

> COME
> HOLY GHOST
> for we can rise
> out
> of this jazz!

Lamantia explained, "You gotta get through this life without getting hung up. That's the whole question – not to get hung up," elaborating that to be "hung up" is to freeze "from others, from yourself, from the Holy Spirit. If you're hung up, you can't love, or care for others." When Wallace asks him why "so many members of the Beat Generation [are] bums and tramps," Lamantia ties the non–hung up vision of love to a specifically Christian one: "Christ says go out and find the bums ... Find the blind and the cripples ... Christ invites everyone, including the outcasts. So there's no contradiction at all between Christ and a bebopper and a hipster." Here Lamantia moves from a vision of a mystical, personal union with Christ to a vision that emphasizes a connection to others, so to embody the Holy Spirit is to "care for others."

While he was doubtless playing up his Beat connections for the story, the arc of *Ekstasis*'s religious vision certainly does represent the Catholic dimension of the movement, and when selecting material for the book, Lamantia seemed determined to cement his association with the other writers on the scene – he remarked later, "With regard to the whole Beat thing, I see it as a matter of karma, really. Or, timing ... I was there and 'on the scene,'" and goes out of his way to associate himself with some of the more well-known Beat names.[43] In "Boobus," for example, he offers a collective portrait in a mirror at Foster's Cafeteria, a bohemian haunt on the ground floor of the Hotel Wentley, the very same place that had lent its name to Wieners's book. Lamantia writes:

> the mirror specks reflect Mike's wife Joanna
> the expanding universe of Foster's on the corner
>   of Polk and Sutter
> A four or five headed portrait of Ginsberg Corso McClure
>   Lamantia Kerouac
> I hope La Vigne paints it.

The specificity here is at once geographic and thematic, for Lamantia wants to count himself part of a Beat hydra at the very center of San Franciscan bohemianism, a move that again marks a turn away from the highly personal poems earlier in the collection (there were a number of Foster's Cafeterias across the city, but the one on Polk and Sutter was favored by those in the know).[44]

As others have noted, the poetry Lamantia wrote during this time was also characterized by "a more vernacular diction," a shift Lamantia himself seems to associate with his influence by or connection with the Beats.[45] Thus in "Füd at Foster's," another poem set at the cafeteria, the titular füd or food isn't as important as the allusions to other work such as the exclamation "NO MORE REALITY SANDWICHES! ! !" which takes us to Ginsberg's poem "On Burroughs' Work" (1954): "A naked lunch is natural to us, / we eat reality sandwiches."[46] Thus similar to the engagements with the Beat scene written around this time by West Coast poets trying to orient their voices relative to the claims of both their fellow writers and mainstream media, "Füd at Foster's" reads like the Beatnik's greatest hits: "My cigarillo's going out in a spanish bedroom / Jazz is for free / . . . Junk's unlimited and sold by agents / . . . Can I make it to windows of fur."[47] As suggested by the double reference to Ginsberg and Burroughs with the invocation of reality sandwiches, the real food at Foster's is intertextuality, so the cafeteria thus becomes a literal geographic instantiation of a movement comprised of the aesthetic sensibilities he cites.

A like-minded declaration of connection to the scene is literalized in another poem, "Immediate Life":

> My name is Philip Lamantia
> And I go around with whoever
> . . .
> junkies, tricks, demi poets, mads, holdupmen, squares,
> priests, monks, professional bums, beat jews, jew haters,
> spade trumpet players, potheads, zen cats.
>
> (Lamantia, *Collected Poems*, 115)

As "Füd at Foster's" and "Immediate Life" demonstrate, not only had Lamantia's associations with other Beat writers nudged his style from densely surreal to colloquial – even as he retained many of the same thematic concerns – he also began to make such connections the subject of his poetry. Thus in "McClure's Favorite," a nod to his fellow poet collected in *Ekstasis*, Lamantia extolls "MADNESS! ABSOLUTE MADNESS!" that would unsettle even the "swift hip reader / super cool cat" (n.p.). The slangy adjectives are a way for Lamantia to both acknowledge and mock the hip scene – if he knows his work will inevitably be measured against other so-called Beat Generation poets, at least he can control the terms of this comparison.

It makes sense, then, that the final poem in *Ekstasis* (the one from which Mike Wallace quoted) is a surreal accounting of the Beat circle in San Francisco. Titled "Binoculars," at first blush the piece appears more like an encyclopedia entry than a poem as it consists of a list of names, under which are elliptical statements apparently connected to those names. The poem lists "GREGORY CORSO," "ALLEN GINSBERG," "CHRISTOPHER MACLAINE," "MICHAEL MCCLURE," "JACK KEROUAC," "JOHN HOFFMAN," "GOGO NESBIT," "GARY SNYDER," "HOWARD

HART," and "PHILIP WHALEN" – the opening lines read, for example: "GREGORY CORSO / mexico a dark mouth terraces burn the morning / the clouds go under / the waves, / Cocaine" (n.p.). The poem's title suggests a tension between a wide-angled view of the figures named and such impressionistic, highly idiosyncratic descriptions under each name (in this way it is comparable to the variations on "funk" in the "blues for bonnie" section of Ray Bremser's *Poems of Madness*). As binoculars are used to render finer detail on things at a distance, Lamantia promises his readers a better view of these figures, but then presents not biographies or texts written but imagistic traces that would probably be fully understood only by the writers themselves or their intimates. Playing on the etymology of the word "binoculars" as two eyes or dual visions, the poem presents a name, then a few lines, leaving readers to determine their connection between intelligible and obscure declarations. For those well known by the Beatnik Era – Corso, Ginsberg, Kerouac, and to a lesser extent McClure, Whalen, and Snyder – Lamantia turns to keywords or themes that might have been associated with them, but recasts such associations via unexplained images. Thus Corso's entry ends with the hanging word "Cocaine," reminding one of his reputation as enfant terrible and causing us to wonder if he is "really" submerged under the influence of the drug. The phrase "God is everywhere" under Ginsberg's name recalls his declaration in "Howl" that "Everything is holy!" and the phrase "the whore in the loin cloth" under Kerouac's suggests the connection between sex and holiness in much of his work, as, say, in *Tristessa* (1960), which describes the title prostitute "pumping with her loins in the air . . . this holy friendship from the sacrificial sick body of Tristessa."[48] These examples at once reinforce popular notions about the Beat Generation's most famous faces, but also make them strangely unfamiliar (how to interpret lines like "the light on the undersea bottle / BLUE" is an open question).

In 1959, some of the other names in "Binoculars" would have been familiar only to the "swift hip reader / super cool cat" in San Francisco or New York, but probably unknown to tourists or devotees of *Time* magazine: Howard Hart was a poet and later playwright locally famous for participating with Lamantia, Kerouac, and David Amram in early jazz-poetry readings in New York; these four performed what Amram later claimed was "the first jazz-poetry reading" in the city.[49] Christopher Maclaine was a poet and filmmaker central to the San Francisco scene but who never made it big and is now unfortunately largely forgotten. Known locally for experimental short films such as *The Man Who Invented Gold* (1957) and *Beat* (1958), his poetry collection from this period, *The Time Capsule* (1960), culminates in a comic though serious defense of "poor heathen beat poets." Maclaine asks: "Will Ma Perkins ever forgive Bob Kaufman? / Will the fuzz ever dig it's part of our religion / and everybody's free to dig Religion?"[50] As mentioned earlier, John Hoffman was central to Lamantia's work, especially in the 1950s, and the elegiac dedication to him – "No one to match you / you went / to watch an albatross," echoes an earlier poem in *Ekstasis* titled "John Hoffman": "road that announced him / road that did not see him / eyes that circles the sun." Such references to Hoffman in *Ekstasis* affirm and extend his position as Beat myth and legend. In the context of the book as a whole, then, "Binoculars" demonstrates Lamantia's movement away from work exploring his idiosyncratic relationships with the divine to work affirming the poet's place in a wider community. Thus despite his interest in surrealism, and his long stretches throughout the 1950s when he was in Mexico or elsewhere, the publication of *Ekstasis* marks Lamantia's contribution to the Beat sensibility, inflected by his particular religious interests.

If such references in *Ekstasis* were not enough to cement his counter-cultural credentials, with the publication of *Narcotica*, also in 1959, Lamantia became legend for those coming to the scene primarily through illicit drug use. In its frankly political railing against drug laws, *Narcotica* is more of a piece with Burroughs's *Junky*, Trocchi's *Cain's Book*, or Kupferberg's "Stimulants" issue of *Birth* than with those Beat texts that use drugs to explore consciousness – although, as we will see below, McClure was inspired by Lamantia in a piece like "Peyote Poem." Alluding to the concept of Moloch from "Howl," Lamantia writes in *Narcotica*:

> DROP DEAD WITH YR ASSHOLE MAMMON MOLOCH MONEY MOTIVATED LAWS ... I DEFY YOU TO SAY IT IS NOT MY HUMAN RIGHT TO USE ANY GOD GIVEN HERB PLANT AND POWDER FOR MY PHYSICAL AND PSYCHIC WELL BEING.
> (Lamantia, *Collected Poems*, 107)

In this view, drugs use is not finally about pleasure or even the expansion of consciousness, but about the fundamental right to individual autonomy freed from the mandates of legislation. Such a perspective would of course become far more common in the 1960s, which helps explain why *Narcotica* became Lamantia's most infamous work (and the cover photographs of the poet shooting up heroin didn't hurt either).

Michael McClure: Powerful Knowledge

As may seem fitting given the discussion in the preceding pages, the poet mentioned most frequently in *Ekstasis* is Michael McClure. As explained in Part I, in 1956, McClure co-edited the important Beat-related magazine, *Ark II*

Moby I and released a chapbook, *Passage*, but it was in the latter 1950s that he had a burst of publishing activity, with four works from 1959 to 1961: *For Artaud* (1959), *Hymns to St. Geryon and Other Poems* (1959), *The New Book/A Book of Torture* (1961), and *Dark Brown* (1961). Of these, *Hymns to St. Geryon* is the most significant as it contains some earlier work such as "Poem" ("Linked part to part"), "Point Lobos: Animism," and "For the Death of 100 Whales," all of which he had read at 6 Gallery. In the mid- to late 1950s, McClure had also become fascinated by Antonin Artaud, whose "visionary Gnosticism" he thought "a way beyond the objectism of American poetry ... a way into the open field of poetry and into the open shape of verse and the physicality of thought"; this interest is reflected most clearly in the eight-part poem published as *For Artaud*, but is also evident throughout *Hymns to St. Geryon*.[51] *Hymns to St. Geryon*, on the cusp of the 1960s, moreover indicates how an interest in environmentalism and deep ecology would inform a powerful strand of Beat-associated writing in that decade. McClure would in fact later define the Beat movement in these terms: "Much of what the Beat Generation is about is nature.... Consciousness is a natural organic phenomenon. The Beats shared an interest in Nature, Mind, and Biology – areas that they expanded and held together with their radical political or antipolitical stance."[52] The poems in *Hymns to St. Geryon* explore both McClure's interest in nature – as in the wider natural world of which humans are but one part – and his interest in consciousness as a "natural organic phenomenon." In his work after the early 1960s, McClure would often explore eco-consciousness, sometimes writing in what he called "beast language," guttural, pre-linguistic utterances that he wanted to be intelligible to all beings, not just humans (in 1966, he famously read to lions from his beast language book *Ghost Tantras* [1964]).

While the poems in *Hymns to St. Geryon* do not yet contain beast language, they certainly demonstrate McClure's interest in the natural world, and his sensitivity to the suffering of all living beings. One of the most arresting poems, "For the Death of 100 Whales," begins with a passage taken from a *Time* magazine article (April 1954) explaining how American servicemen stationed at a NATO airbase near the Arctic circle slaughtered 100 killer whales, described as "savage sea cannibals," by rounding them up "with concentrated machine gun fire."[53] Far from celebrating this act as necessary pest control as *Time* does, McClure imaginatively witnesses the whales' suffering: "Gnashed at their tails and brothers / Cursed Christ of mammals / Snapped at the sun. / Ran for the sea's floor" (8). By associating the whales with Christ, McClure makes their experience knowable as something more than an example of what Kerouac called the "sinister new kind of efficiency" that appeared in America during and after the Korean War, an efficiency apparently admired and even marveled at by *Time*.[54] To do so, McClure expands our sense of what counts as knowable reality – "There are no churches in the waves" (8) – imagining the event from the whales' point of view, but also using their experience to help him understand himself. His pointed refusal of the narrative offered by *Time* is part of what makes the poem Beat, especially as it resonates with Ginsberg's plaintive question to America: "Are you going to let your emotional life be run by Time Magazine?"[55]

This interest in exploring the boundaries of reality characterizes the most important poem in *Hymns to St. Geryon*, "Peyote Poem," which records McClure's experience after he took peyote buttons given to him by the experimental artist Wallace Berman in 1958 (according to John Suiter, it was Philip Lamantia who introduced peyote to the San Francisco scene in the early 1950s).[56] Apparently having "near perfect recall" the next day, McClure wrote "Peyote Poem," the first part of which was published that same year as a broadside in Wallace Berman's loose-leaf arts magazine, *Semina*.[57] "Peyote Poem" is a closely observed exploration of the new consciousness as a "natural organic phenomenon." McClure was partly influenced in this poem by Lamantia's idea of "weir," a kind of clarity induced by certain drugs. Giving credit to Lamantia for "his concept of Weir," McClure defines it as "a solid spectral reality of light on particular objects in special moments of vision."[58] It is easy to see this idea at work in "Peyote Poem," which opens with the words "Clear – the senses bright" (39), and moves on to explore the interconnectedness of the poet's consciousness and his body, facilitated by peyote. In the poem there is the recurring mention of the speaker's stomachache, but rather than something negative, the pain is described in potentially productive terms: "The pain in my stomach / is warm and tender. I am smiling. The pain / is many pointed, without anguish" (39–40). This revision of the definition of "pain" as something "without anguish" leads McClure to see the stomachache as evidence of his embodied existence, as an "organic phenomenon" that doesn't stop at pain, but that can rather be viewed as part of his expanded consciousness:

> My belly and I are two individuals
> joined together
> in life.
> THIS IS THE POWERFUL KNOWLEDGE
> we smile with it.
>
> (42)

In an essay about peyote use, McClure put a finer point on this idea: "In the midst of the euphoria of sensory excitement the stomach or solar plexus can become *consciousnesses* themselves. – Then there is an additional euphoria of the liberated half-beings of ourselves."[59] "Peyote Poem" traces the speaker's awareness of this "POWERFUL KNOWLEDGE," and how it allows him to be fully present in the moment, to reject the artificial or arbitrary names for things. In the poem's second and third parts, after repeating that his stomach is "SWOLLEN AND NUMB" (44), the speaker recognizes "that time is a measurement is arbitrary" (44), that "THERE ARE NO CATEGORIES" (49), and that "I am a spirit / of flesh in the cold air. I need no answer" (45). Again echoing the poem, in his essay on peyote use, McClure claims that "Previously formed hierarchies called *levels of being*, made for convenience in mortal life, pass into nothingness. They turn on their heads and flow one into another and they cease . . . ideas of proportion and measurement . . . are gone" ("Drug Notes," 32). The poem charts an attempt to reinvest the body with a biological immediacy distinct from social or cultural constructs – time, categories, answers, "proportion and measurement" – to recognize instead a consciousness that is organically embodied rather than socially formed. For McClure, this is not merely narcissistic navel-gazing, but a good-faith effort to understand consciousness, an understanding that might help him connect to others, as happens in "For the Death of 100 Whales." As he once explained: "The more one discovers one's *bio-self* as opposed to one's *social self*, . . . The more you discover your biological person and your biological functions, the more you find your biological self, and the more you discover your biological self, the more value you can be to yourself. The more value you can be to yourself, the more value you can be to those around you."[60] "Peyote Poem" is an exploration of this notion of "bio-self," a significant concept for understanding his and the wider Beat circle's interest in nature as it suggests how learning to recognize the non–social self leads to a better or more lucid sense of one's own consciousness, which in turn might allow one to be of greater "value" to others in the world.[61] This is the beginning of the political dimensions of the Beat eco-consciousness that McClure and others would develop into the 1960s, when the expansion of embodied consciousness went hand-in-hand with experimentations in language, both of which were thought to have material effects on the real world.

Philip Whalen: Mind Moving

As McClure's work of the period strove to understand the embodied nature of consciousness, such work is likewise taken up by fellow San Francisco poet Philip Whalen, close friend of McClure's and another participant in the 6 Gallery reading in 1955. Having lived with Gary Snyder during their days at Reed College, back in 1949–1951, by the late 1950s, Whalen knew and was close to not only McClure, but also Kerouac, Ginsberg, Rexroth, Lew Welch, Joanne Kyger, and others – as his biographer has put it, his "personal connections *were* the story."[62] Given these connections, Whalen was known on the scene not only for his poems, which had appeared in venues such as *Evergreen Review*, *Black Mountain Review*, *A New Folder*, and *Yugen*, but also through recordings such as *San Francisco Poets* (ca. 1958–1959) and *Jazz Canto: An Anthology of Poetry and Jazz* (1958). But despite his success in these venues, Whalen had some trouble publishing his first full-length books. After initial interest in mid-1958 from Donald Allen at Grove – who would include Whalen in *The New American Poetry* – he wound up publishing two books in quick succession elsewhere: *Memoirs of an Interglacial Age* (1960) with Auerhahn Press, and *Like I Say* (1960) with LeRoi Jones's Totem Press in New York (in 1959, Auerhahn had published the poem "Self-Portrait, from Another Direction" as a fold-out broadside; it was later included in *Memoirs*, a beautifully produced, large format book).[63]

Today, Whalen is perhaps best remembered as a poet-monk, as he became an ordained Buddhist monk in 1973, and would later serve as abbot of Hartford Street Zen Center in San Francisco; his work of the late 1950s certainly displays his knowledge of Buddhism, which as in Snyder's work shaped how he understood language and its relationship to "reality." And like McClure's "Peyote Poem," Whalen often tries to capture "the real" via language that rejects categories and measurement, so his work is filtered through minute explorations of his own consciousness, and is interested in how language impinges on such consciousness when articulated through poetry.

As his friend and fellow poet Leslie Scalapino put it much later, Whalen was interested in "the possibility of freedom from an 'academy' notion of a poem, which he viewed as being narration of subject matter in a preconceived ordering, bound up. Rather, he realized that a reordering of every level can take place in the line and in the sound structure of the language itself."[64] Throughout *Memoirs of an Interglacial Age* and *Like I Say*, one finds an apparent free play of language that challenges the view that internal or external reality is best understood in terms of "preconceived ordering" – a use of language that Scalapino, for one, links to the movement writ large: "The Beats as a movement were undertaking to undo the convention of U.S. 'seeing' that continually reproduces 'being' divided from subject matter *as* subject matter. Whalen undertook that 'undoing' as the process of language itself" (xxxvii).

Although neither is arranged according to strict chronologies, the poems in *Like I Say* were written slightly earlier than the ones in *Memoirs*, from about 1955 to 1958, and include work he read at the 6 Gallery ("Sourdough Mountain Lookout"), while the material in *Memoirs* dates generally from 1958 to 1959. Whalen's interest in the self as a divided subject is evident in both books. For example, *Memoirs of an Interglacial Age* ends with a short piece called "A Press Release," which Whalen had reluctantly dictated to McClure because Elsa Dorfman, then working at Grove Press, was setting up readings for them on the East Coast, and she wanted material for an actual press release prior to their arrival (Dorfman would go on to become a celebrated photographer; her volume *Elsa's Housebook: A Woman's Photojournal* [1974] contains portraits of a number of Beat-associated writers).[65] This press release is a useful way into Whalen's poetry as it offers an account of his method:

> This poetry is a picture or graph of a mind moving, which is a world body being here and now which is history ... and you. Or think about the Wilson Cloud-chamber, not ideogram, not poetic beauty: bald-faced didacticism moving as Dr. Johnson commands all poetry should, from the particular to the general.[...] I do not put down the academy but have assumed its function in my own person, and in the strictest sense of the word – *academy*: a walking grove of trees. But I cannot and will not solve any problems or answer any questions.[66]

This is a poetics invested in recording the workings of the poet's mind just as a cloud chamber makes visible normally imperceptible features of the physical world. Like many a Beat writer discussed in this book, Whalen opposes his work to "the academy," not so much to excoriate it – as might a writer like Tuli Kupferberg – but to make clear his own disparate aims; his "didacticism" is offering a "picture or graph of a mind moving" rather than overtly moralistic teachings. Many of his poems are thus visually striking, ranging over the open field of page as the poet's mind ranges over thoughts, emotions, and sensory encounters.

In this way, Whalen's work is comparable to McClure's in that it reflects embodied consciousness. This is the case, for example, in "Self-Portrait, from Another Direction," which begins:

> Tuned in on my own frequency
> I watch myself looking
> Lying abed late in the morning
> . . .
>
> I think what is thinking
> What is that use or motion of the mind that compares with

A wink, the motion of the belly

. . .

THOUGHT IS NOT SWIFT!
perhaps the mind is slower than this pencil, its rate of motion
nearer that of the heartbeat –
moving slower than the head which turns
    not as quick as a wink.

(24)

The "self-portrait" promised in the poem's title is really an exploration of the speaker's "frequency," a sense of self made up of the texture of his thought, which is deliberate and relentlessly self-reflexive, so that he is able to look at himself looking. The poem thus becomes about the nature of thought – "I think what is thinking" – and takes readers through the workings of the speaker's mind, which cannot properly be called "stream of consciousness," because this term implies a certain speed, a rapid moving from idea to idea, image to image, whereas Whalen wants to slow down the "rate of motion" and compare it to the bodily regulation of a heartbeat. To approximate this deliberate consciousness of thought, the poem moves across the speaker's mind as it interacts with itself and with various external forces ("Rain/wind bulging the window / An Absolute, i.e. what we think of as / 'An Absolute', 'Force', 'Nature'" [25]) to offer a sketch of the speaker's "frequency" rather than a unified sense of self. After all, as Buddhism teaches, the ego itself is illusory, a veil that shields one from apprehending absolute reality. Thus in much of Whalen's work, even seemingly concrete sense perceptions do not point to a unified self, but to a constantly changing mind, always in motion so that with the final line of "Self-Portrait, from Another Direction," we are left with reflections of the ego, many selves present in a single instant: "Into the mirror (NOW showing many men) all of them 'I'" (27).

The Buddhist idea of the ego being always understood as contingent, in quotation marks, characterizes much of Whalen's work during this period. In "Metaphysical Insomnia Jazz," for example, he alludes to the *Mumon-kan*, or *The Gateless Gate*, a classic collection of Zen koans dating from the thirteenth century.[67] One story unfolds:

> Two monks were arguing about a flag. One said: "The flag is moving."
> The other said: "The wind is moving."
> The sixth patriarch happened to be passing by. He told them: "Not the wind, not the flag; mind is moving."

Imagining the scene on a peak in the western Himalayas, Whalen borrows this story and updates it:

fairly near the summit of Nanga Parbat & back again, the wind
flapping the prayer-flags
"IT IS THE WIND MOVING."

"IT IS THE FLAG MOVING."
Hypnotized by the windshield swipes, Mr. Harold Wood:
"Back & forth; back & forth"

. . .

"IT IS THE MIND MOVING."

& now I'm in my bed alone
Wide awake as any stone.

Like the allusion to the concept of absolute reality in "Self-Portrait, from Another Direction," here the reliance on Buddhist concepts allows Whalen explore the illusory nature of the ego and therefore of consciousness. One thing the koan from *Mumonkan* illustrates is that, as the *Dhammapada* puts it, "mind is the forerunner of all actions," and so one must attend to it even when observing and comprehending a seemingly distinct phenomenon such as flags flapping in the wind. Whalen's conclusion, that he is "wide awake," brings us to the insomnia of the title but also to the notion of a Buddha as an awakened one, suggesting that study of Buddhist texts helps one become a little bit more spiritually awakened, even if couched in day-to-day terms, and that such awakening can be as uncomfortable as insomnia.

The force of this poem depends on the interaction of distinct subjectivities, and this is the case in much of Whalen's poetry, for when he explores his own "mind moving," he often does so by asking how it might be connected to or illuminated by others. Thus "Self-Portrait, from Another Direction," is not merely about the poet's own ego, but how this ego bumps up against others, such as the bohemian students from Reed College:

2 Reedies cross-legged on Taylor Street sidewalk
Beards
Waiting for the campus bus

On Broadway another one gets off a trolley
Full pack & walking-shoes dangling

Moral: Not all the younger generation is going to hell.

(26)

The mention of the "younger generation" can't help but connect the poet's ego to the wider social and literary movement with which he was associated. As mentioned in the earlier discussion of his poetry that had appeared in *Yugen* and elsewhere, Whalen habitually sprinkled his work with not only references to anonymous members of the "younger generation" as in this poem, but also more pointed cameos of his fellow writers, as in the "Haiku for Mike" (McClure), or in the causal acknowledgment of Kerouac's legendary drinking abilities in "Prose Take-Out, Portland 13:ix:58" ("I shall know better next time than to drink with any but certified / drunks (or drinker) that is to say like J-L. K., who don't fade away / with first false showing of dawn"), both of which appear in *Memoirs*.[68] *Like I Say* contains poems such as "Homage to Robert Creeley," a short reflection on the distances between perception and reality, and "Harangue from Newport, to John Wieners, 21:ix:57," a meditation on communication, which ends "Notice also that you not only see me clearly / (A MIRACLE!) / You understand everything I say."[69]

Although Whalen was not necessarily above name-dropping for its own sake, his work is generally invested in a deeper recognition of others, as in "20:vii:58, On Which I Renounce the Notion of Social Responsibility," whose title is a jokey repudiation of the caricatured understanding of the Beatnik's social posture:

> The minute I'm out of town
> My friends get sick, go back on the sauce
> Engage in unhappy love affairs
> They write me letters & I worry
> . . .
> In this context: Fenellosa translated NO (Japanese word)
>   as "accomplishment"
>
>   (a pun for the hip?)
> . . .
> If nothing else we must submit ourselves
> To the charitable impulses of our friends
> Give them a crack at being bodhisattvas.
>   (5)[70]

Riffing off the Rexrothian idea of disaffiliation, Whalen imagines a hipster's dictionary that would have the English version of the Japanese word "no," meaning accomplishment. But while the title proclaims the poet's renunciation of "social responsibility," Whalen nonetheless concludes with a reminder of the interconnectedness of all beings, an idea indicative of much of his poetry during this period: it's "a picture or graph of a mind moving," simultaneously aware of the slipperiness of this mind as well as its interdependence with the minds of others.[71]

9.4 Kerouac, Again: Buddhist Goofing

As the work of Lamantia, McClure, and Whalen suggests, the religious strain in Beat writing ran from Christian mysticism to the application of Buddhist principles in a contemporary Western setting. In popular imagination, the Beat interest in Eastern philosophies and religions is distilled in their study of Zen Buddhism, which some writers of course took more seriously than others, but that was packaged and perhaps commercialized in Kerouac's *The Dharma Bums* (1958). Because *The Dharma Bums* is the first book Kerouac wrote after the Beat Generation blew up during the Beatnik Era, its overtly religious dimensions seem an obvious repudiation of the widespread misunderstandings of the movement. The book was written in November 1957 at the behest of Malcolm Cowley, Kerouac's editor at Viking, who assured him that the publishing house would be interested in bringing out another book to follow *On the Road*, and so he banged out *The Dharma Bums* in two and a half months in his sister's kitchen in Florida.[72] Since *The Dharma Bums* was composed in the afterglow of *On the Road*'s success, it can thus be read partly as a product of Kerouac's fame – a topic he would return to in depth in subsequent novels such as *Big Sur*, *Desolation Angels*, and *Vanity of Duluoz*.

Kerouac insisted throughout 1958 and 1959 that the Beat Generation could best be understood as a religious movement, and *The Dharma Bums* is a testament to his vision at the time. Gone are mentions of petty criminality, replaced instead with detailed passages on writing and the nature of reality: if *On the Road* glorified kicks and frenetic travel, and *The Subterraneans* explored jazz, interracial relationships, and the underground scene, *The Dharma Bums* introduced readers to Kerouac's understanding of Buddhism, as filtered through the characters of Japhy Ryder (modeled on Gary Snyder) and Henry Morley (on librarian John Montgomery).[73] Although the book opens with Kerouac's fictionalized version of the 6 Gallery reading, in which Snyder participated, narrator Ray Smith emphasizes that Ryder is both of this group and distinct from them, an outdoorsman whose defining characteristic is that he "knew all the details of Tibetan, Chinese, Mahayana, Hinayana, Japanese and even Burmese Buddhism" (12).

Interested readers can locate denunciations of mainstream culture throughout *The Dharma Bums* – such as the notion that most Americans are "imprisoned in a system of work, produce, consume, work, produce, consume" (97) – but these critiques are not the real point of the book. They are merely a veneer that would satisfy those casual readers who wanted Kerouac to fulfill his role as social and cultural misfit; the novel's real interest is not with such predictable rants against consumerism, but with the nature of language and its ability to accurately represent reality. Such engagement with the limitations of language is informed by Kerouac's understanding of Buddhist philosophy, and helps explain what he thought he was doing with spontaneity in *The Dharma Bums*. Consider, for example, the following:

> one day, my [Smith's] nephew little Lou came with me and I took an object from the ground and raised it silently, sitting under the tree, and little Lou facing me asked "What's that?" and I said "That" and made a leveling motion with my hand, saying "Tathata," repeating, "That . . . It's *that*" and only when I told him it was a pine cone did he make the imaginary judgment of the word "pine cone," for, indeed, as it says in the sutra: "Emptiness is discrimination." (140, ellipses in original)

The key concept in this passage, *tathata*, was explained by Alan Watts, a great popularizer of Buddhism in the West, like this: Mahayana Buddhism has "another term for reality . . . *tathata*, which we may translate as 'suchness,' 'thusness,' or 'thatness' . . . When we say just 'That' or 'Thus,' we are pointing to the realm of nonverbal experience, to reality as we perceive it directly, for we are trying to indicate what we see or feel rather than what we think or say. *Tathata* therefore indicates the world just as it is, unscreened and undivided by the symbols and definitions of thought."[74] Kerouac includes this interaction between Smith and his nephew because it illustrates the way language only clouds the "world just as it is." The irony of course is that this realization is problematic for anyone whose primary mode of communication is language. Earlier in his career, Kerouac had tried to capture "unscreened and undivided" reality with his spontaneous prose of the early 1950s; by 1958, after he had written a respectable stack of Buddhist-inspired texts such as *Some of the Dharma* (written 1953–1956; published 1997), *Wake Up: A Life of the Buddha* (written 1955; published 2008), and *The Scripture of the Golden Eternity* (written 1956; published 1960), it is possible to discern how his ideas of writing spontaneously married well with those aspects of Buddhist thought glossed by Watts.

Probably the most well-known passage in *The Dharma Bums* comes when Smith applies the principles of spontaneity to mountain climbing, which helps him abandon "imaginary judgment" and exist in the present moment. Smith's guide here is Ryder, who teaches him to deal with treacherous terrain by not overthinking it: "The secret of this kind of climbing," Japhy tells Smith, "is like Zen. Don't think" (64). Smith heeds this advice and realizes that "With my sneakers it was as easy as pie to just dance nimbly from boulder to boulder, ... I learned it was better for me to just spontaneously pick my own boulders and make a ragged dance of my own.... Jumping from boulder to boulder and never falling, with a heavy pack, is easier than it sounds; you just can't fall when you get into the rhythm of the dance" (64–65). This insight, that "spontaneously" hiking dangerous areas is preferable to overthinking your path because it puts you in more immediate contact with your environment, reaches a height when Ryder, more expert in Buddhist action than Smith, begins *"running down the mountain* in huge twenty-foot leaps, ... and in that flash I realized *it's impossible to fall off mountains you fool"* (85). Smith's insight is that in such moments, Ryder is in contact with *tathata*.[75]

For Smith-the-writer, achieving such contact through words proves difficult: at various points Ryder in fact dismisses Smith's eagerness to articulate the experiences he's had ("Ah, it's just a lot of words" [169]), and recounts Zen stories meant to illustrate how language occludes deeper understanding of reality: "One disciple came to a Master and answered his koan and the Master hit him with a stick and knocked him off the veranda.... The disciple got up and laughed. He later became a master himself. 'Twasn't by words he was enlightened" (173). Still, Smith believes that a certain kind of writing that proceeds as spontaneously as Ryder's bouncing down the mountain could begin, however paradoxically, to verbalize the nonverbal *tathata* he was trying to show his nephew. In the mountains with Ryder, Smith feels that he "could understand the perfect gems of haikus the Oriental poets had written, ... just going along ... writing down what they saw without literary devices or fanciness of expression" (59). As is the case with his earlier statements on spontaneous prose, the enemy here is what tradition has deemed "literary," what he pejoratively called "craft" in "Essentials of Spontaneous Prose" (*Portable Kerouac*, 485). *The Dharma Bums* is a Buddhist justification for why "craft" does not equal good writing: as the story of the pine cone illustrates, language grafts arbitrary discriminations onto reality, and thus locates reality only in how we perceive it. Although by its nature writing cannot be as purely spontaneous as Ryder's run down the mountain, the novel can be read as Kerouac's contemplative rationale for one strand of his formal experiments, as he tried to edge closer to the apprehension of *tathata* and away from the "device"-laden writing that he thought dominated literary production at the time.

Kerouac took his insights about spontaneity and ran with them in one of his strangest works, *Old Angel Midnight*, a kind of prose-poem he called "an endless automatic writing piece which raves on and on with no direction and no story."[76] Written on and off from 1956 to 1959 and at times called *Lucien Midnight* (after Lucien Carr), as mentioned earlier, the first part of *Old Angel Midnight* took up the most real estate in the first issue of *Big Table* in 1959, with other parts published in *New Directions* (1961) and *Evergreen Review* (1964). Ann Charters has described the work as "an exercise in pure spontaneous composition," and indeed when opening *Old Angel Midnight* readers are confronted by pages of linguistic weirdness on the order of Joyce's *Finnegans Wake* (1939): Kerouac bounces from thought to thought, image to image, often elaborating associations based on the sound or visual appearance of particular words.[77] As such, the work is rife with wordplay, from punny invented words and slant rhyme echoes of recognizable phrases to guttural sounds apparently divorced from any semantic meaning at all. The piece was successful enough that when the first part appeared in *Big Table*, Robert Duncan said to Jack Spicer – who had been carrying on an open disagreement with the Beat phenomenon – "maybe we should jump on this bandwagon." As Joanne Kyger recalled, "I could tell they were excited by this piece of writing, and thought maybe we should just drop our cultural warfare with these Beat writers who're trying to take over the scene."[78]

Despite first appearances, Kerouac isn't only interested in nonsense for nonsense's sake, and reading *Old Angel Midnight* against *The Dharma Bums* helps us see that formal experimentations are a way for him to explore *tathata* via language. *Old Angel Midnight* was begun after *Scripture of the Golden Eternity* – which is a comparatively straightforward meditation on the dharma – and in it Kerouac stretches and deforms language to imagine reality around or beyond language. We see this in an early passage, which begins with standard, comprehensible sentences, and ends with a breakdown of language:

> What does it mean that True Nature is incomprehensibly beyond the veil of our senses and is like empty light? It means that True Nature is incomprehensibly beyond the veil of our senses & is like empty light. If someone were to say to me, Krap, cart your daddy over here & let's hear tarbey? I'd say Wap, how'n you can cray that way when small fot find out all Sond your Oo like Where you like me & You Like Me & OO La Koo Me the onta logical philosizer fonted in the crap ding?[79]

As we know from *The Dharma Bums*, Kerouac understands the first question posed about *tathata* or True Nature to be unanswerable with language, which he illustrates by the baldest of circular logic, thereby suggesting the poverty of reason and the language used to articulate it.

The passage then spins into an imagined dialogue that quickly evacuates legible meaning to revel in the sound of language. As implied by the broken-up reference to ontology at the end of the passage, remixing language, one of the basic ways we access and understand the world, illuminates it anew by emphasizing the ultimate arbitrariness of language's semantic meaning.

Writing about *Old Angel Midnight*, Michael McClure picks up on this idea, quoting Philip Whalen's quick and dirty definition of *tathata*: "thus come, thus gone; suchness; or, as Suzuki-roshi said, 'Things as is.'" According to McClure, "This definition may be useful for understanding the midnight voice" of *Old Angel Midnight*, which is interested in "recordin sounds of universe" (57) as they are, rather than as perceived through the senses and through language.[80] As in *The Dharma Bums*, Kerouac, lover of words, is in a bind from a Buddhist point of view as words are part of what leads to attachment, which in turn causes *dukkha*, or suffering. If "the mirror doesn't show the real right" (31), then highly mimetic language is just as misleading, and so Kerouac's gambit in *Old Angel Midnight* is to distort language as much as possible. In fashioning himself "John Kerouac transliterator of perfect knowing" (30), he constantly invents new modes of expression, creating a kind of alternative reality that seems odd and unsettling exactly because it doesn't follow the rules of language usage. In another mediation on *tathata*, for example, he refers to the Buddhist notion of nonduality – that discriminations among seemingly disparate things are merely perceptive illusions – to claim "T s all the same wavehood . . . all things are no-things but if this bores you it's because you want bricks in your soup" (12). This means that Kerouac's language ought to be just as nondiscriminatory, which of course makes it hard to follow; later anticipating those readers who may be put off by such conclusions and the language it leads to, Kerouac writes: "if ya don't understand s t t and tish, that langue, it's because the langue just bubbles" (21). He knows the language will be boring or incomprehensible to those interested in the solidity of experience, the "bricks in your soup," whereas *Old Angel Midnight* is interested in accessing the "universe of electrical waves" (13).

It is also worth noting that at the same time Kerouac is making these metaphysical claims, he does so within the context of literary history, so that he links the sensibility of the poem to the wider "new consciousness" central to the Beat movement. While the work alludes to or names directly a host of well-known writers, from Shakespeare and Dostoyevsky to Laurence Sterne, Baudelaire, and Emerson, its fluid voice wants to be freed from such influences: "I'm going to die now, breath no more words pain on this silver & worry hatepage, I am the moth I killed in infant desire Hemming & Waying page of teen" (37). The writers most admired are not these mainstays of tradition, but Kerouac's contemporaries, a veritable Who's Who of Beat-associated writers, including Creeley and Rexroth (p. 4), Ginsberg (7), Olson (12), Snyder and Whalen (13), Alene Lee (17), Kaufman (21), Corso (24), Burroughs (41), and Ferlinghetti (51). It's clear that Kerouac views these people as sympathetic to his aesthetic project, and given that *Old Angel Midnight* was published at the height of the Beatnik Era, it makes sense that he should frame them against mainstream perception, as a menacing "Indian Uprising known as the Beat Generation, is going to eat rails & make tire sandwiches of every junkyard misty rust & all old heroes' eyes in barley Soup of time" (51–52). This imagined insurgency of the Beats is lampooned a couple of pages later when Kerouac channels the voice of the sort of solid citizen who might believe the Beatniks are a threat to civilization: "I just cant stand these people I teel you I dont know what I'm going to do about them . . . *him*, with that dressy little deaful foosy on his lap . . . & all that boommusic on the juke box & I dont know I wanted to call the police & get rid of this sandbag pineneedle Bodhi neighbor who is such ugly bearded dirty" (54). (Fans of more academic debates would also appreciate Kerouac's counterpoint here: "Let's go to Trilling & ask him – I gotta wash my conduct – Dont worry about nothin – I love Allen Ginsberg – Let that be recorded in heaven's unchangeable heart" [7]. The pun "wash" for "watch" resonates with New Criticism figured as soap in the pages of *Yugen*; see Figure 7.1.)

In the end, however, *Old Angel Midnight* reads as joyous affirmation of pure spontaneity – and, by association, the new and unsettling work of those writers Kerouac names throughout. Consider, to take one example, this passage: "'Spit on Bosatsu!' says Gregory Corso – 'Oo that's beautiful?' I say – Dash dash dash dash mash crash wash wash mosh posh tosh tish rish rich sigh my tie thigh pie in the sky – Poo on you too, proo the blue blue, OO U Nu, hello Buddha man" (24). The term "Bosatsu" is the Japanese transliteration for Bodhisattva, a person who has attained enlightenment but chooses to remain on earth to help alleviate the suffering of others, and Corso's charge here is a version of the famous Zen dictum that one ought to kill the Buddha if one comes across him – an injunction that stresses the importance of nonattachment, even to the Buddha. Kerouac is delighted by this statement, and incorporates it into the work, once again launching into apparent nonsense language that revels in sound rather than sense, an aesthetic echo of Corso's dismissal of attachment – a couple of pages later this spitting is imagined as a "long mouth sizzle reaching for the thirsts of Azmec" (27).[81]

9.5 Gary Snyder: Words to Things

Whereas *Old Angel Midnight* explores *tathata* through wild form and "letting go," Gary Snyder's work of this period experiments with methodical control to explore the relationship between language and True Nature. His first book of poetry, *Riprap*, was published in Japan in 1959 and distributed in the States by Ferlinghetti. Some of the events described in *Riprap* overlap with those described in *The Dharma Bums* – the poem "Water" recounts a "dizzy hop-and-step descent" across boulders, and "Migration of Birds" meditates on birds as "Jack Kerouac outside, behind my back / Reads the *Diamond Sutra* in the sun."[82] As Kerouac worried about the arbitrary defining power of words, in *Riprap*, Snyder created minutely wrought poetry that invests words with the concreteness of the natural world, of rocks and the manual labor Snyder performed as he wrote the book.

In the collection's earlier poems, words seem to have little relevance in the natural world, as in the often-anthologized poem "Milton by Firelight," which asks "What use, Milton, a silly story / Of our lost general parents, / eaters of fruit?" (9). Although the answer to this rhetorical question seems to be "no use," especially amid the sublime aspect of the mountains ("In ten thousand years the Sierras / Will be dry and dead, home of the scorpion"), the poem ends not with despair at the smallness of human life but with the contented sense of settling into a quiet campsite as the fire becomes "too dark to read" (10). Milton is at once useless and a resource for the poet's mind, one source of contentment as the poet appreciates the solitude of his remote location. Indeed, in many poems in *Riprap*, Snyder hovers teasingly between declaring words meaningless and redoubling his faith in their worth. Thus in "A Stone Garden," he writes:

> Thinking about a poem I'll never write.
> With gut on wood and hide, and plucking thumb,
> Grope and stutter for the words, invent a tune,
> In any tongue, this moment one time true
> Be wine or blood or rhythm drives it through –
> A leap of words to things and there it stops.
>
> (24)

The physical, visceral description of lyrical invention as rooted in blood and guts suggests a desire to concretize or embody words so that they may prove less slippery or misleading. And yet the meditation itself remains unwritten; even as figments, words can only "leap" to things, and as Ray Smith tried to show his nephew in *The Dharma Bums*, using them only sidesteps "thatness" for discrimination.

Despite its tentativeness regarding language, *Riprap* ends on a note that is cautiously positive about the generative power of words. Whereas in *The Dharma Bums* Kerouac argues for spontaneity as a route to writing around and toward *tathata*, Snyder tries to invest his language with the deliberate clarity of meditative practice. This is the case, for example, in the titular poem, "Riprap," which closes the volume, but that he defined on the title page: "*riprap: a cobble of stone laid on steep, slick rock to make a trail for horses in the mountains.*" Such is the context for the poem:

> Lay down these words
> Before your mind like rocks.
>   placed solid, by hands
> In choice of place, set
> Before the body of the mind
>   in space and time:
> Solidity of bark, leaf, or wall
>   riprap of things:
> Cobble of milky way,
>   straying planets,
> These poems, people,
>   lost ponies with
> Dragging saddles
>   And rocky sure-foot trails.
>   . . .
> In the thin loam, each rock a word
>   a creek-washed stone
> Granite: ingrained
>   with torment of fire and weight
> Crystal and sediment linked hot
>   all change, in thoughts,
> As well as things.
>
>   (32)

In this seemingly simple poem, Snyder reinvests words with power by figuring the landscape itself as words, and vice versa. The opening simile compares language to the stones used to make stable paths for horses on uncertain mountain trails. But if the poet's words are to function in a similarly illuminating way, they must be "placed" deliberately, as are the stones in a mountain path. The form of the poem moreover echoes the rhythms of manual labor as it suggests the poet moving back and forth in repetitive motions. In such motion, with the labor of path- and poetry-making collapsed, the poet orients himself to *tathata*, expanding from the very cosmos to the tiniest "ants and pebbles" before him. That all of these things seem to have some relational meaning is possible both by "reading" the stones as words and in creating one's own words that might have the solidity of the stones themselves.

Snyder's conflicted attitudes about how words have been deployed extends to another collection that appeared around this time, *Myths & Texts* (1960), published by LeRoi Jones's Totem Press and containing poems written throughout the 1950s. Like *Riprap*, *Myths & Texts* is informed by Snyder's fluency with Buddhist concepts – he had taken formal vows in 1955 and by 1959 had moved to Japan to intensify his study of Buddhism. *Myths & Texts* in fact lays bare such influences more explicitly as the long poem progresses from the first section, "Logging," reminiscent of *Riprap* insofar as it celebrates manual labor in the woods, through to "Burning," which relies on what Lee Bartlett has called "fairly labyrinthine Eastern and Native American mythology and symbolism."[83] Throughout there is a tension between the power of language to shape reality and embodied physicality represented by riprap in the previous book. Consider, for instance, these lines from part five of *Myths & Texts*:

> Against the ancient, meaningless
> Abstractions of the educated mind.
>   wet feet and the campfire out.
> Drop a mouthful of useless words.
> – The book's in the crapper
> They're up to the part on Ethics now.[84]

In this stanza, the image of "wet feet" interrupts the "meaningless / Abstractions" of a mind filled with "useless words." Borrowing from the basic premise of haiku, which is to capture a flash of insight about the real, Snyder inserts the striking image of tactile physicality in the middle of that which is supposedly more important or high-minded. In fact, this insertion has the effect of opposing the rightness of images like "wet feet" against abstractions such as "word" or indeed "Ethics" so that third-party views on the real are left in the bathroom in favor of the immediacy of lived experience.

Toward the end of the poem, Snyder recalls one of his environmentalist ancestors, naturalist John Muir, who learns a lesson that would have been familiar to Ray Smith in *The Dharma Bums*. Snyder's Muir recounts a climb up Mount Ritter in which he becomes paralyzed by fear: "Unable to move hand or foot / Either up or down. My doom / Appeared fixed. I MUST fall" (39). Muir panics because the immensity of the mountain is overwhelming for a climber trying to conquer it rationally, "picking ... holds / With intense caution." After the moment of terror on the side of the mountain, though, Muir relaxes his mind so that "My limbs moved with a positiveness and precision / With which I seemed to have / Nothing at all to do" (39). Otherwise put, it is only when Muir learns to climb the mountain spontaneously, abandoning "intense caution," that he is truly able to see with "preternatural clearness," to become of a piece with the natural world rather than a rational actor on it. Such clarity is one ambition of the new consciousness attuned to *tathata*, and can be taken as a constant though elusive goal of Snyder's work during this period.

Snyder's interest in and experience with the outdoors informs not only *Riprap* and *Myths & Texts* but most of his work over the next several decades, notably *Turtle Island* (1974), which won the Pulitzer Prize for poetry, and his epic poem, *Mountains and Rivers without End*, which he began in the mid-1950s and published in pieces throughout his career, with the full four-part poem only appearing in 1996. Bound up with his Buddhist study and practice, Snyder's deep interest in the ecological, including but not limited to humankind's place in nature, marks another important aspect of Beat-associated writing, particularly by those writers living on the West Coast. During the Beatnik Era and after, not only Snyder, but Lew Welch, Michael McClure, and Philip Whalen would all explore the power (or limitations) of language to articulate the nature of consciousness, which is always understood by them as part of a larger ecological order not necessarily dominated by human beings.

9.6   Joanne Kyger: Delicious Interpretation

Born north of San Francisco in 1934, Joanne Kyger had moved to the city in 1957, where she ventured into the poetry circle around Jack Spicer and Robert Duncan. In 1958, she presented a poem, "The Maze," at one of the group's Sunday night readings, and the piece was strong enough that it established Kyger as a writer to watch; it would later open her first collection, *The Tapestry and the Web* (1965). Given her early associations with the Spicer circle, sometime rival of the Beats, it might not be all that surprising that Kyger habitually refused identification with the Beat Generation even though she was a poet in San Francisco at the height of the Beatnik Era. In interviews later in life, she often claimed: "I resisted the Beat label during the time I was associated with the Beat writers because they never considered me a Beat writer. I didn't consider myself a Beat writer."[85] Despite this resistance, another event occurred at a Spicer reading that would forever yoke her to the movement: she met Gary Snyder, who had come to read from *Myths & Texts*, and the two soon became romantically involved.[86] By 1960, Kyger and Snyder were married and living in Kyoto, where they remained for the next four years so that he could pursue his Buddhist studies. Kyger and Snyder divorced in 1965, but their relationship during her formative years as a poet meant that although the Beat movement wasn't necessarily the greatest influence on her poetics, she came to know a range of Beat-associated writers, and has been perennially grouped with other "Beat women" on subsequent panels and in anthologies.[87]

Due to these associations in the late 1950s and early 1960s, most discussions of Kyger in the context of the Beat movement tend to focus on *The Tapestry and the Web*, which contains work from 1958 to late 1964, and *Strange Big Moon: The Japan and Indian Journals, 1960–64*, which details her time in those places.[88] *Tapestry* takes its basic inspiration from *The Odyssey*, particularly the story of Penelope waiting for Odysseus to return from his journeys.[89] Figuring the speaker as a contemporary Penelope, Kyger reflects on a range of interconnected themes, from loneliness to the nature of creativity. When the speaker says, "Refresh my thoughts of Penelope again. / Just HOW / solitary was her wait?" it's hard not to see shades of Kyger's own experiences with Snyder, whom she characterizes in her journals as remote and self-absorbed.[90] In the first few pages of *Strange Big Moon*, for example, she writes, "I wish I weren't married at all I feel trapped" (10) and the penultimate entry, four years later, reads: "Wake up saying I HATE YOU to Gary in my dream" (279). Given her evidently strained relationship with Snyder, those moments in *Tapestry* that name him speak to their constitutive differences, as in "Burning the Baby to make him realer": "Gary says of the blond child / tensely crouching on the porch he's / not human / at 2½ an unfaltering / icy blue stare in his eyes he DEMANDS" (41). Although "Gary" tries to make the unruly child seem foreign to the domestic space the couple has established in Japan, the startling charge that this child is "not human" only makes Gary seem cold and distant, one of the connective thematic threads of *Tapestry*. As she writes in one of the later poems, "Oh he is a liar / from the bottom of his heart / But he puts facts together / and has, little rival, and lets no one know" (53). The implication is that the work in *Tapestry* will reveal not only Kyger's poetic personae but also the "real" Snyder, who is figured as obscured behind various kinds of screens.

Given Kyger's persistent refusals to identify herself as a Beat, it may in fact be the case that despite a highly prolific career during which she published more than thirty books, her earliest work, *Strange Big Moon* in particular, is most imbricated with the Beats. These journals are not only a valuable perspective on Snyder and other figures like Ginsberg and Orlovsky (mainly in connection to a lengthy trip the four took through India); they also reveal how, as Mary Paniccia Carden puts it, "'Joanne Kyger' materializes as a palimpsest of intertextual associations, a fluctuating and multifaceted self assembled in and around internal 'tug of wars' provoked in large part by external demands and expectations" (106). The idea of Kyger's self-fashioning as a complex palimpsest speaks to the fact that her life and work is of course hardly reducible to her time as Snyder's wife or observer of the male Beats, and those interested in her writing have a rich body to mine in the material she produced after her divorce from Snyder, when she returned to California and immersed herself in different contexts.

9.7   Lew Welch: No Separation

With respect to the limitations of language as such, Lew Welch's first, short book, *Wobbly Rock* (1960), takes a page from Snyder's playbook and is in fact in explicit dialogue with Snyder's work as it questions the role language plays in shaping what we take to be reality.[91] Welch was an old Reed College roommate of Snyder and Whalen's, and "Wobbly Rock" opens with a quotation from Snyder: "*'I think I'll be the Buddha of this place' / and sat himself / down.*" Like "Riprap," "Wobbly Rock" is written in deliberate, unadorned language, and begins meditatively, reflecting Welch's experiences with Zen meditation, which he was learning from Snyder in the late 1950s.[92] The title refers to a locally famous rock on the edge of a Californian beach that "moves when hit by waves / Actually shudders," hence its name.[93] As in *The Dharma Bums* and *Riprap*, Welch's Buddhism encourages skepticism about the power of words to capture and account for the real. Early in the poem, for instance, he notes a limitation of figurative language: "(the mind getting it all confused again: / 'snow like frosting on a cake' / 'rose so beautiful it don't look real')" (n.p.). In contrast to the slipperiness of language, which so often serves to confuse rather than clarify the nature of experience, Welch is interested in "the real," and yet, like Kerouac and Snyder, he also recognizes the paradox of this position for a writer. Thus the titular Wobbly Rock is at once "a real rock . . . resting on actual sand" and a metaphor for the precariousness of what we experience as reality, something both tangible and solid ("Hard common stone"), *and* tenuous and fleeting so it "shudders," a situation summed up in the final line of part one: "Wobbly tons" (n.p.).

The poem in fact turns on these questions about the ability of language to describe the real, questions which are also about a poet's own complicity as trafficker in words. This is an abiding concern not only of *The Dharma Bums* and *Riprap*, but also of *The Tapestry and the Web*, in which Kyger is ambivalent about whether "delicious interpretation / is the word, HOW CLEVER OF US / An entirely new thing each time" (49). Welch likewise wants to understand how minute attention to language – such as the simile likening snow to cake frosting – can help him see the interconnectedness of all things. In part three he writes that "*I have been a word in a book*" (n.p.), which suggests the importance of textuality in articulating and therefore understanding the real. As the poem unfolds, the speaker moves along the beach, witnessing a fisherman who is described as a "figure" – recalling figurations such as frosting-like snow – who is nonetheless as real as Wobbly Rock, whose apparent connection to his fishing line reminds the speaker that "there is no separation." This idea is repeated in the final part of the poem, after the speaker rides a boat out into the water – a trip that, as Rod Phillips has pointed out, overturns human-centered hierarchies by "placing the human figures inconspicuously afloat amidst eels, rocks, and starfish" (85). In this way, "Wobbly Rock" is an example of Beat eco-consciousness refracted through a particular awareness of language. For in the final part, the speaker notes that "I lost all separation in step with the / Eucalyptus as the trail walked back beneath me," but then comes around again to the power of an act so fundamental as naming. As he writes:

> Standing on a high rock looking way out over it all:
>
> "*I THINK I'LL CALL IT THE PACIFIC*"
> Wind water
> Wave rock
> Sea sand
> (there is no separation).

The capitalized act of naming echoes the quotation from Snyder that serves as dedication and epigraph to the poem: both are deliberative acts of human thought, but by yoking them Welch questions the distinction between sitting down and being the "Buddha of this place" and the very act of naming – both acts involve the ego, which dictates one's subsequent interaction with the world. In "Wobbly Rock," the speaker returns to his own subjectivity, but privileges it in a way that suggests not domination over the ocean but an interconnection with it, so that naming, making a declarative impact on reality via language, renders the separation between seemingly distinct entities illusory.

9.8   Ron Loewinsohn: The Thing Made Real

In *Memoirs of an Interglacial Age*, Whalen includes a poem called "From a Letter to Ron Loewinsohn, 19:xi:58," part of an ongoing dialogue with the younger, up-and-coming poet. As suggested by the inclusion of the poem in Whalen's book, Loewinsohn was very much a part of the new poetry scene in the late 1950s, but has tended to be left out of discussions of the era and therefore may be less familiar to contemporary readers than many of the other poets already discussed. And yet his strong first book, *Watermelons* (1959), and his inclusion in *The New American Poetry* the following year suggest that Loewinsohn is a Beat-associated poet worth discussing. That said, in pausing over *Watermelons*, it becomes quickly apparent that he should be read not merely for his association with other, more well-known Beat writers, but because the poems themselves are very fine, often humorous, closely observed, and frequently turning on what he called "the unnoticed poetry of our lives' fabric."[94]

Published by Totem Press when Loewinsohn was just twenty-one, *Watermelons* enjoyed the full Beat treatment, with an introduction by Ginsberg *and* a letter of support from William Carlos Williams. Ginsberg's admiring introduction credits a poem of Loewinsohn's with inspiring him to write "In the Baggage Room at Greyhound," collected in *Howl and Other Poems* and composed in May 1956. As Kerouac did for Micheline in his introduction to *River of Red Wine*, Ginsberg places Loewinsohn in an alternative tradition of American poetics: "He fitted his prosody to what he wanted to say, began reading Williams to pick up on the half-century old tradition of American measure. It prepared a usable classical medium for him, & he saw it in time to eliminate bullshit."[95] Williams lauded Loewinsohn for being "sensitive, accurate, fresh."[96] Although such advanced praise is hard to live down, the poems are generally successful, incisive musings about those mundane aspects of life that have not traditionally merited poetic consideration. The book's title is explained by a poem that appeared on its dedication page:

> The pieces of watermelon
> lying shattered
> on the black pavement
> resemble strange jewels,
> jade & ruby clumped together,
> but they're only pieces of watermelon.[97]

Here a mundane accident allows us to see everyday objects anew, so that the watermelon shattered in the street comes to "resemble strange jewels."

But such poetic perception does not transform such objects permanently, for despite the imagistic flash in the center of the poem, the end is in the beginning, and they return merely to "pieces of watermelon."

This interest in language's ability to transform "the real" characterizes much of *Watermelons*, as in the opening poem, "The Thing Made Real," a declaration about the force of the imagination:

> The thing made real by
> a sudden twist of the mind:
> relate the darkness to a face
> rather than
> impose a face on the darkness
> which has no face, in reality.
>
> (3)

Recalling the early days of Totem Press – whose first ever title was *Watermelons* – Hettie Jones singles out this poem as bringing "to the reader the act of the art itself" (*How I Became*, 72). So striking was Loewinsohn's mini-manifesto to the Joneses that LeRoi tacked a copy on the window frame, and Hettie writes that she "read those words at all hours ... The poems *were* our lives" (ibid.). The poem ends with the "thing made real" by the mind thundering into "the consciousness / in all its pure & beautiful / absurdity, / like a White Rhinoceros." As Hettie tells it, Loewinsohn remarked to painter Basil King: "'We need an image that'll knock 'em over,'" and King responded by saying, "how about a white rhinoceros" (ibid.). This image, just the right combination of absurdity and power, is a good encapsulation of the Beat aesthetic as practiced in *Watermelons*, for in "The Thing Made Real," Loewinsohn uses the white rhino to emblematize a certain caution with respect to language's potential to "impose" sense onto reality: the rhino stands as both fantastic and enigmatic, perhaps intriguing exactly because of its mystery.[98] Indeed, despite such caution, *Watermelons* is filled with work that revels in the strange powers of language.

Loewinsohn explores language in "The Necessity of Crosswords," which meditates on various cultural and aesthetic objects, from Porsches to Disneyland, to wonder about the "energy dispersion" of poetry. In an apostrophe to for example, a speeding Porsche, for example, the speaker says:

> O coiled auto
> like a trigger
> if I had your stance your
> constant
> miles an hour
> none of this poem'd be necessary.
>
> (9)

Like many in his circle, Loewinsohn proves himself an inheritor of Charles Olson's "Projective Verse" insofar as he wants to invest his poetry with sports car–like energy: "understanding of energy dispersion – crossword puzzles – as opposed to, say, Disneyland which leads us to poison flowers, sophisticated musicals that lull us to unconsciousness, religion that leads us to the grave" (10). What Disneyland or religion or "sophisticated musicals" lack is the "energy" possible in both poetry and crossword puzzles as they allow the recognition of a brief moment that could cause one to understand the world differently, to see broken watermelons as jewels. The poem then offers up some examples of such energy and insight, from boxer Joey Giardello "swinging / blind at his opponent" (11) to mechanics working on a car to Humphrey Bogart in *The African Queen*. These examples are all purposively mundane, again allowing Loewinsohn to invest the everyday with a kind of magic. This is likewise the case, for example, in "Semicolon; for Phil Whalen," in which he imagines the humble punctuation mark as "the head & forearm of a man swimming, the arm in foreshortened perspective, his head looking away" (21); or "The Stillness of the Poem," which Corso included in a collection he co-edited, *Junge Amerikanische Lyrik*, in 1961; or "The Occasional Room," which Williams singled out in his introductory letter as of particular note. After *Watermelons*, Loewinsohn went on to have a long and successful career, but his work is seldom discussed in light of the Beat movement. I hope that this brief tour suggests that he merits further study in this regard.

9.9   David Meltzer: San Francisco Ragas

The thread of poetic connection from Whalen to Loewinsohn continues through to David Meltzer's book, *Ragas* (1959), which includes "Two Poems for Joey Loewinsohn Age: 4 Months, 9 Days," a sweet update to "Mrs. Loewinsohn &c," the love letter to a pregnant Sue Loewinsohn found in *Watermelons*, which opens by asking: "How can a girl with such a big belly be so desirable?" (14). Meltzer's poem to baby Loewinsohn gives us a glimpse both into Meltzer's community and into his values during this time. Born in 1937, Meltzer grew up in Brooklyn, but then moved with his father to Los Angeles in 1952. Lured by the promise of work, Meltzer moved to San Francisco in 1956, and quickly fell in with the bohemian literary and artistic crowds.[99] As he later recalled, "I began to hang out at North Beach, did some poetry readings at the Cellar.... As a kind of arts community, people may have been ideologically opposed in terms of the practice of poetry, but there was still a certain amount of socializing and community."[100] This community was welcoming enough that in 1957, when Meltzer was just twenty, poet Donald Schenker privately printed a short collection of his work, titled simply *Poems* (it was in a volume with Schenker's own work). One poem offers a compressed tour of Greenwich Village that associates it with radicals "waiting for their chance to step out of the line and proclaim an action that never happened ... to free the enslaved; to enslave the enslavers; to do anything, but to do something final: act for the turmoil wanting form inside."[101] Sounding like a mix of Ginsberg's "Howl" and Propper's "The Fable of the Final Hour," Meltzer, himself a folk singer as well as jazz aficionado, imagines "Folk-singing prophets in mid-afternoon, sandle-squeaking [*sic*] in Washington Square ... the nights of the blackened days, benzedrine blues." The final stanzas convert Ginsberg's famous catalogue of the "best minds" from "who" to "we," a change that writes the poet himself into the "kings of the low-world": "we danced in the Waldorf, turned on in the Automat, threw ourselves in front of the A train in order to know motion; we were living visions of weekly suicides, crawling into hangouts with our bandages dripping and our rebellions slipping" (n.p.). Although Meltzer was still finding his voice in *Poems*, the early work there underscores his commitment to a new consciousness that drew inspiration from Wallace Berman as well as those generally associated with the Beats.[102]

Hardly surprising, then, that in the later collection, *Ragas*, Meltzer explicitly engages others on the San Francisco scene, not only Loewinsohn, but also Wieners and Lamantia, and opens with a letter to Berman – a move that declares Meltzer's connection to a wider aesthetic phenomenon that he would explore and rework again and again throughout his long career. In projects like *San Francisco Beat* (2001), his invaluable collection of interviews conducted over many decades, or his remarkable retrospective epic poem about the movement, *Beat Thing* (2004), Meltzer was perennially interested in thematizing the Beat Generation as a collective phenomenon, an interest that has its seeds in *Poems* and *Ragas*.[103] And owing to Meltzer's capabilities as a musician, he often explored connections among music, particularly jazz, and other forms of artistic expression, particularly poetry, a clear concern of *Ragas* – whose very title, after all, names Indian songs – and that filters through much of his work over the next several decades.

As suggested by his poem to baby Loewinsohn, a striking aspect of *Ragas* is Meltzer's celebration of domestic minutiae (the baby's washcloth "smells like a childhood seashore"), an aspect of Meltzer's (and Loewinsohn's) work that challenges the somewhat accepted wisdom that despite their progressive attitudes in other areas, bohemian men shared with their square counterparts the tendency to ignore the home and family matters like raising children.[104] While it is easy to cite countless examples of this dynamic at work in the lives of Beat-associated writers, Meltzer's work pushes back against that narrative, as in a poem to his wife and folk-singing partner, Tina, with its celebration of children and images of eating ice cream in the kitchen. In 1961, Meltzer would publish "Journal of Birth," a meticulous, joyous record of the home birth of his daughter, which helps explain an image used in the poem to baby Loewinsohn in *Ragas*. In that poem, Meltzer imagines a concert of angels playing children's instruments, asking, "Can't you hear them playing, / loud & cornball, / The Stars & Stripes Forever?" The song choice here takes on a different cast when read against "Journal of Birth," which counterpoints Tina's pregnancy in the summer of 1959 with a triumphalist American political culture in which Independence Day celebrations, "Explosions & distant *Stars & Stripes Forever* played by a brassband on the Marina Green," are imagined as extension of a "synthetic A-Bomb fireworks display."[105] The explosive anthem is for Meltzer an incursion of the political sphere into the domestic one, for although he insists that he doesn't want his "spirit to go thru the Politics meatgrinder" (68), he can't help but be "sick & scared" about the "*NY Times's* report on the Neutron Bomb" (73) and what his family might do "when the bombs did fall" (69). Sidestepping political answers to this question, Meltzer figures his baby as a life-affirming antidote to the death symbolized by the bomb, and after she is born healthy – literally over the *New York Times*, which has been spread across the floor (75) – the doctor remarks, "This takes care of the Neutron Bomb, doesn't it?" An emotionally overwrought Meltzer shakes his hand and tries to say "how I love that hand . . . that brings life into the world" (78). Thus, far from a strain on his freedom or creative energies as Jan Kerouac or William S. Burroughs Jr. would be for their fathers, a child is for Meltzer a source of life and joy that marks another version of the Beat experience circa 1959 (at this time Michael McClure was also married with a small child).

Like Lamantia's *Destroyed Works*, there is a fragmentary quality to *Ragas* because it includes excerpts from longer works such as "The Clown" (published as *Semina 6* in 1960), "Night before Morning," and "Hollywood Poem," which is broken into two excerpts across the book. Rather than an unequivocal condemnation of dominant American culture found in seemingly like-minded work by Micheline, Bremser, and others, *Ragas* takes time to pause over and appreciate some nooks and crannies of this culture, so while ultra-patriotism may occasion concern over atomic weapons, the book also provides finely detailed vignettes of classic Americana like local parades: "The Majorette is 12 & breastless. Her kneecaps are greased with dirt & salt." If the ROTC Brass Auxiliary Band still seems to Meltzer to have a whiff of "paratroopers marching thru Roma," there is a profound appreciation for everyday people giving their all in a performance, not only the Majorette, but the "St Francis Parochial Girls School Percussion Band: yellow & green silk & braid." This is likewise the case in "Hollywood Poem," a paean to old theaters and "the Saturday matinee: 2 movies, 5 cartoons, & 10 acts of vaudeville."

But not all of *Ragas* is celebratory, and readers of "Howl" would recognize the sensibility of a work like "Ward Poem," which uses the asylum as a metaphor for the way artists are bound together precisely because they stand apart from everyday society. The speaker begins the poem by asking, "Do I look mad?" and then proceeds to reflect on how a truly visionary artist might remake reality, thereby creating potential for driving himself mad. The first model for such an artist is Constantin Brâncuşi, the great Romanian sculptor who had died in 1957, but Meltzer counts also Pollock, Bosch, de Chirico, and Bruegel as visionaries who "could have entered the worlds that they created." Such powerful remaking of course comes with a cost, whether madness – literal or perceived as such by mainstream culture – or a turning inward, as is the case with Meltzer's friend Philip Lamantia, whose reputation as a respected poet could not mitigate his struggles with drug addiction:

> Lamantia's long shitbrown scarf thrown
> around his neck – running down Grant St
> chasing echoes of the Last Word – scent
> of the ultimate opium den, lassoed
> around his balls.

Meltzer celebrates creativity, yes, but he also sketches the negatives sometimes attached to artistic vision – in Lamantia's case, addiction, which has him by the balls. And yet "Ward Poem" nonetheless sees a kind of redemption in Lamantia's connection to other artists or visionaries precisely through his estrangement from those events like the little local parade. In this way, "Ward Poem" is a meditation on those projects like *The Beats: A Literary History* that are necessarily engaged in categorizing and labeling; Meltzer wonders "how an age vomits itself up / into books that bind / the whole thing together," suggesting that such binding might obscure rather than illuminate.

9.10   Sheri Martinelli: Queen of the Beats

Like Meltzer, Sheri Martinelli had made the move from the East Coast to San Francisco during the Beatnik Era.[106] Born in 1918, Martinelli was older than almost all the Beats, and had known Kerouac and Ginsberg since the early 1950s, when Anatole Broyard lusted after her – his memoir, *Kafka Was the Rage*, is halved into "Sheri" and "After Sheri" – and William Gaddis incorporated some of her letters verbatim into his postmodern masterpiece *The Recognitions*.[107] But it was after moving to San Francisco that she immersed herself most deeply in the Beat scene, and would by 1960 half-ironically dub herself "the Queen of the Beats."[108] For our purposes, I'll accordingly focus on Martinelli's San Francisco period, but it is important to keep in mind that she brought a certain cultural cachet with her, not only as a painter of some renown, but also as a well-known intimate of Ezra Pound, who through much of the 1950s had been incarcerated at St. Elizabeths Hospital. After Pound broke off their relationship in 1958, Martinelli traveled briefly to Mexico with her new husband Gilbert Lee, and then moved to San Francisco, where she promptly wrote to Ferlinghetti, introducing herself as one "curious as to the mind state of the San Franciscan literary world."[109] Martinelli charmed Ferlinghetti with her refined yet playful sensibility, establishing common ground over their mutual admiration of Corso, whom City Lights was then publishing and whom Martinelli claimed as a friend ("I know how his mind works / Gregory's got a sort of revolving mind . . . that EVERYthing in reality hitches onto & darling Gregory aint got ENOUGH time to sort it out").[110] It wasn't long before Martinelli established herself on the North Beach scene, befriending the likes of McClure, Lamantia, and Kaufman, among others. By 1959, she had plugged herself into the circuit that included the Co-Existence Bagel Shop and the Bread & Wine Mission, living in what she called a "hovel in Old Chinatown" where a steady stream of writers would come seeking her "free works of art for the poets" – she would draw and mimeograph countless handbills advertising readings for local poets Pierre Delattre, Richard Gumbiner, and others.[111]

Martinelli was drawn to the literary and artistic energies in and around North Beach, and started her own little magazine in 1959, *Anagogic & Paideumic Review*, printed in very limited runs and sold at City Lights, which also exhibited her paintings.[112] It was in *Anagogic & Paideumic Review* that she first published "Duties of a Lady Female," an essay or prose-poem that has become her best-known piece of writing because it was anthologized in Richard Peabody's *A Different Beat* (1997). I discuss this piece below, but I also want to underscore that Martinelli's connections to the Beat movement are richer and more extensive than indicated by the presence of a single text in a later anthology.

As much as *Anagogic & Paideumic Review* was reflective of Martinelli's idiosyncratic tastes, it also showcased engagements with the Beat scene reminiscent of *Beatitude*, which had been launched within a few months of her magazine's debut. In addition to the handbills advertising readings or the occasional portraits of friends like Bob Kaufman (see Figure 7.5), *Anagogic & Paideumic Review* printed work about the scene that sometimes placed her at its center, as in William Margolis's "Flash Bulb Photo of Poet's Impromptu," set at the Co-Existence Bagel Shop and describing "so many poets holding down the poltergeist tables with their fountain pens ... sitting between Lamantia & La Martinelli, between words like hyphens, & Kaufman like exclamation points."[113] The nickname "La Martinelli" was used as the title for Martinelli's 1956 collection of paintings, and turns up in work by writers advertising their connections to her (see C. V. J. Anderson's "La Martinelli Talks of Ezra").[114] As was true of *Beatitude*, *Anagogic & Paideumic Review* existed in tension with the Beatniks and the media attention that followed them, and so while Martinelli published and promoted Beat work, she also included a teasing "Anthology of Non-Beat Poetry" in a couple of issues. She also printed a "supplement" to *Anagogic & Paideumic Review*, local poet Sam Suzuki's *San Francisco Beat Scene: Poetry*, which featured her sketch of the beret-clad poet slouching near "ye Aulde Bagel Shoppee." In general, Martinelli was sympathetic to the aims of her Beat friends: once, when in the "hate" phase of her love-hate relationship with Pound, she suggested that the older literary generation symbolized by Pound was being eclipsed for her by a younger one symbolized by Ginsberg: "Your [Pound's] paradise is not worth one second of my Allen Ginsberg 'hell' – because no matter what takes place with me or with my intelligence – Mr. Ginsberg will always be there looking sadly at me with those irridescent [*sic*] eyes – but Mr. Pound hath vanished & is no goddamned good to us."[115]

It is in the San Francisco Beat context, then, that we should read the work of Martinelli's that has received the most critical attention, "Duties of a Lady Female" – it was first published in *Anagogic & Paideumic Review* 1.3 (November/December 1959), immediately preceding Margolis's "Flash Bulb Photo of Poet's Impromptu" (for the cover of this issue, see Figure 9.1) Purportedly written to amuse Pound, "Duties of a Lady Female" is half-ironic advice for hipster women, and its pronouncements center on a woman's relationship to others, not only to men but also to

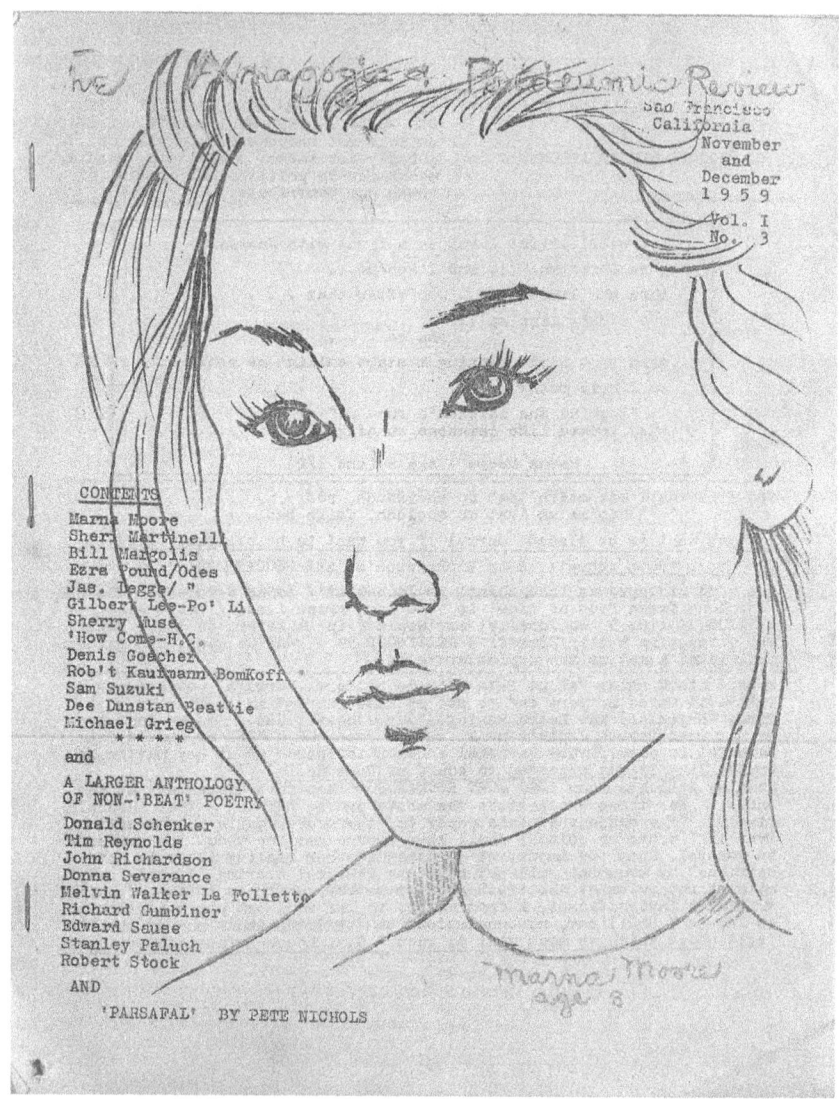

Figure 9.1   Cover for *Anagogic & Paideumic Review* 1.3 (November/December 1959)
drawn by Sheri Martinelli. Note that this issue includes a "Larger Anthology
of Non-Beat Poetry."
Image courtesy of Beinecke Rare Book and Manuscript Library, Yale University

other women. With this conceit, Martinelli reframes the way women found themselves defined always against the desires and judgments of men. The opening line, "Learn HOW to make love," is immediately elaborated into advice for turning oneself into an exotic, perfumed object who might thereby attract male attention. From there the piece continues to measure a woman's success as "lady female" in terms of how a man does or does not feel about her:

> Put into your lover's mind a picture of the KIND of PERSON you feel he secretly thinks he is. Make him love himself & be dependent on you for it. [...]
>
> No high or harsh tones of voice. He is more sensitive than you, to them. [...] If you GOT to cry, do it for him. Example: DONT say: "poor, poor, little baby, you are underprivileged." Tell him: "when I think of all the sufferings that befall a male in this world of survival and chance ... I could weep." Then you can cry. You'll have him weeping with you.
> [...]
> In your love talking put a picture in his mind of something wildly adventurous, suiting his male nature. The Foreign Legion. International Jewel Smuggling. Stalking Through Africa.[...] The result, my sisters, will be this: you'll have no mere male [...] You'll have the bravest Foreign Legionnaire of them all & he'll treat you with the extreme aroused interest of a male used to being predatory, a fine rapacious beastie.[116]

Martinelli's satire is manifest in how perfectly she ventriloquizes a particular sensibility about male–female relationships: the idealized "lady female" does not merely turn herself into a fantasy, she must also convince her man that fantasies about himself are true. In this rendering, a woman's duties are principally to her male lover, and involve sustaining a world of lies at the expense of the disappointing intrusion of reality. Ronna C. Johnson has argued that in this way, "Duties of a Lady Female" is a "revisionary counterpart to 'Howl' that purports to lionize the male while iconographizing the female, just as "Howl" purports a universality that is in actuality male precedence."[117] In other words, whereas "Howl" assumes male experience as universal experience, "Duties of a Lady Female" *appears* to make this assumption, but is really subverting the equation of male with universal by demonstrating the absurdity and pathos required to warrant such a premise.

In the second half of the piece, Martinelli turns attention to how a "lady female" navigates her relationships with other women. As we have seen, many a male Beat writer went out of his way to advertise connections and affinities with other male writers on the scene, a move that seemed to legitimate both the individual writer and the movement *as* a movement. In its fundamental skepticism of this universalizing move, "Duties of a Lady Female" seems to argue that women must constantly be on guard against one another, but actually reveals the fragmentation of female solidarity under such circumstances. This part of the piece begins: "Fraternise with other females. Build a code of behaviour" (155), seemingly reasonable advice soon eclipsed by detailed instructions on how to confront a woman who "EYE BALLS your male": "Raise your voice. Warn her LOUD ... Say: 'you low BITCH get your nose out of him or I'll ruin you'" (156). This cynical stance is followed by guidelines on how to physically fight another woman who doesn't back down, and it is clear that such premises promote absurd notions of masculinity and femininity that debase women by calculating their worth in terms of attention received by men. The piece's straightforward style is ironically what makes it Beat: its advice actually makes perfect sense in the context of conventional or mainstream gender norms, and it is only when such norms are viewed from the outside, when they are shown to be far from universal, does the internal logic of the poem collapse and we can appreciate Martinelli's skewering of such norms.

But if we read "Duties of a Lady Female" against another poem Martinelli published a few months prior, we see that its universalizing claims conceal another layer that relates to the experience of a female artist specifically in the male-dominated enclave of bohemian San Francisco circa 1959. As explained above, "Duties of a Lady Female" opens with "Learn HOW to make love"; the next line is "Books help" (154). In "On Loving Many," a poem published in *Beatitude* in the summer of 1959, Martinelli likewise turns to a book for a helping hand, creating a light-hearted poem in couplets "after Chris Marlowe's translation of Ovid" (she's referring to Ovid's book of love poems, *Amores*).[118] Like "Duties," "On Loving Many" explores gender dynamics, but does so by asserting the speaker's own sexual desires, and announcing at the outset: "here I display my lewd & loose behaviour." This lewdness is illustrated as the speaker describes (imagined?) sex with various male writers, including several associated with the Beat movement:

> Philip Lamantia's coy & he's no clown;
> I think he'd be nimble when he's down.
> . . .
> Beauteous MacLure [McClure] rails at me & that I write,
> Yet I'd grab him, if that I might.
> . . .

Allen sweetly singing, oh then straight I long
To rub on his lips passionately, in song.

. . .

Tall Ferlinghetti, a male Amazon,
Therefore fills the bed he lies upon.

(n.p.)

Also mentioned are other writers such as Pound, Aldous Huxley, Robert Lowell, and "Anatole [Broyard] for his looks" and "young Whalen [who] pleases" (a reference to "Mr. Lowercase" [e. e. cummings] is echoed in the advice in "Duties of a Lady Female" to impress men by quoting "Mr. Lowercase Cummings" [156]). As these examples show, in "On Loving Many," the speaker's sexual desire takes center stage, and it is the men who are sexualized, acted upon, and characterized in terms of their potential to "please" her. In this poem, what matters about the men is not their literary prowess or really any other achievements besides their looks or capacities in the bedroom, an appropriation and reversal of the male logic that saw women as silent Beat chicks. The final couplet in fact declares a classic "love 'em and leave 'em" attitude: "I love them & go on with my job; none do I miss, / I know Rooster-God will send me more Cocks just like this!" In the metonymic collapse of real-life men with their "Cocks," the speaker does not merely assert agency, but does so in terms of her "job," suggesting that these men are no better than distractions from her artistic vocation. "On Loving Many," then, is a revealing addendum to the more-discussed "Duties of a Lady Female" that not only underscores the ironic distance embedded in the latter's advice but lays bare the hip context for said advice.

Taken together with her work on *Anagogic & Paideumic Review* and her many connections to the San Francisco scene, "On Loving Many" reminds us that Martinelli's contribution to the Beat movement was hardly limited to a single text. In fact, she was for a brief period a center of literary activity, acting as what Steven Moore calls "a mother hen to the younger beatniks."[119] However much her sexually charged poetry complicates this maternal metaphor, it is true that the younger writers recognized Martinelli's storied past, and it was she who ultimately grew bored with the city, decamping in the early 1960s. As she explained in "The Last Days of North Beach in San Francisco" (1960), a kind of farewell essay published in *Anagogic & Paideumic Review*, on arriving in the city, she had been "motivated to enlighten & widen the mind-state existing in North Beach" by printing those handbills for "the struggling poets on North Beach."[120] She goes on to describe, however, that many of these "struggling poets" took advantage of her generosity, eating her food and trashing her place, a situation that finally amounted to "one-sided Love," another in a "history of the artist's [Martinelli's] life among her contemporaries."[121] Given such circumstances, she decided it was time to leave North Beach for a literary life of greater solitude on the coast, but had nonetheless left an imprint on the Beat movement that deserves further recognition.

In drawing attention to Martinelli's time in San Francisco, I want echo the work of scholars who have emphasized the role of women in the Beat movement, thereby challenging the general impression that Diane di Prima was the lone Beat woman publishing in the late 1950s. In Part IV, I devote further attention to Beat-associated women writers who were beginning to gain more prominence in the early 1960s and after, but for now I want to follow Martinelli with a discussion of Lenore Kandel, a writer who tends to be invoked in connection to mid- or late 1960s incarnations of Beatness, even though her first work dates from the Beatnik Era.[122]

9.11   Lenore Kandel: Restless Mind

When Kandel turns up in histories of the Beats, it is usually with respect to her graphic and thus controversial *The Love Book* (1966), or to the fact that in *Big Sur* (1962) Kerouac imagined her as Romana Swartz, a "monster beauty ... intelligent, well read, writes poetry, is a Zen student, knows everything."[123] But Kandel was known in bohemian circles prior to this moment as a prolific and powerful poet who preferred to read her work in coffee houses rather than attempt to get them published. This all changed in 1959 when Grover and Rosie Haynes founded the Three Penny Press out of their apartment in Studio City, California. Asserting his interest in the "local barefoot bards," Grover Haynes proudly proclaimed that the work he printed did "not have the GOOD HOUSEKEEPING SEAL OF APPROVAL," a stance that explicitly pitted itself against literature "safe and tested" according to the standards espoused by the New Criticism or practiced by the academic poets.[124] Kandel herself would seize on this same marker of mainstream approval in her poem "First They Slaughtered the Angels," which wonders who is responsible for the repression of "the angels," the marginal or downtrodden: "who raped St. Mary with a plastic dildo stamped with the / Good Housekeeping seal of approval?"[125] The overt anti-establishment stance – magnified in "First They Slaughtered Angels" into violent outrage – marks the general sensibility of Three Penny Press. Like *Yugen* and *The Floating Bear*, it was a small, two-person operation aiming to bring alternative voices in contemporary letters to slightly larger audiences, and drew a direct line to the Beats with titles such as *Beards and Brown Bags* (1959) and *Beat and Beatific II* (1959), collections that included poetry by Kandel and others. In 1959, the Hayneses also published three small books by Kandel: *A Passing Dragon*, *A Passing Dragon Seen Again*, and *An Exquisite Navel*.[126]

True to Grover Haynes's claim that Kandel is "inextricably tied in with coffee houses and the mood that pervades them," the work in her early books is pointedly set in bohemia and explores its "mood."[127] The opening poem in *A Passing Dragon* announces: "All my pockets have holes in the bottoms / and everything I own slides away .... / sooner or later," a passage that cedes the importance of material possessions to an appreciation of the resources of the natural world.[128] The poem concludes: "I filled my pockets with nothing and started again / me and the gray wind." If there is an abiding sensibility of *A Passing Dragon*, it is Kandel's imagining how she might better understand herself through nature, an understanding that her speakers' constitutional impecuniousness only promotes. The poetry in that book uses varied strategies for exploring this connection, including the playful figurations of men as animals that allows her to poke fun at male-centered "preening," as when she writes, "You are like a lion / crashing the bars of your cage / And I am an idiot / Trying to stay you / with / peanuts"; or "Such a tomcat then / sitting there preening his belly fur ... / (so infuriating to a she-cat. ...)." Also characteristic of the volume are the moments when Kandel expresses desire for a mystical connection between her speakers and nature, as in the lines: "The hot wind blows and / I wish I could blow with it" and "I have fallen in love with the wind / I know I can't catch it." In one poem, the speaker becomes literally embodied by nature:

> My love gave me an orange tree
> which would not bear
> I planted it in my belly
> and laid myself down in the soft dark earth
> lapping myself with leaves like a coverlet.

As one can see from this piece's presentation in the original book (see Figure 9.2), the illustration of the woman being wrapped in the roots of a tree interacts with the text of the poem, so the roots become a textual interruption between the first stanza and its final three lines. What seems at first only a bleak metaphorical rendering of unreproductive love – so the tree is "planted" in the speaker's "belly" but is yet unable to bear fruit – is

My love gave me an orange tree
which would not bear
I planted it in my belly
and laid myself down in the soft dark earth
lapping myself with leaves like a coverlet

But our tree bore no fruit
and its roots spread through my body

and pinned me to the barren ground.

I love you.
simpler than that
I can not be.

Figure 9.2   From Lenore Kandel's *A Passing Dragon* (1959). In this original illustration, a woman – the "I" of the poem – physically interacts with a branch or root in a sexually suggestive way.
Photo courtesy of Lafayette College

recontextualized through the final three lines, which assert simple love as a guiding response if not antidote to the aridity in the first stanza. The interconnection of text and image in fact underscores the interconnection of the speaker and nature itself, so being "pinned" to the "barren ground" becomes less a lament about infertility and more a celebration of kinds of growth that are not quite so visible as babies. Being rooted is not a sentence of immobility, but rather a way to bear another kind of fruit, the affirmation of love for the "you" who had planted the original seed.

While *A Passing Dragon* plays with the connectedness of women and the natural world, *An Exquisite Navel* enacts a more familiar Beat resistance to dominant culture that was perceived to foreclose individual expression. The poem "All I have in the world" explores personal subjectivity in a hostile culture in ways reminiscent of work like Ferlinghetti's "Autobiography": "All I have in the world / Dark brown hair and a restless mind / I can feel the earthquakes underneath my feet / Waiting to explode, to erupt, to go boom!"[129] As the poem continues, Kandel's speaker becomes paralyzed by expectations of complacency. In the line that gives the book its title, she claims that "I am tired of my navel, exquisite as it is," and develops her navel's tripartite significance as connected to child-bearing, as object of male desire (in his preface, Haynes approvingly notes that "Lenore worked her way through college as a belly dancer in a Turkish cabaret in New York"), and as site of self-paralysis in the form of navel-gazing. Her body, from her "dark brown hair" to her exquisite navel, is a both a resource and a hindrance to being recognized for her "restless mind." "I am bored with sitting wisely," she writes, "I am tired of being calm." The poem identifies the source of such discontent not only in her being valued just for the exquisiteness of her navel, but also in those "shibboleths and syllogisms" of social regulation that demand fairly narrow ideas of cleanliness or virtue. As a poem like "Howl," "All I have in the world" explores the turmoil beneath the veneer of acceptable society, but does so from a decidedly female perspective, which, like di Prima's work, is not so sure about the distinctions among mainstream and Beat when it comes to gender norms. "All I have in the world" is representative of the poetry in *An Exquisite Navel* in that a witty female sensibility takes on both mainstream culture and its supposed inverse in ways that would be elaborated even more complexly in the coming years, most famously in *The Love Book*, a collection that unites the erotic with the sacred, and that made Kandel's name in the countercultural scene in 1966 when, as happened in connection to "Howl," booksellers in San Francisco were arrested for peddling obscenity.[130]

9.12   Alan Ansen Digs Those Crazy Cats

Just as Kandel was mythologized in *Big Sur*, so too was Alan Ansen in *On the Road* as "wild, ecstatic" Rollo Greb, a figure hip enough that Dean Moriarty himself exclaims, "I want to be like him" (127). Despite his long association with the inner circle, Bill Morgan observes that Ansen has been "virtually forgotten by students of the Beat Generation" (*Typewriter*, 173). Ansen's general absence from Beat literary histories is unfortunate because, as Morgan points out, he was widely admired by the likes of Kerouac, Ginsberg, Burroughs, and Corso from the early 1950s, when he was W. H. Auden's personal secretary.[131] With Ginsberg and Kerouac, Ansen had helped type the manuscript of *Naked Lunch*, and references to him appear all over letters by those in the inner circle. By the Beatnik Era, Ansen had left New York for Venice, Italy, and finally published his own first collection of poetry, *The Old Religion*, in 1959, a book that seems at once Beat and not Beat. In the jacket copy for his second book, *Disorderly Houses* (1961), which incorporates most of *The Old Religion* and adds some new material, Ansen is playfully associated with the Beats: "It would not be accurate to call Mr. Ansen a 'beat' poet, although he has something of the disenchanted attitude and the freedom of language of that school."[132] Like so many of the writers I've been discussing, Ansen insists he isn't Beat while trading on the popularity of that very label.

Disorderly Houses opens with a poem that turns on the poet's relationship with Europe and the United States that could be read as Ansen's declaration of his own poetic voice distinct from any movement. Occasioned by the cruiser USS *Newport News* docking in Venice, the poem reflects:

> Venice, I am not just part of your incomparable poem.
> I have my own poetry and my own past.
> God bless those American angels from the sea
> For reminding me
> "There is one story and one story only."
>
> (3)

The quoted line is from one of Robert Graves's most well-known poems, "To Juan at the Winter Solstice," which compresses his argument about the universalizing nature of poetic myth explicated in his influential book *The White Goddess* (1948).[133] In his poem, Ansen transforms the US military from emblems of violence or regimentation – as happens, for instance, in a poem like Corso's "Army" – into "angels from the sea," modern-day versions of the wandering seafarers of ancient myth who remind the speaker that he is at once individual, with his own poetry and his own past, *and* part of the deeper mythic patterns described by Graves. In its fluency in and reworking of ancient myth, Ansen's poetry may be compared to work such as Kyger's *The Tapestry and the Web*, which, as discussed earlier, rewrites the figure of Penelope from *The Odyssey*. As the very title *The Old Religion* indicates, Ansen's poetry is steeped in tradition, from the use of conventional forms such as a sonnet ("Tennyson") to a contemporary response to Aeschylus' play *Choephoroi*, or *The Libation Bearers* ("Dragon Poem"), once again demolishing the notion that a constitutive feature of Beat writing is triumphant ignorance of literary history (*On the Road*'s version of Ansen, Rollo Greb, "is a great scholar who goes reeling down the New York waterfront with original seventeenth-century musical manuscripts under his arm, shouting," which nicely captures Ansen's deranged erudition [127]).

As "Dragon Poem" updates Aeschylus to "the hour of Campari" (*Disorderly Houses*, 24), so much of the collection explores tensions between old and new, as in the reliance on an ancient form (ode) to describe a modern phenomenon (heroin addiction), as in "Heroin: An Ode," dedicated to Corso.[134] From a Beat point of view, *Disorderly Houses* also touches on some perennial interests, not only drug use, but also Buddhism ("The Wheel"), and mocking the wealthy but vapid, as in "The Party": "My dear! You mean you didn't go? You weren't invited? But how ridiculous! Simply *everybody* was there" (23). Other poems parody the swinging variant of a Beat aesthetic:

> Just because I look as if I were mad
> Or sad
> Or merely dying to be had
> Doesn't mean you can dismiss me as merely a fad
> Of people who neither shit nor get off the pot, who lack the
>   courage to be bad
> But make up for it by cultivating me and think they're quite the lad
> When they watch me upchuck in the street . . .
> Or hum Ethelbert Nevin's "Rosary" in a teahead's pad.
>
> (6)

The use of slang such as "teahead" and "pad" connects the speaker of this poem to the underground, suggesting that the "fad" could as easily refer to the wider Beat phenomenon as it could to the specific experiences named. The punch of rhyme at the end of each line encourages readers to hear the poem's sound, to imagine it being read aloud with musical accompaniment, an idea emphasized by the mention of Nevin, an American composer whose debt and alcoholism-plagued life mark his kinship with the downtrodden teaheads in the poem.

Ansen's play between the old and new is illustrated to comic effect in his use of another apparently outmoded form, the masque, a tradition of courtly entertainment generally associated with sixteenth- and seventeenth-century Europe. Ansen's masque was written in 1959 for his "hostess," well-known patroness of the arts Peggy Guggenheim. By that time Ansen was living what Barry Miles has called a "very comfortable life" in Venice, becoming a "good friend" to the fabulously wealthy Guggenheim (others, including Corso, Ginsberg, and Orlovsky, had also darkened Guggenheim's door).[135] Ansen adopted the masque form to humorously show his appreciation for Guggenheim, and to honor poet James Merrill and his partner David Jackson, who had just returned to Italy from Greece. Performed in Guggenheim's garden in Venice in August 1959, the masque, "The Return from Greece," was divided into ten parts, the most relevant of which for our purpose concern the arrival of four imaginary Beatnik tourists in Venice, and the real-life arrival of Corso.

The first part, the anti-masque, presents a dramatic conversation between a gondolier, a garbage man, and a boy, which is interrupted by a Poet Beatnik, a Nature Boy Beatnik, a Socially Conscious Beatnik, and a Wise Old Sage Beatnik. Seeing them approaching, the boy says, "Ma varda sti tipi mati i che stà a rivar" ("Just look at these oddballs coming up"), and are met with the Beat Poet exclaiming "Dig those crazy cats, man" (71). The balance of the encounter has bemused Italians shaking their heads at the stereotypical Beatniks, whose hipness is played for comic effect so that, for instance, when the Poet Beatnik asks the boy simply, "Rimbaud?" the boy responds by asking for a cigarette. The dismayed poet then fires off a litany of slang that could have been lifted from any of the Beatnik caricatures discussed earlier: "Aw come off that routine, cat. Live poetry. Get high on weed, not that cornball stuff. God, how much I have to teach you" (72). The fun here comes from fulfilling media-created stereotypes and lampooning actual hangers-on who might ramble into a city like Venice behaving like exaggerations of themselves.

This account is followed by a depiction of Corso himself, who often walked that razor's edge of self-caricature. He had blown into Venice that summer from Paris, living with Ansen and stretching himself financially, as he said, to buy "a suit and shoes so that I can go to Peggy Guggenheim's parties" (*Accidental Autobiography*, 201). In fact, Corso became a fixture on the Venice scene that summer, knocking back drinks with painter Willem de Kooning, flirting with Guggenheim, and crashing fancy parties. Much of this spirit is embodied in "The Return from Greece," whose conceit is that thanks to the munificence of "our gracious empress" (Guggenheim), Ansen's players have a gilded space in which to perform the masque. "Rehearse we must the gossip," for Merrill and Jackson have been away for two months (76). While the Beatniks in the earlier part of the masque are cardboard parodies, the sum of media-created clichés, Corso is depicted affectionately, as a perpetually broke rabble-rouser, but a true artist none-theless. Playing on Corso's tendency to beg money in the face of his constant destitution, he is introduced as having a "lust for loot," but still principled aesthetically, unwilling to suffer pretenders like the Beatniks depicted earlier. The action moves to a "waterfront dive" where Corso finds trouble:

> Wassailing ingenuous poets were hogtied,
> Lassoed by Brooklyn buyers out for a good time,

Uninterrupted belches, freedom from conscious verses.
Inundated by dullness, Gregory screamed defiance,
Waterfront dive grew sober, barred the bard the door,
Tawdrily knuckling under to flatulent base chuffs.

(77)

Here a bar full of drunken poets play to those with money, are "hogtied" by touristing New Yorkers, a situation Ansen's Corso finds dull to the point of offensiveness. The ensuing howl of "defiance" represents the historical Corso and his notorious drunken antics such as throwing a glass at a *Life* magazine photographer, but also the defiance of a true poet more aesthetically sophisticated than the caricatures like the Poet Beatnik in earlier section.[136] "The Return from Greece" is thus an example of how a Beat-associated writer like Ansen played the media stereotypes of Beatniks against actual writers, exploring the meaning of the movement in the context of such images, and in the international arena. In this regard, the masque – though a one-off work written for private consumption – resonates with other work published over the next years such as Ferlinghetti's *Her*, Joans's *The Hipsters*, Corso's own *The American Express*, and the collaboration *Minutes to Go*, led by Burroughs and Brion Gysin, texts which were likewise animated by talking back at Beatnik caricatures. These texts are discussed in more detail in Part IV. Ansen, both Beat and his own poet, went on to produce work showcasing his own idiosyncratic vision while maintaining ties to the Beats throughout his life.

CHAPTER 10

Ignus
From the Beat Hotel to *Pull My Daisy*

As evidenced by Ansen's presence in Italy, Beat wanderlust meant that not everyone was headquartered in New York or San Francisco in the late 1950s, and I placed him at the end of a discussion of West Coast writers to suggest Europe as another important site in the geography of the Beat movement. During the post-"Howl" and *On the Road* interest in the Beats, some writers wound up in exile, self-imposed or not (Burroughs, Joans, Harold Norse), or were traveling and living abroad for long periods of time (Ginsberg, Orlovsky, Corso, Snyder, Kyger, Lamantia, Kay Johnson, the Bremsers) – Burroughs wasn't in fact in residence in the United States at all during the Beatnik Era, having moved around in Mexico City, Tangier, and Paris. While each of these cities holds a special place in Beat literary history, only Paris had its own "Beat Hotel," an otherwise unnamed, ramshackle enclave tucked away in the Latin Quarter at 9 rue Gît-le-Coeur, a place that earned its moniker thanks to the concentration of writers and artists who either lived there or passed through for significant amounts of time.[1]

The Beat Hotel was run by a woman named Madame Rachou, who was fond enough of writers, artists, and other bohemian types that they tended to collect there, and the place turned into a commune of sorts. Shabby and cheap, the hotel had a permissive atmosphere that encouraged creativity and experimentation. As Burroughs put it, "Things were happening in every room. People were writing, painting, talking, and planning, and Madame Rachou presided in her little bar with the zinc counter."[2] Among those writing and talking were Ginsberg and Orlovsky, who arrived in October 1957 with Corso not far behind. Burroughs lived there intermittently between 1958 and 1963, when it closed after Madame Rachou's retirement. Other Beat-associated writers who lived at the hotel for extended periods include Brion Gysin, Harold Norse, and Kay Johnson, all of whom later wrote about their experiences there.[3]

The hotel was a significant incubator of Beat writing, and some lasting work was produced within its walls, including parts of Ginsberg's long poem "Kaddish," a lament for his mother that many readers consider among his finest poems, as well as "At Apollinaire's Grave" and "Ignu," all of which were collected in his second book *Kaddish and Other Poems, 1958–1960* (1961).[4] Corso wrote his most famous poem, "Bomb," at the Beat Hotel, and as explained earlier, the fact that the FLN, an Algerian national movement, was detonating actual bombs around Paris at the time suggests a different set of political stakes lurking between its lines. It was also at the hotel that Burroughs and others assembled the sprawling pages of the *Naked Lunch* manuscript for publication, and where Burroughs, Gysin, and mathematician Ian Sommerville constructed their Dreamachine, a cylindrical device with strobe lights intended to mimic certain brainwaves, thereby inducing users into a semi-hypnotic, meditative state.

The most influential aesthetic innovation that emerged from the hotel was the cut-up method, which Gysin discovered in the fall of 1959, and which Burroughs used to great effect in his work throughout the 1960s. Because I see the development of the cut-up method as an important hinge into how the Beat movement developed in the 1960s, I'll reserve an in-depth discussion of it until Part IV, but keep in mind that it is a composition technique on par with Kerouac's spontaneous prose insofar as it changes the game in terms of how meaning can inhere in words, sometimes banishing representation altogether.

An early adopter of Gysin's and Burroughs's technique was Harold Norse, whose book *Beat Hotel* (1983) collects cut-up work he had written at the hotel during the Beatnik Era. Born in Brooklyn in 1916, Norse had been what he later called a "charter member of the 'Beat Generation,'" as Ginsberg had met him even before Kerouac and Burroughs.[5] Although he hadn't been a part of the libertine circle at Columbia – he had already graduated from Brooklyn College in 1938 – he was familiar with the blurred lines between the queer and emergent Beat undergrounds described in Part I, but his ties are easier to recognize in the latter 1950s and after. Norse lived, for instance, at the Beat Hotel in the late 1950s, and later with Paul and Jane Bowles in Tangier, and when he moved back to the States permanently in the early 1970s, his publishing ventures helped to solidify the legacy of the Beat movement, particularly the short-lived little magazine *Bastard Angel* (1972–1974), which focused on work by Beat-associated writers (see in particular issue 3 [fall 1974], which featured beautiful prints of "Beat Generation Poets" by Peter Le Blanc as well as lots of energetic poetry). Likewise in *Beat Hotel*, a compendium of cut-up work and essays about the hotel, Norse characterized the hotel as ground-zero for Beat literary production, noting that "the walls … were acting strangely. Instead of being exclusive, shutting in and out, erecting barrier or frontier, as walls are supposed to do, they behaved like conductors of electricity" (62). In this way, Norse suggests that the very physicality of the building encouraged collaboration and tore down barriers, a situation that he sees as laying the groundwork for the countercultural explosion of the 1960s in both France and the States. Reflecting, for example, on the events of May 1968, in which students and others staged widespread protests throughout Paris, events he called a "revolutionary movement against authority and tradition" (72), Norse linked the spirit of this movement to the electricity of the Beat Hotel, making the bold claim that the radical though seemingly hermetic aesthetic experiments there in fact opened possibilities for different kinds of political engagement in the later 1960s and after, something that we will see in Part IV came to characterize the Beat movement writ large during the decade.[6]

A fitting coda to the Beatnik Era is the short film *Pull My Daisy* (1959), which features Ginsberg, Orlovsky, and Corso more or less playing themselves with a voiceover narration "ad-libbed" by Kerouac.[7] The twenty-eight-minute film was directed by Alfred Leslie with camera work by Swiss photographer Robert Frank, shot in early 1959, and premiered that November.[8] Before moving into an discussion of the film, it's worth noting that while *Pull My Daisy* is the most studied Beat film, others merit further attention. I suggest in particular Christopher Maclaine's shorts *The Man Who Invented Gold* (1957) and *Beat* (1958), as well as Ron Rice's *The Flower Thief* (1960), set in bohemian San Francisco and featuring appearances by Bob Kaufman and others, and *The Brink* (1961), a visual adaptation of ruth weiss's poem of the same name.[9]

Pull My Daisy's plot was inspired by an evening back in 1955 when Carolyn and Neal Cassady had invited an eccentric bishop they knew to meet Kerouac, Ginsberg, and Orlovsky; as Carolyn Cassady later recalled, this bishop "accepted reincarnation and the universality of all religious doctrines [and] . . . favored the teachings of Sri Aurobindo," and so he seemed just the sort of character who might appeal to the circle's sensibility.[10] The ensuing meeting at the Cassadys' home was part theological discussion and part madcap happening, during which they explored, among other topics, the synergies among Buddhism and Christianity. Perhaps inevitably, Ginsberg asked the bishop about his views on sex while Kerouac drank too much, splaying himself on the floor and declaring his love for the bishop. Kerouac first wrote about the evening in 1957, in a play he called *Beat Generation*. It was never produced, but he revisited the material again with *Pull My Daisy*, which opens with a title card: "Written and Narrated by Jack Kerouac." In the film, the characters act out the meeting but viewers don't actually hear them talking; instead, Kerouac narrates over them, doing different voices to match the characters speaking, a strange effect that, as Jack Sargeant observes, means Kerouac is "commenting on events transpiring . . . [and] speaking for all the protagonists" (*Naked Lens*, 22).

The film takes place in the apartment of Milo and his wife (that's the only way she's described in the film), and centers on the encounter between the bishop and Milo's wild friends. Like Neal Cassady, Milo is a railroad brakeman, and he comes home after a hard day's work trailed by Orlovsky, only to find Ginsberg and Corso bouncing around his apartment "bursting with poetry" (22), much to the annoyance of Milo's long-suffering wife (the poets all play themselves). Although Milo's wife tries to tidy up in preparation for the bishop's visit, there is no containing the poets, and when the bishop and his mother finally do arrive, the stage is set for a series of zany encounters. The interactions among the bishop and the free-spirited poets give the film much of its energy, but what is perhaps most charming about *Pull My Daisy* is the way it captures the natural movements and gestures of those in the Beat circle, and achieving a sense of spontaneity was indeed a large part of the point. When Leslie approached musician-writer David Amram to both score the film and appear in it, Leslie stressed that Amram should just behave as he would normally: "You're not supposed to act," Leslie said, "None of you should try to act."[11] The resulting film *feels* very spontaneous, as though the actors are merely extemporaneously being themselves, even though Kerouac's script was in place and Leslie always maintained that "the actual 'narration'" of the film came from his editing and shaping the mass of footage after the fact – he later insisted that "the whole film, since it has been made, has been misread and misinterpreted partially because Robert [Frank] would tell people 'we just all sat around, and I just pointed the camera.'"[12] The tension to which Leslie alludes, between the necessarily planned nature of film production and the spontaneous aesthetic championed by Kerouac et al., can in fact be understood as fundamental to much Beat literature, which, as we have seen throughout this book, prized spontaneity while representing it via methods that could never be purely spontaneous. It is therefore more accurate to think of the film as an example of performed spontaneity, and it is in this apparently contradictory idea that we can see how it reacts to and comments on the ways in which something called the Beat Generation was circulating in American culture at the end of the 1950s.

Given that *Pull My Daisy* was produced amid the widespread mischaracterizations of the Beats as Beatniks, I tend to see its representation of the Beat lifestyle as an elaborate put-on regarding what outsiders might expect a Beat inside to look like. There is thus a voyeur-like quality to the film, as though a curtain is being pulled to reveal the private lives of these Beatnik characters who were so much in the news at the time – a 1999 documentary even noted of *Pull My Daisy* that "at the height of Beatnik mania, a film that authentically portrayed the Beat Generation was released."[13] I think that rather than promising authenticity, the film recognizes the observer's hunger for authenticity only to tease access to it, a notion that explains why, early on, Kerouac says that Corso and Ginsberg's work amounts to "secret scatological thought. That's why everybody wants to see it." The "everybody" here doesn't refer to others in the circle, but everyone else on the hunt for the serious authentic Beat Generation, those who accordingly see Beat writing sociologically, as manifestations of abjection, rather than as texts worthy of serious aesthetic attention.

Likewise, *Pull My Daisy* appears to grant viewers special access to the real or authentic Beat Generation, but does so by recirculating preoccupations and images that were already well worn by 1959, such as an interest in hot jazz, Buddhism, and shocking the bourgeoisie. The questions the poets put to the bishop even echo the Beat Generation's most famous poem, as when Orlovsky asks: "Is everything holy, is alligators holy, bishop? Is the world holy? Is the basketball holy?" and so on, which only seeks to confirm Ginsberg's assertion in "Footnote to Howl" that "The world is holy! ... Everything is holy!" (*Howl: Original*, 8). Thus, the supposedly "authentic" Beats are behaving in exactly the same way an outside observer might expect – at one point, Milo even tells Corso to comb his hair, a particular sticking point, recall, for unimpressed critics and journalists. While the film seems spontaneous, then, in the context of the Beatnik Era – images of which I've discussed throughout Part III – viewers are never quite sure whether they are seeing performance or authenticity, or a little of both, and this very unsettling and uncertainty is, as we have also seen, utterly bound up in the Beat sensibility.

Kerouac again points to uncertainty surrounding who the Beats are and how they are portrayed when Corso asks the bishop:

> is it true that all the ignus that come falling inside the magic beer bottle magian candle stick – he says, I'm awfully sorry, I'm goofing there.
> The bishop says, Goofing?
> He says, yes, goofing means I'm playing around with words. (27)

In a film ostensibly about the real Beats, the joke is that Corso looks to the bishop to confirm whether it is "true" that "ignus" behave in a given way, a moment that amounts to the insider asking the outsider about the inside. Along with "goofing," "ignus" is the key word in this exchange. "Goofing" we know from prior discussions of spontaneous prose and texts like *Old Angel Midnight*. "Ignus" is a bit more opaque, but relates to anyone's capacity – whether the bishop's or the makers of *Pull My Daisy* – to really know and therefore represent a phenomenon known as the Beat Generation. According to Ginsberg, Kerouac had coined the word back in 1948 or 1949 to mean a "gnostic ignoramus" or "a great bullshit artist."[14] Although Kerouac reprises the word in *Pull My Daisy*, it was Ginsberg who had written a whole poem about it, using the word as a synonym for "Beat" insofar as it named like-minded people whom Ginsberg knew.

In mid-November 1958, about six weeks before shooting began on *Pull My Daisy*, Ginsberg wrote Kerouac, mentioning that he was about to "settle in to type last couple years scribbled poetry, ignus, etc."[15] One resulting poem, "Ignu," uses that term to think through what the Beat Generation was coming to mean in the Beatnik Era. The poem opens: "On top of that if you know me I pronounce you an ignu / Ignu knows nothing of the world" (*Collected Poems*, 211). The assertion here is two-fold, claiming first that to be an ignu is to be associated with Ginsberg, and second that the "ignu knows nothing," a reference to – and inversion of – Norman Podhoretz's take-down of the Beats, "The Know-Nothing Bohemians," which had appeared that spring. With "Ignu," then, Ginsberg is not merely making assertions about his circle, but is so doing against hostile misperceptions that defined them negatively, as thoughtless hoodlums. Readers discover that "Ignu has knowledge of the angel indeed ignu is angel in comical form" or that "Ignu goofs nights under bridges and laughs at battleships" (211). But what finally seems to be the defining feature of ignus is that they recognize their own kind: "All ignus know each other in a moment's talk and measure each other up at once / as lifetime friends romantic winks and giggles across continents" (212). With such an idea in mind, it's possible to see that when in *Pull My Daisy* Corso asks the bishop about what ignus really do, he is not soliciting wisdom so much as making fun of the bishop for what he cannot know, a move underscored by his simultaneous goofing, an ignu technique likewise opaque to the bishop.

Despite an outside viewer's expectations of *Pull My Daisy*, then, it doesn't exactly represent the "natural" Beats as they are, but rather a performative approximation of that naturalness. Although on the one hand this is obvious – it's a film, after all – the way the Beats had been received during the Beatnik Era means that *Pull My Daisy* has been revered as a timely record of spontaneous action, just as *On the Road* or "Howl" have been understood as unrevised accounts of "what really happened." In this way, *Pull My Daisy*, like many Beat texts, comes attached to expectations about what it must mean or be *in terms of Beatness*, an attachment that ironically suggests that to recognize the artistry or complexity is to some-how erase what is Beat about it, when in fact the inverse is true. Such a double bind is perhaps why David Amram, poignantly reflecting on the film's successful wrap, could see *Pull My Daisy* as the end of an era: "The 1950s were over. The company store had bought up our ideas and repackaged them into an image so specious that we realized we were no longer welcome unless we wanted to join the charade" (84).

PART IV

Beat Politics (1962–1969)

CHAPTER 11

The Women Who Said Something

An aspect of *Pull My Daisy* that opens another window onto the Beat movement is the domestic drama that plays out as Milo and his poet friends become increasingly rowdy while his wife becomes increasingly irate. Although viewers are told she is a painter, Milo's wife isn't depicted as a bohemian free spirit so much as a joyless shrew whose mission in life is to tamp down the men's exuberance. The film in fact ends with the men fleeing the apartment to go off to do Beat-like things, while the wife is left at home, embittered and alone. The implication, of course, is that men have the true Beat attitude whereas women, even artistic ones, are finally square killjoys bent on regulating male creativity.

This dynamic is a fitting encapsulation of a broader feature of the Beatnik Era: despite all the media attention lavished on the variously defined "Beat Generation" during these years, women were conspicuously absent from public discourse. As Diane di Prima characterized her position in the late 1950s: "As a woman, I was invisible. I took that as a matter of course" (*Recollections*, 238). And yet, as I hope has been evident thus far, such invisibility isn't an indicator of a lack of women writing, but of a lack of recognition or acknowledgment of this writing. Subsequent scholars have tried to address this gendered myopia with anthologies and critical work focused exclusively on Beat women, work that has been essential to the story I'm trying to tell in this book.[1] In fact, there were a number of writers who are also women in the Beat underground in the 1950s who began publishing noteworthy work then and especially over the first half of the 1960s. These writers include, in addition to di Prima and the others discussed in Part III, Joyce Johnson, Elise Cowen, Janine Pommy Vega, Kay Johnson, Barbara Moraff, and Carol Bergé. Figures such as Johnson, Cowen, and Pommy Vega were important parts of the Beat social scene, but didn't necessarily publish substantive work at the time (while Johnson published a novel in 1962, Cowen's poetry, for example, wasn't collected in book form until 2014). There were likewise figures such as Hettie Jones, who as discussed in Part III was an essential editorial force connected to *Yugen* (1958–1962) as well as other projects like *Poems Now* (1966), but was not fully appreciated as a Beat-associated writer until the publication of her brilliant memoir, *How I Became Hettie Jones* (1990). Barbara Moraff was a widely admired regular on the Lower East Side coffee house circuit, and yet her work has been largely ignored. Kay Johnson is a fascinating artist and writer who has been all but erased from literary history. As this list attests, women were present not only as muses and girlfriends, but as poets, prose writers, dramatists, and editors. That their body of work is smaller in quantity and today less well known than that of their male counterparts is partly a by-product of the gendered biases of the 1950s, which has at times been reified by subsequent generations of readers and scholars. And yet if we want to understand the Beat movement's complexities and contradictions, it is absolutely essential to first acknowledge the elision of female voices, and second to attend to not only their historical presence but their considerable literary achievement.

Drawing attention to the work of these writers necessarily pushes back against contemporaneous depictions of the Beats – whether by the male writers themselves or in the media distortions described in the previous chapters – which tended to insist that they were a "boy gang," as Ginsberg put it, thereby relegating women to secondary roles as mute girlfriends or hangers-on. Even in comparatively sympathetic accounts such as Alfred Aronowitz's *New York Post* series from spring 1959, women were portrayed as floating in and out of the Beat scene, as party girls or fellow travelers, but almost never as writers in their own right. Such bias is particularly striking in this account of a Beat happening:

> The party was held ... behind a large ... door which was opened for us by a young woman wearing black stockings, a matching skirt, a sweater which seemed to have more button holes than buttons, and a moon-like face that was kept in partial eclipse behind long, stringy hair. She was the hostess, a printer's daughter of 23, who had gone to Barnard, written a novel, received a $500 advance and befriended, in an intimate sort of way, Jack Kerouac.
> "I don't consider myself beat," she told us, adding later, after some thought: "My book is about a girl who has become alienated emotionally from the world. I mean she can't get excited about *anything*."[2]

The unnamed young woman is characterized first by her black stockings and clothes (a version of the "cool" female hipster Kerouac described as "girls [who] say nothing and wear black" [*Portable Kerouac*, 569–570]), second by her physical appearance, and third by the fact that she herself has a book contract, a detail less important for Aronowitz than that final one, her romantic connection to Kerouac. In fact, when the young woman mentions her novel about an emotionally alienated girl, Aronowitz shows little interest, dismissing her with a kind of rhetorical nudge-nudge to his audience: "We nodded politely, asked where the fire escape was and then stepped out into the parlor."[3]

Although readers in 1959 could not have known from Aronowitz's patronizing description, the young woman was in the thick of the Beat scene throughout the mid- to late 1950s, and would in subsequent decades become one of the most important contributors to and chroniclers of the Beat literary experience. Her name was Joyce Glassman (later Johnson). She was indeed romantically linked to Kerouac, and is known to students of Beat lore insofar as she was present when Kerouac first read with disbelief that glowing *New York Times* review that would change his life; as she later wrote, "The ringing phone woke him the next morning and he was famous."[4] But as we consider Johnson's place in the Beat movement, we should view her "intimate sort of" attachment to Kerouac as a beginning rather than end point, focusing instead on her version of the new consciousness that was informed by her experience as a woman navigating bohemia.

11.1 Joyce Johnson: Moments of Triumph

The novel Aronowitz alluded to is *Come and Join the Dance*, published in January 1962, and retrospectively described by Ronna C. Johnson as "the first Beat generation novel by and about a Beat woman."[5] Johnson had begun the novel in 1955 in a writing workshop taught by Hiram Haydn, editor-in-chief at Random House, and worked on it throughout the late 1950s. Haydn was so impressed by the pages he read that in July 1957, Johnson was issued a contract with Random House, along with the $500 advance mentioned by Aronowitz. The timing here is important as it means that far from being merely a silent Beat chick, Johnson had her own book contract two months before *On the Road* was published, even though she would not finish the novel until 1961 – in part because of her tumultuous relationship with Kerouac from 1957 to 1958.[6] Throughout the Beatnik Era, Johnson returned to her manuscript about a college student, Susan Levitt, who is drawn to the subterranean world of "outlaws, part of a mysterious underground brotherhood," unsure about embarking on the respectable path expected of a young woman of her generation.[7] This period is described in rich detail in her memoir *Minor Characters* (1983) – written under her married name, Joyce Johnson – still among the finest first-person accounts of bohemian New York before and after the publication of *On the Road*.

Come and Join the Dance is set in the mid-1950s, after Susan was supposed to have graduated from Barnard College (an indescribable malaise has kept her from attending gym class so she cannot technically graduate, an experience Johnson herself had).[8] After she dumps her earnest, *New Yorker*–reading boyfriend, Susan is pulled further into the world of three bohemians: college dropout Kay Gorman (modeled on Elise Cowen); eighteen-year-old poet Anthony Leone; and twenty-nine-year-old "perpetual student" (20) Peter, modeled roughly on Donald Cook, a young Columbia instructor. Set as it is before the media-fueled interest in the Beat Generation, *Come and Join the Dance* never uses the term, although its "outlaw" characters sometimes embody what had become cartoon Beatness by 1962, when the novel was finally published: an affected hipster, Peter makes a big show of how he lights out on the road on the slightest pretext. "Oh," he says when readers first encounter him, "I disappeared for a few days – I do that now and then" (18). There are other moments when Peter's language seems to channel Sal Paradise in *On the Road*, as when he drives around frantically trying to find a "mad Puerto Rican bar ... the greatest place in New York" (75). Anthony and Peter constantly blare jazz, the soundtrack of the underground, and the novel even describes Peter's physical movements in musical terms: "The jazz sounded like the way he walked, the shambling, uneven steps, the forward thrust of his head" (56). While Sal Paradise famously "shambles" after those who interest him, Peter just shambles aimlessly, voicing at various moments what passed for common sense in Beat circles, as when he complains that "the system is inescapable" (66), or when Susan, who has been lending him money throughout the novel, suggests he get a job, and Peter responds, "I knew you'd come out with some bourgeois moral thing like that" (58).

Indeed, while *Come and Join the Dance* includes references to the clichéd markers of bohemia – the music, the casual sex, even the distinctive drinks (Pernod) – a crucial thing to recognize is what it sidesteps, how it *doesn't* describe the "Beat Generation" as such. At least one reviewer picked up on this, observing that the novel "reminds us that youth is no fixed identity or state with an all-explaining adjective."[9] As we have seen throughout this book, a hallmark of the male inner circle of Beat writers is a constant referencing of one another, and a continual rewriting of episodes made well known by such repetition, whether Ginsberg dedicating *Howl and Other Poems* to Kerouac, Burroughs, Cassady, and Carr; or Kerouac writing about the 6 Gallery reading in *The Dharma Bums*. Johnson is less interested in valorizing male figures or male-centered events and more engaged in fundamentally reimagining the scene from a female perspective.[10] While writing *Come and Join the Dance*, Johnson was a lively participant in subterranean networks, exchanging letters with Kerouac about publishing and breathlessly referring to the inner circle of writers (this passage is typical: "Have the boys [Ginsberg and Orlovsky] arrived yet? Have you met Burroughs, Anson [Alan Ansen]? ... Has poor Gregory [Corso] recovered his letters? ... Give him, Allen and Peter my love").[11] The novel, by contrast, is much more restrained stylistically and does not obviously exploit the media interest in the Beats by offering portraits of recognizable figures such as Kerouac, Ginsberg, or Corso.

Like much of Diane di Prima's early work, *Come and Join the Dance* is a long way from a whole-hearted endorsement of a bohemian lifestyle, and skewers some of the more recognizable Beat characteristics. As Susan tries to achieve her own version of "freedom," for example, she navigates both the square world represented by staid college administrators and her parents' suburban values, which amount to "disdainful puzzlement over any behavior that was out of the ordinary" (14), and the noncommitted, nonworking, free-love world represented by Kay, Anthony, and Peter. Early in the novel, Kay tells Susan about a dream she had about being locked up "in some kind of home for girls – sort of an army camp or prison – and running around trying to find out the rules of the place" (41). The dream not-so-subtly speaks to the special worry of a female nonconformist, that violating the conventional middle-class "rules" of her parents would lead to imprisonment in a home for girls (this is what happened, recall, to Diane Lattimer in Mandel's *Flee the Angry Strangers*). In this way, *Come and Join the Dance* echoes another, more famous novel first published just a year after and set in New York City at the same time: Sylvia Plath's *The Bell Jar* (1963). Just like Susan Levitt, Plath's Esther Greenwood has aspirations to be a writer, but is surprised to find that she does not cotton to the rigid gender norms she finds rampant in New York City after she travels there for an internship at a women's magazine. The titular bell jar, Plath's metaphor for the suffocation Esther feels as she tries to perform the roles expected of her, sinks down over her life and clouds her sense of reality; this is a version of Kay's institutional nightmare – and indeed, in *The Bell Jar* Esther is eventually institutionalized by her mother. *Come and Join the Dance* and *The Bell Jar* are thus of a particular cultural moment when proto-feminist writers held out for public scrutiny those norms that dictated what they could or could not do.[12]

Whereas *The Bell Jar* depicts a relatively homogenous New York City, Johnson is interested in the divide between the mainstream and what she calls the "outlaw." *Minor Characters* explains how Johnson awakened to this divide at age thirteen, when traveling for the first time from the Upper West Side to Greenwich Village, a place of "romance and adventure" where the sheltered young girl found herself mingling with "the ranks of the unconventional" (26, 31). In *Come and Join the Dance*, the "outlaw" first seems promising as a viable alternative to her parents' stifling middle-class values, but what finally makes the novel Beat is not that Susan ultimately chooses the bohemian orbit, but that she refuses both the terms set by her parents *and* those set by Peter and Anthony. If there is a developmental arc, it is Susan's learning to exact what she herself needs from both spheres – whether her realization that she "wanted to march in the [graduation] procession" despite Kay's argument that not graduating has "a kind of symbolic beauty" (115), or her having sex with Anthony as an "experiment," an act described as "an astonished moment of triumph" (93).

Susan's exploitation and refusal of both spheres amounts to Johnson's rewriting of the male-centered Beat narrative already well-developed by the early 1960s. The last three chapters of the novel are partly a critique of *On the Road* in which Sal and Dean prioritize movement and their own male bonding over the women they leave in their wake.[13] Moreover, by 1958, Johnson's relationship with Kerouac was dissolving, and he was increasingly put off by her earnest declarations of love; as he wrote her in the summer of 1958: "I don't wanta be 'Steadies' with anybody, now if this hurts you why? . . . Don't OWN me, just be my nice little blonde friend and don't be sad because I'm a confirmed bachelor & hermit."[14] The final part of *Come and Join the Dance* is best understood not just as a rebuke of Kerouac and his famous novel, but rather as an affirmation of Susan's autonomy and sexuality free from the constraints or definitions of the male characters, whether her strait-laced father or bohemian Peter.

In those last three chapters, Peter promises to take Susan on a Kerouac-esque road trip, only to make it just a few hours from New York City before his car breaks down: "The night had transfigured the road" (161), writes the narrator, and the aborted road trip helps to transfigure Susan as well. As night falls on Susan and Peter's relationship, his broken car symbolizes a rebuke of the mobility championed in *On the Road*, which is characterized in *Come and Join the Dance* as a sophomoric desire to "just keep going" (164). Demoralized and emasculated, Peter limps back to the Bronx in his ailing car, so that he is physically bound to New York City, desperately trying to drown out his collapsing world with loud jazz.

The contrast to the Kerouac-inspired world could not be more clear: "On the road, before, he hadn't been afraid of silence" (167). Peter's loss of mobility magnifies his fears of intimacy and connection, and the moment after the car is sold for scrap, Susan recognizes that his desire for autonomy has compromised his ability to engage emotionally with others: "How far away from her he had chosen to stand, how separate they were from each other. But I know who you are, she thought, I know who you are" (173). In the novel's final pages, Susan recognizes Peter for the damaged loner that he is, but still elects to sleep with him on her own terms, as she had with Anthony. In bed together in the silence Peter dreads, Susan feels the bell jar lifting in the form of an open window: "The world was returning to her – coming in through the open window" (175). A working title for the novel was "Broken Windows," and with this final metaphor Susan decides not to continue in Peter's bohemian terms, but to instead strike out to Paris as planned, autonomous and "clear-eyed" (177) about herself and the future – as Johnson later recalled, by fictionalizing her experiences with Cook (Peter), "I took away his power to hurt me" (*Minor Characters*, 117). As Susan beats Peter at his own game, *Come and Join the Dance* is at once Beat and feminist, a crucial text for understanding the widening of the movement in the 1960s and after, especially as it related to women who were progenitors of Beat sensibilities.

11.2 Elise Cowen: Beat Fragments

One such woman was Elise Cowen, the model for Kay Gorman in *Come and Join the Dance,* and a significant although lesser-known Beat figure. Just as *On the Road* can be read as an elegy for Neal Cassady, Johnson's later *Minor Characters* is an elegy for Cowen, and her prominence in the memoir encourages readers to see her as both enigmatic heroine and tragic figure, a person at once central and peripheral to the inner circle in the mid- to late 1950s. *Minor Characters* is still the best available source of information about Cowen's brief life, as Johnson weaves Cowen's story in with her own, offering impressions and vignettes, from their first meeting as Barnard undergraduates to Cowen's suicide in February 1962. Cowen is depicted as a brilliant, avowedly nonconformist woman prone to intense love affairs and deep depressions, forever worried that "she will never be found acceptable, never never fit, be outcast even among outcasts" (*Minor Characters*, 77). In Cowen's entanglements with men, Johnson sees reflections of her own experiences, and the lesson that "just as girls guarded their virginity, boys guarded something less tangible which they called

Themselves" (56). A constant navigation of such guardedness underlies not only Johnson's relationship with Kerouac, by turns thrilling and frustrating, but also Cowen's relationship with Ginsberg, which Johnson sees as one of the most significant in her life: "Elise speaks of Allen in a surprising way ... 'Allen is my intercessor,' she says.... That was the meaning of Allen in Elise's life, from the very beginning ... Elise was a moment in Allen's life. In Elise's life, Allen was an eternity" (76–78).

Minor Characters treats this imbalance biographically and thematically, reading it as emblematic of how women were relegated to the peripheries by the male Beats, quoting with wry disdain Ginsberg's remark that "The social organization which is most true of itself to the artist is the boy gang" (79). Of course, works like *Minor Characters* deflate such notions – as does taking seriously female "minor characters" – and yet as the memoir vividly demonstrates, the perpetual blindness of the "boy gang" construct and its tendency to render Cowen invisible had very real effects on her. She floats in and out of Johnson's memoir, sometimes disappearing, "atomized into the windy blue spaces between New York and San Francisco" (200), and yet is as fundamental to the book's texture as she was to the Beat scene at this time. Beyond Johnson and Ginsberg, Cowen knew a wide range of Beat-associated writers, including Kerouac, Huncke, Leo Skir, Irving Rosenthal, John Wieners, and Janine Pommy Vega, all of whom would write about her in later years, thus contributing to a kind of subterranean legend that now surrounds her: "Suicide made Elise mythic," writes Johnson (258).[15]

For years, Cowen was known to students of the Beats not through her own writing but through "mythic" glimpses of her presence on the scene. None other than the original hipster Herbert Huncke contributed to this aura, publishing a sketch of a "mystical" night in March 1961 he spent doing drugs and philosophizing in the apartment Cowen shared with Pommy Vega.[16] Huncke's Cowen has a "strange beauty," is obstinate, difficult to really know, though "she truly loved" Ginsberg (52–53). Huncke also memorably has her skeptical of dubious male artist-intellectuals as she idly toys with "a handful of small items – two gold plated lead figures – of Indian or Tibetan Gods" (51).

In the immediate years after her death, other writers gilded the Cowen legend, sometimes attributing language to her, as in a Wieners poem that appeared in *Pa'Lante*, a one-shot avant-garde collection edited by Cowen's friend Howard Shulman; Wieners has "Elise drunk at the end of the bed" and screaming "*I don't have balls.... But like I don't need them.*"[17] Likewise in Irving Rosenthal's underrated masterpiece *Sheeper*, readers are treated not only to Cowen's words but to glimpses of her writing. In a short chapter called "The Death of Elise," Rosenthal writes that he had saved a small notebook "to remember her by," blank except for three lines: "*My brother! My brother! / Where is my shining brother? / Lost behind the stairs.*"[18] For years interested readers had to be satisfied with fragments such as these, unsure even if Rosenthal is actually providing Cowen's real work; or else they had to seek out the smattering of poetry that had been published after her death in little magazines such as *City Lights Journal* (1964), *Fuck You* (1965), and *El Corno Emplumado* (1966). This changed in 1996 when several of Cowen's poems appeared in *Women of the Beat Generation*, suddenly making some of her work more widely accessible.[19]

The work collected in *Women of the Beat Generation* came from another notebook that had been saved by Cowen's friend, Leo Skir – and this one was filled with poetry.[20] The slim volume has proven a valuable Beat artifact since, as Tony Trigilio explains, Cowen, like Emily Dickinson, "kept her poetry private in her lifetime, rarely sharing her work with others; ... most of her work is destroyed, and what remains is a mixture of completed poems and evocative fragments."[21] These "remains" consti-tute the notebook rescued by Skir, and it wasn't until 2014, some fifty-two years after her death, that Trigilio was able to edit and annotate this material, publishing it as *Poems and Fragments*. Dating from 1959 to 1960, the work in this volume, even in its often-fragmentary state, is a necessary addition to Beat letters as it represents not the hazy myth as recalled by others, but Cowen speaking for herself.[22]

In his introduction to *Poems and Fragments*, Trigilio suggests four broad ways we might understand Cowen's work: through its "revisionary response to matters of the sacred, ... its simultaneous continuity and revision of literary tradition, ... its affinities with the form and content of Beat Generation literature, ... [and] its frank portrayals of the psyche" (xix). Since there is very little scholarship on Cowen, this taxonomy is especially useful for mapping the general concerns and contours of her work. For our purposes, I'll focus on those poems or fragments that resonate most loudly with other Beat-associated writing – with the familiar reminder that such resonance cannot account for the sum of Cowen's work, however small the surviving number. For example, in comparing Cowen's work to that of her Beat peers, we find a tendency to name other writers, but can see this technique operating on its own register since she never intended to publish her work. Thus when she refers to Johnson or Ginsberg or Orlovsky, she does so not to advertise her connections to a scene already famous by 1959 for the benefit of a broader audience, but rather to punctuate her intensely private interrogations of big topics like love, death, or identity. In this way, we find Cowen characterizing Johnson's travails in love as a wholesome inverse to her own, which are clouded throughout *Poems and Fragments* with despair and self-recrimination. Referring to Johnson – whose middle name is Alice – she writes: "ReJoyce these days with Alice hair & Bardot pout / Falling, falling through the crazy life chute / Looking for love with true girl humility."[23] A distorted reversal of Johnson's use of Kay Gorman as the greater "outsider" in *Come and Join the Dance*, here Cowen casts her friend as Alice in Wonderland, romanticizing Johnson's "true girl" amorous adventures relative to her own.

At other moments, Cowen's fragmentary work is stripped of poetic adornment so that references to her circle are reduced to workmanlike lists of those she would harm if she went through with suicide. In one poem reproduced in both *Minor Characters* and *Women of the Beat Generation*, for example, Cowen offers what Johnson sees as "messages to me and all the rest of us confused bystanders who only thought we knew her" (*Minor Characters*, 257). Asserting that "Twenty-seven years is enough," this poem has direct addresses to "Peter – Holy rose youth," as well as messages to "Allen – I'm sorry" and "Joyce – So girl beautiful" (116). Ending as it does with the chilling lines "Let me out now please – / – Please let me in" (116), this piece was composed under very different circumstances from the ones that gave rise to seemingly comparable poems discussed earlier such as Ray Bremser's "blues for bonnie" or Philip Lamantia's "Binoculars," both of which include lists of Beat writers. Cowen is not interested in demonstrating insider knowledge to a wider readership but rather in weighing the consequences of taking her own life in perhaps the most intimate way possible. Unlike Bremser's and Lamantia's poems, the relative fame of some people on the list is incidental, and what matters is not their position on the literary scene, but their connection to Cowen's personal life. In the context of Beat literary history, then, we might read this poem as an example of a female writer searching her private experience without justifying its importance via a connection to the public sphere. As we have seen throughout this book, many male writers had learned to do the opposite, to elevate a private experience precisely insofar as it could stand for the experience of an entire generation. Cowen's work can thus be read as documenting a private Beat experience, a version of Kerouac's "furtive" generation that isn't always constantly looking up to check in on this generation.

Perhaps unsurprisingly given both Cowen's depressive mental state in the last years of her life and her artistic debt to Dickinson, many of the pieces in

Poems and Fragments concern death. One mannered meditation on the subject tackles the problem of the unknown by trying to domesticate it:

> Death, I'm coming
> wait for me.
> I know you'll be
>   at the subway station
>   loaded with galoshes, raincoat, umbrella, babushka
> and your single simple answer
>   to every meaning.
> Incorruptible institution,
> Thoughtful killjoy of fingerprints
> Listen to what she said
> "There's a passage through the white cabbages."
>
> (105)

In a conceit that wouldn't be out of place in a Dickinson poem, death is personified as an elderly woman outfitted against the elements, patiently waiting to offer an all-encompassing "answer" to the riddle of life. What's puzzling about this is the enigma of the final, quoted line: is this death speaking? is it perhaps from a Dickinson poem – after all, it *seems* very Dickinsonian? Given the fragmentary quality to this and other pieces from Cowen's notebook, the poem doesn't offer an answer to the question, and if we stay just in the poem, the final lines serve to ironically reinvest death with mystery. After familiarizing the abstraction through an image evoking a kindly grandmother, the final quotation, while seemingly referring to the experience of death as a "passage" through whiteness, finally leaves it strange and unfamiliar.

But if we move outside the poem, it is possible to learn that the "she" here refers not to death but to Cowen's friend and sometime roommate, Janine Pommy Vega. Vega's much-later poem, "Elise" (1996), describes the experience of encountering Cowen's poem for the first time, "Thirty-five years after the fact / I read your poem, addressed to Mr. Death / a love song you never showed me."[24] Pommy Vega goes on to recall that the genesis of the poem was in a bus ride back from an "all night psychedelic journey" and sees it as a "coded message" difficult to decipher:

> that there are no misfits, no stragglers,
> no one left out of that effulgence
> *There's a passage through the white cabbages*
> you said I said,
>
> a cryptic communiqué mailed
> from the psyche to the girl who traveled
> and the way she envisioned was a way we walk

in the life or out
a pathway back to where we came from

you were so eager to wipe out the traces
to hurl yourself through the plate glass window
. . .
It was something you had to do.
Now thirty-five years later, you are the young one,
the twenty-nine year old, angry at herself
who could not believe she knew
the way home.

(256–257)

In this retrospective analysis of Cowen's poem, Pommy Vega writes herself
into its very center –not to solve the mystery posed by Cowen but rather to
thicken the description of this mystery. Although Pommy Vega apparently
recalls the origins of the cabbage line, her poem crucially doesn't exactly
explain Cowen's, but dwells instead on its cryptic indeterminacy, even
hesitating to definitively claim that she herself did in fact utter this line,
instead emphasizing the fragility of memory, that "you said I said." Taking
a cue from the unresolved quality of Cowen's original poem, Pommy Vega
derives meaning from the "cryptic" or "coded" nature of the cabbage line
by foregrounding its indecipherability and seeing it as a virtue uniting two
psyches on an intuitive, nonrational level. Rather than purporting to grant
readers insider access to what Cowen "really" meant, in other words,
Pommy Vega testifies to the poem's transformative power, using it as an
occasion to reflect on the idea that two writers were connected in ways she
did not quite comprehend. "Elise" then finally underscores the importance
of Cowen's original line: even as it is fundamentally indecipherable inside
the poem, the notion of passing through white cabbages resonated with
Cowen in 1960 as it resonated again for Vega some thirty-five years later.

For all the ways she populates the work of other writers and for her own
distinctive poetic voice now collected in a bound volume, Cowen is and
should remain an important Beat figure. As a writer, she falls into that
category of people who didn't pursue publishing and thus had to be
"recovered" later. And as attested over the thirty-five years from Johnson's
Come and Join the Dance to Pommy Vega's "Elise," she made a profound
impression on those who knew her, and as readers we can only lament the
paucity of her surviving work. But with Poems and Fragments, Tony
Trigilio has given us a strong foundation on which to build future work,
and I hope that on the strength of this slim, fragmented volume, Cowen's
poetry will be seen in a better kind of light.

11.3   Janine Pommy Vega: Paying Dues

Cowen's roommate, Janine Pommy Vega, was born in New Jersey in 1942 and had been so transfixed by *On the Road* in high school that she couldn't shake the allure of the life it described. When she finally ventured across the river to the Cedar Tavern in search of the Beats she had read so much about, she almost immediately ran into Corso, who in time introduced her to Ginsberg, Orlovsky, Huncke, and Kerouac himself. At just sixteen, she was drawn into the Beat circle; as she later recalled, "The bohemian lifestyle of readings, museums, parties and intellectual discussions seemed exactly what I wanted for myself," and the day of her high school graduation party (she was valedictorian), Pommy Vega left her old life in New Jersey to move into an apartment with Cowen, with whom she would live for the next year and a half.[25] Like many women in the Beat circle of the late 1950s, Pommy Vega was, as she put it, "writing . . . listening . . . imbibing . . . reading" – but she didn't show her work to others at the time, except Huncke.[26] Her first book of poetry wouldn't in fact appear for another decade, when City Lights published *Poems to Fernando* in 1968.

Poems to Fernando is dedicated to – and written for – Fernando Vega, a Jewish Peruvian painter Pommy Vega had met in New York. After six months together, the couple left for Jerusalem, where they would live for the next eighteen months, and then for Paris, where Fernando's struggles with drug addiction ultimately got the better of him, and he died in November 1965. *Poems to Fernando* was therefore written in places such as Jerusalem, Paris, Ibiza, New York, and San Francisco, and is divided into two parts, the poems to Fernando, written between 1963 and 1966, and "Other Poems," mostly written in 1967, and reflecting Pommy Vega's involvement in the San Francisco countercultural scene at the time. The earliest poems in the book exhibit the keen eye for cultural observation that informs much of Pommy Vega's later travel writing, and the ones written after Vega's death tend toward searching and highly intimate elegies for her husband. As she writes, "I speak to *you*, always as I would speak before or write letters," the italicized pronoun underscoring the degree to which Pommy Vega wanted to write "for them about them personally," as Paul Goodman had so memorably put it.[27] These poems track Pommy Vega's profound sense of loss, but also explore her need to make sense of herself through travel and immersion in different cultures: "Why is it I travel this road, . . . / Still alive, & yet to learn, or I would not / be here still / penetrating pain itself to find you" (23). As Nancy M. Grace argues, "These delicate elegies to her husband are also a portrait of the woman artist coming into poetry ... [and represent] a crucial moment of enfranchisement in which the woman Beat writer exercises the capacity to transform herself from object to subject."[28] In this regard, the book's subject is both Fernando and Pommy Vega's perceptions of and feelings regarding him, so that he has meaning through images constructed from the poet's memories.

The second half of the book moves from specific addresses to Fernando to explorations of poetry and figurations of poetic communities in the latter 1960s, particularly in San Francisco. These poems offer pithy statements on the nature of poetry ("poem in its footsteps on the page / has a power / to make known its own secret, chattering in the / Ancient tongues" [47]), as well as commentary on the scene that had by that time exploded into near-caricature of bohemian literary posturing. In "Poem against Endless Mass Poetry Readings," for example, Pommy Vega adopts a more wry and humorous tone than in the earlier elegies, lamenting the "tyranny of assembled poets / beleaguering ears & the shoulder muscles," and finally asserting "O pay yr dues before ye lord it over / me" (48), a remark on the frenzied nature of the San Francisco arts scene during the Summer of Love that perhaps explains why Pommy Vega had waited so long to publish her own first book, her "dues" compounding in her travels and personal struggles.

An illustration of Pommy Vega's ongoing connections to the Beat movement, *Poems to Fernando* also contains two poems addressed to Ray Bremser, whom she had come to know in the 1960s. In "Poem to the Old Man," she writes:

> the poems I read you, begotten in secret, are born into power
> / made manifest Being Known
>   by you/
>   springing out clear
>
>   (49)

Such lines are finally testament to poetic community that can be generative – as opposed to the "endless mass poetry readings" ridiculed in other poems – for, as she writes, "this electric communing is holy" (49). Her electric communion with Bremser is echoed in "Junk(& the old man) Changes," which asserts "respect for another soul in its / preciousness also / respect for your own" (51). Thus although her relationship with Fernando Vega was the motivating occasion for *Poems to Fernando* as a whole, its shift from the younger, seemingly more naïve speaker-poet in the first part to the well-traveled and wiser person toward the end suggests the way in which Pommy Vega kept growing and exploring, partly through her ties to the Beat movement. Pommy Vega in fact maintained the Beat spirit throughout her life by striking out on her own in the years after *Poems to Fernando* was published, living in a remote island in Lake Titicaca on the border between Peru and Bolivia, an experience that inspired *Journal of a Hermit* (1974).[29]

11.4 Kay Johnson: Battle for Existence

While Joyce Johnson, Cowen, and Pommy Vega have all received some measure of critical attention, Kay Johnson has slipped through the cracks in literary histories. If a figure like Cowen has remained somewhat obscure even for *Minor Characters* and Trigilio's later recovery efforts, Johnson is even more so, as she has never been vividly recalled in a memoir or recovered in a new scholarly edition. An artist who worked in dance and painting as well as poetry and prose, Johnson sometimes published under the pen name Kaja, adding another complicating factor for those interested in locating her work – as she wrote in 1960, "have no name left but kaja. the other names all died."[30] Although some of Johnson's work appeared intermittently throughout the 1950s, her association with the Beat movement came in the early 1960s, first with her involvement with the New Orleans–based little magazine *Outsider*, and second when she moved to the Beat Hotel in Paris, reputedly out of long-distance admiration for Corso, who affectionately but patronizingly described her to Ferlinghetti as his "female find."[31] Perhaps through Corso, Johnson began a correspondence with Ferlinghetti, and City Lights eventually published her first and only book, *Human Songs*, in 1964. When the Beat Hotel closed in 1963, Johnson found her way to Greece, living on Hydra until 1967. By January 1968, she had wound up in San Francisco after what she described as "4 agonizing Homeless Months, wandering."[32] If these facts seem like broad strokes, they are: Johnson's life is difficult to pin down because she was resolutely peripatetic, and because she was, by most accounts, homeless in the later years of her life (for a likeness of Johnson, see Figure 11.1).[33]

But we do know that in 1960–1961, Johnson was living in New Orleans amid a burgeoning artistic and literary community that one observer has likened to what had blossomed in San Francisco in the middle 1950s.[34] The spirit of this scene is captured most brilliantly in the pages of *Outsider* (1961–1968/1969), a magazine conceived by Jon Edgar and Louise "Gypsy Lou" Webb, then owners of a small art press in New

Figure 11.1   Snapshot of a painting of Kay Johnson by Noel Rockmore (May 1961).
Image courtesy of Bancroft Library, UC-Berkeley

Orleans called Loujon. The Webbs advertised the first volume in the pages
of the *Village Voice* and *Yugen*, where one ad announced: "The Outsider:
International No-Taboo Quarterly Out of New Orleans for the Newest in
New-from-Everywhere Poetry and Prose."[35] When the first issue appeared
in the fall of 1961, it included varied examples of "the newest in new
poetry and prose," boasting an impressive roster of Beat luminaries such as
Corso, Ginsberg, di Prima, Snyder, Orlovsky, Ferlinghetti, Ray Bremser,
McClure, LeRoi Jones, Kupferberg, Burroughs, and Moraff. The Beats were
thus certainly the most identifiable constituency in the magazine, a visibility
magnified by the inclusion of an essay by British pundit Colin Wilson on
Beat sexuality ("Some Comments on the Beats and Angries") as well as
an extended, visually striking excerpt from Burroughs's cut-up experiment,
The Soft Machine, prefaced by a detailed drawing by Jon Edgar Webb.

It was in this context that Johnson published excerpts from a longer
work titled "the emerald city," dedicated to Corso, three fragments of
which appeared in as many issues of *Outsider*. Like its namesake from *The
Wizard of Oz*, Johnson's emerald city is a fantastic realm, but one in which
irrational things happen so that the poet might make the everyday
"strange." In the excerpt published in the last issue of *Outsider* (1968/
1969), for example, Johnson likens her emerald city to the imaginary

world of Don Quixote: "Oh slow moving turtle, oh wooden world, oh fantastic windmills and clocks run by fire – Don Quixote, spare that tree! Ah strange city, we are strangers here!"[36] As in much of Corso's poetry, the strangeness itself is the point as it forces the "we" of the poem to see the world anew – another excerpt makes its inheritance from Corso even more explicit: "Oh ye dead who waken in the underground tombs / of Death's most unhappy birthday," a repurposing of Corso's title *The Happy Birthday of Death* for Johnson's particular vision.[37] Her interest in Corso was so acute that in 1960 she reported to Tuli Kupferberg that she had read *Happy Birthday* "about 6 times, all night long, each time with a different colored pencil, and STILL can't get enough of him ... if you haven't had Corso i am about to buy him at a bookstore here and send him to you i love him this much."[38] For Johnson, Death's birthday is presumably "unhappy" because in the emerald city life is reshuffled and therefore reinvigorated: "Polka-dots have a hard time being born, especially when the / mothers are off at some card party pretending to be spots" (51). Such lines do not make rational sense, and the poem encourages readers to pause over the surreal reimagining of categories. Johnson finally suggests that such a realm is most accessible to children, who have not yet formed their adult prejudices: "Surely the Kingdom of Love is made for children! / The corridors are sick from being stuffed with refrigerated grown-ups" (51). In this regard, "the emerald city" poems reverberate with the youth-oriented strain of Beat writing that expresses distrust of "refrigerated grown-ups" – think Corso's line "I HATE OLD POETMEN!" (*Gasoline*, 42), Kupferberg and Topp's magazine *Swing*, or Johnson's own "An Adolescent Song" in *Human Songs* ("All the grown-ups / we looked up to, how strange / to see *them* disappear" [14]).[39]

Johnson's most obviously "Beat" poems were published in the next issue of *Outsider*, after she had left New Orleans to live in the Beat Hotel, where she sought out Corso's old room, what she called "a true Paris garrett."[40] Beyond the kinship she felt with Corso, Johnson also reveled in her newfound contact with writers such as Harold Norse and William Burroughs, and worked to spread the word about *Outsider* to Paris's literary community.[41] In two "poems from paris" – "experience of 7 consecutive hours" and "heaven at 9 Git-Le-Coeur" – Johnson explores her new life at one epicenter of the Beat-associated avant-garde. In the latter poem, the Beat Hotel is likened to heaven where "Everyone has a dream. / They talk from their souls," and where creativity is so encouraged that "I can type here any hour. / I can paint without comment." In an environment in which creative expression is viewed as a basic good, life itself is affirmed such that "everybody in this Hotel lives. / Nobody ever dies."[42]

While this hymn to bohemian togetherness can be attributed to the excitement that comes with discovering a community of like-minded people, "experience of 7 consecutive hours" offers a more nuanced and revealing depiction of what it could be like as an unknown in that very community. As exhilarating as it might be to rub shoulders with writers whose work Johnson knew and loved, it could also be potentially alienating to live in a space that might reify those notions of "inside" versus "outside" we have seen throughout this book. Indeed, "experience of 7 consecutive hours" questions the virtues of poetic community insofar as the speaker constantly measures herself against the opinion and values of others; as she writes: "I wanted poet-friends to confirm my being" and "Don't some people make me smaller?"[43] This conflicted desire for communal validation leads to an escalating series of self-recriminations as the speaker tries to imagine a model of personhood not tied to the approval of others. The poem opens with a paean to the Paris of bohemian godfather Paul Verlaine as well as Gregory Corso's writings about Greece:

> Paris! My feet are cold and I feel better,
> An hour in Paris with Verlaine,
> In Greece another hour with Gregory Corso
> On the Rue de Seine –
> And it's home with a book of Zen – and two gold apples.
> Paris, I love you again!
>
> (29)

This opening stanza certainly seems to promise a kind of heaven for an artistically inclined sensibility, but as the poem unfolds we start to see the potential negative effects of a poetic community for a person predisposed to measuring herself against others. In one particularly dark stanza, Johnson writes:

> A bad picture of myself – i cringed two days
> Got so small that i could hardly speak:
> Dwindled, shrunken old head of myself, so dim.
> How could i face the World? No Self Respect.
> Didn't i lose my battle for existence?
>
> (30)

In such moments, the poem becomes less an unequivocal celebration of Paris and more a mediation on the speaker's "battle for existence" in this new environment. As she recounts the "experience of 7 consecutive hours," the speaker moves from the highs of the opening stanza to the lows of the one quoted above to finally imagine herself on a footing equal to those figures she has long admired: "Now shoulder to shoulder, tall as they, / ... I'm on the level with lovers, happy / I'm not ashamed looking into their faces" (31). Although the poem ends on a positive note, as a whole it suggests Johnson's ambivalence about being connected to any community, as such a (potential) connection is also bound up in her own sense of self, what she calls her "battle for existence."

Beyond these two Paris poems (probably her best known since they are collected in *A Different Beat*), much of Johnson's work concerns her "battle for existence" – the Paris poems just remind us that this battle was informed by her relationship to other poets and artists of the Beat underground. This relationship is strikingly illustrated in a letter she wrote to Jon Edgar Webb from the Beat Hotel around the time she composed the poems just discussed:

> Yes, Jon, Burroughs is here ... he doesn't like women; well, i don't blame him – so i told him i was Henry Miller (actually i do think i look like Miller in the mirror a bit ... altho some kids here say i remind them of Allen Ginsberg) – well the next time we met, he said "HELLO, MILLER" ... and we shook hands warmly – and now he smiles at me on the stairs ... and asked if I'd heard from you.[44]

Johnson's playful allusion to her androgyny is significant as it relates to a fundamental "battle for existence" found in much of her writing. As she imagines herself reflected in the image of famous male writers, she implies a rejection of identity as rooted in normative assumptions about gender, an idea that she develops to greater effect in *Human Songs*.

Although her book did not appear until 1964, Johnson had been in contact with Ferlinghetti about the possibility of publishing a collection since at least 1960. She first pitched him the book, then called "Human Songs and the Ballads of St. Stupid," as doing

> what Whitman meant to, communicates to *every* human soul ... Human songs is a sort of edgar lee masters of the SOUL, in that i become everyone I see and write what they are, say, cry, first person.
> song of lesbian, song of the young father, song of the virgin, etc.
> idea stolen from Rilke's song of idiot, widow, suicide, etc.[45]

From this initial premise to take on the voices of a range of human subjectivities – following the example of Masters's *Spoon River Anthology* (1915) – Johnson went on to refine her selections, eventually dropping the "Ballads of St. Stupid" from the collection. The final book, *Human Songs*, is remarkable for how fluidly it moves through varieties of human experiences, but here I want to focus specifically on how such fluidity allows Johnson's speakers to evade the straitjacket of normative gender binaries. This evasion is well illustrated in "A Non-Sexual Song," which declares: "In this world / where you should belong clearly / to one camp or another / I'm not at home in any!"[46] The poem echoes the sense of dislocation articulated in "experience of 7 consecutive hours," but expresses it through frustration with gender "camp" – the word choice here is probably not incidental – which forces people to identify with one or the other. And just as "experience of 7 consecutive hours" refers to the "battle for existence," in *Human Songs*, Johnson expands a martial metaphor into a number of variations, as for example in "Split Personality," which describes "combat within" (20), or "In the Kitchen of My Spirit," which imagines a "hectic courtship" between the speaker's male and female sides:

> I'm a woman and a man
> and i live all alone together
> in wedded bliss
> after a hectic courtship.
>
> When someone comes over
> to where I am working or meditating,
> which is the man in me,
> I get right up to put the fire
> under the coffee pot,
> which is the woman in me.
>
> Now in my household
> where once no fire was lit,
> the woman cooks the food,
> the man eats it.
>
> But when the Holy Ghost shall come
> to grace this household,
> we are one.
>
> (23)[47]

In an echo of her jokey performance as Henry Miller for Burroughs's amusement, in this poem Johnson explores how gender expression is affected by the presence of other people. In the opening stanza, the speaker asserts, "I'm a woman and a man," a harmonious situation impinged on by visitors to the "kitchen," a space of course conventionally coded as female. Playing on such gender associations, the speaker's male side works and meditates, while the female side tends to the home fires. Once a visitor arrives, the "wedded bliss" of being both man and woman is compromised. Forced to choose a singular expression, the speaker behaves "just" as a woman, with all the retrograde subservience that womanhood has conventionally been assigned: "the woman cooks the food / the man eats it." The hopeful final allusion to Christian ideas about the Trinity, in which the godhead is conceived as three parts that are at once unified and distinct, provides a model for a future time when humans – not just gods and spirits – might be similarly distinct yet unified. Such a concept may shed light on why Johnson switched between publishing under her given name and the pen name Kaja; as one contributor's note in *Outsider* put it: "KAY JOHNSON & kaja are two different persons, in one body."[48]

The final turn of "In the Kitchen of My Spirit" in fact displays two broad preoccupations of Johnson's work that merit further study: not only the evasion of gender norms discussed above, but also her reimagining of the sacred in this context. We have seen how Johnson questions gender expression in various poems in *Human Songs*; in other work from this period, she does so by appropriating sacred concepts, forms, or language. This is the case, for example, in *Eat Me, Drink Me*, a chapbook of "psalms" she self-published while still in New Orleans; one poem, "My Three Christs," elevates the likes of Rilke and Walt Whitman to Christlike status, the speaker claiming, "What I am ... [is] because of the poems he [Whitman] wrote / personally for me."[49] Or in "LSD-748," a lengthy, dense excerpt from a larger project published in Daniel Richter's short-lived magazine *Residu* (1965). That poem uses Johnson's experiences with hallucinogenic drugs to recalibrate her understanding of the real in ways she likened to religious illumination, as she included footnotes from texts such as Timothy Leary's *The Psychedelic Experience: A Manual Based on the Tibetan Book of the Dead* (1964). At some moments she again channels Corso, whose poem "Under Peyote" describes "a new light / a bannister of music" (*Happy Birthday of Death*, 18). Johnson likewise writes, "EVERYONE i see is enlightened ... keep an awareness not of structure, form, name, BUT LIGHT!"[50] Where she departs from Corso (or McClure's more famous "Peyote Poem") is precisely in the ways in which LSD helps her to understand gender as something extrinsic to one's true self. As in the human song "In the Kitchen of My Spirit," in "LSD-748" "god" is associated with that which is both male and female, at once distinct yet the same, and the LSD helps her apprehend what she calls in another poem "substances within substances" – that is, a deeper kind of meaning beyond the assumed or expected.[51]

The preceding discussion only sketches the complexity of work we do have from Johnson, almost all of which is relatively difficult to access because it is far-flung in little magazines and in self-published chapbooks of very limited runs; her surviving letters indicate a wealth of other writing that has likely been lost.[52] It would be a great service to Beat studies were someone to do for Johnson what Tony Trigilio did for Elise Cowen: collect her work with a full scholarly apparatus so as to make it physically more accessible, thereby allowing a woman who might be the Beatest Beat poet of them all to occupy a more prominent place in twentieth-century letters.

11.5 Barbara Moraff: Hip Song Mistress

In 1962, LeRoi Jones's Totem Press published *Four Young Lady Poets*, collecting the work of Carol Bergé, Barbara Moraff, Rochelle Owens, and Diane Wakoski. This collection marks a significant moment in Beat literary history because it represents a comparatively early focus on women, and because these writers were not expressly identified as "Beat." This may seem a counterintuitive claim to make in a book about the Beats, but if we view the volume as part of a matrix of avant-garde writing in the 1960s that included but was not limited to the Beats, we find that though its contents clearly have a broadly Beat ethos, the contributors were at times connected to the Beats and at others to different literary coteries, particularly a group Carol Bergé would call the Light Years poets. Although in later life Bergé would be especially insistent in cordoning off the Light Year poets from the Beats, as we have seen, lines demarcating one "school" from another were always permeable and ever-shifting.[53] If nothing else, *Four Young Lady Poets* is worth pausing over as it marks the first publication in book form for Bergé, Moraff, and Wakoski (Owens's first book of poetry, *Not Be Essence That Cannot Be,* was published just the year before).[54]

Of the writers collected in *Four Young Lady Poets*, Barbara Moraff, born in 1939, was the youngest and the one most consistently linked to the Beats, a self-described "hip song mistress."[55] As her author note to *Four Young Lady Poets* explains, she was famous on the Village scene for her association with "celebrity" poets: "At 18, she was already part of the thriving New York poetry scene, reading at the famous 1958-59 Seven Arts coffee shop readings which included Gregory Corso, Allen Ginsberg, Paul Blackburn and other now well known poets."[56] Despite her youth, Moraff's work appeared in various issues of *Yugen* and in anthologies such as John Mitchell's *Poetry of the Beat Generation*, Stanley Fisher's *Beat Coast East*, Elias Wilentz's *The Beat Scene*, as well as the *Beatitude Anthology*.[57] Moraff was so esteemed that in 1963, when Kerouac was asked for a list of writers who would be essential to *Poesia degli ultimi americani* (1964), a dual Italian–English anthology of Beat writers, he dubbed Moraff the "best girl poet" (and di Prima the "other best girl poet"; only di Prima wound up in the anthology).[58] Even with such praise from Kerouac, like some other writers invested most in orality, putting together a book was not a priority for Moraff – in fact she wouldn't publish a full-length poetry book until the early 1980s.

Like many of her fellow writers interested in the new consciousness, Moraff's poetry often explores the way individualized subjectivity is of a piece with *tathata* or ultimate reality in the Buddhist sense, what she calls in one poem "the Superb Reality/Mind." The conflation here is not incidental as many of Moraff's poems from this period question the boundedness of one's consciousness, so that to understand "Superb Reality" is to probe consciousness beyond the ego. Consider, for example, this thought experiment:

> Let us suppose the mind
> to be a reversible tea-kettle
>   NO
> rather, let us assume it
> as being a coil of electricity
> which, when provoked (say by Spring-dawn)
> will extend an outer portion of itself
>
> as a moth would extend
> its furry antennae, its white feeler
> to examine the light
> coiling about the rim of a silver bowl.
>
> Perhaps this
> is the Superb Reality/Mind
> being a coil of electricity,
>
> able to extend
> – thereby
> proclaiming the outer worlds
> comparable animation to be
> (in that its substance is critically crystal)
> Reflector . . .
>   of the soul . . .
>
> Notice the moth. pale creature
> whose frail tissue wings flutter
> a purple vibrancy (nervous!) of soul
> when, extending its antennae it discovers
> not god
>   but its own miracle.
>   (*Four Young Lady Poets*, n.p., ellipses in original)

The poem first rejects an unusual metaphor for the mind – "reversible tea-kettle" – to wonder instead if it isn't like a "coil of electricity," a shift that emphasizes how an individual consciousness resonates with the wider universe, for a reversible tea-kettle would merely dissipate steam into the ether, whereas a coil of electricity evokes a tangible if shocking connection to that which is beyond the mind, the "outer portion of itself." In the subsequent comparison of the electrical coil to a moth's antennae, which allow the creature to sense its environment, the poem suggests that a mind is best understood when it is "able to extend" – that is, when one recognizes that the mind and "outer worlds" are in fact one. This is an essentially Buddhist view of the universe, and Moraff's work is sprinkled with references to various Buddhist traditions, as in the final poem collected in *Four Young Lady Poets*, which quotes "om mane padme hum," the most famous Buddhist mantra.[59] In this interest in Buddhist-inspired conceptions of the consciousness and its interconnectedness with all living beings, we can view Moraff's work of the early 1960s as sharing a broad sensibility with some other writers discussed in Part III, notably Snyder, McClure, Welch, and Whalen.

Much of Moraff's poetry from the early 1960s looks at how one's self might be connected to things beyond it – and yet in the course of exploring this idea, she often ends up affirming the value of the self as an acting subject. For example, in "Pome" – collected in the *Beatitude Anthology* – the opening line declares simply, "i'm sitting on an old treestump," but then pushes this physical connection into an off-kilter meditation on God and the universe:

> here i am
> i as me, sitting on the treestump of the universe
> watching stars to float at my fingertips
>   stars? no dragon flutes
> after all maybe god is an unemployed comedian
> who takes tea at moondumb teatime with the ghost
> of that duke princely of winds or
> on the outside trauma of a peacocks womb
> immortality (thats an image!)[60]

The awkward phrase "i as me" at once disassociates the speaker's sense of self from her ego while ironically reinforcing the perceptive power of her idiosyncratic consciousness. As in the poem discussed above, which demands attention to a moth as a route to reconceptualizing the mind, so in "Pome" does the speaker's concentration on the "stump rooted in silence" (83) allow her not only to track her own experience but also to imagine a wild conception of God and the universe that collapses distinctions among inner and outer, the self and the universe. The poem ends with a deliberately casual line that bestows the poet with a great deal of generative power: "as for me – hmm / i'm content to sit here on this treestump / gunung api flicking my cigareet so you may have stars" (84). Still rooted on the tree stump, the speaker uses her imaginative connections to the universe to figure herself Gunung Api, an Indonesian volcano, her cigarette ashes like the molten lava flows that can literally create new topographies on the earth.[61] In "Another Plain Poem" – which made its way into the progressive though relatively mainstream weekly magazine *The Nation* in 1962 – Moraff likewise collapses the distinction between the self and the universe:

> imagine a star is
> your skin.
>> you are a star a galaxy
>> of happenings
>> all the animals & birds
>> & so on.[62]

This poem celebrates the self by rendering it indistinguishable from the "galaxy" – a paradox only when the mind is conceived from a non-Buddhist point of view. And were one inclined to read such poetry in terms of gender, one might conclude that the impulse to preserve idiosyncratic agency is a feminist one, however couched such preservation is in esoteric depictions of the universe in the self.

Not all of Moraff's work is about metaphysical inquiry; like di Prima, she sometimes uses humor to poke fun at aspects of contemporary culture, from hipster intellectuals to bloviating academics. In *Four Young Lady Poets*, there is the affectionate sketch of "tom, the existentialiste" who "drives, off, in his / white Eldorado, top, down, too" (n.p.). The poem follows Tom to Cambridge, where he attempts, unsuccessfully, to impress his friends by ordering in German at a restaurant (he just mouths "bad phone ehticks"), and where he goes "under the table prac / tising his existentialism haha." The account of "tom the existentialiste" is also rife with allusions that prize a poet like Whitman over a poet like Eliot, as the speaker notes she spilled "cafeaulait all over eliot," figuratively obscuring the snooty writer just as they arrive "not too far from lilacsyard," a compressed reference to one of Whitman's most famous poems, "When Lilacs Last in the Dooryard Bloom'd," his pastoral elegy for slain President Lincoln. And despite all the racing around until 4 o'clock in the morning,

Tom doesn't seem to make much progress, and the poem ends where it began, with the hapless existentialist driving off in his white Cadillac, suggesting the final futility of that en vogue philosophical posture.

The facing poem likewise zooms through a landscape that would have been familiar to Whitman – the "lolling meadows of newjersey" – where the speaker mishears the lyrics of a popular children's song, turning its sense of forward momentum into an image of violent change: "the wheel goes round gores round / the ground shakes like a circumlocuting pedagogue ubless i /amb the sun code in duh mental node i roundround go gore / round with the wind wildly whoops birds bursting moonspasms" (*Four Young Lady Poets*, n.p.). The puns link the sing-songy rhythm of "The Wheels on the Bus" to the poetry championed by a "circumlocuting pedagogue," who blesses not the "I" but the "iamb," the classical metrical foot put to annoying use in that song. Moraff mocks the pedagogue for whom the iamb is "the sun code in duh mental node" not just riffing on the children's song but introducing a crucial change ("go" to "gore") and breaking the word "iamb" across two lines, which releases it from its connection to prosody into a pun on "I am." Thus the speaker, the "I" of the poem, becomes the "sun code" that can change up how we perceive the world precisely by mixing up language. As these poems attest, Moraff is a consummate Beat poet as her work demonstrates the close relationship between the new consciousness and the new poetry. Her explorations of subjectivity and selfhood require new modes of expression, and her images and lyricism are more successful than her neglected reputation suggests.

11.6   Carol Bergé: Light Years Ahead

While Moraff was in the early 1960s associated with the Beats by those who took the trouble to label literary movements, Carol Bergé moved in different circles simultaneously, and so is a good example of a writer who can seem Beat from one perspective, but was connected also to other communities. We have seen the cross-pollination among the Beats and the Black Mountain or New York School poets throughout the 1950s; by the early 1960s, other avant-garde groups were beginning to gain traction on the nonacademic literary scene, and Bergé was connected to a circle of some thirty-five poets who gathered to give weekly readings at Les Deux Megots coffee house in New York and other venues. Thinking back on this period, Bergé insisted that this group was distinct from the Beats, "a unit discrete from other non-academic arts groups in New York and from other groups of writers" (*Light Years*, 2). This group came to be known as the Light Years poets, a label that apparently drew inspiration from Jackson Mac Low's "light poems" and from a remark by "another writer [who] labeled the group as 'light years ahead of the contemporary culture.'" Bergé's insistence notwithstanding, others would recall a more fluid movement, and she would also admit that "The Beat poets represented by Allen Ginsberg and Gregory Corso, were also part of a clique, simply because their fame preceded their arrival on the Deux Megots poetry scene" (*Light Years*, 330). But in general, Bergé was invested in arguing for a distinct group at which she was the center, especially later in life as she was retrospectively accounting for all her literary achievement.

There was some precedence for this walling-off of the Light Years circle from the Beats, and in fact the first anthology of Light Years work was explicitly set against the Beats. The collection, *Seventh Street: Poems from Les Deux Megots* (1961), appeared the year before *Four Young Lady Poets*, and included both Bergé and Wakoski, among fifteen others, notably Howard Ant, Don Katzman, Jackson Mac Low, and Robert Nichols. In the foreword to the piece, it is clear these poets wanted to distinguish themselves from what one poet called the "commercialism" of "the Beat deluge."[63] The writers associated with Les Deux Megots defined themselves in part by their distance from the Beats, whom they considered sellouts or stooges forced to play to "tourist hordes" incapable of appreciating serious aesthetic exchange. Although "completely democratic," the Deux Megots readings were, in contrast to readings in places like the Gaslight or Café Bizarre, subject to rigorous critique from the audience, a kind of workshop model implied to lend a seriousness to the proceedings that the commercialized Beats lacked. According to this argument, by 1961, to be associated with the Beats was to be a sellout, so the new authenticity in poetry was to declare yourself anti-academic but not Beat. As Diane Wakoski put it, "while we did represent new things in poetry, not the academic poetry that was being written by college professors, at the same time we were snobs and not really interested in street poetry either."[64]

And yet despite the rigid divide that was claimed to exist, the shared anti-academic stance meant that the Light Years poets are broadly comparable to the Beats, and even Bergé's own work from the period seems to radiate a Beat sensibility. In "tessa's song," for example, Bergé sketches the story of a "shy girl" whose journey from the country into the streets of Greenwich Village is marked by sexual encounter: "the pretty one / slipping by the trees / faster he runs / she runs." From this bucolic setting, the scene moves to bohemian New York, where Tessa is about to have her fifth child by a fifth man, and is suffering from poverty and a heroin addiction.[65] The "doe eye" girl in the first section has been transformed into a hard-nosed realist:

> i talk filth and energy
> pissing at them the vacant horror
> of my lofts and days
>
> . . .
>
> from my slackjaw eyes
> the fifth boybaby will fall soon
> they come at me and fill me with child
> and i cannot stop this
> it speaks of love five fathers
> old sweater on my fat wondering belly
> and my white skinny arms full of holes.
>
> (*Four Young Lady Poets*, n.p.)

In this unflinching depiction of a woman who has been used for her body, Bergé levels the sort of gender critique we saw with di Prima's poetry, as well as in other work in *Four Young Lady Poets*, such as the Moraff poem in which the speaker describes a violent sexual encounter: "he is upon me / . . . raw ignorant lunge . . . / do i bare white teeth like a bird?" Tessa's song is a cautionary tale about the ugly gender dynamics at work in contemporary society that are ironically made even starker by the sexually open social realm marked in the poem by "8th street," a space that renders Tessa a wraith-like stalker in the Village: "all cold except my loose bellyfolds / my world is flat." Whether Tessa was an exaggerated version of Bergé's more conventional, "stifling" experiences – after the birth of her son, she described herself as "trapped in suburbia, as Typical Young Married Housewife and Mother" – her interest in taking on the voice of downtrodden, socially marginalized figures is a basic political commitment that would characterize counter-cultural writing throughout the rest of the 1960s.[66]

Bergé also uses this imaginative voicing of the "Other" in her work in the *Seventh Street* anthology; one poem, for example, merges hipster argot with the figure of a Jewish person devastated by the Holocaust:

> i mean, i really cant believe in a god.
> what with auschwitz and all. but, dig,
> with this nose, these eyes, the forehead,
> how can i come on
>
> . . .
>
> 　　　　　this way it moves
> my hat and my beard. but man, you dig,
> it isn't easy.
>
> (8–9)

The teasing conflation of the Orthodox Jewish beard with the hipster's allows Bergé to make a serious point about the nature of cultural isolation and the damage wrought by seeing people as types or objects – also an interest of "tessa's song." The appropriation of clichéd street language reminds us that, in the early 1960s at least, Bergé was engaged aesthetically in the Beat milieu, even as the poem deploys it ironically. She is thus a figure who at once moved with and admired Beat writers – as evidenced, for instance, in work like "An Answer to One of the Other Women," dedicated to David Ready, Lenore Kandel, and Ed Sanders, and published in *Fuck You* (1963) – but who also actively resisted being counted among them, especially in later years.

Such admiration was publicized in 1964 with *The Vancouver Report*, her critical account of a now-famous three-week poetry conference held at the University of British Columbia in the summer of 1963. Written at the behest of Ed Sanders for his Fuck You Press, the report was Bergé's opportunity to set the record straight regarding what she took to be the most arresting and original poetry on the contemporary scene. The report opens with a list of the "Big Names in Poetry Today" in attendance: Creeley, Duncan, Olson, Ginsberg, Levertov, and Canadian poet Margaret Avison, and the ensuing report records various discussions about poetry and poetics held by these and other participants. At one point, Bergé finds fault with those whom she deems overly derivative, who "rely on the form or method of those who preceded them. *I resent a poem which looks like WCW wrote it, if WCW didn't.*"[67] Following this declaration, she names three poets who are in her opinion producing original work: "See McClure for a brilliant form/content breakthrough; see Whalen's 'Like I Say' for a way to let the self rise to the top and be respected; see John Wieners' 'Hotel Wentley Poems' for the clear voice of a human whose sources are not hidden but exceeded" (11). Despite her retroactive dismissal of Beat writers, then, in the early 1960s, Bergé pointed to three of them as exemplars of how to create "form/content breakthrough" (she probably has McClure's "Rant Block" or "Peyote Poem" in mind here), of how to plumb the new consciousness, and how to write honestly about one's decidedly heterodox experiences.

The Vancouver Report also illustrates Bergé's changing opinion of Ginsberg's work, as she would describe his reading of "Kaddish" as gripping, "the flow carries, this is AG, man who can reach inmost to himself and thereby to us – ... such work of humanity ... am again crying, ... this Kaddish! This poet" (9). And yet by 2006 her evaluation of Ginsberg was unequivocally negative: "Allen G was a weak poet, a Poetry Clown; his rhythms were somewhere between Freud and davening and mantras, not original" ("Remembrance," 85). This about-face demonstrates the deep ambivalence about the Beats on Bergé's part, at least with respect to how she characterized their work in her own writing, another example of the paradoxical lure and repulsion of the Beats for those on the movement's peripheries.

Bergé is one of those figures who seems Beat at certain times and from certain angles, but who can also be profitably understood in other contexts. Her presence in these pages is meant to signal the diversity of a sensibility and aesthetic that could still be recognizably Beat. And as I hope my wider discussion of women writers suggests, as the Beatnik Era shaded into something else, there emerged many other kinds of literary production that complicate the notion that the Beats are best considered as a small, circumscribed group of male writers. Bill Morgan has argued, "We should think of the Beat Generation as a social circle created by Allen Ginsberg and his friends instead of as a literary movement. This will explain why so few women writers are identified with it, Di Prima being the exception."[68] Morgan goes on to note that many male Beats "saw women only as sex objects, providers, and mothers, and rarely did they believe that they could write as well as their male counterparts," and while such a narrative about mid-century gender assumptions is broadly accurate, there is no reason to carry such assumptions into our present moment when writing retrospectively about the Beats. I have tried to show throughout this book that we should indeed think in terms of a Beat literary movement, and I hope this attention to women in particular demonstrates that there were far more diffuse energies than suggested in Morgan's characterization, which in turn might encourage us to be more capacious in considering who or what might fly under the Beat banner.

CHAPTER 12

Liberating Language

By the early 1960s, the media fixation on the Beats as Beatniks was so entrenched that some writers began to thematize this distortion as they further experimented with language and the limits of representation. In order to illustrate more specifically how this worked, I want to turn to four texts that simultaneously reimagine the Beat image while rethinking the relationship between language and representation: Lawrence Ferlinghetti's novel *Her* (1960); Gregory Corso's novel *The American Express* (1961); Ted Joans's *The Hipsters* (1961), a strange book he called "a black humor first visual comment on my worthy constituents of the Beat Generation"; and *Minutes to Go* (1960), a collaborative cut-up text by William Burroughs, Brion Gysin, Sinclair Beiles, and Corso.[1] While these texts were all published during what I'm calling the Beatnik Era, I'm placing them in this section because I see them as bridges into the latter 1960s, when Beat investment in the personal became more stridently political. Although Ferlinghetti and Corso are known primarily as poets, *Her* and *The American Express* are their forays into new genres, and both jettison conventional markers of the novel in order to explore the demarcations between reality and fantasy. Likewise, *The Hipsters* is a humorous work of collage that pokes fun at figurations of Beats, Beatniks, and "the unhip and the squares" ("Je Me Vois," 230). *Minutes to Go* is the most significant text of this grouping insofar as it showcases the first sustained use of Gysin and Burroughs's cut-up method, which seeks to radically rethink how words work, dislodging them from denotative meaning in order to access alternative visions of the real. Taken together, these disparate texts, produced as they were as the Beatnik Era waned, represent a radical refocusing of language informed if not inspired by the widespread caricatures of the Beatnik.

12.1 *Her:* Headlines of Pure Poetry

In 1960, after the success of *A Coney Island of the Mind*, Ferlinghetti published his first novel, *Her*, a Joycean revel in language that wears its

345

literary influences on its sleeve, and that is flagrantly more concerned with wordplay than with character or plot.[2] Parts of *Her* were published in 1959 in *Big Table* 3 and *Beatitude* 8; and the fact that the excerpts make as much sense as stand-alone pieces as they do as part of a book suggests the degree to which *Her* is perhaps more akin to a prose poem than a conventional novel.[3] The plot, such as it is, follows Andy Raffine, an overweight American painter, "Brooklyn's baby," living in Paris, as he lusts after an unnamed woman, the "her" of the title.[4] In a parody of a mythic quest or boy-meet-girl plot, *Her* records the digressive inner workings of Raffine's mind, which is assailed by a range of existential doubts, from the meaning of his own life to whether it is possible to create original art, two questions brought together as he imagines scenes from his own life as a clichéd painting: "It was a scene I had already painted in all its parts.... I had already painted everybody else's painting of the same subject.... It had all already happened" (14–15). This sort of aesthetic paralysis – Raffine's twinned anxieties about his life and his art – form the core of the work, and relate to the Beat movement insofar as Ferlinghetti wonders whether there is really anything new about the "new writing."

Since *Her* is not among the more well-known Beat works, comparatively few critics have written about it, but those who have tend to emphasize its mythic resonances and playful self-awareness. As Michael Skau points out, for example, part of Raffine's paralysis comes from his "reluctant recognition of his role as a fictional character" – in other words, his existential crisis stems not merely from pondering the meaning of life, but the meaning of his life as a character in a novel written by "some hack" (Skau, *"Constantly Risking Absurdity,"* 41; *Her*, 61). In such self-reflexiveness, the novel demonstrates its indebtedness to such Modernist masters as Djuna Barnes, for as Ferlinghetti once told David Meltzer, *Her* is "full of all kinds of stuff I stole from *Nightwood* [1936]," a debt signaled in the novel when Raffine describes himself "walking through those nightwood streets of his own youth" (94).[5] Joyce and Eliot are also central influences on the novel, as seen in the mash-up of the final line of *Ulysses* and the opening ones of *Finnegans Wake*: "pressing down on me until I too and night and hot I yes and riverrun and Tiber run down to the sea" (105), or the double reference to *The Waste Land* and Dante's *Inferno*: "I had not known fat had undone so many" (15), or the constant parody of the Fisher King, a controlling figure in *The Waste Land*: "the fishy king none other than myself" (27).

Intermixed with such reworkings of the highbrow canon are allusions to the work of Ferlinghetti's contemporaries – even his protagonist's name was borrowed from Corso, who came up with "Andalous Raffine," explaining that "Andalous came from a can of fish soup, and Raffine from a box of salt. So there. The entire mad meaning of your proposed hero. Salty Fish."[6] Raffine also appears versed in Burroughs, as when he refers to his mind as "this no-mind noman's land my interzone" (144), an allusion to *Naked Lunch*'s nightmare Interzone, where, recall, "Hipsters with smooth copper-colored faces lounge in doorways twisting shrunk heads on gold chains."[7] Or Kerouac, whose concept of "bookmovie" seems to Raffine a way to articulate his own experiences: "I had not heard the funky bird stop singing in my turning head at a turning point of that endless bookmovie that some hack had adapted from an endless parade of figures who might have been myself in a parody of my life which was itself based upon and endless sexual fantasy" (61). It is significant that Ferlinghetti borrows these particular terms, for Interzone and bookmovie were used by Burroughs and Kerouac to describe contemporary experience in new ways – as Kerouac wrote in 1962, "anybody can write, but not everybody invents new forms of writing," and he called the bookmovie "the movie in words, the visual American form."[8] And as explained in Part II, Burroughs's famous Interzone was modeled on Tangier when it was an International Zone administrated by Great Britain, France, and Spain; "it was an Interzone," he recalled in 1966, "it was no country."[9] By reviving the interzone in *Her*, Ferlinghetti doesn't just idly allude to Burroughs, he does so to suggest that Raffine's mind can be understood partly through *Naked Lunch*, whose characters are similarly unhinged from linear progress. In *Her*, Ferlinghetti thus draws on forms of writing or cultural critique that the Beats thought of as innovative or particularly apt for articulating the contemporary experience, and uses them as a way to confront the anxiety that one is merely repeating older forms, an anxiety Kerouac, for one, often manifested, as when he proclaimed, "Gertrude Stein invented a new form of writing and her imitators are just 'talents'" with the implication that he himself was as inventive as Stein ("Are Writers," 489).

But just as *Her* is about being paralyzed by literary history, published as it was at the tail end of the Beatnik Era, it also contends with the ways the media defined the image of the Beat writer. In one of the more memorable moments in the novel, Raffine runs into "a wailing wild ragged band of American poets from the Rue Git-le-Coeur" – the residents of the famed Beat Hotel. In their impromptu parade-performance, these poets rush "out of a side street into the middle of the boulevard ... singing and shouting that the Poetry Police were coming to save them, the Poetry Police were coming to save them all from death, Captain Poetry was coming to save the world from itself" (42). The passage goes on to explain that the Poetry Police "were about to land simultaneously in the central squares of forty-two major cities" to force libraries, newspapers, and publishing houses to "print nothing henceforth but headlines of pure poetry and menus of pure love" (43).

The idea for the Poetry Police seems to have come from Corso and Burroughs, who while living on Rue Gît-le-Coeur planned to start a new literary magazine named *Interpol*, a mocking reference to the International Criminal Police Organization headquartered in France. Corso tried to solicit material from Ferlinghetti in September 1958: "Bill and I are set on doing a magazine, *Interpol* 'the poet is becoming a policeman' – and our content will be of the most sordid vile vulgar oozing seeping slime imaginable.[...] here is Bill Burroughs word: 'When the Human Image is threatened, the poet dictates forms of survival ... Dream police of poetry protect us from The Human Virus.'"[10] In *Her*, Ferlinghetti has the Corso-like "wailing wild ragged" poets shouting about a Poetry Police who will, as in Corso and Burroughs's model, create "forms of survival" in the face of the "rapidly deteriorating world situation" (43). This is a turning point in the novel: most of the time Raffine is lost in his own head, but when the residents of the Beat Hotel launch their Happening, they do so in order to radiate out into the world, to effect the sort of social and political change that Burroughs claimed could be achieved through poetry. Thus the Poetry Police fantasizes it will spread to the world's great cities with the aim of deciding what "the shape of the table should be at all future peace conferences," a fantasy that presages the growing interest in explicit political engagement that would mark the work of Ferlinghetti and many other Beat-associated writers throughout the 1960s (43).

As promising as this sounds, the very moment Raffine is swept up in the wellspring of fellow feeling, believing that "the Poetry Revolution was growing, the Poetry Revolution was shaking, transforming existence and civilization," another group appears: "crowds of black berets and herds of sandals came floating and staggering and flying out of the Café Mabillon and the Pergola to join the much-belated Poetry Revolution" (45). These crowds do not represent Beat writers but Beatnik hangers-on (as signaled by the reference to berets and sandals), and almost as soon as it begins, the Poetry Revolution collapses under the very weight of Beat fame as "the original small band of mad poets scattering true apocalyptic visions was lost and drowned in the swelling parade of humanity and inhumanity" (45). Once the "snowballing mob of liberated man" (46) makes it to the Right Bank, they are met with a "solid cordon of nine thousand mercenaries, Royalists, and gendarmes" (47), representatives of dominant culture looking to quell revolution. Thus rather than finally dictating new "forms of survival," as suggested by Burroughs, the poets cause "newly startled citizens" to flee, and Raffine himself is "trampled underfoot in the surging throngs" (47, 48).

After the revolution falters, Raffine continues to mope around Paris lusting after "her," and at a certain point finds himself caught between the potentially generative poetics of the Rue Gît-le-Coeur crowd and the Beatnik cartoons come to life, the latter of which, like the great aesthetic works of prior generations, he finds himself replaying. He moves around the city "looking like a beat boulevardier" – thereby suggesting he is not *really* a beat boulevardier, but is rather a fraud, scarcely better than the beret-and-sandal set who overwhelmed the "true" poets (96). Indeed, Raffine remarks that he has become one of those people who do "the opposite of what is popular and acts very strange in society . . . and wears wild beards and tries to live in the future while the present is going on which is how the true hung-up free cat is de-scribed in the press . . . [while] the true beat paint-poet . . . [awaits] the Poetry Police [who] are still coming to carry you all away" (96). So like his friend Lubin, a bohemian whose very lifestyle seems to Raffine derivative, as though he were "a bent character out of those Twenties books, one of those American-in-Paris books, still hanging on to haunt another generation" (65), Raffine's generation is characterized by those who live out media caricatures that ignore actual artists, the "true beat paint-poet," by "de-scribing" – de-writering – their accounts. Ultimately, Raffine remains paralyzed not only by the earlier achievements of Modernism but also by the current Beat-associated work and how it has been characterized by the media, so his final recourse, after much navel-gazing and varied searching for "her," is to commit suicide.

12.2   *The American Express*: Good Language for the New Consciousness

Not long after *Her* was published, Corso wrote to James Laughlin, then his editor at New Directions, to say, "I like Ferl's *Her*, but all poets when writing first prose . . . Experiment with words – as if to say – 'see, even in prose, I'm still a poet.' I passed that pitfall and done a straight *Peyton Place* kind of book with a difference."[11] The book Corso is talking about was his first and only foray into novel writing, *The American Express* (1961). In favorably comparing his book to a steamy best-seller, Corso did not mean to indicate that his novel was likewise filled with sex, but rather that in contrast to the densely allusive linguistic complexity of *Her*, his book was written in simple everyday language, was what he called an "undercover kids classic" (even as the final product isn't exactly easy to understand).[12] Given that Corso inspired the Poetry Police passages in *Her*, it makes a certain sense that when he turned his attention to fiction with *The American Express* he should imagine a revolution of words locked in struggle against a revolution of bombs. Originally to be titled "All Things Are Sustained in Being" or "Oatmeal," *The American Express*, like *Her*, has a surreal quality to it, but it also reads like a farce as it contains a number of outsized characters with little psychological depth.

The novel opens when a motley group of characters disembark from a ship called *Here They Come* in an unnamed, probably European city.[13] They subsequently spend most of the novel debating the pros and cons of two vague, roughly opposed plans proposed by characters named Mr. D and Hinderov. Both men recognize a world in crisis, that "the human experiment has failed" (as another character puts it), and suggest differing strategies for addressing this situation.[14] Hinderov, who we might say loosely corresponds to the American status quo, wants to distribute bombs around the world in order to annihilate humankind, thereby solving its problems; his perverse logic is that "Once everybody gets his own bomb then there will be no more demand for bombs!" (38). The American Express office is crucial for Hinderov's purposes because the company already has a worldwide network he can exploit to distribute his bombs: "I will make this place the capital of the world!" he says. "From here I will direct all forces! I will conduct conquests!" (152).[15] Mr. D, on the other hand, thinks language the better vehicle for change, and that by deforming or changing language, one might correct the failed human experiment. As Corso glossed the novel for Ginsberg, *The American Express* is "about the war between the old and the new. I give Hinderov the old, he … incorporates American Express, sells bombs, distributes war, etc.… And Mr. D. as Bill Burroughs, in a way, who seeks to give the new consciousness a new language, and so I have him go around seeking to buy one – and I give him victory at end of book. I have the wordman prevail."[16] If Raffine in *Her* is at once extraordinarily facile with and paralyzed by language, Mr. D in *The American Express* thinks "language," with all its slippery profusion and irreducibility, might be the salvation of a world on the edge of destruction.

In order to counteract Hinderov's bombs, Mr. D plans to "find a good language for the new consciousness" (43), and travels to various places in time and space attempting to literally buy words from particular cultures. For example, he goes to England, seemingly transported to pre-modern times, and asks clansmen, "What kind of words you got for sale?" with the explicit goal of "outdo[ing]" Hinderov (42). Read in figurative terms,

Mr. D represents those writers like Burroughs whose radical experimentations with language encourage us to understand the world in different ways; as Mr. D. remarks: "With the word goes all meaning and all meaninglessness ... When the word uncreates itself, nothing will remain, not even 'nothing will remain'" (142). Like *Her*, *The American Express* insists on the power of the new language and the new consciousness at a moment when the Beat Generation was being roundly ridiculed, and so although both Corso and Ferlinghetti were decidedly ambivalent about the phenomenon, they put their own surreal spins on the general Beat project of remaking consciousness by remaking language.

12.3   *The Hipsters*: Black Humor First Visual Comment

Characterizing the Beats in subplot or subtext in *Her* and *The American Express* moves to take center stage in Ted Joans's odd but irresistible book, *The Hipsters* (1961), a surreal mix of collage and text that holds a distorted mirror to the ways the Beats had been put through the critical and cultural wringer. In the summer of 1960, Joans was in Venice, Italy, doing things like giving readings with Alan Ansen and so had the benefit of a wider-angle perspective on the scene back home. As Ferlinghetti and Corso had in their new work, Joans ventures away from poetry in *The Hipsters*, and the result is not a novel or even really fiction in any recognizable sense, but rather a kind of hipster satire of work like *The Real Bohemia: A Sociological and Psychological Study of the "Beats"* (1961) that was then beginning to appear.[17] To dismantle the force of such work, *The Hipsters* is comprised of Dadaesque collages of drawings from Victorian-era works of history, anthropology, and the like, with equally old-fashioned medical or entomological reference illustrations meant to satirize the documentary impulse found in work like *The Real Bohemia*. There are even detailed renderings of "The Anatomy of the Hipster," in which "the small numbers indicate his unique characteristics – tremendous sex drive and outstanding intellect."[18]

Consider the set piece shown in Figure 12.1 referring to a "beat-poet publisher" reminiscent of Ferlinghetti or Kupferberg (elsewhere in *The Hipsters* "a young statutory lovely" is depicted reading "Ferlinghetti's latest book of poems"). The interplay between text and image mocks the Beatnik caricature by first seeming to confirm it: the written description informs us that the poet reads to the accompaniment of bongos while decked out in a beret and sandals, the must-have gear for the stereotypically shaggy Beatnik. Yet it's pretty hard to take the caption seriously given the collage it supposedly explains, which satirizes the way dominant culture views the

Meanwhile a beat poet-publisher reads his own written works from
his own published books while a fellow hipster thumps sensually
on a double headed bongo. Such small bongo drums can also be
used to summon police in any town in the United States; if you
doubt it, tonight you should try it. (Notice the conventional clitordectomial vision overhead.)

Figure 12.1   From Ted Joans's *The Hipsters* (1961).
Image courtesy of Lafayette College

Beats as uncivilized. The main image is a circle of North African "natives" listening to a Westerner holding forth, which is juxtaposed with an illustration from a medical reference work, glossed as "the conventional clitordectomial vision." It's unclear at first what the circle and the medical procedure have to do with each other – until we realize that there is perhaps a kind of regulatory violence embedded in characterizing the Beats as bongo-playing primitives, a suggestion echoing the droll aside, that bongo playing will summon unsympathetic police.

The Hipsters has only the faintest suggestion of plot, so a good way to think about the book is as a series of thematically linked routines, as in *Naked Lunch*, except with text and image. Each page has one such routine or set piece that bears loose relation to the book's overall structure, which mocks well-made literary texts such as three-act plays by offering two introductory sections titled "The Scene" and "Dramatis Persona." Following those sections, the text is divided into three acts, "Act 1: That Day," "Act 2: That Night," and "Act 3: The Flight." There are no central characters or linear action to speak of; instead, the "plot" is motivated by the arrival on the scene of those who might be interested in conducting anthropological fieldwork among the bohemians: "From the four corners of the earth arrive four foreign emissaries all bearing some kind of nutty bit to turn everyone on to. They're on a Rockerfeller Brothers grant to study hipsterism and the dilemma of modern man" (n.p.). The coming of these academic-types is mainly a pretext for Joans to take readers through various set pieces like the one pictured in the figure to skewer not only media understandings of the Beats, but also the various character types found on the scene.

The opening section, "The Scene," plays on the word both in the sense of a dramatic setting and in the sense of the social and literary scene – recall that Joans had been prominently featured in Elias Wilentz's *The Beat Scene* the year before. In *The Hipsters*, the scene is illustrated with a line drawing of an African tribal village – playing on the home of the native hipster, Greenwich Village – with an image of a gigantic lobster and lobster claws zanily superimposed. The text reads: "Here is Greenwich Village, New York, the home of the hipster, hipnick, beat, beatnik, flip, flipnik, etc., where several thousand top people of all races, creeds and colors work, play and live in sometimes peace and sometimes harmony and all try to enjoy the lofty fruit of U.S. democracy" (n.p.). From there, Joans goes on to catalogue the nuances of various kinds of Village residents. One finds, for instance, "Cool" and "Extra Cool Hipsters", the "Jivey Leaguer" (who wants to "be a part of everything which he puts down or cashes-in-on as it suits his eternal search for girls"), the "Creepnik" ("always on the scene, digging lonely young chicks ... and other valuables he can steal"), "Folkniks" (who "carry musical instruments and long loose flowing hair as they sit on the steps of the hip folklore music shop"), the "Hipstressnik" ("poet's-little-mistressnik: the most lovable, the most soft, the most quiet, the most wise, the most-in-cooking, the most-in-inspiration, the most-in-bed, the most-in-travel, and the most-cool-in-times-of-stress"), and the "Hipper-than-Thounik" ("overread writer or painter of sort who speaks as an astute authority on every subject, even sex, which she knows only from books"). Readers also encounter "Touristniks": "Fascinated, they point and stare at the natives." These different types move through the scene during the day of Act I and the night of Act II giving poetry readings, listening to jazz, running from "a well known photographer for fear of being seen in a beatnik book that might shock uncool parents" (n.p.). In other words, they comport themselves in much the same way that Joans recommended in his poem "The Sermon," which likewise presented hip characters as wavering between Beat and Beatnik. Does Joans think these are legitimate categories of hip characters? Or is he exaggerating square perceptions? Or is the whole impulse to categorize what is antithetical to hipness as such, which would mean the very premise of *The Hipsters* is a put-on?

However much the book draws readers into these questions without gesturing toward serious answers, I do think that Joans is associating the demonization of bohemia with a longer, historical process of "civilizing." This is why so many set pieces use illustrations of colonial encounter: the pages are filled with Europeans in pith helmets out among the "natives," as well as with clinical renderings of darker-skinned populations that were meant to be representative of a particular ethnic or racial stock for classification purposes. As is the case in his poetry, Joans is finely tuned to the racial element of the fascination/marginalization of bohemia, which is why, for example, the illustration for the "Touristnik" scene mentioned above depicts a wealthy white family, complete with boater hats and parasols, pointing at a black couple in a window, the woman dressed like a housekeeper and holding a feather duster. The cumulative effect is the sense that the mores of the bohemian scene and the shocked attitudes of those interlopers who come to view them are part of a much older story about progress and evolution and enlightenment, which are so often borne on the backs of comparatively powerless populations, from indigenous peoples to domestic workers on the Lower East Side, a basic theme that Joans would return to in later work such as *Afrodisia* (1971).

12.4 The Cut-Up Method of *Minutes to Go*

While Joans lambasted those who exploited hipsters via representation by turning that very representation in on itself, Brion Gysin and William Burroughs were conducting even more radical experiments that would fundamentally challenge how language can mean. Even readers unfamiliar with the particulars may have come across the term "cut-up," a method of composition with which Gysin and Burroughs began working at the Beat Hotel in the fall of 1959. Gysin later explained the birth of cut-ups like this:

> While cutting a mount for a drawing in room #15, I sliced through a pile of newspapers with my Stanley blade and thought of what I had said to Burroughs some six months earlier about the necessity for turning painters' techniques directly into writing. I picked up the raw words and began to piece together texts that later appeared as "First Cut-Ups" in "Minutes to Go." At the time I thought them hilariously funny and hysterically meaningful.[19]

When Gysin alludes to "painters' techniques," he's thinking in terms of both what he calls "things as simple and immediate as collage or montage" and the ability of, say, an abstract work to exist without having to represent something external to itself (n.p.). Abstract Expressionism had been seen as a revolution in what the visual arts could mean or be, but writing seemed to be lagging in this regard. For Gysin, the accidental slicing of newspapers liberated "raw words" from being "chain[ed] . . . in phrases," which in turn suggested new senses of how these words could be "meaningful."

Burroughs took Gysin's discovery and developed it into a whole theory of writing and representation. He recognized the generative potential of approaching composition with a fundamentally different set of assumptions about what words are or can do. For Burroughs, the cut-up method became a way to foreground the visual character of words over their semantic or representational meaning (he called cut-ups "abstract literature"), and a way to access a deeper, more networked sense of reality by accounting for the simultaneities of lived experience.[20] If, as Burroughs speculated in *Naked Lunch*, "the word" had the potential for control and the distortion of reality, then cut-ups tried to reject such control and reflect a deeper sense of reality.

In an early explanation of the technique, "The Cut-Up Method of Brion Gysin," Burroughs focused primarily on the process itself: "Method is simple: Take a page or more or less of your own writing or from any writer living and or dead. Any written or spoken words. Cut into sections with scissors or switch blade as preferred and rearrange sections. Looking away. Now write out result."[21] When Burroughs expanded this piece for inclusion in *The Third Mind* (1978), a collaboration with Gysin some fifteen years in the making, he framed the utility of cut-ups in terms of their ability to reflect a more complex sense of "reality." He contextualizes cut-ups in a history of other avant-garde movements, notably Dada and Tristan Tzara creating work by pulling words randomly from a hat. It is further suggested that Burroughs's Nova Trilogy – *The Soft Machine* (1961, 1966, 1968), *The Ticket That Exploded* (1962, 1967), and *Nova Express* (1964), which he composed using cut-ups and related techniques – "disconnects the concept of reality that has been imposed on us and then plugs normally dissociated zones into the same sector – eventually escapes from the control of its manipulator."[22] While at work on the Nova Trilogy, Burroughs put it like this: "cut-ups make explicit a psycho-sensory process that is going on all the time anyway. Somebody is reading a newspaper, and his eye follows the column in the proper Aristotelian manner, one idea and sentence at a time. But subliminally he is reading the columns on either side and is aware of the person sitting next to him. That's a cut-up."[23] For Burroughs, then, liberating words from their semantic and syntactic chains not only frees them "from the control of its manipulator" (the author), but in so doing allows the manipulator to glimpse the simultaneity of reality, the meaning latent in the arranged words but rendered invisible by their dominant or intended meaning.

As he worked further with cut-ups, Burroughs became particularly interested in their ability to reflect reality anew, which is why in a later version of "The Cut-Up Method of Brion Gysin," published in *The Third Mind*, Burroughs begins with the same straightforward explanation of process, but then recommends some especially generative source material: "Sometimes," he writes, the cut-up will say "much the same thing [as the source text]. Sometimes something quite different – cutting up political speeches is an interesting exercise – in any case you will find that it says something and something quite definite.... The words have lost meaning and life through years of repetition" (*Third Mind*, n.p.). Here Burroughs empha-sizes the democratic nature of cut-ups – "Poetry is for everyone," he repeatedly asserts – as well as their ability to invigorate stale language politicians and others rely on to make questionable positions seem palatable (ibid.).

Indeed, with the recommendation to use "political speeches" as source material, Burroughs suggests that far from being idle aesthetic exercises, cut-ups can have a political function if they challenge how reality has been constructed by those in power. Political speeches are of course among the more obvious ways language can be degraded in the service of dubious masters (think Orwellian Doublespeak), and as we will see in the next chapter, in the mid-1960s and after, the basic observation that politics and language are mutually infectious grew into a pillar of Beat engagement with the Vietnam era public sphere. For example, in "Wichita Vortex Sutra," one of his most influential works of the 1960s, Ginsberg would assert "The war is language, . . . formulas for reality."[24] Although Burroughs would not go down the same road to political activism as Ginsberg and others, he did share the same insight about how corrupt language could distort reality, and both he and Ginsberg imagined ways to recuperate the word.

Beyond their potential to undo "political speeches," there is also a way to see cut-ups in the context of texts like *Her* and *The Hipsters*, which are energized partly by talking back to Beatnik Era representations of Beats. This idea is illustrated by the first cut-up text, *Minutes to Go* (1960). Put together at the Beat Hotel, *Minutes to Go* was published in Paris as a collaboration among Burroughs, Gysin, Corso, and poet Sinclair Beiles – but it was certainly dominated by Burroughs and Gysin.[25] For example, although Corso did collect "things to cut-up" – which included, among others, fragments of poetry by Ginsberg, Percy Shelley, and himself, as well as *Naked Lunch* and Kerouac's *Old Angel Midnight* – he participated in the project "unwillingly *and* willingly." As he explained in a "post-script": "Unwillingly because the poetry I have written was from the soul and not from the dictionary; willingly because if it can be destroyed *or* bettered by the 'cut-up' method, then it is poetry I care not for and should be cut-up."[26] Stuck on the old Romantic notion that poetry is divined from lone geniuses struck by the muse, Corso wasn't totally prepared to sign on to the cut-up project.

One among the "First Cut-Ups" Gysin alluded to when describing the method's origins appears at the beginning of *Minutes to Go*, a piece titled "Open Letter to Life Magazine," a cut-up of Paul O'Neil's 1959 *Life* magazine feature, "The Only Rebellion Around."[27] As discussed in Part III, O'Neil's article was one of the most visible attacks on the Beats, and went a long way in causing them to be perceived as bongo-playing Beatniks rather than legitimate writers. In this way, the article is a consequential example of how the corrupting force of language can lead to perception being confused with reality. Moreover, in the sort of striking coincidence that would mean so much to Burroughs, *Life* staffers had arrived at the Beat Hotel to interview and photograph him for this piece on October 1, 1959, the very day Gysin first cut through those newspapers, so it is fitting that the article should become a source for one of the earliest cut-ups.[28] Here is a sample:

Sickle moon terror nails replica in tin ginsberg. Replicas of Squaresville –
grey piebald pigeons – pointedly questioned, mimic each other. The wet
concrete square – a boy wit police – is ate by lierat birds. Pitiful personal
lives of suspension, flapping frantic, come to stare. An opium eater and a
Vincent-visitors bathe their feet in San Francisco market-deal of the world's
art-compacted-feathers.... Man's hideous professional crouch, the beat
movement, embackwards on an old man's members of north bea. Sockets
stare dedicated in seamed conferlinghetti of ginsbergs kerouacs & badly
blown clarinet-shimmer off the glossy bone. A great deal of their verbal
hearse is skull with surprised china fuzz. But oddly blu seekers after
coolness – solemen accountants, kers, loafers, passive little con men – loan
them sir a Harvard man off the last skimpy surplus of cop-haters. Exhibitionists abused Burroughs. (np)

The first thing to note about this or any cut-up is that it cannot be
analyzed according to the norms of the New Criticism – as we know,
one of the antagonists of the Beat project. In reading a cut-up, one can't –
and shouldn't – try to account for every word or phrase in terms of New
Critical "unity," since the very method throws unity out the window. Yet
the resulting language can still have meaning, and "Open Letter to Life
Magazine" does make a certain sense against O'Neil's original article,
which seems revealed as misinformed fluff that traffics in hollow "replicas"
rather than the real thing. Hence the opening image of the "terror in tin
ginsberg," suggesting that O'Neil's tin ear yields flimsy tin cut-outs of
Ginsberg that are merely imagined caricatures of him from a square point
of view – "Replicas of Squaresville." The piece proceeds, as Burroughs put
it in *The Third Mind*, to disconnect "the concept of reality that has been
imposed on us and then plugs normally dissociated zones into the same
sector" by deforming the semantic and syntactic regularity of the *Life*
article, which only serves to repeat, like pea-brained pigeons mimicking
each other, ungenerous and inaccurate received wisdom about the Beats. If
the cut-up is coherent, it is so in suggestive, imagistic bursts. For example,
O'Neil's critical posture, his "hideous professional crouch," seems
threatened by "the beat movement," which contorts things – bodies,
language – such that its "members" in North Beach become indistinguishable from an old man's sexual member. In its emphasis on "replicas,"
"Open Letter to Life Magazine" underscores the way in which the Beats
have been reproduced and disseminated according to the perceptions of
others, whether critics like O'Neil or those tourists who "come to stare" at
the supposed antics of the Beatniks: "Sockets stare dedicated in seamed
conferlinghetti of ginsbergs kerouacs & badly blown clarinet-shimmer off
the glossy bone." The ultimate effect of O'Neil's article is summed up in

one of the clearest fragments in the cut-up: "Exhibitionists abused Burroughs." This line came from cutting a passage about Burroughs with O'Neil's summative thoughts on the Beats: "They are talkers, loafers, passive little con men, lonely eccentrics, mom-haters, cop-haters, exhibitionists with abused smiles and second mortgages on a bongo drum – writers who cannot write, painters who cannot paint, dancers with unfortunate malfunction of the fetlocks."[29] In reading "Open Letter to Life Magazine," it's pretty clear that Burroughs felt abused by the way he was exhibited in the *Life* article, and comparing the pieces shows that the former inverts one of the latter's most invidious characterizations so that it is O'Neil, not the Beats, who becomes the true exhibitionist.[30]

What the cut-up method does is kick the question of authorial intention way down the road of meaning. Did Burroughs *intend* the meaning explicated above? Did it merely emerge accidentally via the cut-up method, and if so can it really be said to "mean" what I suggest? These are questions that cut-ups invite but never answer – they put readers into uneasy positions: in reading the previous paragraph, a fair response would be that I am reading too much into the *Life* magazine cut-up – and yet the reading makes intuitive sense, and is strangely fitting. In this way, the cut-up method unsettles reality not only with respect to the constructions in an article like "The Only Rebellion Around" – which makes claims to account for the real in ways obviously distorted by the author's distaste for the Beats – but also in the reader's experience of engaging cut-ups, which forces one onto unstable footing and into semantic uncertainties.[31]

CHAPTER 13

The Vietnam Effect

While Burroughs was busy distorting reality in garrets in Paris and London, the terms of reality back in the States seemed to be constantly shifting with the various narratives connected to the Vietnam War that were dominating cultural conversations. The war and attendant flowering of the underground into a widespread social and political phenomenon were indeed the events that had the most far-reaching impact on the direction of Beat writing in the 1960s. Looking back on the decade, Ed Sanders put it evocatively: "the war in Vietnam throbbed like an ever-seething soul sore. However much we partied, shouted our poetry, . . . we could never quite get the war out of our minds."[1] In such an environment, it became harder and harder to deny that "the personal is political," as the well-known feminist slogan went, and thus harder to view language, even as used in the putatively sacrosanct realm of poetry, as innocent of political exigencies. While in earlier years, the Beat movement was widely held to be apolitical, by the mid- to late 1960s, many Beats were channeling their aesthetic energies into work with explicitly political aims. That is, many – though not all – Beat writers invested themselves in causes ranging from antiwar activism, support for anticolonial regimes abroad and civil rights for racial minorities and gay people at home, free speech, marijuana legalization, the expansion eco-consciousness, and the ongoing campaign against nuclear proliferation.

Examples of such commitment are everywhere in Beat writing of the Vietnam era, as we saw for instance in *The Floating Bear*'s increasingly political content over the course of the 1960s. Other magazines that sprung up in the decade were founded on the premise that aesthetics and politics could not be untangled, notably the *Journal for the Protection of All Beings* (1961–1978), *Yeah* (1961–1965), and *Fuck You/A Magazine of the Arts* (1962–1965). *Journal for the Protection of All Beings*, jointly edited by Michael McClure, Lawrence Ferlinghetti, and David Meltzer, was intended to be an "open place where normally apolitical men may speak uncensored ... in a world which politics had made."[2] After *Birth*, Kupferberg launched *Yeah*, a magazine that published poetry alongside collages made from other kinds of language use: clippings from newspapers, magazines, advertisements, and the like. As he explained at the time, "As the editor of a satirical magazine, one of my tasks is to survey the daily press for items suitable for reprinting. The task of selection becomes harder and harder and I am often tempted to simply reprint the entire issue of the New York Times as the greatest satirical journal being published today. That is to say 'society' has become a travesty of itself."[3] In recontextualizing and printing language from the "daily press," Kupferberg extends the basic sensibility of the cut-up method, and to leaf through *Yeah* is to be hit in the face with an onslaught of what society deems acceptable, as in the collage titled "Are Our Leaders Suicidal Lunatics?" (see Figure 13.1). The political energy comes from the ironic juxtapositions which suggest social patterns of violence and intolerance, as in a line from one of the clippings: "One RAF man said they had all been told that

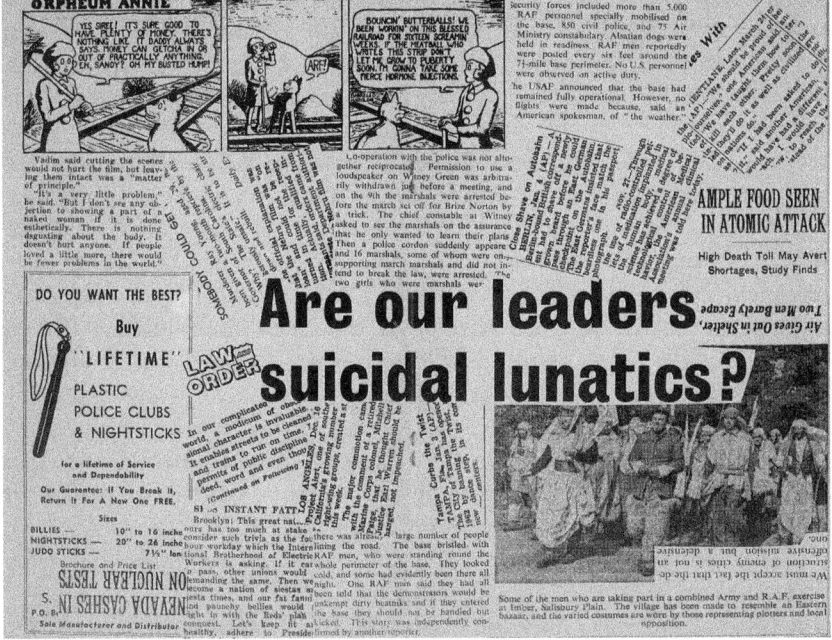

Figure 13.1   A typical collage of "daily press" clippings from Tuli Kupferberg's *Yeah* 2 (February 1962).
Image courtesy of Princeton University Library

the demonstrators would be unkempt dirty beatniks and if they entered the base they should not be handled but kicked."

Writers from di Prima to Ferlinghetti to McClure shared Kupferberg's sense that society had "become a travesty of itself," and were increasingly prone to writing work that directly engaged in political questions, especially as the Vietnam War dragged on and on – as Philip Whalen's "Dear Mr. President" put it in 1965: "Love & Poetry / Win – Forever: / War is Always / A Great Big Lose" (*Collected Poems*, 410).[4] During this era, Bob Kaufman took a ten-year vow of silence in protest of the Vietnam War. Diane di Prima edited the antiwar collection *War Poems* (1968). Kupferberg himself wrote *Fuck Nam: A Morality Play* (1966), in which language from the daily press punctuates a surreal farce that has characters breaking out in song: "You need napalm, and I need napalm, all de debil's chilluns need napalm, Stalin Johnson Hitler love their napalm, lovable lovable napalm."[5] Burroughs, always one to strike his own path, was living in Paris and London for much of the 1960s, and while his engagements with politics tended to remain in the realm of deforming language via cut-ups and related techniques, even he became involved with the counterculture's political activism when *Esquire* sent him to cover the 1968 Democratic National Convention in Chicago. The event became notorious for the particularly brutal way police engaged activists, and in an attempt to make sense of what was happening, Burroughs's *Esquire* piece proposed five issues that were especially pressing for those activists: the Vietnam War, "Alienated Youth," "Black Power," "Our Police and Judicial System," and "The Disappearing Dollar." Analyzing each of these issues, Burroughs claimed that "The youth rebellion is a worldwide phenomenon that has not been seen before in history. I don't believe they will calm down and be ad execs at thirty as the establishment would like to believe. Millions of young people all over the world are fed up with shallow unworthy authority running on a platform of bullshit."[6] Although Beat-associated writers and artists were only a part of this "worldwide phenomenon," throughout the 1960s, some played highly visible roles in this phenomenon or influenced the thinking of younger leaders who came to epitomize the decade's counterculture sensibilities.

The prominent exception in this regard was Kerouac, who in the 1960s struggled with the net of fame and moved to isolate himself from a world which seemed to make impossible demand after impossible demand. Over the course of the decade, Kerouac became increasingly conservative and an even heavier drinker, publishing books like *Big Sur* (1962) (about his battles with alcohol addiction intensified by his celebrity), *Desolation*

Angels (1965) (partly about his experiences around the time *On the Road* was published), and *Vanity of Duluoz* (1967) (a reevaluation of his early days with the libertine circle). In an essay published the month he died, "After Me, the Deluge," Kerouac unleashed a torrent of criticism on the contemporary incarnation of the counterculture, insisting that he was not "the great white father and intellectual forebear who spawned a deluge of alienated radicals, war protestors, dropouts, hippies."[7] If Kerouac's death in October 1969 symbolized the passing of an era – Neal Cassady had died the year before, walking down some train tracks in Mexico – he had already spent much of the 1960s distancing himself from those who would insist on collapsing the distinctions between aesthetic and political expression.

13.1 Countering the Black Magic: Ginsberg's Vietnam Era Poetics

Allen Ginsberg's journey in the 1960s, on the other hand, encapsulates broader changes in Beat literary production as many – though, as Kerouac demonstrates, not all – Beat-associated writers became increasingly politically engaged during the decade. In Ginsberg's case, a turn toward activist politics can be explained partly by his travels abroad, particularly to India, where he and Orlovsky spent fourteen months in 1962–1963. Thanks in part to his interactions with the so-called Hungry Generation, a circle of young Bengali poets in and around Calcutta whose work abandoned hard distinctions between poetry and political protest, when Ginsberg returned to the States in 1963, he embarked on a career of public activism that would make him one of the more well-known antiwar figures of the 1960s.[8] As suggested throughout this book, Ginsberg's poetry had often been laced with political undercurrents prior to this period, but in the Vietnam era, he devoted much of his energy to acts of highly visible public protest, and his poetry changed apace as he tried to find routes away from the corrupted language that politicians and the media used to justify what he considered an unjustifiable war. His two major collections of the era, *Planet News, 1961–1967* (1968) and *The Fall of America: Poems of These States, 1965–1971* (1972), showcase Ginsberg the political poet, and as such they are like a barometer of larger shifts in Beat writing toward the more avowedly political.

Ginsberg's 1960s-era poetry intervenes in political concerns by questioning how language means in ways directly inspired by what Burroughs and Gysin were doing with cut-ups. As in the example of the *Life* magazine cut-up, which exposes what Jon Savage has called the "stock phraseology and tired worldview of mainstream journalism," Ginsberg took the basic spirit of the cut-up method and applied it to what he took to be ethically dubious political rhetoric.[9] Consider, for example, these lines from "Kansas City to St. Louis" (1966) in *The Fall of America*:

> "Torture . . . tear gas legitimate weapons . . .
> Worries language beyond my comprehension" the radio
>   commentator says himself.
> Use the language today
>   ". . . a great blunder"
>   in Vietnam, heavy voices,
> "A great blunder . . . once you're in, uh,
>   one of these things, uh . . ."
> "Stay in." Withdraw,
>   Language, language, uh, uh
>   from the mouths of Senators, uh
>   trying to think on their feet
>   Saying Uhh, politely
>
> Shift linguals, said Burroughs, *Cut the Word Lines!*
> He was right all along.[10]

This is a good illustration of how Ginsberg's Vietnam-era poetry would sometimes incorporate language from political speeches, newspaper articles, radio advertisements, and the like, drawing it into a poem, the effect of which was not merely to question the distinctions between those linguistic fields, but to recontextualize public language, to reveal what it covers up. In these lines, the euphemistic language of "legitimate weapons" and "blunder" are isolated to expose the violence and destruction they conceal in plain sight, while attention to the filler word "Uhh" reverses the criticisms of those who would disparage the Beats for their degraded language. This particular stanza also draws a direct line to Burroughs's explication of the cut-up method (the phrase "cut the word lines" is found in *The Exterminator* [1960], among other places).[11]

Ginsberg had in fact always understood the cut-up method in starkly political terms, as a way to see through the fog of political rhetoric. As he later explained:

> if you take a speech by Nixon in which he's manipulating your mind and you cut up the speech and rearrange it, as Burroughs suggests, you find out what he is actually saying.... most writing, most political writing and journalistic writing, is manipulative in the sense that it is trying to convince you of something, some kind of bullshit, some hot air. If you want to make the manipulative phrasing of it stand out like a sore thumb, just cut it up and rearrange it. (*Best Minds*, 200–201)

Ginsberg adapts this aspect of cut-ups in numerous poems he wrote throughout the 1960s, notably, "These States, into L.A.," which strives to "Cut-Up

Sounds that fill Aether" (*Fall*, 13), "Hiway Poesy LA-Albuquerque-Texas-Wichita," "Chicago to Salt Lake by Air," and, most importantly, "Wichita Vortex Sutra." In these and other poems collected in *Planet News* and *Fall of America*, Ginsberg borrows the logic of cut-ups to radically recontextualize fragments of public language, stripping it down so its status as "manipulative phrasing" is exposed, an endeavor that began to crack the façade of reality built on the "planet thoughtwaves" of politicians and others in power.[12]

The specific place-names in these and other poems point to the fact that many were written as Ginsberg traveled through the Midwest in 1966 in a Volkswagen bus driven by Orlovsky, and as such can be viewed as a kind of rewriting of *On the Road* that attempts to capture where American culture was headed nearly twenty years after Kerouac had taken his road trips with Cassady. Writing with particular reference to "Wichita Vortex Sutra," Eliot Katz observes that "as Ginsberg notices and records newspaper headlines and radio commentaries, he also presents memories, analyses, and information which his empirical perceptions trigger. This technique of spontaneous recording exhibits a willingness to allow his poem to take its shape from its material, rather than fit his observations into a predetermined formal package."[13] By privileging his own "direct experience," Katz argues, Ginsberg reimagines who has authority to write a poem about the experience of war: traditionally, such authority was reserved for soldiers or others who had experienced war first-hand (think Wilfred Owen's great poem "Dulce et Decorum Est" [1917]), and yet Ginsberg subverts this notion and turns it inside out by capturing "the reality of an antiwar poet and activist experiencing the war through direct reception of mainstream media accounts" (143). This emphasis on Ginsberg's own "direct experience" with the fog of language propping up the war allows him to illustrate the effects of such language while simultaneously trying to undo it.

"Wichita Vortex Sutra," a twenty-three-page tour de force through the American heartland, is, in my view, Ginsberg's most successful poem of the 1960s. In it he reprises a mantra that he had written on his very first political protest sign:

> The war is language,
>   language abused
>   for Advertisement,
>   language used
>   like magic for power on the planet:
> Black Magic language,
>   formulas for reality.
>
> (*Planet*, 119)[14]

Although claiming "the war is language" may seem at first to trivialize the very suffering and absurdity that Ginsberg wants to witness, he elsewhere catalogues particularized instances of violence (such as site bombings or specific deaths) in "Wichita Vortex Sutra" and throughout *The Fall of America*. His primary interest, however, was in the rhetorical structuring of the war, a "Black Magic language" which he figures as corrupting reality itself, supplanting the real with deceitful, unethical representations. "Wichita Vortex Sutra" details exactly how Ginsberg sees this happening:

> Time Mutual presents
>   World's Largest Camp Comedy:
>   Magic in Vietnam –
> reality turned inside out
>   changing its sex in the Mass Media
>   for 30 days, TV den and bedroom farce
> Flashing pictures of Senate Foreign Relations Committee room
>   Generals faces flashing on and off screen
>   mouthing language
> State Secretary speaking nothing but language
> MacNamara [*sic*] declining to speak public language
>   The President talking language
>   Senators reinterpreting language.
>
>   (*Fall*, 120)

Ginsberg here unites those politicians responsible for policy decisions pertaining to the Vietnam War with "Mass Media" corporations ("Time Mutual") and outlets (TV) to suggest that the power of such language does not inhere only in the actual language itself – which Ginsberg has elsewhere shown is irrational, immoral, and self-contradictory at best – but in the widespread dissemination and subsequent cultural saturation of this language. Therefore what Secretary of Defense Robert McNamara, President Lyndon Johnson, and Congress are doing with language becomes the "planet thoughtwaves" that amount to global theater: the nod to the satirical styles of farces and camp comedies underscores Ginsberg's perceptions of this "reality turned inside out," which is nonetheless deadly serious, not only for the Vietnamese being bombed or US soldiers being killed, but also for ordinary Americans seemingly removed from the war in remotest Wichita, people who are in fact subjected to the warped reality that has framed the war as a political or military necessity. This is one of the poem's abiding claims, that if you buy into the "Black Magic language" underwriting the war, you are implicated in its perpetuation even while being physically removed from it.

With such claims about the power of language in place, the arc of "Wichita Vortex Sutra" moves from acknowledging "Black Magic language" to imagining a counter-language that Ginsberg himself can summon:

> I lift my voice aloud,
> > make Mantra of American language now,
> > > I here declare the end of the War!
> . . .
> Let the States tremble,
> > let the Nation weep,
> > > let Congress legislate its own delight
> > > > let the President execute his own desire –
> this Act done by my own voice,
> . . .
> The War is gone,
> > Language emerging on the motel news stand,
> > > the right magic
> > > Formula, the language known
> in the back of the mind before, now in black print
> > > > daily consciousness.
> > > > > (*Fall*, 127–129)

These are the most well-known lines from what is probably Ginsberg's most well-known poem of the 1960s: here the poet asserts the power to stop the war simply by declaring it so, a statement that may seem naïve or just plain dumb from a rational point of view. But this is precisely the point. Ginsberg later glossed this moment by saying that he had wanted to "counteract and ultimately overwhelm the force field of language pronounced out of the State Department and out of Johnson's mouth . . . Where they say 'I declare – We declare war,' . . . their mantras are black mantras. . . . They pronounce these words, and then they sign a piece of paper, of other words, and a hundred thousand soldiers go across the ocean. So I pronounce *my* word, and so the point is, how strong is my word?" (*Composed on the Tongue*, 46–47). Otherwise put, Ginsberg wants to deform and recontextualize language with a version of what Burroughs and Gysin were doing with cut-ups; and once this language is exposed as strange "black magic" – and what is stranger than signing a piece of paper and people being killed some 8,000 miles away? – he counters this with his own performative declaration that disrupts the "planet thoughtwaves" by flagrantly disregarding the version of reality these thoughtwaves circumscribe. While of course the war does not literally end with Ginsberg's declaration, the assertion does subvert the whole reality system by creating a context for thinking outside what he calls the "war psychology," and imagines a world that, as Katz puts it, is "mutable, potentially open to change" (232).[15] This stance, that the best way to protest the war was to simply stop playing the reality game as constituted by the "Black Magic language" of those in power, is what became more pervasive in the mid-1960s and after, with the widespread adoption of theatrical activist tactics that seemed to reject terms of "the real" itself.

13.2 Ed Sanders, Fuck You Press, and Theatrical Activism

Among the more influential inheritors of Ginsberg's performative and nonrational political activism was Ed Sanders, co-founder of the rock band The Fugs, proprietor of the Peace Eye Bookstore, and owner of Fuck You Press. Given his energy and eclectic interests, Sanders became a highly visible figure who helped adapt and change the Beat sensibility into the 1960s and after, largely through what he called "perf-po" or performance poetry. Born in Missouri in 1939, Sanders had made the move to New York by the late 1950s, and over the next decade fashioned himself into one of the lodestars of counterculture. Thanks in part to its provocative title, Sanders's *Fuck You/A Magazine of the Arts* (1962–1965) became one of the more notorious little magazines to emerge from the New York underground scene in the 1960s, and his work with The Fugs, which blended poetry and folk-rock, made him a minor celebrity in the counterculture burgeoning beyond the Lower East Side.

As Sanders explains in his memoir of the period, *Fug You* (2011), his literary "hero" at the time was Ginsberg – his "mentor" was Charles Olson – and he had memorized "Howl" back in the Midwest (3, 94). The two poets would later become lifelong friends, and in 2000, Sanders even published a book-length "narrative poem," *The Poetry and Life of Allen Ginsberg*, an admiring but thorough account of Ginsberg's life and achievements.[16] The opening of Sanders's memoir is framed by Ginsberg's influence on him, which has the effect of casting Sanders's own poetry and editorial work as the younger generation's extension of the Beat sensibility. Sanders explains, for instance, that he founded *Fuck You* after he had seen Ginsberg in a short independent film, *Guns of the Trees* (1961), directed by Jonas Mekas. The film is set in the Village hipster scene, and at one point Ginsberg chants the line, "I dreamt that J. Edgar Hoover groped me in a silent hall of the Capitol." This line struck Sanders as so evocative that he "transformed the fragment into the dedication for [his] soon-to-be published magazine" (4). This ever-mutating dedication read, in part, to "Pacifism, National Defense thru Nonviolent Resistance, Guerilla Love-fare, Anarchia the Goddess ... and all those groped by J. Edgar Hoover in the silent halls of Congress," thus advertising the magazine's political commitments as filtered through Ginsberg.[17] (And the line migrated: in Tuli Kupferberg and Robert Bashlow's *1001 Ways to Beat the Draft* [1966], the first item on the list is "Grope J. Edgar Hoover in the silent halls of Congress.")[18]

Fuck You grew from this kernel to become a self-conscious link between the Beat sensibility that flourished in the 1950s and the antiwar, civil rights–minded countercultural sensibility that flourished in the 1960s.[19] If being groped by Hoover was a metaphor for being violated by those powerful ministers of the national security state, Sanders's appropriation casts the sense of general violation into specific political positions. As discussed in Part I, similar pledges to pacifism stretched at least as far back as William Everson's *War Elegies* (1944) and the manifesto prefacing the work in *The Ark*, which set the stage for politically engaged work once Ginsberg and others came to San Francisco. Building on such work, *Fuck You* announced an explicitly Leftist, politically committed version of the counterculture, and purposively printed work of the earlier Beat cohort, including Ray and Bonnie Bremser, Burroughs, Cowen, Corso, Creeley, di Prima, Ferlinghetti, Ginsberg, Huncke, LeRoi Jones, Kaufman, Kandel, Kupferberg, Lamantia, McClure, Moraff, O'Hara, Olson, Orlovsky, Pommy Vega, Snyder, Solomon, Whalen, and Wieners (in the summer of 1964, Sanders also ran a reading series at Le Metro Café featuring the likes of Huncke and Solomon). The work *Fuck You* printed by these and other writers tended to focus on themes of free love, free speech, drug use, and other indices of the counterculture, and in the context of the magazine, work using taboo language such as Kandel's "to fuck with love – phase II" (which became part of *The Love Book* [1966]) or McClure's "Fuck Essay" ("FUCK, say FUCK, say Cunt, say SHIT. Say FUCK GOD as a holy prayer") are political acts insofar as they test the limits of free speech.[20]

Beyond work championing free love or relishing the use of expletives, many contributions to *Fuck You* were directly political, from Sanders's own "Song of the Eye-Heart Mind," written on the occasion of the "Nashville-Wash DC Walk for Peace" in 1962 (issue 3), and "Notes from *On Guerilla Lovefare*" (issue 4) to Kupferberg's "Pacifist Primer" ("All armies are asinine") (issue 3) and "Black & White Manifesto: Thoughts on the White Problem" (issue 5.5) to McClure's "Poisoned Wheat," an antiwar poem later issued as a stand-alone book (5.9). Issue 5.7 opens with Sanders's lengthy "Position Paper" titled "Resistance to Goon Squads," which excoriates "old line totalitarian fuckhaters ... who shudder at the thought of a guiltless freak-cock grooved into a moist cunt ... but love it when a bazooka blasts off the head of a gook in South Vietnam, *ARE STILL IN POWER*!!"[21] The use of explicit language and graphic sexual description is typical of the work in *Fuck You*, which as this line attests was often framed in terms of a broad opposition to the Vietnam War. "Resistance to Goon Squads" even offers specific tactics for antiwar activism, quoting at length from Ginsberg ("Generalissimo Allen Ginzap" of "the N.Y. Guerilla Assault Corps"), who says that "I still think *Gentle Mass Movements* on Times Square could end the Vietnam War. (Violence gives them an excuse to ban demonstrations)" (n.p.). In *Fug You*, Sanders includes numerous examples of direct political action such as a letter he wrote to Lyndon Johnson in 1964, in which he claims that "Allen Ginsberg and I, poets and residents of the lower east side of New York City," might be able to persuade 1,500–2,000 new voters to support him were his policies on Vietnam clarified to their satisfaction (93).

Sanders took Ginsberg's recommendation for theatrical, performative activism and ran with it, both as editor of *Fuck You* and in his own performance poetry that often doubled as activism. His first stand-alone publication, *Poem from Jail* (1963), was written in 1961 after he had illegally boarded a Polaris submarine in what he called a "Guerilla Love-fare peace set."[22] Written while serving a jail sentence for this act, the poem figures Sanders's experiences as representative of contemporary America's fascination with destruction and control: "I have crawled / thru the forest / near the Doom's Day Machine, / puking blood."[23]

In 1962, Sanders met Tuli Kupferberg when the latter was hawking copies of his little magazine, *Birth*. Sanders had recognized Kupferberg from his appearance in anthologies of Beat writing, and the two poets soon became friends and collaborators (*Fug You*, 107–108). Their most significant project together was the founding of The Fugs (named after the euphemism for "fuck" Norman Mailer had used in *The Naked and the Dead* [1948]), a band that was as apt to set William Blake's poetry to music as it was to belt out irreverent protest songs against the Vietnam War and other social and political issues.[24] Sanders later recalled that The Fugs were inspired by a "long and varied tradition going all the way back to the dances of Dionysus . . . and moving forward to . . . the *poèmes simultanés* of the Dadaists in Zurich's Cabaret Voltaire in 1916, to the jazz-poetry of the Beats, to Charlie Parker's seething sax" (ibid., 114). At first, The Fugs played in various small venues around New York City, including a "three day fug-festival" at the East End Theatre run by di Prima and her husband Alan Marlowe, but went on to release records – *The Village Fugs Sing Ballads of Contemporary Protest, Points of View, and General Dissatisfaction*

(Broadside, 1965) (later released by ESP-Disk as *The Fugs First Album*) and *The Fugs* (ESP-Disk, 1966) – and by 1968 were successful enough to tour Europe. But The Fugs were best known for their involvement in political demonstrations, and Sanders planned their first cross-country tour to coincide with the Vietnam Day Committee (VDC) demonstrations in Oakland in October, 1965. After driving across the country, stopping to pay homage to Burroughs's birthplace, The Fugs played numerous benefit concerts around the Bay Area that fall (ibid., 164–170). With songs like "Kill for Peace" and "CIA Man," The Fugs became perhaps *the* key example of theatrical protest that characterized the 1960s counterculture and antiwar activism.

Of course, the fact that Sanders and Kupferberg were performing their poetic protest in a rock band suggests the explosion of folk and rock music as vehicles for activism in the 1960s. While the varied ties between the Beats and these music scenes is too complex to pursue fully in the context of this book, it is generally accepted wisdom that the Beat sensibility was again picked up and transformed by many a musician, most notably Bob Dylan, who had come to New York from Minnesota thinking that *On the Road* was his "bible."[25] After meeting in the early 1960s, Dylan and Ginsberg became close, with Ginsberg famously appearing behind Dylan as he cycled through cue cards containing the lyrics of "Subterranean Homesick Blues" (1965) in the opening of D. A. Pennebaker's documentary about Dylan, *Dont Look Back* (1967) (the song's title was a nod to Kerouac's *The Subterraneans*). Dylan, who shared the Beat attitude that, as he put it, "mainstream culture [was] lame as hell" (35), became the musical voice of sixties counterculture with anthems such as "The Times They Are a-Changin'" (1964), which resonates enough with the sort of work discussed in this book that Ann Charters claimed it and others as Beat in *The Portable Beat Reader*.

From the Human Be-In in San Francisco in 1967, which featured the likes of Ginsberg, Ferlinghetti, Snyder, McClure, and Kandel alongside bands such as Jefferson Airplane and the Grateful Dead, to the National Mobilization Committee to End the War in Vietnam's plan to levitate and exorcise the Pentagon, a theatrical, pugnaciously irrational vision of protest took hold in the American counterculture that was inspired by or directly tied to the Beat sensibility. The Pentagon exorcism, for example, was intended to immediately halt the war, and although Yippie activists Jerry Rubin and Abbie Hoffman are often given credit for the demonstration, it was in fact Sanders who actually first conceived of it (while even the best account of this event, Norman Mailer's *Armies of the Night* [1968], notes that The Fugs served as "theatrical medium," it fails to say that Sanders authored a famous mimeographed declaration of exorcism).[26]

By the late 1960s, the Beat disaffiliation of the 1950s had given way to a kind of hyper-affiliation with ideas, attitudes, and language far beyond what Ginsberg called the "formulas for reality" underwritten by those in power, a shift that Rubin, for one, had traced back to Ginsberg's influence and his "pre-yippie, acid ideas."[27] In his widely read (and stolen?) *Steal This Book* (1971), Hoffman, like Rubin, took a page from Ginsberg by insisting that "Often the critical element involved [in political demonstrations] is the theater. Those who say a demonstration should be concerned with education rather than theater don't understand either and will never organize a successful demonstration."[28] These and other statements and stunts of the late 1960s Yippie era suggest the great distance between 1965, when Ginsberg would introduce ideas about language and theater descended from the Beat aesthetic, and 1971, when such public theater resolutely "OUTSIDE the war psychology," as Ginsberg put it, had become a core tactic of many strands of antiwar protest. The Beat sensibility, always mutating and adapting, had found another life in the 1960s incarnation of youth culture.

Coda

Other books remain to be written about what happened in the 1970s and after when the Beat sensibility fractured and morphed into different kinds of literary, cultural, and political expression – even as figurations of "Beat" never vanished entirely. Such books could indeed explore what exactly it means for "Beat" to not have vanished. I can imagine an obvious answer, which would inevitably include the idea that the Beats must be relevant because they are still popular, selling enough books and related merchandise that the Big Three, though dead, are somehow still releasing "new" uncollected work, while lesser-known figures are being recovered or discovered *because* they are labeled Beat. This sort of circular thinking may account for the admiring feature films, documentaries, websites, and festivals that continue to appear with some regularity, as well as small wonders like the Beat Museum, equal parts event space, reliquary, and gift shop, that opened in San Francisco in 2003. Remember that Bob Dylan, who had advertised his connections to and sympathies with the Beats on his early albums – notably *Bringing It All Back Home* (1965), the back cover of which has photographs of Dylan and Ginsberg symbolically modeling the same top hat – won the 2016 Nobel Prize for Literature, and you have good evidence of the movement's staying power.

On the other hand, I often encounter undergraduates who have never heard of Kerouac or Ginsberg or Burroughs, let alone others discussed in this book. Maybe this is because these writers, so transgressive to those born in the 1920s, seem passé and thus not particularly interesting to those coming of age in the 2020s. Such a paradox might point to the less obvious ways the Beats haven't vanished, that they can seem old hat precisely because they were successful influencers, that even those who have never heard of them are still their inheritors. This claim would elaborate something about progressive social attitudes, and show how the new consciousness rooted and took hold so that it flowered into contemporary consciousness. This version of the story would emphasize that the Beats were champions of individual liberties, that they were on the right side of censorship battles, and that they dared to write about things that seemed radical or even crazy at mid-century, but that are now relatively normal or mainstream.

Such a claim seems intuitively true not only regarding once-taboo topics like, say, same-sex relationships or drug use, but in the very idea that the self is an extravagant enough subject to sustain thousands of pages of writing (looking at you, Knausgaard). Indeed, think of the moment autofiction is having: this is a genre that, as Christian Lorentzen puts it, invites "readers to imagine they might be reading something like a diary, where the transit from real life to the page has been more or less direct. But that effect, whatever the truth of it, is an illusion."[1] It would be difficult to account for this trend – which is, incidentally, the special province of what we now call "literary fiction" – were it not for the Beats, who seemed to invite readers to experience nakedly evocative expressions of self, but whose pretenses to truth were, if not "illusory," then certainly more conflicted than they might first appear. And this elevation of a self always fussily concerned with its representation could easily a suggest a line from the Beats to not only autofiction but to popular culture as manifest in social media, which is predicated on the notion that the self must be presented at all costs. Or a line back to those last bastions of old-fashioned literary culture, poetry magazines: pick one up and you'll find the preponderance of work is searchingly personal, that it mines subjectivities via figurations of race, ethnicity, sexuality, and the like, markers of difference that allow the poet to articulate the self in obsessive nuance.

The final (ironic) inheritance of the Beats, then, might be that everyone can always have their say, which in turn means that hardly anyone is differentiated. It's not necessarily the case that the walls between the dominant culture and the underground have been permanently breached, but that those categories can't really make sense any more. Even in the 1950s, "dominant culture" was as fictitious a monolith as "the underground" – and yet it was still the case that in the States there were three major television networks and a handful of large publishing houses and distributors of national media, and consensus was widely believed to be a virtue. If free expression was guaranteed by the Constitution, there just didn't seem to be many outlets for such expression. This is why sociologist C. Wright Mills famously warned that American culture was drifting toward becoming a "mass society," where "far fewer people express opinions than receive them."[2] The Beats, of course, were never short on opinions, nor on ways to express them, and as they forged ahead with their writing, they did eventually infiltrate the big publishing houses and even television – or else they started their own presses or little magazines, launching new ways of distributing expression, which presaged the inexorable splintering of culture in our age of mass media and social media. As inheritors of that splintered culture, we now have seemingly unlimited ways to express opinions and articulate the self. While it isn't quite right to say our contemporary moment is the opposite of the one Mills worried about in the 1950s, the age of social media does seem like a perverse Beat utopia where nothing is taboo and we can all be celebrities in our own fictional universes.

Notes

Preface

1 Oliver Harris, *William Burroughs and the Secret of Fascination* (Carbondale: Southern Illinois University Press, 2003), 3.

Chapter 1 The Wild Outré Gang of Columbia Campus

1 Allen Ginsberg, *The Book of Martyrdom and Artifice: First Journals and Poems, 1937–1952*, ed. Juanita Liebermann-Plimpton and Bill Morgan (Cambridge, MA: Da Capo Press, 2006), 63.
2 Aaron Latham, "The Columbia Murder That Gave Birth to the Beats," *New York Magazine* (April 19, 1976): 41–53; quotation on 53; Bill Morgan, *The Typewriter Is Holy: The Complete, Uncensored History of the Beat Generation* (New York: Free Press, 2010), 1. In 2012, Latham debuted a play about the murder: *Birth of the Beats: Murder and the Beat Generation*. See also Ronald K. L. Collins and David M. Skover, *Mania: The Story of the Outraged & Outrageous Lives That Launched a Cultural Revolution* (Oak Park, IL: Top 5 Books, 2013).
3 For a discussion of how *Kill Your Darlings* represents the murder and those involved, see Fiona Paton, "Angel Tendencies and Gratuitous Acts: *Kill Your Darlings* and the Legacy of Lucien Carr," in *Beat Drama: Playwrights and Performances of the "Howl" Generation*, ed. Deborah R. Geis (London: Bloomsbury, 2016), 327–343.
4 Allen Ginsberg, *Howl: Original Draft Facsimile*, ed. Barry Miles (New York: Harper Perennial, 2006), 5. On one of Ginsberg's teachers calling "Bloodsong" "smutty," see Ginsberg, *Martyrdom*, 115.
5 Carr to Ginsberg (September 21, 1944), in Ginsberg, *Martyrdom*, 75.
6 Kerouac to Caroline Kerouac Blake (March 14, 1945), in *Selected Letters of Jack Kerouac, 1940–1956*, ed. Ann Charters (New York: Penguin, 1995), 86.
7 For a discussion of literary movements – including the Lost Generation and the Beats – as "generations," see Michael Soto, *The Modernist Nation: Generation, Renaissance, and Twentieth-Century American Literature* (Tuscaloosa: University of Alabama Press, 2004).
8 "I Wish I Were You" is published as an "Appendix" to *The Unknown Kerouac: Rare, Unpublished & Newly Translated Writings*, ed. Todd Tietchen and trans.

Jean-Christophe Cloutier (New York: Library of America, 2016). Although this unfinished work is attributed solely to Kerouac in *Unknown Kerouac*, Tietchen considers it still a collaboration with Burroughs, and notes that Kerouac credited Burroughs on the original title page (email communication with Todd Tietchen, October 15, 2017).

9 Jack Kerouac, *Visions of Cody* (1972; New York: Penguin, 1994), 201.

10 In the later, annotated version of "Howl," Ginsberg glosses the "great suicidal dramas" line quoted above by pointing readers to "a story told in Jack Kerouac's fiction, *Vanity of Duluoz*, Book 12, Chap. VIII" (*Howl: Original*, 133).

11 William S. Burroughs, *Interzone*, ed. James Grauerholz (1989; New York: Penguin, 1990), 85.

12 A prominent exception is Véronique Lane, who argues that *Hippos* reveals "seeds and signs of their [Kerouac and Burroughs's] later more experimental creative work" (Lane, *The French Genealogy of the Beat Generation: Burroughs, Ginsberg, and Kerouac's Appropriation of Modern Literature, from Rimbaud to Michaux* [New York: Bloomsbury, 2017], 25–26).

13 Carr to Ginsberg (October 24, 1962), in Michael Schumacher, *Dharma Lion: A Biography of Allen Ginsberg* (New York: St. Martin's, 1992), 720.

14 Ted Berrigan, "The Art of Fiction: Jack Kerouac," reprinted in *Conversations with Jack Kerouac*, ed. Kevin J. Hayes (Jackson: University Press of Mississippi, 2005), 60.

15 James Grauerholz, "Afterword," in Jack Kerouac and William S. Burroughs, *And the Hippos Were Boiled in Their Tanks* (New York: Grove Press, 2008), 186.

16 Michiko Kakutani, "When a Real-Life Killing Sent Two Future Beats in Search of Their Voices," *New York Times* (November 10, 2008): C7.

17 John Tytell, *Naked Angels: Kerouac, Ginsberg, Burroughs* (New York: Grove, 1976), 59. For an account of Kammerer's murder that argues that it was in fact Kerouac and Carr's increasing "closeness" that sparked the fatal argument, see Ellis Amburn, *Subterranean Kerouac: The Hidden Life of Jack Kerouac* (New York: St. Martin's Press, 1998), 86–90. Although he does not discuss *Hippos* at length, a goal of Amburn's book is to make a case for Kerouac's repressed homosexuality or bisexuality and its effect on his work.

18 Gerald Nicosia, *Memory Babe: A Critical Biography of Jack Kerouac* (1983; Berkeley: University of California Press, 1994), 127; Schumacher, *Dharma Lion*, 28.

19 Joyce Johnson, *The Voice Is All: The Lonely Victory of Jack Kerouac* (New York: Viking, 2012), 167.

20 Kerouac and Burroughs, *Hippos*, 161.

21 There is a large body of work concerning homosexuality in postwar American culture, particularly once the Cold War got underway and a "Lavender Scare" accompanied anti-Communist hysteria, as gay people were seen as especially susceptible to seductive foreign agents; see David K. Johnson, *The Lavender Scare: The Cold War Persecution of Gays and Lesbians in the Federal Government* (Chicago: University of Chicago Press, 2004), and Robert Corber, *Homosexuality in Cold War America: Resistance and the Crisis of Masculinity* (Durham, NC: Duke University Press, 1997).

22 In 1960, Kenneth Rexroth argued that "Duncan was, and still is, the undisputed leader" of "a whole new literary temper, a new way of writing and looking at life" (Kenneth Rexroth, "Robert Duncan," *San Francisco Examiner* [December 11, 1960]; see www.bopsecrets.org/rexroth/sfe/1960/12.htm#Duncan).

23 "Lonergan Alibi: Twisted Sex," *New York Daily News* (October 28, 1943): 1.

24 Robert Duncan, "The Homosexual in Society," *Politics* (August 1944): 210.

25 Frank S. Adams, "Columbia Student Kills Friend and Sinks Body in Hudson River," *New York Times* (August 17, 1944): 1, 13; quotations on 13.

26 Barry Miles, *Call Me Burroughs: A Life* (New York: Twelve, 2014), 112.

27 Arnold Prince, "Student-Slayer Wins Leniency," *Daily Mirror* (October 7, 1944): 5.

28 Maria Damon, *Postliterary America: From Bagel Shop Jazz to Micropoetries* (Iowa City: University of Iowa Press, 2011), 62.

29 Dick Hebdige, *Subculture: The Meaning of Style* (New York: Methuen, 1979), 3, 15.

30 John Clellon Holmes, "This Is the Beat Generation," *New York Times Magazine* (November 16, 1952): 22.

Chapter 2 Write for Them about Them Personally

1 See, e.g., Steven Belletto, "Introduction," *American Literature in Transition, 1950–1960*, ed. Belletto (New York: Cambridge University Press, 2018), 1–14; and David Lehman, *The Last Avant-Garde: The Making of the New York School of Poets* (New York: Doubleday, 1998), 10.

2 Alan Golding, *From Outlaw to Classic: Canons in American Poetry* (Madison: University of Wisconsin Press, 1995), 121.

3 Stephen Voyce, *Poetic Community: Avant-Garde Activism and Cold War Culture* (Toronto: University of Toronto Press, 2013), 4.

4 For more on this point, see Andrew Epstein, *Beautiful Enemies: Friendship and Postwar American Poetry* (New York: Oxford University Press, 2006), 17, 12.

5 Jimmy Fazzino, *World Beats: Beat Generation Writing and the Worlding of U.S. Literature* (Hanover, NH: Dartmouth College Press, 2016), 33.

6 Those versed in critical theory will recognize that Fazzino is relying on Gilles Deleuze and Félix Guattari's concept of the "rhizome," which, as they say, "connects any point to any other point, and its traits are not necessarily linked to traits of the same nature; it brings into play very different regimes of signs, and even nonsign states. The rhizome is reducible neither to the One nor the multiple" (Deleuze and Guattari, *A Thousand Plateaus: Capitalism and Schizophrenia*, trans. and foreword by Brian Massumi [Minneapolis: University of Minnesota Press, 1987], 21). Robin Lydenberg has claimed, "The closest American parallel to the radical theory of Deleuze and Guattari is the 'hipsterism' movement" (Lydenberg, *Word Cultures: Radical Theory and Practice in William S. Burroughs' Fiction* [Urbana: University of Illinois Press, 1987], 191 n. 12). See also Voyce, *Poetic Community*, 89.

7 Lytle Shaw, *Frank O'Hara: The Poetics of Coterie* (Iowa City: University of Iowa Press, 2006), 8.

8 Ann Douglas, "'Telepathic Shock and Meaning Excitement': Kerouac's Poetics of Intimacy," *College Literature* 27.1 (Winter 2000): 14.

9 See Paul Goodman, *Growing Up Absurd* (1960; New York: New York Review of Books, 2012).

10 Paul Goodman, "Advance-Guard Writing 1900–1950," *The Kenyon Review* 13.3 (summer 1951): 363, 366.

11 Mark McGurl, *The Program Era: Postwar Fiction and the Rise of Creative Writing* (Cambridge, MA: Harvard University Press, 2009), 230.

12 John Ciardi, "Epitaph for the Dead Beats," *Saturday Review* (February 6, 1960): 11–13, 42; quotation on 11.

13 Michael Davidson, *The San Francisco Renaissance: Poetics and Community at Mid-Century* (New York: Cambridge University Press, 1989), 5.

14 Kerouac to Ginsberg (late March 1952), in *Jack Kerouac and Allen Ginsberg: The Letters*, ed. Bill Morgan and David Stanford (New York: Viking, 2010), 158.

15 Kaplan Harris, "Black Mountain Poetry," in *The Cambridge Companion to Modern American Poetry*, ed. Walter Kalaidjian (New York: Cambridge University Press, 2015), 156.

16 For one account of the relationship between Black Mountain and the Beats that emphasizes a shared aesthetics and poetics of spontaneity, see Daniel Belgrad, *The Culture of Spontaneity: Improvisation and the Arts in Postwar America* (Chicago: University of Chicago Press, 1998), 123–124, 199–204.

17 Martin Duberman, *Black Mountain: An Exploration in Community* (New York: Dutton, 1972), 372–373.

18 See Charles Olson, *"Projective Verse vs. the Non-projective," Poetry New York* 3 (1950): 13–22.

19 Charles Olson, "Projective Verse," in Olson, *Collected Prose*, ed. Donald Allen and Benjamin Friedlander (Berkeley: University of California Press, 1997), 240.

20 Robert Duncan, "Early Poetic Community" (with Ginsberg), in *Allen Verbatim*, ed. Gordon Ball (New York: McGraw-Hill, 1974), 134; "Writing One's Body: Interview with Michael McClure," *Amerikastudien/American Studies* 32.3 (1987): 364; Joanne Kyger, *Strange Big Moon: The Japan and India Journals: 1960–1964* (1981; Berkeley: North Atlantic Books, 2000), 60. Little wonder, then, that Kerouac would later emphasize the importance of Olson's famously large body to his writing: "If I was six foot six," he remarked in 1967, "I could write anything, couldn't I?" (*Conversations*, 72).

21 Allen Ginsberg, "Improvised Poetics," in *Composed on the Tongue*, ed. Donald Allen (Bolinas, CA: Grey Fox Press, 1980), 40–41. See also Daniel Belgrad, *Culture of Spontaneity*, 196–221; W. T. Lhamon, *Deliberate Speed: The Origins of a Cultural Style in the American 1950s* (Washington, DC: Smithsonian Institution Press, 1990), 151–192; and David Need, "Spontaneity, Immediacy, and Difference: Philosophy, Being in Time, and Creativity in

the Aesthetics of Jack Kerouac, Charles Olson, and John Cage," in *The Philosophy of the Beats*, ed. Sharin Elkholy (Lexington: University of Kentucky Press, 2012), 195–210.

22 Ginsberg to Richard Eberhart (May 18, 1956), in *The Letters of Allen Ginsberg*, ed. Bill Morgan (Boston: Da Capo, 2008), 136.

23 See Duberman, *Black Mountain*, 386–393.

24 Robert Creeley, "On *Black Mountain* Review," in *The Little Magazine in America: A Modern Documentary History*, ed. Elliott Anderson and Mary Kinzie (Yonkers, NY: Pushcart Press, 1978), 248–261; quotation on 260.

25 Allen Ginsberg, "America," *Black Mountain Review* 7 (1957): 25–29; quotations on 29.

26 Olson, *Collected Prose*, 240.

27 Ginsberg to Kerouac (August 20, 1958), in *Kerouac and Ginsberg: The Letters*, 403. Edward Marshall, "Leave the Word Alone," *Black Mountain Review* 7 (1957): 38–51; quotation on 47.

28 William Lee [William Burroughs], "from Naked Lunch, Book III: In Search of Yage," *Black Mountain Review* 7 (1957): 144–148; quotation on 144.

29 Another important little magazine dating from this period that consciously fused Black Mountain and Beat aesthetics is *Measure* (no. 1, summer 1957; no. 2, winter 1958; no. 3, winter 1962), edited by poet John Wieners. I discuss Wieners and *Measure* in more detail later, but for now I would just note that as the first issue of *Measure* was in preparation, Ginsberg recognized that it was "trying to draw all threads together" – that is, the threads of Black Mountain and Beat aesthetics (Ginsberg to Robert LaVigne [June 8, 1957], in *Letters*, 154).

30 Davidson, *San Francisco*, 3.

31 Todd F. Tietchen, "On the Waldport Fine Arts Project and the Aesthetics of Estranged Being," *Mosaic: An Interdisciplinary Critical Journal* 42.3 (September 2009): 19–38; quotation on 21–22.

32 William Everson, *War Elegies* (Waldport, OR: Untide Press, 1944), n.p. This work appeared later in *New Directions* 9 (New York: New Directions, 1946) as William Everson, "Waldport Poems" (146–155). In 1951, Everson joined the Dominican Order and was known as Brother Antoninus until 1969; for representative work, see *The Crooked Lines of God* (1959), *An Age Insurgent* (1959), and *The Hazards of Holiness* (1962). See also *Benchmark & Blaze: The Emergence of William Everson*, ed. Lee Bartlett (Metuchen, NJ: Scarecrow Press, 1979).

33 Schumacher, *Dharma Lion*, 184.

34 See also *Circle* (1944–1948), a little magazine edited by George Leite, out of Berkeley, which also featured many of these writers, including Lamantia, Everson, Parkinson, Rexroth, Duncan, and Harold Norse; and *Contour Quarterly* (1947–1949), edited by Christopher Maclaine, also out of Berkeley, and featuring many of these same writers.

35 "Editorial," *The Ark* (spring 1947): n.p. [3]. Note that no editor is stated, but the "editorial board is open to all interested in active work on the ARK" (n.p. [2]).

36 See, e.g., Kenneth Rexroth, *An Autobiographical Novel* (1964; Santa Barbara, CA: Ross-Erikson, 1978), in which he notes of his circle, "All of us ... unlike the Proletarians of the Thirties, were interested in upholding and defending the rights and standards of the arts against the pretension of the pompous and ignorant bureaucracy, which is, probably by definition, characteristic of all Bolshevism" (208).

37 Eastside High School, *Eastside High School Yearbook* (Paterson, NJ: Graduating Class of 1943, 1943), n.p.

38 Allen Ginsberg, *Howl and Other Poems* (San Francisco: City Lights, 1956), 42.

39 Michael McClure and James Harmon, eds., *Ark II Moby I* (1956–1957), n.p.

40 Neeli Cherkovski, *Ferlinghetti: A Biography* (Garden City, NY: Doubleday, 1979), 79.

41 Tietchen, "Waldport," 36.

42 Lehman, *Last Avant-Garde*, 2.

43 Ann Charters and Samuel Charters, *Brother-Souls: John Clellon Holmes, Jack Kerouac, and the Beat Generation* (Jackson: University Press of Mississippi, 2010), 6.

44 Frank O'Hara, "Personism: A Manifesto," *Yugen* 7 (1961): 28–29.

45 O'Hara quoted in Brad Gooch, *City Poet: The Life and Times of Frank O'Hara* (New York: Knopf, 1993), 187.

46 Epstein, *Beautiful Enemies*, 30.

47 O'Hara, "Personism," 28.

48 Note also that *Lunch Poems* ends with one "dedicated to the health of Allen Ginsberg"; see Frank O'Hara, *Lunch Poems* (1964; San Francisco: City Lights, 2014), 67.

49 Frank O'Hara, "Personal Poem," *Yugen* 6 (1960): 51.

50 Allen Ginsberg, "The Visions of a Great Rememberer," in *Visions of Cody*, 410.

51 For an excellent interactive illustration of literary networks that transcend labels such as Beat and Black Mountain, see the "Networking the New Poetry" project: https://danowski.digitalscholarship.emory.edu/nnap/network/.

Chapter 3 Hipsters in the Zoo

1 Jack Kerouac, *On the Road* (1957; New York: Penguin, 1991), 54; William S. Burroughs, *Naked Lunch: The Restored Text*, ed. James Grauerholz and Barry Miles (New York: Grove, 2001), 3.

2 See, e.g., Ralph Gleason's review of *On the Road*, in which he calls Sal Paradise a "Broyardian hipster" ("Kerouac's Beat Generation," *Saturday Review* 41 [1958]: 75).

3 Anatole Broyard, "A Portrait of the Hipster," *Partisan Review* 15.6 (June 1948): 721.

4 LeRoi Jones, *The Dead Lecturer* (New York: Grove, 1964), 76.

5 Regina Weinreich, "Queer" (interview with William Burroughs), in *Burroughs Live: The Collected Interviews of William S. Burroughs, 1960–1997*, ed. Sylvère Lottinger (Cambridge, MA: Semiotext(e), 2001), 618.

6 Milton Klonsky, "Greenwich Village: Decline and Fall," in *The Scene before You: A New Approach to American Culture*, ed. Chandler Brossard (New York: Rinehart, 1955), 26. The essay originally appeared in *Commentary* in 1948.

7 John Clellon Holmes, "The Name of the Game," in *Nothing More to Declare* (New York: E. P. Dutton, 1967), 107.

8 See W. H. Auden, *The Age of Anxiety* (1947; Princeton: Princeton University Press, 2011). Note that the Beats had read "The Age of Anxiety"; see Jack Kerouac, *Vanity of Duluoz* (1967; New York: Penguin, 1994), 261. See also Irving Howe, "The Age of Conformity," *Dissent* (1954), and Alan Valentine, *The Age of Conformity* (Chicago: Regnery Press, 1954).

9 Peter Matthiessen and George Plimpton, "The Art of Fiction 5: William Styron," *Paris Review* 5 (spring 1954): 47.

10 Holmes quoted in Kerouac, *Selected Letters, 1940–1956*, 226.

11 Jack Kerouac, "Beatific," in *Portable Kerouac*, 568.

Chapter 4 The Rise of the Beat Novel

1 Tim Hunt, *The Textuality of Soulwork: Jack Kerouac's Quest for Spontaneous Prose* (Ann Arbor: University of Michigan Press, 2014), 34. My discussions of Kerouac build on Hunt's work, not only *Textuality*, but also his indispensible foundational study, *Kerouac's Crooked Road: The Development of a Fiction* (1981; Berkeley: University of California Press, 1996).

2 Allen Ginsberg, *The Best Minds of My Generation: A Literary History of the Beats*, ed. Bill Morgan (New York: Grove, 2017), 93–95. See also Nicosia, *Memory Babe*, 302–303.

3 Jack Kerouac, *The Town and the City* (1950; New York: Harcourt Brace, 1970), 115.

4 Robert Lowry, "Is This the Beat Generation?," *American Mercury* 76 (1953): 16–17. This article first appeared under the title "Don Quixotes without Windmills," *American Mercury* 71 (1950), but after Holmes's "This Is the Beat Generation" (1952) generated mild interest in the Beats, it was reprinted with the title reference that does not otherwise appear in the text. For more on the eccentric Lowry, who had glancing connections with the Beats, see James Reidel, "Robert Lowry," *Review of Contemporary Fiction* 25.2 (summer 2005): 46–83.

5 For more on this context, see George Cotkin, *Existential America* (Baltimore: Johns Hopkins University Press, 2003).

6 Marshall McLuhan, "The Psychopathology of *Time* & *Life*," *Neurotica* 5 (autumn 1949): 9; Seymour Krim, "Our Middle-Aged 'Young Writers': The Avant-Garde at a Dead End," *Commentary* 14.4 (October 1952): 339–344; quotation on 343. Kerouac was prescient in his rebuke of the *New Yorker* as it would later pan his books and run John Updike's satire of *On the Road* titled "On the Sidewalk" (*The New Yorker* [February 21, 1959], 32). For a later example of Beat-associated writers poking fun at the *New Yorker*, see Ed Sanders's *Fuck You/A Magazine of the Arts* 5.1 (December

1962), which features a parody of the *New Yorker* feature "Talk of the Town": Sanders appropriates the familiar *New Yorker* drawings and reimagines it as "Fuck You: The Talk of the Town."

7 Jack Kerouac, "Outline of Subsequent Synopsis," in *The Haunted Life and Other Writings* (Boston: Da Capo, 2014), 145.

8 Kerouac to Ginsberg (June 20, 1960), in *Jack Kerouac and Allen Ginsberg: The Letters*, 452. Kerouac pointed to these latter chapters in *The Town and the City* as evidence that he had published Beat material before others; as he complained to Ginsberg: "Oh yes, John Holmes they said in the *Times* that I was a disciple of his and [Anatole] Broyard and [Chandler] Brossard in 1952 (forgetting 1950 *Town and City* hipster chapters)" (ibid.).

9 Jonah Raskin, *American Scream: Allen Ginsberg's Howl and the Making of the Beat Generation* (Berkeley: University of California Press, 2004), 127; Hilary Holladay, *Herbert Huncke* (Tucson: Schaffner Press, 2013), 78–79.

10 See *Portable Kerouac*, 569–570.

11 For accounts of these first meetings, see David Sandison and Graham Vickers, *Neal Cassady: The Fast Life of a Beat Hero* (Chicago: Chicago Review Press, 2006), 77–80; and William Plummer, *The Holy Goof: A Biography of Neal Cassady* (New York: Paragon, 1981), 31–40.

12 See, e.g., Charles Jackson's *The Lost Weekend* (1944), and Nelson Algren's novel of morphine addiction, *The Man with the Golden Arm* (1949), which had recently won the National Book Award.

13 "H Is for Horse," *Time* (May 5, 1952): 120.

14 George Mandel, *Beatville, U.S.A.* (New York: Avon, 1961).

15 George Mandel, *Flee the Angry Strangers* (New York: Thunder's Mouth Press, 2003).

16 L.V., "Among the New Books," *San Francisco Chronicle* (July 27, 1952): 12.

17 George Mandel, *Flee the Angry Strangers* (Indianapolis: Bobbs-Merrill, 1952), 28.

18 Orville Prescott, "Books of the Times," *New York Times* (April 29, 1952): 25.

19 Chandler Brossard, "Tentative Visits to the Cemetery: Reflections on *My* Beat Generation," *Review of Contemporary Fiction* 7.1 (spring 1987): 7–8. The most useful critical work on Brossard is the special number of *Review of Contemporary Fiction* in which this essay appears; see, in particular, Steven Moore's "Chandler Brossard: An Introduction and Checklist" (58–86) and his wide-ranging "An Interview with Chandler Brossard" (38–57). A version of the former is reprinted in Steven Moore, *My Back Pages: Reviews and Essays* (Los Angeles: Zerogram Press, 2017), 452–485.

20 Miles, *Call Me*, 97.

21 See Grauerholz, "Afterword," in Kerouac and Burroughs, *Hippos*, 209.

22 Samuel Charters, "Chandler Brossard," in *The Beats: Literary Bohemians in Postwar America, Part I*, ed. Ann Charters (Detroit: Gale, 1983), 44.

23 Jacket copy for first edition of Chandler Brossard, *Who Walk in Darkness* (New York: New Directions, 1952), n.p.

24 Chandler Brossard, *Who Walk in Darkness* (1952; New York: Harrow Books, 1972), 114. Unless I am pointing to specific differences found in the

published 1952 edition, I will hereafter quote from the 1972, "suppressed original version" of *Who Walk in Darkness* since it better reflects Brossard's vision at the time of composition, and because it is readily available to interested readers.

25 Brossard, "Tentative," 23–24. Many reviewers thought that the most striking thing about the book was its obvious debt to Hemingway's *The Sun Also Rises*; see Schwartz and Isaac Rosenfeld, "Rough and Delicate," *New Republic* (May 5, 1952): 19. Recent scholars have echoed this assessment; see William Crawford Woods, "The 'Passed' White Negro: Brossard and Mailer at the Roots of Hip," *Contemporary Review of Fiction* 7.1 (spring 1987): 100.

26 Delmore Schwartz, "Fiction Chronicle: The Wrongs of Innocence and Experience," *Partisan Review* 19.2 (May–June 1952).

27 William Gaddis, *The Recognitions* (1955; New York: Penguin, 1993), 305. Moore mentions that Gaddis and Brossard were once roommates; see *My Back Pages*, 456.

28 "The Counterfeiters," *Time* (March 14, 1955), 112.

29 See "Chandler Brossard," *Review of Contemporary Fiction*, 178.

30 For a discussion of this history, see Steven Moore, *My Back Pages*, 454–457.

31 Brossard, *Who Walk in Darkness* (1952 edition), 7, 180.

32 Chandler Brossard, "Plaint of a Gentile Intellectual," in *Scene before You*, 88–89.

33 [John] Clellon Holmes, "Tea for Two," *Neurotica* 1.2 (summer 1948): 36–43; quotation on 43. All nine issues of *Neurotica* are collected in *Neurotica: The Authentic Voice of the Beat Generation, 1948–1951*, ed. Jay Landesman (London: Jay Landesman, 1981), which features an introduction by Holmes.

34 Jay Landesman, [Editorial Statement], *Neurotica* 1.1 (spring 1948), 3.

35 Jay Landesman, "Tales of a Cultural Conduit," in *Tales of a Cultural Conduit & The Nervous Set* (Richmond, UK: Tiger of the Stripe, 2006), 23. *Tales* is a useful if somewhat self-aggrandizing account of the cultural and literary circumstances of *Neurotica*'s founding. *The Nervous Set* is a novel that Landesman wrote in 1952 but didn't publish until 2006. It concerns his alter-ego in New York City and elsewhere in the late 1940s and early 1950s, and follows his courting of Jan (modeled on Landesman's wife, Fran), and his entanglements with other women. A generally slighter novel than the others discussed in this section, *The Nervous Set* is of interest for Landesman's perspective on the scene (its memorable ending has Jan being killed in an ambulance crash and the driver associated with rival literary circles: "Blood was dripping over a copy of the *Partisan Review* that was lying next to him, like a bible" [253]). Landesman used the title *The Nervous Set* later in the decade for an off-Broadway musical about Beatniks, produced in 1959.

36 Brossard, "Tentative," 24.

37 R. J. Ellis, "'Little ... Only with Some Qualification': The Beats and Beat 'Little' Magazines," *The Oxford Critical and Cultural History of Modernist Magazines: Volume II: North America 1894–1960*, ed. Peter Brooker and Andrew Thacker (Oxford: Oxford University Press, 2012), 1002–1003. See also Seymour Krim, "A Backward Glance o'er Beatnik Roads," in *The Little Magazine in America: A Modern Documentary History*, ed. Elliott Anderson and Mary Kinzie (New York: Pushcart, 1978), 325–337.

38 John Clellon Holmes, "July 4th Weekend 1948: Two," in *Representative Men: The Biographical Essays* (Fayetteville: University of Arkansas Press, 1988), 79.

39 Holmes quoted in Ann Charters and Samuel Charters, *Brother-Souls*, 64. Given his importance to Beat literature, there is a surprising lack of scholarship on Holmes. *Brother-Souls* is by far the most exhaustive account of his place in Beat literary history, and I've relied on it for my discussion of Holmes's introduction to the inner circle. The book is also useful as it quotes liberally from Holmes's unpublished journals and letters. For a general assessment of Holmes's role in the Beat movement, see, in addition to *Brother-Souls*, Robert Winford Bunce, "The Beat Vision of John Clellon Holmes," PhD diss., University of Mississippi, 1995. Alan Harrington's novel *The Secret Swinger* (New York: Knopf, 1966) covers some of the same events as *Go*, notably the death of Bill Cannastra, fictionalized as Bill Genovese (52–53). Note also that in *On the Road*, a character modeled on Harrington appears as Hal Hingham, a name borrowed from the protagonist of Harrington's first novel, *The Revelations of Dr. Modesto* (1955), a satire on mid-century conformity.

40 John Clellon Holmes, "Introduction," in Holmes, *Go* (1952; New York: Thunder's Mouth Press, 1997), xviii.

41 For a discussion of *Go*'s composition history in relation to *On the Road*'s, see *Brother-Souls*, 173–196.

42 G.M. [Gilbert Millstein], "The 'Kick' That Failed," *New York Times* (November 9, 1952): BR50.

43 Tim Hunt, "Interview with John Clellon Holmes," in *The Beat Journey*, ed. Arthur Knight and Kit Knight (*unspeakable visions of the individual* 8) (California, PA: unspeakable visions, 1978), 148. See also Gregory Stephenson's assessment of Agatson and Stofsky as the "poles of *Go* ... nihilism and vision" (Stephenson, *The Daybreak Boys: Essays on the Literature of the Beat Generation* [Carbondale: Southern Illinois University Press, 1990], 91).

44 Nicosia, *Memory Babe*, 342.

45 See Nicosia, *Memory Babe*, 342–343. Dennis McNally claims that Kerouac "reviled" *Go*; see *Desolate Angel: Jack Kerouac, the Beat Generation, and America* (New York: McGraw-Hill, 1979), 165.

46 Kerouac to Ginsberg (late March 1952), in *Kerouac and Ginsberg: The Letters*, 158.

47 John Clellon Holmes, "This Is the Beat Generation," *New York Times Magazine* (November 16, 1952): 10.

48 John Clellon Holmes, "The Name of the Game," in *Nothing More to Declare* (New York: E. P. Dutton, 1967), 107.

49 Ann Charters, "*Go* in 1952," in Holmes, *Go*, n.p.

50 Seymour Krim, "Afterword," in Holmes, *Go*, n.p.

51 Cynthia Hamilton, "The Prisoner of Self: The Work of John Clellon Holmes," in *The Beat Generation Writers*, ed. A. Robert Lee (London: Pluto Press, 1996), 117.

52 Cassady to Kerouac (July 3, 1949), in Neal Cassady, *Collected Letters, 1947–1967*, ed. Dave Moore (New York: Penguin, 2004), 118–119.

53 In a kind of coda to this earlier depiction of Cassady's domestic violence, in *Desolation Angels* (1965), Kerouac notes a moment in the late 1950s when Cassady was sentenced to prison for marijuana possession, but asserts that the "real reason" for this punishment was "I once saw him belt his daughter across the room . . . and that's why his Karma devolved that way" (Kerouac, *Desolation Angels* [1965; New York: Perigee Books, 1980], 364).

54 William S. Burroughs, *The Letters of Williams S. Burroughs, 1945–1959*, ed. Oliver Harris (New York: Penguin, 1993), 23.

55 See Harris, *Secret*, 65–67.

56 William S. Burroughs, *Junky: The Definitive Text of Junk*, ed. Oliver Harris (New York: Penguin, 2003), 139.

57 William Burroughs, "Introduction to the 1985 Edition," in *Queer*, 135. For a discussion of this claim, see Oliver Harris, "Introduction," in *Queer*, ix–xiii.

58 For an exhaustive account of *Junky*'s publication history, including an explanation of why the book has appeared with the title *Junkie* (1953), *Junk* (1977), and *Junky* (2003) for the 50th anniversary "definitive" edition, see Oliver Harris, "Introduction," *Junky*; Harris also describes the textual differences in these three editions. Over the last couple of decades, Harris has been absolutely tireless in sorting through the often-confusing textual histories of Burroughs's work, and Beat studies has benefited enormously from his meticulous archival sleuthing and editorial work, so we may now work from authoritative editions of *Junky: The Definitive Text of "Junk"* (2003), *The Yage Letters Redux* (2006), and *Queer: Twenty-Fifth Anniversary Edition* (2010) – all of which are, as Harris has shown, complexly interrelated. Thus while there may be legitimate reasons to approach these texts – and *Naked Lunch* – discretely and without reference to the "Beat context," for the purposes of this book I rely on Harris's editions and accordingly follow him in underscoring the importance of this context as well as the permeability of these various texts.

59 Burroughs to Kerouac (April 1952), in *Letters, 1945–1959*, 115.

60 See Harris, "Introduction," *Junky*.

61 Burroughs to Kerouac (March 26, 1952), in *Letters, 1945–1959*, 108.

62 Harris, "Introduction," xii. For references to "Bill Lee," see *Letters, 1945–1959*, 125.

63 Burroughs to Ginsberg (December 24, 1952), in *Letters, 1945–1959*, 145.

64 *Kerouac and Ginsberg: The Letters*, 189. This press release was never actually sent because Kerouac refused to lend his name to it.

65 See also the "hauser and o'brien" chapter of *Naked Lunch*, in which two detectives are tasked with tracking down William Lee in "the Hotel Lamprey. 103 just off B' way" (175). In *Go*, Albert Ancke, the character modeled on Herbert Huncke, complains, "I couldn't seem to score with anyone, not even my usual connection on One Hundred and Third Street" (236).

66 Note also that later in *Junky*, Lee contrasts his "generation" (124) to "The young hipsters [who] seem lacking in energy and spontaneous enjoyment of life. The mention of pot or junk will galvanize them like a shot of coke. They jump around and say, 'Too much! Crazy! Man, let's pick up! Let's get loaded.' But after a shot, they slump in a chair like a resigned baby" (123–124).

67 William S. Burroughs, "Introduction to the 1985 Edition," in Burroughs, *Queer*, ed. Oliver Harris (New York: Penguin, 2010), 128.

68 In 1985, Jennie Skerl argued that *Junky*'s depictions of the underground are an ironic critique of dominant culture, an argument that has since become widely accepted: "Deviant society mirrors the dominant society, exposing a predatory, amoral social order and individuals without 'character' or free will whose identities are wholly formed by needs and social functions" (Jennie Skerl, *William S. Burroughs* [Boston: Twayne, 1985], 28). In this reading, junk is the ultimate commodity, and to explore junk addiction is to explore the dehumanizing effects of capitalism, for as Lee observes: "The kick of junk *is* that you have to have it. Junkies run on junk time and junk metabolism.... You cannot escape from junk sickness any more than you can escape from junk kick after a shot" (81). A commodity that changes an addict on the cellular level, junk is so all-consuming that life telescopes into acquiring it, and this acquisition becomes the sole purpose in a junky's life. See also Timothy S. Murphy, *Wising Up the Marks: The Amodern William Burroughs* (Berkeley: University of California Press, 1997).

69 Oliver Harris, "Introduction," in William S. Burroughs, *Junky: The Definitive Text of "Junk"* (1953; New York: Penguin, 2003), xi.

70 Kerouac and Burroughs, *Hippos*, 21. James Grauerholz notes that Danny Borman is "based on 'Hoagy' Norman, or Norton," suggesting that Burroughs is referring to the same person in the opening of *Junky* (Grauerholz, "Afterword," in *Hippos*, 209).

71 Burroughs uses this technique throughout his subsequent work; see, to name a few examples, the "Lee's Journals" sections of *Interzone*, which open: "Lee's face, his whole person, seemed at first glance completely anonymous. He looked like an FBI man, like anybody" (63); *Naked Lunch*, in which "Bradley the Buyer," the "Best narcotics agent in the industry. Anyone would make him for junk," declares, "Squares on both sides. I am the only complete man in the industry" (14–15); and *The Soft Machine* (New York: Grove, 1966), in which Lee says, "I am a public agent and don't know who I work for" (31).

72 Burroughs to Ginsberg (April 26, 1952), in *Letters, 1945–1959*, 122; Burroughs to Ginsberg (March 20, 1952), 105.

73 William S. Burroughs, *Queer*, ed. and intro Oliver Harris (New York: Penguin, 2010), 65.

74 Ted Morgan, *Literary Outlaw: The Life and Times of William S. Burroughs* (1988; New York: Avon Books, 1990), 185–187; Miles, *Call Me*, 197–198. Note that Morgan only refers to Marker as the pseudonymous Allerton.

75 Alan Ansen, "Anyone Who Can Pick Up a Frying Pan Owns Death," *Big Table* 2 (summer 1959): 39.

76 For a discussion of the complex origins of *The Yage Letters*, see Oliver Harris, "Introduction," in William Burroughs and Allen Ginsberg, *The Yage Letters Redux*, ed. Harris (San Francisco: City Lights, 2006), ix–lii.

77 For other examples, see *Queer*, 46, 50.

78 Barry Miles writes that "Marker was not homosexual ... had never been enthusiastic about the sexual aspect of their relationship, but he ... found Bill's exaggerated humor funny" (*Call Me*, 198).

79 See Johnson, *The Lavender Scare*; Corber, *Homosexuality in Cold War America*; and Michael Davidson, *Guys Like Us: Citing Masculinity in Cold War Poetics* (Chicago: University of Chicago Press, 2004). In *Interzone*, Burroughs offers a pithy list of enemies of the American state: "communism, queers, drug addicts" (123). *Naked Lunch* features "Dr. Berger's Mental Health Hour" (114), which boasts a "cured homosexual" (115); Dr. Berger is a reference to psychoanalyst Edmund Bergler, author of *Homosexuality: Disease or Way of Life?* (New York: Hill and Wang, 1956).

80 Burroughs to Ginsberg (March 20, 1952), in *Letters, 1945–1959*, 105–106.

81 Burroughs to Ginsberg (April 22, 1952), in *Letters, 1945–1959*, 119–120.

82 Such a technique might lead logically to Dr. Benway's perverse claims in *Naked Lunch*: "You can make a square heterosex citizen queer with this angle ... that is, reinforce and second his rejection of normally latent homosexual trends – at the same time depriving him of cunt and subjecting him to homosexual stimulation" (*Naked Lunch*, 24, ellipses in original).

83 The question of Burroughs's imperial tendencies is an important one, but I will nonetheless refrain from exploring it in depth in this book. Oliver Harris, for one, suggests that "Burroughs played the Ugly American ambiguously, at times blind to its operation, at others holding the identity up for coruscating critique" ("Introduction," *Yage Letters Redux*, xxx). See also Brian T. Edwards, *Morocco Bound: Disorienting America's Maghreb, from Casablanca to the Marrakech Express* (Durham, NC: Duke University Press, 2005), 158–197; Allen Hibbard, "William S. Burroughs and U.S. Empire," in *The Transnational Beat Generation*, ed. Nancy M. Grace and Jennie Skerl (New York: Palgrave, 2012), 15–30; and Eric Strand, "The Last Frontier: Burroughs's Early Work and International Tourism," *Twentieth Century Literature* 59.1 (spring 2013): 1–36.

84 James Grauerholz, "Introduction," in William Burroughs, *Interzone*, ed. Grauerholz (New York: Viking Penguin, 1999), x. This introduction offers a valuable overview of *Interzone*'s contents, as well as its publication history, including its relationship to *Naked Lunch*; see also Jimmy Fazzino, *World Beats*, 128–161.

85 Burroughs to Kerouac (August 18, 1954), *Letters, 1945–1959*, 227; Burroughs to Ginsberg (September 29, 1957), 367.

86 For a useful summary of *Naked Lunch* criticism up to 2009, see Jennie Skerl, "The Book, the Movie, the Legend: *Naked Lunch* at 50," in *Naked Lunch@50: Anniversary Essays*, ed. Oliver Harris and Ian MacFayden (Carbondale: Southern Illinois University Press, 2009), 168–171. This is an updated and more compact version of some insights found in Jennie Skerl and Robin Lydenberg, *William S. Burroughs at the Front: Critical Reception, 1959–1989* (Carbondale: Southern Illinois University Press, 1991). Note that, in contrast to the critical tradition sketched above, other critics have emphasized *Naked Lunch*'s literary ancestors; Barry Miles, for example, underscores that the "book uses the oldest format in the world, the picaresque" (*Call Me*, 352).

87 Robin Lydenberg, *Word Cultures*, xi. See also Gilles Deleuze and Félix Guattari, *A Thousand Plateaus*.

88 See also Murphy, *Wising Up*, 77.

89 Oliver Harris, "The Beginnings of '*Naked Lunch*, an Endless Novel,'" in *Naked Lunch@50*, 14.

90 William S. Burroughs, "Deposition: Testimony Concerning a Sickness," in *Naked Lunch: The Restored Text*, 199.

91 Like many Burroughs texts, *Naked Lunch* has an unusually complex material history. Excerpts from *Naked Lunch* were first published in *Black Mountain Review* 7 (1957), *Yugen* 3 (1958), and *Big Table* 1 (1959). The true first edition was *The Naked Lunch* (Paris: Olympia Press, 1959) (note the definite article), which was different from the first American edition: *Naked Lunch* (New York: Grove, 1962). In 2001, Grove published "the restored text," edited by James Grauerholz and Barry Miles. Rather than detail the differences from edition to edition, for our present purposes, I quote from this restored version and treat it as a bounded text – with the caveat that it isn't exactly the same as the 1959 or 1962 versions, a fact that underscores *Naked Lunch*'s mutations over time. For an account of the book's genesis and publication history, see James Grauerholz and Barry Miles, "Editor's Note," in William S. Burroughs, *Naked Lunch: The Restored Text*, 233–248.

92 Murphy, *Wising Up*, 4; see also 76–77.

93 See Michael Sean Bolton, *Mosaic of Juxtaposition: William S. Burroughs' Narrative Revolution* (Amsterdam: Rodopi, 2014).

94 Corso to Ginsberg (October 11, 1959), in *An Accidental Autobiography: The Selected Letters of Gregory Corso*, ed. Bill Morgan (New York: New Directions, 2003), 217.

95 Norman Mailer, *Advertisements for Myself* (1959; Cambridge, MA: Harvard University Press, 1992), 472. In 1962, Mary McCarthy wrote a famously positive review; see "Burroughs' *Naked Lunch*," in *The Writing on the Wall* (New York: Harcourt Brace, 1970), 42–53.

96 Ann Charters, "Introduction," in Jack Kerouac, *On the Road* (1957; New York: Penguin, 1999), ix.

97 Kerouac, *On the Road,* jacket copy. For a discussion of the internal debates at Viking regarding the merits of *On the Road,* see James Campbell, *This Is the Beat Generation: New York – San Francisco – Paris* (Berkeley: University of California Press, 2001), 162–167.

98 Gilbert Millstein, "Books of the Times" (review of *On the Road*), *New York Times* (September 5, 1957): 27.

99 See Ann Douglas, "Telepathic Shock."

100 See, e.g., R. J. Ellis, *"Liar, Liar": Jack Kerouac – Novelist* (London: Greenwich Exchange, 1999); Michael Hrebeniak, *Action Writing: Jack Kerouac's Wild Form* (Carbondale: Southern Illinois University Press, 2006); Nancy M. Grace, *Jack Kerouac and the Literary Imagination* (New York: Palgrave, 2007); and Tim Hunt, *Kerouac's Crooked Road* and *The Textuality of Soulwork,* all of which analyze *On the Road* in the context of Kerouac's other work.

101 Matt Theado, "Revisions of Kerouac: The Long, Strange Trip of the *On the Road* Typescripts," in *What's Your Road, Man? Critical Essays on Jack Kerouac's on the Road,* ed. Hilary Holladay and Robert Holton (Carbondale: Southern Illinois University Press, 2009), 11.

102 Isaac Gewirtz, *Beatific Soul: Jack Kerouac on the Road* (New York: New York Public Library, 2007), 76.

103 Selections from this vast archive have been published in Jack Kerouac, *Windblown World: The Journals of Jack Kerouac, 1947–1954,* ed. Douglas Brinkley (New York: Penguin, 2004); and Jack Kerouac, *The Unknown Kerouac: Rare, Unpublished, & Newly Translated Writings,* ed. Todd Tietchen and trans. Jean-Christopher Cloutier (New York: Library of America, 2016). Where possible, I quote from these sources so readers may more easily locate the references.

104 On Kerouac's use of spontaneity, see, in addition to Hunt, Regina Weinreich, *Kerouac's Spontaneous Poetics: A Study of the Fiction* (New York: Thunder's Mouth Press, 1987); Hrebeniak, *Action Writing*; Joyce Johnson, *The Voice Is All*; and Hassan Melehy, *Kerouac: Language, Poetics, and Territory* (New York: Bloomsbury, 2016).

105 Tim Hunt, *Textuality,* 2.

106 Jack Kerouac, "Essentials of Spontaneous Prose," in *Portable Kerouac,* 485.

107 Another significant novel Kerouac composed around this time was *Doctor Sax* (written 1952; published 1959), a strange, dreamy book inspired by his boyhood in Lowell. For a useful discussion of *Doctor Sax*'s importance in the context of Kerouac's development as a writer, see Fiona Paton, "Reconceiving Kerouac: Why We Should Teach *Doctor Sax*," in *The Beat Generation: Critical Essays,* ed. Kostas Myrsiades (New York: Peter Lang, 2002), 121–153.

108 See Gewirtz, *Beatific Soul,* 123; the bracketed words are written over in pencil in the typescript.

109 Jack Kerouac, *On the Road: The Original Scroll,* ed. Howard Cunnell (New York: Viking, 2007), 110.

110 Kerouac elaborated this description in *Visions of Cody*, calling the Cassady figure (now named Cody) "a Nietzchean hero of the pure snowy wild West" (338). Ginsberg, who had read both *On the Road* and *Visions of Cody* in manuscript, picked up on this depiction of Cassady as "hero" in his 1953 poem "The Green Automobile," which reads, in part: "Neal, we'll be real heroes now" (*Collected Poems*, 94).

111 See, e.g., Hunt, *Kerouac's Crooked Road*, which begins from the premise that Kerouac "deliberately exploits the naiveté of his narrator" (3); Melehy, who, following Hunt, calls Sal a "dreamy, Candide-like naïf" (69); and R. J. Ellis, "Jack Kerouac's *On the Road* and Visions of Cody," *in* The Beat Generation Writers, *203*.

112 Nancy M. Grace, *Jack Kerouac*, 82.

113 Joan Haverty Kerouac, *Nobody's Wife: The Smart Aleck and the King of the Beats* (Berkeley: Creative Arts, 1990), 202–203. It is illuminating to compare *On the Road* to "The Mexican Girl": although the basic plots are the same, there are some key changes, notably with respect to how Kerouac underscores Sal's exoticization of Terry insofar as she wears "dark glasses with authority" but also has a "noble nose, almost hawk-like Indian nose ... and Aunt Jemima Skirt teeth, mud nowhere on her but was imprinted in the pigment of the Mongol skin" ("The Mexican Girl," *Paris Review* 11 [winter 1955]: 11–32; quotation on 18). Here Terry's status as a hipster – marked by her authoritative sunglasses – is connected to her exotic physical features which Kerouac has Sal associate with racial caricature, a metaphor that resonates with Sal's later romanticization of cotton-picking slaves in *On the Road*, echoed also by the mud imprinted on Terry's skin, making it both literally and figuratively darker. Kerouac made these and other changes to the original scroll manuscript but elected not to incorporate them into the published version of *On the Road*.

114 See, e.g., Manuel Luis Martinez, *Countering the Counterculture: Rereading Postwar American Dissent from Jack Kerouac to Tomás Rivera* (Madison: University of Wisconsin Press, 2003), 89; María Josefina Saldaña-Portillo, "'On the Road' with Che and Jack: Melancholia and the Legacy of Colonial Racial Geographies in the Americas," *New Formations* 47 (2002): 87–108; and Rachel Ligairi, "When Mexico Looks like Mexico: The Hyperrealization of Race and the Pursuit of the Authentic," in Holladay and Holton, *What's Your Road*, 139–154.

115 Note, e.g., how Martinez assumes a collapse of author and narrator: "Kerouac/Paradise jettisons the Mexican girl, her family, and his wish to be Mexican when a communal domesticity threatens" (*Countering*, 96).

116 Burroughs to Ginsberg (November 30, 1948), in *Letters, 1945–1959*, 25.

117 James Baldwin famously called *On the Road*'s romanticization of black people "absolute nonsense"; see James Baldwin, "The Black Boy Looks at the White Boy," in *Collected Essays* (New York: Library of America, 1998), 278.

118 For a detailed discussion of Kerouac's racial politics, see Melehy, *Kerouac: Language, Poetics, Territory*, 7, 66, passim.

119 When *On the Road* was still forthcoming, Kerouac published the section about the Mexican brothel under the title "A Billowy Trip in the World," in *New Directions in Prose and Poetry 16*, ed. James Laughlin (New York: New Directions, 1957), 93–105.

120 Ann Charters, *Kerouac: A Biography* (1973; New York: St. Martin's, 1994), 124–125. The full eighteen-page letter was presumed lost for about sixty years, but it resurfaced in 2017 and is now housed at Emory University. As of this writing, the complete 16,000-word letter has not been published, but an excerpt has been public since 1964, when it appeared in the little magazine *Notes from the Underground* 1 (1964), and made more widely available when it was included as one of the "fragments" appended to Cassady's unfinished autobiography, *The First Third* (San Francisco: City Lights, 1971), 145–160; see also *Neal Cassady: Collected Letters, 1944–1967*, 244–255; and *The Portable Beat Reader*, 197–208. The letter's freewheeling style is particularly striking in contrast to the comparatively staid prose of *The First Third*. For a discussion of how the letter was lost, see Dave Moore's note in *Neal Cassady: Collected Letters*, 244 n. 61 (but note Moore was writing before the letter's rediscovery). The feature film *The Last Time I Committed Suicide* (1997) is based on incidents described in the letter.

121 Cassady to Kerouac (December 17, 1950) ["Joan Anderson Letter"], in *Neal Cassady: Collected Letters*, 251.

122 Kerouac later referred to both *On the Road* and *The Dharma Bums* as "real muscular prose" (*Selected Letters, 1957–1969*, 87).

123 Kerouac, "Essentials of Spontaneous Prose," in *Portable Kerouac*, 484.

124 Two classic discussions of Kerouac's spontaneous prose are Warren Tallman's "Kerouac's Sound" (1959), reprinted in *Beat Down Your Soul*, 545–560; and George Dardess, "The Logic of Spontaneity: A Reconsideration of Kerouac's 'Spontaneous Prose Method,'" *boundary 2* 3.3 (spring 1975): 729–746. Outstanding recent discussions of spontaneous prose include Tim Hunt's *The Textuality of Soulwork* and Michael Hrebeniak's *Action Writing*.

125 Jack Kerouac, *Lonesome Traveler* (1960; New York: Grove, 1988), 37.

126 Kerouac to Sterling Lord (March 4, 1957), in *Selected Letters, 1957–1969*, 11.

127 Ginsberg to Kerouac (June 12, 1952), in *Kerouac and Ginsberg: The Letters*, 176–177.

128 See Jack Kerouac, *Visions of Cody* (New York: New Directions, 1960) (this book was printed in December 1959, so sometimes the publication date is given as 1959); and Kerouac, "Manhattan Sketches," in *The Moderns: An Anthology of New Writing in America*, ed. LeRoi Jones (New York: Corinth, 1963), 266–277. Kerouac tried, unsuccessfully, to publish the complete *Visions of Cody* all through his later life; see, e.g., Kerouac to Ginsberg (June 4, 1968), in *Selected Letters, 1957–1969*, 452.

129 Allen Ginsberg, "The Visions of a Great Rememberer," *Visions of Cody*, 427.

130 Ginsberg to Kerouac (June 12, 1952), *Kerouac and Ginsberg: The Letters*, 177.

131 For detailed analyses of how these opening sketches work, see Weinreich, *Kerouac's Spontaneous Prose*, 62–73; and W. T. Lhamon, *Deliberate Speed*, 159–161.

132 Tim Hunt offers an excellent analysis of this part; see *Textuality*, 118–127.

133 I discuss this moment at some length in "Kerouac His Own Historian: *Visions of Cody* and the Politics of Historiography," *Clio* 37 (spring 2008): 193–218. See also James Riley, "'I Am a Recording Angel': Jack Kerouac's *Visions of Cody* and the Recording Process," *Electronic Book Review* (19 December 2006), http://electronicbookreview.com/essay/i-am-a-recording-angel-jack-kerouacs-visions-of-cody-and-the-recording-process/; and John Shapcott, "'I Didn't Punctuate It': Locating the Tape and Text of Jack Kerouac's *Visions of Cody* and *Doctor Sax* in a Culture of Improvisation," *Journal of American Studies* 36.2 (2002): 231–248.

134 *Pull My Daisy*, text ad-libbed by Jack Kerouac for the film by Robert Frank and Alfred Leslie (New York: Grove, 1961), 27.

135 For more detailed discussions of Kerouac's use of allusion in *Visions of Cody*, see Hrebeniak, *Action Writing*, passim.

136 For another analysis of why Kerouac follows the Stooges section with an Eliot quotation, see Ellis, "Jack Kerouac," 54–55.

Chapter 5 The Rise of Beat Poetry

1 Donald Allen, "Preface," in *The New American Poetry*, ed. Allen (New York: Grove, 1960), xi.

2 For discussions of *The New American Poetry* as an oppositional volume – and the critical problems that attend such a view – see John R. Woznicki, "The New American Poetry: Fifty Years Later," in *The New American Poetry Fifty Years Later*, ed. Woznicki (Bethlehem, PA: Lehigh University Press, 2014), 1–14; and Alan Golding, "The New American Poetry Revisited, Again," *Contemporary Literature* 39.2 (summer 1998): 180–211.

3 On this point, see Ben Lee, "LeRoi Jones/Amiri Baraka and the Limits of Open Form," *African American Review* 37.2–3 (June 2003): 371–387.

4 Robert Lowell, "Robert Lowell, Winner of the 1960 Poetry Award for Life Studies," National Book Foundation, www.nationalbook.org/robert-lowells-accepts-the-1960-national-book-awards-in-poetry-for-life-studies/. For a discussion of Lowell's dichotomy in the context of the Beats, see Fiona Paton, "The Beat Movement," in *American Literature in Transition, 1950–1960*, 228.

5 Schumacher, *Dharma Lion*, 140.

6 Marianne Moore to Ginsberg (July 4, 1952), in *On the Poetry of Allen Ginsberg*, ed. Lewis Hyde (Ann Arbor: University of Michigan Press, 1984), 14. See Schumacher, *Dharma Lion*, 142–143.

7 For a discussion of the relationship between Williams's work and Ginsberg's, see Alexandre Ferrere, "Mechanics and Poetics: William Carlos Williams and

Allen Ginsberg," *Beatdom* (March 24, 2018), www.beatdom.com/mechanics-poetics-william-carlos-williams-allen-ginsberg/#_ftnref15.

8 Louis Simpson, *A Revolution in Taste* (New York: Macmillan, 1978), 65.

9 For Ginsberg's further thoughts on these two poems, see *Best Minds*, 371–378.

10 For a detailed analysis of Williams's triadic line, see Eleanor Berry, "William Carlos Williams' Triadic-Line Verse: An Analysis of Its Prosody," *Twentieth Century Literature*, 35.3 (autumn 1989): 364–388.

11 Allen Ginsberg, "Foreword," in *The Beat Book: Writings from the Beat Generation*, ed. Anne Waldman (Boston: Shambala, 1999), xiv.

12 Poet Elise Cowen was by the mid-1950s associated with the Beat circle, and became infatuated with Ginsberg, referencing "green automobiles" in at least two poems, likely as a way to signal her dismay at Ginsberg's crush on Cassady. See, in particular, "I Had a Dream of Mercy," in Cowen, *Poems and Fragments*, ed. Tony Trigilio (Boise: Ahsahta Press, 2014), 88.

13 For discussions of Orlovsky's life and his writing in the context of the Beat movement, see Ann Charters, "Peter Orlovsky," in *The Beats*, 433–439; Charters, "Foreword," in *Peter Orlovsky: A Life in Words*, ed. Bill Morgan (Boulder: Paradigm Publishers, 2014), xi–xix; and Bill Morgan, "Introduction," in *Peter Orlovsky*, xxiii–xxxi. I have drawn on these sources for my brief sketch of Orlovsky's life; beyond this work, there is very little scholarship on Orlovsky's writing as such. Note also that Robert Frank's film *Me and My Brother* (1969) stars (and is about) Orlovsky and his brother Julius.

14 See also Allen Ginsberg and Peter Orlovsky, *Straight Hearts' Delight: Love Poems and Selected Letters*, ed. Winston Leyland (San Francisco: Gay Sunshine Press, 1980).

15 Alfred Aronowitz, "The Beat Generation, Part IV," *New York Post* (March 12, 1959): 22.

16 Paul O'Neil, "The Only Rebellion Around," *Life* (November 30, 1959): 114–116ff.; quotation on 123.

17 Kerouac to Ginsberg, Orlovsky, and Corso (December 10, 1957), in *Selected Letters, 1957–1969*, 88; Ray Bremser, "Biographical Notes," in *The New American Poetry*, 428.

18 "Editorial," *Wagner Literary Magazine* (spring 1959): 2–7; quotation on 3.

19 Peter Orlovsky, *Clean Asshole Poems & Smiling Vegetable Songs* (San Francisco: City Lights, 1978), 11.

20 Although the work Orlovsky published during his lifetime retains his unconventional spellings, Bill Morgan regularized the spelling in *Peter Orlovsky: A Life in Words* because, he suggests, Orlovsky's spelling may have been attributable more to dyslexia than conscious creative choice; see "Introduction," xxix–xxxi. When *Yugen* published Orlovsky's first and second poems (titled "First Poem" and "Second Poem"), their spellings were regularized, although they appear with misspellings in *Clean Asshole Poems* (see Orlovsky, "First Poem," *Yugen* 3 [1958]: 19; and Orlovsky, "Second Poem," *Yugen* 4 [1959]: 4).

21 Gregory Corso, "Introduction to Peter Orlovsky's Poems," in Orlovsky, *Clean Asshole Poems*, 7–8; quotation on 7.

22 See Bill Morgan, "Editor's Introduction," in *Accidental*, xiii.

23 Kerouac to Ginsberg (July 14, 1955), in *Kerouac and Ginsberg: The Letters*, 306; Ginsberg quotation on 303.

24 See Gregory Corso, "Note on My Play," *Encounter* 18.1 (January 1962): 90.

25 See *A Bibliography of Works by Gregory Corso, 1954–1965*, complied by Robert A. Wilson (New York: Phoenix Book Shop, 1966).

26 Nora Sayre, *Previous Convictions: A Journey through the 1950s* (New Brunswick, NJ: Rutgers University Press, 1995), 202–203. The chapter titled "The Poet's Theater and the Beats" is a rich discussion of Sayre's involvement with the Poet's Theater when Corso was in Cambridge.

27 John Tytell, "Review of *Beat Drama*," *Journal of Beat Studies* 5 (2017): 226.

28 Murray Robinson, "Gregory Sends Us Poems That We Don't Get," *New York World Telegram and Sun* (June 15, 1955): 27.

29 Gregory Corso, *Gasoline & The Vestal Lady on Brattle* (San Francisco: City Lights, 1992), 103. *The Vestal Lady on Brattle* was originally published by Richard Brukenfeld (Cambridge, MA, 1955), but this edition is very scarce, so I quote from the City Lights edition later combined with *Gasoline*.

30 Allen Ginsberg, *Best Minds*, 282.

31 Gregory Stephenson, *Exiled Angel: A Study of the Work of Gregory Corso* (London: Hearing Eye, 1989), 11.

32 See Ronna C. Johnson, "Gregory Corso's Dada-Surrealist-Absurd Beat Plays," in *Beat Drama*.

33 Gregory Corso, "In This Hung-Up Age," *Encounter* 18.1 (January 1962): 83–90.

34 In *The Needle* 1.2 (July 1956), for instance, readers would find work by Gary Snyder, Kenneth Patchen, Ron Loewinsohn, and Paul Goodman, while Corso makes an appearance in issue 1.3 (November 1956).

35 Headnote, *The Miscellaneous Man* (summer 1954), n.p.

36 W. J. M. [William J. Margolis], "Manacle … or Man?," *The Miscellaneous Man* (summer 1954): n.p. For a contemporaneous discussion of *The Miscellaneous Man* and Margolis as "with the Beat Generation but not of [it]," see John G. Roberts, "The Frisco Beat," *Mainstream* (July 1958): 24.

37 The best critical discussion of *Mexico City Blues* is James T. Jones's *A Map of Mexico City Blues: Jack Kerouac as Poet* (Carbondale: Southern Illinois University Press, 1992), which offers a detailed analysis of how the book is the "fulfillment of Kerouac's spontaneous poetics" (12).

38 Jack Kerouac, *San Francisco Blues* (New York: Penguin, 1995), n.p.

39 Jack Kerouac, *Mexico City Blues* (1959; New York: Grove, 1990), 49.

40 Loren Glass, *Countercultural Colophon: Grove Press, the Evergreen Review, and the Incorporation of the Avant-Garde* (Stanford: Stanford University Press, 2013), 24. This is the best cultural history of *Evergreen Review* and Grove Press, and I rely on it for my discussion of the "San Francisco Scene" issue.

41 Lawrence Ferlinghetti, *Pictures of the Gone World* (San Francisco: City Lights, 1955), n.p.

42 Ferlinghetti to Ginsberg (October 13, 1955), in Ferlinghetti and Ginsberg, *I Greet You at the Beginning of a Great Career: The Selected Correspondence of Lawrence Ferlinghetti and Allen Ginsberg, 1955–1997*, ed. Bill Morgan (San Francisco: City Lights, 2015), 1.

43 See Bill Morgan, *The Works of Allen Ginsberg, 1941–1994*, 231.

44 Gregory Corso, "The Literary Revolution in America," *Litterair Paspoort* (November 1957): 194.

45 Jack Kerouac, *The Dharma Bums* (1958; New York: Penguin, 1986), 10.

46 On this point, see Jonah Raskin, *American Scream*, 14; and Davidson, *San Francisco*, 3. *American Scream* is one of the best accounts of the 6 Gallery reading specifically and of the impact of "Howl" more generally, and I rely on it throughout this book (for Raskin's description of the 6 Gallery reading, see 13–24). For another participant's detailed recollections of the evening, see Michael McClure, *Scratching the Beat Surface* (San Francisco: North Point Press, 1989), 11–34.

47 For a range of reactions to "Howl" and Ginsberg more generally, see *On the Poetry of Allen Ginsberg*. For uniformly positive assessments, see *Best Minds: A Tribute to Allen Ginsberg*, ed. Bill Morgan and Bob Rosenthal (New York: Lospecchio Press, 1986).

48 Amiri Baraka, *The Autobiography of LeRoi Jones* (New York: Freundlich Books, 1984), 150.

49 John Hollander, "Poetry Chronicle," *Partisan Review* 24.2 (spring 1957): 296–297.

50 Ginsberg to John Hollander (September 7, 1958), in *Letters*, 205.

51 Jonah Raskin, *American Scream*, 185–186. See Richard Eberhart, "West Coast Sounds," *New York Times Book Review* (September 2, 1956); the review is reprinted in *To Eberhart from Ginsberg* (Lincoln, MA: Penmaen Press, 1976), a stand-alone book with commentaries by both Eberhart and Ginsberg.

52 Bill Morgan, *Letters*, 131.

53 Ginsberg to Richard Eberhart (May 18, 1956), in *Letters*, 131.

54 Eliot Katz, *The Poetry and Politics of Allen Ginsberg* (United Kingdom: Beatdom Books, 2016), 68.

55 Anatole Broyard, "Village Café," in *New Directions in Poetry and Prose 12*, ed. James Laughlin (New York: New Directions, 1950), 398–401; quotation on 398.

56 Kenneth Rexroth, "Thou Shalt Not Kill," in *The Complete Poems of Kenneth Rexroth*, ed. Sam Hamill and Bradford Morrow (Port Townsend, WA: Copper Canyon Press, 2003), 570–571. Despite the similarities between "Thou Shalt Not Kill" and "Howl," the standard critical line is, as Sam Hamill puts it: "Both Ginsberg and Rexroth are on record ... denying that Rexroth's poem influenced 'Howl' ... [but] Whether Rexroth liked it or not, his name would be associated with the Beats for the rest of his life" (Hamill, "The Poetry of Kenneth Rexroth," in *The Complete Poems of Kenneth Rexroth*, xvii–xxxvi; quotation on xxv).

57 For Solomon's own reflections on psychiatric hospitals, see Carl Solomon, *Mishaps, Perhaps* (San Francisco: City Lights, 1966), 6–7, 36–50.

58 Raskin, *American Scream*, 139.

59 T. S. Eliot, *The Annotated Waste Land with Eliot's Contemporary Prose*, 2nd edition, ed. Lawrence Rainey (New Haven, CT: Yale University Press, 2005), 72, 74.

60 Ginsberg quoted in Gordon Ball, "'Howl' and Its Influences," in *The Poem That Changed America: "Howl" Fifty Years Later*, ed. Jason Shinder (New York: Farrar, Straus and Giroux, 2006), 97.

61 Marjorie Perloff, "'A Lost Battalion of Platonic Conversationalists': 'Howl' and the Language of Modernism," in *The Poem That Changed America*, 33.

62 For a discussion of what she calls a "problematic division of his [Ginsberg's] readers into insiders and outsiders" which "comes surprisingly close to limiting the proper audience of his poem to poets with X-ray eyes," see Lane, *French Genealogy*, 146. On Ginsberg's tendency to name his intimates, see John Muckle, "The Names: Allen Ginsberg's Writings," in *Beat Generation Writers*, 10–36.

63 Ginsberg, *Howl: Original*, 23. This edition contains five drafts of part I, eighteen for part II, five for part III, and seven for part IV ("Footnote to Howl"). As Barry Miles points out, there are many more variant drafts now scattered in different libraries and private collections; for the purposes of this book, I follow the drafts available in *Howl: Original Draft Facsimile*, which readers can easily consult (Miles, "A Note on the Manuscript," in *Howl: Original*, xiv).

64 Cleanth Brooks, *The Well Wrought Urn: Studies in the Structure of Poetry* (London: Dennis Dobson, 1947), 175.

65 For a compelling reading of the differences between "Howl" as packaged in the 1956 City Lights edition and as packaged in the *Original Draft Facsimile* edition, see Lane, *French Genealogy*, 127–141.

66 See Raskin, *American Scream*, 211–223; and *Howl on Trial: The Battle for Free Expression*, ed. Bill Morgan and Nancy J. Peters (San Francisco: City Lights, 2006), 1–3. *Howl on Trial* is the best single resource for information about the obscenity trial; it includes invaluable contextual information as well as lengthy transcripts from the trial itself, as does a much earlier volume, *Howl of the Censor*, ed. J. W. Ehrlich (San Carlos, CA: Nourse Publishing, 1961). For the film dramatization, see *Howl*, dir. Rob Epstein (2010).

67 "Allen Ginsberg's *Howl*: A Chronology," in *Howl on Trial*, 1–3.

68 John G. Fuller, "Trade Winds," *Saturday Review of Literature* (October 5, 1957): 5–7; quotation on 5 (unbracketed ellipses in original).

Chapter 6 The Establishment Strikes Back

1 Herb Caen's coining of the term "beatnik" dates specifically from his "Pocketful of Notes," *San Francisco Chronicle* (April 2, 1958): sec. 2, p. 15. For a more detailed investigation into the early use of the term, see Clinton Robert Starr, "Bohemian Resonance: The Beat Generation and Urban Countercultures in

the United States during the Late 1950s and Early 1960s," PhD diss., University of Texas-Austin, 2005, 39 n. 13.

2 "The Cool, Cool Bards," *Time* (December 2, 1957): 71.

3 "Blazing and the Beat," *Time* (February 2, 1958): 104; "Fried Shoes," *Time* (February 9, 1959): 16.

4 "Bam; Roll on with Bam!," *Time* (September 14, 1959): 28.

5 "The Bored, the Bearded and the Beat," *Look* (August 19, 1958): 65–68; quotation on 65.

6 O'Neil, "The Only Rebellion Around," 116.

7 Richard Appignansei and Chris Garratt, *Introducing Postmodernism* (Cambridge: Icon Books, 2004), 55. Appignansei and Garratt are glossing Jean Baudrillard's much more complex theory of simulacra.

8 Quoted in the editorial note provided in *Beat Down Your Soul*, 431.

9 Herbert Gold, "How to Tell the Beatniks from the Hipsters," *Noble Savage* (spring 1960): 132–139; quotation on 132.

10 See also Richard E. Geis's *Like Crazy, Man* (1960), and *Bongo Drum* (1966).

11 Harold Norse, *Memoirs of a Bastard Angel* (New York: William Morrow, 1989), 119.

12 Bonnie Golightly, *Beat Girl* (New York: Avon, 1959), 63.

13 See *Beatsville*, ed. Martin McIntosh (Melbourne: Outre Gallery Press, 2003), 52.

14 Albert B. Feldstein, ed., *Like, MAD* (New York: Signet, 1960).

15 George Mandel, *Beatville, U.S.A.* (New York: Avon, 1961); William F. Brown, *Beat Beat Beat* (New York: Signet, 1959).

16 William Raymond Smith, "Hepcats to Hipsters," *The New Republic* (April 2, 1958): 18–20; quotation on 19.

17 See also Dan Jacobson, "America's 'Angry Young Men': How Rebellious Are the San Francisco Rebels?," *Commentary* (December 1957): 475–479; Sam Hynes, "The Beat and the Angry," *Commonweal* (September 5, 1958): 559–561; and Harry Roskolenko, "The Sounds of the Fury," *Prairie Schooner* 33.2 (summer 1959): 148–153.

18 Cleanth Brooks and Robert Penn Warren, *Understanding Fiction* (New York: Appleton Century Crofts, 1943), 107–108.

19 Cleanth Brooks and Robert Penn Warren, *Understanding Fiction*, 2nd edition (New York: Appleton Century Crofts, 1959), 80.

20 John G. Roberts, "The 'Frisco Beat," *Mainstream* (July 1958): 11–26; quotation on 16.

21 Roberts quotes part of this passage on 19; it is found in Kerouac, *The Subterraneans*, 75.

22 Jack Kerouac, "Essentials of Spontaneous Prose," in *Portable Kerouac*, 484–485; quotation on 484; Kerouac to Cassady (December 27, 1950), in *Selected Letters, 1940–1956*, 243.

23 Jack Kerouac, "The Last Word," *Escapade* (June 1959), reprinted in Kerouac, *Good Blonde and Others*, ed. Don Allen (San Francisco: Grey Fox, 1994), 145.

24 In addition to these names, Kerouac also lists "Phil Whalen, Gary Snyder, Denise Levertov, Robert Creeley, in fact e. e. Cummings, Auden, James Jones, Algren, etc." (147).

25 John Sisk, "Beatniks and Tradition," *Commonweal* (April 17, 1959): 75–77; quotation on 77.

26 The essay is collected, for example, in Seymour Krim's *The Beats* (1960), one of the first anthologies of Beat writing, as well as more contemporary anthologies such as *Beat Down Your Soul* (2001).

27 Norman Podhoretz, "The Know-Nothing Bohemians," in *Doings and Undoings: The Fifties and After in American Writing* (New York: Noonday Press, 1964), 143–158; quotation on 155. The essay originally appeared in *Partisan Review* 25.2 (spring 1958).

28 Ginsberg to John Hollander (September 7, 1958), in *Letters*, 203.

29 Kenneth Rexroth, "San Francisco Letter," *Evergreen Review* 1.2 (1957): 11.

30 Norman Mailer, "The White Negro," in *Advertisements for Myself*, 337–358; quotation on 341.

31 Norman Podhoretz, "Where Is the Beat Generation Going?," *Esquire* (December 1958): 147–150; quotation on 150.

32 Richard Ryan, "Of the Beat Generation and Us," *Catholic World* (August 1958): 347; Hynes, "The Beat and the Angry," *Commonweal* (September 5, 1958): 560; "Poet of the New Violence," *The Nation* (February 23, 1957): 162; and James Dickey, "From Babel to Byzantium," *The Sewanee Review* (July–September 1957): 509.

33 Jack Kerouac, "Lamb, No Lion," in *Portable Kerouac*, 562–565; quotations on 563, 564. This article originally appeared in *Pageant* (February 1958).

34 "The Sound of Beat: Three New Poems from Three Leading Beatnik Poets," *Playboy* (July 1959): 44–45.

35 "Beat Playmate," *Playboy* (July 1959): 47.

36 Alfred Aronowitz, "The Beat Generation, Part 1," *New York Post* (March 9, 1959): 4, 40; quotation on 40.

37 Alfred Aronowitz, "The Beat Generation, Part 8," *New York Post* (March 17, 1959): 88.

38 Alfred Aronowitz, "The Beat Generation, Part 9," *New York Post* (March 18, 1959): 64.

39 Alfred Aronowitz, "The Beat Generation, Part 2," *New York Post* (March 10, 1959): 4, 64.

40 Aronowitz, "The Beat Generation, Part 4," 22.

41 Advertisement for *The Holy Barbarians, New York Times* (May 25, 1959): 27.

42 Suzanne Kiplinger, "This Hip-Historian Knows a Man's Pad Is His Castle," in *The Village Voice Reader*, ed. Daniel Wolf and Edwin Fancher (New York: Grove, 1963), 245. For another detailed evaluation of Lipton's work, see Seymour Krim, "The Holy Barbarians," *Evergreen Review* 3.9 (1959): 208–214.

43 Advertisement for *The Holy Barbarians*, 27.

44 Kerouac to Ginsberg (May 19, 1959), in *Kerouac and Ginsberg: The Letters*, 431.

45 Although I won't pursue the Venice scene in this book, there were indeed significant Beat-associated energies there; see, e.g., John Maynard, *Venice West: The Beat Generation in Southern California* (New Brunswick, NJ: Rutgers University Press, 1991).

46 Lawrence Lipton, *The Holy Barbarians* (New York: Julian Messner, 1959), 49.

47 Lipton, *Holy Barbarians*, 296.

48 Lipton, *Holy Barbarians*, 149.

49 Rexroth quoted in Lipton, *Holy Barbarians*, 294.

50 Warren Tallman, "Kerouac's Sound," in *Beat Down Your Soul*, edited by Ann Charters (New York: Penguin, 2001), 545–560; quotation on 547.

51 See also Allen Ginsberg, Review of *The Dharma Bums*, *Village Voice* 4.3 (November 12, 1958), www.villagevoice.com/news/allen-ginsberg-on-the-dharma-bums-6714721.

52 "Editorial," *Wagner Literary Magazine* (spring 1959): 2–7; quotation on 3. For a contemporaneous discussion of this issue, see "Every Man a Beatnik?," *Newsweek* (June 29, 1959): 83.

53 Another contributor worth special mention is Daisy Aldan, a poet, translator, and editor who had moved in Beat-associated circles throughout the 1950s, and who by 1959 had included Beat writers – grouped together as such – in her anthology of contemporary poetry and visual art titled *A New Folder/ Americans: Poems and Drawings*; as she noted at the time, these writers seemed to her "new in the sense that they continue to 'favor what the supercilious do not favor,' and they are not afraid to dare as they sing of what is brutal, real, sweet, sad, unforgiving, and mad in America today" (Aldan, "Note to This Book," in *A New Folder/Americans: Poems and Drawings*, ed. Aldan [New York: Folder Editions, 1959], 127).

54 Ted Joans, *The Hipsters* (New York: Citadel Press), n.p.

Chapter 7 Little Magazines and Subterranean Networks

1 Hettie Jones, *How I Became Hettie Jones* (New York: Grove, 1990), 44. To be accurate, from 1958 on, occasionally a Beat writer did slip into the pages of *Partisan Review* – see, e.g., Ginsberg's "Ready to Roll" (winter 1958), Alan Ansen's memorial to William Cannastra, "Dead Drunk" (fall 1959), or Corso's "In the Fleeting Hand of Time" (spring 1958), ironically in the same issue as "The Know-Nothing Bohemians."

2 Amiri Baraka, *The Autobiography of LeRoi Jones* (New York: Freundlich, 1984), 117.

3 Barry Miles, *The Beat Hotel: Ginsberg, Burroughs, and Corso in Paris, 1958–1963* (New York: Grove Press, 2000), 64.

4 Ginsberg to Richard Eberhart (October 20, 1959), in *Letters*, 225; Burroughs to Ginsberg (November 10, 1960), in *Rub Out the Words: The Letters of*

William S. Burroughs, 1959–1974, ed. Bill Morgan (New York: Penguin, 2012), 59.

5 Corso to Paul Blackburn (May 20, 1958), in *An Accidental*, 104; Corso to Diane di Prima (September 15, 1958), in *An Accidental*, 139.

6 David Ossman, "LeRoi Jones: An Interview on *Yugen*" (1960), in *Conversations with Amiri Baraka*, ed. Charlie Reilly (Jackson: University Press of Mississippi, 1994), 3–4.

7 Jim Burns, "Yugen," *Poetry Information* 16 (winter 1976–1977): 39–41; quotation on 39; Jones, *How I*, 53–54; Miles, *Beat Hotel*, 64.

8 Philip Whalen, "Takeout, 4:ii: 58," *Yugen* 1 (1958): 3.

9 Philip Whalen, "Soufflé," *Yugen* 3 (1958): 10.

10 R. J. Ellis, "Little," 1020. Note also that Ian Paterson discusses *Yugen* in his chapter "New York Poets: *Folder* (1953–6); *Neon* (1956–60); and *Yugen* (1958–62)," in *The Oxford Critical and Cultural History of Modernist Magazines*, vol. 2, 983–1000. For more background on avant-garde little magazines of this era, see Alan Golding, "Little Magazines and Alternative Canons: The Example of *Origin*," *American Literary History*, 2.4 (winter 1990): 691–725.

11 Gary Snyder, "On Vulture Peak," *Yugen* 6 (1960): 34.

12 Diane di Prima, "The Lovers," *Yugen* 2 (1958): 15–16.

13 Diane di Prima, *Recollections of My Life as a Woman: The New York Years* (New York: Viking, 2001), 222.

14 LeRoi Jones, "Putdown of the Whore of Babylon," *Yugen* 7 (1961): 4.

15 Michael McClure, "Rant Block," *Yugen* 5 (1959): 23–24.

16 McClure, *Scratching*, 89. McClure also singles out "Rant Block" in a much earlier essay, "Revolt"; see *Meat Science Essays* (San Francisco: City Lights, 1963), 57–75.

17 For a discussion of *Understanding Poetry*'s influence, see Alan Golding, *From Outlaw to Classic: Canons in American Poetry* (Madison: University of Wisconsin Press, 1995), 102–113.

18 Capote quoted in Gerald Clarke, *Capote: A Biography* (New York: Simon and Schuster, 2010), 315.

19 Title page, *Beatitude* 1 (May 9, 1959): n.p. There are conflicting accounts about who exactly founded the magazine; as R. J. Ellis has put it, *Beatitude*'s "messy production . . . was matched by its messy stream of editors, including Bill Margolis, Bob Kaufman, and Chester Anderson" ("Little," 1023). In 1960, material from *Beatitude* was collected for an anthology published by City Lights, and that volume's headnote claimed that "The original *Beatitude* magazine was conceived by Allen Ginsberg, Bob Kaufman and John Kelly or someone at Cassandra's coffee house in May 1959" (*Beatitude Anthology* [San Francisco: City Lights Books, 1960], n.p.). But in *Beatitude*'s twentieth-anniversary issue in 1979, Neeli Cherkovski asserted that "The original editors were John Kelley [*sic*], John Richardson, William J. Margolis, Bernie Urono-witz, and Bob Kaufman" ("Editorial Notes," *Beatitude* 29 [1979]: n.p.). Although Ginsberg's work appeared frequently in all the early issues, editorial

energies were certainly concentrated around Kelly, Margolis, and Bob Kaufman and his wife, Eileen. See Eileen Kaufman, "Introduction," *Beatitude Vol. II* (1992) www.beatitudepoetry.com/introd.html.

20 Remaining coy about the editorship was part of the fun; for instance, *Beatitude* 4 (May 30, 1959) announced that it was "edited & produced on a kick or miss basis by a few hardy types who sneak out of alleys near Grant Avenue – the only responsible party being: John Kelly" (n.p.).

21 Two more issues appeared in the late 1960s, and the magazine was revived under new editorship in the mid-1970s; see, e.g., issue 21 (1975), edited by Luke Breit; issue 22 (1975), edited by Neeli Cherkovski and Ken Wainio; and issue 23 (February 1976), edited by Jack Hirschman and Kristen Wetterhahn. These later issues do not read as overwhelmingly Beat, but the "Twentieth Anniversary Issue," *Beatitude* 29 (1979), edited by Cherkovski, is of interest as it is dedicated to Bob Kaufman and features his work as well as retrospective tributes. For a "photographic history" of those connected to these later issues, see Thomas Rain Crowe, ed., *Beatitude Magazine & the 1970s San Francisco Renaissance* (Cullowhee, NC: New Native Press, 2014).

22 Pierre Delattre, *Episodes* (St. Paul, MN: Graywolf Press, 1993), 59.

23 Unsigned endnote, *Beatitude* 7 (July 4, 1959): n.p.

24 John Kelly, "Publisher's Letter," *Beatitude* 2 (May 16, 1959): n.p.

25 Title page, *Beatitude* 1 (May 9, 1959): n.p.

26 William J. Margolis, "Poem to My Self – But I'll Clue You In, Too," *Beatitude* 1 (May 9, 1959): n.p.

27 Margolis adopts a like strategy in "Olé," dedicated to Bob Kaufman, "ancestor of the beat," a poem written in the immediate aftermath of a now-infamous incident in which Kaufman lost a toe after a violent encounter with a cop; see Bill Margolis, "Olé," *Beatitude* 8 (August 15, 1959): n.p.

28 joy, "to sociologists and publicists of the beat generation," *Beatitude* 8 (August 15, 1959): n.p.

29 francine & alice, "Beat Congo," *Beatitude* 6 (n.d. [summer 1959]): n.p.

30 Anonymous, "open letter to the beats from a spy deep in enemy territory," *Beatitude* 16 (June 17, 1960): 19.

31 Maria Damon, "Introduction," *Callaloo* 25.1 (winter 2002): 105–111; quotation on 105. Damon has been a vocal academic champion of Kaufman's work over the years, and has been instrumental in reviving critical interest in him. This issue of *Callaloo* is a good introduction to scholarship on Kaufman; see also Damon's *The Dark End of the Street: Margins in American Vanguard Poetry* (Minneapolis: University of Minnesota Press, 1993) and *Postliterary America*; and David Henderson, "Bob Kaufman: Beat, Surreal, Buddhist, and Black," in *Beats at Naropa*, ed. Anne Waldman and Laura Wright (Minneapolis: Coffee House Press, 2009), 117–134.

32 Aldon Lynn Nielsen, "'A Hard Rain': Looking at Bob Kaufman," *Callaloo* 25.1 (winter 2002): 135–145; quotation on 137.

33 For biographical sketches of Kaufman, see A. D. Winans, "Bob Kaufman," *The American Poetry Review* (May/June, 2000): 19–20; David Henderson,

"Introduction," in *Cranial Guitar: Selected Poems by Bob Kaufman*, ed. Gerald Nicosia (Minneapolis: Coffee House Press, 1996), 7–28; and Steve Abbott, "Hidden Master of the Beats," *Poetry Flash* 155 (February 1986): 1, 12–14.

34 Eileen Kaufman, "Who Wouldn't Walk with Tigers," in *Women of the Beat Generation*, ed. Brenda Knight (Berkeley, CA: Conari Press, 1996), 107–114; quotation on 113.

35 See also Kaufman, *Cranial Guitar*.

36 Ted Joans, "Bird Lives & Bob Still Gives," *Beatitude* 29 (1979): 57.

37 Bomkauf [Bob Kaufman], "Notes Dis- and Re- Garding Abomunism," *Beatitude* 2 (May 16, 1959): n.p.

38 "Publisher's Letter," *Beatitude* 3 (May 23, 1959): n.p.

39 Bob Kaufman, "Abomunist Manifesto," in *Solitudes Crowded with Loneliness* (New York: New Directions, 1965), 77–78. For ease of reference, I'll quote now from the readily obtainable later collection. Note that there are Abomunist-related pieces in *Beatitude* written by people other than Kaufman; see, e.g., bimgo [William Margolis], "Abomunistorical Oddities," *Beatitude* 10 (October 1959): n.p.

40 Bob Kaufman, "Excerpts from the Lexicon Abomunon," in *Solitudes Crowded with Loneliness*, 80–81. The "Lexicon Abomunon" is tagged "Compiled by BIMGO" – Bill Margolis (81).

41 Richard Lewis, *Poor Richard's Guide to Non-Tourist San Francisco* (San Francisco: Unicorn Publishing, 1958), 19, 20.

42 For David Meltzer's rejoinder to "Bagel Shop Jazz," a prose-poem that sketches many of the personalities that passed through its doors, see Meltzer, "Untitled," *Callaloo* 25.1 (winter 2002): 201–202.

43 Martinelli to Ferlinghetti (October 24, 1958), "City Lights Books Records, 1953–1970," Box 8, Folder 23, Bancroft Library, UC-Berkeley.

44 "Bagel Shop Jazz" originally appeared in *Beatitude* 3 (May 23, 1959): n.p., but note that the punctuation in the *Beatitude* version is slightly different from the one in *Solitudes* (14–15).

45 Damon, *Postliterary*, 60. Damon offers a nuanced reading of this poem that turns, in part, on who *isn't* depicted as frequenting the Bagel Shop: queer men, despite the fact that Kaufman was at the time "actively enmeshed in a triangle involving queer men" (64); see Damon, *Postliterary*, 57–71.

46 William J. Margolis, *The Anteroom of Hell* (San Francisco: Inferno Press, 1957), 5–6, 10.

47 *Beatitude/east* 17 (February 6, 1961): n.p.

48 C. V. J. Anderson, *Colloquy* (San Francisco: Bread & Wine Press, 1960), n.p.

49 C. V. J. Anderson, *A Liturgy for Dragons* (New York: Chas. P. Young Company, 1961), 5. For further work in *Liturgy for Dragons* that explicitly engages other writers on the scene, see "Marginalia," a response to Jack Spicer's "Four Imaginary Elegies" (11), "Chant/Pioneers," for Pierre Delattre (19), and "Seven Landscape," for Diane Wakoski (20–23).

50 C. V. J. Anderson to Pierre Delattre (September 10, 1959), *Beatitude* 10 (October 1959): n.p.

51 Ibid.

52 See also C. V. J. Anderson's poetic manifesto, "Obvious Statements: Tentative Notes toward a Theory," *Beatitude* 13 (February 1960): n.p. Anderson makes pronouncements such as "Poetry should partake of magic" and "All poetry is religious," statements that underscore his core belief that "Poetry is not sane, and cannot be used sanely." This echoes the epigraph used in both *Colloquy* and *Liturgy for Dragons*: "Logic is a method, not a goal" (n.p.).

53 "c.v.j.a." [C. V. J. Anderson], "How Much Does a Cop Cost?," *Underhound* 1.4 (1960): 12–13; quotation on 13.

54 For a photograph of an advertisement for the "Beatnik Kit," see Alfred Aronowitz, "The Beat Generation, Part VI," *New York Post* (March 15, 1959): M6.

55 Padriec O'Sullivan, *Weep Not My Children* (n.p., n.d; probably 1959), n.p.

56 Another writer connected to *Beatitude* was Richard McBride, an employee at City Lights Books; see McBride, *Oranges* (San Francisco: Bread & Wine Press, 1960), a beautifully hand-set volume with illustrations by Victor Wong and several charming poems about San Francisco.

57 Diane di Prima, "Introduction," in *The Floating Bear: A Newsletter, Numbers 1–37, 1961–1969*, ed. Diane di Prima and LeRoi Jones (La Jolla, CA: Laurence McGilvery, 1973), x–xi. This volume collects all issues of *The Floating Bear* and includes an invaluable introduction and notes by di Prima (which underscore the *Bear*'s Beat connection; see viii–x).

58 A. B. Spellman, *The Beautiful Days* (New York: Poets Press, 1965), n.p.

59 See Irving Rosenthal, *Sheeper* (New York: Grove, 1967), 217–237; quotation on 236.

60 For a useful introduction to Trocchi, *Merlin*, and *Cain's Book*, see Fiona Paton, "*Cain's Book* and the Mark of Exile: Alexander Trocchi as Transnational Beat," in Grace and Skerl, *The Transnational Beat Generation*, 201–217. Paton shows how Trocchi was "firmly connected to the Beat milieu" (202) and reads *Cain's Book* in terms of the emerging transnationalism of the Beat movement. See also Allen Campbell and Tim Niels, eds., *A Life in Pieces: Reflections on Alexander Trocchi* (Edinburgh: Rebel, 1997).

61 Alexander Trocchi, *Cain's Book* (1960; New York: Grove, 1992), 60, 59.

62 Even in the early days, Jones was generally viewed as the more important editor, a fact that speaks to the male Beats' tendency to ignore contributions by women; as di Prima puts it, "though Roi and I coedited the *Bear*, and often it was he who got the credit for the whole thing, most of the actual physical work devolved upon me and those friends I could dig up to help me . . . It was just the natural division of labor/credit" (*Recollections*, 253).

63 See di Prima, *Revolutionary Letters: Expanded Edition* (San Francisco: City Lights, 2019); and *War Poems*, ed. di Prima (New York: Poets Press, 1968).

64 In 1963, New York artist Soren Agenoux, a figure about whom little is known, started a mimeographed newsletter called *The Sinking Bear*, which began as a parody of *The Floating Bear* and its tendency to print a small circle of insiders. While *The Floating Bear* used letters and in-jokes to signal an

artistic community, *The Sinking Bear* printed mostly overheard conversations, witticisms from people Agenoux and other editors encountered, or snippets from other publications, thereby drawing attention to these otherwise throwaway lines and elevating them to objects worthy of critical reflection. Original issues of *The Sinking Bear* are difficult to locate, but interested readers may consult a limited edition of the complete run that was published in 2013; see *The Sinking Bear: A Newsletter*, ed. Johan Kugelberg, Phil Aarons, and Adam Davis (New York: Boo-Hooray, 2013). In his preface to this volume, Davis notes that *Sinking Bear* "arose out of the shared gossip of a loose circle of artists, most of them gay, who were associated with a number of scenes in downtown New York" (*Sinking*, n.p.). In *Recollections*, di Prima explains that she had sublet her apartment to Agenoux after her move to California, describing him as "a dilettante hustler who made various kinds of collage and photo art, and wrote a little" (329). See also Soren Agenoux, "A Movie Review" and "12 Leçons de Tenebres," *The Floating Bear* 24 (September–October 1962).

65 Mabley quoted in Albert Podell, "Censorship on the Campus: The Case of the *Chicago Review*," *San Francisco Review* 1 (spring 1959): 71–89; quotation on 73. Podell was an editor at *Chicago Review* at the time of its suppression; my summary of the incident is taken from his account.

66 *Big Table* 1 (spring 1959): front cover.

67 Tuli Kupferberg, "The Man with the Scissors," *Fuck You* 4 (August 1962): n.p.

68 Douglas Woolf, "Work in Flight Grounded," in *The Moderns*, ed. LeRoi Jones (New York: Corinth, 1963), 84; Lawrence Ferlinghetti, *Her* (New York: New Directions, 1960), 92; Allen Ginsberg, *Collected Poems*, 280–281.

69 For a discussion of the particular contents of these and subsequent anthologies, see Steven Belletto, "Introduction: The Beat Half-Century," in *The Cambridge Companion to the Beats*, ed. Belletto (New York: Cambridge University Press, 2017), 7–17.

70 There are many other significant little magazines that I'm neglecting in this book, notably *Kulchur* (1960–1965/1966), *Journal for the Protection of All Beings* (1961–1978), and *City Lights Journal* (1963–1966), but these and other periodicals certainly do merit further attention.

Chapter 8 The Opening of the Field

1 See Corso, "Variations on a Generation," in Charters, *Portable Beat Reader*, 182–185. This piece was first published in *Gemini* (spring 1959).

2 Gregory Corso, *Gasoline & The Vestal Lady on Brattle* (San Francisco: City Lights, 1992), 42.

3 Allen Ginsberg," Introduction," in Corso, *Gasoline & The Vestal Lady on Brattle*, 13.

4 Ginsberg, *Best Minds*, 308.

5 Gregory Corso, *The Happy Birthday of Death* (New York: New Directions, 1960), 28.

6 Ginsberg, *Best Minds*, 310.

7 Gregory Stephenson, *The Daybreak Boys*, 75.

8 Corso, "Variations on a Generation," in Charters, *Portable Beat Reader*, 182.

9 Gavin Selerie, "Introduction," in *Gregory Corso: The Riverside Interviews* (London: Binnacle Press, 1982), 15.

10 See Corso, *Accidental*, 185.

11 Corso to Ferlinghetti (July 28, 1958), in *Accidental*, 111.

12 Paul Boyer, *By the Bomb's Early Light: American Thought and Culture at the Dawn of the Atomic Age* (New York: Pantheon, 1985), 22.

13 Frances Ferguson, "The Nuclear Sublime," *Diacritics* 14.2 (summer 1984): 7.

14 Tim Armstrong, "Poetry and Science," in *A Companion to Twentieth Century Poetry*, ed. Neil Roberts (London: Blackwell, 2001), 85.

15 Gavin Selerie, "The Interview" (with Corso), in *Riverside Interviews*, 29.

16 For an exhaustive argument about how Corso imagines the bomb taking the place of God, see Christine Hoff Kraemer, "The Brake of Time: Corso's Bomb as Postmodern God(dess)," *Texas Studies in Literature and Language* 44.2 (summer 2002): 211–228.

17 Corso to Orlovsky (September 2, 1958), in *Accidental*, 136.

18 Corso to Allen (September 2, 1958), in *Accidental*, 136.

19 Corso to Gary Snyder (September 24, 1958), in *Accidental*, 142.

20 See Fazzino, *World Beats*, 3–4.

21 Versions of some material found in this section appear in Steven Belletto, "Five Ways of Being Beat, circa 1958–59," in *Cambridge Companion to the Beats*, 92–109.

22 Allen Ginsberg, *Journals: Early Fifties Early Sixties*, ed. Gordon Ball (New York: Grove, 1977), 80.

23 Lawrence Ferlinghetti, "A Non-Introduction by Way of Introduction," in Diane di Prima, *This Kind of Bird Flies Backward* (1958; New York: Paper Book Gallery, 1963), n.p.

24 For other work from this period, see also Diane di Prima, *Earthsong, Poems 1957–59* (New York: Poets Press, 1968).

25 Diane di Prima, *Memoirs of a Beatnik* (1969; New York: Penguin, 1998), 175.

26 "Pieces of a Song" (interview with di Prima), in *Breaking the Rule of Cool: Interviewing and Reading Women Beat Writers*, ed. Nancy M. Grace and Ronna C. Johnson (Jackson: University Press of Mississippi, 2004), 97.

27 Ronna C. Johnson, "Mapping the Women Writers of the Beat Generation," in Grace and Johnson, *Breaking*, 38.

28 "A New Voice on the American Literary Scene," in Diane di Prima, *Dinners & Nightmares* (New York: Corinth Books, 1961), n.p.

29 Di Prima, *Dinners & Nightmares*, 13–14.

30 See also Diane di Prima, *The New Handbook of Heaven* (San Francisco: Auerhahn Press, 1963). Dedicated to LeRoi Jones, the book chronicles the dissolution of their relationship by amplifying many of the themes in *Dinners & Nightmares*, as for instance in the final poem, "The Jungle" (for "Roi"), which dispassionately states "dont palm off yr deaths head on me, man," and

sketches the collapse of the once-intense relationship between the two writers (n.p.).

31 A. Robert Lee, "The Beats and Race," in *The Cambridge Companion to the Beats*, 202. Despite this critical tendency, there are also those who similarly lament the "benign neglect" of Jones by scholars writing about "ethnic writing and the ethnic self"; see, e.g., Patrick Roney, "The Paradox of Experience: Black Art and Black Idiom in the Work of Amiri Baraka," *African American Review* 37.2–3 (summer/fall 2003): 407.

32 In this regard, I am building on the position of Andrew Epstein, who argues in *Beautiful Enemies* that "Baraka stood at the very center of the social and artistic universe that came to be known as the New American Poetry" (167). As Epstein notes, this position revises the notion that Baraka's career is best understood as "one big conversion narrative," an idea elaborated in earlier studies of his work such as Kimberly Benston's *Baraka: The Renegade and the Mask* (1976) and William Harris's *The Poetry and Politics of Amiri Baraka: The Jazz Aesthetic* (1985). See also Aldon Lynn Nielsen, *Black Chant: Languages of African American Postmodernism* (Cambridge: Cambridge University Press, 1997), which argues that Jones is centrally important to the New American Poetry.

33 Baraka, *The Autobiography of LeRoi Jones*, 127.

34 LeRoi Jones, *Preface to a Twenty Volume Suicide Note* (New York: Totem Press, 1961), 18.

35 See Isabel Eberstadt, "King of the East Village," *New York Herald Tribune* (December 13, 1964): 14–15, 18, 20.

36 The Shadow was so important to Kerouac that he served as the inspiration for Dr. Sax; see Erik Mortenson, *Ambiguous Borderlands: Shadow Imagery in Cold War American Culture* (Carbondale: Southern Illinois University Press, 2016), 72–84.

37 K. C. Harrison, "LeRoi Jones's Radio and the Literary 'Break' from Ellison to Burroughs," *African American Review* 47.2–3 (summer/fall 2014): 358.

38 Jones qtd. in Werner Sollors, *Amiri Baraka/LeRoi Jones: The Quest for a "Populist Modernism"* (New York: Columbia University Press, 1978), 45.

39 See Walton Muyumba, "Improvising over the Changes: Improvisation as Intellectual and Aesthetic Practice in the Transitional Poems of LeRoi Jones/Amiri Baraka," *College Literature* 34.1 (winter 2007).

40 Jones qtd. in Sollors, *Amiri Baraka*, 62.

41 Don Katzman, "Coffeehouse Poetry on the Lower East Side," in *Light Years: An Anthology on Sociocultural Happenings (Multimedia in the East Village, 1960–1966)*, ed. Carol Bergé (New York: Spuyten Duyvil, 2010), 330.

42 Jack Kerouac, "Introduction," in Jack Micheline, *River of Red Wine* (1958; Sudbury, MA: Water Row Press, 1986), 7.

43 Micheline quoted in Fred McDarrah, "Anatomy of a Beatnik," in McDarrah and Gloria McDarrah, *Beat Generation: Glory Days in Greenwich Village* (New York: Schirmer Books, 1996), 6–7. The essay was originally published in *Saga* (August 1960).

44 Micheline, *River of Red Wine*, 10.

45 Jack Micheline, "Statement of a Poet," in *In the Bronx and Other Stories* (New York: Sam Hooker Press, 1965), viii.

46 Tuli Kupferberg, "Greenwich Village of My Dreams," in *The Beat Scene*, ed. Elias Wilentz (New York: Corinth, 1960), 67.

47 Charles Kuralt, "William Morris at the Gaslight Café," CBS News (June 9, 1959), http://gvh.aphdigital.org/items/show/227.

48 For this photograph of William Morris, see Wilentz, *Beat Scene*, 98.

49 William Morris, *4* (n.p., 1959), n.p.

50 O'Neil, *Only Rebellion*, 129.

51 Although William Morris is seldom mentioned in scholarship on the Beats, he is discussed in Jim Burns, *Radicals, Beats and Beboppers* ([Preston]: Penniless Press, 2011). For a photograph of Morris and Kerouac, see Gerald Nicosia and Anne Marie Santos, *One and Only: The Untold Story of on the Road* (Berkeley: Viva Editions, 2011), 155.

52 Sean Wilentz, *Bob Dylan in America* (New York: Anchor, 2011), 57.

53 Jack Micheline, "We Walked the Rebel Sun," in *Poetry of the Beat Generation*, ed. John Mitchell (New York: John Mitchell, n.d.; probably 1958 or 1959), 37–38.

54 Clinton Nichols, "The Little Prophet," in Mitchell, *Poetry of the Beat Generation*, 47.

55 Claus Stamm, "The Triolet," in Mitchell, *Poetry of the Beat Generation*, 59.

56 Barbara Moraff's first published broadside was "Mister" (New Haven, CT: Penny Poems, 1959).

57 Seymour Krim, "Review of *The Holy Barbarians*," *Evergreen Review* 3.9 (1959): 211.

58 Dan Propper, *The Fable of the Final Hour and Other Poems* (Queens, NY: Energy Press, n.d.; probably 1960), n.p. "The Fable of the Final Hour" itself dates from 1958 or 1959.

59 Damon, *Postliterary America*, 68.

60 Stephen Tropp, *Mozart in Hell* (New York: Poets Union Press, 1959), n.p.

61 Alfred Aronowitz, "The Beat Generation, Part 9," *New York Post* (March 18, 1959): 64.

62 Ginsberg to Kerouac (November 13, 1957), in *Kerouac and Ginsberg: The Letters*, 372.

63 See Notes on Contributors, *Fuck You/A Magazine of the Arts* 5.2 (December 1962): n.p. Bremser was published with some regularity in *Fuck You* (issues 4, 5.2, 5.3, 5.6); see, in particular, Bremser, "Lacerations Manuscript," *Fuck You/A Magazine of the Arts* 4 (August 1962): n.p. (a six-page tour de force); and Bremser, "Two Poems from the Tombs," *Fuck You* 5.2 (December 1962): n.p. (among the poems he wrote while in prison). For a discussion of the "Open House for Ray Bremser," see Ed Sanders, *Fug You* (Boston: De Capo, 2011), 26–27.

64 Charles Plymell, note accompanying "November 3, 1998 Dark Afternoon," *Evergreen Review* 102 (1998), www.evergreenreview.com/102/poetry/plymell2.html.

65 Ray Bremser, "Part III (Poems of the City Madness)," *Yugen* 3 (1958): 21.

66 Ray Bremser, *Poems of Madness* (New York: Paper Book Gallery, 1965), 1.

67 Drag turns up in another important poem published in *Yugen*, "backyards & deviations," in which Bremser explores childhood memories of being dressed up as a girl by his sister, and the as-yet-unprocessed impact this experience had on his sexuality. "backyards & deviations" was included as the lead poem in Bremser's later collection, *Blowing Mouth: The Jazz Poems, 1958–1970* (Cherry Valley, NY: Cherry Valley Editions, 1978).

68 Ray Bremser, *Angel* (New York: Tompkins Square Press, 1967), 24, 30–31.

69 Allen Ginsberg, "Ray Bremser and His Poetry," in *Poems of Madness*, n.p.

70 Kerouac, *Mexico City Blues*, 80; *The Collected Poems of Philip Whalen*, ed. Michael Rothenberg (Middletown, CT: Wesleyan University Press, 2007), 126.

71 Orlovsky, *Clean Asshole Poems*, 61.

72 Michael McClure, *Ghost Tantras* (1964; San Francisco: City Lights, 2013), 5.

73 For another example of Bremser thematizing his connections to other writers, see "Story of My Life: First 2 Nights Out of Jail," *Hearse* 5 (n.d.; probably 1959), which describes a telegram from Diane di Prima.

74 Mary Paniccia Carden, *Women Writers of the Beat Era: Autobiography and Intertextuality* (Charlottesville: University of Virginia Press, 2018), 64.

75 Bonnie Bremser, *Troia: Mexican Memoirs* (Champaign, IL: Dalkey Archive Press, 2007), 1. Bonnie's poetry of the early 1960s can be stylistically reminiscent of Ray's; see, e.g., Bonnie Bremser, "Fowl-Play," *Fuck You* 5.1 (December 1962): n.p.

76 "Artista" (Nancy M. Grace interviews Brenda [Bonnie] Frazer [Bremser]), in *Breaking*, 115.

77 Bremser, *Troia*, 39. *Troia* was first published in the United States in 1969 by Croton Press, and then in the United Kingdom as *For Love of Ray* (1971). Bremser had changed her name from Brenda Frazer to Bonnie Bremser, and subsequently changed it back, so that one finds her name represented in different ways in the scholarship. Since she published *Troia* under the name "Bonnie Bremser," I refer to her as such when discussing that text.

78 For a detailed analysis of how, in comparison to Kerouac, Bremser claims a "spiritual alliance with the indigenous population of Mexico," see Kurt Hemmer, "The Prostitute Speaks: Brenda Frazer's *Troia: Mexican Memoirs*," *Paradoxa* 18 (2003): 99–117; quotation on 100.

79 Nancy M. Grace, "Snapshots, Sand Paintings, and Celluloid: Formal Considerations in the Life Writing of Women Writers from the Beat Generation," in *Girls Who Wore Black: Women Writing the Beat Generation*, ed. Ronna C. Johnson and Nancy M. Grace (New Brunswick, NJ: Rutgers University Press, 2002), 168.

80 For discussions of the various registers of the word "troia," see Ann Charters, "Introduction," in *Troia: Mexican Memoirs*, by Bonnie Bremser (Champaign, IL: Dalkey Archive Press, 2007), i–vii; Hemmer, "Prostitute," 102; and Carden, *Women Writers*, 63.

81 For more on this point, see Hemmer, "Prostitute."

82 Note that Bremser asserts that she is "violently afraid of the United States and Texas" (78) and that "Texas is the most vicious atmosphere I have ever suffered" (105).

83 See Ted Joans, "Je Me Vois (I See Myself)," in *Contemporary Authors Autobiography* 25 (Detroit, MI: Gale Research, 1996), 219–258.

84 This flier is reproduced in McDarrah, *Beat Generation*, 94.

85 McDarrah, *Beat Generation*, 211.

86 Lee, *Modern American Counter Writing*, 62.

87 Robert Reisner, "Intro," in Ted Joans, *Jazz Poems* (New York: Rhino Review, 1959), n.p.

88 For a reproduction of this photograph and its rendering on the cover of *Like Crazy, Man*, see McIntosh, *Beatsville*, 52–53.

89 Jack Kerouac, "The Roaming Beatniks," *Holiday* (October 1959): 82–86; quotation on 82.

90 See Gerald Nicosia, "A Lifelong Commitment to Change: The Literary Non-Career of Ted Joans," in Joans, *Teducation: Selected Poems* (Minneapolis: Coffee House Press, 1999), i–vii.

91 Many bibliographies list an earlier book, *Beat Poems* (Deretchin, 1957), but I have been unable to locate a copy, and I am unsure that it actually exists. Probably confusion has arisen because *Jazz Poems* was printed with different titles, including *Beat Funky Jazz Poems* and *Funky Jazz Poems*. The most widely available book of this period was *All of Ted Joans and No More*, which collected the work in *Jazz Poems* (without the collages) and added more material, notably the long poems "It Is Time" and "Travelin'." Some of this work was later collected in Ted Joans, *Teducation: Selected Poems* (Minneapolis: Coffee House Press, 1999), but much of Joans's writing remains unpublished.

92 Ted Joans, *All of Ted Joans and No More* (New York: Excelsior Press, 1961), n.p. "The Sermon" appeared in different forms in different books; in *Jazz Poems* (New York: Rhino Review, 1959), for example, these lines are "you must have a copy of on the road / Kerouac on your shelf and know thou self by reading Norman Mailers / "WHITE NEGRO" / . . . You should read / Gregory Corso's poem Marriage before ever doing that bit" (n.p.).

93 For an analysis of "The Sermon" that doesn't take irony into account, see Robert Fox, "Ted Joans and the (B)reach of the African American Literary Canon," *Melus* 29.3–4 (fall/winter 2004).

94 For Joans's retrospective reflection on "The Sermon," see Knight, *Women of the Beat Generation*, 331.

95 Amiri Baraka, "Black Art," *The Liberator* (January 1966).

96 Joans to Kupferberg (1991), Tuli Kupferberg and Sylvia Topp Papers; MSS.385; box 42, folder 52; Fales Library and Special Collections, New York University Libraries.

97 Tuli Kupferberg, "The Hip and the Square" (1967), Tuli Kupferberg and Sylvia Topp Papers; MSS.385; box 8, folder 31; Fales Library and Special Collections, New York University Libraries.

98 Tuli Kupferberg, *The Rub-Ya-Out of Omore Diem* (New York: Birth Press, 1962), n.p.

99 Tuli Kupferberg, *Beating* (New York: Birth Press, 1959), n.p.

100 See also *Birth* 3 (autumn 1960), titled "Stimulants: An Exhibition," which, as Kupferberg writes, aims "to expose the fear of joy which interferes with the rational (and joyous irrational) evaluation of many of these substances" (2–3).

101 Tuli Kupferberg, *Snow Job* (New York: Birth Press, 1959), n.p. See also a similar parody: Kupferberg, "A Funny Thing Happened to Me Today on the Way to the Crematorium": "*Monsters of all countries unite! /* You have nothing to lose but your genes!" (*Yeah* 3 [June 1962]: 3).

Chapter 9 Revisions of the Real

1 Although Marie Ponsot has at times been identified as a Beat writer via her connection to Ferlinghetti, as she later remarked, if you allowed her poetry to "shape your definition of what Beat is, you might come to another, extremely comical conclusion" about what that word means (interview with Marie Ponsot by Benjamin Ivy, *Bomb* (April 2003), https://bombmagazine.org/articles/marie-ponsot/).

2 See jacket copy for the nineteenth printing: Lawrence Ferlinghetti, *A Coney Island of the Mind* (1968; New York: New Directions, 1958), n.p.

3 See Michael Skau, *"Constantly Risking Absurdity": The Writings of Lawrence Ferlinghetti* (Troy, NY: Whitson Publishing Co., 1989).

4 Lawrence Ferlinghetti, *A Coney Island of the Mind* (New York: New Directions, 1958), 30.

5 Skau, *Constantly*, 85.

6 David Kherdian, *Six Poets of the San Francisco Renaissance* (Fresno: Giligia Press, 1967), 3.

7 Alan Watts, *The Way of Zen* (1957; New York: Vintage, 1989), 67.

8 See Lawrence Ferlinghetti, *One Thousand Fearful Words for Fidel Castro* (San Francisco: City Lights, 1961), and *Tyrranus Nix?* (New York: New Directions, 1969). See also Ferlinghetti, *Poetry as Insurgent Art* (New York: New Directions, 2007).

9 Preston Whaley, *Blows like a Horn: Beat Writing, Jazz, Style, and Markets in the Transformation of U.S. Culture* (Cambridge, MA: Harvard University Press, 2004), 50.

10 Nancy M. Grace, "ruth weiss's *DESERT JOURNAL*: A Modern-Beat-Pomo Performance," in *Reconstructing the Beats*, 57–71. Grace notes that weiss spells her name in lowercase "to protest the German convention of capitalizing the first letter of certain nouns" (71).

11 "Single Out" (interview with weiss), in Grace and Johnson, *Breaking*, 64. See also Horst Spandler, "ruth weiss and the American Beat Movement of the '50s and '60s," in ruth weiss, *Can't Stop the Beat: The Life and Words of a Beat Poet* (Studio City, CA: Divine Arts, 2011), xi–xii.

12 ruth weiss, *Can't Stop the Beat: The Life and Words of a Beat Poet* (Studio City, CA: Divine Arts, 2011), 17, 75–76.

13 In fact, as mentioned elsewhere, by that time City Lights' Pocket Poets series had already published Marie Ponsot's *True Minds* (1956) and Denise Levertov's *Here and Now* (1957).

14 ruth weiss, *Steps* (San Francisco: Mel and Ruth Weitsman, 1958), n.p., ellipses in original.

15 Primarily known as painter and visual artist, Sutter Marin also wrote poetry that has claims for being classed as Beat; see, e.g., Marin, *113 Semi-Simple Poams [sic] for the Simple Minded* (San Francisco: Peace & Pieces Books, 1973). Note that "*[sic]*" is in the title of the book.

16 ruth weiss, *For These Women of the Beat* (San Francisco: 3300 Press, 1997), n.p.

17 I say Tarlow's poetry is very Beat because it works with many of the tropes found in other associated work, as in her poem "CONTACT IN A WORLD OF ANIMATION," which looks for evidence of the divine in unlikely places: "WONDER WORDS / can be found anywhere / like / lying near butts on the floor" (Idell [Aya Tarlow], *Poems for Selected People* [Berkeley: Kether Press, 1961], n.p.). See "REVELATION ONE," in *Poems*, a corollary to weiss's *GALLERY OF WOMEN*; and Tarlow, *Zen Love Poems* (Topanga, CA: Love Press, 1967).

18 See ruth weiss, *DESERT JOURNAL* (Boston: Good Gay Poets, 1977).

19 Haselwood quoted in Alastair M. Johnston, *A Bibliography of the Auerhahn Press & Its Successor Dave Haselwood Books* (Berkeley: Poltroon Press, 1976), 6.

20 Johnston, *Bibliography of Auerhahn*, 7.

21 See Robert Dewhurst, "Measure: A Quarterly to the Poem, 1957–1962," *Let the Bucket Down* (2013): 17.

22 Ginsberg to Robert LaVigne (June 8, 1957), in *Letters*, 154.

23 For more on the connections among Black Mountain and Beat in little magazines, see Tim Woods, "Black Mountain and Associates: *Origin* (1951–2007) and *The Black Mountain Review* (1954–7)," in Brooker and Thacker, *The Oxford Critical and Cultural History*, 977.

24 Jack Kerouac, "From Mexico City Blues," *Measure* 2 (winter 1958): 18.

25 Al Filreis, "On the *Hotel Wentley Poems*," *Jacket* 2 (March 7, 2011) http://jacket2.org/commentary/hotel-wentley-poems.

26 Foye quoted in Pamela Petro, "The Hipster of Joy Street: An Introduction to the Life and Work of John Wieners," *Boston College Magazine* (fall 2000): 46.

27 John Wieners, *Stars Seen in Person: Selected Journals*, ed. Michael Seth Stewart (San Francisco: City Lights, 2015), 148.

28 John Wieners, *The Journal of John Wieners Is to Be Called 707 Scott Street for Billie Holiday* (Los Angeles: Sun & Moon Press, 1996), 18.

29 John Wieners, "From a Journal," in *The New American Poetry*, ed. Donald Allen (New York: Grove, 1960), 425.

30 John Wieners, *The Hotel Wentley Poems* (San Francisco: Auerhahn Press, 1958), n.p.

31 See Michael Wilding, "John Milton: The Early Works," *Cambridge Companion to English Poetry, Donne to Marvell*, ed. Thomas N. Corns (Cambridge: Cambridge University Press, 1993), for a discussion of how the younger Milton was obsessed with the image of the music of the spheres, which was supposed to correlate with the "proper subject of poetry" (221).

32 Quoted in Johnston, *Bibliography of Auerhahn*, 8.

33 John Wieners, "Memories of You," *Fuck You* 5.9 (June/July 1965): 15–16.

34 Wieners to Olson quoted in Dewhurst, "Measure," 15.

35 For Lamantia's account of a yahnah ceremony, see his interview with Meltzer in *San Francisco Beat: Talking with the Poets*, ed. David Meltzer (San Francisco: City Lights, 2001), 144. See also his *Collected Poems*: "I see *you* ghost of the scorpion that God bless it bit me / Scorpion that drove me in a poisonous 24 hr circuit" (166). In *Troia*, Bonnie Bremser describes visiting Lamantia in Mexico, noting that "P [Philip] has been held at nighttime superstitious bay by nearby Teotihuacán pyramid of the sun and tells us of hidden spearheads" (126).

36 Garrett Caples, Andrew Joron, and Nancy Joyce Peters, "High Poet: The Life and Work of Philip Lamantia," in *The Collected Poems of Philip Lamantia*, ed. Caples, Joron, and Peters (Berkeley: University of California Press, 2013), xxxvii. This introduction is an excellent overview of Lamantia's life and work.

37 Garrett Caples, "A Note on Tau," in Lamantia, *Tau* by Philip Lamantia and *Journey to the End* by John Hoffman, ed. Caples (San Francisco: City Lights, 2008), 6.

38 Paul Carroll to Lamantia (May 23, 1959), quoted in Joshua Kotin, "Philip Lamantia's Practical Politics," *Colloquium* (October 18, 2012), https://lucian.uchicago.edu/blogs/colloquium/2012/10/18/philip-lamantias-practical-politics/#_edn13.

39 Johnston, *Bibliography of Auerhahn*, 9; see also Lamantia interview with Meltzer, 144.

40 Philip Lamantia, *Ekstatis* (San Francisco: Auerhahn Press, 1959), n.p.

41 "Philip Lamantia: Last Interview," conducted by Garrett Caples (2001). www.angelfire.com/poetry/thepixelplus/nhlamantia.html.

42 "Beat Mystics," *Time* 71.5 (February 3, 1958): 58.

43 "Philip Lamantia: Shaman of the Surreal," interview conducted by Thomas Rain Crowe, http://209.172.130.121/LAMANTIA.html. See original in *Rain Taxi Review of Books* 10.2 (summer 2005).

44 Thomas Albright, *Art in the San Francisco Bay Area, 1945–1980: An Illustrated History* (Berkeley: University of California Press, 1985), 85. This poem was printed in *Poesia degli ultimi americani*, ed. Fernanda Pivano (Milan: Feltrinelli, 1964), a dual Italian–English anthology of Beat writing, and includes an editorial note that "Boobus" was a nickname for McClure's daughter (265).

45 Caples et al., "High Poet," xxxiii.

46 Allen Ginsberg, *Reality Sandwiches* (San Francisco: City Lights, 1963), 40.

47 This poem was originally published in *Beatitude*; see Philip Lamantia, "Füd at Foster's," *Beatitude* 9 (September 18, 1959): n.p.

48 Jack Kerouac, *Tristessa* (1960; New York: Penguin, 1992), 53.

49 David Amram, www.davidamram.com/kerouac.html (from *Evergreen Review*, 1969).

50 Christopher Maclaine, *The Time Capsule* (San Francisco: Adler Press, 1960), n.p.

51 McClure, *Scratching*, 24.

52 McClure, *Scratching*, 11.

53 Michael McClure, *Hymns to St. Geryon and Other Poems* (San Francisco: Auerhahn Press, 1959), 7.

54 Jack Kerouac, "About the Beat Generation," in *Portable Kerouac*, 560. Compare "For the Death of 100 Whales" with a moment in Kerouac's *Visions of Cody* that pauses over the "final capture of Moby Dick around February 1952, by the crew of a Scandinavian whaler equipped with a harpoon cannon ... tragic" (348).

55 Ginsberg, *Collected Poems*, 155.

56 John Suiter, *Poets on the Peaks: Gary Snyder, Philip Whalen and Jack Kerouac in the North Cascades* (Washington, DC: Counterpoint, 2002), 114.

57 McClure, *Scratching*, 6. Wallace Berman was close to McClure and a crucial presence on the San Francisco arts scene during this time. He produced *Semina* intermittently from 1955 and 1964, a periodical important to Beat literary history as it published some of the most well-known Beat-associated writers in beautifully crafted formats: each poem was printed on individual cards in different fonts and inks so they became stand-alone art objects. Sometimes entire issues were devoted to a single poem, as is the case with "Peyote Poem" and David Meltzer's "The Clown" (*Semina* 6 [1960]). Like little magazines such as *Yugen*, *Semina* was not limited to Beat writers, nor did Berman conceive of it as an expressly Beat project, but there are some clear Beat energies, particularly in issue 4 (1959), which contains work by Ginsberg, Burroughs, Ray Bremser, Ron Loewinsohn, John Wieners, Philip Lamantia, and Bob Kaufman; and issue 5 (winter 1959), with more work by these last three as well as David Meltzer, John Hoffman, Kirby Doyle, ruth weiss, and William Margolis (in *Semina* 5, Wieners published his own "Peyote Poem").

58 McClure quoted in "High Poet," xliii.

59 Michael McClure, "Drug Notes: Peyote," in *Meat Science Essays* (San Francisco: City Lights, 1963), 25.

60 Harald Mesch, "Writing One's Body: Interview with Michael McClure," *Amerikastudien/American Studies* 32.3 (1987): 361.

61 See also Michael McClure, "Lines from a Peyote Depression," *Beatitude* 5 (June 6, 1959): n.p.

62 David Schneider, *Crowded by Beauty: The Life and Zen of Poet Philip Whalen* (Berkeley: University of California Press, 2015), 57; quotation on 188.

63 Schneider, *Crowded by Beauty*, 188.

64 Leslie Scalapino, "Language as Transient Act, the Poetry of Philip Whalen," in Whalen, *Collected Poems*, xxxii.

65 See David Meltzer, "Interview with Philip Whalen," in Meltzer, *San Francisco Beat*, 345.

66 Philip Whalen, *Memoirs of an Interglacial Age* (San Francisco: Auerhahn Press, 1960), 49, unbracketed ellipses in original. In *Mexico City Blues*, Kerouac writes "nothing there but the picture / in the movie of your mind" (67).

67 In the *Collected Poems*, this poem is titled "Metaphysical Insomnia Jazz. Mumonkan XXIX" (96).

68 Whalen, "Prose Take-Out, Portland 13:ix:58," *Memoirs of an Interglacial Age*, 9.

69 Philip Whalen, *Like I Say* (New York: Totem Press, 1960), 25.

70 Whalen's "20:vii:58, On Which I Renounce the Notion of Social Responsibility" first appeared in *Beatitude* 12 (December 1959): n.p.

71 Schneider's *Crowded by Beauty* is a rich discussion of Whalen's Buddhism and how it was reflected in his poetry.

72 Charters, *Kerouac*, 293.

73 For Montgomery's reflections on Kerouac and on Montgomery's own place in the Beat scene, see the contemporaneous essay by John Montgomery, "Report from the Beat Generation," *Library Journal* 84.12 (June 15, 1959): 1999–2000; the later *Jack Kerouac* (Fresno, CA: Giligia Press, 1970); and *Kerouac West Coast* (Palo Alto, CA: Fels & Firn Press, 1976).

74 Watts, *Way of Zen*, 67.

75 Preston Whaley has suggested that this spontaneous sprint down the mountain can be associated with the musical spontaneity of bop, "in the way a solo may take unusual 'leaps' from one note to the next . . . At another moment the solo may seem to be 'running' in orderly fashion through diatonic arpeggios or scales, or chromatic runs. Jazz solos seem to 'bounce' as they syncopate or swing the beat in a particular way" (*Blows*, 32–33).

76 Kerouac to Holmes (May 27, 1956), *Selected Letters, 1940–1956*, 580.

77 Ann Charters, "'Letting Go' in Writing," in Jack Kerouac, *Old Angel Midnight* (San Francisco: Grey Fox Press, 1993), x.

78 Joanne Kyger, interview with Linda Russo, "Particularizing People's Lives," *Jacket 2* no. 11 (April 2000), http://jacketmagazine.com/11/kyger-iv-by-russo.html.

79 Kerouac, *Old Angel Midnight*, 13.

80 Michael McClure, "Jack's *Old Angel* Midnight," in Kerouac, *Old Angel Midnight*, xvii.

81 See also Philip Whalen's *Goofbook* (1961; Pacifica, CA: Big Bridge Press, 2001), an experiment in spontaneous prose he called a "book for Jack, saying whatever I want to say, whatever I feel like saying" (1). As in *Old Angel Midnight*, Whalen uses spontaneous composition as an opportunity to explore what happens when we give "a name to _____ a state beyond description the suchness, TATHATA" (22).

82 Gary Snyder, *Riprap and Cold Mountain Poems* (Washington, DC: Shoemaker & Hoard, 2004), 12, 19. *Riprap* was originally published by Origin Press (1959), and "Cold Mountain Poems," Snyder's translations of work attributed

to the semi-legendary Chinese poet Han-Shan, appeared in *Evergreen Review* 6 (1958).

83 Lee Bartlett, "Gary Snyder's *Myths & Texts* and the Monomyth," *Western American Literature* 17.2 (summer 1982): 137.

84 Gary Snyder, *Myths & Texts* (New York: Totem, 1960), 7.

85 "Places to Go," in Grace and Johnson, *Breaking*, 140.

86 "Joanne Kyger," in Knight, *Women*, 198.

87 See, e.g., the "Women and the Beats" panel at Naropa University in 2000, the transcripts of which are in *Beats at Naropa*, ed. Anne Waldman and Laura Wright (Minneapolis: Coffee House Press, 2009), 45–60; Kyger is included in *Girls Who Wore Black*, *Breaking the Rule of Cool*, and *Beat Down Your Soul*.

88 See, e.g., Carden, *Women Writers*, 105–135.

89 For a detailed analysis of how Kyger rewrites the epic in *Tapestry*, see Linda Russo, "To Deal with Parts and Particulars: Joanne Kyger's Early Epic Poetics," in *Girls Who Wore Black*, 179–204.

90 Joanne Kyger, *The Tapestry and the Web* (San Francisco: Four Seasons Foundation, 1965), 31.

91 For other representative work from this period, see Lew Welch, *Hermit Poems* (San Francisco: Four Seasons Foundation, 1965), and *On Out* (Berkeley: Oyez, 1965). Welch's body of work may be found *Ring of Bone: Collected Poems* (San Francisco: City Lights, 2012).

92 Rod Phillips, *"Forest Beatniks" and "Urban Thoreaus": Gary Snyder, Jack Kerouac, Lew Welch, and Michael McClure* (New York: Peter Lang, 2000), 80.

93 Lew Welch, *Wobbly Rock* (San Francisco: Auerhahn Press, 1960), n.p.

94 Ron Loewinsohn, *Watermelons* (New York: Totem Press, 1959), 22.

95 Allen Ginsberg, "Introduction," in Loewinsohn, *Watermelons*, 1.

96 William Carlos Williams to Loewinsohn (April 8, 1958), in Loewinsohn, *Watermelons*, 2.

97 This poem also appeared in *Semina* 4 (1959), reproduced in Wallace Berman, *Semina 1955–1964 Art Is Love Is God*, ed. Johan Kugelberg (New York: Boo-Hooray, 2013), 79.

98 Throughout his career, Ted Joans also used the rhino as something like a personal watermark, and in work like "Sanctified Rhino" underscores the Beat inheritance from surrealism: "The rhinos roots a baby goose / while the marvelous candles glow / the owl howls the Ginsberg address / that only the hipster would know" (*Jazz Poems*, n.p.).

99 Simon Warner, *Text and Drugs and Rock 'n' Roll* (New York: Bloomsbury, 2013), 289–299. Warner conducted extensive interviews with Meltzer, and *Text and Drugs* provides a detailed overview of Meltzer's early days in San Francisco, including his meeting with Bob Dylan, which Warner thinks is the first personal contact Dylan had with the Beat writers.

100 Meltzer quoted in Warner, *Text*, 299.

101 David Meltzer, in Meltzer, *Poems*, and David Shenker, *Poetry* (San Francisco: Donald & Alice Schenker, 1957), n.p.

102 In the late 1950s, Meltzer was also working on "Notes for a History," a lengthy poem published across some issues of *Beatitude*. See, e.g., *Beatitude* 11 (November 2, 1959), which contains "From: Notes for a History," in part a nostalgic look at Max Bodenheim, the "original" Greenwich Village bohemian.

103 *Beat Thing* is a brilliant meditation on the elusive phenomenon the title names; Meltzer explores questions of marketing, commercialization, sensationalism, and fandom, among others, across the decades, only to recognize the ultimate arbitrariness of the label "Beat": "who's beat now & then / who keeps score / who're the gatekeeper guys & gals who bar office doors / you need a password a look a book an agent & / good connections" (Meltzer, *Beat Thing* [Albuquerque: La Alameda Press, 2004], 44).

104 David Meltzer, *Ragas* (San Francisco: Discovery Books, 1959), n.p.

105 David Meltzer, "Journal of Birth," *Journal for the Protection of All Beings* 1 (1961): 69.

106 The best discussion of Martinelli's biography is Steven Moore, "Sheri Martinelli: A Modernist Muse," in *My Back Pages*, 535–566. I rely on Moore here.

107 See Anatole Broyard, *Kafka Was the Rage* (New York: Vintage, 1993). Broyard disguises Martinelli as "Sheri Donatti," but she is otherwise quite recognizable; he writes that she was "her own avant-garde" (3).

108 Martinelli to Charles Bukowski (July 6, 1960), in *Beerspit Night and Cursing: The Correspondence of Charles Bukowski and Sheri Martinelli, 1960–1967*, ed. Steven Moore (Santa Rosa, CA: Black Sparrow Press, 2001), 54.

109 Martinelli to Ferlinghetti (October 2, 1958), "City Lights Books Records, 1953–1970," Box 8, Folder 23, Bancroft Library, UC-Berkeley.

110 Martinelli to Ferlinghetti (October 13, 1958), "City Lights Books Records, 1953–1970," Box 8, Folder 23, Bancroft Library, UC-Berkeley.

111 Sheri Martinelli, "The Last Days of North Beach in San Francisco," *Anagogic & Paideumic Review* 1.6 (1960): n.p. This issue also collects some of the handbills she had drawn for local poetry readings.

112 Steven Moore explains that "'anagogic' is a spiritual interpretation of a text, and 'paideumic' derives from *paideuma*, a term Pound picked up from Frobenius to describe 'the tangle or complex of the inrooted ideas of any period' (or, more simply, the culture taught by educators)" ("Modernist Muse," 556).

113 William Margolis, "Flash Bulb Photo of Poet's Impromptu," *Anagogic & Paideumic Review* 1.3 (November/December 1959): n.p.

114 C. V. J. Anderson, "La Martinelli Talks of Ezra," *Beatitude* 16 (September–October 1960): n.p. For other work about Martinelli, see Philip Lamantia, "Sheri," in *Ekstasis* (1959); and Allen Ginsberg, "Iron Horse" (1966), which describes his visit to "Sheri Martinelli's little house with combs and shells / Since February fear, she saw LSD / Zodiac in earth grass"; in *Collected Poems*, 468. In 1959, Lamantia wrote to Martinelli: "I love you because I love you. Because you are a GODDESS! And because you are *the* Painter NOW! THE

Artist!" (Lamantia to Martinelli, [April 16], 1959, Sheri Martinelli papers, 1905–1980, Box 16, "Lamantia" folder, Yale Collection of American Literature, Beinecke Rare Book and Manuscript Library, Yale University).

115 Sheri Martinelli, "The Case against Ezra Pound & Confucius & Christ," Sheri Martinelli papers, 1905–1980, Box 25, "Anagogic & Paideumic Review" folder, Yale Collection of American Literature, Beinecke Rare Book and Manuscript Library, Yale University. See also Martinelli, "For Allen," in *Best Minds: A Tribute to Allen Ginsberg*, ed. Bill Morgan and Bob Rosenthal (New York: Lospecchio Press, 1986), 190.

116 Sheri Martinelli, "Duties of a Lady Female," *Anagogic & Paideumic Review* 1.3 (November/December 1959): n.p., unbracketed ellipses in original. This version is identical to the one printed in *A Different Beat*, 154–158, so I will quote from that so readers may easily locate the references; this quotation in Peabody, *A Different Beat*, 154–155.

117 Ronna Johnson, "Beats and Gender," in Belletto, *Cambridge Companion to the Beats*, 168–169.

118 La Martinelli [Sheri Martinelli], "On Loving Many," *Beatitude* 6 (n.d. [summer 1959]): n.p.

119 Moore, "A Modernist Muse," 558.

120 Sheri Martinelli, "The Last Days of North Beach in San Francisco," *Anagogic & Paideumic Review* 1.6 (1960): n.p.

121 Martinelli notes at the end of the essay that Bob Kaufman, Padriec O'Sullivan, William Margolis, and Sam Suzuki are "exempted from all above comments."

122 For example, Kandel is not discussed at length in *Girls Who Wore Black* or *Women Writers of the Beat Era*, nor is she included in *The Portable Beat Reader*. *Reconstructing the Beats* contains essays on Kandel's *The Love Book*.

123 Jack Kerouac, *Big Sur* (1962; New York: Bantam, 1963), 61.

124 Grover Haynes, untitled afterword, in Lenore Kandel, *A Passing Dragon* (Studio City: Three Penny Press, 1959), n.p.

125 Lenore Kandel, "First They Slaughtered Angels," in *Beatitude Anthology*, 80.

126 *A Passing Dragon* and *A Passing Dragon Seen Again* are essentially the same book, but with a few minor changes: Grover Haynes slightly revised his introductory statement (from "About the Poet" in *A Passing Dragon* to "Preface" in *A Passing Dragon Seen Again*), and there are a couple more poems in *A Passing Dragon Seen Again*.

127 Haynes, "About the Poet," in Kandel, *A Passing Dragon*, n.p.

128 Lenore Kandel, "I have chosen for my guide the gray wind," in *A Passing Dragon*, n.p. Unless otherwise noted, the poems in Kandel's early books are untitled, so I refer to them by their first lines.

129 Lenore Kandel, "All I Have in the World," in *An Exquisite Navel* (Studio City: Three Penny Press, 1959), n.p.

130 See Lenore Kandel, *The Love Book* (San Francisco: Stolen Paper Editions, 1966).

131 One notable exception is Steven Moore, who has written a very useful sketch of Ansen's life and works; see Moore, "The Legend of Alan Ansen," in *My Back Pages*, 486–505.

132 Alan Ansen, *Disorderly Houses* (Middleton, CT: Wesleyan University Press, 1961), n.p. Steven Moore notes that *Disorderly Houses*, which contains most of the material in *The Old Religion*, is "the principal volume by which Ansen's work as a poet was known until the 1989 publication of *Contact Highs*" ("Legend of Alan Ansen," 500). Since most of *The Old Religion* is incorporated into *Disorderly Houses*, Ansen's more well-known volume, I quote from that book. See also Ansen, *Contact Highs: Selected Poems 1957–1987* (New York: Dalkey Archive Press, 1989).

133 Philip Whalen's undergraduate thesis, "The Calendar: A Book of Poems" (1951), was based on Graves's translation of the old Welsh "Song of Amergin," which appeared in *The White Goddess*. See Whalen, *Collected Poems*, 817–826.

134 In a poem in turn dedicated to Ansen, Corso claimed Venice was "Aging my modern vision"; see Corso, "I Where I Stand," in *Long Live Man* (New York: New Directions, 1962), 41.

135 Miles, *Beat Hotel*, 76.

136 See Corso, *Accidental Autobiography*, 210.

Chapter 10 Ignus

1 The most comprehensive account of the Beat Hotel is Barry Miles's *The Beat Hotel*. I rely on Miles for my brief account of the hotel; for photographs of the hotel and its residents during this period, see Harold Chapman, *The Beat Hotel* (Geneva: Gris Banal, 1984). There is also a documentary worth watching: *The Beat Hotel*, dir. Alan Govenar (2012).

2 William S. Burroughs, "Foreword," in Harold Norse, *Beat Hotel* (San Diego: Atticus Press, 1983), n.p.

3 See Brion Gysin, *The Last Museum* (New York: Grove, 1986); Harold Norse, *Memoirs of Bastard Angel* (New York: William Morrow, 1989), 330–380; Norse, *The Beat Hotel*; and Kay Johnson, *Human Songs* (London: City Lights/ Villiers, 1964). See also Jean-Jacques Lebel, "Burroughs: The Beat Years," in Harris and MacFayden, *Naked Lunch@50*, 84–90.

4 For a discussion of how "Kaddish" came into being, see Bill Morgan, "Some Words on Allen Ginsberg's Kaddish," in Ginsberg, *Kaddish and Other Poems, 1958–1960*, expanded edition (1961; San Francisco: City Lights, 2010), 101–125.

5 Norse, *Memoirs of a Bastard Angel*, 139.

6 See also Norse, "calling all geniuses" (Norse, *In the Hub of the Fiery Force: Collected Poems 1934–2003* [New York: Thunder's Mouth Press, 2003], 80–81), "the death of 9 rue gît-le-coeur" (332–333), "beat hotel, 9 rue gît-le-coeur" (511), and Norse, *Hotel Nirvana* (San Francisco: City Lights, 1974), which proceeds "from the beat hotel where I cut up my life" (1).

7 *Pull My Daisy* (New York: Grove, 1961). This volume includes a transcript of Kerouac's narration, as well as numerous stills from the film. Although Kerouac did speak the voiceover spontaneously, it was not completely ad-libbed on the spot insofar as the characters and some of the dialogue were drawn from a play he had written; see Kerouac, *Beat Generation* (New York: Thunder's Mouth Press, 2005).

8 For a description of the film's production, see Jack Sargeant, *Naked Lens: An Illustrated History of Beat Cinema* (London: Creation Books, 1997), 13–23. Although the opening title card announces that "Robert Frank and Alfred Leslie Present" *Pull My Daisy*, there was some disagreement between the two men as to who "really" directed the film; for their differing perspectives, see "An Interview with Alfred Leslie," 34–35; and "An Interview with Robert Frank," 44–45, both in Sargeant, *Naked Lens*.

9 For good discussions of Beat film, see Sargeant, *Naked Lens*; and David Sterritt, *Mad to Be Saved: The Beats, the '50s, and Film* (Carbondale: Southern Illinois University Press, 1998).

10 Carolyn Cassady, *Off the Road* (New York: Penguin, 1990), 264.

11 David Amram, *Offbeat: Collaborating with Kerouac* (New York: Thunder's Mouth Press, 2002), 49. Amram, an important Beat musician and writer, offers the most detailed insider's account of the making of *Pull My Daisy* (48–84). Note that in *Offbeat*, one keyword is "natural," as for example when he notes that "The collaboration that Jack Kerouac and I began in 1956 happened naturally" (v) or that "Collaborating with Kerouac was as natural as breathing" (3).

12 "An Interview with Alfred Leslie," in Sargeant, *Naked Lens*, 37.

13 *Rebels: A Journey Underground*, dir. Kevin Alexander (1999).

14 Allen Ginsberg reading "Ignu" at Salem State University 1973. Available online: www.youtube.com/watch?v=ZxIOMtR-byY.

15 Ginsberg to Kerouac (November 17, 1958), in Kerouac and Ginsberg, *The Letters*, 418.

Chapter 11 The Women Who Said Something

1 See, in particular, *Women of the Beat Generation* (1996), *A Different Beat* (1997), *Girls Who Wore Black* (2002), *Out of the Shadows: Beat Women Are Not Beaten Women*, ed. Frida Forsgren and Michael J. Prince (Kristiansand, Norway: Portal Books, 2015), and *Women Writers of the Beat Era* (2018).

2 Alfred Aronowitz, "The Beat Generation, Part 4," *New York Post* (March 12, 1959): 4, 22; quotation on 4.

3 Aronowitz, "The Beat Generation, Part 4," 4.

4 Joyce Johnson, *Minor Characters: A Beat Memoir* (1983; New York: Penguin, 1994), 135.

5 Ronna C. Johnson, "'And Then She Went': Beat Departures and Feminine Transgressions in Joyce Johnson's *Come and Join the Dance*," in Johnson and Grace, *Girls Who Wore Black*, 70.

6 Jack Kerouac and Joyce Johnson, *Door Wide Open: A Beat Love Affair in Letters, 1957–1958* (New York: Viking, 2000), 6, 39.

7 Joyce Johnson, *Come and Join the Dance* (1962; New York: Open Road, 2014), 63. This novel was first published under the name Joyce Glassman, but since the writer has subsequently been known professionally by her married name, Joyce Johnson, I use that name throughout this book.

8 According to *Minor Characters*, Susan's collegiate career mirrors Johnson's own (94); see also Susan's physical description (10–11), which resonates with Aronowitz's description of Johnson.

9 Gerald Walker, "Fugitive from Girlhood," *New York Times* (January 28, 1962): 217.

10 Nevertheless, Kerouac wanted to view *Come and Join the Dance* in terms of his own aims and methodologies; as he wrote to Ginsberg in 1958, Johnson was "going to write a big VISIONS OF ELISE just for me (then publish it later as is, tho she doesn't believe it)" (Kerouac to Ginsberg [January 21, 1958], in Kerouac and Ginsberg, *The Letters*, 391).

11 Johnson to "Sheila" (September 16, 1957), in Kerouac and Johnson, *Door Wide Open*, 71.

12 Note also that in 1960, Barbara Probst Solomon had borrowed the term "beat" for her novel *The Beat of Life* (1960), a move at least one reviewer thought "unfortunate" because "its claim and disclaimer of 'Beat'" made the book "self-consciously representative of this year's generation" (John Thompson, "Other People's Affairs," *Partisan Review* 28.1 [January–February 1961]: 119). Solomon was, like Johnson, a Barnard student in the late 1950s, and like *Come and Join the Dance* Solomon's novel follows a female protagonist from the Upper West Side who comes to move in the more bohemian circles in the Village and elsewhere. See Solomon, *The Beat of Life* (1960; New York: Great Marsh Press, 1998).

13 See Ronna C. Johnson, "And Then She Went," for an elaboration of this reading. Johnson's essay is, to my knowledge, the only detailed scholarly treatment of *Come and Join the Dance*.

14 Kerouac to Johnson (mid-August 1958), in Kerouac and Johnson, *Door Wide Open*, 161.

15 See also Allen Ginsberg, "A Dream," *GNAOUA* 1 (spring 1964): 31–32.

16 Herbert Huncke, "Beware of Fallen Angels," in *Huncke's Journal* (New York: Poets Press, 1965), 49.

17 John Wieners, "Monday (In the jungle," in *Pa'Lante*, ed. Howard Shulman (New York: League of Militant Poets, 1962), 56–57.

18 Irving Rosenthal, *Sheeper* (New York: Grove Press, 1967), 253.

19 When Cowen's work was included in *Fuck You*, editor Ed Sanders, known for his flamboyant characterizations in the contributors' notes, wrote: "ELISE COWAN [*sic*] was flashed to heaven in 1962 when she threw her body out of her parents New York apartment. A friend of Ginzap [Ginsberg], Huncke, Orlovsky, she has published in Things, City Lights Journal #2, & other publications" ("Notes on Contributors," *Fuck You* 5.8 [March 1965]: n.p.).

20 See Leo Skir, "Elise Cowen: A Brief Memoir of the Fifties," in Knight, *Women of the Beat Generation*, 143–158. For Skir's take on same-sex desire set against the backdrop of the changing Beat scene, see his novel, *Boychik* (New York: Winter House, 1971). Early on, the main characters head off to see "'the girlfriend of one of the leading beat poets' ... 'Is *she* a beatnik?' [said Boychik]. 'They don't call themselves beatniks,' I said. 'But she is'" (18).

21 Tony Trigilio, "Introduction," in Cowen, *Poems and Fragments*, xiv–xv.

22 For a bibliography of Cowen's known publications, see Cowen, *Poems and Fragments*, 170–172. As Trigilio explains, the poems printed in earlier anthologies rely on corrupt copies; in *Poems and Fragments*, by contrast, Trigilio works from the original notebook, the result of which is that some of the poems are represented quite differently in that volume than in those anthologies; for this reason I'm quoting from the versions in *Poems and Fragments*.

23 Cowen, *Poems and Fragments*, 51.

24 Janine Pommy Vega, *Mad Dogs of Trieste* (Santa Rosa: Black Sparrow, 2000), 256.

25 Janine Pommy Vega, *Tracking the Serpent: Journeys to Four Continents* (San Francisco: City Lights, 1997), 3. The first part of *Tracking*, called "Seeds of Travel," is the best succinct overview of Pommy Vega's early life, including when she met Fernando Vega. See also Pommy Vega's interview with Nancy M. Grace in Grace and Johnson, *Breaking*, 235–253.

26 "Tracking the Serpent," in Grace and Johnson, *Breaking*, 244, 247–248.

27 Janine Pommy Vega, *Poems to Fernando* (San Francisco: City Lights, 1968), 15.

28 Grace and Johnson, *Breaking the Rule of Cool*, 232.

29 See J. Vega, *Journal of a Hermit* (Cherry Valley, NY: Cherry Valley Editions, 1974); another edition, *Journal of a Hermit &*, was published by Cherry Valley Editions in 1979 and included some extra material.

30 Johnson to Kupferberg (1960), Tuli Kupferberg and Sylvia Topp Papers, MSS.385; box 42, folder 59, Fales Library and Special Collections, New York University Libraries.

31 Corso to Ferlinghetti (ca. July 15, 1961), in Corso, *Accidental Autobiography*, 290.

32 Johnson to Ferlinghetti (January 27, 1968), City Lights Books Records, Box 6, Folder 37, Bancroft Library, UC-Berkeley.

33 For reminiscences about Kay Johnson by those who knew her, see www.emptymirrorbooks.com/beat/kaja.html.

34 Jeff Weddle, *Bohemian New Orleans: The Story of Outsider and Loujon Press* (Jackson: University Press of Mississippi, 2007), 57.

35 "The Outsider" advertisement, *Yugen* 7 (1961): n.p.

36 Kay Johnson, "the emerald city," *Outsider* 2.4–5 (winter 1968/1969): 188.

37 Kaja [Kay Johnson], "the emerald city," *Outsider* 1.2 (summer 1962): 50.

38 Johnson to Kupferberg (July 25, 1960), Tuli Kupferberg and Sylvia Topp Papers, MSS.385; box 42, folder 59, Fales Library and Special Collections, New York University Libraries.

39 See also "A Serious and Sad Poem," in Kaja (Kay Johnson), *The Impossible Possible* (New Orleans: New School Press, 1960), 5.

40 Johnson to Ferlinghetti (December 8, 1961), City Lights Books Records, 1953–1970, Box 6, Folder 37, Bancroft Library, UC-Berkeley.

41 See Weddle, *Bohemian New Orleans*, 72–73.

42 Kay Johnson, "in Heaven at 9 Git-Le-Coeur," *Outsider* 1.2 (summer 1962): 32, 33. See also "Where I Live," in Johnson, *Human Songs* (London: City Lights/Villiers, 1964), 16. For another account of Johnson's experience at the Beat Hotel, see her letter to Ferlinghetti (December 8, 1961).

43 Kay Johnson, "experience of 7 consecutive hours," *Outsider* 1.2 (summer 1962): 29, 30.

44 Quoted in Weddle, *Bohemian New Orleans*, 73.

45 Johnson to Ferlinghetti (July 24, 1960), City Lights Books Records, 1953–1970, Box 6, Folder 37, Bancroft Library, UC-Berkeley.

46 Johnson, *Human Songs*, 9.

47 For other poems in *Human Songs* that challenge normative gender binaries, see "In Heaven, It's Publicly Intimate" and "Many a Male."

48 Kay Johnson contributor's note, *Outsider* 1.2 (summer 1962): n.p.

49 Kaja [Kay Johnson], *Eat Me, Drink Me* (New Orleans: New School Press, 1960), 7.

50 Kay Johnson, "LSD – 748," *Residu* 1.1 (spring 1965): 81.

51 Kay Johnson, "from: the fourth hour," *Outsider* 1.2 (summer 1961): 9.

52 In the rambling and disjointed letters Johnson wrote to Ferlinghetti throughout the 1960s, she often refers to a startling range of projects in progress, amounting to at least "3 army trunks full" of novels and other writing (Johnson to Ferlinghetti, July 28, 1964). In 1961, she claimed that "Olympia Press wants to see my novel about the man who thought he was a loaf of bread ... called I AM IN THE BELLY OF THE WHALE" (Johnson to Ferlinghetti, December 8, 1961). And in 1963, she informed him that "i am now writing several lonely novels: but they are all the same novel," and that "i am writing a new novel called BEAN SOUP or THE WOMAN WHO WAS AFRAID TO BE GOD; ... It is for D.H. Lawrence. as i am his re-incarnation" (August 20 to September 5, 1963). All letters in City Lights Books Records, 1953–1970, Box 6, Folder 37, Bancroft Library, UC-Berkeley.

53 After 1962, Bergé, Owens, and Wakoski would go on to long and distinguished literary careers, but none has been consistently linked to the Beats, even as their early work appeared in some of the little magazines discussed earlier: *Beatitude/East* (Bergé), *Yugen* (Owens), and *Beatitude* (Wakoski).

54 Diane Wakoski's first poetry collection, *Coins and Coffins*, was published later in 1962 by poet Jerome Rothenberg's Hawk's Well Press. As a student at UC-Berkeley in the late 1950s, she had edited a magazine, *Occident*, which had published her poem "God Damn It, I Hate War," as a broadside in 1960.

55 Barbara Moraff, "im a hip song mistress," *Fuck You* 5.4 (n.d.; between May and December, 1963): n.p.

56 LeRoi Jones, "Note on the Authors," in *Four Young Lady Poets,* ed. Jones (New York: Totem Press, 1962), n.p.

57 See Barbara Moraff, "Poem for Theo," *Yugen* 2 (1958): 12–13; "Poem for Tamara," "In a Hospital Room from a Halfclosed Lid," and "Wednesday Understands That," all in *Yugen* 3 (1958): 6–7; "poem," *Yugen* 5 (1959): 30. Although Moraff was included in a later anthology of women Beat writers, Richard Peabody's *A Different Beat* (1997), she tends not to figure in other studies of Beat women, including Knight's *Women of the Beat Generation,* Grace and Johnson's *Breaking the Rule of Cool* or *Girls Who Wore Black,* or Mary Paniccia Carden's *Women Writers of the Beat Era.*

58 Kerouac quoted in Amy L. Friedman, "'I Say My New Name': Women Writers of the Beat Generation," in Lee, *The Beat Generation Writers,* 203.

59 See Robert E. Buswell Jr. and Donald S. Lopez Jr., *The Princeton Dictionary of Buddhism* (Princeton: Princeton University Press, 2014), 603. The conventional English transliteration is: "om mani padme hum," meaning "homage to the Jewel-Lotus one" in Sanskirt.

60 Barbara Moraff, "Pome," *Beatitude* 9 (September 18, 1959): n.p. It was reprinted in *Beatitude Anthology,* 84. Compare Moraff's line "who takes tea at moondumb teatime" with a line in Kerouac's *Old Angel Midnight:* "The moon is a piece of tea" (8).

61 This image echoes one in Lenore Kandel's poem "All I have in the world," in which Kandel connects herself to volcanoes as a way of asserting power: "I would like to sit on mountain tops / and watch the lava flow" (*Exquisite Navel,* n.p.).

62 Barbara Moraff, "Another Plain Poem," *The Nation* (June 9, 1962): 523.

63 No author [Howard Ant], "Les Deux Megots," in *Seventh Street: Poems from Les Deux Megots* (New York: Hesperidian Press, 1961), x–xi. See Bergé, *Light Years,* 18, for the attribution of this unsigned foreword to Ant.

64 Diane Wakoski, "Remembering the New York 1960s Coffee House World of Poetry," in Bergé, *Light Years,* 573.

65 For a contemporaneous poem about a similarly attired Tessa, see Elise Cowen, "Tessa Flaps through My Door," in Cowen, *Poems and Fragments,* 78.

66 Carol Bergé, "Remembrance of Things to Come," in Bergé, *Light Years,* 77.

67 Carol Bergé, *The Vancouver Report* (New York: Fuck You Press, 1964), 10–11. Note in her chapbook of the same year, *The Vulnerable Island* (Cleveland, OH: Renegade Press, 1964), Bergé included a poem, "Scene," subtitled "in memoriam: WCW." For more on the conference, see *The Line Has Shattered: Vancouver's Landmark 1963 Poetry Conference,* dir. Robert McTavish (2013).

68 Morgan, *Typewriter,* 155.

Chapter 12 Liberating Language

1 Joans, "Je Me Vois," 230.

2 Ferlinghetti sometimes insisted *Her* was not a novel, but at other times referred to it as such; see Skau, *"Constantly Risking,"* 50 n. 5.

3 See Ferlinghetti, "Page of Writing from *HER*," *Beatitude* 8 (August 15, 1959): n.p.

4 Lawrence Ferlinghetti, *Her* (1960; New York: New Directions, 1988), 24.

5 Ferlinghetti, *San Francisco Beat*, 85

6 Corso quoted in *I Greet*, 65.

7 Burroughs, *Naked Lunch: The Restored Text*, 89.

8 Kerouac, "Are Writers Made or Born?," in *Portable Kerouac*, 489; Kerouac, "Belief & Technique for Modern Prose," in *Portable Kerouac*, 483.

9 Conrad Knickerbocker, "White Junk" (interview with William Burroughs), in William S. Burroughs, *Burroughs Live: The Collected Interviews of William S. Burroughs, 1960–1997*, ed. Sylvère Lotringer (Cambridge, MA: Semiotext(e), 2001), 94.

10 Corso to Ferlinghetti (September 24, 1958), in Corso, *Accidental Autobiography*, 141, unbracketed ellipses in original.

11 Corso to James Laughlin (ca. December 1960), in Corso, *Accidental Autobiography*, 269.

12 Corso to Allen Ginsberg (ca. November 30, 1960), in Corso, *Accidental Autobiography*, 267.

13 In 1961, Corso wrote to Ginsberg about his "European beatniking forth" (Corso, *Accidental Autobiography*, 276).

14 Gregory Corso, *The American Express* (Paris: Olympia, 1961), 28.

15 For more on Corso's use of the American Express office, see Merve Emre, "Ironic Institutions: Counterculture Fictions and the American Express Company," *American Literature* 87.1 (March 2015): 107–136.

16 Corso to Ginsberg (ca. December 14, 1960), in Corso, *Accidental Autobiography*, 270.

17 See Francis J. Rigney and Douglas L. Smith, *The Real Bohemia: A Sociological and Psychological Study of the "Beats"* (New York: Basic Books, 1961).

18 Ted Joans, *The Hipsters* (New York: Corinth Books, 1961), n.p.

19 William S. Burroughs and Brion Gysin, *The Third Mind* (New York: Viking, 1978), n.p.

20 Burroughs to Dave Haselwood (June 24, 1960), in Burroughs, *Rub Out*, 33.

21 William S. Burroughs, "The Cut Up Method of Brion Gysin," in Parkinson, *A Casebook on the Beat*, 105.

22 Gérard-Georges Lemaire, "23 Stitches Taken," in *Third Mind*, n.p." Emphasizing the importance of material history, Oliver Harris points out that analyzing this trilogy is particularly tricky because it "became so garbled by new editions that the first title has become the last text and the last title the earliest text. This peculiar trilogy has managed to reverse beginnings and ends, to lose its center, and for lack of due attention to *which* edition they are reading, to confuse the critics" (Harris, *Secret*, 244–245). In this way, the strange textual history of the Nova Trilogy reflects, in a more global way, the evasive tactics of discrete cut-ups.

23 Knickerbocker, "White Junk," 67. See also Burroughs, "Introductions," in *The Third Mind*, n.p.

24 Allen Ginsberg, *Planet News* (San Francisco: City Lights, 1968), 119.

25 For an account of the cut-up method's origins and the genesis of *Minutes to Go*, see Miles, *Call Me*, 362–366. Note that as *Minutes to Go* was being prepared for publication, Burroughs had sent another cut-up collaboration with Gysin to Dave Haselwood in San Francisco, who published it as Burroughs and Gysin, *The Exterminator* (San Francisco: Auerhahn, 1960). Burroughs wanted to immediately publish another cut-up collaboration, "Exterminator II," with Auerhahn, but the project never came to fruition.

26 Sinclair Beiles, William S. Burroughs, Gregory Corso, and Brion Gysin, *Minutes to Go* (Paris: Two Cities Editions, 1960), n.p.

27 In *Minutes to Go*, Burroughs specifies that "Open Letter to Life Magazine" is a "Cut-up of 'Beat Generation' Life Magazine Dec-5 1959." In fact, it is a cut-up of Paul O'Neil's "The Only Rebellion Around," *Life* (November 30, 1959).

28 This is according to Bill Morgan; see his editor's note in Burroughs, *Rub Out*, 10.

29 O'Neil, "Only Rebellion Around," 119.

30 The *Life* article includes a photo of Burroughs sitting forlornly on an iron bed at the Beat Hotel, and describes him as "a pale, cadaverous and bespectacled being who has devoted most of his adult life to a lonely pursuit of drugs and debauchery" (124).

31 See Jon Savage, "Cut-Ups Go Pop: William S. Burroughs and a Mashed-Up Future," in *Cut-Ups, Cut-Ins, Cut-Outs: The Art of William S. Burroughs*, ed. Colin Fallows and Synne Genzmer (Vienna: Kunsthalle Wien, 2012). This volume is the catalogue accompanying an exhibit on Burroughs in Vienna in 2012, and is a good introduction to his experimental work, including cut-ups and fold-ins; numerous photographs offer a visual sense of this work.

Chapter 13 The Vietnam Effect

1 Sanders, *Fug You*, 277.

2 "Editors Statement," *Journal for the Protection of All Beings* 1.1 (1961): n.p.

3 Tuli Kupferberg, "The Function of Bohemia" (1962), Tuli Kupferberg and Sylvia Topp Papers, MSS.385; box 8, folder 10, Fales Library and Special Collections, New York University Libraries.

4 See, among many other examples, Diane di Prima, *Revolutionary Letters* (1968; San Francisco: City Lights, 2019); Lawrence Ferlinghetti, *Routines* (New York: New Directions, 1964); and Michael McClure, *Poisoned Wheat* (San Francisco: privately printed, 1965).

5 Tuli Kupferberg, *Fuck Nam: A Morality Play* (New York: Birth Press, 1966), 14.

6 William S. Burroughs, "The Coming of the Purple Better One," *Esquire* (November 1, 1968), https://classic.esquire.com/article/1968/11/1/the-coming-of-the-purple-better-one.

7 Kerouac, "After Me, the Deluge," in *Portable Kerouac*, 573.

8 For more on the connections between the Beats and the Hungry Generation, see Steven Belletto, "The Beat Generation Meets the Hungry Generation:

U.S.–Calcutta Networks and the 1960s 'Revolt of the Personal,'" *Humanities* 8.3 (January 2019): 1–17.

9　Savage, "Cut-Ups Go Pop," 38–39.

10　Allen Ginsberg, *The Fall of America* (San Francisco: City Lights, 1972), 32, ellipses in original.

11　See William Burroughs and Brion Gysin, *The Exterminator* (San Francisco: Auerhahn, 1960), 5; and Burroughs, "The Cut-Up Method of Brion Gysin," in *The Third Mind*, n.p.

12　The focus on Wichita draws attention to Kansas as a locus of Beat-related activity. See in particular the work of Charles Plymell; as Ginsberg wrote in his introduction to Plymell's first book of poetry, *Apocalypse Rose* (1966), "Plymell and friends inventing the Wichita *Vortex* contribute to a tradition stretching back from Lamantia ... to Poe" (Ginsberg, "Plymell's Qualities," in Charles Plymell, *Apocalypse Rose* [San Francisco: Dave Haselwood, 1966], n.p.).

13　Eliot Katz, *The Poetry and Politics of Allen Ginsberg* (United Kingdom: Beatdom Books, 2016), 146.

14　See Belletto, "The Beat Generation Meets the Hungry Generation," 12–14.

15　Allen Ginsberg, "Demonstration or Spectacle as Example, as Communication; or How to Make a March/Spectacle," in *Deliberate Prose: Selected Essays, 1952–1995,* ed. Bill Morgan (New York: Perennial 2000), 10.

16　See Ed Sanders, *The Poetry and Life of Allen Ginsberg: A Narrative Poem* (Woodstock, NY: Overlook Press, 2000).

17　*Fuck You* 5.4 (1963): n.p. Note that major Beat writers were such an important influence on Sanders that *Fuck You*'s first issue (February 1962) is devoted mostly to his own "Soft-Man Poems," which as he recalled, were "a kind of semireligious text inspired by William Burroughs's novel *The Soft Machine*" (*Fug You*, 8). These poems later opened Sanders's second book of poetry, *Peace Eye* (Buffalo, NY: Frontier Press, 1965). A "2nd enlarged edition" was published by Frontier Press in 1967.

18　Tuli Kupferberg and Robert Bashlow, *1001 Ways to Beat the Draft* (New York: Oliver Layton Press, 1966), 3.

19　For a more detailed discussion of *Fuck You*, see Daniel Kane, *All Poets Welcome: The Lower East Side Poetry Scene in the 1960s* (Berkeley: University of California Press, 2003), 64–79.

20　Michael McClure, "Fuck Essay," *Fuck You* 5.4 (1963): n.p.

21　Ed Sanders, "Resistance to Goon Squads," *Fuck You* 5.7 (August 1964): n.p.

22　Editorial notes, *Fuck You/A Magazine of the Arts* 5.3 (May 1963): n.p.

23　Ed Sanders, *Poem from Jail* (San Francisco: City Lights, 1963), 10.

24　Other regular members included Ken Weaver, Steve Weber, and Peter Stampfel.

25　Bob Dylan, *Chronicles: Vol. 1* (New York: Simon & Schuster, 2004), 57. For more on the connections between the Beats and rock music, see Warner, *Text and Drugs*.

26　Norman Mailer, *Armies of the Night* (1968; New York: Plume, 1994), 120.

27 Jerry Rubin, *Do It! Scenarios of the Revolution* (New York: Simon & Schuster, 1970), 45.
28 Abbie Hoffman, *Steal This Book* (1971; New York: Thunder's Mouth Press, 2002), 147.

Coda

1 Christian Lorentzen, "Sheila Heti, Ben Lerner, Tao Lin: How 'Auto' Is 'Autofiction'?," *Vulture* (May 11, 2018), www.vulture.com/2018/05/how-auto-is-autofiction.html.
2 C. Wright Mills, *The Power Elite* (1956; New York: Oxford University Press, 2000), 304.

Bibliography

Note: Individual poems are cited in the notes.

BEAT-ASSOCIATED LITTLE MAGAZINES

Anagogic & Paideumic Review, ed. Sheri Martinelli (1959–1960)
Ark II Moby I, ed. Michael McClure and James Harmon (1956–1957)
Bastard Angel, ed. Harold Norse (1972–1974)
Beatitude, ed. John Kelly, Bob Kaufman, et al. (first run: 1959–1960)
Big Table, ed. Irving Rosenthal and Paul Carroll (1959–1960)
Birth, ed. Tuli Kupferberg (1958–1960)
Black Mountain Review, ed. Robert Creeley (1954–1957)
Circle, ed. George Leite (1944–1948)
City Lights Journal, ed. Lawrence Ferlinghetti (1963–1966)
Contour, ed. Christopher Maclaine (1947–1949)
Evergreen Review, ed. Barney Rosset (first run: 1957–1973)
The Floating Bear, ed. Diane di Prima and LeRoi Jones (1961–1969)
Fuck You/A Magazine of the Arts, ed. Ed Sanders (1962–1965)
Journal for the Protection of All Beings, ed. Michael McClure, Lawrence Ferlinghetti, David Meltzer, and Gary Snyder (1961–1978)
Kulchur, ed. Mark Schleifer, Lita Hornick, et al. (1960–1966)
Measure, ed. John Wieners (1957–1962)
Miscellaneous Man, ed. William J. Margolis (first run: 1954–1959)
Outsider, ed. Jon Edgar Webb (1961–1968/1969)
Semina, ed. Wallace Berman (1955–1964)
Yeah, ed. Tuli Kupferberg (1961–1965)
Yugen, ed. LeRoi Jones and Hettie Cohen (Jones) (1958–1962)

PUBLISHED AND UNPUBLISHED WORKS

Abbott, Steve. "Hidden Master of the Beats," *Poetry Flash* 155 (February 1986): 1, 12–14.
Adams, Frank S. "Columbia Student Kills Friend and Sinks Body in Hudson River," *New York Times* (August 17, 1944): 1, 13.

Albright, Thomas. *Art in the San Francisco Bay Area, 1945–1980: An Illustrated History*. Berkeley: University of California Press, 1985.

Aldan, Daisy. "Note to This Book," in *A New Folder/Americans: Poems and Drawings*, ed. Aldan. New York: Folder Editions, 1959.

Allen, Donald. "Preface," in *The New American Poetry*.

ed. *The New American Poetry*. New York: Grove, 1960.

Amburn, Ellis. *Subterranean Kerouac: The Hidden Life of Jack Kerouac*. New York: St. Martin's Press, 1998.

Amram, David. *Offbeat: Collaborating with Kerouac*. New York: Thunder's Mouth Press, 2002.

Anderson, C. V. J. *Colloquy*. San Francisco: Bread & Wine Press, 1960.

A Liturgy for Dragons. New York: Chas. P. Young Company, 1961.

Ansen, Alan. "Anyone Who Can Pick Up a Frying Pan Owns Death," *Big Table* 2 (summer 1959).

Disorderly Houses. Middleton, CT: Wesleyan University Press, 1961.

Appignansei, Richard and Chris Garratt. *Introducing Postmodernism*. Cambridge: Icon Books, 2004.

Armstrong, Tim. "Poetry and Science," in *A Companion to Twentieth Century Poetry*, ed. Neil Roberts. London: Blackwell, 2001.

Aronowitz, Alfred. "The Beat Generation, Parts I–XII," *New York Post* (March 9–21, 1959).

Auden, W. H. *The Age of Anxiety*. 1947. Princeton: Princeton University Press, 2011.

Baldwin, James. "The Black Boy Looks at the White Boy," in *Collected Essays*. New York: Library of America, 1998.

"Bam; Roll on with Bam!" *Time* (September 14, 1959): 28.

Baraka, Amiri. *The Autobiography of LeRoi Jones*. New York: Freundlich Books, 1984.

Transbluecency: The Selected Poetry of Amiri Baraka/LeRoi Jones: 1961–1995. Venice: Marsilio, 1995.

See also Jones, LeRoi.

Bartlett, Lee, ed. *Benchmark & Blaze: The Emergence of William Everson*. Metuchen, NJ: Scarecrow Press, 1979.

Bartlett, Lee, "Gary Snyder's *Myths & Texts* and the Monomyth," *Western American Literature* 17.2 (summer 1982).

"Beat Mystics," *Time* 71.5 (February 3, 1958): 58.

"Beat Playmate," *Playboy* (July 1959).

Beatitude Anthology. San Francisco: City Lights, 1960.

Beiles, Sinclair, William S. Burroughs, Gregory Corso, and Brion Gysin. *Minutes to Go*. Paris: Two Cities Editions, 1960.

Belgrad, Daniel. *The Culture of Spontaneity: Improvisation and the Arts in Postwar America*. Chicago: University of Chicago Press, 1998.

Belletto, Steven, ed. *American Literature in Transition, 1950–1960*. New York: Cambridge University Press, 2018.

"The Beat Generation Meets the Hungry Generation: U.S.–Calcutta Networks and the 1960s 'Revolt of the Personal,'" *Humanities* 8.3 (January 2019): 1–17.

ed. *The Cambridge Companion to the Beats*. New York: Cambridge University Press, 2017.

"Five Ways of Being Beat, circa 1958–59," in *The Cambridge Companion to the Beats*.

"Introduction," in *American Literature in Transition, 1950–1960*.

"Introduction: The Beat Half-Century," in *The Cambridge Companion to the Beats*.

"Kerouac His Own Historian: *Visions of Cody* and the Politics of Historiography," *Clio* 37 (spring 2008): 193–218.

Bergé, Carol, ed. *Light Years: An Anthology on Sociocultural Happenings (Multimedia in the East Village, 1960–1966)*. New York: Spuyten Duyvil, 2010.

"Remembrance of Things to Come," in Bergé, *Light Years*.

The Vancouver Report. New York: Fuck You Press, 1964.

The Vulnerable Island. Cleveland, OH: Renegade Press, 1964.

Bergler, Edmund. *Homosexuality: Disease or Way of Life?* New York: Hill and Wang, 1956.

Berman, Wallace. *Semina 1955–1964 Art Is Love Is God*, ed. Johan Kugelberg. New York: Boo-Hooray, 2013.

Berrigan, Ted. "The Art of Fiction: Jack Kerouac," reprinted in *Conversations with Jack Kerouac*, ed. Kevin J. Hayes. Jackson: University Press of Mississippi, 2005.

Berry, Eleanor. "William Carlos Williams' Triadic-Line Verse: An Analysis of Its Prosody," *Twentieth Century Literature*, 35.3 (autumn 1989): 364–388.

"Blazing and the Beat," *Time* (February 2, 1958): 104.

Bolton, Michael Sean. *Mosaic of Juxtaposition: William S. Burroughs' Narrative Revolution*. Amsterdam: Rodopi, 2014.

"The Bored, the Bearded and the Beat," *Look* (August 19, 1958): 65–68.

Boyer, Paul. *By the Bomb's Early Light: American Thought and Culture at the Dawn of the Atomic Age*. New York: Pantheon, 1985.

Bremser, Bonnie. *Troia: Mexican Memoirs*. 1969. Champaign, IL: Dalkey Archive Press, 2007.

Bremser, Ray. *Angel*. New York: Tompkins Square Press, 1967.

Blowing Mouth: The Jazz Poems, 1958–1970. Cherry Valley, NY: Cherry Valley Editions, 1978.

Poems of Madness. New York: Paper Book Gallery, 1965.

Brooker, Peter and Andrew Thacker, eds. *The Oxford Critical and Cultural History of Modernist Magazines: Volume II: North America 1894–1960*. Oxford: Oxford University Press, 2012.

Brooks, Cleanth. *The Well Wrought Urn: Studies in the Structure of Poetry*. London: Dennis Dobson, 1947.

Brooks, Cleanth and Robert Penn Warren. *Understanding Fiction*. New York: Appleton Century Crofts, 1943.

Understanding Fiction, 2nd edition. New York: Appleton Century Crofts, 1959.

Brossard, Chandler. "Plaint of a Gentile Intellectual," in *The Scene before You*.

ed. *The Scene before You: A New Approach to American Culture*. New York: Rinehart, 1955.

"Tentative Visits to the Cemetery: Reflections on *My* Beat Generation," *Review of Contemporary Fiction* 7.1 (spring 1987).

Who Walk in Darkness. New York: New Directions, 1952.

Who Walk in Darkness. 1952. New York: Harrow Books, 1972.

Brown, William F. *Beat Beat Beat.* New York: Signet, 1959.

Broyard, Anatole. *Kafka Was the Rage.* New York: Vintage, 1993.

"A Portrait of the Hipster," *Partisan Review* 15.6 (June 1948).

"Village Café," in *New Directions in Poetry and Prose 12*, ed. James Laughlin. New York: New Directions, 1950, 398–401.

Bunce, Robert Winford. "The Beat Vision of John Clellon Holmes." PhD diss., University of Mississippi, 1995.

Burns, Jim. *Radicals, Beats and Beboppers.* [Preston]: Penniless Press, 2011.

"Yugen," *Poetry Information* 16 (winter 1976–1977): 39–41.

Burroughs, William S. *Burroughs Live: The Collected Interviews of William S. Burroughs, 1960–1997*, ed. Sylvère Lotringer. Cambridge, MA: Semiotext(e), 2001.

"The Coming of the Purple Better One," *Esquire* (November 1, 1968).

"The Cut Up Method of Brion Gysin," in Parkinson, *A Casebook on the Beat.*

"Deposition: Testimony Concerning a Sickness," in *Naked Lunch: The Restored Text.*

"Foreword," in Norse, *Beat Hotel.*

[as William Lee]. "from Naked Lunch, Book III: In Search of Yage," *Black Mountain Review* 7 (1957): 144–148.

Interzone, ed. James Grauerholz. 1989. New York: Penguin, 1990.

"Introduction to the 1985 Edition," in *Queer.*

Junky: The Definitive Text of Junk, ed. Oliver Harris. New York: Penguin, 2003.

The Letters of Williams S. Burroughs, 1945–1959, ed. Oliver Harris. New York: Penguin, 1993.

The Naked Lunch. Paris: Olympia Press, 1959.

Naked Lunch. New York: Grove, 1962.

Naked Lunch: The Restored Text, ed. James Grauerholz and Barry Miles. New York: Grove, 2001.

Queer, ed. Oliver Harris. New York: Penguin, 2010.

Rub Out the Words: The Letters of William S. Burroughs, 1959–1974, ed. Bill Morgan. New York: Penguin, 2012.

The Soft Machine. New York: Grove, 1966.

Burroughs, William S. and Allen Ginsberg. *The Yage Letters Redux*, ed. Oliver Harris. San Francisco: City Lights, 2006.

Burroughs, William S. and Brion Gysin. *The Exterminator.* San Francisco: Auerhahn, 1960.

The Third Mind. New York: Viking, 1978.

Buswell, Robert E. and Donald S. Lopez. *The Princeton Dictionary of Buddhism.* Princeton: Princeton University Press, 2014.

Caen, Herb. "Pocketful of Notes," *San Francisco Chronicle* (April 2, 1958).

Campbell, Allen and Tim Niels, eds. *A Life in Pieces: Reflections on Alexander Trocchi*. Edinburgh: Rebel, 1997.

Campbell, James. *This Is the Beat Generation: New York – San Francisco – Paris*. Berkeley: University of California Press, 2001.

Caples, Garrett. "A Note on Tau," in Lamantia, *Tau* by Philip Lamantia.

"Philip Lamantia: Last Interview," 2001, www.angelfire.com/poetry/thepixel plus/nhlamantia.html.

Caples, Garrett, Andrew Joron, and Nancy Joyce Peters. "High Poet: The Life and Work of Philip Lamantia," in Lamantia, *The Collected Poems of Philip Lamantia*.

Carden, Mary Paniccia. *Women Writers of the Beat Era: Autobiography and Intertextuality*. Charlottesville: University of Virginia Press, 2018.

Cassady, Carolyn. *Off the Road*. New York: Penguin, 1990.

Cassady, Neal. *Collected Letters, 1947–1967*, ed. Dave Moore. New York: Penguin, 2004.

The First Third. San Francisco: City Lights, 1971.

Chapman, Harold. *The Beat Hotel*. Geneva: Gris Banal, 1984.

Charters, Ann, ed. *Beat Down Your Soul: What Was the Beat Generation?* New York: Penguin, 2001.

ed. *The Beats: Literary Bohemians in Postwar America, Parts I and II*. Detroit: Gale, 1983.

"Foreword," in Orlovsky, *Peter Orlovsky*.

"Introduction," in Kerouac, *On the Road*.

"Introduction," in Bremser, *Troia: Mexican Memoirs*.

Kerouac: A Biography. 1973. New York: St. Martin's, 1994.

"'Letting Go' in Writing," in Kerouac, *Old Angel Midnight*.

"Peter Orlovsky," in *The Beats*.

ed. *Portable Beat Reader*. New York: Penguin, 1992.

Charters, Ann and Samuel Charters. *Brother-Souls: John Clellon Holmes, Jack Kerouac, and the Beat Generation*. Jackson: University Press of Mississippi, 2010.

Charters, Samuel. "Chandler Brossard," in Charters, *The Beats*.

Cherkovski, Neeli. *Ferlinghetti: A Biography*. Garden City, NY: Doubleday, 1979.

Ciardi, John. "Epitaph for the Dead Beats," *Saturday Review* (February 6, 1960): 11–13, 42.

Clarke, Gerald. *Capote: A Biography*. New York: Simon and Schuster, 2010.

Collins, Ronald K. L. and David M. Skover. *Mania: The Story of the Outraged & Outrageous Lives That Launched a Cultural Revolution*. Oak Park, IL: Top 5 Books, 2013.

"The Cool, Cool Bards," *Time* (December 2, 1957): 71.

Corber, Robert. *Homosexuality in Cold War America: Resistance and the Crisis of Masculinity*. Durham, NC: Duke University Press, 1997.

Corso, Gregory. *An Accidental Autobiography: The Selected Letters of Gregory Corso*, ed. Bill Morgan. New York: New Directions, 2003.

The American Express. Paris: Olympia, 1961.

Gasoline & The Vestal Lady on Brattle. San Francisco: City Lights, 1992.

The Happy Birthday of Death. New York: New Directions, 1960.

"In This Hung-Up Age," *Encounter* 18.1 (January 1962).

"Introduction to Peter Orlovsky's Poems," in Orlovsky, *Clean Asshole Poems.*

"The Literary Revolution in America," *Litterair Paspoort* (November 1957).

Long Live Man. New York: New Directions, 1962.

"Note on My Play," *Encounter* 18.1 (January 1962).

"Variations on a Generation," in Charters, *Portable Beat Reader.*

Cotkin, George. *Existential America.* Baltimore: Johns Hopkins University Press, 2003.

"The Counterfeiters," *Time* (March 14, 1955): 112.

Cowen, Elise. *Poems and Fragments*, ed. Tony Trigilio. Boise, ID: Ahsahta Press, 2014.

Creeley, Robert. "On *Black Mountain* Review," in *The Little Magazine in America: A Modern Documentary History*, ed. Elliott Anderson and Mary Kinzie. Yonkers, NY: Pushcart Press, 1978, 248–261.

Crowe, Thomas Raine, ed. *Beatitude Magazine & the 1970s San Francisco Renaissance.* Cullowhee, NC: New Native Press, 2014.

"Philip Lamantia: Shaman of the Surreal," *Rain Taxi Review of Books* 10.2 (summer 2005). http://209.172.130.121/LAMANTIA.html.

Damon, Maria. *The Dark End of the Street: Margins in American Vanguard Poetry.* Minneapolis: University of Minnesota Press, 1993.

"Introduction," *Callaloo* 25.1 (winter 2002): 105–111.

Postliterary America: From Bagel Shop Jazz to Micropoetries. Iowa City: University of Iowa Press, 2011.

Dardess, George. "The Logic of Spontaneity: A Reconsideration of Kerouac's 'Spontaneous Prose Method,'" *boundary 2* 3.3 (spring 1975): 729–746.

Davidson, Michael. *Guys Like Us: Citing Masculinity in Cold War Poetics.* Chicago: University of Chicago Press, 2004.

The San Francisco Renaissance: Poetics and Community at Mid-Century. New York: Cambridge University Press, 1989.

Delattre, Pierre. *Episodes.* St. Paul, MN: Graywolf Press, 1993.

Deleuze, Gilles and Félix Guattari, *A Thousand Plateaus: Capitalism and Schizophrenia*, trans. and foreword by Brian Massumi. Minneapolis: University of Minnesota Press, 1987.

Dewhurst, Robert. "Measure: A Quarterly to the Poem, 1957–1962," *Let the Bucket Down* (2013).

di Prima, Diane. *Dinners & Nightmares.* New York: Corinth Books, 1961.

Earthsong, Poems 1957–59. New York: Poets Press, 1968.

"Introduction," in di Prima and Jones, *The Floating Bear: A Newsletter.*

Memoirs of a Beatnik. 1969. New York: Penguin, 1998.

The New Handbook of Heaven. San Francisco: Auerhahn Press, 1963.

Recollections of My Life as a Woman: The New York Years. New York: Viking, 2001.

Revolutionary Letters: Expanded Edition. San Francisco: City Lights, 2019.

This Kind of Bird Flies Backward. 1958. New York: Paper Book Gallery, 1963.

ed. *War Poems.* New York: Poets Press, 1968.

di Prima, Diane and LeRoi Jones, eds. *The Floating Bear: A Newsletter, Numbers 1–37, 1961–1969.* La Jolla, CA: Laurence McGilvery, 1973.

Dickey, James. "From Babel to Byzantium," *The Sewanee Review* (July–September 1957).

Douglas, Ann. "'Telepathic Shock and Meaning Excitement': Kerouac's Poetics of Intimacy," *College Literature* 27.1 (winter 2000).

Duberman, Martin. *Black Mountain: An Exploration in Community.* New York: Dutton, 1972.

Duncan, Robert. "Early Poetic Community" (with Ginsberg), in Ginsberg, *Allen Verbatim.*

"The Homosexual in Society," *Politics* (August 1944).

Dylan, Bob. *Chronicles: Vol. 1.* New York: Simon & Schuster, 2004.

Eastside High School. *Eastside High School Yearbook.* Paterson, NJ: Graduating Class of 1943, 1943.

Eberhart, Richard. "West Coast Sounds," *New York Times Book Review* (September 2, 1956).

Eberhart, Richard and Allen Ginsberg. *To Eberhart from Ginsberg.* Lincoln, MA: Penmaen Press, 1976.

Eberstadt, Isabel. "King of the East Village," *New York Herald Tribune* (December 13, 1964).

"Editorial," *The Ark* (spring 1947).

"Editorial," *Wagner Literary Magazine* (spring 1959).

"Editorial Notes," *Beatitude* 29 (1979).

"Editors Statement," *Journal for the Protection of All Beings* 1.1 (1961).

Edwards, Brian T. *Morocco Bound: Disorienting America's Maghreb, from Casablanca to the Marrakech Express.* Durham, NC: Duke University Press, 2005.

Ehrlich, J. W. *Howl of the Censor.* San Carlos, CA: Nourse Publishing, 1961.

Eliot, T. S. *The Annotated Waste Land with Eliot's Contemporary Prose,* 2nd edition, ed. Lawrence Rainey. New Haven, CT: Yale University Press, 2005.

Elkholy, Sharin, ed. *The Philosophy of the Beats.* Lexington: University of Kentucky Press, 2012.

Ellis, R. J. "Jack Kerouac's *On the Road* and *Visions of Cody,*" in Lee, *The Beat Generation Writers.*

"Liar, Liar": Jack Kerouac – Novelist. London: Greenwich Exchange, 1999.

"'Little . . . Only with Some Qualification': The Beats and Beat 'Little' Magazines," in Brooker and Thacker, *The Oxford Critical and Cultural History.*

Emre, Merve. "Ironic Institutions: Counterculture Fictions and the American Express Company," *American Literature* 87.1 (March 2015): 107–136.

Epstein, Andrew. *Beautiful Enemies: Friendship and Postwar American Poetry.* New York: Oxford University Press, 2006.

Everson, William. *An Age Insurgent.* San Francisco: Blackfriars, 1959.

Crooked Lines of God. Detroit: University of Detroit Press, 1959.

The Hazards of Holiness. Garden City: Doubleday, 1962.

War Elegies. Waldport, OR: Untide Press, 1944.

"Every Man a Beatnik?," *Newsweek* (June 29, 1959): 83.

Fazzino, Jimmy. *World Beats: Beat Generation Writing and the Worlding of U.S. Literature*. Hanover, NH: Dartmouth College Press, 2016.

Feldman, Gene and Max Gartenberg, eds. *The Beat Generation and the Angry Young Men*. New York: Dell, 1958.

Feldstein, Albert B., ed. *Like, MAD*. New York: Signet, 1960.

Ferguson, Frances. "The Nuclear Sublime," *Diacritics* 14.2 (summer 1984).

Ferlinghetti, Lawrence. *A Coney Island of the Mind*. New York: New Directions, 1958.

    Her. New York: New Directions, 1960.

    "A Non-introduction by Way of Introduction," in di Prima, *This Kind of Bird Flies Backward*.

    One Thousand Fearful Words for Fidel Castro. San Francisco: City Lights, 1961.

    Pictures of the Gone World. San Francisco: City Lights, 1955.

    Poetry as Insurgent Art. New York: New Directions, 2007.

    Routines. New York: New Directions, 1964.

    Tyrranus Nix? New York: New Directions, 1969.

Ferlinghetti, Lawrence and Allen Ginsberg. *I Greet You at the Beginning of a Great Career: The Selected Correspondence of Lawrence Ferlinghetti and Allen Ginsberg, 1955–1997*, ed. Bill Morgan. San Francisco: City Lights, 2015.

Ferrere, Alexandre. "Mechanics and Poetics: William Carlos Williams and Allen Ginsberg," *Beatdom* (March 24, 2018), www.beatdom.com/mechanics-poetics-william-carlos-williams-allen-ginsberg/#_ftnref15.

Filreis, Al. "On the *Hotel Wentley Poems*," *Jacket* 2 (March 7, 2011), http://jacket2.org/commentary/hotel-wentley-poems.

Forsgren, Frida and Michael J. Prince, eds. *Out of the Shadows: Beat Women Are Not Beaten Women*. Kristiansand, Norway: Portal Books, 2015.

Fox, Robert. "Ted Joans and the (B)reach of the African American Literary Canon," *Melus* 29.3–4 (fall/winter 2004).

"Fried Shoes," *Time* (February 9, 1959): 16.

Friedman, Amy L. "'I Say My New Name': Women Writers of the Beat Generation," in Lee, *The Beat Generation Writers*.

Fuller, John G. "Trade Winds," *Saturday Review of Literature* (October 5, 1957): 5–7.

Gaddis, William. *The Recognitions*. 1955. New York: Penguin, 1993.

Geis, Deborah R., ed. *Beat Drama: Playwrights and Performances of the "Howl" Generation*. London: Bloomsbury, 2016.

Gewirtz, Isaac. *Beatific Soul: Jack Kerouac on the Road*. New York: New York Public Library, 2007.

Ginsberg, Allen. *Allen Verbatim*, ed. Gordon Ball. New York: McGraw-Hill, 1974.

    The Best Minds of My Generation: A Literary History of the Beats, ed. Bill Morgan. New York: Grove, 2017.

    The Book of Martyrdom and Artifice: First Journals and Poems, 1937–1952, ed. Juanita Liebermann-Plimpton and Bill Morgan. Cambridge, MA: Da Capo Press, 2006.

Collected Poems, 1947–1997. New York: Harper Perennial, 2006.

Composed on the Tongue, ed. Donald Allen. Bolinas, CA: Grey Fox Press, 1980.

Deliberate Prose: Selected Essays, 1952–1995, ed. Bill Morgan. New York: Perennial 2000.

The Fall of America. San Francisco: City Lights, 1972.

"Foreword," in Waldman, *The Beat Book*.

Howl and Other Poems. San Francisco: City Lights, 1956.

Howl: Original Draft Facsimile, ed. Barry Miles. New York: Harper Perennial, 2006.

"Improvised Poetics," in *Composed on the Tongue*.

"Introduction," in Corso, *Gasoline*.

"Introduction," in Loewinsohn, *Watermelons*.

Journals: Early Fifties Early Sixties, ed. Gordon Ball. New York: Grove, 1977.

Kaddish and Other Poems, 1958–1960. 1961. San Francisco: City Lights, 2010.

The Letters of Allen Ginsberg, ed. Bill Morgan. Boston: Da Capo, 2008.

Planet News. San Francisco: City Lights, 1968.

"Plymell's Qualities," in Plymell, *Apocalypse Rose*.

"Ray Bremser and His Poetry," in Bremser, *Poems of Madness*.

Reality Sandwiches. San Francisco: City Lights, 1963.

"The Visions of a Great Rememberer," in Kerouac, *Visions of Cody*.

Ginsberg, Allen and Peter Orlovsky. *Straight Hearts' Delight: Love Poems and Selected Letters*, ed. Winston Leyland. San Francisco: Gay Sunshine Press, 1980.

Glass, Loren. *Countercultural Colophon: Grove Press, the Evergreen Review, and the Incorporation of the Avant-Garde*. Stanford: Stanford University Press, 2013.

Gleason, Ralph. "Kerouac's Beat Generation," *Saturday Review* 41 (1958).

Gold, Herbert. "How to Tell the Beatniks from the Hipsters," *Noble Savage* (spring 1960): 132–139.

Golding, Alan. *From Outlaw to Classic: Canons in American Poetry*. Madison: University of Wisconsin Press, 1995.

"The New American Poetry Revisited, Again," *Contemporary Literature* 39.2 (summer 1998): 180–211.

Golightly, Bonnie. *Beat Girl*. New York: Avon, 1959.

Gooch, Brad. *City Poet: The Life and Times of Frank O'Hara*. New York: Knopf, 1993.

Goodman, Paul. "Advance-Guard Writing 1900–1950," *The Kenyon Review* 13.3 (summer 1951).

Growing Up Absurd. 1960. New York: New York Review Books, 2012.

Grace, Nancy M. "Artista" (interview with Bonnie Bremser), in Grace and Johnson, *Breaking the Rule of Cool*.

Jack Kerouac and the Literary Imagination. New York: Palgrave, 2007.

"Pieces of a Song" (interview with Diane di Prima), in Grace and Johnson, *Breaking the Rule of Cool*.

"ruth weiss's DESERT JOURNAL: A Modern-Beat-Pomo Performance," in *Reconstructing the Beats*, ed. Jennie Skerl. New York: Palgrave, 2004, 57–71.

"Single Out" (interview with ruth weiss), in Grace and Johnson, *Breaking the Rule of Cool*.

"Snapshots, Sand Paintings, and Celluloid: Formal Considerations in the Life Writing of Women Writers from the Beat Generation," in Johnson and Grace, *Girls Who Wore Black*.

Grace, Nancy M. and Ronna C. Johnson, *Breaking the Rule of Cool: Interviewing and Reading Women Beat Writers*. Jackson: University Press of Mississippi, 2004.

Grace, Nancy M. and Jennie Skerl, eds. *The Transnational Beat Generation*. New York: Palgrave, 2012.

Grauerholz, James. "Afterword," in Kerouac and Burroughs, *And the Hippos Were Boiled in Their Tanks*.

Gysin, Brion. *The Last Museum*. New York: Grove, 1986.

"H Is for Horse," *Time* (May 5, 1952): 120.

Hamill, Sam. "The Poetry of Kenneth Rexroth," in Rexroth, *The Complete Poems of Kenneth Rexroth*.

Hamilton, Cynthia. "The Prisoner of Self: The Work of John Clellon Holmes," in Lee, *The Beat Generation Writers*.

Harrington, Alan. *The Secret Swinger*. New York: Knopf, 1966.

Harris, Kaplan. "Black Mountain Poetry," in *The Cambridge Companion to Modern American Poetry*, ed. Walter Kalaidjian. New York: Cambridge University Press, 2015.

Harris, Oliver. "The Beginnings of "*Naked Lunch*, an Endless Novel," in Harris and MacFayden, *Naked Lunch@50*.

"Introduction," in Burroughs, *Junky*.

"Introduction," in Burroughs, *Queer*.

"Introduction," in Burroughs and Ginsberg, *The Yage Letters Redux*.

William Burroughs and the Secret of Fascination. Carbondale: Southern Illinois University Press, 2003.

Harris, Oliver and Ian MacFayden, eds. *Naked Lunch@50: Anniversary Essays*. Carbondale: Southern Illinois University Press, 2009.

Harrison, K. C. "LeRoi Jones's Radio and the Literary 'Break' from Ellison to Burroughs," *African American Review* 47.2-3 (summer/fall 2014).

Haynes, Grover. Untitled afterword, in Kandel, *A Passing Dragon*.

Hebdige, Dick. *Subculture: The Meaning of Style*. New York: Methuen, 1979.

Hemmer, Kurt. "The Prostitute Speaks: Brenda Frazer's *Troia: Mexican Memoirs*," *Paradoxa* 18 (2003): 99–117.

Henderson, David. "Bob Kaufman: Beat, Surreal, Buddhist, and Black," in *Beats at Naropa*, ed. Anne Waldman and Laura Wright. Minneapolis: Coffee House Press, 2009, 117–134.

"Introduction," in Kaufman, *Cranial Guitar*.

Hibbard, Allen. "William S. Burroughs and U.S. Empire," in Grace and Skerl, *The Transnational Beat Generation*.

Hoffman, Abbie. *Steal This Book*. 1971. New York: Thunder's Mouth Press, 2002.

Holladay, Hilary. *Herbert Huncke*. Tucson: Schaffner Press, 2013.

Holladay, Hilary and Robert Holton, eds. *What's Your Road, Man? Critical Essays on Jack Kerouac's On the Road*. Carbondale: Southern Illinois University Press, 2009.

Hollander, John. "Poetry Chronicle," *Partisan Review* 24.2 (spring 1957).

Holmes, John Clellon. *Go*. 1952. New York: Thunder's Mouth Press, 1997.

The Horn. 1958. New York: Thunder's Mouth Press, 1988.

"Introduction," in *Go*.

"July 4th Weekend 1948: Two," in *Representative Men: The Biographical Essays*. Fayetteville: University of Arkansas Press, 1988.

"The Name of the Game," in *Nothing More to Declare*. New York: E. P. Dutton, 1967.

"Tea for Two," *Neurotica* 1.2 (summer 1948): 36–43.

"This Is the Beat Generation," *New York Times Magazine* (November 16, 1952).

Howe, Irving. "The Age of Conformity," *Dissent* (January 1, 1954).

Hrebeniak, Michael. *Action Writing: Jack Kerouac's Wild Form*. Carbondale: Southern Illinois University Press, 2006.

Huncke, Herbert. *Huncke's Journal*. New York: Poets Press, 1965.

Hunt, Tim. "Interview with John Clellon Holmes," in *The Beat Journey*, ed. Arthur Knight and Kit Knight (*unspeakable visions of the individual* 8). California, PA: unspeakable visions, 1978.

Kerouac's Crooked Road: The Development of a Fiction. 1981. Berkeley: University of California Press, 1996.

The Textuality of Soulwork: Jack Kerouac's Quest for Spontaneous Prose. Ann Arbor: University of Michigan Press, 2014.

Hyde, Lewis, ed. *On the Poetry of Allen Ginsberg*. Ann Arbor: University of Michigan Press, 1984.

Hynes, Sam. "The Beat and the Angry," *Commonweal* (September 5, 1958): 559–561.

Ivy, Benjamin. "Interview with Marie Ponsot," *Bomb* (April 2003), https://bombmagazine.org/articles/marie-ponsot/.

Jacobson, Dan. "America's 'Angry Young Men': How Rebellious Are the San Francisco Rebels?," *Commentary* (December 1957): 475–479.

Joans, Ted. *All of Ted Joans and No More*. New York: Excelsior Press, 1961.

The Hipsters. New York: Citadel Press. 1961.

Jazz Poems. New York: Rhino Review, 1959.

"Je Me Vois (I See Myself)," in *Contemporary Authors Autobiography* 25. Detroit: Gale Research, 1996, 219–258.

Teducation: Selected Poems. Minneapolis: Coffee House Press, 1999.

Johnson, David K. *The Lavender Scare: The Cold War Persecution of Gays and Lesbians in the Federal Government*. Chicago: University of Chicago Press, 2004.

Johnson, Joyce. *Come and Join the Dance*. 1962. New York: Open Road, 2014.

Minor Characters: A Beat Memoir. 1983. New York: Penguin, 1994.

The Voice Is All: The Lonely Victory of Jack Kerouac. New York: Viking, 2012.

Johnson, Kay. *Eat Me, Drink Me*. New Orleans: New School Press, 1960.
    Human Songs. London: City Lights/Villiers, 1964.
    The Impossible Possible. New Orleans: New School Press, 1960.
Johnson, Ronna C. "'And Then She Went': Beat Departures and Feminine Transgressions in Joyce Johnson's *Come and Join the Dance*," in Johnson and Grace, *Girls Who Wore Black*.
    "Beats and Gender," in Belletto, *The Cambridge Companion to the Beats*.
    "Gregory Corso's Dada-Surrealist-Absurd Beat Plays," in Geis, *Beat Drama*.
    "Mapping the Women Writers of the Beat Generation," in Grace and Johnson, *Breaking the Rule of Cool*.
Johnson, Ronna C. and Nancy M. Grace, eds. *Girls Who Wore Black: Women Writing the Beat Generation*. New Brunswick, NJ: Rutgers University Press, 2002.
Johnston, Alastair M. *A Bibliography of the Auerhahn Press & Its Successor Dave Haselwood Books*. Berkeley: Poltroon Press, 1976.
Jones, Hettie. *How I Became Hettie Jones*. New York: Grove, 1990.
Jones, James T. *A Map of Mexico City Blues: Jack Kerouac as Poet*. Carbondale: Southern Illinois University Press, 1992.
Jones, LeRoi. *The Dead Lecturer*. New York: Grove, 1964.
    ed. *Four Young Lady Poets*. New York: Totem Press, 1962.
    ed. *The Moderns: An Anthology of New Writing in America*. New York: Corinth, 1963.
    Preface to a Twenty Volume Suicide Note. New York: Totem Press, 1961.
    See also Baraka, Amiri.
Kakutani, Michiko. "When a Real-Life Killing Sent Two Future Beats in Search of Their Voices," *New York Times* (November 10, 2008).
Kandel, Lenore. *Collected Poems of Lenore Kandel*. Berkeley: North Atlantic Books, 2012.
    An Exquisite Navel. Studio City: Three Penny Press, 1959.
    The Love Book. San Francisco: Stolen Paper Editions, 1966.
    A Passing Dragon. Studio City: Three Penny Press, 1959.
Kane, Daniel. *All Poets Welcome: The Lower East Side Poetry Scene in the 1960s*. Berkeley: University of California Press, 2003.
Katz, Eliot. *The Poetry and Politics of Allen Ginsberg*. United Kingdom: Beatdom Books, 2016.
Katzman, Don. "Coffeehouse Poetry on the Lower East Side," in Bergé, *Light Years*.
    ed. *Seventh Street: Poems from Les Deux Megots*. New York: Hesperidian Press, 1961.
Kaufman, Bob. *Abomunist Manifesto*. San Francisco: City Lights, 1959.
    The Ancient Rain, Poems 1956–1978. New York: New Directions, 1981.
    Cranial Guitar: Selected Poems by Bob Kaufman, ed. Gerald Nicosia. Minneapolis: Coffee House Press, 1996.
    Golden Sardine. San Francisco: City Lights, 1967.
    Solitudes Crowded with Loneliness. New York: New Directions, 1965.

Kaufman, Eileen. "Introduction," *Beatitude Vol. II* (1992), www.beatitudepoetry
.com/introd.html.

"Who Wouldn't Walk with Tigers," in Knight, *Women of the Beat Generation.*

Kelly, John. "Publisher's Letter," *Beatitude* 2 (May 16, 1959).

Kerouac, Jack. "About the Beat Generation," in *Portable Kerouac.*

"After Me, the Deluge," in *Portable Kerouac.*

"Are Writers Made or Born?," in *Portable Kerouac.*

Beat Generation. New York: Thunder's Mouth Press, 2005.

"Beatific," in *Portable Kerouac.*

"Belief & Technique for Modern Prose," in *Portable Kerouac.*

Big Sur. 1962. New York: Bantam, 1963.

"A Billowy Trip in the World," in *New Directions in Prose and Poetry* 16, ed.
James Laughlin. New York: New Directions, 1957, 93–105.

Desolation Angels. 1965. New York: Perigee Books, 1980.

The Dharma Bums. 1958. New York: Penguin, 1986.

Doctor Sax. 1959. New York: Penguin, 2012.

"Essentials of Spontaneous Prose," in *Portable Kerouac.*

Good Blonde and Others, ed. Don Allen. San Francisco: Grey Fox, 1994.

"I Wish I Were You," in *Unknown Kerouac.*

"Introduction," in Micheline, *River of Red Wine.*

"Lamb, No Lion," in *Portable Kerouac.*

Lonesome Traveler. 1960. New York: Grove, 1988.

"Manhattan Sketches," in Jones, *The Moderns.*

Mexico City Blues. 1959. New York: Grove, 1990.

"The Mexican Girl," *Paris Review* 11 (winter 1955): 11–32.

Old Angel Midnight. San Francisco: Grey Fox Press, 1993.

On the Road. 1957. New York: Penguin, 1991.

On the Road: The Original Scroll, ed. Howard Cunnell. New York: Viking,
2007.

"Outline of Subsequent Synopsis," in *The Haunted Life and Other Writings*, ed.
Todd Tietchen. Boston: Da Capo, 2014.

The Portable Jack Kerouac, ed. Ann Charters. New York: Viking, 1995.

"The Roaming Beatniks," *Holiday* (October 1959): 82–86.

San Francisco Blues. New York: Penguin, 1995.

Selected Letters, 1940–1956, ed. Ann Charters. New York: Penguin, 1995.

Selected Letters, 1957–1969, ed. Ann Charters. New York: Viking, 1999.

The Town and the City. 1950. New York: Harcourt Brace, 1970.

Tristessa. 1960. New York: Penguin, 1992.

The Unknown Kerouac: Rare, Unpublished, & Newly Translated Writings, ed.
Todd Tietchen and trans. Jean-Christopher Cloutier. New York: Library of
America, 2016.

Vanity of Duluoz. 1967. New York: Penguin, 1994.

Visions of Cody. 1972. New York: Penguin, 1994.

Windblown World: The Journals of Jack Kerouac, 1947–1954, ed. Douglas
Brinkley. New York: Penguin, 2004.

Kerouac, Jack and Allen Ginsberg. *Jack Kerouac and Allen Ginsberg: The Letters*, ed. Bill Morgan and David Stanford. New York: Viking, 2010.

Kerouac, Jack and Joyce Johnson. *Door Wide Open: A Beat Love Affair in Letters, 1957–1958*. New York: Viking, 2000.

Kerouac, Jack and William S. Burroughs. *And the Hippos Were Boiled in Their Tanks*. New York: Grove Press, 2008.

Kerouac, Joan Haverty. *Nobody's Wife: The Smart Aleck and the King of the Beats*. Berkeley: Creative Arts, 1990.

Kherdian, David. *Six Poets of the San Francisco Renaissance*. Fresno: Giligia Press, 1967.

Kiplinger, Suzanne. "This Hip-Historian Knows a Man's Pad Is His Castle," in *The Village Voice Reader*, ed. Daniel Wolf and Edwin Fancher. New York: Grove, 1963.

Klonsky, Milton. "Greenwich Village: Decline and Fall," in Brossard, *The Scene before You*.

Knickerbocker, Conrad. "White Junk" (interview with William Burroughs), in Burroughs, *Burroughs Live*.

Knight, Brenda, ed. *Women of the Beat Generation*. Berkeley, CA: Conari Press, 1996.

Kotin, Joshua. "Philip Lamantia's Practical Politics," *Colloquium* (October 18, 2012), https://lucian.uchicago.edu/blogs/colloquium/2012/10/18/philip-lamantias-practical-politics/#_edn13.

Kraemer, Christine Hoff. "The Brake of Time: Corso's Bomb as Postmodern God(dess)," *Texas Studies in Literature and Language* 44:2 (summer 2002): 211–228.

Krim, Seymour. "Afterword," in Holmes, *Go*.
  "A Backward Glance o'er Beatnik Roads," in *The Little Magazine in America: A Modern Documentary History*, ed. Elliott Anderson and Mary Kinzie. New York: Pushcart, 1978, 325–337.
  ed. *The Beats*. Greenwich, CT: Fawcett Gold Medal, 1960.
  "The Holy Barbarians," *Evergreen Review* 3.9 (1959): 208–214.
  "Our Middle-Aged 'Young Writers': The Avant-Garde at a Dead End," *Commentary* 14.4 (October 1952): 339–344.

Kugelberg, Johan, Phil Aarons, and Adam Davis, eds. *The Sinking Bear: A Newsletter*. New York: Boo-Hooray, 2013.

Kupferberg, Tuli. *Beating*. New York: Birth Press, 1959.
  Fuck Nam: A Morality Play. New York: Birth Press, 1966.
  "The Function of Bohemia" (1962). Tuli Kupferberg and Sylvia Topp Papers.
  The Rub-Ya-Out of Omore Diem. New York: Birth Press, 1962.
  Selected Fruits & Nuts. New York: Birth Press, 1959.
  Snow Job. New York: Birth Press, 1959.

Kupferberg, Tuli and Robert Bashlow. *1001 Ways to Beat the Draft*. New York: Oliver Layton Press, 1966.

Kuralt, Charles. "William Morris at the Gaslight Café," *CBS News* (June 9, 1959), http://gvh.aphdigital.org/items/show/227.

Kyger, Joanne. *Strange Big Moon: The Japan and India Journals: 1960–1964.* 1981. Berkeley: North Atlantic Books, 2000.

The Tapestry and the Web. San Francisco: Four Seasons Foundation, 1965.

Lamantia, Philip. *The Collected Poems of Philip Lamantia*, ed. Garrett Caples, Andrew Joron, and Nancy J. Peters. Berkeley: University of California Press, 2013.

Ekstatis. San Francisco: Auerhahn Press, 1959.

Tau by Philip Lamantia and *Journey to the End* by John Hoffman, ed. Garret Caples. San Francisco: City Lights, 2008.

Landesman, Jay. Editorial Statement, *Neurotica* 1.1 (spring 1948): 3.

ed. *Neurotica: The Authentic Voice of the Beat Generation, 1948–1951.* London: Jay Landesman, 1981.

Tales of a Cultural Conduit & The Nervous Set. Richmond, UK: Tiger of the Stripe, 2006.

Lane, Véronique. *The French Genealogy of the Beat Generation: Burroughs, Ginsberg, and Kerouac's Appropriation of Modern Literature, from Rimbaud to Michaux.* New York: Bloomsbury, 2017.

Latham, Aaron. "The Columbia Murder That Gave Birth to the Beats," *New York Magazine* (April 19, 1976): 41–53.

Lebel, Jean-Jacques. "Burroughs: The Beat Years," in Harris and MacFayden, *Naked Lunch@50.*

Lee, A. Robert, ed. *The Beat Generation Writers.* London: Pluto Press, 1996.

"The Beats and Race," in Belletto, *The Cambridge Companion to the Beats.*

Modern American Counter Writing: Beats, Outriders, Ethnics. New York: Routledge, 2010.

Lee, Ben. "LeRoi Jones/Amiri Baraka and the Limits of Open Form," *African American Review* 37.2–3 (June 2003).

Lehman, David. *The Last Avant-Garde: The Making of the New York School of Poets.* New York: Doubleday, 1998.

Lemaire, Gérard-Georges, "23 Stitches Taken" in Burroughs and Gysin, *Third Mind.*

Lewis, Richard. *Poor Richard's Guide to Non-tourist San Francisco.* San Francisco: Unicorn Publishing, 1958.

Lhamon, W. T. *Deliberate Speed: The Origins of a Cultural Style in the American 1950s.* Washington, DC: Smithsonian Institution Press, 1990.

Ligairi, Rachel. "When Mexico Looks like Mexico: The Hyperrealization of Race and the Pursuit of the Authentic," in Holladay and Holton, *What's Your Road, Man?*

Lipton, Lawrence. *The Holy Barbarians.* New York: Julian Messner, 1959.

Loewinsohn, Ron. *Watermelons.* New York: Totem Press, 1959.

"Lonergan Alibi: Twisted Sex," *New York Daily News* (October 28, 1943): 1.

Lorentzen, Christian. "Sheila Heti, Ben Lerner, Tao Lin: How 'Auto' Is 'Autofiction'?," *Vulture* (May 11, 2018), www.vulture.com/2018/05/how-auto-is-autofiction.html.

Lowell, Robert. "Robert Lowell, Winner of the 1960 Poetry Award for Life Studies," National Book Foundation, www.nationalbook.org/nbaaccept speech_rlowell.html#.VzNGjHn2aP8.

Lowry, Robert. "Is This the Beat Generation?," *American Mercury* 76 (1953).

L.V. "Among the New Books," *San Francisco Chronicle* (July 27, 1952).

Lydenberg, Robin. *Word Cultures: Radical Theory and Practice in William S. Burroughs' Fiction.* Urbana: University of Illinois Press, 1987.

Maclaine, Christopher. *The Time Capsule.* San Francisco: Adler Press, 1960.

Mailer, Norman. *Advertisements for Myself.* 1959. Cambridge, MA: Harvard University Press, 1992.

    Armies of the Night. 1968. New York: Plume, 1994.

    "The White Negro," in *Advertisements for Myself.*

Mandel, George. *Beatville, U.S.A.* New York: Avon, 1961.

    Flee the Angry Strangers. Indianapolis: Bobbs-Merrill, 1952.

Margolis, William J. *The Anteroom of Hell.* San Francisco: Inferno Press, 1957.

Marin, Sutter. *113 Semi-Simple Poams [sic] for the Simple Minded.* San Francisco: Peace & Pieces Books, 1973.

Martinelli, Sheri. "The Case against Ezra Pound & Confucius & Christ." Sheri Martinelli Papers.

    "Duties of a Lady Female," *Anagogic & Paideumic Review* 1.3 (December 1959).

    "For Allen," in Ginsberg, *Best Minds: A Tribute to Allen Ginsberg.*

    "The Last Days of North Beach in San Francisco," *Anagogic & Paideumic Review* 1.6 (1960).

    "On Loving Many," *Beatitude* 6 (n.d. [summer 1959]).

Martinez, Manuel Luis. *Countering the Counterculture: Rereading Postwar American Dissent from Jack Kerouac to Tomás Rivera.* Madison: University of Wisconsin Press, 2003.

Matthiessen, Peter and George Plimpton. "The Art of Fiction 5: William Styron," *Paris Review* 5 (spring 1954).

Maynard, John. *Venice West: The Beat Generation in Southern California.* New Brunswick, NJ: Rutgers University Press, 1991.

McBride, Richard. *Oranges.* San Francisco: Bread & Wine Press, 1960.

McCarthy, Mary. "Burroughs' *Naked Lunch*," in *The Writing on the Wall.* New York: Harcourt Brace, 1970.

McClure, Michael. "Drug Notes: Peyote," in *Meat Science Essays.*

    "Fuck Essay," *Fuck You* 5.4 (1963).

    Ghost Tantras. 1964. San Francisco: City Lights, 2013.

    Hymns to St. Geryon and Other Poems. San Francisco: Auerhahn Press, 1959.

    "Jack's *Old Angel Midnight*," in Kerouac, *Old Angel Midnight.*

    Meat Science Essays. San Francisco: City Lights, 1963.

    Poisoned Wheat. San Francisco: privately printed, 1965.

    Scratching the Beat Surface. San Francisco: North Point Press, 1989.

    "Writing One's Body: Interview with Michael McClure," *Amerikastudien/American Studies* 32.3 (1987).

McDarrah, Fred and Gloria McDarrah. *Beat Generation: Glory Days in Greenwich Village.* New York: Schirmer Books, 1996.

McGurl, Mark. *The Program Era: Postwar Fiction and the Rise of Creative Writing.* Cambridge, MA: Harvard University Press, 2009.

McIntosh, Martin, ed. *Beatsville.* Melbourne: Outre Gallery Press, 2003.

McLuhan, Marshall. "The Psychopathology of *Time* & *Life*," *Neurotica* 5 (autumn 1949).

McNally, Dennis. *Desolate Angel: Jack Kerouac, the Beat Generation, and America.* New York: McGraw-Hill, 1979.

Melehy, Hassan. *Kerouac: Language, Poetics, and Territory.* New York: Bloomsbury, 2016.

Meltzer, David. *Beat Thing.* Albuquerque: La Alameda Press, 2004.

Poems. San Francisco: Donald & Alice Schenker, 1957.

Ragas. San Francisco: Discovery Books, 1959.

ed. *San Francisco Beat: Talking with the Poets.* San Francisco: City Lights, 2001.

Micheline, Jack. *In the Bronx and Other Stories.* New York: Sam Hooker Press, 1965.

River of Red Wine. 1958. Sudbury, MA: Water Row Press, 1986.

Miles, Barry. *The Beat Hotel: Ginsberg, Burroughs, and Corso in Paris, 1958–1963.* New York: Grove Press, 2000.

Call Me Burroughs: A Life. New York: Twelve, 2014.

"A Note on the Manuscript," in Ginsberg, *Howl: Original Draft.*

Mills, C. Wright. *The Power Elite.* 1956. New York: Oxford University Press, 2000.

Millstein, Gilbert. "Books of the Times" (review of *On the Road*), *New York Times* (September 5, 1957).

"The 'Kick' That Failed" (review of *Go*), *New York Times* (November 9, 1952).

Mitchell, John, ed. *Poetry of the Beat Generation: As Read at the Gaslight.* New York: John Mitchell, n.d.; probably 1958 or 1959.

Montgomery, John. *Jack Kerouac.* Fresno, CA: Giligia Press, 1970.

Kerouac West Coast. Palo Alto, CA: Fels & Firn Press, 1976.

"Report from the Beat Generation," *Library Journal* 84.12 (June 15, 1959): 1999–2000.

Moore, Steven, ed. *Beerspit Night and Cursing: The Correspondence of Charles Bukowski and Sheri Martinelli, 1960–1967.* Santa Rosa, CA: Black Sparrow Press, 2001.

"An Interview with Chandler Brossard," *Review of Contemporary Fiction* 7.1 (spring 1987): 38–57.

My Back Pages: Reviews and Essays. Los Angeles: Zerogram Press, 2017.

Moraff, Barbara. *Mister.* New Haven, CT: Penny Poems, 1959.

Morgan, Bill. "Editor's Introduction," in Corso, *Accidental Autobiography.*

"Some Words on Allen Ginsberg's Kaddish," in Ginsberg, *Kaddish.*

The Typewriter Is Holy: The Complete, Uncensored History of the Beat Generation. New York: Free Press, 2010.

The Works of Allen Ginsberg, 1941–1994: A Descriptive Bibliography. Westport, CT: Greenwood Press, 1995.

Morgan, Bill and Nancy J. Peters, eds. *Howl on Trial: The Battle for Free Expression.* San Francisco: City Lights, 2006.

Morgan, Bill and Bob Rosenthal, eds. *Best Minds: A Tribute to Allen Ginsberg.* New York: Lospecchio Press, 1986.

Morgan, Ted. *Literary Outlaw: The Life and Times of William S. Burroughs.* 1988. New York: Avon Books, 1990.

Morris, William. *4.* n.p., 1959.

Mortenson, Erik. *Ambiguous Borderlands: Shadow Imagery in Cold War American Culture.* Carbondale: Southern Illinois University Press, 2016.

Muckle, John. "The Names: Allen Ginsberg's Writings," in Lee, *Beat Generation Writers.*

Murphy, Timothy S. *Wising Up the Marks: The Amodern William Burroughs.* Berkeley: University of California Press, 1997.

Muyumba, Walton. "Improvising over the Changes: Improvisation as Intellectual and Aesthetic Practice in the Transitional Poems of LeRoi Jones/Amiri Baraka," *College Literature* 34.1 (winter 2007).

Myrsiades, Kostas, ed. *The Beat Generation: Critical Essays.* New York: Peter Lang, 2002.

Need, David. "Spontaneity, Immediacy, and Difference: Philosophy, Being in Time, and Creativity in the Aesthetics of Jack Kerouac, Charles Olson, and John Cage," in Elkholy, *The Philosophy of the Beats.*

Nicosia, Gerald. "A Lifelong Commitment to Change: The Literary Non-career of Ted Joans," in Joans, *Teduction.*
   Memory Babe: A Critical Biography of Jack Kerouac. 1983. Berkeley: University of California Press, 1994.

Nicosia, Gerald and Anne Marie Santos, *One and Only: The Untold Story of On the Road.* Berkeley: Viva Editions, 2011.

Nielsen, Aldon Lynn. *Black Chant: Languages of African American Postmodernism.* Cambridge: Cambridge University Press, 1997.
   "'A Hard Rain': Looking at Bob Kaufman," *Callaloo* 25.1 (winter 2002): 135–145

Norse, Harold. *Beat Hotel.* San Diego: Atticus Press, 1983.
   Hotel Nirvana. San Francisco: City Lights, 1974.
   In the Hub of the Fiery Force: Collected Poems 1934–2003. New York: Thunder's Mouth Press, 2003.
   Memoirs of a Bastard Angel. New York: William Morrow, 1989.

O'Hara, Frank. *Lunch Poems.* 1964. San Francisco: City Lights, 2014.
   "Personism: A Manifesto," *Yugen* 7 (1961): 28–29.

Olson, Charles. *Collected Prose,* ed. Donald Allen and Benjamin Friedlander. Berkeley: University of California Press, 1997.
   "Projective Verse," in *Collected Prose.*
   "Projective Verse vs. the Non-projective," *Poetry New York* 3 (1950): 13–22.

O'Neil, Paul. "The Only Rebellion Around," *Life* (November 30, 1959).

Orlovsky, Peter. *Clean Asshole Poems & Smiling Vegetable Songs.* San Francisco: City Lights, 1978.

Peter Orlovsky: A Life in Words, ed. Bill Morgan. Boulder: Paradigm Publishers, 2014.

Ossman, David. "LeRoi Jones: An Interview on *Yugen*" (1960), in *Conversations with Amiri Baraka*, ed. Charlie Reilly. Jackson: University Press of Mississippi, 1994.

O'Sullivan, Padriec. *Weep Not My Children*. n.p., n.d.; probably 1959.

Parkinson, Thomas, ed. *A Casebook on the Beat*. New York: Thomas Y. Crowell, 1961.

Paton, Fiona. "Angel Tendencies and Gratuitous Acts: *Kill Your Darlings* and the Legacy of Lucien Carr," in Geis, *Beat Drama*.

"The Beat Movement," in Belletto, *American Literature in Transition, 1950–1960*.

"*Cain's Book* and the Mark of Exile: Alexander Trocchi as Transnational Beat," in Grace and Skerl, *The Transnational Beat Generation*.

"Reconceiving Kerouac: Why We Should Teach *Doctor Sax*," in Myrsiades, *The Beat Generation: Critical Essays*.

Peabody, Richard, ed. *A Different Beat: Writings by Women of the Beat Generation*. London: Serpent's Tail, 1997.

Perloff, Marjorie. "'A Lost Battalion of Platonic Conversationalists': 'Howl' and the Language of Modernism," in Shinder, *The Poem That Changed America*.

Petro, Pamela. "The Hipster of Joy Street: An Introduction to the Life and Work of John Wieners," *Boston College Magazine* (fall 2000).

Phillips, Rod. *"Forest Beatniks" and "Urban Thoreaus": Gary Snyder, Jack Kerouac, Lew Welch, and Michael McClure*. New York: Peter Lang, 2000.

Pivano, Fernanda, ed. *Poesia degli ultimi americani*. Milan: Feltrinelli, 1964.

Plummer, William. *The Holy Goof: A Biography of Neal Cassady*. New York: Paragon, 1981.

Plymell, Charles. *Apocalypse Rose*. San Francisco: Dave Haselwood, 1966.

Note accompanying "November 3, 1998 Dark Afternoon," *Evergreen Review* 102 (1998).

Podell, Albert. "Censorship on the Campus: The Case of the *Chicago Review*," *San Francisco Review* 1 (spring 1959): 71–89.

Podhoretz, Norman. "The Know-Nothing Bohemians," in *Doings and Undoings: The Fifties and After in American Writing*. New York: Noonday Press, 1964.

"Where Is the Beat Generation Going?" *Esquire* (December 1958): 147–150.

Prescott, Orville. "Books of the Times," *New York Times* (April 29, 1952).

Prince, Arnold. "Student-Slayer Wins Leniency," *Daily Mirror* (October 7, 1944): 5.

Propper, Dan. *The Fable of the Final Hour and Other Poems*. Queens, NY: Energy Press, n.d.; probably 1960.

Pull My Daisy, text ad-libbed by Jack Kerouac for the film by Robert Frank and Alfred Leslie. New York: Grove, 1961.

Raskin, Jonah. *American Scream: Allen Ginsberg's Howl and the Making of the Beat Generation*. Berkeley: University of California Press, 2004.

Rebels: A Journey Underground, dir. Kevin Alexander (1999).

Reidel, James. "Robert Lowry," *Review of Contemporary Fiction* 25.2 (summer 2005).

Reisner, Robert. "Intro," in Joans, *Jazz Poems*.

Rexroth, Kenneth. *An Autobiographical Novel.* 1964. Santa Barbara, CA: Ross-Erikson, 1978.

   The Complete Poems of Kenneth Rexroth, ed. Sam Hamill and Bradford Morrow. Port Townsend, WA: Copper Canyon Press, 2003.

   "Robert Duncan," *San Francisco Examiner* (December 11, 1960).

   "San Francisco Letter," *Evergreen Review* 1.2 (1957).

Rigney, Francis J. and Douglas L. Smith. *The Real Bohemia: A Sociological and Psychological Study of the "Beats."* New York: Basic Books, 1961.

Riley, James. "'I Am a Recording Angel': Jack Kerouac's *Visions of Cody* and the Recording Process," *Electronic Book Review* (December 19, 2006), http://electronicbookreview.com/essay/i-am-a-recording-angel-jack-kerouacs-visions-of-cody-and-the-recording-process/.

Roberts, John G. "The Frisco Beat," *Mainstream* (July 1958): 11–26.

Robinson, Murray. "Gregory Sends Us Poems That We Don't Get," *New York World Telegram and Sun* (June 15, 1955).

Roney, Patrick. "The Paradox of Experience: Black Art and Black Idiom in the Work of Amiri Baraka," *African American Review* 37.2–3 (summer/fall 2003).

Rosenfeld, Isaac. "Rough and Delicate," *New Republic* (May 5, 1952).

Rosenthal, Irving. *Sheeper.* New York: Grove, 1967.

Roskolenko, Harry. "The Sounds of the Fury," *Prairie Schooner* 33.2 (summer 1959): 148–153.

Rubin, Jerry. *Do It! Scenarios of the Revolution.* New York: Simon & Schuster, 1970.

Russo, Linda, "To Deal with Parts and Particulars: Joanne Kyger's Early Epic Poetics," in Johnson and Grace, *Girls Who Wore Black*.

   "Particularizing People's Lives," *Jacket 2* 11 (April 2000), http://jacketmagazine.com/11/kyger-iv-by-russo.html.

Ryan, Richard. "Of the Beat Generation and Us," *Catholic World* (August 1958).

Saldaña-Portillo, María Josefina. "'On the Road' with Che and Jack: Melancholia and the Legacy of Colonial Racial Geographies in the Americas," *New Formations* 47 (2002): 87–108.

Sanders, Ed. *Fug You.* Boston: De Capo, 2011.

   Peace Eye. Buffalo, NY: Frontier Press, 1965.

   Poem from Jail. San Francisco: City Lights, 1963.

   The Poetry and Life of Allen Ginsberg: A Narrative Poem. Woodstock, NY: Overlook Press, 2000.

   "Resistance to Goon Squads," *Fuck You* 5.7 (August 1964).

Sandison, David and Graham Vickers. *Neal Cassady: The Fast Life of a Beat Hero.* Chicago: Chicago Review Press, 2006.

Sargeant, Jack. *Naked Lens: An Illustrated History of Beat Cinema.* London: Creation Books, 1997.

Savage, Jon. "Cut-Ups Go Pop: William S. Burroughs and a Mashed-Up Future," in *Cut-Ups, Cut-Ins, Cut-Outs: The Art of William S. Burroughs*, ed. Colin Fallows and Synne Genzmer. Vienna: Kunsthalle Wien, 2012.

Sayre, Nora. *Previous Convictions: A Journey through the 1950s*. New Brunswick, NJ: Rutgers University Press, 1995.

Scalapino, Leslie. "Language as Transient Act, the Poetry of Philip Whalen," in Whalen, *Collected Poems of Philip Whalen*.

Schneider, David. *Crowded by Beauty: The Life and Zen of Poet Philip Whalen*. Berkeley: University of California Press, 2015.

Schumacher, Michael. *Dharma Lion: A Biography of Allen Ginsberg*. New York: St. Martin's, 1992.

Schwartz, Delmore. "Fiction Chronicle: The Wrongs of Innocence and Experience," *Partisan Review* 19.2 (May–June 1952).

Selerie, Gavin, "Introduction," in *Gregory Corso: The Riverside Interviews*. London: Binnacle Press, 1982.

Shapcott, John. "'I Didn't Punctuate It': Locating the Tape and Text of Jack Kerouac's *Visions of Cody* and *Doctor Sax* in a Culture of Improvisation," *Journal of American Studies* 36.2 (2002): 231–248.

Shaw, Lytle. *Frank O'Hara: The Poetics of Coterie*. Iowa City: University of Iowa Press, 2006.

Shinder, Jason, ed. *The Poem That Changed America: "Howl" Fifty Years Later*. New York: Farrar, Straus and Giroux, 2006.

Simpson, Louis. *A Revolution in Taste*. New York: Macmillan, 1978.

Sisk, John. "Beatniks and Tradition," *Commonweal* (April 17, 1959): 75–77.

Skau, Michael. *"Constantly Risking Absurdity": The Writings of Lawrence Ferlinghetti*. Troy, NY: Whitson Publishing Co., 1989.

Skerl, Jennie. "The Book, the Movie, the Legend: *Naked Lunch* at 50," in Harris and MacFayden, *Naked Lunch@50*.

William S. Burroughs. Boston: Twayne, 1985.

Skerl, Jennie and Robin Lydenberg. *William S. Burroughs at the Front: Critical Reception, 1959–1989*. Carbondale: Southern Illinois University Press, 1991.

Skir, Leo. *Boychik*. New York: Winter House, 1971.

"Elise Cowen: A Brief Memoir of the Fifties," in Knight, *Women of the Beat Generation*.

Smith, William Raymond. "Hepcats to Hipsters," *The New Republic* (April 2, 1958): 18–20.

Snyder, Gary. *Myths & Texts*. New York: Totem, 1960.

Riprap and Cold Mountain Poems. Washington, DC: Shoemaker & Hoard, 2004.

Sollors, Werner. *Amiri Baraka/LeRoi Jones: The Quest for a "Populist Modernism."* New York: Columbia University Press, 1978.

Solomon, Barbara Probst. *The Beat of Life*. 1960. New York: Great Marsh Press, 1998.

Solomon, Carl. *Mishaps, Perhaps*. San Francisco: City Lights, 1966.

Soto, Michael. *The Modernist Nation: Generation, Renaissance, and Twentieth-Century American Literature*. Tuscaloosa: University of Alabama Press, 2004.

Spandler, Horst. "ruth weiss and the American Beat Movement of the '50s and '60s," in weiss, *Can't Stop the Beat.*

"The Sound of Beat: Three New Poems from Three Leading Beatnik Poets," *Playboy* (July 1959): 44–45.

Spellman, A. B. *The Beautiful Days.* New York: Poets Press, 1965.

Starr, Clinton Robert. "Bohemian Resonance: The Beat Generation and Urban Countercultures in the United States during the Late 1950s and Early 1960s." PhD diss., University of Texas-Austin, 2005.

Stephenson, Gregory. *The Daybreak Boys: Essays on the Literature of the Beat Generation.* Carbondale: Southern Illinois University Press, 1990.

Exiled Angel: A Study of the Work of Gregory Corso. London: Hearing Eye, 1989.

Sterritt, David. *Mad to Be Saved: The Beats, the '50s, and Film.* Carbondale: Southern Illinois University Press, 1998.

Strand, Eric. "The Last Frontier: Burroughs's Early Work and International Tourism," *Twentieth Century Literature* 59.1 (spring 2013).

Suiter, John. *Poets on the Peaks: Gary Snyder, Philip Whalen and Jack Kerouac in the North Cascades.* Washington, DC: Counterpoint, 2002.

Tallman, Warren. "Kerouac's Sound" (1959), reprinted in Charters, *Beat Down Your Soul.*

Tarlow, Aya [writing as Idell]. *Poems for Selected People.* Berkeley: Kether Press, 1961.

Zen Love Poems. Topanga, CA: Love Press, 1967.

Theado, Matt. "Revisions of Kerouac: The Long, Strange Trip of the *On the Road* Typescripts," in Holladay and Holton, *What's Your Road, Man?*

Thompson, John. "Other People's Affairs," *Partisan Review* 28.1 (January–February 1961).

Tietchen, Todd F. "On the Waldport Fine Arts Project and the Aesthetics of Estranged Being," *Mosaic: An Interdisciplinary Critical Journal* 42.3 (September 2009): 19–38.

Trigilio, Tony. "Introduction," in Cowen, *Poems and Fragments.*

Trocchi, Alexander. *Cain's Book.* 1960. New York: Grove, 1992.

Tropp, Stephen. *Mozart in Hell.* New York: Poets Union Press, 1959.

Tytell, John. *Naked Angels: Kerouac, Ginsberg, Burroughs.* New York: Grove, 1976.

"Review of *Beat Drama*," *Journal of Beat Studies* 5 (2017).

Updike, John. "On the Sidewalk," *The New Yorker* (February 21, 1959).

Valentine, Alan. *The Age of Conformity.* Chicago: Regnery Press, 1954.

Vega, Janine Pommy. *Journal of a Hermit.* Cherry Valley, NY: Cherry Valley Editions, 1974.

Mad Dogs of Trieste. Santa Rosa: Black Sparrow, 2000.

Poems to Fernando. San Francisco: City Lights, 1968.

Tracking the Serpent: Journeys to Four Continents. San Francisco: City Lights, 1997.

Voyce, Stephen. *Poetic Community: Avant-Garde Activism and Cold War Culture.* Toronto: University of Toronto Press, 2013.

Wakoski, Diane. "Remembering the New York 1960s Coffee House World of Poetry," in Bergé, *Light Years*.

Waldman, Anne, ed. *The Beat Book: Writings from the Beat Generation*. Boston: Shambala, 1999.

Walker, Gerald. "Fugitive from Girlhood," *New York Times* (January 28, 1962).

Warner, Simon. *Text and Drugs and Rock 'n' Roll*. New York: Bloomsbury, 2013.

Watts, Alan. *The Way of Zen*. 1957. New York: Vintage, 1989.

Weddle, Jeff. *Bohemian New Orleans: The Story of Outsider and Loujon Press*. Jackson: University Press of Mississippi, 2007.

Weinreich, Regina. *Kerouac's Spontaneous Poetics: A Study of the Fiction*. New York: Thunder's Mouth Press, 1987.

"Queer" (interview with William Burroughs), in Burroughs, *Burroughs Live*.

weiss, ruth. *Can't Stop the Beat: The Life and Words of a Beat Poet*. Studio City, CA: Divine Arts, 2011.

DESERT JOURNAL. Boston: Good Gay Poets, 1977.

For These Women of the Beat. San Francisco: 3300 Press, 1997.

GALLERY OF WOMEN. San Francisco: Adler Press, 1959.

Steps. San Francisco: Mel and Ruth Weitsman, 1958.

Welch, Lew. *Hermit Poems*. San Francisco: Four Seasons Foundation, 1965.

On Out. Berkeley: Oyez, 1965.

Ring of Bone: Collected Poems. San Francisco: City Lights, 2012.

Wobbly Rock. San Francisco: Auerhahn Press, 1960.

Whalen, Philip. *The Collected Poems of Philip Whalen*, ed. Michael Rothenberg. Middletown, CT: Wesleyan University Press, 2007.

Goofbook. 1961. Pacifica, CA: Big Bridge Press, 2001.

Like I Say. New York: Totem Press, 1960.

Memoirs of an Interglacial Age. San Francisco: Auerhahn Press, 1960.

Whaley, Preston. *Blows like a Horn: Beat Writing, Jazz, Style, and Markets in the Transformation of U.S. Culture*. Cambridge, MA: Harvard University Press, 2004.

Wieners, John. "From a Journal," in Allen, *New American Poetry*.

The Hotel Wentley Poems. San Francisco: Auerhahn Press, 1958.

The Journal of John Wieners Is to Be Called 707 Scott Street for Billie Holiday. Los Angeles: Sun & Moon Press, 1996.

Stars Seen in Person: Selected Journals, ed. Michael Seth Stewart. San Francisco: City Lights, 2015.

Wilding, Michael. "John Milton: The Early Works," in *The Cambridge Companion to English Poetry, Donne to Marvell*, ed. Thomas N. Corns. Cambridge: Cambridge University Press, 1993.

Wilentz, Elias, ed. *The Beat Scene*. New York: Corinth, 1960.

Wilentz, Sean. *Bob Dylan in America*. New York: Anchor, 2011.

Wilson, Robert A. *A Bibliography of Works by Gregory Corso, 1954–1965*. New York: Phoenix Book Shop, 1966.

Winans, A. D. "Bob Kaufman," *The American Poetry Review* (May–June 2000): 19–20.

Woods, Tim. "Black Mountain and Associates: *Origin* (1951–2007) and *The Black Mountain Review* (1954–7)," in Brooker and Thacker, *The Oxford Critical and Cultural History*.

Woods, William Crawford. "The 'Passed' White Negro: Brossard and Mailer at the Roots of Hip," *Contemporary Review of Fiction* 7.1 (spring 1987).

Woolf, Douglas. "Work in Flight Grounded," in Jones, *The Moderns*.

Woznicki, John R. "The New American Poetry: Fifty Years Later," in *The New American Poetry Fifty Years Later*, ed. Woznicki. Bethlehem, PA: Lehigh University Press, 2014, 1–14.

Index

453

Printed in the USA
CPSIA information can be obtained
at www.ICGtesting.com
LVHW080619221123
764620LV00007B/501